WORLD WAR II

A Student Companion

Student Companions to American History
WILLIAM H. CHAFE, GENERAL EDITOR

WORLD WAR II
A Student Companion

William L. O'Neill

Oxford University Press
New York

Oxford University Press

Oxford   New York
Athens   Auckland   Bangkok   Bogotá   Buenos Aires   Calcutta
Cape Town   Chennai   Dar es Salaam   Delhi   Florence   Hong Kong   Istanbul
Karachi   Kuala Lumpur   Madrid   Melbourne   Mexico City   Mumbai
Nairobi   Paris   São Paulo   Singapore   Taipei   Tokyo   Toronto   Warsaw
and associated companies in
Berlin   Ibadan

Copyright © 1999 by William L. O'Neill
Published by Oxford University Press, Inc.
198 Madison Avenue, New York, New York 10016
Website: www.oup.com

Oxford is a registered trademark of Oxford University Press

Library of Congress Cataloging-in-Publication Data

O'Neill, William L.
World War II : a student companion / William L. O'Neill.
p.   cm.
Includes bibliographical references and index.
ISBN 0–19–510800–0
1. World War, 1939–45—Juvenile literature. I. Title.
II. Title: World War Two. III. Title: World War 2.
d743.7.049   1999
940.53—dc21   98-54918

9 8 7 6 5 4 3 2 1

Printed in the United States of America
on acid-free paper

On the cover: (top left) Dwight D. Eisenhower; (top right) Adolf Hitler;
(bottom) USS *Bunker Hill* bombarded by kamikazes off Kyushu,
Japan, May 11, 1945

Frontispiece: Private Paul Oglesby of the 30th Infantry stands at the altar of
a bombed-out church during the Italian campaign, September 23, 1943.

CONTENTS

Servicemen put out a fire aboard the USS West Virginia during the Japanese attack on Pearl Harbor.

PREFACE

The Second World War was the most deadly and costly military struggle ever fought. It is estimated that some 60 million people died as a result of it, most of them civilians. But this figure is only a guess. Some countries did not want to admit the full extent of their losses. The Soviet Union, for example, always used to claim that about 20 million soldiers and civilians died because of the war. But when he was still president of the USSR Mikhail Gorbachev admitted that as many as 29 million Soviet citizens may have perished. Even this number could still be too low.

Despite the war's frightful cost, the Soviet Union and the Western democracies had no choice except to resist the forces of Imperial Japan and Nazi Germany. To start with, of course, they fought to save themselves. But there was more at stake than simple survival. Japan intended to enslave the peoples of East and Southeast Asia, whom the Japanese regarded as racially inferior. The Nazis also viewed most of the people of Europe as racially inferior to the Aryan, or Nordic, "race," of which they believed Germans to be members. The Nazi plan was to rule Europe, at the very least, and to exterminate not only Jews, but Gypsies and millions of Slavs. The wars against Germany and Japan were, in this sense, wars against particularly murderous forms of racism. They were also wars fought to save democracy and freedom. It was for good reason that General Dwight D. Eisenhower called his autobiography *Crusade in Europe*.

War is never the best way to handle political problems. And wars, even when they end in victory, cannot cure every ill. After World War II Americans were unhappy that Eastern Europe, and later China and other nations, came under Communist rule. That could not be helped. Without the Soviet Union Nazi Germany could not have been defeated, and the Soviets could not be denied the spoils of victory. Neither could the Communists in China be prevented from taking advantage of the opportunity that the defeat of Japan gave them. But over the long term Communism has proved to be less of a threat to freedom than Nazi Germany and Imperial Japan. It has shown itself to be capable of reform, as in China, and even of being overturned, as in Russia and Eastern Europe.

World War II remains, therefore, a struggle that was not less noble for being imperfect. It was fought at times with methods that are hard to defend today. It failed to solve all the problems of humanity. But what it did do was save a large part of the world from tyranny, and make possible the salvation of other parts of the world in the future. Every Allied nation can take pride in what it sacrificed for this great outcome. No subject is more worth studying today for what it teaches us about the meaning of freedom and democracy.

The articles in this book have been designed to explain the war as accurately as possible. Many of the topics covered remain controversial to this day, so no attempt has been made to present this material as the last word on any subject. Readers will have to decide for themselves whether this policy or that program was wise, or moral, or effective. Although the facts are correct to the best of my knowledge, the opinions expressed are my own. They are products of long study and reflection and are as well-reasoned as I could make them, but scholars with impressive qualifications have often come to different conclusions. That is the nature of history as a field, and part of its glory.

Each entry is meant both to provide essential information and to lead readers on to further study by pointing to other entries, suggested readings, and significant films and videos. A general bibliography at the end lists some of the most important books on World War II, but the subject is so vast that a complete listing would require a separate volume.

HOW TO USE
THIS BOOK

The articles in this *Companion* are arranged alphabetically, so you can look up words, concepts, or names as you come across them in other readings. You can then use the SEE ALSO listings at the end of an article to find entries about related subjects. Sometimes you may find that the *Companion* deals with information under a different article name than what you looked up. The book will then refer you to the proper article. For example, if you look up Paratroops, you will find the notation "SEE Airborne Warfare." If you cannot find an article on a particular subject, look in the index to guide you to the relevant articles.

All people are listed alphabetically by last name; for example the entry for Harry Truman is listed under T as Truman, Harry S. In the case of military figures the rank or position given is the highest they held during the war. For example the entry for Omar N. Bradley names him as Commander of the 12th U.S. Army Group, although he held many other positions and would rise after the war to become chief of the Joint Chiefs of Staff.

You can also use this *Companion* topically, by reading all the articles about a particular aspect of World War II. Below are several groupings of topics around common themes.

Battles and events: The names of battles and events are those most commonly used, for example Bulge, battle of the; D-Day; Dresden, bombing of; Malmedy massacre.

Countries: Information on the war at home for Britain, Canada, France, Germany, Italy, Japan, Poland, and the Soviet Union can be found in the articles named for those countries. American life during the war is listed separately under "Home front." Other articles on domestic matters include "Financing the war," "Labor," "Mobilization," and "Motion Pictures."

Military organizations: The United States spells out or abbreviates major units as follows: Fleets, armies and air forces are spelled out; for example, Fifth Fleet, Third Army, Eighth Air Force. Units below them were assigned roman numerals; for example, IV Corps or XX Bomber Command. More basic units were given Arabic numbers; for example, Task Force 58, 4th Armored Division. Army companies were assigned letters, such as Company C, also known as Charlie Company. Battalions and regiments were numbered, as in 2nd Battalion, 354th Regiment.

American historians often apply American terms to foreign units, except when they had distinctive names, such as Luftwaffe for the German Air Force. If confusion sets in remember that the important thing is to get the number right, whether Arabic, roman, or spelled out.

Notable individuals: If you want to know about a particular military or civilian figure in the war look up his or her last name. There are also topical articles on particular groups, such as African Americans and Japanese Americans.

Ordnance: Individual weapons or weapons systems sometimes have their own entries, for example the V-1 flying bomb and the German U-boat (submarine). If you do not find the weapon you are looking for under its own entry try looking under general headings such as Small arms, Artillery, and Bombers.

Origins of the war: The origins of the war with Germany and the war with Japan are explained in the articles on each country. But their surrenders are treated in separate articles, for example "Japan, surrender of".

Theaters of war: Theater is an old term for a region of military operations. However, in World War II the United States used theater only in the war against Germany, as in the European Theater of Operations (ETO). In the Pacific War theaters were called areas. Except for the Southwest Pacific Area, which was an Army theater commanded by General Douglas

Members of the 41st Engineers stand in formation at Fort Bragg, N.C.

MacArthur, the rest of the Pacific was under the command of Admiral Chester Nimitz and known collectively as the Pacific Ocean Area (POA). It was subdivided into the South, Central and North Pacific Areas, each being a separate theater. The article Pacific War covers all the fighting against Japan from Pearl Harbor in 1941 through the first half of 1942. Thereafter combat operations are described in separate articles named for each area.

Further Reading: If you want to know more about a specific topic, you can use the FURTHER READING entries at the end of each article as well as the Further Reading guide at the end of the book, which lists more general sources.

Museums and historic sites: A partial list of museums and historic sites is included. Some of these, such as the Arlington Cemetery in Washington, D.C., are not limited to World War II, but all bear importantly on the war experience. As a rule museums and sites do not provide a great deal of information, but they often give impressions or provide a sense of time and place that cannot be found elsewhere.

Websites: There are a growing number of internet sites devoted to aspects of World War II. The Further Reading section in the back of this book provides links to internet addresses and resources. Web pages for the museums and historic sites listed in Appendix 2 have been included when available.

African Americans

Negroes, the term used to describe African Americans for most of the 19th and 20th centuries, were the largest racial minority in the United States and suffered from segregation and discrimination during the war just as they had before it. Yet manpower shortages and President Franklin D. Roosevelt's need for black votes combined to temper white intolerance. More important, gains made by blacks during the war set the stage for the civil rights revolution that would follow it.

Blacks in the Services Because the leadership of the armed forces was prejudiced against blacks, the mobilization plan of 1940 called for only about half as many blacks as whites to be drafted in proportion to their respective populations. Blacks were to be confined largely to service rather than combat units and be excluded entirely from the Army Air Corps and Marines, and from the Navy except as waiters. However, military discrimination became a political issue in the 1940 election, and to hold the black vote Roosevelt forced the Army to say that it would become 10 percent black, giving roughly the same ratio of blacks to whites as in the general population.

This did not go far enough for white liberals and black activists, and in response to further pressure the Army announced that it would form a number of black combat units, promote a black colonel to the rank of brigadier general, and appoint black advisors to Secretary of War Henry Stimson and the Selective Service chief, Brigadier General Lewis B. Hershey. These actions kept black voters in the Democratic party, even though blacks continued to serve in segregated units.

In 1942 African Americans were still underrepresented in the military, which was not only politically unwise but a waste of manpower. Roosevelt ordered the Navy, much against its will, to enlist blacks for general service. The Army General Staff suggested that racially integrated units be formed. This proved to be too radical a step, even though it was more expensive to build segregated training camps. However, in all the service branches except the Army Air Corps, officer candidate schools were integrated to save money.

At the end of 1944 there were more black officers than could be placed, because of the Army's rule that only whites were to command black units. Another rule was that no black could be ranked higher than the lowest-ranked white in any unit, which meant that few blacks could rise above first lieutenant. This was justified on the grounds that black troops were said to prefer white officers, which was untrue, particularly because so many white officers were southerners with racist attitudes offensive to African-American troops.

White officers seldom wished to be assigned to black units. If white officers were hard on the troops, charges of discrimination typically resulted, but if they stood up for their men they were often scorned by their peers and accused of being "nigger lovers."

To police African-American barracks, and prevent violence directed against black soldiers by whites, white officers often had to take on extra patrol duties because commanders would not entrust black officers with doing this. In the South, white officers of black units were discriminated against socially. Almost everyone believed that they were assigned to command black troops as a punishment.

In addition, black soldiers were often victims of violence, especially in the South; scores were killed or wounded during the war. Often these cases resulted from fights between black soldiers and white soldiers and civilians, but even minor violations of local racial codes could prove fatal. In March 1942, for example, Sergeant Thomas B. Foster of the black 92nd Engineers Battalion was shot to death by Little Rock, Arkansas, police for questioning the methods being employed by military police in arresting a drunken black soldier.

Race riots and fights between black and white servicemen broke out all over the world, not just in the South. These hurt the morale of black troops, and the problem was not helped when Assistant Secretary of War John McCloy blamed poor morale on black oversensitivity and a fault-finding Negro press. Since the pressure did not go away, in 1944 he ordered the desegregation of all facilities on military posts—an edict that was widely ignored.

As late as the spring of 1943, only 79,000 out of a total of 504,000 black soldiers were overseas, because they were not wanted as combat troops. The Army's solution was to train them as service troops, who were accepted—especially for menial work. Representative Hamilton Fish (Republican–N.Y.), who had commanded black fighting men in World War I, asked Secretary of War Stimson to explain this policy and was told that blacks "have been unable to master efficiently the techniques of modern weapons." Stimson flatly lied when he said that the War Department was not trying to keep blacks out of combat. Thus, only one black division, the 92nd Infantry, was ever in combat.

The Navy assigned blacks to labor units only after it was pressured to stop using them exclusively as waiters. It was not until after riots broke out that the Navy began to integrate a handful of noncombat ships.

Small- to medium-sized black com-

bat outfits in the Army and Army Air Forces were relatively few in number but disproved charges that African Americans could not, or would not, fight. The black 99th Pursuit Squadron, which was a great success, became the core of an entire black fighter group—known as the Redtails because of their aircrafts' markings—who were much in demand as escorts throughout the 15th Air Force because they never lost a bomber to enemy fighters.

A number of black ground units also performed well. The 761st Tank Battalion had a brilliant record, while the 969th Field Artillery Battalion won a Distinguished Unit Citation. During the Battle of the Bulge, African Americans in the Army Service Forces were allowed to volunteer for infantry platoons, and after six weeks of training, the 2,500 who were accepted performed well in combat. The tiny Coast Guard—which totaled only 240,000 men compared to the Navy's millions—gave African Americans a chance to serve; it commis-

An African-American Coast Guardman demonstrates the assembly and operation of a 20 mm gun to his fellow sailors.

sioned 700 black officers to the Navy's 58. But, on the whole, blacks were neglected by the military in World War II, which, given the manpower shortage, was a blunder as well as an injustice.

Despite everything, the black war experience had long-term benefits in addition to the fact that African-American veterans took advantage of the GI Bill of Rights. The war gave black veterans a larger view of the world and of their own abilities. Many who were drafted from southern states never returned to the region that had discriminated against them most fiercely. By 1950 more than half of all black veterans were living in a different part of the country from where they had been born, compared to about a third of blacks in the same age group who had not served in the military.

Studies show that military service benefited veterans after the war. In 1949 each additional year of age added $75 to the annual income of whites nationwide, but only $20 to that of blacks in the South. If they had moved to the North, their income increase was the same as that of whites. For whites each year of military service was worth as much to their later earning power as an additional year of education. But for blacks each year of service was worth up to three years of education. One of the few good things about the war was that the military, which did not want blacks and discriminated against them severely, benefited African Americans just the same.

On the home front For black civilian workers, World War II opened up a host of new opportunities. This too was unintentional, for, like the armed services, industry had not intended to recruit blacks. In 1940 there were 5,389,000 employed blacks, of whom 3,582,000 were male, almost none of whom had high-paying defense jobs. A survey made by the U.S. Employment Office found that more than half of the responding defense contractors had no intention of hiring blacks.

This situation outraged A. Philip Randolph, president of the Brotherhood of Sleeping Car Porters, the only Negro union of any importance, who issued a call for a black march on Washington to protest job discrimination. Randolph was the leading spokesman for black workers because the two most important labor organizations had no black officers. The American Federation of Labor, an older establishment consisting of unions that organized workers by craft—plumbers, mechanics, and carpenters, for example—actively discriminated against blacks. The Congress of Industrial Organizations, which enrolled its members industrywide, did have black members, but, because it was only a few years old, no prominent black officers. Because the all-black Brotherhood of Sleeping Car Porters was large and established, both it and Randolph commanded great respect among African Americans.

Despite the requests of Mayor Fiorello LaGuardia of New York and others not to hurt the defense effort or embarrass President Roosevelt, Randolph went forward with his plans for the march. It was expected that 50,000 African Americans would turn out on July 1, 1941. Four days before the scheduled march, FDR invited a group of leaders, including Randolph and Walter White, president of the National Association for the Advancement of Colored People (NAACP), to meet with him.

The result was Executive Order 8802, which established what became the Fair Employment Practices Commission (FEPC), an agency that worked on behalf of African Americans, Jews, aliens, naturalized citizens, Asians, Hispanics, and Native Americans. It would enjoy considerable success, aided greatly by labor shortages that forced employers to lower old barriers. By 1944 blacks held 7.5 percent of all jobs in war industries. This was less than their share of the population but a great improvement over 1940.

The industries that resisted hiring blacks, or hired them only at the lowest levels, were usually those dominated by racist labor unions. The machinists and boilermakers represented 30 to 40 percent of airframe workers and more than 20 percent of shipyard employees, but the machinists were lily white and the boilermakers segregated blacks in powerless locals. Of the 31 national unions that openly discriminated against blacks, 19 were in the railroad industry. Almost all of them refused to change their practices despite FEPC orders and court rulings. White workers frequently went on strike to protest the hiring or promotion of blacks. When white workers at the Philadelphia Transit Company went on strike to protest the upgrading of eight black porters to drivers, the company had to be taken over by the Army in order to keep the trains and buses running.

Job discrimination was bad, but racial violence was even worse. Attacks on blacks were frequent in the South, where lynchings continued throughout the war. They also became common elsewhere. A series of racial clashes occurred in 1943. Fights between white and black gangs in Newark, New Jersey, caused the death of one black. A black soldier was killed during a race riot in Centreville, Mississippi. In El Paso, Texas, a riot among soldiers caused two deaths. At Camp Stewart, Georgia, gunfire was exchanged between black soldiers and military policemen that resulted in five casualties, one fatal. After 12 blacks were promoted at a shipyard

in Mobile, Alabama, white workers rioted, seriously injuring 20 blacks. Two blacks were killed and 50 injured during a race riot in Beaumont, Texas.

On June 15 and 17, 1943, there were minor race riots in the Detroit area, where black workers had flocked for automotive industry jobs, worsening an already acute housing shortage. Sunday, June 20, was unusually hot, and crowds of people jammed Belle Isle in the Detroit River seeking relief. Many fights broke out and by 11:00 p.m. the fights had turned into mob violence. Downtown, a black mob, inflamed by rumors, seems to have rioted first, after which whites retaliated, hunting down and killing blacks, with police support and approval.

Federal troops were finally called in to restore order, by which time some 35 people, a majority of them black, were dead, more than 700 wounded, and 1,300 under arrest. Seventeen blacks were shot by the police, all of them supposedly looters. Whites looted and burned, too, but none were shot by policemen.

In light of the appalling amount of racial violence during the war, some of it caused by blacks to be sure, but most of it a result of white racism, there was no reason to be optimistic about an

Adam Clayton Powell, Jr., addresses the Negro Freedom Rally at Madison Square Garden in New York City, June 26, 1944.

improved climate for racial relations in the United States. Even so, amid the turmoil, momentous changes were developing. Black voters were gaining strength in 17 northern states with a total of 281 votes out of 531 in the electoral college.

In New York City's Harlem district, Adam Clayton Powell, Jr., was already an emerging leader. In 1944 he would be elected to Congress, becoming the first black to represent an urban ghetto. Then, too, rising wages and an increased political awareness were leading blacks to join the NAACP in huge numbers. That organization would multiply tenfold during the war, achieving a dues-paying membership of half a million in 1945.

During the war there were some 230 black newspapers with 2 million readers (among them one daily, the *Atlanta Daily World*). There was also a black news service, the Associated Negro Press of Chicago. The black press now played a crucial role, because the white media habitually ignored news of interest to African Americans. Many small changes were taking place locally that together would prove to be important. In Little Rock, after the murder of Sergeant Foster, eight black officers were hired despite local resistance. Later, as the result of a lawsuit, the federal court of appeals ordered Little Rock to pay white and black school teachers equally. These were small steps, but little by little segregation was being eroded.

Another important element, which people took for granted then but was a source of strength that would be greatly missed in later years, was that a majority of black children were still being raised in two-parent families. Blacks were poor, but they lived in wholesome communities and had a strong family system. These resources, in addition to wartime progress, would make the civil rights revolution possible.

SEE ALSO
GI Bill of Rights

FURTHER READING
Buchanan, Albert Russell. *Black Americans in World War II*. Santa Barbara, Calif.: ABC-Clio, 1977.
Clark, John. *Black Soldier*. Garden City, N.Y.: Doubleday, 1968.
Dalfiume, Richard. *Desegregation of the U.S. Armed Forces: Fighting on Two Fronts, 1939–1953*. Columbia: University of Missouri Press, 1969.
Moore, Brenda L. *To Serve My Country, To Serve My Race: The Story of the Only African American WACS Stationed Overseas during World War II*. New York: New York University Press, 1996.
Motley, Mary, ed. *The Invisible Soldier: The Experience of the Black Soldier, World War II*. Detroit: Wayne State University Press, 1975.
Trotter, Joe William, Jr. *From a Raw Deal to a New Deal? African Americans 1929–1945*. New York: Oxford University Press, 1996.

Afrika Korps

In January 1941 Adolf Hitler was disturbed by Italian defeats at the hands of British forces in the western desert of Egypt and what is today Libya. In February he named Major General Erwin Rommel to take command of a hastily assembled German force and bail the Italians out. Rommel arrived in October to head a command that, despite its impressive title—Deutsches Afrika Korps (German Africa Corps)—consisted of nothing more than two randomly assigned German divisions, assorted Italian units, and, later on, detachments from the German Air Force, the Luftwaffe.

Rommel turned this motley crew into a tightly integrated, highly loyal, superb fighting unit that would hand the British a string of defeats. Although Rommel's command expanded to become an entire army group, the Afrika Korps remained its most valuable asset. The Korps won its last victory at the Kasserine Pass southwest of Tunis in February 1943, against inexperienced U.S. troops, and was one of the last German units to surrender in May when Tunisia fell to the Allies.

SEE ALSO
North African campaign; Rommel, Erwin

FURTHER READING
Forty, George. *Afrika Korps at War.* New York: Scribners, 1978.
Editors of Time-Life Books. *Afrikakorps.* Alexandria, Va.: Time-Life Books, 1990.
Lewin, Ronald. *The Life and Death of the Afrika Korps.* London: Batsford, 1977.

Airborne warfare

The idea of surprising an enemy by jumping out of a plane and landing behind its lines arose as soon as aircraft large enough to carry troops were developed in the 1920s. Germany was the first nation to employ highly trained parachutists in battle, dropping small numbers of them during its 1940 campaigns before staging a major drop on the Mediterranean island of Crete in May 1940.

Because of the success of the Crete campaign, the British Army, and later the U.S. Army too, spent a great deal of money training and equipping elite airborne divisions, which were used in the Mediterranean and European theaters. This decision was an expensive mistake. Extremely costly to build and maintain, airborne divisions were easy to destroy, because jumping was so dangerous and, because once on the ground, lightly armed parachutists were no match for regular infantry and armored divisions. A quarter of the German parachutists who landed on Crete were killed, with the rest so battered that Germany never staged a mass drop again. It would have been wise of the Allies to follow suit.

Allied parachutists played a small role in North Africa and a larger one in Sicily, where units of a U.S. airborne force were mistakenly fired on by Allied gun-

Waves of paratroopers are dropped from planes during operations in Holland.

ners, taking serious casualties even before reaching their drop sites. The most successful Allied drops were made on the night of June 5–6, 1944, as the spearhead of Operation Overlord, the code name for the invasion of Normandy. One British and two U.S. divisions (the 82nd and 101st Airborne) succeeded in taking most of their objectives, more or less justifying themselves—although there is no question but that Overlord would have succeeded without them.

The greatest loss experienced by paratroopers took place during Operation Market Garden when, beginning on September 17, 1944, one British and two U.S. airborne divisions, plus a Polish brigade, landed behind enemy lines in Holland. The plan was to secure bridges, especially over the Rhine, but it proved to be too ambitious, and heavy Allied casualties produced few returns.

Thereafter, except for an uneventful two-division drop behind the Rhine in March 1945, most Allied paratroopers fought as regular infantrymen. Even the famed U.S. XVIII Airborne Corps, which was brilliantly led by Major General Matthew B. Ridgway, a paratroop commander, consisted largely of regular infantry and armored units. Though they did a superb job, the use of trained parachutists as ordinary infantrymen was in effect an admission that large-scale airborne operations were not cost effective. Apparently they still are not, for although the U.S. Army continues to maintain airborne divisions, it has not staged a mass combat drop since World War II.

SEE ALSO
D-Day

FURTHER READING
Ambrose, Stephen E. *Band of Brothers: E Company, 506th Regiment, 101st Airborne: From Normandy to Hitler's Eagle's Nest.* New York: Simon & Schuster, 1992.
Gavin, James M. *On to Berlin: Battles of an Airborne Commander.* New York: Viking, 1978.
Huston, James Alvin. *Out of the Blue: U.S. Army Airborne Operations in World War II.* West Lafayette, Ind.: Purdue University Press, 1972.
Ridgway, Matthew B. *Soldier: The Memoirs of Matthew B. Ridgway.* New York: Harper, 1956.

Air Corps, U.S.

SEE United States Army Air Forces (USAAF)

Aircraft

More than anything else, what distinguished World War II from previous conflicts was the massive use of aircraft. Germany's *blitzkriegs* (lightning wars) were made possible by powerful air attacks on enemy units, and on the communication and supply lines behind them. The defeat of Britain and France in 1940 resulted in large part from their having lost control of the air.

No nation made greater use of aircraft than the United States. The Japanese Navy was defeated almost entirely by U.S. naval warplanes. General Douglas MacArthur was able to bypass strongly defended Japanese-held islands in the Southwest Pacific because they were completely cut off by the Army Air Forces and could not launch attacks or be reinforced or supplied.

The Axis forces in North Africa were defeated after Allied air power isolated them from their sources of supply in Europe. The Allies gained control of the air over Western Europe even before the invasion of Normandy and maintained it afterward. Because the Ger-

TBF Avengers (torpedo bombers) fly in formation during exercises over Norfolk, Virginia.

mans could only travel on land at night and in bad weather, their operations were severely limited. When pressure from Allied ground forces threw them into retreat, and therefore into the open, slaughter resulted.

Air transportation was vital as well. China was supplied entirely by air for most of World War II. U.S. forces were able to fight all over the world because of the mighty U.S. Air Transport Command (ATC), whose fleet of two- and four-engine planes served as freighters, troop carriers, ambulances, and tankers as needed. With a peak strength of 3,700 aircraft, the ATC was an asset unmatched by any other power and envied by all.

Fighter-bombers and medium bombers served both the Allied and Axis powers well. But the American and British investment in heavy four-engine bombers was a poor one. Heavy bombers were, according to air marshals and generals, supposed to win the war against Japan but never produced the expected results or justified the resources devoted to them. They were more useful in the Pacific, where Japanese air defenses were light, but the strategic bombing of Japan was essentially a failure. It was irrelevant, too, as the blockade of Japan had already stopped the wheels of Japanese industry when the air campaign got under way.

SEE ALSO

Bombers; Japanese Army; Japanese Navy; Luftwaffe; Royal Air Force; Strategic bombing; United States Army Air Forces; United States Navy

Aircraft carriers

When the United States went to war, the U.S. Navy possessed seven fleet carriers (CVs). Two, *Lexington* and *Saratoga,* had been built on the hulls of battle cruisers, and with a displacement of almost 34,000 tons were the largest ships in the fleet. None of the other five was larger than 18,000 tons. Under construction were the first of the *Essex*-class aircraft carriers, which displaced 24,500 tons and would begin joining the fleet in 1942. Because their flight decks were not armored, protection having been sacrificed for speed and carrying capacity, all were capable of speeds in excess of 30 knots. The older carriers held about 70 warplanes, whereas *Essex*-class carriers had room for more than 100.

Before the war most admirals had believed that battleships would continue to be the decisive weapons of naval warfare. Carriers were seen as auxiliaries that would scout ahead of the battle line, achieve air superiority, attack enemy ships, and perform other useful services. But Pearl Harbor and Midway established the carrier's primacy. Thereafter, battleships served as auxiliaries.

Because the carriers of the Pacific Fleet were heavily outnumbered by those of Japan, an emergency class of

Construction on the Essex-class carriers began when the war broke out. Although the flight decks were not armored, the carriers were faster and held more planes than the Navy's previous carriers.

nine light carriers (designated CVL) were built on cruiser hulls and entered service in 1943. Although they carried only about 30 aircraft apiece, they were as fast as the fleet carriers and fought alongside them.

A third type, the small escort or "jeep" carrier (designated CVE), proved vitally important to the war effort. The first few of these escorts were built on the hulls of cargo ships, but the later classes were designed as carriers from the keel up. They ranged from 7,000 to 17,000 tons in size and could carry up to 36 aircraft, but their slow speed made them unusable in fleet actions.

Airplanes based on escort carriers became the most effective antisubmarine weapons, though land-based aircraft and surface warships remained important. This was Roosevelt's doing, for if Admiral Ernest J. King had gotten his way, there would not have been enough escort carriers to go around. King favored CVs, so that in June 1942 when the industrialist Henry J. Kaiser proposed building 30 escort carriers, the Navy rejected his offer. Kaiser had

enough clout that he did not have to take no for an answer. He went directly to Roosevelt, who reversed the decision. In time Kaiser's shipyards would be producing one of these ships every week. Escort carriers were immensely valuable to the Allies and, thanks to Roosevelt, they joined the fleet when most needed.

Deadly hunter-killer groups were built around the escort carriers, groups that played havoc with German Admiral Doenitz's U-boats. In the Pacific they were useful too, providing close support to amphibious troops from inshore waters, where the fleet carriers dared not go. Ultimately even King recognized their value and they were built in large numbers, especially the *Casablanca* class, of which 49 were launched. In the Battle of Leyte Gulf, escort carriers would engage a Japanese battleship force and save the invasion fleet.

The Royal Navy and the Imperial Japanese Navy were the only other services besides the U.S. Navy with large carrier fleets. Japanese carriers were constructed along the same lines as those of the U.S. Navy: big, fast, lightly armored, carrying large air groups. The British carriers were different, having heavily armored flight decks and smaller air groups—no more than 60 aircraft. Although both Japan and the United States equipped their carriers with modern single-wing aircraft, Britain entered the war with obsolete planes. The Swordfish, its primary torpedo bomber, was a slow biplane similar in appearance to those used in World War I. Fortunately for the Swordfish, neither Germany nor Italy possessed any usable aircraft carriers, which made it possible for Swordfish to help sink the *Bismarck* and destroy three Italian battleships at anchor. The Royal Navy contributed a carrier task force equipped with modern aircraft to the Battle of Okinawa. Thanks to their armored flight decks they stood up to the Japanese suicide attacks, while eight thin-skinned U.S. carriers had to be withdrawn from combat when their flight decks were penetrated by kamikazes.

SEE ALSO

Battleships; Kamikaze; Leyte Gulf, Battle of; Midway, Battle of; Okinawa, Battle of; Pearl Harbor, attack on; Philippine Sea, Battle of the

FURTHER READING

Hough, Richard. *The Longest Battle: The War at Sea, 1939–45.* New York: Morrow, 1986.
Miller, David. *Carriers: The Men and the Machines.* New York: Salamander, 1991.
Poolman, Kenneth. *Allied Escort Carriers of World War Two in Action.* New York: Blandford, 1988.
Reynolds, Clark G. *The Carrier War.* Alexandria, Va: Time-Life Books, 1982.
Y'Blood, William T. *The Little Giants: U.S. Escort Carriers Against Japan.* Annapolis, Md.: Naval Institute Press, 1987.

Air Force, U.S.

SEE United States Army Air Forces

Allies

Following the World War I model, all states at war with, or occupied by, the Axis powers became known during World War II as the Allies. The principal member states were China, France, Britain (also known as the United Kingdom) and its empire and commonwealth, the Soviet Union, and the United States. Because the Western Allies and the Soviet Union conducted entirely separate war efforts, in common speech the term *Allies* sometimes referred only to the West. When making a point of

including the Soviet Union, the term Grand Alliance was frequently used. The Allies were also called the United Nations well before the United Nations organization was formed in 1945.

SEE ALSO

Britain; China; France; Soviet Union; United States

America First Committee

The America First Committee led the fight to keep the United States from entering World War II. Because antiwar sentiment was particularly strong on college campuses, it was hardly surprising that the America First Committee (AFC) grew out of a student group organized at Yale University by Kingman Brewster (a future president of Yale) and R. Douglas Stuart, a law student. Business and political leaders responded enthusiastically to this student initiative, and on September 4, 1940, the AFC was launched in Chicago with Robert Wood, chairman of Sears Roebuck and Company, as national chairman and Stuart as national director.

At its peak the AFC had some 800,000 members, the largest enrollment

Bicycle riders in Vale, Oregon, proudly display their patriotism and America First allegiance in a July 4th parade, 1941.

of any antiwar organization. More important, its members were to a large extent influential business and professional people and included national leaders such as Senator Burton K. Wheeler and Charles A. Lindbergh—at that time considered to be the greatest American hero.

Although dedicated to neutrality, the AFC favored a strong defense, which annoyed pacifists. This position led Harold Ickes, Roosevelt's sharp-tongued secretary of the interior, to rename the group "America Last." By this he meant that if the AFC had succeeded in its aims, the United States would not have gone to war until all its potential allies had been beaten.

Although well financed and respectable, America First lost much support as a result of Lindbergh's speech in Des Moines, Iowa, on September 11, 1941, in which he accused the Jewish people of "agitating for war." Thus the AFC was already in decline on December 7, 1941, when Japan's attack on Pearl Harbor put an end to it.

SEE ALSO
Isolationists

FURTHER READING

Cole, Wayne S. *Charles A. Lindbergh and the Battle Against Intervention in World War II.* New York: Harcourt, Brace, 1974.
Doenecke, Justus D., ed. *In Danger Undaunted: The Anti-Interventionist Movement of 1940–1941 As Revealed in the Papers of the America First Committee.* Stanford, Calif.: Hoover Institution Press, 1990.
Stenehjem, Michele Flynn. *An American First: John T. Flynn and the America First Committee.* New Rochelle, N.Y.: Arlington House, 1976.

American Federation of Labor

SEE Mobilization

Anzio, Battle of

A central mystery of the Italian campaign is why the Allies did not exploit their control of sea and air to land behind Germany's powerful defense lines. Then they would have been attacking from the rear, where the Germans were weak, instead of always launching costly frontal attacks. Operation Shingle, the one effort to do so, offers a partial answer.

The repeated failure of Allied offensives led President Roosevelt in December 1943 to support British prime minister Winston Churchill's plan for an amphibious landing behind the enemy's Gustav Line in south central Italy by providing 56 of the all-important Landing Ships Tanks (LSTs), as well as two divisions.

At first, Operation Shingle, as the landing at Anzio was code named, seemed off to a promising start. The U.S. VI Corps achieved complete surprise when it went ashore at Anzio, near Rome, on January 22, 1944. But its objectives were unclear, it moved out too slowly, and a supporting attack by the U.S. Fifth Army failed to break the Gustav line, which lay only about 40 miles south of Anzio. Field Marshal Albert Kesselring reacted to Shingle with lightning speed, containing the beachhead with six divisions and almost driving the VI Corps into the sea.

A stalemate followed until late spring when the Gustav Line was finally breached, enabling the VI Corps to break out of its beachhead at Anzio and link up with the Fifth Army. Allied casualties in Anzio came to about 43,000, of which 7,000 were fatalities. Another 44,000 troops were lost to sickness and injury. Although the primary reason that Shingle failed seems to have been that the attacking force was too small to do the job it had been assigned, no further efforts were made to exploit Allied sea power. For the rest of the war Allied forces inched their way up the Italian peninsula by means of costly frontal assaults.

SEE ALSO

Italian campaigns

FURTHER READING

D'Este, Carlo. *Fatal Decision: Anzio and the Battle for Rome.* New York: Harper-Collins, 1991.
Sheehan, Fred. *Anzio, Epic of Bravery.* Norman: University of Oklahoma Press, 1964.
Verney, Peter. *Anzio 1944: An Unexpected Fury.* London: Batsford, 1978.

Appeasement

Appeasement is a term used to negatively characterize the Anglo-French policy of attempting to prevent a European war by agreeing to Hitler's demand for additional territory—particularly Austria and the western tip of Czechoslovakia. In 1938 appeasement climaxed at the Munich conference. There an agreement was negotiated, primarily by Hitler and British Prime Minister Neville Chamberlain, although France and Italy participated as well. The Munich agreement gave the western end of Czechoslovakia to Germany, in return for Hitler's promise to end his demands. His failure to live up to its terms meant the end of appeasement and, soon, to the outbreak of war.

SEE ALSO

Chamberlain, Neville; Germany; Munich agreement

FURTHER READING

De Bedts, Ralph F. *Ambassador Joseph Kennedy 1938–1940: An Anatomy of Appeasement.* New York: P. Lang, 1985.

Robbins, Keith. *Appeasement.* Malden, Mass.: Blackwell, 1997.
Taylor, Telford. *Munich: The Price of Peace.* Garden City, N.Y.: Doubleday, 1979.

Arcadia conference

Arcadia was the code name for the first summit meeting held by the Americans and the British after Pearl Harbor. Churchill and his chiefs met with Roosevelt and his advisors in Washington from December 22, 1941, to January 14, 1942. Among the decisions they made was to confirm their prewar commitment to give the defeat of Germany top priority. For the first time, they seriously discussed an invasion of North Africa. The course of the war was reviewed and the U.S. agreed to much higher production quotas than those established when it was still neutral. A unified command in the Far East called ABDA (American, British, Dutch, Australian) was formed. Roosevelt created the Joint Chiefs of Staff as a counterpart to the British body already in existence, and the Combined Chiefs of Staff, which consisted of the British and American chiefs to oversee the war as a whole, was created.

SEE ALSO

Chiefs of Staff, Combined; Chiefs of Staff, Joint

Ardennes campaign

SEE Bulge, Battle of the

Armor

In 1939 the Allies had thousands of tanks and the Soviets even more. Germany had fewer tanks than Britain and France, and not very good ones at that. But instead of using tanks as infantry support weapons, in the manner of other armies, the German army employed them as the armored spearhead of its attack force, deploying them in massive formations to breach or encircle enemy lines. This produced the blitzkrieg (lightning war) victories against Poland in 1939 and the Western Allies in 1940.

These battles were won chiefly with the aid of lightly armored and gunned medium tanks known as the Mark III and Mark IV (also called the Pz III and IV). But the Soviet Union was already working on new models that would make these German tanks obsolete. One was the heavy 43-ton KV 1B, the other the 26-ton T34, one of the outstanding tanks of the war. The KV was so heavily shielded that even the legendary German 88 mm could not penetrate it, and the T34 was fast and well armored for its size.

Germany's first response was to upgrade its Mark IIIs and IVs with more armor and better guns. Improvements enabled Germany to continue using these prewar models, but its real answers were the Panther and Tiger tanks. These were superb weapons. The Panther weighed 45 tons and had a highly effective 75-mm gun with an extra-long barrel. The Tiger weighed 56 tons and was armed with the 88-mm gun. Germany's problem, one it never solved, was that it lacked the capacity to produce these formidable weapons in sufficient quantities.

Early in the war, American tanks were few and pitiful. To buy time, the U.S. Army fielded the Grant tank first. It was already obsolete, because its 75-mm gun was mounted in a side housing instead of on the turret and had a limited field of fire. By 1943 the United States was producing a good medium tank, the Sherman, which became the mainstay of both the British and U.S. armies.

Unfortunately for the crews, what was a good tank in 1943 became a bad one a year later. When the Allies went ashore in Normandy their Shermans were hopelessly outclassed by the German Panthers and all but helpless when faced with their Tigers. Apart from its power turret, the Sherman had no advantage over German tanks except that it could be manufactured in immense quantities.

German and Soviet tanks were regularly upgraded. Germany's incredible Tiger II, for example, weighed 68 tons and was practically invulnerable. Americans tinkered with the Sherman, but the improvements were usually minor or involved only a small number of units. It was almost a crime that the much superior Pershing tank was not rushed into production. And if the U.S. Army had given every Sherman a heavier gun, as the British did with their Shermans, thousands of lives might well have been saved.

American Sherman tanks such as this one were outclassed by German Panthers in Europe, but the United States did little to upgrade them.

SEE ALSO

De Gaulle, Charles; Eastern front; France, Battle of; France, fall of; Guderian, General Heinz

FURTHER READING

Dunnigan, James F. *How to Make War: A Comprehensive Guide to Modern Warfare.* New York: Morrow, 1982.
Dupuy, Trevor Nevitt. *The Evolution of Weapons and Warfare.* Indianapolis: Bobbs-Merrill, 1980.

Foss, Christopher, and Ian Hogg. *Battlefield: The Weapons of Modern Land Warfare.* London: Orbis, 1986.

Arnold, Henry H.

CHIEF OF THE U.S. ARMY AIR FORCES, 1941–46

- *Born: June 15, 1886, Gladwyne, Penn.*
- *Education: U.S. Military Academy, 1903–07*
- *Military service: U.S. Army—2nd lieutenant, 1907–13; 1st lieutenant, 1913–16; captain, 1913–17; major 1917; colonel 1917–20; major, 1920–31; lieutenant colonel, 1931–34; brigadier general, 1934–38; major general, 1938–41; lieutenant general, 1941–43; general, 1943–44; general of the army, 1944–49; general of the air force, 1949; chief of the U.S. Army Air Corps, September 29, 1938; deputy chief of staff for air, October 30, 1940; chief of the U.S Army Air Forces, 1941–46; seated as member of Joint Chiefs of Staff, February 9, 1942*
- *Died: January 13, 1950, Valley of the Moon, Calif.*

Known to his peers and superiors as "Hap," Arnold presented a different face to those who worked under him and were familiar with his quick temper and ruthlessness. He was a "bomber baron," one of those air commanders who believed that strategic bombing could win the war and who pushed relentlessly for the men and aircraft needed to lay waste to military and civilian targets in Europe and Japan. He took no interest in grand strategy, which he was happy to leave to the Army's chief of staff, General George C. Marshall. But he exercised tight control over those parts of the air force that were engaged in major bombing campaigns.

When the B-29 Superfortress, which could carry twice the load of a B-17 and take it twice as far, became operational, Arnold, fearing that all theater comman-

ders would want this aircraft, thwarted them by having every B-29 assigned to the Twentieth Air Force. He then persuaded the Joint Chiefs of Staff to take command of the Twentieth and assign him to act as their executive agent. Thus he ensured that nearly all Superfortresses would be used to bomb Japan.

When high-altitude precision bombing proved to be impractical, Arnold made it known that low-level fire raids would do. He did not favor using atomic bombs against Japan, because he believed that fire bombing alone would be enough to force Tokyo to surrender. In this he was almost certainly wrong, because nearly every city in Japan had been burned out by August 6, 1945, when Hiroshima was destroyed, but the Japanese government was not much closer to surrendering than it had been in March, when the incendiary raids began.

SEE ALSO

Atomic bombs; Strategic bombing

FURTHER READING

Coffey, Thomas M. *Hap: The Story of the U.S. Air Force and the Man Who Built It, General Henry H. "Hap" Arnold.* New York: Viking, 1982.
Copp, DeWitt S. *A Few Great Captains: The Men and Events that Shaped the Development of U.S. Air Power.* Garden City, N.Y.: Doubleday, 1980.
DuPre, Flint O. *Hap Arnold: Architect of American Air Power.* New York: Macmillan, 1972.

Henry H. Arnold sits at his desk in the War Department in Washington, D.C. After completing his military training at West Point, Arnold was taught to fly by the Wright Brothers.

Artillery

Field guns were critical to the U.S. Army's success, inflicting more casualties on the enemy than all other ground weapons combined. American infantry divisions were equipped with superb 105-mm and 155-mm guns that poured devastating fire on enemy positions. American gunners excelled at their technical art, guided by forward spotters who flitted about in tiny aircraft. Their specialty was the "TOT," or time-on-target concentration, in which all available guns would commence firing at intervals, depending on their range and distance from the target, so that the first round from every gun arrived simultaneously. After that the gunners would fire at will until a specified time limit had been reached. The resulting storm of fire that broke without warning was the American tactic that German soldiers feared most.

The principles that made U.S. artillery so formidable had been developed before the war, although the Army then had almost none of the equipment it would need to make them work. Lacking modern guns, vehicles with which to move them, reliable communications, and much else, artillery officers planned as if everything would be available when needed. Thus they invented the principles and techniques that helped make the U.S. division an artillery-infantry team of enormous power.

In addition to developing TOT, the Artillery School at Fort Sill, Oklahoma, had worked hard to make field artillery both mobile and highly accurate. When the real war came, along with real weapons, trucks, radios, and other equipment, artillery officers had the doctrine and training to make the most of what they were given.

When it came to smaller guns, however, the army was not so fortunate. It never developed a good antitank gun, and the tank destroyers that were supposed to make antitank guns unnecessary were no match for German panzers. The basic tank destroyer was an open half-tracked vehicle on which a low-velocity 75-mm gun had been bolted. The gun could not penetrate German armor, and the vehicle was so top-heavy that great care was needed to prevent it from tipping over. Better tank destroyers were devised as the war went on, but as the Germans developed better tanks, tank destroyers never caught up. Their best use, it turned out, was to serve as mobile assault guns in support of infantry attacks.

American soldiers would have given much to have a weapon like the German 88-mm gun. It had been designed as an antiaircraft, or "flak," gun, a role in which it excelled. But, with its penetrat-

Artillerymen lay down a barrage of fire on Japanese artillery positions in Balete Pass, Luzon, Philippine Islands.

ing power and accuracy, it also proved to be the best antitank gun of the war as well as one of the best tank guns.

Although Germany and the Soviet Union produced large numbers of self-propelled (SP) assault guns—artillery pieces mounted on tank bodies—the United States and Britain did not, believing that ordinary towed guns provided the infantry with sufficient fire support. Perhaps this was so, but the employment of tank destroyers as assault guns, a use for which they had not been designed and one that put crews at high risk, suggests that a fully armored, large-caliber American SP gun would have been valuable in Europe.

Antiaircraft (AA) guns were of two types: light weapons for use against low-flying planes and heavier guns designed to reach high altitudes. The American 90-mm gun was a good example of the latter, especially when firing rounds equipped with "proximity" fuses. These were, in effect, tiny radar units that exploded AA rounds in the neighborhood of the target. First used in 1943 against Japanese aircraft in the Pacific, proximity fuses were eventually directed against ground as well as aerial targets in both Europe and the Pacific. Its ability to enable gunners to destroy their targets without making a direct hit made the proximity fuse a great asset.

A German innovation was the "flak tower," a reinforced concrete structure bristling with AA guns that was almost impossible to destroy from the air. After the war, they proved so hard to level that in Berlin one was finally covered with earth to make an artificial hill.

By 1944 U.S. air superiority above the battlefield was so great that the number of AA units could be sharply reduced, freeing up a substantial number of men for service in the infantry, where they were desperately needed. Germany, on the other hand, fired its massed AA

guns against the great Allied bomber fleets to the bitter end.

FURTHER READING

Baldwin, Ralph Belknap. *The Deadly Fuze: The Secret Weapon of World War II.* San Rafael, Calif.: Presidio Press, 1980.

Batchelor, John, and Ian V. Hogg. *Artillery.* New York: Scribners, 1972.

Blackburn, George G. *The Guns of Normandy: A Soldier's Eye View, France 1944.* Toronto: McClelland & Stewart, 1995.

Hogg, Ian V. *British & American Artillery of World War II.* New York: Hippocrene, 1978.

Perret, Geoffrey. *There's a War to Be Won: The United States Army in World War II.* New York: Random House, 1991.

Atlantic, Battle of the

Of all the battles fought in World War II, the Battle of the Atlantic was the most important. If it had been lost, there would have been no aid to Britain, no Allied invasion of France, no Lend-Lease convoys to Russia, and therefore no victory. Shipping was critical to every Allied operation and the greatest number of ships lost went down in the North Atlantic. Yet, despite the life-and-death struggle that Britain was waging against Hitler's U-boats, the U.S. military had made no preparations of its own to conduct antisubmarine warfare (ASW) before Pearl Harbor. As a result, the Western Hemisphere became a happy hunting ground for U-boat captains, beginning on December 31, 1941, when they first reached U.S. waters.

During the next several months, 61 ships were sunk off the East Coast; in February and March, 42 ships went down in the Caribbean and 8 in the Gulf of Mexico. U-boats struck at will, attacking on the surface even in broad

U-boats stalked ships along coastal waters and convoy routes in the Atlantic. Groups of U-boats were called "wolf packs."

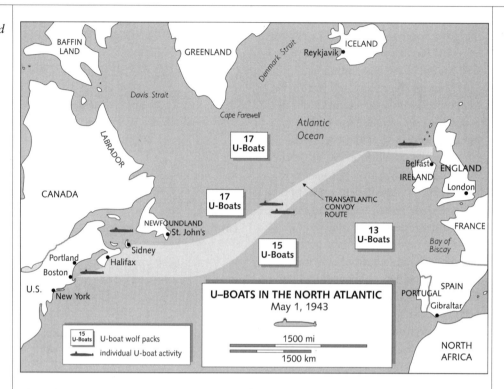

daylight. For ASW operations along the East Coast of the United States, the Navy had available perhaps 20 vessels, not one of which was fast enough to catch a U-boat running on the surface. It also had about 100 aircraft, none suited to ASW or capable of long patrols.

The Army Air Forces (AAF) threw in 100 two-engine aircraft, 9 B-17 bombers, and a handful of other planes whose crews had no ASW training and which were not equipped to track, much less destroy, enemy submarines. Luckily, Germany was not building many U-boats, but even the handful it deployed were tremendously effective. If Hitler had seen their value in time, the war might have gone far worse for the Allies.

Gradually, under pressure from oil company executives alarmed by tanker losses, some obvious and overdue steps were taken. In March 1942 the Civil Air Patrol began making offshore flights and gradually the AAF's 1st Bomber Command acquired the means to fight U-boats. By early April the Navy had established a limited convoy system. By the middle of May a coastal blackout (needed because ships silhouetted by lights on shore were easy targets) was in force—despite numerous complaints that it would damage the tourist season.

Yet after six and a half months, the United States had sunk only 8 U-boats while losing more than 360 merchant ships. As late as June 15, two U.S. merchant vessels were torpedoed off Virginia Beach in full view of bathers. Finally, by late summer enough ASW small boats and aircraft had been assembled to force the U-boats to relocate to the western Caribbean. By the end of September, 173 merchantmen had been sunk there. On October 15, 1942, the 1st Bomber Command became the Army Air Forces's Antisubmarine Command (AAFAC). The Air Forces had discovered that the Very Long Range Liberator (VLR Liberator) was its best weapon against the U-boat, and also that searching out U-boats was more effective than simply escorting convoys—though that had to be done as well. Its views were opposed by the Navy, which wanted the VLR Liberators itself and still preferred to escort convoys.

This interservice bickering and competition took place against a background of rising ship losses. Although waters in the Western Hemisphere grew safer, the mid-Atlantic became increasingly dangerous. After January 1943 no merchant ship was destroyed within a 600-mile radius of any Allied air base, yet the overall loss rate soared. This was the work of Admiral Karl Doenitz, head of the U-boat force and, since January 30, commander in chief of the German Navy. His promotion was a result of Hitler's decision to forget the surface fleet and concentrate on submarines.

Fortunately for the Allies, Hitler did so too late, but Doenitz still managed to wreak havoc by concentrating his vessels in a patch of the North Atlantic that was beyond the reach of land-based aircraft. As many as 80 U-boats at a time worked the area, with devastating results. In the first three weeks of March 1943 alone, the Allies lost 750,000 tons of shipping, a rate that if continued for long would have destroyed their merchant fleets, or at least those of Britain.

In 1942 the amount of U.S. shipped goods to the British doubled, while Britain transported many U.S. troops and significantly increased the number of warships that protected Atlantic convoys. Nonetheless, in 1942 Britain lost almost 6 million tons of shipping, a third more than in 1941, while U.S. losses came to fewer than 2.5 million tons. In the same year American shipyards turned out vessels able to carry almost 4 million tons of shipping, giving the United States a net gain of 1.5 million tons, while Britain suffered a net loss in excess of 2 million tons. This combination of shipping losses and a great increase in military cargo crippled Britain's merchant fleet. In January 1943 imports fell to the lowest level of the war, leaving Britain with no more than a few months' supply of food.

Roosevelt had already agreed, on November 30, 1942, to assign Britain 2.5 million tons of shipping. But much of it was yet to be built. In the meantime sinkings continued to rise while the needs of the Mediterranean were proving to be greater than expected. Military operations in North Africa were supposed to require only 66 ships a month for a four-month period, but they actually used more than 400—much of the excess provided by Britain. In January, Churchill took the extreme step of switching to Atlantic routes 52 of 92 monthly sailings scheduled for India. Despite such drastic measures Britain remained short of merchant vessels at a time when Americans were making ever greater demands on them. The gap between what American planners wanted and Britain could provide came to about 6 million tons, more than a quarter of the entire volume of cargo destined for U.S. forces overseas that year.

Troop and cargo movements from

After 85 days on a raft, three survivors of a torpedoed merchant ship are rescued off the coast of Brazil by a Navy patrol boat on January 24, 1943.

the United States to Britain almost ceased, thanks to the Allied invasion of Africa and the great upsurge in U-boat activity. On March 12, 1943, Britain revealed its shipping requirements to the U.S. service heads. The figures seemed to indicate that if 27 million tons of goods were shipped to Britain, the least it could get by with, there would be almost no merchant vessels left to support U.S. forces. The U.S. Joint Chiefs demanded that Britain provide more ships anyway, but Britain had none to spare. Although no one questioned the necessity of having the United States meet its own shipping needs, if Britain's basic requirements were not met, the British national war effort—and therefore the Allied one—would collapse. The Joint Chiefs refused to admit this, however, insisting that the shipping agreements made at the Casablanca conference in January 1943, when shipping losses were not so great, be carried out anyway.

Only Roosevelt could break the deadlock, which he was able to do because the U.S. War Shipping Administration (WSA) believed that the Joint Chiefs were asking for too much. The WSA's figures indicated that, thanks to increased shipbuilding, a modest cutback in military shipping during the third quarter of 1943 would make it possible to meet the essential needs of Britain at little expense to the U.S. war effort. FDR accepted this analysis and took one of his bigger gambles.

Overruling the Joint Chiefs, Roosevelt stood by his promise to assign Britain 2.5 million tons of shipping. In May he directed the WSA to provide Britain with 150 to 200 merchant ships over a 10-month period. From a low point of 4.5 million tons in the first quarter of 1943, British imports rose to 7.5 million tons in the second, exceeding requirements. And, as it turned out, the

Army could not fully use even the reduced tonnage made available to it, having asked for too much in the first place.

Roosevelt won his gamble not only because more shipping was built than anticipated but because ASW weapons became better and more numerous. Also, the navy became more cooperative. But success was, in addition, a result of decisions about how weapons should be deployed that Roosevelt made personally. This involved managing details of the war that Hitler, Stalin, and Churchill did all the time but was unusual for Roosevelt, who gave the service chiefs a high degree of freedom. In this respect, one reason for Germany's success was that the U-boats were directed by a single commander while the various Allied services often worked at cross-purposes, each going its own way using different methods and failing to cooperate or share information.

Of all the Allied military shortcomings, the intelligence failure was the most serious, for by 1943, ULTRA, Britain's code-breaking operation, was turning out a steady flow of decrypted enemy radio messages. ULTRA was a great help in locating U-boats, not only so that they could be attacked but also because convoys could be rerouted away from U-boat "wolf packs," easily the most effective way of defending them. However, for lack of coordination, the priceless data did not always reach those who needed them. Further, the U.S. Navy retained operational control over army air units and exercised it constantly, rather than laying down policy and allowing air officers to carry it out, the procedure followed with much success by the Royal Navy and Royal Air Force Coastal Command.

Admiral Ernest J. King, the hardnosed U.S. naval chief, finally admitted that the Battle of the Atlantic was being lost, and on March 1, 1943, at his invi-

Servicemen on the deck of the U.S. Coast Guard cutter Spencer *watch the explosion of a depth charge aimed at destroying a German U-boat trying to break into the center of a large convoy off the American coastline.*

tation, a secret Washington convoy conference opened with 100 participants representing the armies and navies of the United States, Britain, and Canada. At the end of 12 days they agreed to divide the oceans into zones of responsibility for ASW purposes.

King then formed what was called the Tenth Fleet, an advisory group within his own headquarters that became the nerve center of the U.S. ASW campaign. Improved coordination and communication were accompanied by, among other measures, more sophisticated detection devices, better use of ULTRA decryptions, and an increase in land-based aircraft and escort vessels, including small carriers.

An important change was ordered by Roosevelt himself. In 1943 the most desperately needed ASW aircraft was the VLR Liberator, a modified B-24 heavy bomber. The Navy had 112 of these, most of which King was hoarding in the Pacific. AAFAC had two squadrons, but they were operating in North Africa. This left only 18 VLRs in the Royal Air Force's Coastal Command to cover the

entire Atlantic. Somehow Roosevelt, who almost never concerned himself with tactics, learned of this. On March 18, 1943, during the worst month of the U-boat war, he asked for the exact locations of every VLR Liberator. Upon being informed that they were mostly in the wrong places, he ordered what proved to be a crucial transfer. Roosevelt's lifelong interest in naval matters would now greatly benefit the Allied cause.

By mid-April, 41 VLRs were flying above the North Atlantic, and U-boats could no longer surface without risk anywhere in it. The issue of which service should command ASW aircraft was finally resolved, too. In the summer of 1943, air and naval officers agreed that the Army should withdraw from the antisubmarine war entirely, while the Navy would give up the idea of strategic bombing in exchange.

Admiral King vetoed the deal at first, wanting to keep his heavy bomber force, but he relented in the end. and a trade was agreed to. AAFAC gave its VLR Liberators to the Navy in return for conventional B-24s. Its pride satisfied, the Navy finally admitted that the AAFAC doctrine of search and destroy was more effective than simply escorting convoys. By mid-May escort carriers could give air protection to convoys everywhere in the Atlantic. During April and May 1943, Admiral Doenitz lost 56 boats, a casualty rate so high that he was forced temporarily to abandon the North Atlantic. The British, who had been fighting U-boats much longer than the United States, contributed immensely to this outcome, yet Roosevelt's interventions may have provided the margin of victory.

It had taken only five weeks to eliminate the U-boat menace. Two figures sum things up. In April, Allied shipping losses amounted to 245,000 tons, but in June only 18,000 tons. It was the most important defeat for German arms since World War I. Soon U.S. shipyards were producing in volume, and by October 1943 all the shipping capacity lost since 1939 had been replaced. Doenitz came back later with more and better U-boats, but the Allies kept ahead of him. By 1944, despite a great increase in Allied traffic, the tonnage—not the number of vessels but their combined weight—of U-boats lost exceeded that of all Allied merchant ships destroyed.

Of 1,162 U-boats commissioned during the war, 941 were sunk or captured. Seventy-five percent of those who fought the undersea war for Hitler became casualties, a rate unmatched by any other fighting service of any belligerent nation. Thanks to Roosevelt personally, to the U.S. Navy, which awoke to the U-boat menace just in time, to those who fought the German submarines, and to the dedicated civilian sailors of the Allied merchant fleets—thousands of whom gave their lives—the Allies won control of the Atlantic and, with it, the cause of freedom.

SEE ALSO
Aircraft carriers; U-boats

FURTHER READING
Bateman, Robert. *Race Against the U-Boats*. London: Cape, 1963.
Burland, Brian. *A Fall from Aloft*. London: Barrie and Rockcliff, 1968.
Hough, Richard. *The Longest Battle: The War at Sea 1939–45*. New York: Morrow, 1986.
Mason, John T., ed. *Atlantic War Remembered: An Oral History Collection*. Annapolis, Md.: Naval Institute Press, 1990.
Morrison, Samuel Eliot. *History of United States Naval Operations in World War II*. Vol. 4. *Coral Sea, Midway and Submarine Actions. May 1942–August 1942*. Boston: Little, Brown, 1949.
———. *History of United States Naval Operations in World War II*. Vol. 10. *The Atlantic Battle Won. May 1943–May 1945*. Boston: Little, Brown, 1956.

Atlantic Charter

On August 4, 1941, at a time when the United States was not yet at war with Germany or Japan, President Franklin D. Roosevelt slipped quietly out of New London, Connecticut, transferring at sea to the cruiser *Augusta* for a rendezvous with Britain's prime minister Winston Churchill. They met at Argentia Bay in Newfoundland to pursue somewhat different agendas. Churchill hoped for U.S. promises of additional support, especially against Japan. Roosevelt wanted a joint statement of principles that would establish the basis for a democratic war effort. Both believed that the United States would soon be at war, even though neither knew how this would come to pass.

The result of their meeting, a document that became known as the Atlantic Charter, was not very important, although it would be cited repeatedly

Franklin Roosevelt (left) and Winston Churchill discuss wartime goals on board the Augusta. *The resulting Atlantic Charter was endorsed by the Soviet Union and 14 other Allied states.*

throughout the war as having established the "Four Freedoms"—freedom of speech and religion, freedom from want and fear—as Allied war aims. It declared eight principles to be the goals of the war effort, including self-determination of subject peoples (Churchill, who still hoped to save the British Empire, bet that he would not have to live up to this part of the agreement at the end of the war), freedom of trade, freedom of the seas, disarmament, and eventually some kind of permanent alliance.

Roosevelt was vague about Japan, but having already decided to do so, he could promise the prime minister a U.S. convoy system to protect marine shipments from German U-boats on the passage across the Atlantic. Roosevelt's interest in supporting the Soviet Union also received much encouragement, from Churchill and from events on the eastern front itself where the Soviets seemed to be holding their own.

Because the conference was largely symbolic, its value depended on the weight given to its pronouncements. To Roosevelt and his supporters, the Argentia meeting was a great success, which may have been true so far as publicity went. To the British, who had hoped for more definite commitments, the conference was disappointing, although as usual Churchill put the best possible face on things. To isolationists, the charter was a mask behind which

Roosevelt had secretly agreed to invade Europe. This was one claim that had no basis at all in fact.

FURTHER READING

Brinkley, Douglas and David R. Facey-Crowther. *The Atlantic Charter*. New York: Macmillan, 1994.
Wilson, Theodore A. *The First Summit: Roosevelt and Churchill at Placentia Bay, 1941*. Lawrence: University Press of Kansas, 1991.

Atomic bombs

Research conducted in the 1920s and 1930s by physicists specializing in ultra-high energy, most of them European, opened up the possibility of unleashing a nuclear chain reaction that would produce tremendous amounts of energy. By September 1939 Nazi Germany, where nuclear fission had been discovered the previous year, was developing an atom bomb project based on this research. At the same time in the United States, refugee scientists, led by Leo Szilard of Hungary, who had been driven from Europe by Nazi anti-Semitism, were attempting to persuade American officials of the need for such a program.

Things went slowly at first, but in September 1942 Major General Leslie Richard Groves, an officer in the U.S. Army Corps of Engineers, which had just finished building the Pentagon, was assigned to oversee the nuclear development program. In October he appointed J. Robert Oppenheimer as director of research for what was to be called the Manhattan Project. Oppenheimer, who would one day be seen as the father of the atom bomb, was a theoretical physicist with joint appointments at the Cali-

This implosion-type plutonium bomb, called "Fat Man," was dropped on Nagasaki on August 9, 1945.

fornia Institute of Technology and the University of California at Berkeley. Although he was a brilliant scientist, Oppenheimer had never run a large laboratory and—unlike the leading scientists of the Manhattan Project—had never won the Nobel Prize.

Major General Groves insisted on making this appointment, overriding objections from scientists and Army counterintelligence, who opposed naming someone whose former fiancée, wife, brother, and sister-in-law had all been members of the Communist party, and perhaps still were. In doing so, Groves made his greatest contribution to the bomb project, for Oppenheimer, who had what a colleague described as "intellectual sex appeal," was able to enlist hundreds—and eventually thousands—of scientists and engineers to work on a program he could not reveal to them in advance for security reasons. Further,

most of them would be required to live on a remote mesa in New Mexico where the scientific work was to be consolidated at the Los Alamos Laboratory. Oppenheimer also turned out to be a natural leader, able to keep his collection of geniuses and prima donnas hard at work under spartan conditions.

To make the fuel for an atomic bomb, an entire industry had to be built from scratch, at a cost of some $2 billion—a gigantic sum at the time, especially because Congress could not be told what it was appropriating the money for. The manufacturing work was concentrated in two places—Oak Ridge, Tennessee, and Hanford, Washington—each of which had the abundant supply of electrical power required to make an atomic bomb. But otherwise the manufacturing centers were completely different, for the Manhattan Project's goal was to make not one type of atomic bomb but two radically different weapons.

Soldiers examine the devastating effects of the atomic bomb dropped on Hiroshima.

Oak Ridge had the easier job of refining uranium 235 until it achieved the level of purity that would cause a chain reaction when two pieces of it collided. This was accomplished by fitting them into a barrel and firing one piece at another. The theory behind this weapon was so convincing that scientists did not even field test the device. The first uranium-based explosion took place over Hiroshima, Japan, on August 6, 1945, the product of a bomb known as Little Boy. The plane that carried the bomb was *Enola Gay,* named after the pilot's mother. It was estimated that the force of Little Boy equaled an explosion of 12,500 tons of TNT. In the future, nuclear weapons would be designated according to the number of such kiloton (one thousand tons) units of force they would release. Little Boy is believed to have killed between 70,000 and 200,000 people. The highest figure includes those who died years, and in some cases many years, after the blast and is probably exaggerated.

Late in 1942, at the University of Chicago, a team led by Enrico Fermi, a Nobel laureate from Italy, built the first atomic reactor. At Hanford, Washington, five reactors modeled on this prototype created an artificial element called plutonium by bombarding uranium 238 with neutrons. After many difficulties, sufficient plutonium was produced to set off a chain reaction. This was achieved by surrounding pure plutonium with high explosives that, when detonated, compressed the material, causing a chain reaction faster and more efficiently than could be done in a gun barrel. In effect, the plutonium was imploded to produce a gigantic eruption. However, because of its complexity, the implosion device had to be tested. This was done at the Alamogordo Bombing Range in New Mexico on July 16, 1945.

After the first atomic explosion in history had taken place, the scientists left their bunkers to see the soon-to-become-familiar giant, boiling, mushroom-shaped cloud rising toward the heavens. Careful calculations revealed that the plutonium weapon had a force of 18.6 kilotons, four times what had been expected.

It was a plutonium bomb, known as Fat Man, that exploded over Nagasaki, Japan, on August 9, 1945, with a force estimated at 22 kilotons. Because of high winds, Fat Man had to be dropped several miles from the intended site, and it was therefore less destructive than Little Boy, killing somewhere between 40,000 and 140,000 people.

The extensive damage done to the human body by the radiation effect, which caused people to die long after a nuclear explosion, and which partially accounts for the wide variation in casualty estimates, was not anticipated by scientists. It would be years before the Los Alamos scientists and others involved with the U.S. nuclear weapons program would come to grips with what many regarded as the ugliest feature of nuclear warfare. Although few questioned the decision to wage nuclear war at the time, a controversy developed later that continues to this day.

SEE ALSO
Japan, surrender of

FURTHER READING
Cooper, Dan. *Enrico Fermi and the Revolutions of Modern Physics.* New York: Oxford University Press, 1999.
Goodchild, Peter. *J. Robert Oppenheimer: Shatter of Worlds.* Boston: Houghton Mifflin, 1980.
Hersey, John. *Hiroshima.* 1946. Reprint, New York: Knopf, 1985.
Maruki, Toshi. *Hiroshima No Pika.* New York: Lothrop, Lee, and Shepard, 1982. Fiction.
Rhodes, Richard. *The Making of the Atomic Bomb.* New York: Simon & Schuster, 1986.
Wyden, Peter. *Day One: Before Hiroshima and After.* New York: Simon & Schuster, 1984.

Axis

In 1936 Italy and Germany established by treaty what became known as the Rome–Berlin Axis. Later, Japan associated itself with the Axis, and in 1940 the "Tripartite Pact" allied the three states. Germany's client states, Romania, Bulgaria, and Hungary, were also considered Axis powers.

Bataan death march

On April 9, 1942, some 78,000 U.S. and Philippine troops surrendered to the Japanese on the Bataan Peninsula of Luzon in the Philippine Islands. These men had fought magnificently—and for much longer than the Japanese had expected.

Outgunned by the Japanese and abandoned by the United States, including at the end by General Douglas MacArthur, and with little ammunition, less food, and almost no medical care,

they surrendered in the end due to starvation, disease, and a near-total lack of supplies. The Japanese were unprepared for the large number of prisoners they took and, despising prisoners of war (POWs) in any case—they themselves rarely surrendered—cared little whether the men lived or died. They forced their exhausted prisoners to walk 65 miles to the nearest prison camp, killing those who fell by the way, usually with great cruelty. No one knows the exact number of those who died, but it certainly ran to the thousands. By 1943 news of the death march reached the United States, further inflaming public opinion against the Japanese and contributing to the extreme brutality that marked the Pacific war.

SEE ALSO

MacArthur, Douglas; Pacific war; Southwest Pacific Area

FURTHER READING

James, D. Clayton. *The Years of MacArthur.* Vol. 2. Boston: Houghton Mifflin, 1975.
FitzPatrick, Bernard T. *The Hike into the Sun: Memoir of an American Soldier Captured on Bataan in 1942 and Imprisoned by the Japanese until 1945.* Jefferson, N.C.: McFarland & Co., 1993.
Villarin, Mariano. *We Remember Bataan and Corregidor: The Story of the American & Filipino Defenders of Bataan and*

American prisoners carry fallen comrades on their march in Bataan. This captured Japanese photograph testifies to the cruelty with which POWs were treated.

Corregidor and Their Captivity. Baltimore: Gateway Press, 1990.

Battleships

In 1939 most navies regarded the battleship as their primary weapon of war. In the event of war with Japan, the U.S. Navy had long planned to meet the enemy's "battle line" (a line or column of battleships) at sea and destroy it with gunfire. When the United States entered the war, most battleships in service, designated BBs, had been built during or just after World War I, mounted 10 or 12 14-inch guns, and had a top speed of some 20 knots per hour. This meant they could not keep up with the newer aircraft carriers, which had speeds in excess of 30 knots. But because carriers were considered auxiliary ships, this did not seem a major problem.

After the Japanese attack in December 1941 on Pearl Harbor, during which all the battleships of the Pacific Fleet were sunk or badly damaged, and the all-carrier Battle of Midway, it was clear that the battleship was now the auxiliary and the carrier the main instrument of naval warfare. Thereafter, the slower battleships were used only to bombard enemy-held islands.

Two fast battleships mounting 16-inch guns and with a top speed of about 27 knots entered service in 1941. In 1943 and 1944 they were joined by four more of the *Iowa* class, bigger ships that could make 33 knots. This handful of fast battleships fought a number of surface engagements in the Solomon Islands campaign, but their primary work for most of the Pacific war was to provide antiaircraft protection for the carriers and fire support for amphibious landings. This outcome was a cruel disappointment for the once-dominant "battleship admirals," who had scorned aircraft carriers before the war, only to find that the "air admirals" were right and battleships and bat-

The USS Iowa *conducts a battle drill, 1944.*

tleship tactics obsolete.

Britain had a large battleship force, its *King George* class being comparable to the United States's fast BBs. Because Germany built very few large ships, British battleships fought mainly against U-boats, although they did engage in a handful of surface actions, notably the sinking of the powerful German battleship the *Bismarck,* on May 27, 1941. The Royal Navy's darkest day came on December 8, 1941, when the battleship *Prince of Wales* (and its escort, the battle cruiser *Repulse*) was sunk by Japanese aircraft. This forced even the most conservative admirals to admit that a battleship without the support of an aircraft carrier could not defend itself against serious air attacks.

No nation invested more in battleships than Japan, which not only built a large number of them but also had two super-battleships, *Yamato* and *Musashi,* which were in a class of their own. These enormous vessels displaced 64,000 tons, compared to 46,000 for the *Iowa,* and mounted nine 18.1-inch guns, making them far and away the biggest and most powerful surface ships in the world. Nonetheless, even these behemoths were no match for U.S. naval aviators. The *Musashi* was sunk on October 24, 1944, during the Battle of Leyte Gulf, the *Yamato* on April 7, 1945, while making a suicide run for Okinawa.

FURTHER READING

Dulin, Robert O. *Battleships: United States Battleships in World War II.* Annapolis, Md.: Naval Institute Press, 1976.

Garzke, William H. *Battleships: Axis and Neutral Battleships in World War II.* Annapolis, Md.: Naval Institute Press, 1985.

Gray, Edwyn. *Hitler's Battleships.* London: L. Cooper, 1992.

Kennedy, Ludovic Henry Coverly. *Pursuit: The Chase and Sinking of the Bismarck.* New York: Viking, 1974.

Yoshida, Mitsura. *Requiem for Battleship Yamato.* Seattle: University of Washington Press, 1985.

Bazookas

The bazooka was a recoilless rocket launcher, aimed and fired by one man; a second man served as loader. It was first used as an antitank weapon in 1942, with some success, but by 1944 the bazooka was all but useless in that role because its small warhead (2.36 inches) could not penetrate the thick armor of Germany's late-model tanks.

The Germans copied and improved the bazooka. Their *panzerschreck* (tank terror) fired a 3.4-inch rocket grenade capable of penetrating 8.25 inches of armor, which was more than enough power to hole any Allied tank. The somewhat smaller and more portable Panzerfaust (tank fist) was almost as effective. The British PIAT (Projector Infantry Anti-Tank) was inferior to the bazooka and, like it, was useful only as an infantry rather than antitank weapon. Allied troops used captured Panzerfausts whenever they could in preference to their own inferior weapons.

Berlin, bombing of

Air Marshal Sir Arthur Harris, who headed the Royal Air Force's Bomber Command, was obsessed with Berlin, so much so that on November 3, 1943, he wrote to Prime Minister Winston Churchill as follows: "We can wreck Berlin from end to end if the USAAF will come in on it. It will cost between 400–500 aircraft. It will cost Germany the war."

This statement was ridiculous on several counts. For one, U.S. air generals at this stage of the war were dead set against area bombing (indiscriminate attacks on entire cities). And even if they had wanted to cooperate with Harris, the U.S. Eighth Air Force was reeling from terrible losses in August and October that had, in effect, forced it to give up bombing German cities until it could be supplied with long-range fighter escorts. What's more, even if it had had more bombers and fighters, daylight attacks on one of the most heavily defended cities in Europe would have been very costly, a fact that was proven the following March when the Eighth Air Force did attack Berlin—with a powerful fighter escort—but still suffered heavy losses. Further, the small bomb-load capacity of U.S. heavy bombers, which had been designed for precise attacks on industrial sites rather than entire cities, meant that they would contribute relatively little to the destruction of a great urban area like Berlin.

It is a mystery why Harris, or anyone else, believed that leveling the capital of Germany would cause the Nazi government to surrender, since the great bulk of Germany's industrial might would remain untouched. It says much about the general pointlessness of the Allied bombing offensives that Harris was allowed to act on this ill-conceived campaign anyway. What Harris called the Battle of Berlin started on August 23, 1943, and ended in the spring of 1944, when Bomber Command was forced to concentrate on D-Day targets.

The Battle of Berlin ended in failure for the Allies; the German capital continued to function, even though the Eighth Air Force staged daylight attacks on Berlin during the last days of the war. Harris lost 492 bombers during this campaign, the United States fewer because of its later start. Nothing much was learned from this defeat, because the Allies were by now so committed to

the air war that second thoughts could not be permitted.

SEE ALSO
Royal Air Force; Strategic bombing; United States Army Air Forces

FURTHER READING
Cooper, Alan W. *Bombers over Berlin: The RAF Offensive, November 1943–March 1944.* Wellingborough: P. Stephens, 1989.
Hastings, Max. *Bomber Command.* New York: Dial, 1979.
Hawkins, Ian L., ed. *Courage*Honor*Victory, B-17s Over Berlin: Personal Stories from the 95th Bomb Group.* Washington, D.C.: Brassey's, 1995.
Middlebrook, Martin. *The Berlin Raids: R.A.F. Bomber Command Winter, 1943–44.* New York: Viking, 1988.

Berlin, fall of

Winston Churchill and Joseph Stalin both regarded Berlin as a highly valuable prize that would give whichever nation captured it great prestige and a degree of political benefit as well. For this reason Churchill put heavy pressure on General Dwight D. Eisenhower, commander in chief of Allied forces, to take Berlin before the Soviets could. It is not clear whether

Two Russian officers salute a photographer of the American Signal Corps in Berlin after its capture.

this would have been possible, since by late April 1945, the Red Army was closer to Berlin than the U.S. forces were.

In any case, Eisenhower decided not to try, believing that Berlin had little military value and that the prestige gained would not be worth the lives that would be lost storming the German capital. That left the way open for the Soviets, who surrounded Berlin on April 25. Hitler killed himself on April 30, and the city surrendered on May 2.

Eisenhower's decision was much criticized, then and later, but the Soviets did not gain any benefits they would not have gotten anyway under the terms of the Yalta agreement in February 1945 that divided up postwar Germany. The Soviets are believed to have suffered 100,000 casualties taking Berlin, more than the United States sustained in the Battle of the Bulge, the biggest engagement ever fought by the U.S. Army. It was Soviet practice to squander lives for the flimsiest of reasons, but that was not Eisenhower's way, and thousands of GIs therefore owed their lives to him.

SEE ALSO

Germany, surrender of; Yalta conference

FURTHER READING

Ambrose, Stephen E. *Eisenhower and Berlin, 1945: The Decision to Halt at the Elbe.* New York: Norton, 1967.
Brett-Smith, Richard. *Berlin '45: The Grey City.* London: Macmillan, 1966.
Parrish, Thomas. *Berlin in the Balance, 1945–1949: The Blockade, the Airlift, the First Major Battle of the Cold War.* Reading, Mass.: Addison-Wesley, 1998.
Read, Anthony. *The Fall of Berlin.* London: Hutchinson, 1992.
Studnitz, Hans-Georg von. *While Berlin Burns: The Diary of Hans-Georg von Studnitz, 1943–1945.* Englewood Cliffs, N.J.: Prentice-Hall, 1965.

Blacks

SEE African Americans

Blitzkrieg

Germany's attacks on Poland in 1939 and the Allies in 1940, spearheaded by fast-moving panzer (armored) divisions supported by light and medium bombers, were called blitzkriegs (lightning wars), because of the German Army's speed and power. These wars were also like lightning in being violent and brief.

After the invasion of Greece in 1941, there were no more blitzkriegs. Operation Barbarossa, the German invasion of the Soviet Union in 1941, began with blitzkrieg-style victories, but unlike France and Poland, the Soviet Union could not be made to surrender. Although Germany would launch major armored assaults in 1942, 1943, and as late as December 1944, the blitzkrieg era was over.

Russia could trade land for time for as long as it took to create additional powerful armies, which meant that Germany's armored attacks could no longer be decisive. Once Germany was forced to retreat in Russia, Africa, and France, the fast, light tanks of the blitzkrieg years were increasingly replaced by heavily armored models. These were extremely useful for defensive purposes but too slow for the rapid maneuvers that blitzkriegs required.

SEE ALSO

France, fall of; Soviet Union (USSR)

FURTHER READING

Delaney, John. *The Blitzkrieg Campaigns: Germany's 'Lightning War' Strategy in Action.* London: Arms and Armour, 1996.
Wernick, Robert, and the editors of Time-Life Books. *Blitzkrieg.* New York: Time-Life Books, 1976.

Bombers

Three types of bombers were used by the great powers—heavy, medium, and light (also called dive-bombers and, later, fighter-bombers). Only Britain and the United States employed four-engine heavy bombers, mainly in costly offensives against Germany and Japan. They were also used in the Atlantic against German U-boats, and the United States used them against Japanese targets in the Southwest Pacific.

"Heavies" operated at high altitudes (above 20,000 feet) and carried the largest bombloads. In Europe the B-17 Flying Fortress was the premier U.S. heavy bomber, although the more vulnerable B-24 Liberator was used extensively as well. On long missions both typically carried bombloads of 4,000 pounds. Britain's best heavy, the Lancaster, was less well armed and armored and could carry a bombload in excess of 10,000 pounds. The greatest heavy of the war was the Boeing B-29 Superfortress. It was used exclusively against Japan, could operate above 30,000 feet, and was notable for its long range and large bombload.

Two-engine medium bombers were employed by all the great powers. Because they operated at 10,000 to 15,000 feet, they were more accurate and versatile than heavy bombers. Typically they bombed behind enemy lines,

This B-25 takes off from the deck of the USS Hornet to take part in the first U.S. air raid on Japan.

striking at supply dumps, headquarters, and other facilities. The best German medium was the Junkers 88, which could serve as a dive-bomber in addition to making level attacks. The United States's best medium was the B-25 Mitchell, which in the Pacific was sometimes equipped with up to eight 50-caliber machine guns mounted in the nose. This made it a formidable gunship able to destroy both ground targets and small vessels.

In the Pacific both the U.S. and Japanese navies employed dive and torpedo bombers throughout the war. Because of torpedo defects the U.S. Navy relied mainly on dive-bombers, while the Japanese, who had a superb torpedo, made very good use of it. In Europe Allied fighter-bombers attacked all kinds of targets with great success and were especially useful in support of ground troops.

The leading U.S. fighter-bomber was the P-47 Thunderbolt, which carried a large and varied arsenal of weapons. The British Typhoon was a great tank-killer and the first fighter-bomber to be armed with air-to-ground rockets. The Soviets made extensive use of fighter-bombers as well. The famous German Stuka dive-bomber, already obsolete when the war broke out in September 1939, was useful only against nations with weak air defenses. When they were employed in the Battle of Britain, so many were destroyed that the Stuka had to be grounded. Neither Germany nor Japan used fighter-bombers to the same degree as the Allies, partly because they favored medium bombers and partly because by 1943 they had lost control of the air over most battlefields.

SEE ALSO
Atomic bombs; Strategic bombing

Bourke-White, Margaret

PHOTOJOURNALIST

- *Born: June 14, 1906, New York, N.Y.*
- *Education: Columbia University, University of Michigan, Cornell University, 1927*
- *Died: August 27, 1971, Stamford, Conn.*

A pioneer photojournalist, Margaret Bourke-White was best known before the war as a photographer of industry. The first issue of *Fortune* magazine in 1929 featured her pictures. In 1930 she became the first foreign photographer allowed to shoot pictures of Soviet industry and social conditions. In 1936 she was one of the first staff photographers to be hired by *Life* magazine. She also collaborated with her husband, the writer Erskine Caldwell, on several documentary books.

Bourke-White's reputation soared during the war when she toured the battlefronts for *Life*. She was the first woman to be accredited as a photographer by the U.S. Army Air Forces and the first to fly a combat mission. She became one of the best, and best known, of the war's great photojournalists. And unlike most of her male colleagues, she made a point of covering women's contributions to the war as well as combat operations. She recorded, for example, the experiences of female nurses and WACs (Women's Army Corps) when the troopship they were on was torpedoed on its way to Africa. She was among the first Western journalists to cover the liberation of the Nazi death camps, which resulted in her powerful book *Dear Fatherland, Rest Quietly* (1946).

SEE ALSO
Women

FURTHER READING
Ayer, Eleanor H. *Margaret Bourke-White: Photographing the World*. New York: Maxwell/Macmillan, 1992.
Bourke-White, Margaret. *The Photographs of Margaret Bourke-White*. Sean Callahan, ed. Greenwich, Conn.: New York Graphic Society, 1972.
Bourke-White, Margaret. *Portrait of Myself*. New York: Simon & Schuster, 1963.
Daffron, Carolyn. *Margaret Bourke-White*. New York: Chelsea House, 1992.
Goldberg, Vicki. *Margaret Bourke-White: A Biography*. New York: Harper & Row, 1986.
Keller, Emily. *Margaret Bourke-White: A Photographer's Life*. Minneapolis: Lerner, 1996.
Silverman, Jonathan. *For the World to See: The Life of Margaret Bourke-White*. New York: Viking Press, 1983.

Bradley, Omar N.

COMMANDER OF U.S. 12TH ARMY GROUP

- *Born: February 12, 1893, Clark, Mo.*
- *Education: West Point, 1911–15*
- *Military Service: U.S. Army—second lieutenant, 1915; first lieutenant, 1916; captain, 1918; major 1924; lieutenant colonel, 1936; brigadier general, 1941; major general, 1941; commander of II Corps, 1943; commander of U.S. First Army, 1943; commander 12th U.S. Army Group, 1944–45, lieutenant general, 1944; general, 1945; five-star general of the army, 1950*
- *Died: April 8, 1981, New York, N.Y.*

A capable and soft-spoken man, Omar N. Bradley had the confidence and trust of his superiors, which is why he rose so high in the Army. After Bradley had commanded two divisions in training, Chief of Staff General George C. Marshall sent him to North Africa in 1942 as a troubleshooter for Lieutenant General Dwight D. Eisenhower, who was the Allied supreme commander in the Mediterranean. Bradley was assistant commander of the II Corps under Lieutenant General George C. Patton in Africa, and then served as its commander in Africa and Sicily.

Although not the most brilliant of soldiers, Bradley was reliable and diplomatic. Patton was more gifted, but he did not always control his temper and disliked the British intensely. Therefore, when General Eisenhower left the Mediterranean to become supreme commander in Europe, he chose Bradley to be First Army commander instead of Patton; this was because the job meant planning and working closely with the British, especially the very difficult General Sir Bernard Law Montgomery.

On D-Day, June 6, 1944, Bradley commanded America's soldiers in France as head of First Army, while Montgomery was the overall commander of Allied ground forces. On August 1 the 12th Army Group became operational and Bradley assumed command, the First Army going to Lieutenant General Courtnay Hodges. On September 1 Eisenhower moved his headquarters to France and took direct control of the ground war. Montgomery ceased being Allied ground commander, while retaining his 21st Army Group. "Brad" and "Monty," as everyone called them, were now equals, both reporting to Eisenhower.

Bradley's group would eventually include 4 armies—the First, Third, Ninth, and Fifteenth (which arrived late and saw little action)—and number between 1.2 and 1.3 million men. It was the largest field command ever held by a U.S. general.

After D-Day the Allies bogged down in Normandy, whose hedgerows (high earthen walls around farm fields held together by the roots of bushes and trees) were powerful natural defenses, which the Germans used well. Gradually, the Americans learned how to fight in the hedgerows, but the going was slow and the costs heavy. In order to achieve a breakthrough Bradley drew up plans for Operation Cobra. This attack in the south of Normandy would begin with a huge saturation bombing attack on the German lines. After delays and a false start, it took place on July 26. The Germans held out for a few days longer against repeated ground attacks, but by the 28th their lines were crumbling.

Bradley then unleashed Patton's Third Army, and the breakthrough turned into a breakout, with two of Patton's corps racing east, then north. Most of the Germans in France were now in danger of being caught between British and U.S. forces in the Falaise "pocket." Two of Montgomery's divisions, which were to close the pocket, moved out slowly. Patton wanted to close the Falaise pocket himself, but Bradley would not hear of it. As a result most of the Germans got away, although some 50,000 were still in the pocket when it finally shut.

This was Bradley's most criticized decision. If Patton had been allowed to proceed, most of the Germans in France might have been taken. Nothing would have stood between the Allies and a sweep into Germany, for its West Wall (a line of frontier fortifications) was in need of repair and weakly held.

Bradley restrained Patton because he thought that the Third Army was overextended and its lead elements would be crushed by the retreating Germans. That may have been so, but had Patton failed to close the gap, at worst a division or two might have been lost. If he had succeeded, the war in the West would have been practically over. In hindsight, it appears to have been a risk worth taking.

All the same, the breakout was, on its own terms, a triumph. The Germans

were driven from most of France and much of Belgium. The River Seine was easily crossed and Paris liberated.

On September 4 the British took the great Belgian port of Antwerp intact. This should have solved what were becoming very serious Allied supply problems, as everything was still coming in over the beaches of Normandy and being trucked for longer and longer distances as the armies advanced. However, British delay enabled German troops to fortify their side of the Scheldt Estuary, a 60-mile-long waterway that linked Antwerp to the North Sea. It took Canadian troops months to clear the Scheldt, seriously handicapping Allied operations. Further, the retreating Germans had dug in and rebuilt the West Wall, so the war of movement was over, and it was back to wearing the enemy down again.

By December 1944 the Germans had cut Bradley's headquarters in Luxembourg off from his First and Ninth armies, which came temporarily under British command. In January he regained the First Army, but the Ninth Army stayed with Montgomery to beef up his 21st Army Group, which was much smaller than Bradley's and not getting any reinforcements. The Americans were having manpower problems too, but a few more divisions were still on their way to the front. And infantry replacements were found by taking men from antiaircraft units and from non-combat jobs behind the lines. Bradley would not have all the men he wanted, but he would have enough.

In February the Allied combined chiefs of staff agreed to Eisenhower's plan for final victory. Montgomery's 21st Army Group was supposed to be the main assault force, driving across the Rhine and the north German plain toward Berlin. The U.S. 6th Army Group—which consisted of the U.S. Sev-

Omar Bradley discusses strategy with General Dwight Eisenhower.

enth Army and the French First Army—and Bradley's 12th Army Group would play supporting roles by making local attacks in their areas.

All this changed on March 7, when units of the First Army seized an intact bridge at Remagen on the Rhine. Eisenhower allowed Bradley to expand his bridgehead on the east bank of the Rhine, and on March 22 Patton's Third Army crossed the Rhine also, giving Bradley two solid bases from which to expand. Montgomery crossed on the 24th as planned, but Bradley's forces were moving so much faster that Eisenhower changed his plans.

When the First and Ninth armies met on April 1, the German Army Group B in the Ruhr was surrounded. On April 4 the Ninth Army rejoined the 12th Army Group and Bradley was given the job of ending German resistance in the west. Montgomery's 21st Army Group, now much smaller, would guard his northern flank, with 6th Army Group doing the same to his south. The race for glory would be won by the Americans rather than the British.

Bradley formed his three armies along a 140-mile front running north to south. By April 7 nearly all his forces were in motion. The Ninth Army reached its stop line, the Elbe River, on April 11, having traveled 226 miles in 19 days. The First Army linked up with the Soviets, who were advancing from the east, on April 25. Patton's Third Army reached the former Czechoslovakia at the beginning of May, stopping to wait for the Soviets, who would occupy the reborn state after the war. In the north, Montgomery moved forward with his usual caution.

Seeing that all the German fronts were collapsing and Berlin was under attack by the Soviets, Hitler killed himself on April 30. On May 7 the Germans formally surrendered to Eisenhower in Reims, France.

These were Bradley's salad days, which would in time bring him a fifth star, making him equal in rank to Eisenhower and other senior commanders. As head of the largest army group in the West, he certainly deserved this honor. Although some historians have been critical of Bradley for being overly conservative, his style meshed well with Eisenhower's broad front strategy.

Bradley remained in the Army after World War II, becoming chief of staff in 1948 and chief of the Joint Chiefs of Staff in 1949. He held this position throughout the Korean War (1950–53), and in its final months served again under Eisenhower, who had been elected President. He retired from military service after a truce agreement with China and North Korea was signed in the summer of 1953.

Britain

In 1940 Britain had a population of 48 million. It was one of the world's great powers, a leading industrial state, and possessed a vast empire that spanned the globe and occupied about one-fourth of it. Although the army was relatively small, the Royal Navy was the largest in the world, as was the British merchant fleet. In Europe the Royal Air Force took second place only to the German Luft-waffe. Together with those of France, which was also a wealthy industrial state with a huge land army and a modern fleet, these assets gave the Allies superior-ity over the Wehrmacht (Germany's com-bined military forces) on paper.

But, although it was superior to the German armed forces in sheer numbers, the Allies did not have the advantage in quality, as was demonstrated when Ger-many attacked to the west in May 1940. By the end of June it had conquered France and driven Britain out of Europe. The British Army survived and returned home, thanks to the "miracle of Dunkirk" in which civilian vessels joined the military to save many British troops beached on the French coast. But the Army arrived in England minus its vehicles and heavy weapons.

Britain now found itself alone fac-ing a triumphant Third Reich that pos-sessed or controlled almost the entire continent of Europe. Little wonder some in Britain believed that with all hope of defeating Hitler apparently lost, the time had come to make peace. Hitler, prepared to deal, proposed that in return for peace he would allow Britain to retain its independence and its empire. Britain would still rule the waves, while he would continue to rule Europe.

Britain alone Thanks to inspired leadership by Winston Churchill, Britain's new prime minister, and their native stubbornness, the British stood firm and saved their island from inva-sion by winning the Battle of Britain. The Royal Air Force (RAF) prevented German troops from landing, but if it had failed, the invaders would not have been met by the British Army alone. A "Home Army" of poorly armed overage men, mostly veterans of World War I, was mobilized as well. As there was no invasion, they served the rest of the war in capacities where combat-ready sol-diers were not required. Even so, the willingness of aging and unprepared men to fight was a measure of Britain's

These English policemen escort a mother and her chil-dren from an area where an unexploded German bomb waits to be defused.

This photograph of a London railway station captures the British mobilization effort. As troops arrive for training and defense, children hurry to a reception room where they await evacuation from the capital.

spirit in the dangerous summer of 1940.

At this stage of the war, everything was at stake, not just for Britain but for democracy—even for the United States, although many Americans refused to admit this. Had Britain fallen, there would have been no D-Day—in 1944, or ever—for the United States could not have liberated Europe alone. Without Britain, the United States would have been the only surviving democratic great power in a world dominated by police states.

Could the United States have survived in such a world? Would it have been able to remain democratic? These are questions that have never had to be answered, because the RAF and the British people won out in what Churchill would rightly call their "finest hour."

It remained true in 1940, however, that while Hitler had lost the battle, he still seemed to have won the war. Britain therefore adopted the only possible course of action, a strategy announced in plain words by Churchill. It would, he declared, hang on by the skin of its teeth and keep fighting Germany as best it could until the United States entered the war. Churchill knew that sooner or later the United States would have to

fight, for it would only be a matter of time before an all-powerful Germany threatened U.S. interests and even its national security. As no one could say how long this would take, the British soldiered on and did their best. It would prove to be more than enough.

Mobilization for war Britain was the most fully and efficiently mobilized of all the great warring powers. It mobilized so well because it had to, of course, but except for the United States, all the other great powers would eventually find themselves in similarly desperate positions. None would match Britain's achievement. Britain's success was based partly on the relative speed but also on the thoroughness with which it mobilized its resources—especially its womanpower.

Every nation drafted men and, except for the United States again, most controlled the male labor force as well. But only the British actually conscripted women. Single females between 19 and 30 years old were drafted and given a choice between serving in uniform or working in a war industry. In practice Britain mobilized every woman younger than 40, except those with large family responsibilities or ones who had to care for war workers assigned to their homes.

Women labored in the fields and did every sort of industrial job, however dangerous or dirty, except coal mining, a male area that few, if any, women cared to enter.

The result was that although 22 percent of the country's workforce, male and female, served in the armed forces, an even larger group, 33 percent, labored in war industries. This enabled production to reach amazing heights. Aircraft production rose from 3,000 machines built in 1938 to 15,000 by January 1940. During the next two years, 30,000 aircraft were built, and by March 1944, another 60,000 had gone into service. This was an incredible production feat that equaled, and may even have exceeded, Germany's effort. Between 1939 and early 1944, when Britain was building 105,000 planes, Germany turned out about 118,000 aircraft; however, only a handful of Germany's planes were four-engined, as opposed to thousands of Britain's.

Because it was an island nation, Britain built a huge number of ships. This was an area in which Germany could not compete, because the British destroyed most of its small surface fleet and swept German merchant ships from the seas as well. Britain, on the other hand, was building major warships at the rate of more than 100 a year by 1942, and merchant shipping was well in excess of 1 million tons annually. Because Britain had the smallest population of any great power and had to import every raw material it needed except coal, this was a stunning achievement.

In World War II, Britain introduced rationing at once, remembering its experience in World War I when it waited too long to start conserving. Gasoline was rationed in September 1939; meat, butter, and sugar early in 1940; clothing in 1941. By 1942, when the U-boats had made the shortages most acute, an adult was allowed about one pound of meat a week, four ounces of bacon and ham, eight of sugar, and eight of cheese. During an eight-week span, a consumer could have a packet of dried eggs, equal in theory (though not in taste) to a dozen real ones. This rationing was far more strict than that practiced in the United States, but it was widely accepted as fair.

Food rationing did not really take hold in the United States until March 1943, and there was actually a meat surplus that year because beef and pork production rose while rationing cut into sales. Victory gardens, not possible in crowded England, produced huge quantities of fresh vegetables. At various times coffee, sugar, whiskey, cigarettes, and other goods were in short supply. But gasoline rationing ended on August 15, 1945, and most other forms ended soon after. For Britons rationing continued well into peacetime.

Surprisingly, the nation as a whole ate better under rationing than it had before the war. In the 1930s high unemployment and low wages during the worldwide Depression had combined to leave many working-class families short of food. But under rationing, and with real wages rising because of the labor shortage, workers could buy more expensive foods and often ate in factory lunchrooms where food was wholesome and plentiful. Cheap new restaurants also sprang up in which food was "off the ration." Because of better nutrition, civilian death rates in Britain actually declined during the war.

British taxation, though heavy, was fair also. Britain financed 55 percent of its war effort through income rather than borrowing, which was the highest rate in the world. (Even the United States paid only 45 percent of its war costs through tax revenue.) The basic income tax rate, which had been 50 percent, rose to 95 percent for the wealthy. This program brought the rich and the poor closer together, because while wages rose during the war, unearned income—money gained from stocks, bonds, and the like—declined.

Life in wartime Unlike the United States, which found the war to be within its means, Britain could not afford to fight on the scale that was required. British economic recovery from the war would be long and slow as a result, a measure of what the nation sacrificed for the Allied cause.

Housing in Britain during the war was in short supply because of heavy German bombing and because workers moved into industrial areas with inadequate housing stocks. Some idea of the resulting chaos may be gained from the fact that a civilian population of 38 million registered 60 million changes of address between 1939 and 1945. By 1942 some 300,000 families were living in buildings that by prewar standards would have been seen as unfit for use. In that year two and a half million families lived in bomb-damaged quarters that had been hastily repaired. By the war's end perhaps another million families found themselves in the same boat.

Violent crime decreased in both Britain and the United States, although juvenile delinquency rose. There were fewer suicides. In both countries the birth rate, at an all-time low in the 1930s, began to rise. Many of these additional babies were illegitimate, traditional morals giving way to the pressures and excitement of wartime.

After the war, as also in the United States, there was a rush to marry and start families. Britons had an additional reason for their baby boom, though, one not felt in the United States. Some 60,000 civilians died as a result of bombing attacks, compared to about 260,000 men in uniform who lost their lives during the war.

British morale ebbed and flowed. It

was probably highest in 1940 and 1941 when the German blitz of London and other areas brought out the best in people, as crisis often does. It may have been lowest in 1944, when to war weariness was added the strain of a new German bombing attack featuring V-1 "buzz bombs" and V-2 rockets. These killed fewer civilians than had died during the blitz but were in some respects more frightening. The buzz bomb had wings and was powered by a small jet engine. As long as you could hear the bomb you were safe. But when the engine cut out, the bomb began to fall, so that an eerie silence would precede the impact, followed by a large explosion.

The V-2 rockets went faster than the speed of sound and gave no warning at all, which was also highly frightening, since each breath you drew could be your last—especially if you lived in London, where the majority of these rockets were targeted. Unlike conventional bombing attacks, when air raid warnings provided time to find shelter, V-bomb attacks often caught people in the open, another of their dismal features.

Britons kept up their morale in part not only by shared risks and sacrifices but by government reforms. Unlike in the United States, no general elections were held in Britain for the duration of the

Firefighters engage in war exercises at the Greenwich fire station. Fires erupting during German air blitzes were a serious concern.

war. Thus, the Conservative Parliament elected in 1935 sat for 10 years, instead of the usual maximum of 6. But, although it was dominated in name by Conservatives, Britain was actually run by a coalition government that in 1940 consisted of 15 Conservative ministers, 4 from Labour, and 1 representing the Liberal party. Although Churchill focused on war issues and his party, the Conservatives, did not like social reforms, popular demand forced the government to introduce them while the war was still on.

In 1942 a committee of civil servants issued a paper on social insurance that became known as the Beveridge Report. Its call for a full-scale welfare state met with widespread approval, as 9 out of 10 persons interviewed by the Gallup poll said it should be enacted. This great a response could not be ignored. Therefore, in November 1943 Churchill appointed a minister of reconstruction to plan for the future.

In 1944 a ministry of national insurance was created. The Education Act of that year guaranteed a secondary education for every British youth. Work was also begun on a program for full employment after the war, the payment of family allowances, and the building of a national health service.

The Conservative party itself became a casualty of the public's demand for social insurance. Churchill had wanted the general election delayed until after Japan had been defeated. But the Labour party insisted on holding it after victory was won in Europe. Although Churchill's popularity as a war leader was great, a majority of Britons did not trust the Conservatives to build the welfare state.

On July 26, 1945, while he was at the Potsdam conference in Germany with Soviet Premier Joseph Stalin and U.S. President Harry Truman, Churchill learned that the Conservatives had lost and promptly resigned as prime minister.

To Americans this election seemed to reflect a lack of gratitude for his outstanding leadership. However, the British were looking ahead. They would always respect Churchill, who would have a last turn as prime minister in the 1950s. But they had suffered much during the war and as a reward wanted a better Britain than they thought the Conservatives could provide. To most Britons, World War II was a "people's war," and after it they wanted a people's state that would protect them from cradle to grave.

The great British historian A. J. P. Taylor would later write of the British in 1945 that they were the only people who had gone through both world wars from beginning to end. (He is technically correct: France surrendered to the Germans in 1940, and Germany surrendered to the Allies in May 1945, but the war did not end until that following August.) In doing so they had not lost their best national traits of tolerance, patience, and generosity. Yet, while they remained a civilized people, they had changed. Taylor described the British people as they were in August 1945: "Traditional values lost much of their force. Other values took their place. Imperial greatness was on the way out: the welfare state was on the way in. The British empire declined: the condition of the people improved. Few now sang 'Land of Hope and Glory.' Few even sang 'England Arise.' England had risen all the same."

SEE ALSO

British Army; Churchill, Winston Spencer; France, battle of; France, fall of; Germany; Royal Air Force; Royal Navy

FURTHER READING

Calder, Angus. *The People's War: Britain 1939–45*. London: Jonathan Cape, 1969.
Churchill, Winston. *History of the Second World War*. Boston: Houghton Mifflin, 1948–54.
Taylor, A. J. P. *English History, 1914–1945*. New York: Oxford University Press, 1965.

Britain, Battle of

After France fell to Germany in June 1940 and the British Expeditionary Force had been evacuated from Dunkirk, Hitler had expected that Britain would negotiate a settlement with him. When Britain decided to fight on instead, Hitler ordered an invasion of England, code named Operation Sea Lion. If it was to succeed, Germany had to gain control of the air over the English Channel and the invasion beaches, so on August 15, 1940, the Luftwaffe (German air force) launched an all-out attack on the Royal Air Force (RAF), attacking its airfields, radar sites, headquarters, and the aircraft factories that supplied the RAF. The Luftwaffe came close to driving the RAF out of southeastern England. Unaware of this, and in need of a quick victory before the weather turned bad, on September 7 the Luftwaffe turned to bombing London, thinking that would force RAF fighters into a massive air battle that they would lose. The climax came on September 15, thereafter known as Battle of Britain Day, when Germany threw every plane it had into the air and suffered heavy losses. Two days later Operation Sea Lion was indefinitely postponed. About 2,500 RAF pilots fought the Battle of Britain, leading Winston Churchill to say, "Never in the field of human conflict was so much owed by so many to so few." But, while fighter pilots were the cutting edge, it was the British people as a whole—steadfast in their defiance of Hitler—who provided the sword. It was, as Churchill also said, their finest hour.

SEE ALSO
Britain; Royal Air Force

FURTHER READING
Parkinson, Roger. *Summer 1940: The Battle of Britain*. New York: David McKay, 1977.

The Allied Relief Fund's mobile canteens provided food and drink to London's air raid victims.

British Air Force

SEE   Royal Air Force

British Army

In September 1939 the British Army was divided between the active duty regular armies and a reserve force known as the territorial armies, similar to the U.S. National Guard. All were commanded by the chief of the Imperial General Staff, who also sat on the Chiefs of Staff Committee, which coordinated British military operations and advised the prime minister and his cabinet.

The Home Guard In May 1940, after Germany launched its great offensive on the western front, Britain formed what became known as the Home Guard as a last line of defense. It consisted at first of overaged males who, although they were not called on to fight (except to man antiaircraft batteries), performed useful service as lookouts, guards, and checkpoint and roadblock soldiers. In 1942 the Home Guard trained boys aged 17 and 18 before they were drafted for active duty. At its peak, the Home Guard consisted of 1.75 million men, whose average age was less than 30. In December 1944, the need for it having passed, the Home Guard was dissolved.

The British Army Because a partial draft had been in effect since April 1939, the Army had almost 900,000 men when war broke out in September that year, but many of them were stationed in India and elsewhere throughout Britain's still vast empire. Further, the Army did not as yet have a single armored division, the Royal Armored Corps, which included all armored divi-

sions, having been created only the previous year. At its peak the army would have 2.92 million men and 191,000 women. Its combat forces ultimately consisted of 11 armored divisions, 34 infantry divisions, and 2 airborne divisions. Because the empire had to be guarded and policed, two armored and nine infantry divisions—the equivalent of an entire field army—never saw action. When the Army developed a manpower shortage after D-Day in 1944, these divisions would be sorely missed. The Army suffered 570,000 casualties during the war, of which 144,000 were fatalities.

The British Army, like that of the United States, was organized from the bottom up, by companies forming battalions, battalions making up regiments, regiments joined as divisions, divisions assigned to corps, corps assembled into armies, and two or more armies becoming an army group. Unlike the U.S. Army, however, the British Army, its infantry in particular, was based on the regiment.

Many regiments had hundreds of years of tradition behind them and their own distinctive badges and customs. The individual soldier was encouraged to identify with his regiment. Solidarity was further enhanced by the fact that regiments were locally based and drew their replacements from the immediate geographic area. When casualties were high, regiments had to take what they could get, so men often found themselves assigned to strange regiments. On the whole, however, this was an effective system that did much to strengthen unit cohesion and morale. The drawback, as with the U.S. National Guard, was that when a regiment sustained heavy losses, the town or county where it was based would receive more than its share of suffering.

General Bernard Montgomery leads British troops in the campaign to liberate North Africa.

Like all armies, the British Army did not always make the best use of its resources. It disdained tanks before the war and never developed the doctrine and tactics that would have enabled its armor and infantry to work closely together. A British infantry division had more vehicles than those of any other army, although most of them had only two powered wheels. This put them ahead of the Germans, whose regular infantry divisions depended on horses and oxen for transport, but behind the U.S. Army, nearly all of whose vehicles had four-wheel drive and could go off-road.

Britain relieved its front-line troops more often than the United States did. Some historians feel that Britain in fact took its soldiers out of the line too often for maximum efficiency, but it seems more likely that Britain erred, if at all, on the right side, whereas U.S. troops were relieved only seldom and then briefly.

Another criticism is that the British were not aggressive enough. When the forces were commanded by Bernard Law Montgomery, this was certainly true. But Britain, the weakest of the three great Allied powers, was the only one to fight the war from beginning to end and had good reason to conserve its limited manpower.

SEE ALSO
Britain; Montgomery, Bernard

FURTHER READING
Fraser, David. *And We Shall Shock Them: The British Army in World War II.* London: Hodder & Stoughton, 1983.
War Department, U.S. *The British Army in World War II: A Handbook.* Novato, Calif.: Presidio, 1990.

British Navy

SEE Royal Navy

Bulge, Battle of the

The U.S. Army would meet its supreme test in the Ardennes Forest of Belgium in December and January 1944–45. The Battle of the Bulge—named for the large indentation made in the U.S. Army's line—was the greatest clash on the western front, and the biggest engagement the United States has ever fought, ranging over an area that was roughly 60 miles wide and 30 miles deep. Some 600,000 U.S. soldiers were involved, and they took proportionate casualties: 20,000 killed, 20,000 captured, and 40,000 wounded. Two U.S. infantry divisions were all but wiped out, and 800 tanks were destroyed.

Terrible though these losses may seem, Germany's were worse, totaling perhaps 100,000, or a third of their attacking force. At the Bulge, Hitler used up his manpower reserves, hastening Germany's defeat.

Hitler began planning his final counteroffensive in northwest Europe, aimed at splitting the Allies and recapturing Antwerp, Belgium, in late July 1944. At the time, he had just lost 25 divisions on the eastern front, and the Allies were bursting out of Normandy and had already taken Rome. The 25 Volksgrenadier (People's Army) divisions Hitler raised during the fall consisted largely of teenagers and Hitler youth who were poorly trained but highly motivated. The Germans also assembled ten panzer brigades (larger than a regiment but smaller than a division), each with 40 new tanks, including many enormous Tigers and Panthers, both of which outgunned and outclassed the United States's weakly armed Shermans.

In its final form, the attacking force would consist of three armies amounting to some 300,000 men, 1,900 artillery pieces, and 970 tanks and armored assault guns. In the east these armies would have been swallowed up, but on the smaller western front they might make a difference. Probably they would not, but Hitler had nothing to lose by trying.

The idea was to drive a wedge between the U.S. 12th and British 21st Army groups where their fronts joined in Belgium. SS general Josef "Sepp" Dietrich's Sixth SS Panzer Army was to drive through the Ardennes Forest, cross the Meuse River as the Germans had done in 1940, then wheel north to Antwerp. Supporting it on the left would be the Fifth Panzer Army, while the Seventh Army would hold open the southern shoulder of the bulge against General George Patton's expected counterattack. The Germans counted on bad weather to ground the Allied fighter-bombers, unleashing Germany's armor.

When Germany struck the U.S. forces would have only a cavalry group, one armored division, and four infantry

divisions holding the Ardennes front. Two of the infantry divisions were green and two exhausted from the Battle of the Huertgen Forest, which had cost the U.S. First Army 34,000 casualties. The Germans expected to overrun these raw or worn-out divisions. The Germans hoped to achieve a rout that would cause U.S. morale to collapse, Allied bickering to reach new heights, and the Grand Alliance to fall apart. Whether anyone actually believed this is hard to say. However, because Hitler would not surrender and could not be replaced, the Wehrmacht (consisting of all German ground forces) had to obey orders.

Although the strategy behind this attack was poor, the tactics and logistics to carry it out were up to the usual German standards. Three armies were assembled in the Eifel Mountains of Germany without Allied intelligence's knowledge, a remarkable feat considering that the men and supplies had to brought from as far away as Austria and Denmark.

General Dwight D. Eisenhower, the Allied supreme commander, knew that the Ardennes sector was weak, but he could not reinforce it except at the expense of limited offensives taking place elsewhere.

American infantrymen of the 290th Regiment fight in fresh snow near Amonines, Belgium, in January 1945.

Those offensives were part of his broad-front strategy, which was already being executed with too few troops to provide a margin of safety. On December 16 the entire U.S. reserve consisted of the 82nd and 101st Airborne divisions, both of which were being refitted after suffering heavy losses. Although they would play important roles in the Bulge, a reserve consisting of two undermanned divisions—which even at full strength had only 10,000 men apiece, no armor, and few guns—was close to being no reserve at all.

After a short artillery barrage, the Germans attacked on December 16 along an 85-mile front, taking Allied Supreme Headquarters by surprise. But what should have been easy became terribly difficult, thanks to the undaunted if greatly outnumbered Americans. Most remarkable was the defense put up by the 99th Infantry Division, a new outfit that had seen little action. Like other divisions in the Ardennes, it occupied a stretch of line that ought to have been held by a corps, the next larger unit, which equaled two or even more divisions. Although caught off guard, the men of the 99th fought back furiously, to the point of calling friendly artillery fire down on their own positions.

The 99th was the northernmost division to be attacked. Behind it lay Elsenborn Ridge, high ground covering two critical road junctions without which the Sixth SS Panzer Army could not advance. Though Dietrich did not know it, quite by chance the veteran U.S. 2nd Infantry Division was attacking just above him. As the 99th's situation worsened, Major General Leonard T. Gerow of the V Corps, which was responsible for the northern Ardennes, put the 2nd Division's reserve regiment in front of Elsenborn Ridge.

On December 17, Lieutenant General Courtney H. Hodges of the First Army gave Gerow a free hand. Gerow immediately ordered the 2nd Division to break off its attack and join its 23rd Infantry Regiment at Elsenborn. Hodges ordered up the famed 1st Infantry Division, "the Big Red One," from Aachen, where it too was recuperating. The 2nd disengaged itself from the enemy in an extremely difficult operation that it executed smoothly, evidence of how good the Army had become since coming ashore in France.

Meanwhile, the 99th's battered parts disengaged and passed through the 23rd Infantry to regroup and dig in on Elsenborn Ridge, where the 2nd and 9th divisions would join them. By December 18 Elsenborn was proving its worth. U.S. artillery laid down murderous barrages from the ridge. Protected by fog and darkness, U.S. tanks and guns were lying in wait along narrow roads, striking panzers from the side and rear, where even the Tigers were vulnerable. On the 18th, brute force having failed, Dietrich attempted to bypass Elsenborn, but his attacking force was prevented from reaching the strategic Malmedy Road by elements of the Big Red One, which had arrived just in time.

Together these four divisions, the 2nd and 99th in the center and the 9th and 1st on their flanks, created an unbreakable line by December 20. As a result of their determined stand the German counteroffensive was spoiled after only five days of battle. Dietrich realized this and wanted to settle for limited gains, but Hitler insisted on continuing the attack even though Elsenborn Ridge barred the Sixth Panzer Army from Antwerp. This was sheer stubbornness on his part, as the operation now lacked any strategic purpose.

Most accounts of the fighting turn on the 101st Airborne and its defense of Bastogne, which was indeed remarkable. But the key position in the Battle of the Bulge was Elsenborn Ridge. The holding of it by the 2nd and 99th Infantry divisions, the latter often fighting in small units out of touch with higher command against attackers who outnumbered them five or more to one, was the outstanding achievement of the battle. In the critical early days, these two divisions repelled an entire German corps, the elite First SS Panzers.

At the southern end of the front the Germans were also in trouble. Although Germany's Seventh Army greatly outnumbered the veteran U.S. Fourth Infantry Division, which had taken 6,000 casualties in the Huertgen Forest and was still recovering, the 4th put up a tremendous defense, slowing down the German advance and gaining time for reinforcements to move up. As a result another unbreakable line was established, which forced the Germans to narrow their attack to the central Ardennes, in which there was little room to maneuver.

The Fifth Panzer Army was now playing the part originally assigned to the Sixth. Things were going much better for Germany in the central Ardennes, because of outstanding leadership by Lieutenant General Hasso von Manteuffel. His plan of attack did not rely on brute force but was marked by stealth and speed, with deep-penetration units racing through the U.S. lines without benefit of artillery support. These and other enterprising methods smashed the veteran U.S. 28th Infantry Division and wiped out the 106th, which had just arrived in the Ardennes and was an outfit that had been built from scratch by cannabilizing other units. Further, it was deployed in a position from which it could not retreat. As a result it was cut to pieces. In addition to heavy casualties, at least 7,000 men became prisoners of war (POWs)—the largest number of U.S. POWs ever taken by Germany in a single action.

However, while Manteuffel had effectively destroyed two divisions, it had taken him longer than he could afford. Before the 28th and the 106th went under they fought hard. The time they won enabled Eisenhower to rush support to the pivotal crossroad villages of St. Vith and Bastogne. At St. Vith the 7th Armored Division held up an entire German corps for three days, ruining Manteuffel's schedule and giving the U.S. generals time to gain control of the battle. During this critical period Eisenhower was drawing men and supplies from other sectors of the front and pouring them into the Ardennes. He moved 250,000 men and 50,000 vehicles in the first week, a performance that no other army in history has ever equaled.

Although surrounded, Bastogne remained in U.S. hands, thanks to the 101st Airborne, Combat Command B of the 10th Armored Division, and the crack 705th Tank Destroyer Battalion. With the aid of breaks in the weather that permitted air support and resupply, this mixed force held out until General Patton's relief column could reach it on December 27. That same day, survivors of the 2nd Panzer Division gave themselves up, having almost reached the Meuse before being blocked by the U.S. 2nd Armored Division. That proved to be as far as the Germans would get.

As great as the U.S. victory was, the Battle of the Bulge might have been greater still. Eisenhower had reacted quickly to the German attack, sending the 7th and 10th Armored divisions to Middleton's sector on December 16 despite General Omar Bradley's reservations. Hitler had told his generals that it would take at least two days for Eisenhower to realize the trouble he was in, then two or three more to receive permission from Roosevelt and Churchill to call off his offensives and reinforce the Ardennes. By then he intended that the Germans would be across the Meuse

THE BATTLE OF THE BULGE
November 8, 1942

50 mi

100 km

←	German Armies
→	U.S. corps and divisions
- - - -	front line, Dec. 16th

them to the north at right angles across his own lines of communication.

On December 20, with Bradley separated from his First and Ninth armies by the German penetration, Eisenhower gave temporary command of them to Montgomery, leaving Bradley with only the Third Army under his immediate control. This decision, a result of Bradley's comparative isolation in Luxembourg, was a major mistake by Eisenhower that would have serious consequences. For one, although Ike was eager to begin enveloping the Bulge, Montgomery, as always, dragged his feet. Further, when he did attack, he wanted to push the Bulge back into Germany rather than cut it off. After a meeting on the 28th, Eisenhower believed that he had gotten Montgomery's promise to attack on January 1. But then Eisenhower was informed that Montgomery would not jump off until January 3 or later.

Eisenhower was furious with Montgomery, forcing Freddie De Guingand, Montgomery's chief of staff, to shuttle back and forth between Supreme Headquarters and the 21st Army Group. While the debate was raging over what Montgomery had promised to do, he sent Eisenhower a letter demanding to be put in complete charge of the land battle, which under his direction would feature a single thrust to Berlin—a blatant attempt to take advantage of the crisis and impose his overall strategy upon Eisenhower. Instead, Eisenhower returned the First Army to Bradley with orders to pinch off the Bulge and prepared for a showdown with Monty. Montgomery did advance on January 3, though not as strongly as Eisenhower wanted and not in the right direction. So passed an opportunity to destroy three German armies, a result of Montgomery's obsession with a single-front strategy. Under pressure from both ends,

and on their way to Antwerp. Hitler's mistake was to assume that the Allied commanders were as tightly controlled as his own, and he did not understand that Eisenhower had real authority—even over British troops, although Montgomery did all he could to limit it.

On December 17, Eisenhower sent more men to the Ardennes and put a stop to Allied offensives elsewhere in preparation for his retaliatory strokes. On the 18th, he met with his top commanders and told them to view the Bulge as an opportunity, not a problem. Once the Germans were further extended, he wanted to attack both their flanks and capture the whole force. By the 19th, preparations for this double envelopment were under way and Patton was beginning an intricate process of pulling three divisions out of his front and advancing the Germans withdrew slowly in good order, inflicting maximum damage. The Battle of the Bulge was declared at an end on January 28, though the old lines were not restored until February 7.

SEE ALSO
Eisenhower, Dwight D.; France, Battle of; Montgomery, Bernard Law; Patton, George S., Jr.

FURTHER READING
Ambrose, Stephen A. *Citizen Soldiers.* New York: Simon & Schuster, 1997.
———. *Eisenhower, 1890–1952.* New York: Simon & Schuster, 1983.
Bradley, Omar N., and Clay Blair. *A General's Life: An Autobiography by General of the Army Omar N. Bradley.* New York: Simon & Schuster, 1983.
MacDonald, Charles B. *A Time for Trumpets: The Untold Story of the Battle of the Bulge.* New York: Morrow, 1985.

Burma

A British colony when the Pacific war broke out on December 7, 1941, Burma was invaded by Japanese forces one week later. The Japanese aims were to protect their position in Malaya, to cut the Burma Road, which was the principal supply route to Nationalist China, and to use Burma as a staging area for possible operations against India. After fierce fighting, Britain was driven from Burma in May, its troops making the longest fighting retreat in the history of the British Army. The fight for Burma would be Britain's longest campaign of the war, ending only when the Japanese Empire laid down its arms.

Apart from a desire to avenge its defeat, Britain's objective in fighting so hard and at such length in the terrifying mountains and jungles of Burma was never entirely clear. The strategic impor-

tance of the Burma Road was that without it supplies for China had to be flown in over the dreaded "Hump," a series of high mountain ranges that lay between India and Kunming, China. Because the United States regarded keeping China in the war essential to victory, the loss of Burma forced it to open an air route to China that was extraordinarily expensive and dangerous to maintain, yet could deliver only a fraction of the goods China needed. In January 1945, for example, a total of only 15,000 tons was ferried to China, at a cost to the U.S. Air Transport Command of 36 lives. (This was about equal to the monthly tonnage moved over the Burma Road in 1941, but more than half of it was for American use.) In that same month an alternative route to China, the Ledo Road, was completed, after which the United States, its strategic goal having been met, largely withdrew from Burma.

Although the Allies discussed a variety of more imaginative ways in which Burma might be retaken, in whole or in part, the actual process involved grueling land campaigns supported by air power. The first offensive began in October 1942. It achieved modest gains but ended in a stalemate. A long-range penetration by 3,000 British, Gurkha, and Burmese troops (called Chindits) under the colorful Brigadier Orne Wingate fought behind enemy lines, supplied entirely by air, from February into April of 1943. The raid was highly publicized and did prove that troops could fight in this way, but the losses were so great (almost a third of Wingate's force) and the results so disappointing that it is hard to see why another such raid was authorized.

Nonetheless, in February 1944 the British began flying in another long-range penetration force of 9,000 men. After Wingate was killed in a plane crash in March, in April his force fell into a conventional role, supporting a Chinese offensive under U.S. General Joseph Stilwell. By August, when it was airlifted back to India, the group had sustained 3,600 casualties. A U.S. force, called Merrill's Marauders after its commander, Major-General Frank Merrill, was based on the Chindit model and suffered comparably in support of Stilwell's operations.

In the end the fight for Burma took place by conventional means. North Burma, including the vital town of Myitkyina, was taken by an Allied mixed but mostly Chinese force under Stilwell in 1944. Western, southern, and central Burma fell to Britain's largely Indian Fourteenth Army, commanded by General Sir William Slim, regarded by many as Britain's best field commander, in 1944 and 1945. Portions of eastern Burma remained in Japanese hands until August 28, 1945, when the Burmese garrison surrendered. British and Commonwealth casualties in Burma came to 71,200, Japanese to 106,000. The fighting in Burma was as fierce as anywhere else in the war, the environment equally difficult. As Burma was of little strategic value, most of this effort was misplaced. A limited campaign in the north to seize and hold the territory through which the Ledo Road was to cross was probably all that was needed. Yet even that limited aim might have been too much, because the road was completed so late in the war that it did little to benefit China.

SEE ALSO
Chiang Kai-shek; China; China-Burma-India theater

FURTHER READING
Allen, Louis. *Burma: The Longest War, 1941–1945.* New York: St. Martin's, 1984.
Bidwell, Shelford. *The Chindit War: Stilwell, Wingate, and the Campaign in Burma, 1944.* New York: Macmillan, 1980.

Chan, Won-loy. *Burma, the Untold Story.* Novato, Calif.: Presidio, 1986.
Grounds, Tom. *Some Letters from Burma: The Story of the 25th Dragoons at War.* Tunbridge Wells: Parapress, 1994.

Byrnes, James F.
U.S. SECRETARY OF STATE, 1945–47

- *Born: May 2, 1879, Charleston, S.C.*
- *Political party: Democratic*
- *Education: Parochial school*
- *Government service: House of Representatives (Democrat–S.C.), 1910–24; U.S. Senate (Democrat–S.C.), 1930–41; U.S. Supreme Court justice, 1941–42; director, Office of Economic Stabilization, 1942–43; director, Office of War Mobilization, 1943–45; secretary of state, 1945–47; governor of South Carolina, 1951–55*
- *Died: January 24, 1972, Columbia, S.C.*

Jamess F. Byrnes was a conservative Democrat, an early supporter of Franklin D. Roosevelt for President and a friend of the New Deal during his years in the Senate. An able administrator, he, perhaps more than anyone else, was responsible for imposing order on the chaotic mobilization process and was sometimes referred to by journalists as the "assistant president," a term Roosevelt hated.

As senators, Byrnes and Harry S. Truman had been allies and friends, so much so that in 1944 Byrnes asked Truman to nominate him for Vice President at the 1944 Democratic National Convention. Truman agreed to do so, but when Roosevelt made clear his preference for Truman, Byrnes withdrew, saving Truman considerable embarrassment.

Truman, who placed great weight on friendship, asked Byrnes to serve as secretary of state within hours of taking his oath of office. According to the law at that time, Byrnes, as secretary of state, would have succeeded to the presidency had anything happened to Truman. On the face of it, friendship apart, there did not seem to be any particularly good reason for putting Byrnes, a man without experience in foreign affairs, in charge of the State Department. One theory is that Truman wanted Byrnes, who had been a court reporter in his youth, because he had the only verbatim stenographic record made by any American at Yalta. It was an incomplete record, because Roosevelt, with his usual shrewdness, had allowed Byrnes to sit in on only those discussions that would play well in the United States. As, in effect, Roosevelt's salesman for Yalta, Byrnes did a good enough job to make Truman think he would be highly useful at the State Department.

President Truman gave Byrnes a free hand at first, so he bore considerable responsibility for the Potsdam conference and the subsequent negotiations with Japan that ended World War II. But the strong-willed Byrnes and President Truman soon fell out after the war, and Byrnes secretly resigned in April 1946, although the volume of work still to be done required him to stay on until January 1947. Byrnes was out of his depth as secretary of state and one of Truman's weakest appointments.

SEE ALSO

Japan, surrender of; Truman, Harry S.; Yalta conference

FURTHER READING

Clements, Kendrick A., ed. *James F. Byrnes and the Origins of the Cold War.* Durham, N.C.: Carolina Academic Press, 1982.
Messer, Robert L. *The End of an Alliance: Byrnes, Roosevelt, Truman, and the Origins of the Cold War.* Chapel Hill: University of North Carolina Press, 1982.
Robertson, David. *Sly and Able: A Political Biography of James F. Byrnes.* New York: Norton, 1994.

Ward, Patricia Dawson. *The Threat of Peace: James F. Byrnes and the Council of Foreign Ministers, 1945–1946.* Kent, Ohio: Kent State University Press, 1979.

Canada

By the time of World War II, Canada had long been a colony of Britain and then a self-governing dominion of the British Commonwealth. In 1931 Britain's Parliament enacted the Statute of Westminster, which gave Canada and the other dominions control of their foreign policies as well as domestic affairs. This meant that Canada was not obliged to follow Britain's lead in declaring war upon Germany, but it did so anyway. On September 9, 1939, Canada's government, reflecting the views of its English-speaking population, asked King George VI to issue a declaration of war on its behalf. On September 10, a week after Britain, Canada was at war.

Although geographically one of the largest countries in the world, Canada then had a population of only 11.5 million, most of it concentrated within 60 miles of the U.S. border. A third of the population was of French descent and lived primarily in the province of Quebec. Because Francophones, as French-speaking Canadians are called, had resented being drafted in World War I, Prime Minister Mackenzie King promised that draftees would not be sent abroad without their consent. Those who refused service overseas—not all of them French Canadians—were deeply resented by the volunteers serving in fighting units, who called them "zombies." Riots at home against conscription by these so-called zombies were deeply resented at the front. Despite resistance to the war at home and a

Canadian soldiers, driving hard toward the Rhine and the defeat of Germany, take a break from their duties for mail call.

leisurely initial approach to mobilization, Canada threw itself into war work after the fall of France in June 1940.

Even though it had relatively few workers compared to the United States, Canada was amazingly productive. It had not built a single merchant ship before the war, but ultimately constructed 345. And, in addition to thousands of aircraft, Canada manufactured 707,000 military cars and trucks and 45,710 armored vehicles. All this was achieved by a mere 1.2 million workers. A large majority of the weapons and equipment Canada produced, some 70 percent, was used not by Canadian forces but given to its allies, Britain in particular. This program, called Canadian Mutual Aid, was similar to the United States's Lend-Lease, except that Canada devoted a larger share of its budget to aiding its allies than the United States did.

Before the war Canada was virtually unarmed. The Royal Canadian Navy (RCN) had fewer than 2,000 men on active duty and 10 small warships, while the Army consisted of 4,260 officers and men, a few trucks, and 2 light tanks. The Royal Canadian Air Force's strength amounted to slightly more than 3,000

men operating 37 usable aircraft. Yet, by war's end, more than 1 million men and women had served in the Canadian armed forces, of whom 42,000 were killed, 54,000 wounded, and 9,000 taken prisoner. This high casualty rate resulted from the deployment of Canadian troops on some of the most dangerous battlefields in Italy—where a quarter, an enormous percentage—of the 93,000 Canadian troops became casualties, and on the western front.

After D-Day (June 6, 1944), the First Canadian Army took so many casualties that Prime Minister King was forced to break his promise that he would not send draftees to Europe against their will. But this decision was fiercely resisted and few conscripts were forcibly sent to Europe. More than in other Allied countries, therefore, the burden of combat was born by a relatively small proportion of eligible males.

Canada's efforts at sea and in the air were especially important to the Allied war effort. Although the Royal Canadian Navy started with only 4 modern destroyers, it would have 365 ships by 1945, including 2 heavy cruisers and 2 aircraft carriers, and would be the third largest Allied navy. Convoying merchant ships along the vital North Atlantic lifeline, where it sank 33 U-boats, was probably the RCN's most important job, but it was also active in the English Channel and, to a much smaller extent, in the Pacific. Twenty-four Canadian warships were lost during the war.

Perhaps the greatest contribution made to the air war by Canada was the British Empire Air Training Scheme. At Britain's request Canada agreed in December 1939 to establish a large aircrew training program. The plan was for Canada to provide the facilities and training for British and other dominion air crews as well as for its own, who would be in a minority. Originally Canada promised to turn out 20,000 pilots and 30,000 other specialists and to provide more than half of the $607 million it was believed the plan would cost. This was a great deal to ask of a small population and its tiny air force, but Canada succeeded beyond all expectations. In the end, Canada graduated 168,600 flying personnel, of whom more than 75,000 were pilots. Moreover, it paid almost three-quarters of the total cost of $2.2 billion, a remarkable feat. Commonwealth fliers were trained in Australia, New Zealand, South Africa, and Rhodesia, too, but the majority were produced by Canada.

In addition, Canada was an important participant in the Royal Air Force (RAF) Bomber Command's war on German cities. Its first bomber squadron was made up Canadians who had served in the RAF. But ultimately the Royal Canadian Air Force (RCAF) sent 94,000 men and 48 squadrons of aircraft overseas. One-eighth of all the bombs dropped by Bomber Command fell from Canadian planes. Counting accidents, 17,000 members of the RCAF were killed during the war, which equaled the Canadian army's losses in

the European theater. For Canada, more than any other nation, the theory that making war by air would be cheaper in lives than fighting on the ground proved to be an illusion.

In many ways the Canadian war effort resembled the U.S. experience. Inflation was brought under control, and the combination of full employment and relatively high wages meant a rising standard of living during the war with continued prosperity after it. Unlike the United States, however, where domestic policy was conservative during the war, Canada's moved leftward. In September 1943 its Liberal party government announced that it would create a welfare state. Partly this was intended, through heavy government spending, to prevent a recession after the war. In part this change was forced on the Liberal party by the two opposition factions, both of which had been advocating social welfare measures with considerable success. Although the idea of the welfare state would continue to be despised in the United States, Canada proceeded to pay monthly family allowances to mothers for every child and spend very large sums for housing while the war was still on.

Before the war, although diplomatic and economic relations with the United States were close, Canada had tried to keep its mighty southern neighbor at arm's length. But the war changed that. A Joint Canadian–U.S. Defense Board was established in 1940, more than a year before U.S. entry into the war. After Pearl Harbor was attacked in December 1941, the U.S. and Canadian economies became tightly integrated, and their military activities, especially in the U-boat war, were closely linked. Canada provided more support for the atomic bomb project than any other country except Britain.

Inevitably, as the United States and Canada grew closer together, Canada and Britain drew further apart. After the war, Canada and the United States would become each other's closest friends and biggest trading partners. The United States could not have asked for, or dreamed of, a better neighbor and ally.

SEE ALSO

Atlantic, Battle of; France, Battle of; Italian campaigns; Lend-Lease; Strategic bombing; Royal Air Force

FURTHER READING

Barris, Theodore. *Days of Victory: Canadians Remember, 1939–1945*. Toronto: Macmillan Canada, 1995.

Douglas, William A. B. *Out of the Shadows: Canada in the Second World War*. New York: Oxford University Press, 1977.

Granatstein, J. L., and Peter Neary, eds. *The Good Fight: Canadians and World War II*. Toronto: Copp Clark, 1995.

Kirkconnell, Watson. *Canada, Europe, and Hitler*. London: Oxford University Press, 1940.

Minns, John A., ed. *The Cinderella Army: Canada's First Army in Europe, 1944*. Barrie, Ont.: RAM Press, 1993.

Morton, Desmond. *Canada and War: A Military and Political History*. Toronto: Butterworths, 1981.

Carriers

SEE Aircraft carriers

Casablanca conference

President Franklin D. Roosevelt and Prime Minister Winston Churchill met at Casablanca, Morocco, from January 14 to January 24, 1943. This conference, code-named Symbol, resulted in several important decisions. It was decided there to give the highest priority to the Battle of the Atlantic, which the Allies were losing at the time. Britain and the United States agreed that the U.S. Army Air Force would bomb targets on the European continent by day while the RAF's Bomber Command would continue its nighttime area-bombing (indiscriminate air attacks on German cities). Under Operation Pointblank, as this program was called, the United States would conduct its own air war instead of joining forces with Bomber Command, as Churchill and the British had hoped.

Roosevelt announced at the conference that the Allies would accept nothing less than the unconditional surrender of the Axis powers. This would prove to be a controversial decision that, critics argued, lengthened the war. The French generals Charles de Gaulle and Henri Giraud were forced, despite being political antagonists, to join forces in what became the French National Committee for Liberation. The Combined Chiefs of Staff, consisting of the U.S. and British chiefs, agreed on Operation Husky, the invasion of Sicily in July, and established August 1, 1943, as the target date for invading France. Husky, to no one's surprise, forced that date to be pushed back, first to May 1944, and ultimately to June.

Apart from giving the Battle of the Atlantic high priority—a very important step—the decisions reached at Casablanca have been criticized by many historians for delaying the invasion of Normandy and thereby lengthening the war. Operation Pointblank, also known as the Combined Bomber Offensive, was, at the very least, premature. Both the U.S. and British bomber offensives would be defeated, heavy losses causing them to be suspended until 1944. The effort, largely inspired by Roosevelt, to make Giraud equal to de Gaulle also ended in failure. By the end of the year it would be de Gaulle who commanded the Free French.

SEE ALSO

Atlantic, Battle of the; de Gaulle, Charles; Italy, surrender of; Roosevelt, Franklin D.; Strategic bombing; Unconditional surrender

FURTHER READING

Armstrong, Anne. *Unconditional Surrender: The Impact of the Casablanca Policy upon World War II.* New Brunswick, N.J.: Rutgers University Press, 1961.
Stoler, Mark A. *The Politics of the Second Front: American Military Planning and Diplomacy in Coalition Warfare 1941–1943.* Westport, Conn.: Greenwood Press, 1977.

Casualties

Figures on the war's human cost are notoriously inaccurate, except where the Western Allies are concerned, mainly because the German, Japanese, and Italian records were destroyed and those of the Soviet Union were carelessly kept. In round numbers China's military casualties are thought to have numbered 3,211,000, of which 1,320,000 were fatal. Millions of civilians were killed by the Japanese or died of starvation because of the war, perhaps 6 million in all, but the actual number of Chinese killed is probably much higher than the official figures suggest. Recently, China claims that its total losses as a result of the Japanese war ran as high as 35 million lives.

German military losses seem to have been something like 4 million dead, and perhaps 700,000 to 1 million civilians were killed by Allied bombers.

Roughly 2 million Japanese soldiers, sailors, and airmen were killed, along with perhaps 1 million civilians.

Soviet losses were so enormous, and so impossible to keep track of because the fighting swept back and forth across huge areas of land, that estimates vary widely. In 1990 the Soviet Union announced that 8,668,000 military personnel had been killed in the Great Patriotic War. However, no one knows how many Soviet prisoners of war died in German camps or were executed after the war by Soviet authorities who considered

Final rites are given during this memorial service for Americans who died during the Japanese raid on Midway Island in June 1942.

surrender by their soldiers as treason. Estimates range from some tens of thousands to, as is more likely, several million, so the official figure is clearly unreliable. At a guess, 10 million Soviet military personnel were killed and another 18 million wounded, of whom 1 million died. The civilian dead may have amounted to another 1 million killed by enemy action. Untold millions more died of malnutrition-related diseases, exposure, and other causes resulting from the war.

When one adds to these gruesome figures the losses of Australia (17,501 dead), Canada (42,000 dead), Italy (over 300,000 dead), the United Kingdom (270,000 military personnel and 60,000 civilians dead), and the United States (405,000 dead), the millions slain in the Holocaust—perhaps 12 million persons, half of them Jewish—and the enormous civilian casualties sustained by Poland and other occupied countries, the total becomes astronomical. A common figure used to account for all deaths in the war is 60 million, a figure so huge that it is hard to grasp; it would be like losing the entire current population of France. Yet even this vast number is probably too low, given the uncertainties of measurement. All one can know for sure is that it was the bloodiest war in history—especially for civilians whose deaths outnumbered those of the military.

SEE ALSO
Medicine

Central Pacific Area

In 1942 the Joint Chiefs of Staff divided the Pacific into four theaters of war, named the Central Pacific Area, the North Pacific Area, the South Pacific Area, and the Southwest Pacific Area. The Southwest Pacific Area (SWPA) was an Army theater; the others belonged to the Navy and were commanded collectively by Admiral Chester Nimitz under the designation Pacific Ocean Area.

Although some ships went to the SWPA and the Navy was heavily engaged in the South Pacific from 1942 to 1944, the Central Pacific became its main theater. This was because Chief of Naval Operations Admiral Ernest King chose to make it so. King believed—wrongly, some have argued—that the best way to defeat Japan was first to take the scattered atolls and islands of the Central Pacific, then land on the coast of China. From bases there, Japan could be bombed into surrendering or possibly be invaded. General Douglas MacArthur, the supreme commander of SWPA, thought that his theater should have gotten the resources that went to the Central Pacific. Many historians have since agreed with him, but King was a power on the Joint Chiefs of Staff, and as a rule, he got his way in the Pacific.

Tarawa Thus, instead of aiding MacArthur, the largest fleet in the world attacked Tarawa and Makin atolls in the Gilbert Islands. On November 21, 1943, after a brief bombardment, U.S. Marines assaulted Tarawa's Betio Island in a bloody three-day engagement. The Japanese had dug in, and the Marines suffered 3,000 casualties, including 1,000 dead, while Japan lost 4,500 men—all on an island of less than three square miles.

Army casualties on Makin were low, but on the fourth and last day a Japanese submarine sank the escort carrier *Liscomb Bay* at a cost of more than 600 lives. Naval officers were not slow to point out that had the Marines been sent to Makin they could have taken it by storm and the *Liscomb Bay* would have been safely at sea when the Japanese sub arrived. This was probably unfair, since Makin was taken according to a timetable agreed to by the Navy.

There is no way to resolve the old Army-Marine controversy over speed and safety; history offers examples to support each argument. However, one thing is certain: the possession of an elite assault force enabled the Navy to stage operations that the Army could not manage. At Tarawa 40 percent of the combat troops became casualties. In other island assaults Marine regiments would lose even more, up to a peak of 81 percent casualties sustained by the 29th Marines on Okinawa. In every case the carnage was to some extent optional, because unlike Bataan, or the Battle of the Bulge, where soldiers had to stand and fight, the island assaults of the Central Pacific were selected from among a range of choices. It is doubtful they would have been made at all had there been no Marine Corps.

The Navy learned a number of lessons at Tarawa, such as the need for heavier artillery bombardments and additional tracked landing vehicles, that it applied to subsequent landings. But the fact remained that assaulting fortified strong points would always be bloody work no matter how well supported the attacking troops were. Such attacks would become routine in the Central Pacific, but not in MacArthur's theater, where geography and a lack of means inspired more creative solutions.

Support for the Central Pacific effort was most marked at the top, thanks to King's driving force and his willingness to make deals. It was a source of great annoyance to him that senior naval officers in the Pacific Ocean Areas command did not share his enthusiasm for Central Pacific operations. But King had the final say and persuaded the Joint Chiefs to back him. In Novem-

Two U.S. officers plant the first American flag on Guam eight minutes after Marines and Army assault troops landed on the island on July 20, 1944.

ber 1943, the British and American Combined Chiefs of Staff (CCS) approved an "Overall Plan for the Defeat of Japan" that called for Nimitz to take the Marshalls in January, the Carolines and Truks in July, and the Marianas in October.

This course was taken over the objections not only of MacArthur but also of Admiral Nimitz plus his second in command, his chief of staff, and his head planner, all of whom preferred to operate in the Southwest Pacific. They met with representatives of Admiral William Halsey, commander in chief of the South Pacific, and MacArthur at Pearl Harbor in January 1944 and agreed that the Central Pacific was the wrong area for a major offensive. They especially did not want to take the Marianas, which had no good harbors, were within the range of Japanese land-based aircraft but beyond that of the U.S. heavy bombers, and had no military value except as B-29 bases. Instead of continuing westward, Nimitz seems to have favored the conference proposal to turn south, take the Palau and Truks, and join up with MacArthur for an assault on Mindanao, the nearest Philippine island. This meant having, if not a unified command in the Pacific, at least unity of action, so that the whole of the United

States's increasing might in the Pacific could be applied to a single purpose.

Defenders of the Central Pacific campaigns argue that the two drives were mutually supportive, yet this was seldom the case. They required two entirely separate lines of communication with much duplication of effort, and they competed with each other for scarce resources, notably landing ships and service personnel. SWPA never had enough service troops, engineers in particular, and the Marianas made things worse, because the great bomber bases established there required large numbers of engineers to build and maintain them.

The plan suggested at Pearl Harbor would have put the Navy's main effort on MacArthur's flank, required only one line of communications to serve both campaigns, and enabled landing ships and carriers to shuttle between the two theaters as needed. These campaigns would have been mutually supportive in fact as well as theory.

There would also have been no more battles like that at Tarawa, for in the Southwest Pacific the enemy strongholds could usually be bypassed and contained with land-based air attacks—as had happened at Rabaul, where 100,000 Japanese troops were dug in behind fearsome defenses. To take Rabaul by storm would have cost more U.S. lives than were expended on Iwo Jima. Instead, it was simply neutralized for the balance of the war. If Iwo Jima and the Marianas had been treated similarly, thousands of lives would have been saved.

Between April and October of 1944, MacArthur's forces advanced 1,000 miles in Indonesia, from Hollandia (now Jayapura) to Morotai, destroying nine Japanese divisions at a cost of 10,000 U.S. casualties, including 1,648 dead. Yet in the Marianas alone that

summer the United States would sustain nearly 23,000 casualties in the process of destroying at most three Japanese divisions.

Saipan and beyond Unhappily for many Marines, Nimitz did not run the Navy. When King, who did, saw the joint report drawn up at the Pearl Harbor conference in January he exploded, leaving Nimitz no choice but to obey orders. It was on to the Marianas and their principal islands, Guam, Tinian, and especially Saipan—which was invaded on June 15, 1944. The Marines fought another bloody battle and suffered heavy losses.

One merit of this campaign, however, was that it drew out the Japanese fleet. The Imperial Japanese Navy had been planning an attack on MacArthur's forces but sailed for the Marianas instead. This resulted in the Great Marinas Turkey Shoot or, as it is more properly called, the Battle of the Philippine Sea. When it was over, Japanese naval aviation was finished as an effective force.

On July 26, 1944, as the Marines fought to clear Guam, Franklin Delano Roosevelt sailed into Pearl Harbor. He was running for office again and wished to impress the electorate by showing his flag as commander in chief. But he also had real work to do, because the time for a final decision on Pacific strategy was fast approaching.

Events had overtaken the old plan approved in 1943. At that time the goal was to reach the South China coast and establish bomber bases there from which to reduce Japan or, perhaps, prepare to invade it. But since then the Japanese had seized more of China, and the Army Air Forces were preparing to launch its B-29 Superfortress bombers from the Marianas. What to do next was becoming the subject of heated debate, with King wanting to invade Formosa, MacArthur the Philippines.

These tank lighters came under fire during the invasion of Saipan in 1944.

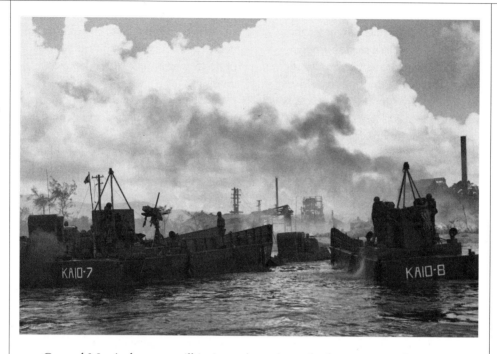

General MacArthur was still insisting that the whole Philippine archipelago had to be liberated, for political as well as military reasons. He argued that the United States would lose face abroad if it allowed the loyal Filipinos to languish needlessly. The voters at home would be unhappy also, because the nation felt guilty about having failed the Philippines in 1942. And not only MacArthur, whose motives were transparently selfish and self-aggrandizing, argued that bases in the Philippines should be established before conducting further operations.

Chester Nimitz thought so too, as did most of his senior commanders. The naval officers' main difference with MacArthur was that they did not agree with him on the need to liberate the entire archipelago. Having the northernmost island of Luzon was essential, however, for aircraft based there could cover the South China Sea and cut off Japan from Southeast Asia. In addition, Manila Bay was far superior as a fleet anchorage to the Marianas.

In Hawaii, Nimitz loyally presented King's argument for the invasion of Formosa as the fastest way to Japan. MacArthur eloquently made the case for Luzon's being slower but surer. MacArthur may in fact have arrived at a tacit agreement with Roosevelt by which the President would support MacArthur's plan while the general issued glowing communiques from his theater in time for the November elections. Whether that was so or not, FDR did endorse the plan, Admiral Leahy—Roosevelt's personal chief of staff—favored it, too, and within six weeks of their conference Nimitz, who required little persuasion, had fallen into line.

In the end even King had to agree, if only because his own planners had found that Formosa could not be taken without a huge number of army service troops. Because they were not available in the numbers required, Formosa was definitely out. But in the Philippines, where sympathetic local troops could be recruited for much of the heavy labor, additional army service workers would not be required.

Iwo Jima and Okinawa In the Philippine Islands the two Pacific wars came together briefly, for the Navy loaned its mighty Third Fleet to MacArthur in support of his invasion of Leyte. But in 1945 the Central Pacific drive resumed its bloody course. In February, U.S. forces invaded Iwo Jima, a small volcanic island about halfway between the Marianas and Japan. There the Marines lost three divisions so that the Army Air Forces could have emergency airfields.

Iwo Jima was a terrible battle, but Okinawa was even worse. After U.S. troops went ashore on April 1, 1945, some of the heaviest fighting in the Pacific war took place. Eighty days later, when the battle finally ended, 7,000 men had been lost on land and 4,900 at sea. In addition, 32,800 men had been wounded. Due to kamikaze (suicide) attacks, 20 percent of all casualties sustained by the U.S. Navy in World War II were taken in the waters off Okinawa. It was a gruesome foretaste of what an invasion of Japan would have caused. Although planning for this operation was far advanced, Okinawa marked the end of the Central Pacific campaign, because the atomic bomb forced a quick Japanese surrender.

SEE ALSO

Iwo Jima, Battle of; Japan; King, Ernest J.; MacArthur, Douglas; Nimitz, Chester W.; North Pacific Area; Okinawa, Battle of; Philippine Sea, Battle of the; Saipan, Battle of; South Pacific Area; Southwest Pacific Area; Tarawa, Battle of

FURTHER READING

Feiffer, George. *Tennozan: The Battle of Okinawa and the Atomic Bomb.* New York: Ticknor & Fields, 1992.
Manchester, William. *Goodbye Darkness: A Memoir of the Pacific War.* Boston: Little, Brown, 1980.
Reynolds, Clark G. *The East Carriers: The Forging of an Air Navy.* New York: McGraw-Hill, 1968.
Ross, Bill D. *Iwo Jima: Legacy of Valor.* New York: Random House, 1985.
Spector, Ronald H. *Eagle Against the Sun: The U.S. War with Japan.* New York: Free Press, 1985.

Chamberlain, Neville
PRIME MINISTER OF BRITAIN

- *Born: March 18, 1869, Birmingham, England*
- *Political party: Conservative*
- *Education: Rugby College, 1882–87*
- *Military service: None*
- *Government service: Lord mayor of Birmingham, 1915–16; member of Parliament, 1918–40; chancellor of the exchequer, 1923, 1931–37; minister of health, 1924–29; prime minister, 1937–40*
- *Died: November 9, 1940, Heckfield, Hampshire, England*

Neville Chamberlain belonged to a prominent political family and was active in business and civic affairs in Birmingham before entering Parliament. As prime minister of Britain from May 1937 to May 1940, he carried out the policy of "appeasing" Hitler. He is best remembered today as the man who sold out Czechoslovakia to Germany at Munich in September 1938, thereby strengthening Adolf Hitler's hand and making a general European war inevitable. However, Chamberlain was well liked and respected by his fellow Tories in Parliament, and what is now called appeasement was then popular with the British people. Most hoped, as Chamberlain did, that it would keep the peace in Europe. His mistake was in believing that Hitler could be trusted to keep his agreements, a belief widely shared at the time.

The disastrous Norwegian campaign, in which Hitler's troops occupied Norway during the spring of 1940, led to public demands that Chamberlain step down. Though the Conservative members of Parliament greatly preferred Chamberlain to Winston Churchill, they also recognized that the nation had lost confidence in him. When the Labour party refused to serve in a coalition government under Chamberlain, he was forced to resign as prime minister, although he remained leader of the Conservatives in Parliament until shortly before his death. He never seems to have doubted his prewar policy, and in one of his last letters defended the Munich agreement as having bought Britain time to rearm.

SEE ALSO

Appeasement; Churchill, Winston S.; Munich agreement

FURTHER READING

Chamberlain, Neville. *The Struggle for Peace.* London: Hutchinson, 1939.
Dilks, David. *Neville Chamberlain.* New York: Cambridge University Press, 1984.
Parker, Robert Alexander Clarke. *Chamberlain and Appeasement: British Policy and the Coming of the Second World War.* New York: St. Martin's, 1993.

Chiang Kai-shek

PRESIDENT AND COMMANDER IN CHIEF, REPUBLIC OF CHINA

- *Born: October 31, 1887, Chi Kou, Zhejiang Province, China*
- *Political party: Kuomintang (Nationalist)*
- *Education: Paoting Military Academy, 1906–07; Preparatory Military Academy (Tokyo), 1907–09*
- *Military and political service: conspired to overthrow Manchu dynasty, 1911; conspired to overthrow the successor government of Yuan Shih-Kai, 1913–16; aide to Sun Yat-Sen, 1917; chief of staff to commander in chief, 1922; commandant of the Whampoa Military Academy and army commander, 1924–28; head of government under various titles and generalissimo in charge of all Chinese Nationalist Forces, 1928–49; leader of rump government in Formosa (Taiwan), 1949–75.*
- *Died: April 5, 1975, Taiwan*

The future generalissimo of China joined the Nationalist party in 1908 and participated in its overthrow of China's last imperial dynasty, the Manchu, in 1911–12. Because China was in constant turmoil, his subsequent career in politics and the military is poorly documented. It is known, however, that in 1922 he had become important enough to hold the position of chief of staff to the commander in chief of the Nationalist army.

Other assignments followed, and Chiang periodically left the army, on one occasion even supporting himself as a broker on the Shanghai stock exchange. In 1924 he served as first commandant of the Whampoa Military Academy in Canton. After the death of Sun Yat-sen, the republic's founding father, in 1925, Chiang had himself put in command of the Northern Punitive Expedition, charged with defeating or at least controlling five major warlords, or regional rulers. As commander of the National Revolutionary Army, he secured 10 provinces in central and south China, including the important cities of Shanghai and Nanking.

A complex power struggle followed between Chiang and his noncommunist rivals in the Nationalist, or Kuomintang, party (KMT). At the same time, he was struggling against communist members of the party. By 1928 the communists, who had tried to seize power by force, had been driven from the KMT. A small remnant under the leadership of Mao Zedong had retreated to the mountains of Kiangsi Province and seemed to pose no threat. Chiang then resumed the Northern Expedition, captured Beijing, the ancient capital, and was named

Although Chiang Kai-shek rose to power quickly, he struggled to control the factions of his own government while engaging in war with Japan.

chairman of the State Council and generalissimo. He established his capital at Nanking, an inland city near Shanghai.

Chiang's rise to power had been rapid, but the power he actually exercised was less than it seemed. He did not replace the leaders he defeated with men loyal to himself, so the warlords were constantly rising against him and having to be defeated or negotiated with. Chiang's actual rule did not extend beyond the provinces of China controlled by his army. The number of provinces varied considerably but may have averaged around 10. The rest of China's 28 provinces were ruled by warlords. Although in theory subordinate to Chiang and the national government, in practice they did as they pleased in their holdings. Beset by the warlords, pressing him from the provinces he did not control; the communists, who began to grow again; and challenges to his rule from within the KMT, Chiang was always at war.

Matters grew worse for him in 1931 when the Japanese seized the territory of Manchuria's warlord, who was aligned with Chiang. Further incidents followed, ending with the outright invasion of China by the Imperial Japanese Army in 1937. During these years Chiang continued to extend his rule and succeeded in driving the communists out of southern China. Late in 1936 Chiang was kidnapped and, while being held captive, agreed to form a joint anti-Japanese front with the communists. The agreement was never formalized, however, and nothing really changed. Chiang does not seem to have been weakened by the experience, as he had actually conceded little.

When Japan invaded, Chiang put into effect a strategy of retreat he had developed earlier, trading space for time until the Japanese were overextended. Events unfolded as he had thought they would. Japan won all the battles and ended up controlling much of the coast and some 170 million Chinese. But it could not catch the retreating Chinese forces or dislodge Chiang from his new capital of Chungking, deep in the interior.

Though cut off from most of the world, except for modest amounts of aid that reached him over the Burma Road or from Soviet Russia, Chiang and his forces survived. The Japanese now found themselves locked in a war of attrition that they could not afford and could not end—except by leaving China. This was out of the question for Japan's militarists, who had planned the invasion and now would have to live with their mistake—one that would ultimately be fatal to them.

In 1941 Japan decided to cut off China from outside aid and strangle Chiang's government. Because this would probably mean war with the United States, Japan seized the initiative by destroying much of the Pacific Fleet at Pearl Harbor, Hawaii, in December and seizing virtually all of Southeast Asia and the western Pacific.

In the years that followed, U.S. aid to Nationalist China increased. Supplies were flown to China from India, and U.S. warplanes operated out of bases on Nationalist soil. Allied forces gradually retook most of Burma, and by 1945 a new road, the Ledo, ran from India to China. Throughout this period Chiang contributed as few troops as possible to the war against Japan, keeping his best units along his northwest frontier with Communist China. This infuriated many Americans who had to deal with Chiang, since their only interest was in defeating Japan. He wanted to see Japan defeated as well, but he was counting on the Allies doing it while he prepared for his postwar showdown with the communists.

Successful in the short run, Chiang would fail in the end because his regime was brutal, incompetent, and corrupt, and because as a leader he fell far short of Mao Zedong, leader of Communist China and a master of intrigue and propaganda. In the postwar struggle for power, Chiang would be outmaneuvered, his popular support would fall away, and army desertions to the communist side would take place on an enormous scale. In 1949 Chiang and the Kuomintang party were driven from China. Chiang spent the rest of his life as the ruler of the island of Formosa (later renamed Taiwan), cherishing futile hopes of one day returning in triumph to the mainland.

SEE ALSO

Chiang Kai-shek, Madam; China; China-Burma-India theater

FURTHER READING

Berkov, Robert. *Strong Man of China: The Story of Chiang Kai-shek.* Freeport, N.Y.: Books for Libraries Press, 1970.
Chiang, Kai-shek. *China's Destiny.* 1947. Reprint, New York: Da Capo, 1976.
Crozier, Brian. *The Man Who Lost China: Chiang Kai-shek.* New York: Scribners, 1976.
Dolan, Sean. *Chiang Kai-shek.* New York: Chelsea House, 1988.

Madame Chiang Kai-shek and her husband laugh during a photo session while visiting the United States in 1940.

Chiang Kai-shek, Madam (Soong Mei-ling)

WIFE OF CHINA'S PRESIDENT

- Born: 1898, Shanghai, China
- Education: Wesleyan College, Macon, GA, 1913–17

Madam Chiang was the third wife of Generalissimo Chiang Kai-shek. Born in 1900 as Soong Mei-ling, she belonged to one of the best-known families in China. Her father, Charles Jones Soong, was a Methodist missionary and merchant who supported Sun Yat-sen, the father of the Republic of China. Soong had three daughters and three sons, the third of whom, T. V. Soong, held a variety of offices under Chiang, including foreign minister and premier.

One daughter, Ch'ing-ling, became the second wife of Sun Yat-sen. Soong Ai-ling, another daughter married H. H. K'ung, a future president of Nationalist China.

In 1927 Soong Mei-ling married Chiang Kai-shek. Charming, beautiful, intelligent, and courageous, she was also hot-tempered and arrogant. However, these less attractive qualities did not prevent her from being a great asset to her husband, particularly during World War II.

After Eleanor Roosevelt, she was the most famous wife of a head of state and was greatly admired in the United States, where she had been educated. She used her celebrity and fluent English to promote China, notably during a highly successful tour of the United States from November 1942 to May 1943. There she spoke effectively at rallies, got her picture on the cover of *Life* magazine (a great distinction at the time), and secured additional aid for China. The willingness of the press to take her at face value helped Nationalist China conceal its defects for a long time.

SEE ALSO

Chiang Kai-shek

FURTHER READING

Eunson, Roby. *The Soong Sisters.* New York: Franklin Watts, 1975.
Seagrave, Sterling. *The Soong Dynasty.* New York: Harper & Row, 1985.
Thomas, Harry J. *The First Lady of China: the Historic Wartime Visit of Mme. Chiang Kai-shek to the United States in 1943.* New York: International Business Machines Corp., 1943.

Chiefs of Staff, Combined (U.K.–U.S.)

The Combined Chiefs of Staff (CCS) committee brought together the chiefs of staff of the British and U.S. military. Prime Minister Churchill and President Roosevelt agreed to form the CCS at the Arcadia conference, which met in Washington during December 1941. The CCS held strategy meetings periodically throughout the war, at which all major Allied operations were decided. The CCS was headquartered in Washington.

The CCS established a Combined Munitions Assignment Board to allocate supplies and weapons. Because the British chiefs would be absent most of the time, a Joint Staff Mission was formed to represent them. Its first head, Field Marshal Sir John Dill, enjoyed particularly close relations with General George Marshall, the U.S. Army's chief of staff. Although meetings of the CCS were often stormy, because the British and U.S. chiefs differed on important strategic issues, as an institution the CCS was highly effective. As a mechanism for coordinating an allied war effort it has never been surpassed.

SEE ALSO
Arcadia conference

Chiefs of Staff, Joint (U.S.)

Before Pearl Harbor there was no institution linking the U.S. Army and Navy. Each service went its own way, a cavalier system that was adequate in peacetime but made little sense during a major war. At Arcadia, the first Allied war conference, which was held in Washington during December 1941, it became evident that the United States needed a counterpart to the British Chiefs of Staff Committee. Accordingly, President Roosevelt created on the spot a body known as the Joint Chiefs of Staff (JCS).

In its final form, the JCS consisted of General George Marshall, the Army's chief of staff; General Henry Arnold, head of the Army Air Forces, which Marshall treated to a large extent as a separate service; and Admiral Ernest King, chief of naval operations. The JCS was chaired by Admiral William Leahy, Roosevelt's personal chief of staff.

While the JCS had its own staff and planners, all important decisions were personally made by the Joint Chiefs, who frequently disregarded the advice given them by their staffs. Often these decisions were the result of hard bargaining and horse trading in which one service would approve an operation of the other in order to gain approval for its own. The military side of the U.S. war effort was, therefore, run by a committee— although General Marshall, its most admired member and the chief of the largest service, was clearly first among equals.

SEE ALSO

Arcadia conference; Arnold, Henry H.; King, Ernest J.; Marshall, George C.

FURTHER READING

Hayes, Grace P. *The History of the Joint Chiefs of Staff in World War II: The War against Japan.* Annapolis, Md.: Naval Institute Press, 1982.

China

When Japan attacked the U.S. naval fleet at Pearl Harbor on December 7, 1941, China had already been at war with Japan for more than four years. Almost without industry and desperately poor, China had survived the Japanese onslaught in 1937 chiefly because of its great size and enormous population. Somewhere between 400 and 500 million people were believed to live in China, making it the most populous nation on earth as well as one of the poorest.

In attempting to seize China, Japan had made a monumental mistake. Although the Japanese Army won every battle and occupied much of the coast and most major cities, it could not catch the Chinese forces, which withdrew into the vast interior. This retreat compelled Japan to fight an endless war on the margins of its conquered lands, as well as against guerrilla forces operating behind Japanese lines. Japan attempted to terrorize the Chinese into surrendering by raping, torturing, and killing them, systematically and at random. But Chiang Kai-shek's national government was located in distant Chungking, which the Japanese could not reach. Nor could they get to the northern region controlled by the Chinese Communist party (CCP). The Chinese people refused to give in, despite a level of suffering not exceeded anywhere.

Chiang Kai-shek ruled Nationalist China from his wartime capital through the Kuomintang party (KMT), just as he had before the war. Although Nationalist China was a one-party state, the KMT was far from unified. It consisted of a strange collection of warlords, landlords, merchants, intellectu-

als, and others. Chiang played the factions in it off against one another to his own advantage.

In retreating to the west Chiang had been forced to abandon the southern and central provinces where he had the most support. But he had always led China from a position of weakness, because the KMT was a fragile political vehicle held together mainly by corruption, self-interest, and fear. There had been frequent power plays against Chiang in the past, and independent warlords always controlled large parts of China during the Kuomintang era. Chiang's power rested on the National Army, which was poorly armed, trained, paid, motivated, and led. However, the warlords' armies were worse, so it usually defeated them.

By virtue of its superior numbers, the National Army had often beaten the communists, but Chiang had never been able to crush the CCP. Under the leadership of wily Mao Zedong it had retreated to Shensi Province in northern China, where it was out of Chiang's reach—and beyond that of the Japanese Army as well. Although technically a part of Nationalist China, Communist China was in fact completely independent.

Circumstances forced the KMT and the CCP to follow similar strategies. From 1937 to about 1942, each was preoccupied with questions of survival. However, once the Allies were at war with Japan, both sides took it for granted that the Allies would win, and they prepared for the struggle to follow. Each side had to take some action against Japanese forces to remain credible to the Allies and the Chinese people. But both the KMT and the CCP viewed anti-Japanese operations in the context of the more critical struggle for power that would follow Japan's defeat.

In the wartime jockeying for position, the communists far exceeded the

A Chinese soldier, age 10, waits to board a plane back to China after fighting on the front lines during the Burma campaign.

Nationalists in ability and success. The KMT was fatally handicapped by its corrupt nature and its unwillingness, or inability, to control the exploitative practices of the landlords, petty warlords, and other camp followers who belonged to it. The National Army was vastly inferior to Japan's forces. And it was hard to get starving, unpaid soldiers—no matter how patriotic—to fight under well-fed officers who were in the habit of pocketing their men's wages.

In contrast, the CCP was scrupulously honest. The peasant populations under its control benefited from communist land reforms and were taxed and treated fairly by Chinese standards. Thus, while the KMT aroused little enthusiasm, communist rule was popular. And the communist army, though relatively small, was well trained and led and highly motivated. Through a skillful combination of policies aimed at civilians, and deft, small-scale military actions, the CCP expanded greatly during the war, laying the foundations for its later success.

In 1937 the CCP had about 40,000 members and governed, in addition to Shensi, parts of two other desperately poor provinces with a total population of 1.5 million. The communists responded to the Japanese invasion and occupation by sending troops and political workers behind Japanese lines to link up with centers of resistance, establish underground governments, and launch guerrilla actions. In the expanding areas they controlled, communists brought the same reforms they had instituted in Shensi. They also cooperated with non-communist elements, encouraged local initiatives, and confiscated and redistributed the assets of wealthy "traitors." The result was that by 1945 the CCP had more than 1.2 million members and governed territories in which, according to Mao, some 96 million Chinese people lived. This is probably an inflated figure, but all the same, communist growth during the war was astonishing, including the building of an army of some 900,000 men.

There was no way that the Nationalist government could equal the communist political success. But Chiang commanded substantial military forces during the war and could draw on a much larger population and resupply base. Nationalist China was poorly located to receive aid, but the relatively small amounts it received were vitally important. Support from Soviet Russia overland through Central Asia, never great, was ended by Stalin in 1940. A trickle of aid, mainly over the Burma Road, came to an end in 1942 when Japan seized Southeast Asia. By 1944 the United States was managing to bring in a fair amount of supplies by air over dangerous mountain ranges known collectively as "The Hump". But much of these went to U.S. forces in China, doing the KMT little good.

U.S. military leaders in China, notably Lieutenant General Joseph W. Stilwell, were infuriated by Chiang Kai-shek's failure to be more aggressive. Americans generally had an exaggerated

This U.S. convoy, which operated between Chen-Yi and Kweiyang, China, ascends the famous 21 curves at Annan, China.

view of Nationalist China's abilities. Reporters in China, both before and during the war, wanted China saved and tended to misrepresent it so as to build support in the United States for the Nationalist government. They emphasized the heroic aspects of China's resistance to Japan, passing over the KMT's numerous failings.

This favorable publicity made China seem morally better and more effective than was actually the case. The truth was that Chiang's forces were never strong enough, or well enough supplied, to carry out major offensive actions. The kind of expansion by infiltration that the communists practiced

was done at the expense of the KMT and could not be practiced by government forces. In any case, Chiang's postwar survival no longer depended on his fighting Japan but rather on being able to beat the communists after Japan was defeated. Wasting his assets by attacking the Japanese would have threatened his survival, a point Americans never understood.

The main contribution Nationalist China made to the war was accomplished simply by surviving. Because it did, and because the communists did, too, Japan had to maintain large forces in China, at a great cost to its war effort. This was no small thing, even if it fell short of what U.S. leaders had expected of Nationalist China.

SEE ALSO

Chiang Kai-shek; China-Burma-India theater; Japan

FURTHER READING

Boyle, John Hunter. *China and Japan at War, 1937–1945*. Stanford, Calif.: Stanford University Press, 1972.
Chi, Hsi-sheng. *Nationalist China at War: Military Defeats and Political Collapse*. Ann Arbor: University of Michigan Press, 1982.
Eastman, Lloyd E. *Seeds of Destruction: Nationalist China in War and Revolution, 1937–1945*. Stanford, Calif.: Stanford University Press, 1984.

China-Burma-India theater

Nowhere else did U.S. policy fail so utterly as in the China-Burma-India theater. This was ironic, because it was for China's sake that the United States had gone to war. Had Roosevelt not made

Japan's withdrawal from China an essential condition for lifting sanctions in 1941, the United States could probably have struck a temporary deal with Japan. To knowingly risk war on its behalf is the most one nation can do for another, yet Americans, including the President, knew almost nothing about the country they were trying to save.

Despite this lack of knowledge there was a large body of support in the United States for China, especially after it was invaded by Japan. Following Pearl Harbor, China became the United States's favorite ally. Most Americans seem to have been at least honorary members of what would later be called the China lobby.

Even though China had been the United States's reason for entering the Pacific war, Washington could do little to help it during the dark days after the attack on Pearl Harbor on December 7, 1941, beyond maintaining a volunteer U.S. fighter group, the Flying Tigers, that had been established there earlier that year. Once the Pacific war broke out, the Flying Tigers became part of the Tenth, then the Fourteenth, Army Air Force. The United States had few weapons to spare at first. And China could not be easily supplied, because Japan controlled all the convenient ports and the Burma Road to India. Nevertheless, Roosevelt was determined to build up Generalissimo Chiang Kai-shek's government and expand his territory as a base from which to invade Japan, and so that China could serve as a useful ally in the postwar era. Much bitterness would result from this unfortunate decision.

The truth about China was that it would never be able to offer much help. But because Americans believed that a strong China was essential to the war effort, truth could not be allowed to stand in the way of policy. Neither could the fact that Washington and Chung-

king, where Chiang had established his wartime capital, had radically different agendas. Whereas Roosevelt meant to strengthen Chiang's government as a weapon against Japan, Chiang was primarily interested in destroying the Chinese Communist Party (CCP). After Pearl Harbor, Chiang's policy was to let the United States beat the Japanese while he prepared for war with the communists. Under intense pressure, Chiang would cooperate militarily with the United States, but on the smallest scale possible.

Despite a stream of negative reports from U.S. diplomatic and military personnel on the incompetence and unpopularity of Chiang's regime, Roosevelt refused to admit that his China policy was fatally flawed. Nor would he accept the view of his ambassador in Chungking, Clarence Gauss, that the country could never be more than a "minor asset" to the United States and had the potential to become a "major liability."

Chiang had skillful representation in the United States and was the China lobby's favorite leader. For political reasons, Roosevelt could not turn his back on Chiang, and the military saw China as the logical springboard from which to invade Japan. Then, too, Roosevelt wanted China to be one of his "Four Policemen," who would maintain peace after the war was over. Necessity thus became the mother of self-deception.

In 1942 U.S. Army Chief of Staff George C. Marshall sent Lieutenant General Joseph W. "Vinegar Joe" Stilwell, an expert on China, where he had served for many years, to command in China and Burma.

Stilwell had been military attaché to the U.S. embassy in Beijing, when Japan attacked in 1937, and sympathized with the Chinese. He was an outstanding field commander, having distinguished himself in prewar maneuvers by his flair and imagination. In addition to his theater command, Chiang named him chief of staff of the Nationalist Chinese Army, an empty gesture, since Chiang had no intention of allowing an American to command his troops. They would not be of much use anyway, for the 3-million-strong National Army of the Republic of China looked impressive only on paper. Most of its 300 divisions were ill trained, malnourished, disease ridden, horribly led, and, for the most part, outside Chiang's jurisdiction. Warlords ran most of these divisions, with Chiang commanding no more than 30. What few resources he did have available went to the 400,000 men who stood guard against the CCP in North China, leaving little for the fight against Japan.

Stilwell reached China in March 1942, just as the Japanese invaded Burma, where the British fought badly and the Chinese worse. Chiang gave Stilwell nominal command of his troops in Burma, but once there, Vinegar Joe discovered that he had no real authority over them. In lightning attacks the Japanese destroyed the Allied front, and Stilwell personally led a column of 114 survivors out of the jungle to India, the only group of escapees to make it without loss of life.

Throughout the campaign, American journalists had published evasive reports. Upon reaching India, Stilwell put things right at a press conference with the blunt statement: "I claim we took a hell of a beating. We got run out of Burma and it is humiliating as hell. I think we ought to find out what caused it, go back and retake it." These remarks made him famous.

Stilwell would spend the next two and a half years trying to build up a Chinese force of 30 divisions able to retake North Burma and defend a new land route from India in place of the old Burma Road. Until then, China could be

supplied only by air over the treacherous Himalayas—called by fliers "The Hump"—an extraordinarily dangerous route that claimed the lives of many. This trickle of supplies, when a torrent was needed, ruled out major operations.

In his effort to open Burma, Stilwell found his greatest enemy to be Generalissimo Chiang Kai-shek, whom he privately called Peanut, and his next greatest Claire Chennault, who led the Flying Tigers and its successor, the U.S. Fourteenth Air Force. Chennault, who wanted to be independent of Stilwell, was making absurd promises to defeat Japan if he were provided with 147 aircraft.

The actual situation, as Stilwell pointed out, was that if Chennault annoyed the Japanese too much they would simply take his airfields. He argued that the correct strategy was to secure a land route to India first, then undertake more ambitious land and air operations. However, Roosevelt favored Chennault's idea—because Chiang liked it and because it would be easier to supply a small air force than a large ground army. At the Trident conference in May 1943 in Washington, Churchill and Roosevelt produced a compromise, dividing the supplies sent to China between Stilwell and Chennault, although Chennault had the higher priority.

In March 1944 Japan launched two major offensives that prompted important changes. One drive along the Burma–India frontier threatened the Chinese "X-Force" operating in Burma under Stilwell's command. This drive finally led Washington to warn Chiang that all U.S. aid to him would be cut off unless he put the companion "Y-Force" under Stilwell also. Chiang had been accepting aid but keeping most of his troops out of battle, which could no longer be tolerated.

Chiang complied, permitting a

Sino–Anglo–United States offensive to take place in Burma. This drive, which was ultimately successful, served no strategic purpose once the Joint Chiefs of Staff decided not to use China as a staging area from which to invade Japan. This decision came too late to call off the Burma campaign, thus fully justifying Britain's persistent lack of enthusiasm for it. So did Japan's new offensive in southeastern China, which overran many of Chennault's airfields. Constructed and supplied at enormous cost, in the end they accomplished nothing.

Japan's offensive proved that Stilwell had been right about Chennault's bases being indefensible. It also gave Roosevelt an interest in utilizing the Chinese communists, a step Chiang feared and that he had thus far prevented. On July 6, at Marshall's urging, FDR cabled Chiang that the crisis made it imperative for Stilwell to take "command of all Chinese and U.S. forces . . . including the communist forces."

Apart from the military advantages, Roosevelt apparently hoped that a unified command might enable the KMT and the CCP to settle their differences. Chiang agreed in principle but took no other action, so in September Washington said there would be no more aid unless Stilwell was empowered at once. Vinegar Joe delivered the message to Chiang personally and with great relish, writing doggerel verses afterward to celebrate having kicked Peanut in the pants.

Stilwell's elation proved to be premature, however, for instead of giving in to official U.S. pressure, Chiang forced FDR to choose between him and Stilwell. By this time, U.S. military leaders had lost faith in China and, with the war going well in the Pacific, no longer saw it as essential to Japan's defeat. Ironically, because the China-Burma-India theater no longer mattered, it was

unnecessary to keep Stilwell as theater commander. His special abilities would not be required for what was now a routine assignment.

Accordingly, on October 18, 1944, Roosevelt recalled Stilwell and replaced him with Lieutenant General Albert C. Wedemeyer. This pleased the generalissimo, who failed to understand the real reason why the change had come about.

Stilwell's recall led to a flood of stories at home detailing, almost for the first time, the manifold shortcomings of Chiang and the ruling Kuomintang (KMT) party. Although the China lobby would continue to exercise great influence, the U.S. love affair with China was over. Thereafter, Wedemeyer and the U.S. ambassador to China made certain that there would be no aid to the CCP and no political concessions made to it. U.S. aid to Chiang increased substantially in 1945, even though the KMT made little effort to combat the Japanese, and the Reds, too, were husbanding their strength for the coming civil war.

The British would retake much of Burma by war's end, aided by substantial U.S. forces, including a famous unit called Merrill's Marauders that operated behind Japanese lines. Chennault's air force made a modest contribution too,

Chinese soldiers train in foxholes for combat on the frontlines. China preferred to leave fighting the Japanese to the Americans, holding soldiers in reserve to fight a civil war against the Communists instead.

but the entire China-Burma-India theater never justified the resources that
were, with such difficulty, devoted to it.

SEE ALSO
Chiang Kai-shek; China

FURTHER READING
Sun, Youli. *China and the Origins of the
Pacific War, 1931–1941.* New York: St.
Martin's, 1993.
Tuchman, Barbara W. *Stilwell and the U.S.
Experience in China, 1911–1945.* New
York: Macmillan, 1971.

Churchill, Winston Spencer

*PRIME MINISTER OF BRITAIN,
1940–45*

- *Born: November 30, 1874, Blenheim
  Palace, England*
- *Political parties: Union, Liberal,
  Conservative*
- *Education: Harrow, 1886–92; Royal
  Military College at Sandhurst, 1893–94*
- *Military service: British cavalry 2nd
  lieutenant, 1895–1900; major, 1915;
  lieutenant colonel of infantry, 1915–16*
- *Previous government service: House of
  Commons, 1900–1904; undersecretary
  of state for the colonies, 1905–1908;
  president of the Board of Trade,
  1908–10; home secretary, 1910–11;
  first lord of the Admiralty, 1911–15;
  minister of munitions, 1917–18;
  secretary of state for war and air,
  1918–21; secretary for the colonies,
  1921–22; chancellor of the exchequer,
  1924–29; first lord of the Admiralty,
  1939–40*
- *Died: January 24, 1965, London,
  England*

Winston S. Churchill is best known in
the United States as Britain's wartime
prime minister, particularly for his heroic leadership in 1940 and 1941 when
Britain stood alone against Germany.
But Churchill had been a major figure in
British politics since the early years of

the century and was very well known
both at home and abroad.

Early life Although Churchill was
the grandson of a duke, he was technically a commoner, because titles of
nobility passed only to eldest sons. His
father, Lord (a courtesy title) Randolph
Churchill, was the third son of the seventh duke of Marlborough and therefore did not inherit the dukedom. Lord
Randolph was a Conservative politician
of note, rising to become chancellor of
the exchequer (in charge of the treasury). He married Jennie Jerome, an
American heiress, but her money never
came down to Winston, who was obliged to earn his living by his pen for
most of his adult life.

After attending prep school at Harrow, which he hated, and the military
academy at Sandhurst, which he liked,
Churchill joined the cavalry and served
in India, Cuba, and the Sudan. He had
many adventures during these years,
most of them as a journalist on leave
from his regiment in India, where little
was happening. At the 1898 Battle of
Omdurman in Sudan during Britain's
war with the Dervishes, Churchill took
part in the last great cavalry charge
made by the British Army. He also covered the Boer War in South Africa as a
reporter, was captured by the Boers, and
then escaped, which made him an
instant celebrity.

Churchill resigned his commission in
1900 and stood for Parliament as a Conservative. His own fame, augmented by
already extensive writings, and his
famous name, ensured his election. In
1905 he bolted the Conservative party
and became a Liberal, a step perhaps
even more rare in Britain than in the
United States. As a Liberal he quickly
rose to become civilian head of the Royal
Navy, which, because Britain still ruled
the waves, made him a world figure. He
championed the doomed Gallipoli,

Turkey, campaign in 1915, and its failure seemed likely to end his career in politics. But, after service in the trenches, he was brought back into government by Prime Minister David Lloyd George, a former cabinet colleague and now head of the wartime coalition government.

After World War I Churchill "re-ratted," as he put it, becoming a Conservative again, and was rewarded with the chancellorship of the exchequer in the first postwar Conservative government. He lost his job when the Conservatives were defeated in 1929, and although they regained power later, he was not offered another post. Most Conservatives disliked and mistrusted Churchill, with the result that he did not hold office again until after World War II broke out.

During his "wilderness years," Churchill earned a great deal of money by writing numerous books and articles, including a four-volume biography of the first duke of Marlborough. He had to, because his opulent style of life on his country estate, Chartwell, required constant infusions of cash.

Churchill had a reputation for being politically untrustworthy, which he did not improve by taking a reactionary stand on self-government for India and other issues. He also backed King Edward VII's attempt to marry a divorced American woman without giving up his throne, which most of the British people opposed. When Edward was forced to abdicate, with him went any hope, it appeared, of Churchill's returning to the cabinet.

But there was more to Churchill than his misadventures. He was the first important British politician to warn against the threat of Adolf Hitler. During the 1930s, his was the loudest voice in Britain calling for rearmament. Although only a "backbencher," as a British member of Parliament who does

Winston Churchill speaks before a joint session of the U.S. Congress on December 26, 1941.

not have a leadership position is called, he still had his eloquent tongue and pen. He used them to fight the policy of "appeasement" that the Conservative government of Britain was pursuing, further annoying his party.

Rise to power After the war broke out, Churchill's long record of anti-Nazism forced Prime Minister Neville Chamberlain to bring him back to the cabinet again, once more as head of the Admiralty. After the disastrous 1940 Norwegian campaign, for which Churchill had been as responsible as anyone, Chamberlain was forced to step down. Most Conservative members of Parliament would have preferred almost anyone else to Churchill but, in a rare instance when public opinion forced the issue, were obliged to accept him as Britain's leader.

Churchill became prime minister on May 10, 1940, the very day Germany launched its stunningly successful surprise attack through the Ardennes Forest into France. His first days in office were spent presiding over Britain's defeat on the Continent and the evacuation of

Allied troops from Dunkirk, which was completed June 3.

The British expeditionary force was saved, but all else was lost. The Army returned to Britain minus most of its weapons. France surrendered in June. With Germany having won the Continent, and the United States on the sidelines, there were many in Britain who felt that the time had come to accept Hitler's terms for peace—which were that Britain could keep the Empire while Germany retained Europe. If Britain had dropped out of the war there would have been no way for the United States to intervene in Europe and little chance of defeating Hitler. It was at this critical juncture, with the fate of the world hanging in the balance, that Churchill realized his full promise at last. Insisting on a fight to the finish, he led the British people with never-to-be-forgotten eloquence and force as they stood alone against Hitler's war machine.

On June 4 Churchill addressed the House of Commons, ending with these defiant lines:

"Even though large tracts of Europe and many old and famous States have fallen or may fall into the grip of the Gestapo and all the odious apparatus of Nazi rule, we shall not flag or fail.

"We shall go on to the end. We shall fight in France, we shall fight on the seas and oceans, we shall fight with growing confidence and growing strength in the air, we shall defend our island, whatever the cost may be.

"We shall fight on the beaches, we shall fight on the landing grounds, we shall fight in the fields and in the streets, we shall fight in the hills; we shall never surrender.

"And even if, which I do not for a moment believe, this island or a large part of it were subjugated and starving, then our Empire beyond the seas, armed and guarded by the British Fleet, would carry on the struggle, until, in God's good time, the New World, with all its power and might, steps forth to the rescue and the liberation of the Old."

His listeners were deeply moved, one Labour member writing that the speech "was worth 1,000 guns and the speeches of 1,000 years."

For his leadership in that desperate time, Churchill will always be honored. In a rare moment of modesty, Churchill once said that it was the British people who had the lion's heart; it fell to him only to give the roar. This was to allow himself too little credit, for no other British politician could have rallied the British as he did—none had his command of the language, his ability to summon the past in aid of the present, his faith in Britain's greatness. Who else could have convinced the British when all seemed lost that they were actually enjoying what he would later call "their finest hour"?

Churchill as war leader After the Soviet Union and the United States became allies of Britain, Churchill probably did the war effort more harm than good. As prime minister and minister of defence, he strongly influenced British strategy, often for the worse. No one was more responsible than he for the Royal Air Force's bombing attacks on Germany, which killed hundreds of thousands of civilians and consumed at a minimum 25 percent of Britain's war effort, while contributing little to victory. Like the U.S. air war over Europe, it was not only a crime but a blunder— one which, unlike the United States, Britain could ill afford.

More serious still was Churchill's absolute determination to prevent, or at least delay, the Allied invasion of France, the only way for the Allies to ensure Germany's early defeat and, in addition, minimize the Soviet Union's postwar

Churchill (below foreground lamppost) waves and gives the famous V-for-victory sign to a mob of people on May 8, 1945, after making his V-E Day speech in London.

position in Europe. This was a return to the marginal strategy Churchill had advocated in World War I, which had ended in defeat at Gallipoli. It proved a poor strategy in World War II as well, tying down most of the West's strength in North Africa and Italy while the buildup for the attack across the English Channel languished.

If D-Day, the invasion of France, had taken place in 1943, as General George C. Marshall and other U.S. strategists wanted, Germany would most likely have fallen at least a year earlier than it did, with a great saving of human lives on the battlefield and in the Holocaust. Also, all of central Europe, and maybe part of eastern Europe as well, would have ended up outside the Soviet empire. Conservative Americans used to argue that if only Roosevelt had listened to Churchill there would have been no sellout to Stalin at Yalta. The opposite is more likely true, however: although Churchill's ancient anti-Bolshevism—which dated all the way back to 1917—resurfaced near the end of the war, no one had done more to ensure that communism would rule in the East than he,

by resisting for as long as he could the creation of a second front. It was the postponement of what became Operation Overlord, not Stalin's guile or Roosevelt's innocence, that let the Red Army occupy so much of Europe.

Declining influence After D-Day, Churchill's influence in the Grand Alliance of Britain, the Soviet Union, and the United States diminished. The United States was now providing not only the bulk of Allied military strength in the West and 25 percent of Britain's weaponry but many other forms of aid as well. In the bargaining with Stalin that occupied much of Roosevelt's last months, FDR went his own way—dragging Churchill behind him.

The unkindest blow of all fell on Churchill in July 1945, during a conference of the Big Three in Potsdam, Germany. Britain held its first general election in 10 years and, to the surprise of Americans, threw the Conservatives out. Churchill, preoccupied with war and diplomacy, had failed to recognize that the British people, who had suffered so much, were now determined to have a welfare state, which only the Labour party could give them.

Churchill, though deeply hurt, took his defeat with the greatness of character that always redeemed his quick temper, heavy drinking, and other faults. He was bathing when he got the news, and remarked: "They are perfectly entitled to vote as they please. This is democracy. This is what we have been fighting for." Although entitled to return to Potsdam for the conference's end, Churchill went to Buckingham Palace at the end of election day and gave his resignation to the king. Churchill then issued a statement wishing the new government well. In private, his words carried more bitterness. When his wife remarked that this might be a blessing in disguise, Churchill replied that it seemed "quite effectively disguised."

In recent years British authors have written books highly critical of Churchill. It is true that he had serious faults and made many mistakes, but when he rallied the British in 1940, he, and they, saved everything. Their finest hour is Churchill's monument and his claim to greatness. With his books, articles, and especially speeches, he proved once again that words above all determine the fate of nations. It was not just Britain's good fortune but the world's that when all seemed lost, it was led by a man who could mobilize the full power of the English language in the service of liberty.

SEE ALSO

D-Day; Foreign policy; France, fall of; Italian campaigns; Mediterranean theater; Potsdam conference; Strategic bombing; Yalta conference

FURTHER READING

Churchill, Winston S. *The Second World War*. 6 vols. Boston: Houghton Mifflin, 1948–54.
Gilbert, Martin. *Churchill: A Life*. New York: Henry Holt, 1991.
Kimball, Warren F. *Forged in War: Roosevelt, Churchill, and the Second World War*. New York: Morrow, 1997.
Rose, Norman. *Churchill: The Unruly Giant*. New York: Free Press, 1994.

Civil defense

The office of Civilian Defense (OCD) was established in May 1941 by President Roosevelt, who named the peppery mayor of New York, Fiorello LaGuardia, as its chief. OCD was supposed to coordinate civilian efforts to prepare for war, but its authority was so vague, its mission so unclear, and public enthusiasm for its mandate so slight, that little came of it at first. Then, after the attack on Pearl Harbor in December 1941, a vast tide of civilian enthusiasm overwhelmed the OCD. Citizens committees sprang up everywhere. Hospitals reeled before hordes of people eager to donate blood for the armed forces. In Chicago 23,000 block captains were sworn in at a mass ceremony. OCD's inability to channel this surge of support aroused numerous complaints—that it did not have a women's division, for example—although any civilian effort would have to depend on women to a very large extent.

In time the OCD did make use of female volunteers, especially after the President appointed his wife Eleanor to give LaGuardia a hand. But the OCD never became a major government agency, in large part because the United States was never attacked, making a civil defense effort on the European scale unnecessary. For the most part, civilian contributions to the war effort were handled by other agencies, by a vast number of independent organizations like the Red Cross, or not at all.

The Civilian Air Warning System, amateur aircraft spotters, enrolled a half million members. A partial blackout of the East Coast was imposed in 1942. First aid classes drew hundreds of thousands of students, as did classes on how to survive an air raid. By February 1952 5 million Americans belonged to some type of volunteer civil defense organization. That summer some 11,000 Local Defense Councils carried 10 million volunteers on their rolls, some directly involved in civil defense, others in numerous war-related activities, such as scrap drives and Victory gardens.

Concentration camps

The Nazis began establishing concentration camps for political prisoners soon after coming to power in 1933. The first and most notorious of these was Dachau, located near Munich. These camps were atrocious places and designed to be so. The Nazis meant to terrorize their enemies—and potential enemies—by inflicting inhuman punishments on them, including torturing, beating, and starving them, frequently to death.

At first Nazi Germany had many such camps, but in 1934 the system was reorganized under the Schutzstattel (SS) and put under the supervision of special Death's Head formations. By 1937 there were only three important camps: Dachau, Sachsenhausen, and Buchenwald. The Allied troops who liberated these camps in 1945 were horrified by the mass graves, fiendish instruments of torture, and brutalized inmates they discovered there. But for all their ghastliness, they were small-scale affairs compared to the death camps of the Holocaust, which lay to the east of Germany. The victims of concentration camps numbered only in the tens of thousands, whereas perhaps 12 million people—half of them Jews—perished in the death camps.

SEE ALSO
Holocaust

FURTHER READING
Auerbacher, Inge. *I Am a Star: Child of the Holocaust.* Englewood Cliffs, N.J.: Prentice-Hall, 1986.
Buechner, Howard A. *Dachau: The Hour of the Avenger (An Eyewitness Account).* Metairie, La.: Thunderbird Press, 1986.

Two prisoners (in foreground) support a comrade during a roll call at this German concentration camp because fainting was frequently used as an excuse for guards to "liquidate" useless inmates.

Baldwin, Margaret. *The Boys Who Saved the Children*. New York: Julian Messner, 1981.

Feig, Konnilyn G. *Hitler's Death Camps: The Sanity of Madness*. New York: Holmes & Meier, 1981.

Geehr, Richard S., ed. *Letters from the Doomed: Concentration Camp Correspondence 1940–1945*. Lanham, Md.: University Press of America, 1992.

Phillips, Walter Alfred Peter. *The Tragedy of Nazi Germany*. London: Routledge & Kegan Paul, 1969.

Smith, Marcus J. *The Harrowing of Hell: Dachau*. Albuquerque: University of New Mexico Press, 1972.

Congress, U.S.

Beginning in 1937, Congress, although nominally under Democratic control, was really dominated by a coalition of Republicans and conservative southern Democrats. Because Congress was strongly influenced by isolationism (the desire of most citizens for the United States to stay out of world affairs in general and World War II in particular) before the bombing of Pearl Harbor in December 1941, Roosevelt was reluctant to prepare adequately for war, and slow to aid the Allies after Hitler invaded Poland in September 1939.

Nevertheless, Congress, by very narrow margins, did enact a bill creating the Selective Service System (which administered a military draft) in 1940, extended it in 1941 (by a single vote in the House), and passed the important Lend-Lease Act (which provided war machinery to Britain and its allies) in 1941. Once the United States entered the war, Congress gave Roosevelt an almost completely free hand when it came to defense and foreign policy issues.

In the off-year election of 1942, Republicans made big gains, partly because voter turnout was light and partly because the war had not been going well up to that time. President Roosevelt had hoped that Operation Torch, the invasion of French North Africa, would turn the electorate around. But Operation Torch came on November 8, just a few days after the election. To his credit, Roosevelt did not flinch when informed of the invasion's delay, which he knew would hurt Democrats at the polls. In the new 78th Congress the Republicans were just 13 seats short of a majority in the House and 9 seats behind in the Senate. Because of by-elections held to fill vacated seats, the Democrats actually lost their majority in the House, although it was not reorganized under Republican leadership because the 1944 elections were so near.

Although it continued to support Roosevelt in military and foreign affairs, the new Congress killed off as many New Deal agencies as it could. Young people were hardest hit, losing the National Youth Administration, the Civilian Conservation Corps, and other programs targeted at them. These were not needed during the war, when most young people were in the armed services or at work on a full- or part-time basis. But they would be missed afterward.

Congress would not expand the draft in 1944 when the military manpower crisis hit. It consistently refused to draft women for noncombat jobs, even though public opinion polls showed that most Americans, including young women of draft age, would accept such a measure. It would not pass a national service bill that would have required civilians to work at assigned jobs, although again the polls were favorable. But in 1944 it did pass the GI Bill of Rights, a sweeping program of veterans' benefits that was both very popular and a great success. In the 1944 elections Democrats regained control of Congress again, too late to make any difference to the war effort.

SEE ALSO

Election of 1942; Election of 1944; GI Bill of Rights; Lend-Lease; Selective Service System

FURTHER READING

Burns, James MacGregor. *Roosevelt: The Soldier of Freedom.* New York: Harcourt Brace Jovanovich, 1970.
Colegrove, Kenneth Wallace. *The American Senate and World Peace.* New York: Vanguard, 1944.
Porter, David L. *The Seventy-sixth Congress and World War II, 1939-1940.* Columbia: University of Missouri Press, 1979.
Ritchie, Donald A. *The Young Oxford Companion to the Congress of the United States.* New York: Oxford University Press, 1993.

Coral Sea, Battle of the

In the six months after the bombing of Pearl Harbor in December 1941, the Japanese ran wild in Southeast Asia and the western Pacific, sweeping all before them. Yet at the pinnacle of Japan's success, the tide of war would turn as a result of two crucial sea battles. The first of these, the Battle of the Coral Sea, put an end to Japanese expansion. At Midway its main attack force would be shattered.

These defeats came about partly because in the late spring of 1942 many Japanese officers were suffering from what they came to call "victory disease," the symptoms being euphoria and carelessness. Drunk with success, rather than consolidating its gains after taking the Philippine archipelago, Japan proceeded at once with further offensive actions.

Their first effort was to occupy Tulagi in the Solomon Islands and other points in the region, notably Port Moresby, New Guinea, so as to gain control of the Coral Sea and neutralize Australia. As usual the enemy plan was exceedingly complex, requiring not only great skill on the Imperial Japanese Navy's part but also that U.S. forces would respond as the Japanese expected. Moreover, the Japanese paid little attention to security. That lapse was more dangerous than they knew, because, although it was outnumbered and outgunned, the U.S. Navy had an overwhelming intelligence advantage.

Naval Intelligence was in fact monitoring 60 percent of Japan's radio transmissions over its Mid-Pacific Direction-Finding Net. This chain of stations tracked individual ships over thousands of miles of ocean by a process known as radio traffic analysis. Because of a self-imposed radio silence, the Japanese fleet that had bombed Pearl Harbor had been missed by U.S. Naval Intelligence. However, radio silence was not characteristic of the Imperial Japanese Navy, whose ships were always chattering away, to the great benefit of the U.S. Navy. Navy code breakers were able to decrypt a significant amount of the Japanese Navy's operational code, which yielded invaluable data.

By April 20, 1942, Admiral Chester Nimitz, who commanded the Pacific Fleet, knew that in two weeks' time a Japanese carrier task force would enter

Although the Lexington was hit with Japanese torpedoes and bombs during the Battle of the Coral Sea, it was not until the fleet carrier was heading home that its ruptured gas tanks exploded.

the Coral Sea bound for Port Moresby. Although this area was in General Douglas MacArthur's theater, a divided command arrangement stipulated that fleet carrier operations would remain under Navy control wherever they took place. Accordingly, Nimitz sent Vice Admiral Frank Jack Fletcher to defend the Coral Sea with two fleet carriers, *Lexington* and *Yorktown*. Nimitz had no replacement for these priceless warships, but the Allies could not afford to lose Australia, so the risk had to be taken. At the Coral Sea, Nimitz's courage would be rewarded, and not for the last time.

On May 1 both U.S. carrier groups were in place. They and the Japanese strike force, which included two fleet carriers and one light carrier, blundered back and forth for days, always missing each other. Battle was finally joined on May 7. When it was over, Japanese planes had sunk a U.S. destroyer and an oil tanker and scored numerous but not fatal hits on *Lexington* and *Yorktown*. The "Lady Lex" suffered most, because she had been built on a battle cruiser hull and was less maneuverable than *Yorktown*, a carrier from her keel up. At this point the U.S. Navy was far ahead, the Japanese having lost a light carrier and the use (temporarily) of its big carriers, the *Shokaku* for two crucial months, and the *Zuikaku* until June 12, because of heavy damage to its air group.

But the balance changed when *Lexington* started erupting. She had taken two torpedoes and three bomb hits during the battle, but her crew gained control of the fires, relit her boilers, and she was steaming home at 25 knots when gasoline fumes from her ruptured tanks exploded.

Remarkably, although 36 planes went down with her, only some 200 lives were lost out of a complement of nearly 3,000. The *Lexington,* with *Saratoga,* the biggest combat vessel in the Navy, was famous as a happy ship and was greatly missed by her crew. She was also missed by Admiral Nimitz, for now he was left with only three carriers to face the Japanese onslaught.

The loss of *Lexington* made the battle of the Coral Sea a tactical win for the Japanese, who had inflicted more harm than they suffered. But it remained a strategic victory for the United States, because after the battle Japan was obliged to call off its invasion of Port Moresby for lack of air support. In the Coral Sea the United States's sailors and airmen saved Australia.

The Battle of the Coral Sea was the high-water mark of Japan's advance in the Pacific, as it turned out, and a crucial setback. Because of it, two damaged Japanese fleet carriers would not return to service in time for Midway—much reducing the odds in that all-important engagement. The Coral Sea was the first naval battle fought entirely by aircraft, and both sides made many mistakes. But the Japanese committed more of them, and the U.S. Navy was learning fast. The next time, at Midway, it would do better.

SEE ALSO
Midway, Battle of; Pacific war

FURTHER READING
Hoyt, Edwin Palmer. *Blue Skies and Blood: The Battle of the Coral Sea.* New York: Eriksson, 1975.
Millot, Bernard. *The Battle of the Coral Sea.* London: Allan, 1974.

Cruisers

After battleships and carriers, cruisers were the largest warships in the U.S. Navy. Like most navies, the U.S. Navy had two basic cruiser types, heavy (more than 10,000 tons' displacement), and light. Heavy cruisers were armed usually with 8-inch guns, lights with 5- or 6-inch guns.

Traditionally, cruisers had been scout and fast attack vessels ranging ahead of the battle line. But as World War II progressed, the cruiser's scouting and fast attack roles were taken over by airplanes, and cruisers were increasingly devoted to antiaircraft and antisubmarine work.

Cruisers lost some of their heavy guns and eventually all their torpedo tubes, which were replaced with antiaircraft (AA) guns. As so few fast battleships were built, cruisers, with their high rate of speed (as fast as 38 knots), provided most of the AA support for fast carrier groups.

The *Baltimore* class of heavy cruisers, which began entering service in 1943, were the best of their type in the world. Large (13,600 tons), heavily armed and armored, they were also fast (33 knots) and, thanks to their size, could sail for long distances without refueling. However, because of steel shortages, only six or seven of this class were constructed in time to see action. They were the largest class of cruiser ever built, and would have been larger still had not nine of them been converted to *Independence*-class light carriers.

The mainstay of the light cruiser force was the *Cleveland* class, of which 27 saw service. The best U.S. light cruisers, *Cleveland*s were at least equal to their best foreign counterparts. At 10,000 tons' displacement they were armed with a dozen 6-inch guns in addition to numerous AA guns and made a top speed of 33 knots.

FURTHER READING

Musicant, Ivan. *U.S. Armored Cruisers: A Design and Operational History.* Annapolis, Md.: Naval Institute Press, 1985.

Whitley, M. J. *Cruisers of World War Two: An International Encyclopedia.* London: Arms and Armour, 1995.

D-Day

Operation Overlord, the Allied invasion of France on June 6, 1944, today looks like it would be a sure thing. The Allies had firm control of the sea and air. Only one of the five invasion beaches was hard to take, and at the end of the "longest day" (the term writer Cornelius Ryan used to describe D-Day years later), some 156,000 men were ashore. But Overlord was actually a high-risk operation. Germany had some 55 divisions defending France on D-Day, while the Allies could muster only 35. Because the standard military guideline is that attackers must outnumber defenders, invading France was, on the face of it, a hopeless task.

What the Allied planners counted on were certain advantages they had that they hoped might offset their shortage of troops. For one, Germany could not deploy all its forces on the English Channel, because the rest of France had to be defended as well, especially the Mediterranean coast. Second, the Soviet Union had agreed to launch an offensive at the same time as Overlord, to prevent

A Coast Guard landing boat puts American soldiers on the coast of France under heavy Nazi fire.

Division patch-es were worn on American military uni-forms for quick identification. They were especially use-ful during large operations, such as the Normandy invasion.

the Germans from bringing up rein-forcements from the eastern front.

A third factor favoring the Allies was that they had broken Germany's military codes and could read its radio traffic. ULTRA, as this information was called, had been most useful in Africa, where radio was the principal medium of communications. It would be of less value on the Continent, where secure land lines reduced German radio use. Yet the Allies could usually count on knowing the enemy's strength—referred to in military terms as "the order of battle"—giving them an intelligence advantage.

Preparations Although the Allies' efforts to destroy the German-controlled French rail yards with heavy bombers did not have the hoped-for results, Allied fighter-bomber attacks were highly suc-cessful. By D-Day, Major General Lewis H. Brereton's Ninth Air Force had 11 medium bomber groups, each consisting of 64 aircraft, and 18 fighter groups with 75 planes apiece, which he used to destroy bridges. At the time, critics argued that bridges were poor targets, because they said it would take 1,200 tons of bombs to destroy a single bridge across the Seine. But on May 10, 1944, a flight of P-47 Thunderbolts dropped two 1,000-pound bombs on a rail bridge, completely destroying it.

Supreme Headquarters Allied Expe-ditionary Forces (SHAEF) then drew up a plan to destroy bridges all over north-ern France. They would isolate the Nor-mandy beaches, all the while keeping Germany in the dark as to where the Allied landings would take place. The campaign began on May 24.

By D-Day the U.S. Ninth Air Force and the RAF's Second Tactical Air Force had destroyed all nine Seine railroad crossings and a dozen highway bridges. Allied air units then kept them closed, by bombing repaired structures, boats that

the Germans pressed into service, and temporary bridges. These attacks se-verely limited Germany's ability to move troops and supplies around in France.

Deception Equally important, the Allies leaked false plans that kept Hitler, who made the key decisions, from con-centrating his troops in Normandy. There were 6 primary plans plus 36 sec-ondary ones, entailing leaked informa-tion, guerrilla raids by resistance forces, Allied military actions, and a host of other activities that misled Germany and kept its troops dispersed.

One of the best deception opera-tions was Fortitude North, a low-cost plan that required only a handful of men and women. The Allied command created a fictitious British Fourth Army headquartered at Edinburgh Castle in Scotland and, by pouring out radio mes-sages, convinced German intelligence that the Allies were about to invade Norway, which Germany had occupied since June 1940. As a result, the 27 Ger-man divisions in Norway remained there instead of defending France.

The most important deception plan, code named Fortitude South, had two parts. First it had to persuade Germany that the main Allied effort would be at the Pas de Calais, where the English Channel was narrowest. After D-Day the job of this force was to suggest that the Normandy landings had been intended to mislead, the real target still being Calais.

In a major counterintelligence tri-umph, the British had "turned" an entire German spy network, which was now working for the Allies and giving the Reich a flood of misinformation. But the heart of this massive deception effort was a fake army group supposed-ly consisting of 50 divisions and 1 mil-lion men in the southeast of England commanded by Lieutenant General George S. Patton, Jr. To support the illusion, imitation landing craft were moored in rivers, and what seemed to be ammunition dumps, hospitals, field kitchens, and weaponry of all kinds, including rubber tanks, were scattered over the countryside.

So realistic were the means employed that German intelligence became convinced that the 1st U.S. Army Group did exist and was going ashore at Calais. Accordingly, the Germans braced themselves for an assault by upward of 90 divisions instead of the 35 that were actually on hand.

While deliberately misleading German intelligence, the Allies had available to them a mountain of data gathered by agents in France and from the French resistance, aerial photographs, underwater specialists, and commandos. On the basis of this information, plans could be laid and troops trained with a high degree of precision. Furthermore, for this campaign the British had developed a variety of special armored weapons: amphibious tanks, tanks that could blow up minefields by beating them with chains, flame-throwing tanks, mortar-firing tanks, bridge-laying tanks, and other specially developed weapons.

Although Operation Overlord was the best-planned Allied operation of the war, it was still risky. Everything had to go just right, particularly the deception plans. And the Allies needed to be lucky, for the weather had to meet rigid requirements. There were only three days in each two-week period in June when low tide and first light came together, the conditions that gave landing craft their best chance of survival. And the massive parachute drops that would begin the attack had to take place during a rising full moon—reducing the available days to only three. Further, on these three days the onshore winds could not exceed 12 miles per hour, and the offshore winds 18 miles per hour.

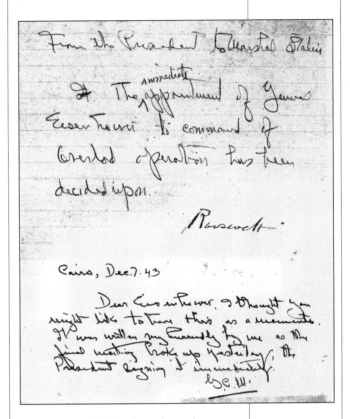

The visibility had to be at least three miles for naval gunfire to be accurate, and the cloud base no lower than 3,000 feet to allow fighter-bomber support.

Eisenhower's big decision It was ultimately the weather that forced General Dwight Eisenhower, who commanded the operation, to make one of the toughest decisions of the war. Overlord had been scheduled for June 5 and the assault troops were already on board ship when a channel storm grounded the all-important air support. At 4:30 a.m. on June 4, Eisenhower ordered a postponement and met again that night with his commanders. He had to decide whether to go ahead on Tuesday, June 6, or stand his forces down until the 19th, the next date when high tide and first light would coincide. It was raining hard at the time, but RAF Group Captain J. M. Stagg, SHAEF's chief meteorologist, reported that an area of decent weather had formed and would shortly provide

President Franklin Roosevelt signed this memo to Marshal Joseph Stalin, informing him that General Dwight Eisenhower was to head Operation Overlord. A Roosevelt aide then sent it to Eisenhower for him to keep it as a memento.

36 hours of reasonably clear air over the Channel.

Weather forecasting depended more on guesswork in 1944 than it does today, but the good weather did exist and was being tracked by Allied planes and radar. Thus, the next morning at 4:15, with the rain still pouring down, Eisenhower ordered the attack to begin.

Within minutes, 5,000 ships were putting out to sea. Ike knew the risk he was taking, since if bad weather continued Overlord would fail. In that case, if the losses were heavy, there might not be time to mount another assault on France in 1944.

Despite the odds, Overlord succeeded. High winds and nervous pilots caused many paratroopers to be dropped outside their landing zones, resulting in heavy casualties. High waves sank dozens of amphibious tanks, whose inflatable canvas covers were never designed for rough water. The casualties at Omaha Beach, where a strong German force poured heavy fire down from high cliffs, ran to several thousand. Of 225 men from the 2nd Ranger Battalion, who climbed the sheer cliffs of Pointe du Hoc under heavy fire, only 90 were still standing by nightfall.

But Fortitude South worked, the landings succeeded, and Germany's subsequent efforts to reinforce the defenders were smothered by Allied air power, naval guns, and French resistance forces, which blew up bridges, cut telephone lines, and attacked road convoys. At sunset on June 6, 1944, the European Theater of Operations at last included the Continent. The Allies were now too strongly entrenched to be driven off the beaches, and the fate of the Third Reich was no longer in doubt.

SEE ALSO

Eisenhower, Dwight D.; European Theater of Operations; France, Battle of

FURTHER READING

Ambrose, Stephen E. *D-Day*. New York: Simon & Schuster, 1994.
Ryan, Cornelius. *The Longest Day*. New York: Popular Library, 1959.

de Gaulle, Charles

COMMANDER, FREE FRENCH FORCES

- *Born: November 22, 1890, Lille, France*
- *Education: Saint-Cyr military academy, second lieutenant, 1912*
- *Military service: Infantry officer, 1912–16; prisoner of war, 1916–18; instructor and staff officer, 1918–37; tank commander, 1937–40*
- *Government service: Undersecretary of war, 1940; leader of Free France, 1940–1944; president of provisional government, 1944–46; president of France, 1958–69*
- *Died: November 9, 1970, Colombey-les-Deux-Eglises, France*

Charles de Gaulle knew even as a child that he was destined for greatness. After graduating from Saint-Cyr, France's equivalent of West Point, de Gaulle served bravely as an officer in World War I, performing heroic feats during the Battle of Verdun, in which he was taken prisoner. As a prisoner of war he made frequent—if vain—escape attempts.

Between the wars, de Gaulle became famous in the army for well-written lectures, articles, and books in which he put forward his ideas about the coming age of armored warfare, arguing that tanks should not be scattered among infantry regiments, as was the French practice, but concentrated as the army's shock force. The failure of France's senior officers to listen to him contributed to France's defeat in 1940.

One of the few French generals to achieve any success during the fall of

Charles de Gaulle is welcomed to Chad in 1942 by Governor-General Felix Eboune, the first African leader to rally to the Free French cause.

France to the Germans in June 1940, de Gaulle was serving as undersecretary of war in the cabinet in 1940 when it decided to ask for an end to the fighting that amounted to total surrender. With his usual farsightedness he had already recognized that France was doomed and saw that the fight must go on overseas. For that to be possible, however, Britain had to survive. This explained de Gaulle's remark to Churchill in 1940 after the prime minister had refused to throw his last fighter squadrons into the hopeless defense of France: "It is you who are right." For this support Churchill was prepared—and would be required—to forgive much.

The French National Committee
Britain took de Gaulle under its wing because he was the only French official of note in 1940 to reject the armistice. However, de Gaulle did not head a government in exile, only an organization called the French National Committee, whose resources consisted initially of the 7,000 French troops evacuated during the June 1940 British escape from Dunkirk who did not return to France. The administrators of a few minor colonies also threw in their lot with Free France, or Fighting France, as it was also called, as did the crews of some small warships and perhaps a quarter of the French merchant fleet.

Refugees excepted, most Frenchmen overseas, including those living in the United States, accepted the legality of the Nazi puppet government headquartered in Vichy. More importantly, so did President Roosevelt, who made his friend Admiral William D. Leahy ambassador to Vichy—which had some authority in southern France, the rest of the country being occupied and directly administered by the Germans.

FDR did so mainly to help Vichy France under Marshal Henri Petain keep its fleet and colonies out of German hands. Roosevelt confirmed Vichy control of French possessions in the Americas (such as Martinique) in return for the continued neutrality of the French forces stationed there. He also assured Marshal Petain—who had saved France during World War I but now was seen by the Free French as a traitor—that the United States would respect Vichy colonies in North Africa as well.

This policy put the United States on a collision course with de Gaulle, who was seizing French possessions wherever he could and was particularly interested in the small islands of Saint-Pierre and Miquelon just off Newfoundland. The British, who were giving de Gaulle financial backing, had no objection to this because a powerful radio station on Saint-Pierre was broadcasting Vichy propaganda. But Washington wanted the seizure to be undertaken by Canada, to spare Vichy feelings. Churchill said much later that de Gaulle had agreed to this arrangement but then, without warning, ordered his little navy to take the islands, which it did just before Christmas 1941.

This action was popular locally—the inhabitants voted overwhelmingly to join Free France—and the U.S. press was favorable, too. Churchill thought de Gaulle's action made little difference, but Roosevelt and Secretary of State Cordell Hull were furious, all the more so because of de Gaulle's refusal to compromise on how the islands should be governed. Although after much protest Hull allowed the issue to die, the Free French's relations with the United States were permanently poisoned by this adventure.

De Gaulle as war leader Charles de Gaulle was an outsized figure even in an age of giants, but unlike other world leaders he was not chief of a great state. De Gaulle started out as the leader of practically nothing, yet through persistence and strength of character, he spearheaded the drive to restore French honor. His insignia, the two-barred Cross of Lorraine, would everywhere come to be seen as the symbol of France's rebirth. It took immense personal powers and unbending determination to accomplish this.

To Roosevelt, and even to Churchill, who was more sympathetic, de Gaulle appeared to have major faults. Utterly dependent on Britain and the United States, he made a habit of biting the hands that were feeding him. Churchill claimed that de Gaulle once said to him that if he were too cooperative he would be regarded by the French as being a tool of the Allies. If that was the danger, he clearly succeeded in avoiding it, leading to Churchill's well-known remark that the heaviest cross he had to bear was the Cross of Lorraine.

The fundamental disagreement between de Gaulle and his allies was that they were determined to treat him as the commander of a small allied force, while he insisted upon being treated as the leader of France. In his outstanding war memoirs, de Gaulle explained his strategy, which he adopted immediately upon reaching England in 1940. Although grateful to Churchill, de Gaulle had reason to feel that the great powers would pursue their war aims at the expense of France if necessary—which he was determined to prevent against all odds.

From the first, de Gaulle's idea was that since he had nothing, he could not give an inch. As he wrote in his memoirs: "Those who, all through the drama, were offended by this intransigence were unwilling to see that for me, intent as I was on beating back innumerable conflicting pressures, the slightest wavering would have brought collapse. In short, limited and alone though I was, and precisely because I was so, I had to climb to the heights and never then to come down."

This proved to be no idle boast but became an exact description of the course he followed. No one less arrogant, unbending, insensitive, ungrateful, and self-confident than de Gaulle could have forced the Allies to accept him as the leader first of North Africa, then of liberated France, and finally the head of a great power entitled to share in the occupation of Germany at the end of the war. Inevitably, this brought down on him the anger of Churchill but especially Roosevelt.

But, however mistaken de Gaulle may have been in matters of detail, as over Saint-Pierre and Miquelon, his devotion to France would make possible its salvation. Few Frenchmen appreciated this at first. Most accepted German rule as final: some passively, many others by actively cooperating with the Nazis. Among the latter "collaborators" were those responsible, among other crimes, for the deaths of many of the 75,000 to 100,000 French Jews who were sent to Nazi death camps. It was de Gaulle's major achievement that, over time, he and his movement made it impossible to be both a good French citizen and a collaborator. This situation first angered and embarrassed many, but finally it became the means to restore the self-respect of the French.

De Gaulle and Roosevelt The combination of his relatively low rank and his high aims made it easy to underestimate de Gaulle at first, as did Roosevelt. In October 1942 he began giving Lend-Lease aid directly to de Gaulle's French

General de Gualle addresses the Algiers Consultative Assembly on June 17, 1944.

National Committee, but while Allied military cooperation improved somewhat, the Free French were not only excluded from the invasion of French North Africa but were not even informed of it. De Gaulle had no doubts about what FDR meant. It was the President's intention, de Gaulle believed, to gain control of French affairs and the Free French army.

This explanation appeared to de Gaulle to be the reason why the Americans had first tried to make General Henri Giraud the leader of French North Africa but then struck a bargain with Admiral Jean Darlan, the commander of Vichy armed forces who had been in North Africa on November 8, 1942, when the Allies invaded it. The so-called Darlan deal made this Nazi collaborator the high commissioner of French North Africa (with Giraud under him as head of the military) in return for ordering the Vichy French forces to lay down their arms.

This deal, which the Allies considered practical, was to de Gaulle merely a crude attempt by Roosevelt to take Free France out of the picture. If so, the policy failed badly. The French authorities in Tunisia defied Darlan's order to surrender, giving Hitler time to rush in troops and prevent an Allied victory. And, after Darlan was assassinated on December 24, 1942, the Allied attempt to replace him with Giraud aroused little enthusiasm.

Throughout the critical year following the North African invasion, de Gaulle played his cards with great shrewdness. He did not blame the Allies for failing to include Free France in their invasion of French territory but instead called on Frenchmen to assist it. Never challenging Roosevelt directly, he continued to extend his influence and build grass roots support.

In time it became clear that the French in North Africa would not accept Giraud and his Vichyites as their lawful rulers. A clumsy power-sharing arrangement with de Gaulle worked no better. Finally, Giraud resigned as co-president of the French Committee for National Liberation—now the umbrella group covering all anti-Vichy Frenchmen—and closed his separate recruiting offices. In 10 months de Gaulle had swallowed him up.

French Committee for National Liberation On November 9, 1943, de Gaulle created a government in exile. From that day on there was one army, one navy, and one leader of all the Free French for the first time since 1940. In his memoirs de Gaulle is honest about how he forced himself and his government upon the reluctant Allies, saying only that they came to terms with what they could not prevent. It was in fact greatly to France's advantage to have de Gaulle in command, for he was a fierce and successful defender of French interests. But the Allied cause did not suffer as a result, despite Roosevelt's reluctance to accept de Gaulle as a legitimate leader.

Roosevelt made a final effort to put de Gaulle in his place before D-Day, when he insisted that de Gaulle's followers not be allowed to govern the liberated areas of France, but this ploy also came to nothing. On June 14, 1944, after the Allied beachhead was established, de Gaulle arrived in Normandy, toured the liberated area, and as he left General Bernard Montgomery's headquarters, said to the British commander that he was leaving an officer behind to "look after the population." With these words Charles de Gaulle established his authority over liberated France, and because it could not be removed except by force, Roosevelt had to accept it.

Under de Gaulle, France made important contributions to the war effort, especially in Italy and on the western front. And de Gaulle proved himself to be genuinely democratic, stepping down from his position as head of state in 1946 when he encountered opposition instead of using the army to stay in power. Thus de Gaulle was well placed in 1958 to save French democracy once again when it was threatened by an armed revolt led by generals determined to win the losing struggle to retain Algeria.

SEE ALSO
France; Mediterranean theater

FURTHER READING
Aglion, Raoul. *Roosevelt and de Gaulle: Allies in Conflict: A Personal Memoir.* New York: Free Press, 1988.
Cogan, Charles G. *Charles De Gaulle: A Brief Biography With Documents.* New York: Bedford, 1995.
Cook, Don. *Charles De Gaulle: A Biography.* New York: Putnam, 1983.
De Gaulle, Charles. *The Complete War Memoirs of Charles De Gaulle.* New York: Simon & Schuster, 1967.
Lacouture, Jean. *De Gaulle: The Rebel, 1880–1944.* New York: Norton, 1990.
Shennan, Andrew. *De Gaulle.* New York: Longman, 1993.

Destroyers

Before the development of destroyer escorts during World War II, destroyers were the smallest naval warships. Fast, maneuverable, armed with naval guns, torpedo tubes, depth charge launchers, and a wide variety of antiaircraft weapons, destroyers were among the most useful of fighting ships.

The most common U.S. destroyer of World War II was the *Fletcher* class, of which at least 175 were built. Capable of making 38 knots, with their five 5-inch guns and 10 torpedo tubes they packed a sizable punch. At first they were less effective than Japanese destroyers, because of seriously defective torpedoes and inferior tactics. But when these faults were corrected, the *Fletcher* class came to be regarded as the best destroyers of the war. They were used in action in both the Atlantic and Pacific oceans.

SEE ALSO
Submarines in the Pacific; U-boats

Destroyer escorts

The enormous demand for ships capable of escorting Atlantic convoys led Britain, and then the United States, to create antisubmarine vessels smaller in size than destroyers but cheaper and easier to build. The United States produced two classes of destroyer escorts.

These two classes ranged in length from 289 to 306 feet. They had a maximum crew size of 208, compared to destroyers, which could be as long as 381 feet and carry up to 340 men.

Destroyer escorts were slow ships compared to destroyers, with top speeds that did not exceed 24 knots. And they were even less comfortable and less seaworthy than their big brothers, the rough-riding "tin cans." Still, they were invaluable in the war against the U-boats. Three hundred seventy-three of them saw active service.

SEE ALSO
Atlantic, Battle of the; U-boats

Diplomacy

SEE Foreign policy

Draft

SEE Selective Service System

Dresden, bombing of

The destruction of Dresden, Germany, from the air on February 13–14, 1945, remains the most controversial attack of the European air war.

A charming old city on the Elbe River in eastern Germany, Dresden had been largely untouched by Allied bombers, because of its military insignificance. Why Dresden was bombed at all is still something of an open question. One reason was that killing German civilians was the number one priority of Air Marshal Sir Arthur Harris, head of the RAF's Bomber Command. He never stopped believing that Germany could be made to stop the war as the result of terror attacks. The fact that Dresden was swollen with refugees would have made it a particularly attractive target from this point of view.

Some historians have argued that the Western Allies wished to impress the Soviets, who were approaching Dresden, with the power of their air arms. However, military concerns came into play as well. The Soviets had asked for air support, and Dresden had recently become a regional command and communications center, meaning that bombing it would impair Germany's defenses in the east. No doubt some combination of these reasons lay behind the decision to attack Dresden.

On the night of February 13, 1945, some 800 RAF *Lancaster* bombers dropped a sufficient number of high-explosive and incendiary bombs to start the intended "firestorm," in which separate fires combine to form one great inferno that sucks oxygen up at such a rate that people untouched by the fire or blast still suffocate in their shelters. On February 14 a daylight raid by Flying

Fortresses of the U.S. Eighth Air Force wiped out Dresden's civil defense workers.

It is not known how many perished in the firestorm, since most of the dead were hurriedly buried in mass graves. At a rough guess, some 50,000 people were killed in Dresden. Prime Minister Churchill, a supporter of this operation at first, backed away from it when critics challenged the morality of making war on civilians.

SEE ALSO

Arnold, Henry H.; Hamburg, bombing of; Strategic bombing

FURTHER READING

Irving, David. *The Destruction of Dresden.* New York: Ballantine, 1963.
McKee, Alexander. *Dresden 1945: The Devil's Tinderbox.* New York: Dutton, 1984.
Vonnegut, Kurt. *Slaughterhouse-Five.* 1959. Reprint, New York: Dell, 1999. Fiction.

Eastern front

The eastern front opened on June 22, 1941, when the Wehrmacht, Germany's armed forces, swept over the country's border into the Soviet Union. Operation Barbarossa, the code name for this assault, was designed to seize European Russia with its coal, oil, and grain fields. These newly conquered territories were to provide Germany with unlimited raw materials and living room (in German, *lebensraum*) beyond what anyone previously had thought possible.

Yet, despite Germany's early successes there, the eastern front would become the graveyard of that army and cost Hitler the war. A single statistic tells it all: In World War II, German forces are believed to have taken more than 13 million casualties (dead, wounded, missing, and cap-

tured). Of these, more than 10 million were sustained on the eastern front.

Hitler and most of his generals underestimated the difficulties they would face in Russia. For one thing, they believed—with good reason—that the Red Army would be easy to beat. Stalin had murdered most of his senior officers during the purges of the 1930s. Then, too, the Red Army had performed badly in its Winter War with Finland in 1939–40. As part of the Stalin-Hitler Pact of August 23, 1939, the Soviets were allowed to invade Finland in that year. Stalin wanted to strengthen Russia's security at Finnish expense by seizing various territories, notably lands north of Leningrad and west of Murmansk. When the Finns refused to give in to Soviet demands, the Red Army attacked on November 30.

The Soviets won in the end, but only at a remarkable cost. Although Finland had some 200,000 troops and the Soviets 1.2 million, the Finns were highly motivated, well trained, and ably led. Leaderless and demoralized, the Red Army floundered, then ground to a halt. A new offensive that began on February 1, 1940, did better, after the Soviet forces had been reorganized and reequipped. They broke the Mannerheim line across Finland's Karelian Peninsula and destroyed the Finns' fallback positions as well.

The armistice concluded on March 12, 1940, gave Stalin just what he had asked for. Even so, 200,000 Russian troops had been killed, while Finnish losses were only one-eighth as great. Understandably, military experts around the world concluded that the Red Army was far more feeble than its huge numbers of men and weapons suggested.

Besides the issue of military might, Germany believed that the Soviet Union was politically fragile. Stalin's rule was based on terror, and many of the Soviet "republics," such as Ukraine and the former Baltic states, were known to want independence. Then, too, the German blitzkrieg (literally, "lightning war") had been so effective against Britain and France, with their much more modern forces, that Germany did not believe the Red Army could stand up to a similar assault.

These arguments inspired Germany to go east, although Britain still remained unconquered on Germany's western front. There would be time enough to deal with Britain later, Hitler thought, which turned out to be another serious mistake.

Barbarossa At first it seemed as if the experts who predicted an easy victory were right. Germany attacked with overwhelming force—some 3.2 million men—including troops from other Axis states, 3,600 tanks, and 2,700 aircraft. Against them stood 2.9 million Soviet troops, 10,000 to 15,000 tanks, and about 8,000 aircraft. But the Soviet troops were unready, Stalin having insisted, despite plenty of warnings from Britain, the United States, and, more importantly, his own spies, that his forces remain on a peacetime footing. Furthermore, nearly all the Soviet tanks were obsolete, as were Soviet aircraft—most of which were destroyed on the ground in any case. As a result, Soviet soldiers—outnumbered, outgunned, and with the Germans breaking through their lines at will, surrendered by the millions.

All the same, victory eluded the Wehrmacht. No doubt it could have taken Moscow had not Hitler insisted on establishing three separate fronts. He divided his troops into Army Groups North, South, and Center, none of them strong enough to achieve their aims. Army Group North was stopped at Leningrad, Army Group South at the Donets Basin, north of the Sea of Azov

and between the Dnieper and Donets rivers. When Army Group Center was finally reinforced and allowed to move in strength against the Soviets, fall rains made the roads useless—and then came winter. Despite the usual victories and mass Soviet surrenders, Army Group Center ground to a halt in December with the spires of Moscow's Kremlin in sight. It was then thrown back by troops from Siberia, which had been kept in reserve for this purpose.

During the winter of 1941–42, Germany held its ground, but the troops suffered greatly. They had been issued no winter gear and were unprepared for days when the temperature dropped to

40 degrees below zero. Water froze in locomotive boilers, oil in crankcases, grease in the army's guns. Wounded German troops died where they fell, victims of shock and frostbite. One hundred thousand horses died over the winter and were eaten by starving troops. The Soviet forces, which were trained and equipped for such weather, were also much closer to their sources of supply and made it through the winter easily.

Although Germany was still far from beaten, apart from its battlefield victories little had gone according to plan. The Soviets' resistance had proven stronger than expected, and the Germans could not take advantage of the anticommunist feelings that ran high in the territories they were occupying. Hitler had ordered that these Slavic peoples be treated brutally as future slaves of the Third Reich. These ethnic minorities, already unwilling Soviet citizens, had believed that no rule could be worse than Stalin's, which, given their experience to date with the Soviets, was perfectly reasonable. On that basis many had welcomed the German troops as liberators at first. But Hitler's forces were even worse than the devil they knew, forcing the Soviet people to fight for their lives, even if this also meant fighting for Stalin.

If Hitler had taken a softer line, which is to say if he had not been a Nazi, the conquered anticommunist ethnic groups might have become German allies and the war would have turned out quite differently. Hitler's racial prejudices, which were central to Nazi ideology, were also his greatest weakness and would bring him down in the end. Stalin cleverly exploited the Nazis' weaknesses, downplaying his own communist ideology and declaring Russia's fight for survival to be the "Great Patriotic War." Hitler had been right in believing that the Soviet Union was politically weak, but by his racial policies, he made it stronger.

Moreover, the German strategists had failed to allow for the vast distances in European Russia and the Soviet Union's enormous manpower reserves. Stalin could, and did, trade land for time, drawing the Wehrmacht deeper and deeper into what would finally become a trap. While he did so, he had many Soviet factories dismantled on the run and relocated behind the Ural Mountains, where Germany could not get them. This feat, which was the equivalent of moving the industrial cities of Detroit and Pittsburgh to California, would have been an incredible accomplishment even in peacetime. Only a people made desperate by the Nazis' savagery could have accomplished such a thing while fighting a terrible war.

But more important than Hitler's political and military errors was his one overwhelming strategic mistake. He failed to see that the Soviet Union was just too enormous to be beaten by military means alone. Even if Moscow had fallen, as it nearly did, Stalin could have retreated to strongholds in and beyond the Urals and continued the war indefinitely.

By the end of 1941 the Soviet Union remained unconquered, even though Germany had won nearly every battle. In doing so, it had sustained almost 1 million casualties, nearly a third of the attacking force. The Soviets' suffering was even worse, with more than 3 million men having become prisoners of war and additional millions killed or wounded. But the Soviet Union could afford its losses; Germany could not. Thus, while the Red Army would grow and improve, the Wehrmacht would never be as strong again as when it had first invaded Russia.

In the spring Germany attacked again, aiming to win the war. For this drive, called Operation Blue, which Hitler had planned himself, he had some 2.5 million troops stretched along a 1,500-

A German motorized column comes under attack by Soviet aircraft during the early weeks of the war on the eastern front.

mile front. Over the winter he sent only 7,500 new vehicles to replace 75,000 that had been lost. Equally serious for an army that still relied on draft animals to transport its infantry, of 180,000 horses and oxen that had been lost, Germany could replace only 20,000. And, because German industry was still on a peacetime footing, Nazi aircraft and tank shortages were also acute.

Meanwhile, Soviet production was booming. Factories—often without heat or even roofs, and staffed by women, old men, and children—were churning out weaponry. By the end of 1942, the Soviet assembly lines were producing 2,000 tanks a month and 30,000 planes per year, whereas Germany would build only 4,000 planes in all of 1942. The aircraft were good, too; the tanks even better. More than half the Soviet tank production consisted of the excellent T-34, which Germany would not match until its Panther was deployed in 1943. And even then, the Panthers would be produced in small numbers compared to T-34s.

Despite these shortages, the German offensive went well at first, resulting in the expected victories. The Crimea, in

the Black Sea, fell at last, and the Germans seized additional territory elsewhere in southern Russia and the Caucasus, between the Caspian and Black seas. But the main German thrust came to grief in the city of Stalingrad.

With 500,000 inhabitants when the war broke out, Stalingrad commanded the Volga River basin and produced more than a quarter of all Soviet tanks and mechanized vehicles. German General Friedrich Paulus and his Sixth Army reached Stalingrad in November 1942, but, although he nearly destroyed the city, he succeeded only in taking part of it. The Soviets launched flanking attacks to the Sixth Army's rear and, on November 23, completely encircled it. Paulus requested permission to break out, but Hitler, relying on Reich Marshal Goering's promise to supply the Sixth Army by air, refused to permit a retreat. The Luftwaffe, or German Air Force, took heavy losses and could not meet the minimum needs of the embattled Sixth Army. Paulus surrendered to the Soviets on January 31, 1943. In a few more days, the Battle of Stalingrad was over. Later in February, the Caucasus was cleared of Germans for good.

Stalingrad proved to be the turning point of the European war. The Red Army emerged from it as a first-class fighting force that would never again suffer a strategic defeat. The Wehrmacht was now forced to fight defensively for the rest of the war. It did launch one last great eastern front assault in 1943, aimed at Kursk in the Soviet heartland. On July 5 the Wehrmacht pushed 700,000 troops, 2,400 tanks and assault guns, and 1,800 aircraft into the Kursk salient, or bulge. It was defended by a Soviet force that included 1.3 million men, 3,400 tanks and assault guns, and 2,100 aircraft. Hitler had not hoped to win the war in the East with so small a force, but rather to slow the Soviet tide. However, with the Red Army well dug in, well armed, and well led, and under attack by a smaller force, the outcome was never in doubt.

On July 12, 1943, the German II SS Panzer Corps met the Soviets' Fifth Guards Tank Army. In the resulting battle the panzers, outnumbered three to one by 900 Soviet tanks, were decisively beaten. This, the greatest single tank fight of World War II, was the end of Germany's last serious offensive. In late July and August, Soviet forces made further advances. A total of 4 million men, 13,000 armored vehicles, and 12,000 aircraft (three-quarters of them Soviet) fought in these engagements, making Kursk one of the largest battles of World War II.

From then on it would be Germany that traded land for time, until it ran out of both. By January 1944 Soviet forces had reached the southeast corner of pre-war Poland and lifted the siege of Leningrad. Germany sustained further losses during the spring, and on June 23, Marshal Georgi K. Zhukov launched a great offensive that took him into the rear of Army Group Center and cost the Germans 350,000 men. In August the Soviets reached Warsaw, pausing (delib-erately, some believed) to allow German forces to crush an uprising in the city of the Polish Home Army. The Poles had hoped to install a national government there before the Soviets arrived, which would have been awkward for Stalin, who had formed a communist government of Poland in Lublin.

However, while Stalin certainly welcomed the destruction of a potential rival, the main reason why the Red Army stopped short of Warsaw seems to have been that it was worn out by its long advance. In any case, the last Polish resistance ended on October 2, by which time Warsaw had been leveled and its entire population of 700,000 were either in concentration and death camps (the vast majority) or else had become slave laborers in Germany.

On September 12 Romania surrendered to the invading Soviets. As part of the terms, it contributed upwards of 16 divisions which fought on the Soviet side for the rest of the war. On September 19, Finland made peace with the Soviet Union, giving up the territories the USSR had first seized in 1940 but had never occupied. By the end of 1944, the Balkans had been largely cleared of Germans and the Baltic states retaken.

Then, on January 12, 1945, Stalin launched the single greatest offensive of World War II, sending almost 4 million troops against German forces that were frequently outnumbered 10 to 1. Although they fought desperately and at times slowed the Soviets, the necessary miracle did not take place. Berlin fell on May 2. The last German troops laid down their arms in the former Czecho-slovakia on May 11.

It is not sufficiently recognized that the largest battles of World War II were fought on the eastern front. Millions of men and hundreds of divisions were employed by each side. To appreciate the difference in scale, on the western front the largest separate command was the army group, consisting of two or more field armies. At their peak the Western Allies deployed three such groups. The Soviet equivalent of an army group was a front, of which the Soviets fielded no fewer than 37 at various times. The distances in the east dwarfed those of the western front as well.

The fighting on the eastern front involved a level of viciousness never exceeded in modern times. This was, for the most part, Germany's fault. Admittedly, Soviet troops committed atrocities at times, and once they reached German soil they developed a reputation for crimes against captured civilians, particularly women. But the Wehrmacht—not just the SS units but the German Army as a whole—pursued a "scorched earth" policy (in which the military destroys property and murders civilians while in retreat) in Russia that defies description.

On the western front, German troops by and large observed the rules of the Geneva convention governing captors' conduct toward prisoners. There, prisoners of war were correctly treated as a rule. Atrocities were rare, almost always committed by Nazi fanatics in the SS and similar formations. But on the eastern front, sadistic violence was commonplace. Villages were torched for no apparent reason, and prisoners and civilians were murdered by the millions, with the Wehrmacht behaving like a barbarian horde rather than a civilized army.

Taught from childhood to regard Jews and Slavs as subhuman, and deprived of their own humanity by Nazi doctrine and the primitive conditions under which they fought, German soldiers behaved worse than beasts. The Holocaust of the death camps is vividly remembered today; the other holocaust, in the East, is not. But it was just as homicidal and equally deserving of remembrance.

SEE ALSO

Poland; Soviet Union; Stalin, Joseph; Stalingrad, Battle of, Zhukov, Georgi K.

FURTHER READING

Bartov, Omer. *Hitler's Army: Soldiers, Nazis, and War in the Third Reich*. New York: Oxford University Press, 1991.
Erickson, John. *The Road to Stalingrad*. New York: Harper & Row, 1975.
Salisbury, Harrison. *The 900 Days: The Siege of Leningrad*. New York: Avon, 1969.
Werth, Alexander. *Russia at War, 1941–1945*. New York: Avon, 1970.

Eisenhower, Dwight D.

SUPREME COMMANDER, ALLIED EUROPEAN THEATER

- *Born: October 14, 1890, Denison, Tex.*
- *Political party: Republican*
- *Education: United States Military Academy, B.S., 1915; U.S. Army Command and General Staff School, 1925–26; Army War College, 1927–28*
- *Military service: U.S. Army—2nd lieutenant, 1915; major, 1918; Office of Assistant Secretary of War, 1929–33; aide to General Douglas MacArthur, Office of Army Chief of Staff, 1933–35; assistant military advisor, Commonwealth of the Philippines, 1935–39; colonel, 1939; major general, 1941; commander of U.S. forces in Europe, 1942; Allied commander for invasion of North Africa, 1942–43; Allied supreme commander in Europe, 1943–45; general of the army, 1945; commander in chief of U.S. armed services as President, 1953–61*
- *Died: March 28, 1969, Washington, D.C.*

Eisenhower was the third son of hard-working, devout, German-American parents in Abilene, Kansas, once a famous cow town but in Eisenhower's youth just another midwestern village

General Eisenhower consults with Free French leader Charles de Gaulle in Normandy.

lacking in diversity, the citizens to a large degree being white, Protestant Republicans with similar ideas about everything. Eisenhower always regarded it as an ideal community just the same, because its class lines were not sharply drawn and there was a strong emphasis on democracy, morality, achievement, and hard work. However, Eisenhower was relatively unprejudiced and had a knack for dealing with all kinds of people. These gifts would help make him the outstanding leader of coalition forces in World War II.

Eisenhower attended West Point for the free education rather than because he dreamed of military glory, and his early career showed little promise. When Eisenhower graduated in 1915, he ranked 61st in a class of 164 and seems not to have impressed anyone. Then in 1922 he was assigned to the Panama Canal Zone as executive officer to General Fox Connor, who changed his life.

Connor, a student of military science and history, became Eisenhower's mentor, leading the young officer through a program of study with a particular aim in mind. Connor believed that there was going to be another world war in which U.S. generals would lead allied forces, and he wanted Eisenhower to be one of these favored commanders. After Eisenhower's three-year tour in Panama was up, Connor used his influence to have Eisenhower admitted into the Command and General Staff School at Leavenworth, Kansas. Attendance at Leavenworth was a requirement for promotion to the highest ranks. After a year of study, Eisenhower graduated at the top of his class of 275 officers, all selected for their ability.

Because in the peacetime army promotion was slow, this achievement, while it made him known to his superiors, did not bring immediate benefits. However, in 1933 Eisenhower became an aide to General Douglas MacArthur, then army chief of staff, whom he served in Manila as well as after MacArthur took command of the Philippine armed forces. In 1940, only a lieutenant colonel after 25 years of service in which he had earned the highest praise from MacArthur as well as Connor, Eisenhower became a regimental executive and battalion commander in the 3rd Infantry Division.

The Army was now on the verge of tremendous growth, and Eisenhower would rise with it. In January 1941 he was made chief of staff to General Walter Krueger's Third Army, receiving much of the credit when Third Army defeated Second in the big Louisiana training maneuvers of August and September. On December 12, 1941, five days after Pearl Harbor, General George C. Marshall summoned Eisenhower to the War Department, and by April Eisenhower had become a major general in charge of planning. On June 11, 1942, he was appointed to command the new European Theater of Operations, which brought him the third of his eventual five stars.

When Britain and the United States decided to invade French North Africa in 1942, Eisenhower was the obvious choice to lead the operation. He knew many of the leading British officers, got along with them well, and was already displaying the political skills that a coalition commander needed to have. The invasion itself was untidy, but luckily the forces of Vichy France put up little resistance. The real problems came when Hitler decided to pour troops into Tunisia, which he imprudently insisted on trying to keep.

It would take until May 1943 to defeat Germany and the Axis powers in North Africa, during which time U.S. soldiers did not always perform well, especially at the beginning. This was only to be expected of raw troops and untried commanders and was not held against Eisenhower by General Marshall, whose opinion meant everything. Another invasion, Operation Husky, the conquest of Sicily, proved more difficult than it should have been, but Eisenhower could not be faulted because the British had done the planning for it. The invasion of Italy in September 1943 was a near disaster, and the U.S. troops that landed near Salerno were nearly driven off the beach. Here Eisenhower showed his military talents for the first time, salvaging the operation with timely reinforcements and troop movements.

By the end of 1943 Eisenhower had behind him not only a fast rise in rank even by wartime standards, but the experience of commanding three amphibious landings on enemy shores. This background made him the logical person to take charge of Operation Overlord, the scheduled invasion of France, which would be the greatest such operation in history. Yet at the time people took it for granted that because he had created the forces that would take part in it, General Marshall would command Overlord. Eisenhower was expected to replace Marshall as chief of staff.

However, on December 5, 1943, President Franklin D. Roosevelt asked his chief of staff what position he wished to have next. Marshall in fact wanted to command Overlord, but he told the President that he would cheerfully do whatever he was asked. Roosevelt then said, "Well, I don't feel I could sleep at ease if you were out of Washington." So it was Eisenhower who won the prize assignment of the war.

FDR's decision turned out to be among his most important. Apart from Marshall's gifts as a leader and military executive, the main argument for giving Overlord to him was as a reward for his services. If Overlord resulted in victory, its commander would be seen as the foremost U.S. general of the war. After building up the U.S. Army from scratch, Marshall had earned the right to lead it in its greatest battles and enjoy the resulting glory.

Otherwise, trading Marshall for Eisenhower had nothing to recommend it. Each would have to learn a new and very different job. Each would lack the experience that had helped make the other successful. Marshall was the military man Congress trusted most, Eisenhower the American in whom Britain had the greatest confidence. Many men had died to qualify Eisenhower for supreme commander. It made no sense to waste their lives and what Eisenhower had learned in those battles to implement what was ultimately a sentimental decision. Roosevelt had the right men in the right jobs and wisely kept them there.

Eisenhower would fully justify the trust that had been placed in him. Overlord, under his direction, was the best-planned Allied operation of the war. Thanks to him, the British and U.S. officers who staffed his Supreme Headquarters Allied Expeditionary Force (SHAEF) in London worked together effectively and with a minimum of friction. When all was ready, Eisenhower made what was, perhaps, the hardest decision required of any U.S. commander in World War II.

The invasion of Normandy, France, was scheduled for June 5, 1944. The men and equipment were aboard their ships on June 4 when bad weather struck the English Channel. Eisenhower delayed the attack for a day, but on June 5 he had to decide whether to give the

Eisenhower, accompanied by General Omar Bradley (middle right), inspects art treasures stolen by the Nazis and hidden in a salt mine in Germany.

go-ahead signal or not. If he ordered the invasion to begin and the weather did not break, Overlord would fail. It would be months before the Allies could try again, and by then the element of surprise would be lost.

At the moment of decision, the German leaders still did not know where the attack would take place and had divided their forces to cover the most likely sites. Once they became sure, however, they could concentrate all their forces in Normandy and very possibly repel the invasion. The temptation must have been strong for Eisenhower to play it safe by waiting for better conditions. But he made the hard choice instead, gambling that the weather would clear in time for his landing craft to make the long passage from their troopships to the enemy shore. In the end, fortune favored the brave: the weather did clear on June 6 for just long enough, and D-Day became a great victory, made possible by Eisenhower's bold decision.

After long, hard fighting the Allies broke out of Normandy in August, crossed the Seine River, and expelled the German forces from most of France. On August 30 General George Patton's Third Army, which had led the U.S. charge, ran out of gas—literally. Because the Allies did not have an intact seaport, their fuel and supplies were being unloaded on the beaches of Normandy. There was not enough of anything to go around, although fuel was in the shortest supply. In a much-criticized decision, Eisenhower gave preference for supplies to the British 21st Army Group at the expense of the U.S. 12th, which included the Third Army. While Patton fumed, the British staged Operation Market-Garden, an effort to seize a bridge that crossed the Rhine in the Netherlands. Market-Garden failed, and the great Allied advance from Normandy came to an end.

From then on, until almost the close of the war in Europe, the Allies pursued Eisenhower's "broad front" strategy, which applied pressure to the Germans all along their newly reformed front. This tactic was, and remains, controversial. General Omar Bradley, commanding all the U.S. ground forces in the European theater, and Field Marshal Bernard Law Montgomery, the British commander, both disliked this strategy. Each would have preferred to have the bulk of the Allied resources committed to his own command for a decisive strike.

In hindsight, it would probably have been best to have concentrated on a narrower front and broken through Germany's western defenses in the fall of 1944. Bradley's command was the logical force for this role, because it was stronger and faster than Montgomery's. But politics appears to have ruled this out. The British would have been furious if Eisenhower had assigned them to a supporting role. For the sake of Allied unity, then, he chose to make a slow advance along a broad front as the practical course, if not the best strategy.

From September 1944 until March 1945, the Allies advanced slowly. Then, late in December 1944, Hitler surprised the Allies by launching one last offensive, through the Ardennes Forest of Belgium, where the U.S. line was weak. Eisenhower was at his best in this crisis, telling his commanders to see this as an opportunity rather than a setback.

Eisenhower pulled men out of the long U.S. front and rushed them in huge numbers to the bulge created by Germany's advance. This engagement, the Battle of the Bulge, was the greatest ever fought by the U.S. Army and ended in victory, as Eisenhower knew it would.

Eisenhower's broad-front approach began paying off in March 1945, when the German lines started to crumble. Although Montgomery was supposed to cross the Rhine River first, units of the U.S. Ninth Army under Bradley's overall command, seized an intact Rhine bridge at Remagen, and Eisenhower gave Bradley free rein to exploit this opportunity.

What followed was another great surge forward like the one after the breakout from Normandy, with U.S. armored units running wild and capturing entire German armies. On May 7, following Hitler's suicide on April 30, Admiral Karl Doenitz, who now commanded the Third Reich, surrendered to Eisenhower at 2:41 a.m. in Reims, France. Eisenhower, the Allies, and the cause of freedom had triumphed.

After the war, Eisenhower would be criticized for failing to take Berlin, which might have been possible. The Soviets had been closer to it than U.S. troops in March, when German resistance in the West began to collapse, but Bradley's troops were more mobile and perhaps could have reached Berlin first. Churchill was all in favor of such a dash, but the territory that would have been gained by it had been promised to the Soviet Union at the Yalta conference in February 1945 and would have had to be turned over to it in any case. Furthermore, Berlin was a political prize but had no strategic value, and taking it would have been very costly. Eisenhower therefore did the sensible thing, notifying Stalin that his forces would stop along the line agreed to at Yalta. Soviet troops then went on to take Berlin, suffering, at the very least, 100,000 casualties for the sake of this empty honor.

SEE ALSO

Bulge, Battle of; D-Day; France, Battle of; Italian campaigns; Marshall, George C.; North African campaign; Patton, George S., Jr.; Sicily, Battle of

FURTHER READING

Ambrose, Stephen. *Eisenhower: Soldier and President*. New York: Touchstone, 1991.
———. *Eisenhower: Soldier of the Army, President-Elect, 1890–1952*. New York: Simon & Schuster, 1983.
Darby, Jean. *Dwight D. Eisenhower: A Man Called Ike*. New York: Lerner, 1989.
Eisenhower, David. *Eisenhower at War, 1943–1945*. New York: Random House, 1986.
Eisenhower, Dwight D. *Crusade in Europe*. Garden City, N.Y.: Doubleday, 1948.
Lee, R. Alton. *Dwight D. Eisenhower: A Bibliography of His Times and Presidency*. Wilmington, Del.: Scholarly Resources, 1991.
Sandberg, Peter Lars. *Dwight D. Eisenhower*. New York: Chelsea House, 1987.

Election of 1942

In 1940 the Democratic party retained control of both houses of Congress. But President Franklin D. Roosevelt was often frustrated by Congress, because many Democrats in it were conservative

southerners who were closer on many issues to the Republican party than to Roosevelt's New Deal program.

In the off-year elections of November 1942, the conservatives won so many seats that during the next two years the legislative branch was, in all but name, a Republican Congress. Because of a light Democratic turnout (possibly caused by a lack of confidence in Roosevelt), and because most of the war news to that point had been bad, the Republicans fell only 13 seats short of a majority in the House and missed controlling the Senate by just 9.

If North Africa had been invaded a week earlier than it was on November 8, the election results might well have been different, for Operation Torch was popular at home, and its impact would have benefited the Democrats. Instead, their margin was so thin that in 1944, just before the general election, the Democrats would lose their majority altogether.

The 1942 election results strengthened the conservative wing of each party. Southern Democrats frequently voted with Republicans, which is how it came about that the 78th Congress ended many New Deal programs. Although Congress normally supported the President in military and foreign affairs, in 1944 it refused to enact a national service bill. This measure would have given the federal government considerable authority over the civilian labor force, so that workers could be kept on the job or sent wherever they were most needed. Congress also refused to increase the military draft when asked to do so. ·

Both congressional decisions hurt the war effort. Congress's failure to expand the draft was especially serious, because in 1944 a military manpower shortage developed. This forced the army to keep fighting men on the line for longer periods than was good for combat efficiency.

Election of 1944

By the fall of 1944, business was booming while abroad one victory followed another. Under these circumstances and with President Franklin D. Roosevelt's reelection a sure thing, it was hard to generate interest in politics.

In 1944, unlike in 1940, Roosevelt made an early announcement of his intention to run, draining the GOP nomination of its value. Thomas E. Dewey, formerly a mob-busting district attorney and now governor of New York, accepted it anyway. Because Dewey represented eastern, internationalist Republicans, the Republicans balanced their ticket by nominating as his running mate the isolationist governor of Ohio, John Bricker, a darling of the party's right wing. Having no fresh ideas, the GOP ran against the New Deal again, exciting few but the party faithful.

The Democratic convention proved to be much more lively, because even though the Presidential nomination had been settled, the choice of a Vice President remained open. The incumbent, Henry A. Wallace of Iowa, was popular among liberal Democrats, but southerners hated him, as did the big-city bosses, who still had great power. FDR was willing to dump Wallace if necessary, and because he ignored his Vice Presidents anyway, he did not have a strong personal preference.

The choice of the party's leaders was Harry S. Truman of Missouri, who had been a little-known U.S. senator until 1941. In that year he became chair of the Senate Special Committee to Investigate the National Defense Program, a job he performed well and that gained him much respect. Truman had voted consistently for New Deal legislation but was personally liked by conservative Senate Democrats, which made him ideal as a compromise figure.

Given FDR's failing health, it must be asked if he was wrong to run again. At the time he stood for reelection, Roosevelt was becoming forgetful because a combination of very high blood pressure, congestive heart failure, anemia, and congestion in his lungs prevented sufficient blood from getting to his brain. Yet his memory lapses, although they had become more frequent, were short-lived. There is no evidence that his mental capacity was otherwise impaired, and his enfeebled condition did not keep the President from hitting the campaign trail hard.

Roosevelt used one of the first important political pollsters, Hadley Cantril, and tailored his campaign according to Cantril's findings. Thus, in the fall, when polls showed that voters had doubts about his health, Roosevelt spoke outdoors in Ebbets Field, home of the Brooklyn Dodgers, then rode for four hours through pouring rain in an open car, exposing himself to both the elements and the voters, after which he gave a major address to the Foreign Policy Association. He exhibited stamina several more times before the election, undermining charges about his ill health, although they were in fact true.

It seems fair to say that if Roosevelt's campaign methods were a little misleading, his motives for wanting a fourth term stand up to examination. By this time the President had enjoyed all the power and glory that a human being might want; what remained was to finish the job. With Germany and Japan losing on the battlefield, the war no longer vitally interested FDR.

The great unfinished task was to secure the peace, which Roosevelt hoped to do by cementing the Grand Alliance of Britain, the Soviet Union, and the United States. No other statesman, he rightly believed, had the experience and skill needed to deal with Churchill and Stalin. Like most great men, Roosevelt believed that no one could replace him, and in truth, even as his powers declined, he was still better qualified to steer the ship of state through troubled waters than any other American.

The election campaign of 1944 plodded slowly along until Roosevelt made a brilliant speech to the Teamsters Union on September 23, indicting the GOP for telling lies about his pet dog Fala. This attack stung Dewey, and from then on, he and Bricker passed up no chances to sling political mud. Dewey claimed that Roosevelt was a left-winger and Truman a Ku Klux Klansman. According to Bricker, New Dealers had gotten the country into the war as a cure for unemployment. But such slander failed to slow the President down. He

In 1944, most Americans felt that Roosevelt should "stay and finish the job," despite doubts about his health.

climaxed the campaign in Boston by making fun of Dewey's desperate tactics, quoting from different speeches given on the same day in which Dewey had accused the President of allowing communists to seize power and of planning to make himself king.

The newspapers anticipated an extremely close election, but Roosevelt led Dewey by 3.6 million ballots and carried 36 states, with a total of 432 electoral votes to Dewey's 99. The election of 1944 was FDR's narrowest margin of victory, although a clear one, which carried over into the House of Representatives, where the Democrats returned to power. Many isolationists went down to defeat at last, easing the path of U.S. entry into the organization later to be known as the United Nations.

Probably the most important circumstance of this election was that in reelecting Roosevelt, the voters were also, without knowing it, choosing Truman as their next President. Although Democratic leaders had selected Truman for narrowly partisan reasons, they, and the country, were in luck, for Truman would be a better President than anyone could have expected, considering his limited experience.

ENIGMA

SEE Intelligence, military

European Theater of Operations

The name *European Theater of Operations* was commonly used to describe the theater of war commanded by General Dwight D. Eisenhower. Initially consisting only of the Britain, after Operation Overlord it grew to include France, the Netherlands, Belgium, and western Germany.

SEE ALSO
Supreme Headquarters Allied Expeditionary Forces (SHAEF)

Fair Employment Practices Commission

When the United States began to mobilize for war in 1940 and 1941, racial minorities, particularly blacks, were denied entry to almost all of the well-paid new jobs in defense industries. To protest the government's failure to correct this injustice, A. Philip Randolph, head of the most important black union, the Brotherhood of Sleeping Car Porters, called for a march on Washington to take place on July 1, 1941. The Roosevelt administration tried to persuade Randolph to call off the march. That failing, the President met with Randolph

A young man receives machine shop training in preparation for work in the defense industry. The Fair Employment Practices Commission ensured that blacks and other minorities would not be denied war-industry positions.

and other black leaders a few days before the scheduled event. The result was that the march was canceled in exchange for FDR's issuing of Executive Order 8802, establishing what became the Fair Employment Practices Commission (FEPC).

The FEPC opened up many defense industries not only to blacks but to Jews, aliens, Hispanics, American Indians, and other groups suffering from job discrimination. Thus, the march on Washington of 1941 that never took place was more successful than most of the actual civil rights marches of later years, which usually failed to produce such immediate and tangible benefits.

SEE ALSO
African Americans

Fascism

Technically, facism was the political doctrine of Benito Mussolini's National Fascist party of Italy. However, it is used as a general term to include all the right-wing totalitarian movements that sprang up after World War I. These included the National Socialists of Germany, the Spanish Falangists, the Romanian Iron Guard, and the Hungarian Arrow Cross parties.

Unlike Marxism, fascism had no central body of theory, but rather certain traits common to its various movements. Fascists were invariably superpatriotic and usually believed that their people were racially superior to others. They were intensely anticommunist. They all put their nation's mission and destiny ahead of individual rights. Fascist parties and regimes were typically brutal,

authoritarian (that is, they did not tolerate differences of opinion or political protest), militaristic, and anti-intellectual.

While these qualities often made them attractive to criminals and ultranationalists, no fascist party ever came to power by means of a free election. And fascist regimes' ultranationalism—their most central trait—also made it difficult for them to cooperate with each other. There was no coalition on the Axis side equal to that of the Anglo-American alliance, which set the standard for joint planning and teamwork.

SEE ALSO
Germany; Hitler, Adolf; Italy; Mussolini, Benito.

FURTHER READING
Griffin, Roger, and W. J. Krazanowski, eds. *Fascism*. New York: Oxford University Press, 1995.
Payne, Stanley G. *A History of Fascism, 1914-1945*. Madison: University of Wisconsin Press, 1995.
Stille, Alexander. *Benevolence and Betrayal: Five Italian Jewish Families Under Fascism*. New York: Penguin, 1993.

Financing the war

Taxation was the government's most important economic tool to pay for the enormous cost of war. An effective inflation fighter, it also raised huge amounts of money. However, taxes were not the only way the federal government could obtain cash. It could sell war bonds directly to individuals and institutions. It could force people to save money, then borrow the funds thus created. The Victory tax of 1942 had a compulsory savings feature which proved so unpopular that Secretary of the Treasury Henry

The artist Thomas Hart Benton created this poster as part of the government's campaign to encourage the purchase of war bonds.

Morgenthau led a successful fight to repeal it the next year.

Far more successful was the Revenue Act of 1942, which revolutionized the tax structure. This act was based on the ideas of Beardsley Ruml, the treasurer of Macy's and something of a financial genius. Ruml led a body of businessmen, called the Committee for Economic Development, who were dedicated to remodeling the federal tax structure. Ruml's group favored lowering the amount of income that would not be subject to tax so as to include the non-paying majority of Americans.

The Revenue Act of 1942 made this change, and the next year Congress adopted another idea of Ruml's, the "collection at the source" or "pay as you go" income tax plan, whereby tax payments were deducted from employees' paychecks. Thus, although only 7 million Americans had filed income tax returns in 1941, in 1944 some 42 million would do so. Not only did this new way of taxing people help finance the war but it was also fair, because it taxed people on the basis of their ability to pay. This tax was "progressive," meaning that the more you made the higher your rate of taxation became.

A national sales tax, on the other hand, which Morgenthau rejected, would have been "regressive," because everyone, rich and poor, would have paid at the same rate. This scheme would have burdened the poor, while the rich would hardly have noticed it.

This is why regressive, or "flat," taxes are generally popular among the rich.

The new tax formula aroused little opposition outside of government, with patriotism being one reason and the psychology of it another. The Internal Revenue Service discovered, as merchants had earlier, that individuals found small installment payments to be fairly painless, compared to having to pay in one large sum. The government made it easier still by its payroll withholding plan. Even people who had never heard of "pay as you earn" liked the idea at once. Gallup pollers found that as late as December 1942 only 44 percent of respondents knew what the Ruml plan was. However, when "pay as you earn" was explained to them, 71 percent endorsed it. By January 1943, when the government's publicity had done its work, 81 percent of Americans knew about the Ruml plan, and 90 percent of them favored it.

Thanks in part to the new income tax, during the war years the distance between high- and middle-income earners narrowed. For instance, in 1937 the richest 5 percent of Americans earned 27 percent of all income, but by 1944 their share had fallen to 16 percent. It was the only time in modern history when this happened.

Borrowing was another important way in which the federal government financed the war. Secretary Morgenthau believed that bonds should be sold in such a way as to inspire support for the war effort. Because to sell bonds was to sell the war, bond drives were aimed at average Americans rather than wealthy investors. This meant in turn drawing heavily on the popular culture. Movie stars played major parts. Hollywood organized tours that played in 300 communities. Dorothy Lamour, the co-star of a series of movies with Bob Hope and Bing Crosby, was credited with selling $350 million worth of bonds. Carole Lombard, a popular movie actress, gave her life to the effort, dying in a plane crash on her way home from a bond tour.

In addition to bonds, war stamps costing only pennies were sold, mainly to children. Every form of marketing was employed in this cause, with few Americans managing to escape it.

It cost the United States $318 billion to wage World War II, of which 45 percent was paid for out of current revenues. In no other American war was such a large share of the cost paid for during the duration. The percentage of national income that went to pay federal taxes rose from 7.1 percent in 1940 to an impressive 24.2 percent in 1945—without inflation or raising interest rates. The way in which government paid for the war was one of its biggest achievements, which contributed in important ways both to winning the war and to increasing the real income of most Americans.

FURTHER READING

Barber, William J. *Designs within Disorder: Franklin D. Roosevelt, the Economists, and the Shaping of American Economic Policy, 1933–1945.* New York: Cambridge University Press, 1996.

Lipsitz, George. *Rainbow at Midnight: Labor and Culture in the 1940s.* Urbana: University of Illinois Press, 1994.

Sutton, Antony C. *Wall Street and FDR.* New Rochelle, N.Y.: Arlington House, 1975.

Vatter, Harold G. *The U.S. Economy in World War II.* New York: Columbia University Press, 1985.

Finland

Finland was the only democracy to fight on the Axis side in World War II. There was a simple reason for this.

On November 30, 1939, the Soviet Union invaded Finland after the Finns refused to hand over territory that the USSR wanted. Some of the frontier land Soviet leader Joseph Stalin demanded was of no great value. But Soviet designs on the province of Karelia, the border of which was only a few miles from Leningrad, required Finland to give up a prosperous and thickly settled region.

Stalin had expected an easy victory, because the heavily outnumbered Finns were poorly armed. Instead, the Finns, who were well trained and tremendously motivated, fought the Soviets to a standstill in the Winter War of 1939–40. The Red Army won in the end, because of its enormous size and firepower compared to that of tiny Finland, and because the other democracies gave Finland little support. Thus the Soviets acquired what they wanted, chiefly the port of Karelia and the north shore of Lake Ladoga. Four hundred thousand Finns became refugees as a result.

After the Winter War, Finland rearmed and, having nowhere else to turn, accepted aid from Germany. When Germany invaded the Soviet Union in June 1941 Finland did, too, regaining most of its lost territory. It then went on the defensive until an armistice with the Soviets could be concluded on September 19, 1944. The terms of this agreement forced Finland to give back what it had regained and provide the Soviet Union with money and goods as compensation for the war.

After Soviet planes bombed this Finnish town, women returned to salvage what they could from their ruined homes.

The two wars cost Finland, which had a population of just 3.6 million in 1938, some 92,000 lives and ruined its economy. But the Finns' valor ("sisu," the national motto) and patriotism seem to have convinced Stalin that Finland as an occupied state would be more trouble than it was worth. As a result Finland remained independent and democratic, the only nation within the Soviet sphere of influence to have achieved this status.

The Soviet Union's Finnish policy ended up costing it dearly. Had Stalin left Finland alone, it would have remained neutral, like its neighbor Sweden. This would have saved the Red Army hundreds of thousands of men and much material that would otherwise have been available to the Soviet Union in 1941 and 1942, when it was fighting for its life and every man and gun was needed. Thus, the Soviet invasion of Finland was not only unjustified but a bad blunder as well.

SEE ALSO

Eastern front

Flamethrowers

A flamethrower functioned by combining the contents of a tank of thickened gasoline with pressurized nitrogen from a second tank. The nitrogen propelled the gasoline, which was ignited as it left the device's nozzle. The introduction of napalm (made from gasoline, other fuels, and a gelling agent consisting of napathenic and palmitic acids) in 1943 made the flamethrower even more terrifying and effective. Those carried by a man had a flame that extended up to 50 yards. Armored vehicles were equipped with much larger flamethrowers that had greater ranges.

Although every army used them, flamethrowers were most often employed by British and U.S. forces in Europe, and by the Americans in the Pacific. The chief defect of the hand-carried version was that it made the user an easy target. Thus flamethrowers were most effective against pillboxes (small, enclosed fortifications) and bunkers that had already been seriously weakened. One-man flamethrowers were, therefore, primarily mopping-up weapons, unlike the armored models, which could be used offensively. Even in mopping-up operations, casualties among those who operated flamethrowers remained high.

Flying Tigers

The American Volunteer Group (AVG) in China was known as the Flying Tigers because of the fangs painted on the long noses of their P-40 fighters.

The AVG was formed by Captain Claire Chennault, a retired U.S. Army flying officer who was an advisor to Generalissimo Chiang Kai-shek. In 1941, when the United States was still neutral, Chennault persuaded Washington to pay for air units in China that would be manned by volunteers from the U.S. Army and Navy. By November 1941 three AVG squadrons consisting of 100 pilots were training in Burma.

When Japan attacked Burma (then still a British colony) in December, the AVG joined with Royal Air Force (RAF) units to put up a remarkable defense. Although heavily outnumbered, the Allied squadrons repeatedly broke up Japanese air attacks, particularly those aimed at Rangoon. These successes enabled the British first to reinforce the Burmese capital and then, when its fall became certain, to withdraw from Rangoon in good order. The Japanese occupied it on March 8, 1942, only because Allied air strength was down to 10 fighters, some barely airworthy.

After leaving Burma, AVG pilots operated from bases in China until their contracts ran out in July 1942. Chennault had hoped that most of the pilots

A Chinese soldier guards a line of American P-40 fighter planes (Flying Tigers) at an unidentified flying field in China. The American pursuit planes had a 12-to-1 victory ratio over the Japanese.

would stay on under his command in what would become the U.S. Tenth Air Force, but only five did so, most preferring to rejoin their old outfits.

Except for delaying the fall of Rangoon and permitting a safe evacuation, the Flying Tigers did not significantly change the course of events. But their courage and skill were legendary and gave both the United States and China something to cheer about in the darkest days of the war.

SEE ALSO
China-Burma-India theater

FURTHER READING

Bond, Charles R. *A Flying Tiger's Diary.* College Station: Texas A&M University Press, 1984.
Chennault, Claire Lee. *Way of a Fighter.* New York: Putnam, 1949.
Howard, James H. *Roar of the Tiger.* New York: Orion, 1991.
Schultz, Duane. *The Maverick War.* New York: St. Martin's, 1987.

Forrestal, James V.
SECRETARY OF THE NAVY

- *Born: February 15, 1892, Beacon, N.Y.*
- *Government service: Undersecretary of the navy, 1940–44; secretary of the navy, 1944–47; secretary of defense, 1947–49*
- *Died: May 22, 1949, Bethesda, Md.*

Beginning as a bond salesman on Wall Street, Forrestal worked his way up to become president of a large brokerage house, Dillon, Read and Co., in 1938. As undersecretary of the navy, he supervised its procurement and production program. He worked closely with Secretary Frank Knox and was a dependable ally in Knox's struggle to keep the arrogant chief of naval operations, Admiral Ernest King, from adding to his already

vast powers. This struggle continued when Forrestal succeeded Knox after the secretary's death on April 28, 1944.

A member of the Urban League, which worked to improve economic opportunities for blacks, Forrestal immediately assigned more blacks to large auxiliary vessels, such as supply ships and tankers. Previously, African Americans had only served in the Navy's most menial jobs. Under Forrestal, many skilled occupations were opened to blacks, and 60 became officers. He also opened the previously all-white WAVES (Women Accepted for Voluntary Emergency Service) to blacks.

Forrestal worked hard to improve the Navy's public relations, despite Admiral King's notorious reluctance to tell the press anything. A frequent visitor to the Navy's far-flung battle areas, he witnessed the Marine Corps's bloody assault on Iwo Jima in February 1945. Forrestal was deeply moved by the sacrifice and suffering he saw on Iwo, and his former mere dislike of war turned to absolute hatred as a result.

Forrestal played a small but important role in the surrender of Japan. On August 10, 1945, after two atomic bombs had been dropped on it and the Soviets had entered the Pacific war, Japan broadcast to the Allies that it would surrender on the condition that "the prerogatives of His Majesty as a Sovereign Ruler" be maintained. Most of Truman's advisors believed that this offer should be accepted because the emperor would, in fact, be subordinate to General Douglas MacArthur, who would head the occupation of Japan. Only Secretary of State James Byrnes insisted that nothing less than unconditional surrender would meet with public approval. Forrestal broke the standoff by suggesting that Japan's condition be accepted, but that its surrender still be called unconditional.

SEE ALSO
King, Ernest J.; Knox, William Franklin

FURTHER READING
Forrestal, James. *The Forrestal Diaries.*
New York: Viking, 1951.
Hoopes, Townsend, and Douglas Brinkley.
*Driven Patriot: The Life and Times of
James Forrestal.* New York: Knopf,
1992.

France

When war broke out in 1939, France was one of the world's great powers and a leading industrial state. It still retained a vast colonial empire, with particularly large holdings in Africa and Southeast Asia. It was also a fully functioning democracy with a greatly admired high culture.

In the late 1930s, France had spent heavily on defense, with the result that it had large, well-equipped armed forces, including the world's fourth-largest fleet and a 5-million-man army. Its frontier with Germany was defended by the Maginot Line, a chain of modern, linked underground forts of unequaled size and strength. The Maginot Line was at the time believed to be impossible to break. Further, France was allied with Britain, an even richer and more powerful state with a larger empire and the world's biggest navy. Unlike the situation in 1914, when it had few troops, Britain was raising a large army.

But France had great liabilities, too. France's population of 41 million was smaller than Britain's and barely half that of Germany. Its empire, like Britain's, was too large to defend—especially French Indochina.

Furthermore, French morale was poor. Unlike Germany, which under Hitler regained its nerve, France had never

Troops in an American armored car parade victoriously past the Arc de Triomphe during the liberation of France.

recovered psychologically from its enormous losses in World War I. The attitude of the French Army reflected this loss of spirit. It thought only in defensive terms, although the best defense is the ability to deliver an effective counterattack. The French Army had done this in 1914, flanking a German host on the Marne River and saving France from defeat.

But there would be no "Miracle of the Marne" in World War II. When the German blitzkrieg (lightning war) struck in May 1940, France and Britain were defeated by an enemy inferior in numbers of men and tanks to the Allied force but superior in just about everything else.

As the western front collapsed, defeatists in the French cabinet refused Prime Minister Winston Churchill's request that the seat of government be moved to North Africa. From there, protected by its own fleet as well as the Royal Navy, and with an empire to draw on for men and material, France could have fought on.

Instead, France abandoned all resistance and signed a humiliating armistice with Germany. Most of France was annexed or occupied by the Germans, and Italy received a small occupation zone in the French Riviera. On July 10, 1940, the French National Assembly voted overwhelmingly to give control of what remained of France to Marshal Philippe Pétain. Petain had been a great hero in World War I, but he would disgrace himself, and France, by collaborating with the Nazis. All that remained of French honor now resided in the tiny forces of Brigadier General Charles de Gaulle, who escaped to Britain. There he set up a government in exile that was recognized by only a handful of small French colonies.

Petain's government was called Vichy France, because of its location in the small resort city of Vichy, in the center of the country, where it had been forced to move when Paris became the seat of the German military government. Petain and his followers regarded collaboration as the only course for France to take, because they assumed that Germany would win the war. In this spirit they faithfully obeyed German directives, passed anti-Semitic laws, and cooperated with the Gestapo (the police department of the SS) in rounding up Jewish refugees and shipping them to death camps. The Vichy government also consented to having 1.6 million French prisoners of war kept in Germany as workers. This amounted to slave labor and was a violation of the rules of war established by the Geneva Convention. And, when French resistance became active, the Vichy state assisted Germany's efforts to suppress it.

The Vichy government, together with French collaborators in the occupied zones, was of immense value to the German war effort, chiefly for economic reasons. By 1943 some 40 percent of France's economic output was going directly to the Germans. At least 55 percent of Vichy revenue went to Germany as payment for occupation costs. Because of its prewar wealth and industry, France became by far Germany's most important supplier of raw materials, manufactured goods, and services.

In addition, about 600,000 French workers were sent to Germany after France surrendered to the Nazis. A larger number were forced to work in French factories and mines whose output also went to the Germans. All told, France's contribution was equal to about one-quarter of the German gross national product. Without French cooperation on this massive scale, Germany would have been defeated much sooner.

Had the French authorities refused to collaborate, or had done so as little as possible, Germany would still have exploited the French economy, but much less effectively. This was demonstrated late in the war when the Vichy government began to collapse.

Despite its initial popularity, Vichy began to lose support as huge transfers of wealth to Germany drove down France's standard of living. The resistance movement grew in spite of savage German punishments. Low-level officials began refusing to obey orders, or in various ways undermined them. By June 1944, when the Allies invaded Normandy, Vichy was all but dead and the Germans were losing their grip on the French economy.

Germany never had the means to govern France directly and had to depend on collaborators for this. But when collaboration became a dirty word, Germany could maintain effective control only over the services essential to its army in France. And once the Allied invasion began, even this became difficult.

After D-Day, June 6, 1944, Charles de Gaulle established a temporary government manned by members of his Free French movement and leaders of the resistance organizations. Although de Gaulle remained firmly in charge, his government was broadly based and widely accepted. Fears that the conservative and highhanded de Gaulle would prevent the return of democracy proved unfounded.

Local elections were held in April and May 1944, a national election in October. De Gaulle accepted the results, even though more than 80 percent of the seats in France's new legislature went to left-wing parties, which opposed him.

At the time of France's liberation, one French army had been fighting with distinction in Italy for the better part of two years. After liberation de Gaulle formed a second army in France, basing it on the resistance fighters of the Maquis, an underground army that had fought the Germans in occupied France. As the First French Army it too fought with distinction as part of the U.S. 6th Army Group.

When the war ended, the French Army had a total of 18 divisions, a respectable force under the circumstances, though small compared to what France had fielded in 1939–40. Still, the French contribution to victory was sufficient for de Gaulle to demand, and be granted, an occupation zone in Germany alongside those of the United States, Britain, and the Soviet Union. He was not invited to the critical Yalta conference in 1945, because France was still more of a dependent state than an equal ally. But in the years after the war France would rise again, thanks largely to de Gaulle, the Free French, and the resistance.

France lost more people in the war than either Britain or the United States, despite their larger populations. All told, including some resistance fighters and 40,000 men from Alsace and Lorraine drafted into the German Army, 210,000 French military personnel died. Added to that figure were 60,000 French civilians killed by bombers—mostly Allied aircraft—and another 90,000 civilians and resistance fighters who were massacred, executed, or otherwise killed by the Germans. Further, 40,000 French prisoners of war died, another 40,000 French workers in Germany were killed, and 160,000 people were deported from France for political or racial reasons. The total French deaths, the majority of them civilians, came to some 600,000.

SEE ALSO

De Gaulle, Charles; France, Battle of; France, fall of

FURTHER READING

Burrin, Philip. *France under the Germans: Collaboration and Compromise.* New York: New Press, 1996.
Paxton, Robert O. *Vichy France: Old Guard and New Order.* New York: Columbia University Press, 1972.
Shirer, William L. *The Collapse of the Third Republic.* New York: Simon & Schuster, 1969.
Tunis, John R. *His Enemy, His Friend.* New York: Morrow, 1967.

France, Battle of

After the Allies landed in Normandy on D-Day, June 6, 1944, the plan was to clear Normandy by June 23, reach the mouth of the Seine River by July 10, and then drive eastward. But, despite Allied air supremacy, the Germans managed to bring in reinforcements and put

A woman cheers the return of the French Army and the liberation of France by the Allies.

up tremendous resistance. British attacks on the key city of Caen were beaten back by Germany's powerful Tiger tanks. U.S. Army assaults bogged down in the hedgerow country of southern Normandy, known as the Bocage.

All the same, inch by inch, in the face of heavy casualties, the Allies expanded their beachhead. On July 25 General Omar Bradley kicked off Operation Cobra, a massive attack designed to break the German front. After five days it was successful, and the Battle of France began.

On the 27th, Bradley had given Lieutenant General George S. Patton, Jr., command of a corps, with the rest of Patton's new Third Army to follow on August 1. On July 30 the 4th Armored Division seized Avranches, at the base of the Cotentin Peninsula, opening up not just Brittany but southern Normandy as well. U.S. Army pressure forced the Germans out of cover during daylight, exposing them to fighter-bomber attacks.

In three days Patton poured seven divisions through the narrow Avranches bottleneck onto open ground beyond it in one of his more amazing feats. Meeting little resistance, he asked for permission to junk the cautious original plan and break out of Normandy to the east. Given his head, Patton unleashed his armor, which raced east, then north, creating one side of a large pocket in which parts of three German armies were trapped. In a week one of his corps was at Le Mans, and by August 13 it was driving for Argentan.

On the 7th, the Germans had launched a desperate counterattack on Mortain, which failed. Now, finding themselves in danger of wholesale capture, they turned around and scrambled frantically to escape the pocket before it could be closed by Patton's troops advancing from the south and Canadians moving down from the north. Fear-

ing that the two Allied armies would end up firing on each other, Bradley prevented Patton from closing what became known as the Falaise gap. Many Germans thus managed to escape, but when the gap was closed on August 21, some 50,000 German troops were captured, with another 10,000 killed in the bloody Falaise pocket.

With the Allies in hot pursuit, the surviving Germans raced for the Seine River, which they crossed in a week. Although they had to leave much equipment behind and were down to a hundred tanks, 240,000 German troops escaped. This was enough, together with reinforcements, to rebuild and defend Germany's West Wall, or Siegfried Line, a belt of fortifications on its western border. Four Allied armies crossed after them, soon to be joined by a fifth. It had landed on France's Mediterranean coast in mid-August and in early September moved into position on Patton's right, completing the Allied front.

The Allies made good progress for a while after crossing the Seine. Patton advanced a hundred miles to the Meuse, Brussels fell to the British, who then took the great port of Antwerp with its docking facilities intact. Unfortunately, British commanders failed to occupy the far side of the Scheldt River, a 60-mile-long estuary that linked Antwerp to the open sea. It would take Canadian troops several months to clear the Germans out, during which time Allied supply problems would end the great advance.

As of September 1944, the Allies did not have a single usable port and were still bringing their supplies in over open English Channel beaches hundreds of miles from the front. The more the Allied armies advanced, the fewer supplies they could receive. Shortages forced Supreme Commander Dwight D. Eisenhower to ration supplies in a way that, as it turned out, was chiefly at Patton's expense. Thus

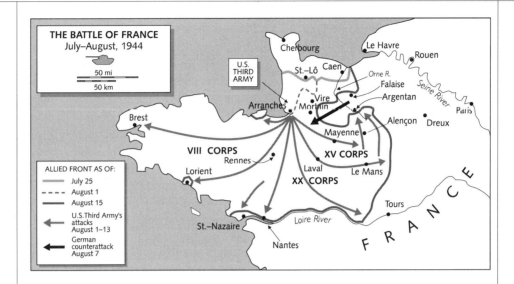

he literally ran out of gas and the Third Army ground to a halt. (The other Allied armies did too, partly because of stiffer German resistance, but mostly from lack of supplies and because their vehicles were wearing out.)

All hope of continuing the drive now rested upon the success of Operation Market-Garden, an ambitious plan to drop Allied airborne divisions deep into enemy territory on crucial river crossings. The farthest of these, the Rhine bridges at Arnheim, Holland, were some 60 miles behind German lines. The plan was that the British Second Army would then drive through the corridor thus created and cross the Rhine.

But this plan, which was exceptionally daring for Field Marshal Sir Bernard Law Montgomery, the normally cautious British commander, exceeded the Allies' ability. British airborne troops, in one of the most remarkable small-unit actions of the war, did seize the end of a bridge at Arnheim, but they could not hold it. The British Second Army failed to break through the German defenses to relieve the paratroopers at Arnheim.

The Allies ground to a halt. In hindsight, it is clear that Operation Market Garden was overly ambitious. As one British officer memorably put it, the operation failed because it tried to go "a bridge too far." The larger problem was that without Antwerp the Allied armies could not be adequately supplied. Although there would be much hard fighting over the winter, the Allies would not roll again until the spring of 1945.

General Omar Bradley's decision to halt Patton at Falaise and Eisenhower's refusal to give Patton the gas he needed to keep moving in September have been severely criticized. There was some risk at Falaise, to be sure. Patton could have closed the gap when he wanted to, but whether he could have held it shut against the desperate Germans will never be known. And it was true that the Allied forces might have accidentally fired at each other as they drew closer together.

But if Patton had succeeded, the Germans would have lost most of their divisional and corps leaders and staffs, making it all but impossible for them to establish a new line of defense. The war would then have been all but over. Here, it seems, was a risk worth taking. Eisenhower's decision, though it was partly political—he could not allow Patton to win more glory by taking supplies away from the British—is easier to defend. The Third Army, attacking on its own, had it gotten into Germany, would have been extremely vulnerable to flank attacks. Because of this perhaps the risk was too great.

The Battle of France, even if it did not bring total victory in the West, was still one of the greatest wins of the war. The Germans had lost half a million men since D-Day and been driven out of France. Germany's final defeat, as all could now see, was but a matter of time.

SEE ALSO

D-Day; Eisenhower, Dwight D.; Germany, surrender of; Montgomery, Sir Bernard; Patton, George S., Jr.

FURTHER READING

Ambrose, Stephen C. *Citizen Soldiers.* New York: Simon & Schuster, 1997.
Eisenhower, David. *Eisenhower at War, 1943–1945.* New York: Random House, 1986.
Knight, Clayton. *We Were There at the Normandy Invasion.* New York: Grosset & Dunlap, 1956.
Ryan, Cornelius. *A Bridge Too Far.* New York: Simon & Schuster, 1974.
Weigley, Russell F. *Eisenhower's Lieutenants: The Campaign of France and Germany, 1944–1945.* Bloomington: Indiana University Press, 1981.

France, fall of

In 1940 the Allies were confident that they could hold the western front. During the winter of 1939–40, known as the "Phony War" because little action took place, France had time to fully mobilize and Britain to send it more than 10 divisions. "Hitler has missed the boat," Prime Minister Neville Chamberlain declared. What he meant was, by the standards of World War I, to which the Allies were still clinging, they had more than enough men and weapons to stop a German attack.

Including Belgium and the Netherlands, known as the Low Countries, which were neutral before the German blitzkrieg (lightning war) began but would fight when invaded, the Allies may have had as many as 4 million men compared to Germany's 2 million. They also had more guns and tanks than Germany, which outnumbered them only in the air.

Few outside Germany believed that you could successfully attack a force up to twice the size of your own. On the contrary, a common rule of thumb was that the assault force had to be twice the enemy's size, because fighting on the defensive was so much easier than attacking.

If Germany had followed its original plan, it probably would have been stopped. The German General Staff's first thought had been to attack through the Low Countries again, as in World War I. But the Allies expected this and placed their forces to meet such an assault. Germany would not attack the mighty Maginot Line along its border with France, they reasoned. And the Ardennes Forest could not be crossed by armored vehicles. Therefore, Germany had no choice except to go through the Low Countries, where the Allies were ready to establish a defensive line as soon as Germany's guns opened up.

Hitler had wanted to invade the West immediately after Poland fell, but bad weather and other problems forced Germany to wait. During that time, the full difficulty of attacking a superior force became obvious and Hitler was persuaded to drop his original plan. The Low Countries would still be attacked, to suck the Allies in, but the main thrust would be through the lightly defended Ardennes. Lieutenant General Hans Guderian, the army's armor expert, was certain his tanks could get through the Ardennes and split the Allied front.

Guderian was right. On May 10, 1940, the Germans struck hard, battering the Belgians and Dutch, then drawing the main Allied formations north just as Hitler wanted. The Netherlands fell in four days, and panzers were soon roaring through Belgium. Meanwhile, unnoticed, the main German armored force was driving carefully through the Ardennes Forest. By May 12 the Germans were on the Meuse River, France's main line of defense in the region. On the 13th they crossed it. By the next day they had opened a hole 50 miles wide in the French line and were driving hard for the English Channel.

Even some Germans were alarmed by their own success, for their attacking panzers had wide-open flanks that were protected only by the Luftwaffe, Germany's air force. A strong French counterattack could slice through the infantry advancing on foot, then roll the panzers up. The German high command, fearing just such a movement, ordered the armor to slow down until the infantry could arrive.

Guderian and his commanders, determined not to miss their chance, asked for permission to send out patrols, then charged ahead full blast. By the time their disobedience became clear, it was too late to stop them. On May 21 German forces reached the coast, cutting off the Allies' northern armies. Guderian had gambled that the French could not mount a flank attack and was proved right.

It turned out that the French were even worse off than Guderian guessed. On May 16 Winston Churchill, the new British prime minister, had flown to Paris. As the attackers were so strung out, he inquired, why did not the French throw their reserves at the open German flank? When Churchill was informed to his horror that there were no reserves, he knew that all was lost.

The encircled British and French armies were ordered to make a 180-

Hitler (center) and top aides parade in triumph before the Eiffel Tower in Paris. The Germans were to hold the city for more than four years.

degree turn and break out of their trap by attacking south. But, disorganized and under heavy air attacks from a Luftwaffe that now ruled the skies, this task was simply beyond them. Thoughts of home now came to Lord John Gort, who commanded the British Expeditionary Force (BEF). He asked for, and received, permission to assemble his troops on the coast where the Navy could pick them up.

Gaining permission turned out to be one thing, removing the men another. At first the Royal Navy thought it would be lucky to return as few as 50,000 troops to England. As it turned out, however, the Navy rescued 215,000 British and about 125,000 French and other Allied troops.

The "miracle" of Dunkirk was made possible because the Germans decided to slow down and isolate the beachhead by air. This could not be done, though, because Churchill risked fighter squadrons that were being saved for the defense of England to rescue the BEF.

Further support came from French and Belgian units left behind that fought a gallant rear-guard action.

And, finally, the British sent everything that could sail to the French coast—fast destroyers, private yachts, ferries, ancient gunboats. The Mosquito Navy, as they called it, was the most peculiar fleet of vessels ever assembled for a military operation. Hundreds of them were lost in the process, but the BEF got home.

The miracle of Dunkirk, which came to an end on June 4, 1940, was a marvelous achievement, good for British morale as well as for Britain's chances of survival. But it resulted from the worst British defeat since 1066, a beating that destroyed the French Army and made Hitler master of Europe. Although the BEF got away, the Germans had no trouble mopping up France's weary troops. The Germans took Paris without a fight on June 14. The Maginot Line was taken from the rear, where it had no weapons. The Italians attacked in the south but were thrown back by a small French force in a victory that changed nothing. On June 22 France signed a truce in the same railway car where the triumphant Allies had accepted Germany's surrender in 1918.

There is much disagreement over the extent to which defeatism and low morale were responsible for the fall of France. At one time they were considered vital to Germany's success. In recent years, however, explanations have focused on a combination of Allied mistakes and German advantages. For instance, almost a third of France's available troops were used to garrison the Maginot Line and therefore missed the decisive battles. If large numbers of them had been placed in a mobile reserve they might have made all the difference.

Furthermore, success would have been even more likely if France had created an armored force instead of distributing its numerous tanks among the infantry. Before the war Charles de Gaulle, France's leading authority on tanks, had begged Premier Leon Blum to insist on such a force. But the French Army ignored de Gaulle's warnings, so when Germany's panzers crossed the Meuse River they were unstoppable. Yet the armored fist that won the battle was made up of only seven armored and two motorized infantry divisions. The rest of the attacking host consisted of slow-moving infantry divisions that advanced on foot and depended on horses and oxen to move their heavy weapons and supplies. De Gaulle's armored force, had it existed, could have stopped them cold. Instead, the panzer attack, together with superior German planning, training, leadership, and tactics, won the day.

The Luftwaffe was important too in the fall of France, for it quickly won the air battle. The British did not have enough modern planes to achieve air superiority over the battlefield and at the same time protect Britain, and the French Air Force performed feebly. Once the Allied front was broken, French leaders lost all confidence and promptly surrendered, rather than ordering the Army to fall back or relocate to North Africa. As a result, after the fall of France, Britain remained the only power still at war with Hitler. Its turn would be next.

SEE ALSO

Britain, Battle of; de Gaulle, Charles; France

FURTHER READING

Gunsburg, Jeffrey A. *Divided and Conquered: The French High Command and the Defeat of the West, 1940.* Westport, Conn.: Greenwood, 1979.

Taylor, Telford. *March of Conquest: The German Victories in Western Europe, 1940.* New York: Simon & Schuster, 1958.

Genocide

The literal meaning of genocide is the effort to deliberately and systematically destroy a race or nation of people. The term seems to have been coined by Raphael Lemkin, a Polish-born legal expert who served during the war as an advisor to the U.S. War Department. He formed it by joining the Greek word *genos* (race or tribe) with the Latin suffix *-cide* (to kill). Lemkin first used it in his book *Axis Rule in Occupied Europe* (1944).

The need for a new term to describe the slaughter of Europe's Jews, Gypsies, and other minority groups was strongly felt at the time, Churchill having called what was then going on "a crime that has no name."

SEE ALSO
Holocaust

German Air Force

SEE Luftwaffe

German Army

At the outbreak of war in 1939, the German Army consisted of 3.74 million men, a figure that would rise to more than 6.5 million in 1943–44. At that time (1943–44) the army was organized into 11 groups, each consisting of two or more field armies, of which there were 26 in all.

A Nazi soldier carries ammunition boxes to the front lines to support the German counter-offensive in December 1944.

The German Army was the best in the world when war broke out and may have remained so as late as 1943. By then, however, the enormous losses sustained on the eastern front compelled Germany to take whatever soldiers it could get as replacements. Not only were under- and over-age Germans drafted, but to fill out the ranks Germany took men from many nations, including Russian prisoners of war and Muslims from Yugoslavia. Even these often reluctant warriors were not enough to keep the German Army up to strength. Whereas in 1939 an infantry division had 17,734 men, by 1944 the typical division was down to 12,700—including 1,700 non-Germans.

The strengths of the German Army, its great size apart, were numerous. German weaponry was always first class, as were German munitions. German planning was unrivaled, enabling major campaigns and offensives to be launched on short notice. A classic example was the Norwegian campaign that began on April 7, 1940. Hitler had not given the order for it until February 21, which meant that his staff officers had only about six weeks to put together an operation that was brilliantly planned and carried out. Of all the armies in the world, only Germany's could have pulled this off. Then, too, German discipline was harsh. On the eastern front some 15,000 troops were executed for cowardice or other failings, frequently on the spot.

Even so, fear was not what drove the German Army. Unlike the myth that German soldiers were mindless robots, individual initiative was prized and encouraged at every level. German commanders had more freedom of action than was usual in the West. Once a mission plan was laid down, they could change it as needed. Divisional commanders led from the front, sometimes with just a radioman and a driver. Hundreds of German generals were killed after putting themselves thus at risk, but the results spoke for themselves.

All ranks were taught the führer, or leadership, principle. Every soldier was encouraged to think two ranks above his own so that if his immediate superior fell, he could step into the open position. More than anything else, this was what kept the German Army together until the very last days of the war. Obedience combined with the führer principle made it possible for the surviving fragments of destroyed divisions to be assembled virtually on the battlefield and returned to combat as effective units. No other army could do this.

Good as it was, the German Army had serious defects. The pool of German manpower was not sufficient for the army to field hundreds of divisions of equal quality. Unlike in the West, where all infantry divisions were more or less similar, German infantry ranged in quality from assault divisions consisting of well-trained, able-bodied men to support and garrison divisions manned with under- and overage men and even the handicapped.

More serious still was the failure of German industry to put the Army on wheels. Of the 304 divisions that it possessed in 1945, only 31 were armored and 13 motorized. Most of the rest relied on horses and oxen to move their supplies, equipment, and heavy weapons. Even the Red Army was more mobile, thanks to the 450,000 vehicles it was provided with by the United States.

And, despite the fact that Germany invented armored warfare, from 1941 onward it never had enough tanks. Because Germany was not equipped to produce tanks in volume, it tried to make up for what it lacked in quantity with superior design. Its Panthers and Tigers were among the best tanks of the war, but for every Panther Germany produced, Russia built two and one-half of its comparable T-34s. The heavy Tiger was king of the western battlefields. However, barely more than 1,000 saw service, a tenth the number that Germany needed.

As the war went on, a lack of mobility and armor and the steadily declining quality of German military manpower drained the army's strength. Although the German Army remained a very tough foe to the end, by 1944 both the U.S. and Soviet armies were superior to it in most respects.

SEE ALSO

Bulge, Battle of the; Eastern front; France, Battle of; Germany, surrender of; SS (Schutzsstaffeln)

FURTHER READING

Bartov, Omer. *Hitler's Army*. New York: Oxford University Press, 1991.
Görlitz, Walter. *History of the German General Staff*. New York: Praeger, 1953.
Guderian, General Heinz. *Panzer Leader*. London: Michael Joseph, 1952.
Manstein, Erich. *Lost Victories*. Chicago: Henry Regnery, 1958.

The original
caption to this
captured Nazi
photograph
reads, "Austria
becomes Ger-
man. Entry of
German police
into Imst."

The original
caption to this
captured Nazi
photograph
reads, "Austria
becomes Ger-
man. Entry of
German police
into Imst."

Germany

The second great European war of this
century grew out of the first. Most Germans regarded the Treaty of Versailles,
which established the conditions under
which Germany would have to live
after World War I, as much too severe.
The treaty, signed on June 28, 1919,
forced the new German republic that
had replaced imperial Germany to
admit all responsibility for the war. It
deprived Germany of its colonies,
restored the provinces of Alsace and
Lorraine to France, and redrew Germany's boundaries to the advantage of
some of its neighbors. The size of Germany's armed forces was strictly limited
by the treaty, and it was required to pay
a large sum (the figure to be arrived at
later) to the victorious Allied nations.

The new democratic Germany,
which moved its capital to the small
city of Weimar, was saddled with heavy
burdens from the start. Extreme German nationalists never accepted their
defeat, claiming that the German Army
had not been beaten on the battlefield
but had been "stabbed in the back" by
Jews, communists, and other disloyal
elements who overthrew the kaiser, or
emperor, of Germany and made a
treacherous peace. The German officers
knew better, however, for the army was
in retreat when the empire collapsed
but wanted to refight the war anyway
in order to reverse its outcome.

The rise of Hitler Shortly after
the war, a former corporal of the German Army, Adolf Hitler, established his
National Socialist German Workers'
(Nazi) party. Hitler's aim was to destroy the Weimar Republic, establish
himself as dictator of Germany, rearm
the German state, and eliminate Germany's Jews, communists, socialists,
and others whom he detested. (He
included the word "socialist" in his
party's name to placate left-wingers.)
He then proposed to lead this newly

strengthened and purified nation in an anticommunist, anti-Slav war that would provide Germans with additional living space.

Far from making a secret of his plans to destroy democracy and subjugate Europe, Hitler laid them out in *Mein Kampf* (My Struggle), a book that other leaders in Germany and the rest of the world failed to take seriously. It was written in 1924, while Hitler was in prison for having attempted to seize control of Munich, the capital of Bavaria, by force. Although his small band of revolutionaries was easily defeated, Hitler's decision to take power legally proved to be all too successful.

Hitler turned his small party into a national movement by exploiting German anti-Semitism, anticommunism, and resentment of the Versailles Treaty. But had it not been for the Great Depression, it is unlikely that he would have been able to seize power.

In the 1928 general election, Hitler's party gained only 800,000 votes. Then, on September 14, 1930, as the German economy was falling apart, the Nazis won 6.5 million votes—more than 18 percent of the total that were cast. On July 31, 1932, with the economy in ruins because of the Great Depression, the Nazis doubled their representation in the Reichstag, Germany's parliament. They won 37 percent of the popular vote and elected 230 of about 545 delegates. They were now the largest German political party. The Weimar Republic had held its last free election. As the economy continued to worsen, Adolf Hitler, through a series of complex political maneuvers, succeeded in having himself appointed chancellor of Germany.

Hitler in power As Germany's chief executive, Hitler rapidly consolidated his power by appointing Nazis to key positions. He also persuaded President Paul von Hindenburg, who was old and politically incompetent, to issue emergency decrees that concentrated all power in Hitler's hands. It was the end of German democracy. After Hindenburg died in 1934 Hitler took over the presidency as well, naming himself to the new office of Führer (leader) and Reich chancellor. Germany was now officially the Third Reich (the first was the medieval Holy Roman Empire; the second, imperial Germany).

In 1935, having turned Germany into a police state, Hitler canceled the military provisions of the Treaty of Versailles and officially launched his rearmament program. On March 7, 1936, he marched troops into the Rhineland section of Germany (on the border with France), which had been demilitarized by the Versailles Treaty. Although his army was very small at this time, Britain, but especially France—which had enough troops to sweep the Rhineland clean of German forces in a matter of days—did nothing. This was the first of Hitler's bloodless victories that would make Germany the dominant power in Europe. Britain and France believed they had to choose between war (which both desperately wanted to avoid) or tolerating German expansion. In the end, they wound up with both.

On March 12, 1938, Hitler's troops marched into the independent state of Austria, absorbing its largely German-speaking population into the Third Reich. Hitler then turned his attention to Czechoslovakia, where about 3 million ethnic Germans lived in the Sudetenland, the area bordering Germany. Although Czechoslovakia had a military alliance with France, Hitler believed, correctly, that the Allies would continue to appease him. He was also correct in thinking that the Allies would continue to ignore the Soviet Union, which, alarmed by Germany's growing appetite, was trying to promote unity of action among the anti-Nazi states of Europe.

Amid a crisis atmosphere, and faced with a Nazi deadline, the leaders of Britain, France, Italy, and Germany met in Munich on September 29, 1938. On the next day it was agreed that Germany was to have the Sudetenland, while Poland and Hungary would also acquire Czech territory. The Czech government, abandoned by its allies, went down without a fight. When he returned home, Prime Minister Neville Chamberlain of Britain waved a copy of the Munich agreement in the air and said, "This means peace in our time." "Our time" lasted slightly less than one year.

Since 1938 Munich has symbolized the wrongness of seeking to buy off aggressors by submitting to their demands. It was the low point of the era of appeasement and the prelude to war. It was also the result of a major failure by the Allies to understand the political and military realities of Europe in 1938. Britain and France did understand that another great war, even if they won it, would finish them as world powers.

What Britain and France did not see was that Hitler's plans could be realized only by another great war and, that being so, the best time to fight him would have been in 1938. Germany's war mobilization plan would not be completed until 1942. At the time of Munich the German Army was far weaker than it would be a year later. Czechoslovakia's army had 35 well-armed divisions, equipped by the mighty Skoda works, the greatest arms manufacturing complex in Europe, and powerful fortifications along its border with Germany. If Britain and France had come to Czechoslovakia's aid, the odds were that Germany would have been beaten.

The German high command was so certain of losing that certain prominent

generals had organized a conspiracy to unseat Hitler, as they obviously would have to do if the Allies stood firm at Munich. Their failure confirmed Hitler as the man who was always right, putting an end to the plot against him. It also deprived the Allies of a vast store of Czech armaments that Germany would use against them.

After promising at Munich that there would be no more annexations, on March 15, 1939, Hitler seized what was left of Czechoslovakia. Britain and France at once gave guarantees of military support to Poland, Romania, Greece, and Turkey, all of which feared military attack by Germany. As it turned out, the promise that mattered most was the one given to Poland.

Poland was the wrong place to draw the line, however, because it had no strongly fortified border with the Reich and was too far away for the Allies to support. There now remained only one more step for Hitler to take before launching a general war.

On August 23, 1939, the world learned that Germany and the Soviet Union had signed a nonaggression treaty, usually known as the Stalin-Hitler Pact. The Allies were stunned, for Hitler's anticommunist views were

On August 23, 1939, Soviet foreign minister Molotov signs the German-Soviet nonaggression pact. Stalin (standing second from right), witnesses the historic event.

widely known, while the Soviets had for years been seeking an alliance with the West. Hitler's motives were obvious. With the Soviet Union out of the way he would not have to fight a two-front war, as Germany had been forced to do in 1914–18. The Soviet's motives were less clear. At the time, communists praised the pact as a master stroke that would give Russia time to rearm. Nonetheless, when war did come to the Soviets in 1941 they were unready for it.

A more likely explanation for the Soviets' signing of this pact is that Stalin had decided that the Allies would not accept him as a partner, which was true at the time, since they feared him as much as Hitler. That being so, a war between the Allies and Germany would probably drag on for years, as it had after 1914. This presented Stalin with an opportunity to grab land, with German permission, in return for Soviet neutrality—without, as he saw it, risking very much. Stalin believed that, as a result of the pact, the Soviet Union would gain a large chunk of Poland, the Baltic states of Latvia, Lithuania, and Estonia, parts of Romania, and—after hard fighting, which Stalin had not expected—Finland. In return, the Soviets were to provide Germany with huge amounts of oil, grain, and other raw materials, a promise Stalin scrupulously kept.

Of all Stalin's blunders this pact was certainly the greatest. But for it, Hitler would not have dared to invade France for fear of a Soviet attack. Or, if he did, he would have had to leave such large forces on his eastern frontier that France would not have fallen. As it was, Stalin's greed very nearly undid the Soviet Union.

The outbreak of war Hitler invaded Poland on September 1, 1939, defeating it in four weeks. On Septem-

ber 28 Germany and the Soviet Union divided Poland between them. The Allies declared war on September 3 but took no real action against the Third Reich, resulting in the so-called "Phony War" of 1939–40. This period ended in April 1940, when Germany seized Denmark and invaded Norway. Allied efforts to aid Norway were futile, and it surrendered on June 9, by which time Germany had driven the British out of Europe and all but defeated France. On June 22, 1941, Germany invaded the Soviet Union.

This was the final result of the Stalin-Hitler Pact, which came close to destroying the Soviet Union. As Winston Churchill said in the memoirs he wrote after the war, these events showed Stalin and his henchmen to be "the most completely outwitted bunglers" of the war. Millions of Soviet citizens would pay with their lives for Stalin's blunders, as would other innocent millions whose graves would cover Europe.

Role of the United States The United States's policy during this period was much the same as that of Britain and France, although it pursued the policy independently, because the United States did not belong to the League of Nations and was not allied with anyone. Public opinion polls, which had become important in the United States by the mid 1930s, showed that a large majority was opposed to fighting in Europe for any reason. Congress responded to this sentiment with a series of Neutrality acts that tied the President's hands. Accordingly, President Roosevelt had little choice except to hope that appeasement would work. When the Spanish Civil War broke out in 1936, he followed the Allied lead in embargoing arms both to the democratically elected government of Spain and the Fascist rebels, as he was required to do by the Neutrality acts. And after the

Munich agreement was signed, Roosevelt congratulated Prime Minister Chamberlain for having kept the peace.

After war broke out, the United States remained neutral, as required by law. However, the Allies were able to purchase commodities and war materials in the United States while Germany could not, because of a British blockade. After the fall of France in June 1940, Roosevelt sent as many weapons as possible to the British Army, which had left most of its arms behind during the evacuation from the northern French port of Dunkirk in June 1940.

By ransacking its arsenals and armories, the United States was able to transfer a total of 970,000 rifles, 87,500 machine guns, and 895 field guns, together with large quantities of ammunition, to the British. Although most of these arms were leftovers from World War I, they were useful for training purposes and for arming Britain's Home Guards—overaged civilians who would fight as a last resort. In September Roosevelt announced that agreement had been reached with Britain to exchange 50 or 60 obsolete U.S. destroyers for the American right to use British bases in the Western Hemisphere.

Roosevelt wished to do more, but U.S. isolationists were already furious with him for the steps he had taken thus far. This mattered, because he had decided to run for an unprecedented third term and could not afford to antagonize any more voters. Once safely elected, though, Roosevelt called for a program to aid Britain and its allies by lending, or leasing, weapons to them that would supposedly be repaid in cash, or in kind (a term that Roosevelt never clarified), after the war. Lend-Lease, as it came to be called, would make a great difference in the end. But it would help Britain very little in the short run, because the United States was underarmed itself and

had little to spare.

What Britain needed to win its lonely war with Hitler was to have the United States as a full-fledged ally, not simply a provider of aid. This remained true even after Germany invaded the Soviet Union in June 1941, as the Soviets were not expected to survive the Nazi onslaught. In fact, now that the Soviet Union had entered the war, it was more important than ever for the United States to get in, too.

Although Germany was not yet in a position to threaten the United States, if it defeated Britain and the Soviets that day would surely come. Waiting for Germany to invade the United States, as polls showed Americans wished to do, would mean battling Germany without Allies, on U.S. soil. Obviously, one would think, the time to fight was while Britain and the Soviet Union were still in the war. And the best place to fight was as far from the United States as possible.

Roosevelt's efforts to join the war
By the summer of 1941, Roosevelt seems to have reached this conclusion, but because the American people had not, he was prepared to take action himself. The result was an undeclared naval war against Germany designed to provoke incidents that would either lead Hitler to declare war on the United States or lead Americans to demand that Congress declare war against Germany.

On July 7, 1941, a U.S. occupation force landed in Iceland, giving the United States a forward base from which it could command the sea-lanes to Britain. In August, Roosevelt met with Winston Churchill and signed a statement of war aims that was called the Atlantic Charter. He was making plans to have U.S. naval ships escort convoys when, on September 4, the destroyer USS *Greer* was torpedoed by a German U-boat. Roosevelt used this

A mass roll call of several of Hitler's armies at a rally in Nuremberg attests to their strength and organization.

incident to begin convoying, while also instructing the U.S. Navy to shoot German warships "on sight."

A Gallup poll in September 1941 showed that, although they still hoped to stay out of the war, 62 percent of Americans supported the President's shoot-on-sight order. But even after a U-boat sank the USS *Reuben James* on October 31, killing 115 sailors, polls showed that the public still would not support a declaration of war against Germany. With Hitler obstinately refusing to take the bait, Roosevelt's strategy had failed. In that dark hour the cause of freedom seemed lost, and it might have been had Japan not attacked U.S. military installations, including the great naval base at Pearl Harbor on December 7. Four days later Hitler, too, declared war on the United States. U.S. entry into World War II had become a reality at last.

German home front In 1939 Germany had a population of 79.5 million

and a geographic area of 226,288 square miles. At the peak of its power in 1941, the Third Reich, having annexed vast territories on all three of its prewar frontiers, had 116 million inhabitants and covered an area of 344,080 square miles.

Even before this great expansion, however, Germany was the largest country west of the Soviet Union and the economic giant of Europe. Thanks to Hitler's rearmament program, there was no unemployment. At the time, many Americans believed that the German state and economy were models of Teutonic precision and police-state efficiency. But in fact the Nazi state was a shambles, remarkable for its overlapping authorities and plagued by bureaucratic chaos. Personalities were vitally important, with favored administrators expanding their little empires at the expense of those outside the magic circle of power.

Germany's economic planning shared these same defects and was further handicapped because the supreme leader did not wish the military mobilization to annoy civilians. Accordingly, although Hitler increased armament production before the war, he resisted stockpiling essential materials. German munitions were produced over and above consumer goods to a much greater degree than might be expected. Germany made up for domestic shortages by plundering captive nations, but robbery had its limits. In 1942 Hitler was obliged to put the economy on a war footing at last.

After the death of Minister of Armaments and War Production Fritz Todt, Hitler installed Albert Speer, his favorite architect, as head of mobilization. In 1942 and 1943, Speer tripled war production. In some areas he did more than that, increasing tank production sixfold in two years, for example. Yet still more could have been done, for Speer never had full control of the domestic war effort. Manpower was directed by another minister, who seldom took account of Speer's requirements. And powerful leaders, such as Nazi party chief Martin Bormann, opposed total mobilization as being harmful to civilian morale.

There were other reasons why Speer was unable to make the best use of Germany's human and material resources. Hitler made a practice of assigning one or more agencies or individuals to perform the same task. "That way," he used to tell Speer, "the stronger one does the job." Another handicap was that Nazi dogma prevented Speer from mobilizing German women. Businessmen showed Speer photographs of workers changing shifts in the same ammunition factory 24 years apart. Yet while in 1918 the employees had been predominantly women, in 1942 most were men. To Speer's disgust they remained so, with Nazi leaders refusing to actively recruit women despite the labor shortage.

Furthermore, the Nazis insisted on maintaining peacetime standards of comfort and luxury. As late as 1944, factories manufacturing such domestic items as rugs and picture frames were still not converted to producing war materials. For these and other reasons Germany's ammunition production never reached World War I levels, though its paperwork was far greater, the Ordnance Office alone having a staff 10 times as big as in the previous war. Captured resources, the exploitation of occupied lands, and widespread use of slave labor (7.8 million forced laborers in 1944, compared to 28.6 million German workers) enabled Germany to carry on for a long time. Even so, there were never enough workers, and by 1944 food, oil, and other essentials were running short as well. After D-Day, Hitler was finally forced to mobilize the Reich fully—a move that came too late in the war to affect its outcome.

The result was that, despite Speer's best efforts, Germany's war production did not meet its needs. During the war, German aircraft plants turned out at most 118,000 aircraft, only about as many as Britain did. The United States had built more than 300,000 planes by war's end.

In tanks, too, Germany was heavily outproduced. During the war years, Germany produced some 64,000 tanks, but few of these were Panthers and Tigers, the best German models. The United States built about 86,000 tanks, most of them comparable to the average German tank, but the Soviets manufactured more than 100,000 assault guns and tanks. Further, the Soviets had medium and heavy tanks that were comparable to Germany's Panthers and Tigers but were produced in far larger numbers.

Nazi Germany was a unitary state. All power was derived from Hitler personally, and his rule was enforced by the SS, which directly controlled all police and internal security agencies. Opponents of the Nazis were executed or sent to concentration camps. Increasingly the country was administered, as well as led, by the Nazi party rather than by government ministries. A shadow and, finally, a real government based on regional party leaders called *gauleiters,* paralleled the departments of state. All Germans were expected to be members of one or more Nazi organizations.

Instead of trade unions, German workers were required to join the German Labor Front. In 1942 it had 25 million members, and its farmers' equivalent, the Reich Foodstuffs Corporation, 15 million. German children between 10 and 18 years of age belonged to Hitler youth organizations. As an administrative body, therefore, the Nazi state was a nightmare and an obstacle to efficiency. As a police state, however, it was highly effective and kept Germany's population in line to the very last day of the war.

SEE ALSO

Atlantic Charter; France, fall of; German Army; Hitler, Adolf; Holocaust; Japan; Luftwaffe; Poland; Soviet Union; SS (Schutzsstaffeln); Stalin, Joseph

FURTHER READING

Bidwell, Shelford. *Hitler's Generals and Their Battles.* New York: Random House, 1998.
Forman, James. *Horses of Anger.* New York: Farrar, Straus & Giroux, 1967.
Haslam, Jonathan. *The Soviet Union and the Struggle for Collective Security in Europe, 1933–39.* New York: St. Martin's, 1984.
Heinrichs, Waldo. *Threshold of War: Franklin D. Roosevelt & U.S. Entry into World War II.* New York: Oxford University Press, 1988.
Hildebrand, Klaus. *The Foreign Policy of the Third Reich.* Berkeley: University of California Press, 1973.
Jäckel, Eberhard. *Hitler's World View: A Blueprint for Power.* Cambridge, Mass.: Harvard University Press, 1981.
Murray, Williamson. *The Change in the European Balance of Power, 1938–1939: The Path to Ruin.* Princeton, N.J.:
Princeton University Press, 1984.
Shirer, William L. *The Rise and Fall of the Third Reich.* New York: Simon & Schuster, 1960.
Speer, Albert. *Inside the Third Reich.* New York: Macmillan, 1970.
Weinberg, Gerhart L. *The Foreign Policy of Hitler's Germany.* Chicago: University of Chicago Press, 1980.

Germany, surrender of

On January 12, 1945, while the Battle of the Bulge was still raging, the Soviets kicked off their long-awaited offensive and the eastern front promptly crumbled. The German economy was on the verge of collapse. Yet with Germany on its last legs, its cities burned out, and the noose around it tightening, the German Army fought on without hope or purpose.

Some veterans would later say that by continuing the war they were attempting to save as much of Germany as they could from being overrun by the Soviets. This argument would be plausible if German resistance on the western front had faltered. Instead, right up to its final days the German Army was still fighting hard in the West, blowing bridges and doing all it could to delay the Allied advance. Desperate as conditions were, however, they might have been worse. Hitler's final orders, which were not carried out because of the obvious madness behind them, were for the Army to destroy everything of value in Germany and then fight to the last man.

While those on the inside could see that Germany was finished, the Allies did not. The Battle of the Bulge seemed to show that Germany could still take offensive action. It was known that German industry was still producing fighter planes in quantity despite all the bombing attacks. Luftwaffe pilots still had plenty of aircraft, which were increasingly jets, while the first Allied jet was not expected to enter service before October—another nine months away.

In addition, General Omar Bradley's "hurry up" offensive, which he launched to take advantage of Germany's retreat from the Bulge, stalled. On February 1, he was up against the West Wall, Germany's lines of defense, and going nowhere fast. At the same time, losses were continuing to mount. The U.S. Army's casualties, including those resulting from illness or injury, totaled 134,400 in December, 136,700 in February, and would come to 101,000 in March.

Meanwhile, on March 3, the last U.S. divisions arrived in Europe. Except for individual replacements, there were no troops left in the States, forcing Eisenhower to consider transferring his newest armored divisions to the infantry. By late January he was short 82,000 infantrymen and the deficit was growing.

Fortunately for all concerned, the war was nearly over. At Malta, on their way to the Yalta conference, U.S. and British chiefs met to plan their final offensives. One last British effort to give Field Marshal Sir Bernard Law Montgomery 16 U.S. divisions for a single thrust into northern Germany, plus command of all land forces, was stopped for good by General George C. Marshall. While Britain cited the Battle of the Bulge as evidence that the Allies were too weak for more than one offensive, Eisenhower had drawn the opposite conclusion. He was convinced that the Allies needed to launch several attacks in order to keep Germany from concentrating all its available forces against a single one. However, Montgomery would still get 12 U.S. divisions, and his next two offensives would be strongly supported.

But whereas Britain wanted the remaining U.S. armies to go over to the

defensive, Bradley would be allowed to mount a secondary advance on Frankfurt-Kassel. He was content with this, certain that Montgomery would attack too late and move too slowly. Moreover, although this was unclear as yet, retraining programs, transferring men from the air forces and rear areas, together with Germany's increasing weakness, would provide sufficient riflemen for a big U.S. push.

Bradley's plan The British commenced Operation Veritable on February 8, 1945, but covered only 17 miles during the next two weeks. Meanwhile,

General George S. Patton's Third Army, which had been ordered to conduct an "active defense," had broken through the West Wall on a 40-mile front. The U.S. Ninth Army and the British 21st Army Group jumped off together on February 23 and made the long-awaited breakthrough, advancing 53 miles in two weeks, capturing 30,000 German troops, and clearing 34 miles of the Rhine's west bank.

Meanwhile, Bradley was working on a plan of attack that would put his own armies on the Rhine as well. This strategy went beyond the supportive role he had been assigned and would enable his armies to cross the Rhine before Montgomery if Montgomery failed to pick up speed. On March 7 both armies reached the Rhine.

Supreme Headquarters planned for Montgomery to cross on March 24 with 32 divisions. But Bradley intended to take advantage of the room Eisenhower was giving him to merge Third and Seventh armies, plus French First, for a massive sweep to Frankfurt. This in turn would enable the U.S. First Army to cross the Rhine and the combined Franco-American force of 40 divisions to drive on to Kassel.

Plunder, the British operation, was supposed to be the main event, with Bradley's, code named Undertow, a secondary operation. If all worked as Bradley expected, however, the U.S. drive would change that.

On the evening of March 7, fate gave Bradley a hand. He received a call from Lieutenant General Courtnay H. Hodges saying that the 9th Armored Division of his First Army had just captured the Ludendorff railway bridge at Remagen, the Germans having failed to blow it. Bradley ordered Hodges to cross in strength and hold the bridge at all costs. Bradley was elated—now he had an opportunity to launch an offen-sive that would rival, and perhaps replace, Montgomery's, which was not to start for two weeks.

Eisenhower, also excited by the turn of events, gave permission to put four divisions over the Rhine. On March 13 Eisenhower instructed Bradley to secure the bridgehead at Remagen and attack toward Frankfurt, junking Operation Undertow. He also approved Bradley's "right hook" plan, knowing full well, or so Bradley believed, that while Plunder was still supposed to be the major operation, the U.S. attack would actually become the main one. Hitler also recognized the importance of losing the Ludendorff bridge. The officers held to be responsible for the loss were shot.

The U.S. offensive On March 13 Patton set off, followed by the Seventh Army. After hard initial fighting they speeded up, capturing 90,000 Germans between them in the largest seizure of prisoners since the Germans lost North Africa. On the 23rd, Patton called Bradley to say he was over the Rhine, having crossed on the fly without even firing an artillery barrage. He was excited over beating Montgomery, who had, as usual, spent too much time making his arrangements. Montgomery crossed easily on the 24th as scheduled. Meanwhile, U.S. troops were pouring across the Rhine on boats and pontoon bridges. Their effort to contain the U.S. Army and conduct the war-winning offensive having failed, the British had no choice but to accept a revised plan that had U.S. forces driving for the Elbe—where the Allies and the Soviets would meet—while Montgomery protected their northern flank. Montgomery's 21st Army Group, having moved too slowly, would now have to play the supporting role.

On April 4 Eisenhower returned the Ninth Army to Bradley, who now commanded four U.S. armies with 48 divi-

An aerial view of the medieval German city of Wurzberg reveals the damage inflicted by an Allied bombing raid on April 1, 1945. Strategic bombing often turned into terror bombing, and many German city centers were completely destroyed.

sions and 1.3 million men, the largest ground force ever commanded by a U.S. general. With it he would promptly win the war in the West.

Originally the Americans, like the British, had seen Berlin as the great prize toward which their efforts should be directed. But at the Yalta conference, Britain took the lead in agreeing to occupation boundaries that put Berlin well within what would become the Soviet zone, although the city itself was to be divided among the victors. In late March, with German resistance crumbling, it suddenly became possible for the 12th Army Group to drive straight for Berlin. But all knew that whoever attacked Berlin would take heavy losses.

Any responsible U.S. commander was bound to shrink from the idea of losing many men for territory that would then have to be given up. Thus, at the end of March, on his own initiative,

Eisenhower notified Stalin that he expected to meet the Soviet forces roughly along the lines established at Yalta. Although this decision was heavily criticized at the time, it now seems that Eisenhower was right to make it. Saving American lives was more important than the empty honor of taking Berlin.

The war ended abruptly. The Ninth Army reached the Elbe River on April 11 after traveling 226 miles in 19 days. On the 16th, Soviet forces attacked Berlin. Two days later German resistance in the Ruhr ended, with the Allies taking 317,000 prisoners. While Montgomery moved carefully across northern Germany, more American troops reached the Elbe and Patton drove into Czechoslovakia.

The German retreat quickly became a rout, with the U.S. 18th Airborne Corps alone capturing 360,000 enemy soldiers. Hitler committed suicide in his

Berlin bunker on April 30. The next day Germany's last units in Italy surrendered. On May 7 Admiral Karl Doenitz, who had taken command of the Third Reich, surrendered it to Eisenhower at 2:41 a.m. in Reims, France. The war in Europe was over.

SEE ALSO

Bulge, Battle of; Eastern front; Eisenhower, Dwight D.

FURTHER READING

Ambrose, Stephen A. *Eisenhower and Berlin: The Decision to Halt at the Elbe.* New York: Norton, 1967.
Benary, Margo. *Dangerous Spring.* New York: Harcourt Brace, 1961.
Montgomery, Rutherford G. *Rough Riders Ho!* Philadelphia: David McKay, 1946.
Ryan, Cornelius. *The Last Battle.* New York: Simon & Schuster, 1966.
Toland, John. *The Last 100 Days.* New York: Random House, 1966.

GI Bill of Rights

The Servicemen's Readjustment Act, popularly known as the GI Bill, was passed by Congress in January 1944. After the Civil War and World War I, Congress had voted cash bonuses for veterans. These benefits had become political footballs, especially the World War I bonuses. When it came time to consider veterans' benefits for World War II, everyone remembered the two "bonus marches" of the Depression era, one of which had ended in violence, when thousands of veterans had marched on Washington demanding early payment of their bonuses.

After World War II, thanks to the GI Bill, there would be no bonus armies, no violence, and no attempts to buy veterans' votes. One feature of the bill provided veterans with $20 a week for up to 52 weeks to ease the transition from war to work. Among other things, the bill provided low-cost, no-down-payment home loans, lent money to start businesses or run farms, and, most important, provided tuition and some living costs for veterans wanting to enroll in high schools, trade schools, and colleges.

Congress had not wanted this bill to be thought of as social legislation. But owing to the huge number of World War II veterans, the GI Bill had the same effect as a major social reform. By 1950 the 16 million veterans and their families made up fully a third of the population. In 1945 there had been a colossal housing shortage. Five years later it was over, thanks largely to the 4.3 million home loans provided by the GI Bill. Nearly 8 million veterans went back to school, learned a trade, or attended college under the bill.

The money spent directly by the federal government rippled through the whole economy, providing jobs in construction, manufacturing, retail sales, and other areas to people who were not veterans. Further, the bill made possible the baby boom, for veterans could now afford to start families while they were still in school, which millions of them did. The soaring birth rate, which rose year by year until the end of the 1950s, created the largest generation in history. These baby boomers had to be housed, fed, and educated, creating additional millions of jobs.

The members of the war generation became the best-educated and most prosperous Americans ever seen up to that time because of a much-deserved tribute to them that benefited the entire nation. The GI Bill showed government at its best, rewarding veterans for their sacrifices and helping them to reach their full potential.

Veterans wore this discharge emblem, which they irreverently called "the ruptured duck," on civilian clothing after the war.

FURTHER READING

Kennett, Lee B. *G.I.: The American Soldier in World War II.* New York: Scribners, 1987.

Linderman, Gerald F. *The World Within War: America's Combat Experience in World War II.* New York: Free Press, 1997.

Great Britain

SEE Britain

Grenades

Grenades were used by all the armies in World War II to lay smoke (as markers) and to kill or knock out the enemy. Antipersonnel grenades were designed to break into pieces, spraying deadly shrapnel. Concussion grenades were hurled by advancing troops to stun the enemy without doing harm to themselves. Rifle grenades could be fired longer distances than a man could throw and packed a greater punch. The U.S. M9A1 armor-piercing grenade was especially good, with many GIs preferring it to the rocket-firing bazooka. Because of their smaller size, U.S. grenades could be thrown farther than German or Japanese ones.

The long-handled German "potato masher" grenade was more powerful and easier to throw accurately than U.S. grenades. Japanese grenades, like so many of their explosives, were frequently duds. There were cases of Japanese soldiers attempting to commit suicide with grenades that only gave them headaches.

Guadalcanal, Battle of

The Solomon Islands are a chain that runs more or less alongside of southeastern New Guinea. Guadalcanal (code named Cactus by the military) is the largest of the southern Solomons.

In 1942 the Japanese were building an airfield on it. The U.S. Navy's chief, Admiral Ernest King, was determined to seize Guadalcanal, although there was no compelling reason to do so. Japan already had a great network of naval and air stations in the region at Rabaul. The airfield on Guadalcanal could never equal Fortress Rabaul, and it was farther from New Guinea, where the Japanese forces were under heavy pressure from General Douglas MacArthur.

The reason King wanted Guadalcanal was probably that otherwise the Navy would have nothing going on in the Pacific in 1942 to match MacArthur's efforts there, putting it at a disadvantage in its continuous rivalry with the Army. The War Department had well-grounded fears that the Navy was too weak to mount such an offensive and would soon be calling for help. Nonetheless, as part of the ceaseless bargaining between the services, it reluctantly gave its consent.

Operation Watchtower, or Operation Shoestring, as the men called it, consisted of three elements. Its landing party was built around the 1st Marine Division, which was not yet fully trained and prepared for combat. The invasion fleet included three of the Navy's four remaining carriers under the command of Rear Admiral Frank Jack Fletcher. The third element, Amphibious Force South Pacific, was made up of the vessels transporting the 1st Marines and their gear. It was commanded by Rear Admiral Richmond Kelly Turner, formerly a planner on King's staff. Known as "Terrible" Turner because of his bad temper and abusive language, he would become the

A mechanic hoists up the tail of this Corsair at an airstrip in Guadalcanal in order to align the plane's guns properly.

navy's leading expert on amphibious operations.

Watchtower nearly failed at the outset because of Fletcher's lack of faith in it and his fear of losing carriers. For these reasons he sailed away only 36 hours after the Marines had landed and before they were half unloaded. He left only cruisers and destroyers to defend the invasion force. Fletcher's career never recovered from this mistake, because even as he fled, Japanese heavy cruisers were storming down the "Slot" formed by the Solomon Islands. At 1:30 a.m. on August 9, 1942, they took the Allied cruisers by surprise, destroying four—three U.S. and one Australian. The Battle of Savo Island, the U.S. Navy's worst defeat at sea, did much to make the Guadalcanal campaign a prolonged nightmare. Since Turner now had no air cover, Amphibious Force South Pacific weighed anchor at noon, leaving the Marines stranded.

As the Allies were stretched so thin, Watchtower might have ended disastrously but for a stroke of luck. The Japanese had nearly finished their airfield on Guadalcanal, which the invading Marines captured. Then on August 20 the Marines received 19 U.S. fighters and 12 dive bombers, the beginnings of the "Cactus Air Force." Its planes controlled the air and sea by day, confining the enemy to night attacks and limited, high-speed, nocturnal supply runs. This "Tokyo Express" enabled Japanese troops to keep fighting on Guadalcanal, but in the race to build up their respective forces Japan would be the loser.

Guadalcanal might have gone the other way if Japan had made a maximum effort. Instead, the Japanese reinforced their position piecemeal, frittering away their troops. Even so, as a direct result of Watchtower, the Navy was reduced at one point to a single carrier in the Pacific. To hold Guadalcanal would cost the United States 24 ships and make the waters between it and Savo and Florida islands—Ironbottom Sound to the Allied sailors—the largest naval graveyard of the war.

The fight to secure Guadalcanal would last for six months, involve six major naval engagements, the loss of six Allied heavy cruisers and two fleet carriers, and the commitment of 60,000 soldiers and Marines. For four of those months, the Marines would be partially isolated, dependent on a handful of pilots and a few blockade-runners. The

Marines hung on by their fingertips, inspiring James Michener to compare the "Canal" to Valley Forge and Shiloh.

After Guadalcanal was secured, it seemed logical to clear the rest of the Solomons, which would take most of 1943 and, like Guadalcanal itself, confer few benefits beyond the destruction of Japanese weapons and personnel. Although the Marines covered themselves with glory in this fight, they endured almost 6,000 casualties on Guadalcanal, of which 1,600 were fatal. Together with the Navy's losses, this was a high price to pay for marginal real estate.

SEE ALSO

Halsey, William F.; South Pacific area; Southwest Pacific area

FURTHER READING

Bergerud, Eric. *Touched with Fire: The Land War in the South Pacific.* New York: Viking, 1996.

Leckie, Robert. *Challenge for the Pacific: Guadalcanal, the Turning Point of the War.* Garden City, N.Y.: Doubleday, 1965.

Merillat, Herbert. *Guadalcanal Remembered.* New York: Dodd, Mead, 1982.

Guderian, Heinz
GERMAN GENERAL AND PANZER COMMANDER

- *Born: June 17, 1888, Germany*
- *Political party: National Socialist*
- *Education: Cadet School, 1907; War School, 1908; War Academy, 1914*
- *Military service: General Staff Corps, 1918; chief of staff of Panzertruppe, 1934; commander, Panzer Group Guderian, 1940; acting chief of staff, Army High Command (OKH), 1944*
- *Died: May 14, 1954, Wurnburg, Germany*

Although Heinz Guderian did not rise to the top of the German Army, as he should have given his genius for war, he was the world's foremost exponent of armored warfare. In that capacity he invented the blitzkrieg form of attack that swept the enemy from the field in Poland and France.

During the years between the world wars, Guderian was one of a handful of prophets of armored warfare, a small group that included Charles de Gaulle of France, J. F. C. Fuller in Britain, and Major Dwight D. Eisenhower and Colonel George S. Patton of the U.S. Army. Most armies then regarded the tank as an infantry support weapon. Only this small group of visionaries realized that the mobility and striking power of an armored force made it capable of spearheading an army's attack. It could then either pierce the enemy's line or flank it, that is, go around it and cut it off, leading to a quick victory in either case.

Unlike the others, Guderian was able to put this idea into practice during the 1930s because he enjoyed the patronage of Adolf Hitler. Although Hitler was eager for war in the 1930s, he understood that Germany did not have the resources to win a war of attrition. It was critical, therefore, that ways be found to neutralize the superiority in manpower and industrial resources that Germany's potential enemies enjoyed.

Hitler believed that part of the answer lay in forming the world's best air force. The rest of the solution, he concluded, could be provided by a tank-led army. Guderian stood out among Germany's tank experts, both because of his ability and because of his book *Achtung! Panzer!*, which drew attention to his ideas when it was published in 1937.

As chief of staff of the Panzertruppe, Germany's first real armored force, which was Guderian's creation, he had been able to prove in practice what he had argued for in theory. As a relatively junior general, and because the high command was not entirely persuaded by his ideas, Guderian was allowed to command only a single corps during the 1939 attack on Poland. In the main, however, the Polish campaign vindicated Guderian's theories. For the attack in the west, Guderian was again given only his XIX Corps, but it was assigned the most important task: to lead the assault through the Ardennes Forest that was to split the Allied line and win a stunning victory.

Guderian and his corps performed brilliantly, breaking through to the English Channel in a matter of days. Had the German advance not been brought to a halt at Hitler's orders, it would certainly have taken the British Expeditionary Force (BEF) and the French First Army. Even though the BEF escaped through the "miracle of Dunkirk" by which civilian and military shipping combined to save many British troops, the victory remained a major achievement that made Guderian famous. In the final assault on French forces, his augmented command, Panzer Group Guderian, advanced south to the Swiss border and captured 250,000 French troops in a series of brilliant maneuvers.

Guderian opposed the invasion of Russia (Operation Barbarossa) in 1941, because Britain had not been defeated yet and he was also concerned about the strength of Soviet armor. All the same, he was given command of Panzer Group 2, which later became the Second Panzer Army, the strongest of Germany's four panzer groups. More brilliant victories followed until in December the German advance came to a halt because of the onset of winter. Guderian, with other officers, argued strongly for a strategic retreat from the gates of Moscow. Denied permission by Hitler, he made such a withdrawal anyway, only to be relieved of his command in the purge of some 30 senior officers that followed. He never led troops in the field again.

In 1943 Guderian was brought out of retirement and made Inspector General of Armored Forces: in effect, Hitler's advisor on tanks. Following a failed coup attempt against Hitler in July 1944, Guderian became acting chief of the army high command, but with German forces everywhere in retreat and under Hitler's suspicious eye there was little he could do. Guderian made every effort to keep Hitler from squandering what remained of the Army's strength but failed even in this. After opposing the Ardennes campaign, or the Battle of the Bulge, Guderian was relieved of duty again in February 1945.

Of all the Nazi generals only a few, notably Guderian and Marshal Erwin Rommel, would be well regarded by Westerners after the war. In Guderian's case, this was in some measure a result of his autobiography, *Panzer Commander* (1952), a best-seller in the United States. However, both were admired for their professionalism, for how they led from the front and being popular with their troops, for not participating in Hitler's crimes, and for having waged war as honorably as possible.

For example, Guderian refused to obey Hitler's infamous order that German soldiers were not to be punished for killing Russian civilians. At the time, Guderian invoked professional reasons for disciplining offending German soldiers, saying that allowing murder would be prejudicial to discipline. After the war he added that murdering civilians was contrary to the "dictates of Christian conscience." Both explanations may well have been true.

SEE ALSO
Bulge, Battle of the; Eastern front; France, fall of

FURTHER READING
Macksey, Kenneth. *Guderian: Panzer General.* London: MacDonald and Janes, 1975.

Halsey, William F.

COMMANDER, U.S. THIRD FLEET, 1943–45

- *Born: October 30, 1882, Elizabeth, N.J.*
- *Education: U.S. Naval Academy, 1904; Naval War College, 1932–33; Army War College, 1933–34*
- *Military Service: midshipman, 1904; ensign, 1906; lieutenant, 1909; lieutenant commander, 1915; commander, 1918; captain, 1927; commander of Saratoga, 1935; commandant, Pensacola Naval Air Station, 1936–38; commander, Aircraft Battle Force, 1940–41; commander, South Pacific force and South Pacific area, 1942–43; commander, Third Fleet, 1943–45*
- *Died: August 15, 1959, Fisher's Island, N.Y.*

William "Bull" Halsey was the most popular U.S. admiral of World War II. Although not the most brilliant fleet officer, Halsey was a hard driver. He won the confidence of his men by his concern for their welfare and by his aggressive leadership and forceful language.

Halsey was a destroyerman for most of his career, not becoming interested in naval aviation until 1934, when he was offered command of the carrier *Saratoga*. Only flying officers were given carrier commands, so Halsey first had to qualify as an aviator. He did so, which meant that he was one of the very few admirals qualified to command carrier task forces once war with Japan broke out.

After Pearl Harbor, Halsey led some of the first carrier raids against Japanese positions. He also led the Doolittle raid, the first air raid on Tokyo using bombers launched from the U.S.S. *Hornet* in April 1942. But Halsey's greatest contribution to victory resulted from his being appointed commander of the South Pacific Area in October 1942.

At the time, U.S. forces were having difficulty holding on to Guadalcanal. Naval action in the Solomon Islands had reduced the United States's carrier strength in the entire Pacific to a single ship. The headquarters of the South Pacific Area reeked of defeatism.

Halsey was supposed to breathe new life into the Solomons campaign, raise morale, secure Guadalcanal, and take the rest of the island chain. As the U.S. forces were still stretched thin, this was no easy assignment, but Halsey filled the leadership gap. Under his direction, and with the aid of reinforcements, the entire South Pacific Area was in Allied hands by spring of 1944.

In September 1944, Halsey took command of the main force of the Pacific Fleet, which included all the fast carriers. Previously, under the command of Admiral Raymond Spruance, it had Fifth Fleet. Thereafter, the two admirals would alternate command, the force being the Third Fleet when Halsey led, the Fifth Fleet under Spruance. This unique command arrangement enabled one admiral to plan the next operation while the other was at sea.

Admiral Marc Mitscher commanded the fast carriers under both men. His unit was designated Task Force (TF) 38 when under Halsey and TF 58 under Spruance.

Halsey led the Third Fleet in many successful actions and one controversial fight. During the Battle of Leyte Gulf (October 24–25, 1944), he fell for a Japanese deception plan. The Imperial Japanese Navy had decided to attack the U.S. amphibious force that was landing on Leyte with most of its remaining cruisers and battleships. Because the Japanese attacking force would have little air support, it was important to draw away TF 38 from Leyte Gulf. The Japanese accomplished this by sending their remaining carriers to the north.

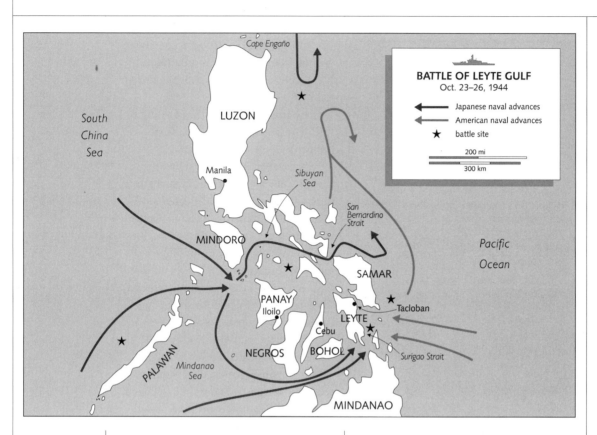

These carriers were harmless, having lost most of their aircraft, but the Americans did not know that.

Halsey took the bait, driving north with all his fast carriers and battleships when the enemy carriers were sighted. This enabled the enemy's battle line to attack the troop and supply ships of the invasion fleet, which were defended by just three task forces built around small escort carriers. The defenders put up such a furious fight, however, that the Japanese commander believed he was under attack by TF 38 and retreated from Leyte Gulf.

Halsey's decision to go after the Japanese carriers has attracted many defenders. He believed that his main duty was not to protect the invasion force but to destroy the Japanese Fleet. Because Halsey reported to the Navy's Admiral Nimitz, while the admiral commanding the invasion reported to the Army's General MacArthur, confusion reigned.

It was the divided command of the Pacific war that was really at fault, not Halsey's decision—even though it put the invasion force at risk. Had he guarded the beaches instead of going after what was thought to be a powerful carrier group, he would have been criticized for that decision too. This had been the fate of Admiral Spruance after the Battle of the Philippine Sea, when he was accused of allowing Japanese carriers to escape, out of a misplaced concern for the Saipan invasion force.

But, while questions may be raised about Halsey's performance at Leyte Gulf and about his seamanship (he twice sailed his fleet into typhoons), his place in history seems secure. He raised U.S. morale in the darkest days of the war with his carrier raids and pugnacity. As commander of the South Pacific Area, he turned a demoralized command into a winning one and led the Third Fleet to numerous victories. Few admirals accomplished as much.

SEE ALSO
Guadalcanal, Battle of; Leyte Gulf, Battle of; South Pacific Area

FURTHER READING
Potter, E. B. *Bull Halsey.* Annapolis, Md.: Naval Institute Press, 1985.

Hamburg, bombing of

The first firestorm (in which separate fires combine to form one great inferno that sucks oxygen up at such a rate that people untouched by the fire or blast still suffocated in their shelters) to result from a bombing attack took place in Hamburg, Germany. On July 24, 1943, the Royal Air Force's Bomber Command launched 791 aircraft. It was the largest attack Bomber Command had made to that date. For the first time, bundles of narrow foil strips, called windows, were employed to confuse German radar. It was highly successful, with 306 bombers of the attacking force dropping their bombs within three miles of the aiming point. For a night operation this was a very good score.

On July 25 and 26, 235 heavy bombers of the U.S. Eighth Air Force attacked Hamburg again, during daylight. And on the night of July 27, with much of Hamburg already in flames, Bomber Command once more attacked. Of 787 planes dispatched, 722 hit Hamburg, 325 of them within three miles of the target. Although Bomber Command attacked Hamburg twice more, it was the raid of July 27 that ignited the firestorm.

Around the aiming point, temperatures exceeded 1,500 degrees Fahrenheit, consuming oxygen at such a rate that 150-mile-per-hour winds arose as air was sucked into the vacuum. People untouched by the flames died of gas poisoning in their homes and air raid shelters for lack of oxygen.

Perhaps 42,000 people perished in Hamburg, and 1 million more fled the city. In one week Bomber Command and U.S. bombers had killed more civilians than the Luftwaffe had slain in its entire eight-month blitz of England in 1940–41. Yet, like other terror raids, this did not drive German morale to the point of surrender, as had been hoped. Nor did it destroy many industrial targets, because most lay outside the devastated city's center. According to some accounts, military production actually rose in greater Hamburg after the raids, because workers previously employed in shops and stores burned out by the attack sought employment in defense industries.

SEE ALSO
Royal Air Force; Strategic bombing

Hirohito
EMPEROR OF JAPAN, 1926–89

- *Born: April 29, 1901, Tokyo, Japan*
- *Education: Peer's School, 1908–20*
- *Military service: none*
- *Previous government service: regent, 1921–26*
- *Died: January 7, 1989, Tokyo, Japan*

Much controversy surrounds the role Hirohito played before and during the Pacific war. In theory he was an absolute ruler and commander in chief of the armed forces. In practice he seldom expressed an opinion when major decisions were being discussed. When he did speak, it was in vague and confusing

Emperor Hirohito (seated, left) accompanies former Qing emperor Pu Yi to an official event. In 1932 the Japanese occupied Manchuria and installed Pu Yi as a Japanese puppet leader.

terms that usually left considerable room for interpretation.

Some emperors before him had been more forceful, exercising real rather than symbolic leadership, but this was not Hirohito's way. His main contribution was to remain passive, as when the Japanese Army seized Manchuria in 1931 and then abolished party government in Japan the following year. He also did not try to prevent the army from launching an ill-fated war with China in 1937.

Yet at times the emperor did assert himself, for example, by failing to make appointments recommended by the cabinet. Some historians have argued that, as he did show initiative on occasion, he would have had the power to prevent Japan from going to war. Since he did not do so, the presumption remains that he actually approved of the wars conducted in his name. It does appear that

Japan's victories over the West, beginning with Pearl Harbor on December 7, 1941, aroused the emperor's enthusiasm. And he still seems to have hoped that peace could be achieved: by force of arms as late as 1943 and by negotiated settlement until 1945.

Critics have judged the emperor harshly for not asserting himself when the tide of war turned against Japan. But to attempt, in his role as commander in chief, to order a cease-fire and negotiations would have been a high-risk strategy. Defenders of the emperor maintain that if he had done so the military would simply have deposed him and put someone more compliant on the throne.

There is little doubt, however, that the two atomic bombs dropped on Japanese cities on August 6 and 9, 1945, spurred the emperor to action. He did assert himself then, while the cabinet was arguing over what course to take, and ordered his government to accept the Allied demand for unconditional surrender. No one can say what would have happened had he done so earlier. But if he had not acted when he did, it is highly probable that the cabinet might well have decided to fight on. Or, if it had voted to surrender, it might have become the victim of an attempt to remove Hirohito staged by fanatical diehard younger officers. Such an effort was indeed made, but the emperor had forced fast action on the government that gave the opposition too little time to come up with an effective plan for seizing power. For this, at least, he deserves considerable credit.

SEE ALSO

Japan; Japan, surrender of

FURTHER READING

Irokawa, Daikichi. *The Age of Hirohito: In Search of Modern Japan.* New York: Free Press, 1995.

Hiroshima

SEE Atomic bombs

Hitler, Adolf

GERMAN FÜHRER, 1934–45

- *Born: April 20, 1889, Braunau-am-Inn, Austria*
- *Political party: National Socialist*
- *Education: Left high school without degree, 1905*
- *Military service: German Army, 1914–20*
- *Previous government service: Reich chancellor, 1933–34*
- *Died: April 30, 1945, Berlin, Germany*

Little in Hitler's early life suggested the man he would become. After flunking out of high school in Linz, Austria, in 1905, he moved to Vienna in 1907. There he dabbled in the arts, barely supporting himself by selling his drawings and paintings. In 1913 he moved to Munich, where he enjoyed a similar lack of success. He did better in the army, where he rose to the rank of corporal and won the Iron Cross, First Class, for bravery, an award seldom given to enlisted men.

After the war Hitler returned to Munich and joined a right-wing organization called the National Socialist German Worker's party (NSDAP)—Nazi party for short. In November 1923 Hitler and the Nazis attempted to seize power in Munich by force. Their "Beer Hall Putsch" was quickly suppressed, and Hitler was convicted of treason. He served only one year of his four-year sentence, time enough to write his political testament, *Mein Kampf* (My Struggle).

The Beer Hall Putsch attempt having been a fiasco, Hitler resolved to take power more conventionally. By 1929 the Nazis had a membership of 178,000 and were winning substantial shares of the vote in provincial elections. But it seems unlikely that Hitler would have prevailed without the aid of the worldwide economic depression of the 1930s. By 1933 one in three German workers was unemployed, and in desperation many turned away from the Social Democratic party to the radical communists. An alarmed middle class looked more and more to the Nazis as the means to restore the German economy and forestall a communist takeover. The German state established after World War I, known as the Weimar Republic, was democratic, but democracy had shallow roots in Germany and would not survive the depression.

In July 1932 the Nazis won 230 seats in the Reichstag, Germany's parliament, which made them the largest political party. They lost 34 of these in a November election, but this setback did not matter because Germany's leaders were planning to scrap the Weimar constitution. It was their intention to establish a new authoritarian government that would eliminate the communist threat. This could not be done without Nazi support, and the price of it was that Hitler be appointed Reich chancellor, the equivalent of prime minister. This was done on January 30, 1933.

Hitler quickly consolidated his power by appointing Nazis to the key positions of government. Paul von Hindenburg, the old and feeble president, was persuaded to issue decrees that allowed Hitler to bypass the Reichstag. In March even this small obstacle was removed. The Reichstag passed an Enabling Act that legalized Hitler's dictatorship. Those opposition parties that did not disband were crushed. Within a year Germany had become a one-party police state. On August 2, 1934, when

President Hindenburg died, Hitler announced that the offices of Reich chancellor and president would be combined in the single office of Führer (leader) and Reich chancellor.

Hitler's rise was astonishing. He had gone from corporal to dictator in a mere 13 years, despite having little education and no civilian job experience except as party leader. Several things explain his climb. Hitler was a great orator, the best German speaker of his age. Hitler was also something of a political genius. He turned a small right-wing party, little different from many others, into a mighty movement. Apart from the Munich fiasco, he made very few mistakes and was a superb judge of what he could get away with and when it was time to act. What he lacked in education he made up for, to an extent, with a nearly photographic memory. He could process huge amounts of information, and was always surprising his generals with his detailed knowledge of weaponry and troop deployments.

But above all, Hitler's power lay in his ability to inspire personal loyalty and devotion. He saw himself as a messiah, a savior of the German nation and he made millions of others see him in that light. The Nazi party was built initially on the fury of young thugs, ultra-nationalists who were enraged by Germany's defeat in the war and who hated democracy. They were hot for revenge—against the Allies, of course, but also against those who had supposedly "stabbed Germany in the back"—Jews, communists, and Social Democrats. However, to these violent men Hitler added a huge following drawn primarily from the middle and farming classes, respectable people who fell under his spell. Worshiped by masses of Germans, he also won over men superior to him in culture and sophistication—men such as Albert Speer. An architect who became

Hitler's minister of munitions, Speer was mesmerized by Hitler and followed him slavishly to the end. Only a figure of unrivaled charismatic power could have won over both the masses and the elite in this way. And only a Hitler could have led Germany into the most lethal of all European wars and to commit the most unspeakable crimes.

In the years that followed Hitler's seizure of power, full employment returned, thanks to massive government expenditures for public works and armaments. The Wehrmacht was expanded far beyond what the Versailles Treaty allowed, Hitler thumbing his nose at France and Britain. In *Mein Kampf*, Hitler had laid out his program for Germany and Europe. It was to make Germany master of the continent, expel the Jews, destroy communism, and acquire *lebensraum* (living room) for the German people to expand into at the expense of Slavic nations. Western leaders tried to dismiss this terrifying shopping list as political propaganda, but it was what Hitler wanted and would almost get.

Always impatient, Hitler got an early start on his program of acquisitions. He failed to seize Austria in 1934 when Mussolini forced him to back off. But in 1935 the Saar region of Germany, which had been under League of Nations's control, voted overwhelmingly to rejoin Germany. On March 7, 1935, Hitler sent troops into the Rhineland, Germany's frontier with France, a move forbidden by the Versailles Treaty, which had demilitarized the region. Although France could easily have crushed Hitler's small force, which had orders to withdraw if attacked, it did nothing. Nor did the Allies respond effectively when Germany seized Austria on March 12, 1938. He then set his sights on the Sudetenland, Czechoslovakia's German-speaking frontier with the Reich. He acquired it in October 1938 after Britain and France pressured the Czechs into giving up the territory.

On October 14–15 Germany seized the rest of Czechoslovakia, in violation of the Munich agreement that had given it the Sudetenland. Britain and France then guaranteed the independence of Poland. They were forced to declare war on Germany in September when it invaded Poland anyway. Hitler moved so rapidly because he was impatient, also because the German economy was in trouble. Rearmament was proceeding at too high a rate. Nazi economic planning was disastrously bad. Forced to choose between retrenchment and expansion, Hitler chose the latter.

As usual, it appeared Hitler could do no wrong. Poland was quickly beaten and divided with the Soviet Union, as provided for by the nonaggression pact with Germany that it had signed in August. In the spring of 1940 Germany took Denmark and Norway. On May 10 it attacked in the west, defeated the French and British armies, occupied France, and moved to invade England. Although defeated in the Battle of Britain, the first to be fought almost entirely by aircraft, Hitler was now master of Europe. In 1941 he ordered his armies to invade the Soviet Union, but after the usual lightning victories, his offensive stalled at the gates of Moscow.

In attacking the Soviets, Hitler had overreached himself, a step that would be fatal to him and his Third Reich. The Soviet Union was simply too vast, and its military potential too great. The Red Army could trade space for time until German forces were overextended. Germany won almost every battle from June 22, 1941, when it rolled into Soviet territory, until November 1942, when its Sixth Army was surrounded at Stalingrad. But in doing so, Germany lost the war. The longer it fought the weaker the Wehrmacht became, while the Soviets

grew stronger and stronger. On February 2, 1943, the Sixth Army surrendered, giving the Soviets a permanent strategic advantage.

Hitler made many other mistakes as well. He declared war on the United States after Japan attacked Pearl Harbor on December 7, 1941. Though allied with the Japanese, he was not required by treaty to take this step, which guaranteed that Germany would be defeated in the west as well as in the east. Hitler did not order full mobilization of the German people and economy until late in the war, when it could no longer make a difference. He squandered Germany's limited manpower and industrial resources on the V-1 buzz bomb, and especially the V-2 rocket. These were purely terror weapons and produced no military benefits.

This list of errors could be extended, for Hitler made many military decisions himself that cost the German

The cult of personality surrounding Adolf Hitler was enormous. Here, crowds gather to cheer him on at a Nazi rally in Nuremberg.

Army dearly—such as his order to the Sixth Army that it hold onto Stalingrad instead of breaking out. But the biggest of all his blunders was to attack the Soviet Union in the first place, and his downfall began there. Slowly the German Army fell back until it was reduced to making hopeless last-ditch stands on the soil of the Reich. After D-Day on June 6, 1944, the Wehrmacht was retreating on two fronts. When the Soviets entered Berlin, Hitler and his mistress Eva Braun committed suicide and their bodies were burned so they could not be put on display. So ended the Third Reich.

SEE ALSO

Britain, Battle of; Eastern front; France, Battle of; France, fall of; Germany; Germany, Battle of; Germany, surrender of; Stalingrad, Battle of

FURTHER READING

Bullock, Alan. *Hitler: A Study in Tyranny.* New York: Harper & Row, 1964.
Fest, Joachim. *Hitler.* New York: Harcourt, Brace, Jovanovich, 1973.

Hobby, Oveta Culp

COMMANDER OF THE WOMEN'S ARMY CORPS

- *Born: January 19, 1905, Killeen, Tex.*
- *Political party: Democratic*
- *Education: Mary Hardin Baylor College, Waco, Tex.*
- *Military service: Women's Army Corps, 1941–45*
- *Died: August 16, 1995, Houston, Tex.*

Oveta Culp Hobby was one of the most able women of her generation, rising from modest middle-class origins to positions of great power and responsibility. The daughter of a small-town lawyer, she dropped out of college when he was elected to the state legislature. In 1925, at the age of 20, she became parliamentarian of the Texas legislature.

Although she owed the job to her father, she made a name for herself by a book she wrote called *Mr. Chairman,* which became a widely used text. She later ran for the legislature herself but was defeated by an opponent who accused her of being a Unitarian as well as a parliamentarian, which many voters appeared to think were disqualifications for office.

In 1931 Oveta Culp married William P. Hobby, a former governor of Texas who was then publisher and subsequently owner of the *Houston Post-Dispatch,* where she worked in the circulation department. Although she owed her first executive position on the paper to her marriage, she demonstrated so much managerial ability that her reputation grew along with the media empire that she and her husband were building. It was this executive experience, which few women had at the time, that the Army wanted. Thus, in 1941 she was asked to serve as commander of the newly formed Women's Auxiliary Army Corps, later renamed the Women's Army Corps (WAC), with the rank of colonel.

Despite having no real precedents to go by, and in the face of tremendous hostility against the WAC inside the Army as well as out, Colonel Hobby made it into a service organization of great usefulness to the Army. Her success led the Navy, which had at first been opposed to enlisting women, to form its

Given the rank of colonel by the U.S. Army, Oveta Culp Hobby led the Women's Army Corps to great accomplishment and praise. General Douglas MacArthur once called the Corps "my best soldiers."

own female branch, known as the WAVES (Women Accepted for Volunteer Emergency Service).

Although most WACs served in the United States, they were greatly appreciated by many overseas commanders, who were pleased to have as many of them as possible. General Douglas MacArthur, for instance, called them "my best soldiers," a view that was widely shared. All told, some 140,000 WACs served in the Army and the Army Air Forces, easing the military manpower shortage, which by 1944 was severe.

The shortage could have been ended altogether if U.S. women had been subject to the draft. Polls showed that women in the draftable age group favored conscription for noncombat jobs by extremely large margins, but Congress refused to pass such a law. This prevented the WAC from achieving the size it needed because, while women were willing to be drafted, they could not easily volunteer for military service. A public campaign waged against women in the military by word of mouth, and by some newspapers, made accusations of promiscuity that were utterly false. WACs in fact had fewer instances of giving illegitimate birth than civilian women their age, but this did not sway public opinion. By the time the war was over, the high quality and superb achievements of the WACs had finally become common knowledge.

In January 1945, Colonel Hobby was awarded the Distinguished Service Medal for her outstanding leadership and service, which was "without guidance or precedents in U.S. military history." She may have made a greater contribution to the war effort than any other woman in the United States. Hobby later served in President Dwight Eisenhower's cabinet as the first secretary of the Department of Health, Education, and Welfare.

Holocaust

Holocaust has become the preferred term to use for the Nazi campaign of extermination directed against Europe's Jews. It is properly called genocidal as well, though genocide refers to all such crimes, while Holocaust is specific to World War II.

Hitler's original intention had been to force Germany's Jews to emigrate by separating them from other Germans and seizing their property. This frequently involved great violence, notably on November 9–10, 1938, called *Kristallnacht* (night of broken glass). During an orgy of destruction, 7,000 Jewish businesses and homes were destroyed, 100 Jews killed, and, afterward, 30,000 imprisoned in concentration camps. As late as 1940, after the fall of France, SS leaders were still thinking in terms of expelling Jews from Europe. One plan involved forcing them to relocate on the island of Madagascar, off the southeast coast of Africa, since no other country would accept Jewish refugees in the number required.

The second phase of Hitler's war against the Jews began in 1941 when Germany invaded the Soviet Union. Special killing teams called Einsatzgruppen fanned out behind the advancing troops, gunning down Jews or gassing them in specially equipped trucks. In 1941 and 1942, 1 million Jews are thought to have been murdered by the Einsatzgruppen.

But mass murder conducted in this way had serious drawbacks from a Nazi point of view. For one, it was a slow process. Many in the Einsatzgruppen were not considered sufficiently dedicated; others found the work sickening. Furthermore, while it was easy to commit butchery and remain more or less undetected in the wide-open spaces of Russia, there was too much risk of exposure in the heavily populated areas of central and western Europe. To avoid bad publicity, murder by stealth was what Hitler wanted.

The answer was what the Nazis called the Final Solution (of the Jewish "problem"), meaning the total annihilation of Europe's Jews. The Jewish victims would be transported to camps located in a remote area for death and disposal. In the summer of 1941, Rudolph Hoss, commandant of the Auschwitz concentration camp in Poland, received orders to expand and transform his facility into a giant death factory. Five other death camps were established in or near the General Government of Poland (as the Nazi-occupied territory was called), but Auschwitz was the most destructive.

Two technical problems needed to be solved before death could be put on an industrial basis. The first was how to kill people on the largest possible scale; the second how to dispose of the millions of bodies. The first problem was solved by building large chambers in which people could be gassed. The second was handled by erecting huge ovens called crematoria to burn the corpses.

Hoss was proud of his methods, which were much more advanced than those employed at Treblinka, a neighboring camp. While Treblinka's 10 gas chambers could hold only 200 people each, at Auschwitz the chambers held 2,000. And, while Treblinka relied on monoxide gas, at Auschwitz zyklon-B (prussic acid), did the killing much more efficiently.

In March 1942 the first shipment of Jews reached Auschwitz, and in the months and years that followed death trains steamed into Poland from the four corners of Europe. The inhumanity

of this did not bother Hitler and the SS. Perhaps more surprisingly, neither did the harm done to the German war effort. The SS was slaughtering able-bodied men and women at a time when German industry was desperately short of labor. Many were taken directly from war plants to Auschwitz. Some victims even worked for a time at real factories in the death camps before being murdered. But as a labor source, these people were largely wasted.

Also wasted were the transportation resources required for the Final Solution, for the death trains had top priority, even over military shipments. It appears that, with defeat staring him in the face, Hitler regarded the Final Solution as his monument. He was determined to see it carried through at whatever cost to the war effort.

Like so many war statistics, the total number of Holocaust victims can only be approximated. The best estimate is that between 5 and 6 million Jews perished in the Holocaust, or about 80 percent of European Jewry. That any survived at all was partly a result of many heroic individuals and groups who rescued Jews from the Holocaust.

Oskar Schindler, a businessman, more or less single-handedly saved 1,300 Polish Jews who were workers in his factory and their families. A Swede, Raoul Wallenberg, with the aid of U.S. funding and a network of assistants, saved at least 100,000 Hungarian Jews. The villagers of Le Chambon, a French town on the Swiss frontier, saved thousands of Jews by hiding them until they could be spirited over the border. Most of occupied Denmark's Jews—some 6,000 of them—were brought to Sweden and safety by boat in a single night.

But most of the Jews who survived were citizens of the lesser Axis states. Mussolini refused to ship Jews to the death camps. His armies protected large numbers of Jews in the areas of France and the Balkans that they controlled. When Germany took direct control of Italy in 1943, the Italian Army was disarmed and the Holocaust reached Italy and the former Italian zones of occupation. Even so, most of Italy's 40,000 Jews survived the war, in part because the Holocaust came to Italy late, but also because Italians hid the Jews from the Germans.

As long as Hungary remained independent, it too refused to send Jews to the slaughter. When Germany occupied Hungary in 1944, the death trains from there began to roll, but again because of the late start, and in this case Raoul Wallenberg's intervention as well, 350,000 of a total population of 750,000 Hungarian Jews survived the war.

Although Romanian troops participated in the killing of foreign Jews, the Romanian government refused to participate in the Holocaust. It succeeded in saving perhaps half of its 600,000 Jews. The Bulgarian government saved all of its Jewish citizens—about 60,000.

The brave men and women who risked, and sometimes lost, their lives in attempts to rescue Jews enable us to retain our faith in human nature. But it remains true that the Holocaust was one of the most atrocious crimes in history and came quite near to complete success. It should be remembered, too, that the victims of the Holocaust were outnumbered by the non-Jews who were starved, shot, or worked to death by German authorities. Forty percent of Europe's 1 million Gypsies, whom the Nazis had marked for total destruction, were killed. So too were 4 million Poles, Ukrainians, and Byelorussians, and perhaps 3 million Soviet prisoners of war. The total figure of non-Jews slain by the Nazis cannot be less than 10 million. In the Holocaust Hitler and his minions unleashed a storm of death over Europe so vast and horrible that the mind cannot comprehend it, the true legacy of the Third Reich, as Hitler meant it to be.

SEE ALSO

Concentration camps; Eastern front; Genocide; Wallenberg, Raoul

FURTHER READING

Aaron, Chester. *Gideon, A Novel.* New York: Lippincott, 1981.

Dawidowicz, Lucy. *The War Against the Jews, 1933–1945.* New York: Holt, Rinehart & Winston, 1975.

Hilberg, Raul. *The Destruction of the European Jews.* New York: Holmes & Meier, 1985.

Lustig, Arnost. *Darkness Casts No Shadow.* Washington, D.C.: Inscape, 1976.

Home front

There were 133.4 million Americans in 1941, of whom 13.7 million were classified by the Census Bureau as "Negro and other." The great majority of black adults were employed as laborers, laundrywomen, domestic servants, and similar unskilled, low-wage occupations. Racial segregation was universal, enforced by law in the southern states and everywhere else by custom.

White women were better off than blacks, but unlike today their choices were limited and most served as full-time housewives. In 1940, of 65.6 million women in the population 13.8 million were employed, and of them, all but 4.2 million were single.

Most working women were young and expected to leave the workforce after marriage. The majority of employed women were unskilled factory operatives, servants, shop clerks, secretaries, and clerical workers. Others served in the helping professions, like teaching and nursing, that were poorly paid and lacked opportunities for advancement.

While the United States had few armed defenders—only 458,000 servicemen in 1939—it was better prepared to make war than it might have looked on paper. Despite hard times, it was the world's foremost industrial nation. It had produced in the previous year 28.7 percent of world manufacturing output, compared to Germany's 13.2 percent and

Japan's 3.8. Beyond that, however, the Americans were a proud people who subscribed to a common culture based on work, family, respect for institutions, and faith in self and nation. It was these qualities, as well as more measurable factors, that the Axis powers failed to take into account when declaring war on the United States.

However, when Pearl Harbor was attacked, on December 7, 1941, the United States was unprepared to fight either Germany or Japan, let alone both. The process of developing a war economy was proceeding at a leisurely pace. Rearmament crawled along too, and although the army had drafted 1 million men beginning in 1940, they were still being trained. The armed forces could not absorb the huge numbers of men who rushed to enlist after Pearl Harbor. Nor was industry ready to absorb the millions of civilian volunteers who also wished to help the war effort.

As government struggled to mobilize, many civilians took matters into their own hands, forming a huge variety of volunteer organizations to serve in civilian defense, roll bandages, sell war bonds, and collect scrap metal, rubber, fats, and many other increasingly scarce items and commodities. Volunteerism became a big part of U.S. life, which helped somewhat to offset government's failure to plan ahead.

Far more than any other warring nation, the United States would depend on volunteers, and especially women, to organize the home front. The Red Cross, with 3.5 million female volunteers, was far and away the most important body engaged in volunteer war work. But many more served in organizations like the Women's Ambulance and Defense Corps of the United States, which also trained volunteers to serve as air raid wardens, security guards, and messengers. There were thousands of war-related volunteer

These giant gears in a machine shop in Massachusetts would become part of U.S. warships. To build even one battleship or aircraft carrier was a monumental task.

groups, which did everything from staging advertising campaigns for the armed forces to collecting scrap metal.

It was civilians who put together the great salvage drives that became such a prominent feature of domestic life. And it was civilians who made successes of the seven war-bond sales campaigns that raised many billions of dollars. With no federal support at all to begin with, the so-called Victory gardens sprouted in backyards, courtyards, parks, and public spaces. Individuals and local governments pitched in to grow vegetables for themselves and their neighbors. This allowed more of the commercial crops to be canned for use by the military and U.S. allies.

During most of the war, polls showed that people were willing to sacrifice even more than the government asked. It was clear that Americans would have accepted a military draft of young women if Congress had passed such a bill. They also supported President Roosevelt's proposal for national service. This would have required all able-bodied adults—with some exceptions, such as mothers of young children—to fill partic-

ular jobs if assigned to them by government. But Congress was afraid to enact what was essentially a labor draft, no matter what the polls reported.

Unquestionably the greatest achievement on the home front was the enormous increase in production that made the United States, as Roosevelt called it, the Arsenal of Democracy. A tanker fleet with a total capacity of 2.5 million tons in 1941 grew to 11.4 million tons in 1945, despite heavy losses in the early war years. To equip the nation's factories, the machine tool industry produced $4.7 billion worth of tools between 1940 and 1945, 20 times what had been made in the previous decade.

When the President asked for 50,000 aircraft in 1940, people thought he was crazy—but by 1945, 300,000 aircraft had been built, 245,000 for the Army and Navy, the rest for the Allies. Other munitions figures were similarly gigantic. From May 1940 to war's end, U.S. industry turned out 8,243 warships, 64,000 landing vessels, and 86,000 tanks. A new type of cargo vessel called the Liberty ship, which was relatively cheap and easy to make, was designed during the war. The U.S. yards built 2,710 of them.

In some industries, such as steel, which had been underused before the war, output could be raised just by going to full production. In 1940 steel mills were running at 82 percent of capacity and pouring 67 million tons a year. In 1945 the mills poured 89 million tons, half the world's total—with the same-size workforce. As a rule, the existing plants and mills could greatly expand their production simply by going to double or triple shifts.

But thousands of facilities had to be greatly enlarged, while others were built from scratch. And about 16 million men served in the military during the war, creating an industrial manpower shortage. It was solved by hiring older men and boys and paying more overtime, but chiefly by recruiting married women. Because 90 percent of the munitions jobs were new and there were few men to fill them, the strong prejudice against hiring women for what were seen as male jobs had to be put aside.

The war changed everything except human needs and desires. Many once-ordinary tasks became fiendishly difficult to perform under wartime conditions. Numerous goods previously taken for granted were replaced by inferior substitutes or simply disappeared altogether. A 48-hour work week and long commutes became the rule for all workers, regardless of gender. Because so many goods and services—including household appliances and supplies, certain types of food, domestic help, and medical care—were in short supply, wives and mothers (whether employed or not) had to devote more time to housework, getting their children to doctors, and shopping, which was further complicated by the use of ration books and the need to go from store to store looking for scarce items.

Shopping has probably never been more difficult. Consumers had to return used toothpaste tubes in order to buy new ones, while tinfoil and cellophane simply disappeared, as did bobby pins, which were replaced by wooden toothpicks and thread. New clothes lacked elastic thread and webbing, metal buttons, zippers, hooks and eyes, silk, nylon, canvas, duck, and sometimes leather. Coats could not have pleats, gussets, bellows, or yokes. A "victory suit," which would have carried economy to the point of eliminating lapels, was ruled out, but to save wool double-breasted suits could not have vests, and no suit could come with more than one pair of pants. Cloth could not go over cloth, eliminating trouser cuffs and patch pockets.

Women's skirts were limited in length and circumference; certain dyes, especially greens and browns, were sometimes unavailable. Girdles, still everyday wear for women, had to be made of bone or piano wire instead of rubber. Shoes, when you could get them, came in only six colors, three of them shades of brown. Almost anything from coffee to canned goods (half the 1943 production went overseas) could run out without notice, and cigarette shortages were hard on this nation of smokers.

A striking feature of the war effort, and a source of many problems, was the enormous increase in the movement of people from one place to another. Including service personnel, 27.3 million people moved from their original county of residence during the war. In the period 1935–40, an unusually active one because men were moving often in their search for work, total civilian mobility amounted to 2.8 million persons a year. But during each of the peak war years it averaged 4.7 million.

With automobile use restricted, most long-distance travel was by train, putting enormous stress on the rail system as well as the passengers—jammed into over-

Black women plant flowers and place flags on graves in the Negro section of Arlington National Cemetery, Va., on Memorial Day, 1943. Esther Bubley took this photograph as part of a government documentary project on racism.

crowded and poorly maintained cars that were slow and often late because of breakdowns, or from having been side-tracked for high-priority troop trains.

Difficult as travel became, starting over in strange places was worse. Adolescents were particularly affected, not only because relocation is emotionally most difficult at that age, but also because so many were also going to work full-time or entering the services. In 1940 the number of employed persons between the ages of 14 and 17 was 1.7 million. In 1944 it came to 4.61 million, of whom 1.43 million were part-time students.

During World War II the decline in child labor was temporarily reversed, as was the trend toward longer periods of education. Total school attendance for the 14- to 19-year-old age group in 1940 came to 9.16 million persons. By 1944 it had fallen to 7.93 million. The number of boys and girls aged 14 to 18 who were employed rose from 1 million in 1940 to 2.9 million in 1944. The number of girls working in mills alone rose from 271,000 to 950,000.

Since so many young males—the principal crime-committing group—were

in uniform, most crimes declined, except possibly rapes, although as they were seldom reported the statistics are not very useful. But the total number of murders in the country, a more reliable figure, fell from 8,329 in 1940 to a low of 6,675 in 1944. Auto thefts went up in 1942 when new cars became unavailable, but the total number of reported crimes followed the same curve as murders, falling after 1940 and rising again only in 1945 when veterans began reentering civilian life. Suicides declined by a third, from a total of about 19,000 in 1940 to some 13,000 four years later. The war, it seems, had made life more worth living.

As there was so little to buy, and life was more difficult than before the war, some of the extra income earned by Americans was spent on entertainment. Movies were, after radio, the most important medium. Most of the 2,500 motion pictures that Hollywood turned out during World War II reflected the demand for amusement. Hollywood never stopped making comedies and musicals, and although after Pearl Harbor war films increased in number, 1943 being the peak year, by 1944 service pictures were becoming fewer and better.

Popular music played a crucial part, too, by entertaining people and lifting morale. For the most part, songs composed for or about the war were not as popular as romantic ballads, or lyrics that spoke to those separated from their loved ones. The biggest hit of the war was Irving Berlin's 1942 song "White Christmas," introduced by Bing Crosby in the movie *Holiday Inn.* It became the first song in a decade to sell more than 1 million copies of sheet music, and led the Hit Parade—music's equivalent of Nielsen ratings in television—nine times, rebounding again during the Christmases of 1943 and 1944.

The most popular song of 1944 was the touching "I'll Be Seeing You," and in that same year "I'll Be Home for Christmas" (with its melancholy ending "if only in my dreams") was a hit also. Songs like this meant much to battle-hardened troops as well as to the folks back home. In memoir after memoir, veterans noted how much popular music meant to them. This was particularly true in Europe, where soldiers with access to a radio could receive American pop songs from the U.S. Armed Services Network, the British Broadcasting Company, and even from German stations.

By 1944 everyone at home smelled victory and saw no need to keep working without a letup, especially since war production was being cut back. Once government began reducing defense orders, no appeal for voluntary sacrifice could be expected to have much effect. Good harvests reduced the incentive to maintain Victory gardens. The wheat yield in 1944 was the largest in American history, the corn crop second only to the record harvest of 1942. People responded accordingly. While in 1943 some 21 million families had planted Victory gardens, in 1945 only 17 million would do so. With plenty of money on hand and no appliances or new housing to buy, consumption of whatever remained was bound to increase. Hence the contradiction that as the war entered its bloodiest phase, at home the good times were rolling.

In 1944 farmers made a total of $20 billion, compared to an average of $8 billion in the late 1930s, although the farm population shrank by more than 8 million people. Workers in 1944 earned $44 billion, as against $13 billion in 1939. Department stores were packed with buyers of luxury goods despite a shortage of salespeople. Restaurants were mobbed, movie and stage theaters teemed, nightclubs flourished.

Hotels were booked solid weeks in advance, even though the best rooms cost as much as $105 a day, a lot of money in the 1940s. New records were constantly being set for tickets sold for shows, trains, horse races—even book purchases were up. All this was a function of the national incomes having reached $150 billion at a time when only $95 billion worth of goods and services was available for purchase. Flush times were the result.

The Battle of the Bulge that began in December 1944 came as a shock to Americans, who were under the impression that Germany had all but been defeated. It provoked a burst of demands for more sacrifices and greater efforts on the home front. In response, government closed the racetracks, ended the reconversion of war plants to consumer goods production, and placed a midnight curfew on bars and nightspots.

Supposedly these steps were to conserve fuel and essential services, but everyone knew that their primary purpose was motivational—and it didn't work. Those most affected by the curfew were servicemen on leave and night-shift workers, who bitterly protested the pointlessness of denying them a little fun. The curfew proved so unpopular that it could not be enforced. Late-night bars reappeared; drinking and sexual relations became more open and commonplace than ever. After three months officials reopened the tracks and lifted the curfew.

Although the Pacific war was approaching its climax, demobilized servicemen were coming home in ever-growing numbers. The halting reconversion to a peacetime economy deprived people of jobs without adding to the war effort. Moralizers blamed people for being self-indulgent, yet the polls did not support this.

A 1943 Gallup poll showed that 78 percent of respondents favored drafting 4Fs (able-bodied men who had escaped military service because of minor physical handicaps) into war plants. After the Battle of the Bulge, 56 percent favored a general labor draft, with only 36 percent of those questioned objecting.

In short, people knew they had it easy. In February 1945 the Gallup organization released a poll in which only 36 percent had answered yes to the question, "Have you had to make any real sacrifice for the war?" The most common reason for an affirmative answer was having a loved one in the armed forces, not any loss of comforts.

There was always more support for a greater war effort than Congress would authorize. It was hard to blame people for letting their Victory gardens go to seed after years of bumper crops, or for buying whatever they could with the surplus income Congress would not tax, or for holding nonessential jobs in the absence of a labor draft. These were policy issues, not questions of conscience. Moreover, it became public knowledge at the end of February 1945 that the army planned to release between 200,000 and 250,000 soldiers a month after the war in Europe was over, which would end the civilian labor shortage. No wonder appeals for sacrifice fell upon deaf ears.

In any case, the American people had nothing to apologize for. Not only had they raised and armed the most powerful military force in the world, more than 12 million strong at its peak, but they had fed and armed their allies as well to a considerable extent.

Furthermore, some 400,000 American men died in the war, almost 300,000 of them in combat. And U.S. support for the war was remarkably high, considering that it was the only great power not fighting for its life. All the others were invaded or, in the cases of Britain and Japan, heavily bombed and in danger of invasion. The threats of invasion had a highly stimulating effect on morale that the United States utterly lacked. The Americans fought the war, as one foreigner put it, on

imagination alone—which, if not literally true, points in the right direction.

Americans could have done more, but what they did do was more than enough. The United States provided the margin of victory in Europe and did more than any other country to defeat Japan. That democracy survived the war was—with all due respect for Britain's vital contribution—a uniquely American achievement. Afterward, the United States would take the lead in rebuilding not only the economies of the Allied states but those of its former enemies too. Seldom, probably never, had civilization owed so much to a single nation.

SEE ALSO

African Americans; Election of 1942; Election of 1944; Financing the war; Japanese Americans; Labor; Mobilization; Women

FURTHER READING

Blum, John Morton. *V Was for Victory: Politics and the American Culture During World War II*. New York: Harcourt, Brace, Jovanovich, 1976.
Brier, Howard M. *Swing Shift*. New York: Random House, 1943.
O'Neill, William L. *Democracy at War: America's Fight at Home and Abroad in World War II*. New York: Free Press, 1993.
Perrett, Geoffrey. *Days of Sadness, Years of Triumph: The American People, 1939–1945*. Madison: University of Wisconsin Press, 1983.

Small flags were displayed in many American windows during the war. The color of the star in the center indicated specific information, such as the death of a son overseas.

Tamar, Erika. *Good-bye Glamour Girl.* New York: Lippincott, 1984.

Hull, Cordell

SECRETARY OF STATE, 1933–44

- *Born: October 2, 1871, Pickett, Tenn.*
- *Political party: Democratic*
- *Previous government service: Tennessee state representative, 1893–97; judge, fifth judicial circuit, Tennessee, 1903–7; congressman, 1907–21, 1923–31; senator, 1931–33*
- *Died: July 23, 1955, Washington, D.C.*

Cordell Hull was appointed secretary of state by President Franklin D. Roosevelt because he believed Hull had influence with southern Democrats and was a moderate internationalist. The President, who intended to be his own foreign secretary, did not often consult Hull. Roosevelt's favorite diplomatic aide was his friend Sumner Welles (the undersecretary of state from 1937 to 1943), a relationship that Hull resented. He also resented Secretary of the Treasury Henry Morgenthau, another friend of Roosevelt, who had much more influence with him than did Hull.

Secretary Hull's chief prewar goal was to sign trade agreements with other nations. After the United States entered the war, Hull's slight authority declined further. According to Hull, he was frequently not even allowed to see the communications between Roosevelt and Prime Minister Churchill.

However, the President did allow Hull a free hand in designing postwar institutions like the United Nations in which the United States would participate. This was probably because Roosevelt had little faith in the UN, and expected instead that peace would be maintained by the victorious great powers acting together. Others took a more hopeful view of the United Nations, which was why Hull received the Nobel Peace Prize in 1945. Hull was a popular secretary and a political asset to Roosevelt, who regretted his resignation. Worn out and frustrated, Hull left office immediately after the 1944 Presidential election.

FURTHER READING

Gellman, Irwin F. *Secret Affairs: Franklin Roosevelt, Cordell Hull, and Sumner Welles.* Baltimore: Johns Hopkins University Press, 1995.
Hull, Cordell. *Memoirs.* New York: Macmillan, 1948.

Imperial Japanese Navy

SEE   Japanese Navy

Inflation

SEE   Wage and price controls

Intelligence, military

Military organizations seek to gather information about the enemy in various ways. Sometimes actual spies are used, like the legendary Mata Hari during World War I. In World War II the Soviets were especially successful in this area. They placed a spy named Richard Sorge in Germany's Tokyo embassy. He provided them, among other things, with exact information about Operation Barbarossa, the German invasion of Russia. The Lucy Ring was a Soviet espionage network in Germany that also provided valuable military intelligence.

However, most intelligence was gathered by means of technology. Much battlefield intelligence was provided by aerial photography. In addition, intelligence officers served near the front, interrogating prisoners and identifying enemy units. And deception operations were important to both sides. The Japanese attack on Pearl Harbor in December 1941 took the United States by surprise in part because deceptive signals and strict radio silence kept U.S. intelligence officers from knowing where the enemy carriers were. Likewise, the Allied landings in Normandy on D-Day surprised Hitler because numerous Allied deception programs had convinced him that the attack would take place farther north. The Germans secretly assembled three armies for their December 1944 assault in the Ardennes Forest (also known as the Battle of the Bulge) without Allied intelligence being any the wiser.

But while both sides enjoyed intelligence victories, the Allies' signals intelligence was better than that of the Axis powers and contributed much to winning the war. Signals intelligence begins by receiving enemy radio messages. It includes tracking the location of enemy broadcasters by means of these interceptions. And it is most valuable when the transmissions can be decoded, or decrypted, and their content analyzed.

Although their Pearl Harbor attack force kept quiet, Japanese radio discipline was usually poor. This enabled U.S. listening stations to acquire considerable information about enemy movements, even before analyzing their messages.

Perhaps the single greatest achievement of U.S. intelligence in World War II was to break the Japanese diplomatic codes and ciphers. This ability provided U.S. leaders with a great deal of intelligence, known by the code name

"MAGIC," that had military as well as political value. Especially revealing was the information gained from reading messages enciphered by a Japanese Foreign Ministry machine which Americans called "Purple." The first Purple text to be deciphered was read on September 25, 1940. From that time until the end of the war, U.S. intelligence was able to read Japan's diplomatic traffic.

Thanks to MAGIC, for example, Washington knew that Japan was trying to use Moscow as a mediator to negotiate an end to the Pacific war in 1945. But the same source revealed that the terms Japan's military leaders were insisting on were so far removed from actual surrender that they were not worth discussing.

U.S. and British intelligence had considerable success in breaking Japanese military codes as well. The information gained in this way was often called MAGIC, too, although, strictly speaking, decrypted military messages should be referred to by the code name ULTRA.

After Pearl Harbor, U.S. code breakers made an all-out attack on the Japanese Navy's operational code, known as JN-25. It was never broken as completely as Japan's diplomatic codes. But when the Japanese were planning their attack on Midway Island in 1942, U.S. Naval Intelligence at Pearl Harbor was able to read a good deal of their radio traffic. Because of this, Admiral Nimitz knew when and where the Japanese planned to strike. That information was what made it possible for a heavily outnumbered U.S. naval force to win the Battle of Midway. In 1942 changes in

The Germans used ENIGMA cipher machines to encode all of thier military radio transmissions. What they did not know was that Polish intelligence had provided the Allies with ENIGMA machines.

the JN-25 code stumped U.S. code breakers, but in 1943 they began reading it again. With some lapses, they would do so for the rest of the war.

Japanese Army messages were harder to crack, and it was not until 1943 that code breakers in the Southwest Pacific Area began to make progress decrypting them. A major breakthrough was finally achieved in January 1944 when the code books of a retreating Japanese division were unearthed. The army's code could then be read for some months. By the time it was changed, code breakers had already learned where a Japanese barge bearing the new code books had been sunk. When divers brought them up, this produced another intelligence triumph.

In the summer of 1945 additional code books were discovered in the Philippines and Okinawa. Decryptions obtained by their use made it clear that Japan's preparations for defending the home islands against an invasion were far stronger than had been thought. It is possible that the planned invasion might have been canceled, therefore, even if the atomic bombs dropped on Hiroshima and Nagasaki had failed to produce a Japanese surrender.

Although British intelligence played an active part in the effort to crack Japanese codes, Americans did the largest share of the work. In the war against Germany, however, these positions were reversed. Britain had been at war with Germany for more than two years before the United States came in, and thus had a significant lead in signals intelligence. British intelligence owed much to the Poles, who had built duplicates of the German "ENIGMA" code machine. All of Germany's armed forces used ENIGMA to encipher their radio communications, believing that its millions of possible combinations made ENIGMA's ciphers unbreakable.

In July 1939, Polish intelligence gave one ENIGMA machine each to Britain and France. Britain proceeded to construct a huge code-breaking operation at Bletchley Park, giving the information derived from breaking ENIGMA ciphers the code name ULTRA. Gathering ULTRA data was a continuous process, as the Germans regularly introduced new keys and made changes to the machine itself. Beginning in January 1944, Americans participated in the work of Bletchley Park, though in a lesser role.

ULTRA was a considerable aid to Britain's Fighter Command during the Battle of Britain. It was also very helpful in the long war Britain fought with German and Italian forces in North Africa. The great British victory at El Alamein, in particular, was made possible by ULTRA.

ULTRA played an important part in the Battle of the Atlantic, enabling the Allies to divert convoys from areas to which U-boats had been ordered. ULTRA also enabled Allied planners to tell whether the elaborate deception plans designed to draw German attention away from Normandy prior to D-Day were working. But ULTRA proved most useful in North Africa and at sea, where the Germans could not communicate by secure land lines.

Throughout the war, German radio traffic generated ULTRA information of considerable value. The Germans never realized that ENIGMA had been broken, thanks in part to incredibly tight Allied security. Indeed, not until the 1970s was the existence of ULTRA made public. This information required the rewriting of many military histories.

SEE ALSO

D-Day

FURTHER READING

Ambrose, Stephen E. *Ike's Spies: Eisenhower and the Espionage Establishment.* Garden City, N.Y.: Doubleday, 1981.

Dulles, Allen Welsh. *From Hitler's Doorstep: The Wartime Intelligence Reports of Allen Dulles, 1942–1945.* University Park: Pennsylvania State University Press, 1996.

Hinsley, F.H., and Alan Stripp, eds. *Codebreakers: The Inside Story of Bletchley Park.* New York: Oxford University Press, 1993.

Kirkpatrick, Lyman B. *Captains Without Eyes; Intelligence Failures in World War II.* New York: Macmillan, 1969.

Lewin, Ronald. *Ultra Goes to War.* London: Hutchinson, 1978.

———. *American Magic.* New York: Farrar, Straus, & Giroux, 1982.

Prados, John. *Combined Fleet Decoded: The Secret History of American Intelligence and the Japanese Navy in World War II.* New York: Random House, 1995.

Internment

Both sides in World War II detained or imprisoned (interned) citizens of the states they warred with. Neutral nations usually interned military personnel of belligerent states who strayed into their territories. Britain interned a large number of German and Austrian nationals, frequently failing to distinguish between Nazis and anti-Nazi refugees.

Harsh conditions in the internment camps, and the death of 661 enemy aliens when a vessel transporting them to Canada was sunk, led to severe criticism of these policies. By the summer of 1942, few aliens remained in British detention camps.

Internment became the fate of every Japanese and Japanese American on the West Coast of the United States who had escaped arrest in the roundup that followed Pearl Harbor. It was the greatest U.S. violation of human rights during the war. Those interned had no charges brought against them. Their only crime

was to be of Japanese descent. Not until after the 1944 elections were the first internees released from their bleak camps. German and Italian aliens were interned as well, but in much smaller numbers.

Although it in no way excuses this unfortunate action by the United States against its own citizens, the fate of enemy civilians who fell into Japanese hands was far worse. They were not treated as savagely as were prisoners of war, but the U.S., British, and Dutch civilians interned in Southeast Asia suffered extreme hardships. Beatings and other forms of mistreatment were common. Food rations diminished as the war went on. Many died before they could be liberated. Those who lived were sometimes as starved as the survivors of Germany's concentration camps. Germany, for its part, interned few civilians. Its policy was simply to murder unwanted noncombatants.

The maltreatment of internees in World War II was hardly remarkable in a war waged to a remarkable degree against civilians. No one knows how many people—in and out of uniform—were killed in World War II, estimates range from 60 to 85 million. But that a majority of the dead were noncombatants is beyond dispute. Gassed, bombed,

The Hirano family was forced to live at the Colorado River Relocation Center, Poston, Arizona. In this ironic family portrait, the Hiranos display their patriotism.

and starved to death by the tens of millions, civilians stood little chance of having their human rights respected in internment camps.

SEE ALSO
Japanese Americans

FURTHER READING
Christgau, John. *"Enemies": World War II Alien Internment.* Ames: Iowa State University Press, 1985.
Collins, Donald E. *Native American Aliens: Disloyalty and the Renunciation of Citizenship by Japanese Americans during World War II.* Westport, Conn.: Greenwood Press, 1985.
Smith, Page. *Democracy on Trial: The Japanese American Evacuation and Relocation in World War II.* New York: Simon & Schuster, 1995.
Taylor, Sandra C. *Jewel of the Desert: Japanese American Internment at Topaz.* Berkeley: University of California Press, 1993.

Isolationists

Americans who were opposed to entering World War II before Pearl Harbor was attacked in December 1941 were called isolationists. After World War I, a majority of Americans, both liberals and conservatives, decided that entering the war had been a mistake. When Hitler dragged Europe into war in 1939 most people failed to understand that, unlike in 1917, the United States had a great deal at stake in the outcome.

In World War I a German victory would not have made much difference to Americans. But a German victory in World War II would have left the United States as the only democratic power in a world of police states and empires. For the United States to adopt a policy of isolationism meant running the risk that democracy, and perhaps the United

States itself, would be able to survive under these conditions. It was a risk Americans should have been unwilling to take. The fact remains that they did.

Democrats and Republicans alike—but the latter more strongly—agreed throughout the prewar years that the United States should not rearm and should stay out of Europe's affairs. No one did more to encourage these beliefs than Charles A. Lindbergh, the greatest American hero of his generation.

The first man to fly solo across the Atlantic, Lindbergh won the nation's heart, not only for the feat itself but for his supposed modesty. He protected his privacy as much as a celebrity could, but Lindbergh had a high opinion of himself and a low one of humankind. The kidnapping and murder of his first child, the media circus surrounding it, and the trial of the boy's killer only deepened his dislike of the masses.

Charles Lindbergh had supported the crusade of his father, Congressman C. A. Lindbergh, against U.S. intervention in World War I, a stand that destroyed the elder Lindbergh's political career. This experience was much on Lindbergh's mind during his own similar campaign a generation later. So too was the idea that another great war, no matter who won it, would destroy Western civilization and leave Soviet communism as the only real victor, a common view among conservative isolationists.

Through the efforts of a U.S. military attaché in Berlin, who hoped Lindbergh would learn something useful, he made several visits to Germany at the invitation of the Nazis. The first was for eleven days in July and August 1936, followed by two others, one of several weeks in 1937, and a final one October 11–29, 1938. During these visits the Nazis managed to fool Lindbergh into thinking that the Luftwaffe (German

Next to a portrait of Adolf Hitler, the American aviator Charles Lindbergh (left) meets with Nazi leader Hermann Göring (right). Lindbergh was perhaps the best-known advocate of American isolationism in the years preceding the war.

Air Force) was so strong as to be unbeatable. Ignorant of history and politics, and with some Nazi sympathies, Lindbergh was an easy mark. Until the war broke out, Lindbergh, who was then living in England, made every effort to encourage the policy of giving in to Hitler that Britain pursued until the spring of 1938.

When war broke out in Europe, Lindbergh severed his informal connection with the Army Air Corps, freeing himself to fight against U.S. intervention. A conservative commentator named Fulton Lewis, Jr., arranged for Lindbergh to air his opinions over the Mutual Radio Network. His talk, which was actually carried by three networks, proved to be one of five nationally broadcast radio addresses Lindbergh would give in the first 15 months of the war. He would also speak at two public meetings, testify before two committees of Congress, write three articles for national magazines, and advise many leaders. All this activity occurred before he joined the America First Committee, a large, well-financed orga-

nization devoted to keeping the United States at peace whatever the cost.

In April 1941 Lindbergh began speaking under the auspices of the America First Committee. Lindbergh and America First lost much of their standing after Lindbergh's speech of September 11 that year in which he accused Jews of conspiring to drag the United States into the war. But, as the polls showed, most Americans were against declaring war on Germany right up to Pearl Harbor. (Curiously, Americans did come to favor declaring war on Japan under certain conditions—apparently because they believed the Japanese would be easy to beat.)

After the fall of France in 1940, Americans supported aid to Britain, which is why President Roosevelt was able to have his Lend-Lease bill pass Congress early the next year. They supported aid to the Soviet Union too, after it was invaded. Still, Americans remained convinced that the time to fight Hitler was when he attacked the United States. The arguments that this would mean waiting until all of the nation's potential allies had been beaten, and that defeat would then be likely, did not carry much weight.

Nor were the advantages of fighting abroad, rather than at home, evident to many. Isolationism was not based on a rational analysis of what course best served the United States's interests. "American boys must not die in foreign wars" was a frequently repeated chant. Few asked why it would be better to have them killed at home, along with many civilians.

SEE ALSO

America First Committee; Germany; Japan

FURTHER READING

Adler, Selig. *The Isolationist Impulse: Its Twentieth-century Reaction.* New York: Abelard-Schuman, 1957.
Cole, Wayne S. *Charles A. Lindbergh and the Battle Against American Intervention in World War II.* New York: Harcourt, Brace, Jovanovich, 1974.
———. *Roosevelt & the Isolationists, 1932–45.* Lincoln: University of Nebraska Press, 1983.
Mosley, Leonard. *Lindbergh: A Biography.* Garden City, N.Y.: Doubleday, 1976.

Italian campaigns

After the capture of Sicily in August 1943, the Allies invaded the Italian mainland, as much out of momentum as for any strategic reason. There had been much discussion as to whether this was a good idea. The British, especially Prime Minister Winston Churchill, his cabinet, and his chiefs of staff, were keenly in favor of "knocking Italy out of the war," as they frequently put it. Their argument was that aircraft based in Italy could strike Germany and targets in the Balkans. Also, taking Italy would make clearing the rest of the Mediterranean simpler, a high priority for the British. With Italy in hand, it would then be easier to open a second front in the Balkans, which the British preferred to invading France.

U.S. planners were unhappy about invading Italy, however, because doing so would not weaken Germany much. Indeed, some argued that Italy in German hands would actually be an Allied asset. Germany would then have to occupy it, tying up more than a few divisions. But if the Allies invaded Italy, they would take unnecessary casualties. And then they would have to supply its civilian population with at least the bare necessities, which would require ships that were needed elsewhere.

The Invasion However, by the time Sicily fell it was too late in the year to organize an invasion of France, while forces already on the island could quickly be moved to the Italian mainland. Thus, on September 3, General Bernard Law Montgomery's Eighth Army crossed the Strait of Messina. U.S. forces were scheduled to invade Salerno and drop from the air on Rome. Mussolini had been arrested in July (he would be rescued later by German commandos) and replaced by Marshal Pietro Badoglio.

On September 8, Badoglio surrendered Italy to the Allies without a struggle. On September 9, General Mark Clark's U.S. Fifth Army, consisting of four divisions plus special forces, went ashore at Salerno (code named Avalanche). There it met with such fierce German resistance that it was almost driven off.

The Germans seized control of

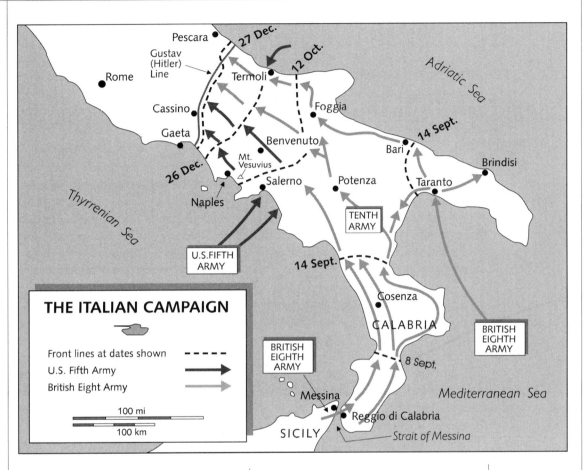

THE ITALIAN CAMPAIGN

Front lines at dates shown — — — —
U.S. Fifth Army ➤
British Eight Army ➤

100 mi
100 km

Rome and most of the country, with Badoglio fleeing south to the protection of Britain's Eighth Army, which was encamped in the toe of Italy's "boot" in the extreme south. The Italian fleet set sail for various Allied ports. Italy's soldiers abroad became German prisoners, while those at home were disarmed and released, or else sent to Germany as slave laborers.

Eisenhower canceled the planned assault on Rome and dropped some of the paratroopers intended for it on Salerno instead. Heavy fire from naval guns and a maximum air effort secured the beachhead. In two weeks the Eighth Army arrived from Calabria, giving the Allies a continuous line across Italy.

Field Marshal Albert Kesselring, commander of Germany's forces in southern Italy, was persuaded by the

Allies' narrow win at Salerno that they could be stopped. Hitler required little persuasion, so the German Army quickly dug in. Now, instead of an easy takeover, the Allies found themselves caught up in a grueling struggle that would go on almost to the day Germany surrendered.

The fight for Italy Italy saw some of the hardest fighting of the entire war. The Germans dug themselves into mountainous positions from which they had to be blasted out by Allied troops fighting uphill. In many places the ground was so rough that supplies had to be delivered by mules. The winter fights were especially cruel. When a German position finally fell, there was always another right behind it.

The Allied buildup was so slow that when winter came to Italy the Germans had 20 divisions in place, the

Allies only 14. Over time, more divisions arrived, giving the Allies a slight numerical advantage. But, because of U.S. reservations and British weakness, the Allies never were strong enough to punch through Germany's lines of defense except with the greatest difficulty.

After a series of failed attacks, the Allies sought to break the Gustav Line by landing above it at Anzio in January 1944. Although the idea behind Operation Shingle was sound, the force that landed was a feeble one and Kesselring easily contained it.

Breaking the Gustav and Gothic lines All that remained was to batter at the German line in hopes it would collapse. In the winter and spring of 1944, the U.S. Fifth and British Eighth armies fought a series of punishing battles to seize Monte Cassino, the key to the Gustav Line. The fighting lasted from January 12 to May 18. After the first attack failed, the Allies decided to bomb a 6th-century monastery that overlooked the town, in the mistaken belief that it had been fortified by the Germans. Not only a crime against culture, the attack was also an outright blunder, because the Germans proceeded to fortify the ruins, making their position even stronger.

Eventually the Polish II Corps took Monte Cassino, the Gustav Line was pierced in several places, and the embattled U.S. VI Corps broke out of Anzio. But, as so often in the war, the Allies moved too slowly, the Germans too fast. Kesselring merely pulled his troops out and retired to the Gothic Line above Rome, so the whole cycle had to be repeated. After another cruel winter of fighting, the Gothic Line was finally broken.

This time, with the Third Reich on the verge of collapse, the German army group did not escape. Harried by fight-er-bombers and with Allied forces having sealed off the Alps, it surrendered on May 2. By then Hitler and Mussolini were already dead. Mussolini had been shot by Italian partisans on April 28, and Hitler had killed himself on April 30.

The Allies sustained 189,000 casualties in Italy, the Germans 435,000. In a strictly numerical sense, therefore, the Italian campaign might be said to have paid for itself. But many of the German casualties were prisoners of war taken at the very end. During most of the fight for Italy, a smaller German force held a larger Allied one at bay. If the Allies had chosen not to invade Italy, the 20-odd Allied divisions stuck there could have hastened the day of Hitler's defeat by fighting on the western front. Meanwhile, the Germans would still have had to keep many divisions in Italy for fear of an Allied attack. Thus the mere threat of an invasion would have weakened Germany at almost no cost. With all respect for the brave men who fought it, the Italian campaign was an error.

SEE ALSO

Anzio, Battle of; Italy; Italy, surrender of; Mussolini, Benito; Sicily, Battle of

FURTHER READING

Blaxland, Gregory. *Alexander's Generals: The Italian campaign, 1944–45.* London: W. Kimber, 1979.

Bluemenson, Martin. *Salerno to Cassino.* Washington, D.C.: Office of the Chief of Military History, 1969.

Botjer, George F. *Sideshow War: The Italian Campaign, 1943–1945.* College Station: Texas A & M University Press, 1996.

Fisher, Ernest F. *Cassino to the Alps.* Washington, D.C.: Office of the Chief of Military History, 1977.

Jackson, W. G. F. *The Battle for Italy.* New York: Harper & Row, 1967.

Shepperd, G. A. *The Italian Campaign, 1943–45, A Political and Military Re-assessment.* New York: Praeger, 1968.

Wallace, Robert. *The Italian Campaign.* Alexandria, Va.: Time-Life Books, 1978.

Italy

From 1861 until 1922, Italy had been a parliamentary democracy with a constitutional monarch. In 1922 Benito Mussolini came to power; in 1925, he abolished democracy but retained King Victor Emmanuel III. At the time, Italy possessed as colonies Libya, Eritrea, and Italian Somaliland, all in Africa, plus the Dodecanese Islands in the eastern Mediterranean. To them Mussolini would add Ethiopia (then called Abyssinia) in 1936 and Albania in 1939.

Italy had a population of 42 million in 1936, making it one of the most populous states in Europe. But it lacked raw materials and the industrial and technical resources of a great power. In 1938 it consumed 13 million tons of coal (all but 1 million of it imported), while France was producing 47 million tons and Britain 230 million tons. The national income of Italy was less than half that of France and only a quarter of Britain's. While motor vehicles were now required to move any army, Italy produced only 71,000 of them in 1939. That same year France manufactured 227,000 vehicles and Britain 445,000.

Moving up through the village of Prato, Italy, men of the 370th Infantry Regiment slowly make their way up the Italian peninsula.

The great differences between Italy's means and Mussolini's aims would be fatal to Italian fascism—and to many Italians. Despite its rich culture and beauty, Italy was a nation of the second or third rank that Mussolini treated as if it were a great power. Among many vainglorious gestures, one may stand for all. In 1936 Italy seized Ethiopia, most of whose people still lived in the Stone Age. Mussolini then announced the birth of a new Roman Empire.

Although he was jealous of Hitler, Mussolini was naturally drawn to an alliance with Germany. It was a fascist police state like Italy and, like Italy again, bent on conquest. The Allies would certainly have accepted Italy, and offered some material benefits to it. But the Allies would not have gone along with Mussolini's expansion plans, while Hitler did. Thus Mussolini forged a "Pact of Steel" with Germany in 1939 and seized Albania. Then, after a prudent interval to make sure that Germany would win the battle, Italy attacked France on June 10, 1940— unsuccessfully, as the French easily drove the Italian Army back. But Hitler rewarded Mussolini all the same by giving Italy an occupation zone in southern France.

The Italian Army's poor showing against France ought to have made Mussolini rethink his position, but did not. In 1940–41 Italy and Britain fought a series of naval battles for control of the Mediterranean, which the British usually won. In an especially bold stroke a handful of obsolete British carrier planes crippled half the Italian fleet at Taranto on November 11, 1940.

On land it was worse. In October 1940 Mussolini's army invaded Greece, which had rejected various unreasonable Italian demands. But after gaining some ground, the Italians were forced back. With British air support, the Greek Army pushed ahead during the winter of 1940–41. This setback, embarrassing for Mussolini, interfered with Germany's plans for the Balkans and forced Hitler to bail Italy out.

To attack Greece, the Germans needed permission to cross Yugoslavia. On March 25, 1941, it was granted by the Yugoslavian government, which also joined the Axis. But the existing government was then promptly overthrown by patriots who reversed the decision. An infuriated Hitler ordered the seizure of Yugoslavia as well as Greece. Ten days later, on April 6, 1941, the German forces struck. Yugoslavia fell almost at once and an armistice was signed on the 17th. Without pausing for breath, the Germans rolled into Greece, and took it in a matter of weeks.

Italy was allowed to occupy most of Greece and part of Yugoslavia. While the Italian Army had failed to distinguish itself in war, it behaved honorably as an occupation force by refusing to implement Hitler's anti-Semitic policies. More than that, Italian officers protected Jews in their zones of occupation. In France the Italian Army prevented Germans and police from the pro-Nazi Vichy government—sometimes at gunpoint—from seizing the 240,000 Jews who were under its protection. In Yugoslavia it saved some 600,000 Jews from anti-Semitic and pro-Nazi Croatian forces.

The seeds of Italy's next defeats had already been sown before it advanced into Greece. In August 1940 an Italian army stationed in Ethiopia easily occupied British Somaliland. The next month Italian units advanced out of Libya about 60 miles into Egypt, which was independent in theory but actually controlled by Britain. In December the British struck back, driving deeply into Libya. After eight weeks of fighting, Italian casualties (mostly prisoners of war) came to

130,000, while the British lost fewer than 2,000 men.

The British could have eliminated the Italians entirely. Instead, the British commander, General Richard O'Connor, was forced by orders from London to halt. Most of his troops were then sent to Greece as part of the vain British effort to save it. This change of plan gave Hitler the opportunity to rescue Mussolini again.

But Italy's humiliation was not yet complete. In May 1940, after a three-month campaign, British forces regained British Somaliland and liberated Ethiopia. Italian losses, chiefly prisoners of war again, came to almost 300,000. The British took 1,200 battle casualties, although 75,000 men caught vicious local diseases, chiefly dysentery and malaria.

This victory was more than offset, however, by British losses in Libya and the western desert of Egypt. To keep the Italians from losing Libya, Hitler sent two divisions there under the command of General Erwin Rommel. At the end of March 1941, Rommel attacked the British, driving them back into Egypt and capturing General O'Connor. It was the start of a two-year struggle during which Rommel, the "Desert Fox" to his enemies, would punish the British severely for having failed to take Libya when they had the chance.

The Italian units under Rommel's command fought better than they had alone, easing somewhat the sting of their earlier defeats. Still, in the end, defeat could not be avoided. When Tunisia, where the Axis forces made their last stand in Africa, fell in May 1943, more than 250,000 men—half of them Italian—became Allied prisoners of war. By the time the Allies took Sicily in August, Mussolini had fallen; Italy would soon be out of the war.

The Italian people and nation suffered terribly as a result of Mussolini's

leadership. Rationing began in 1939 and by 1941 gasoline was no longer available to civilians. Newspapers were limited to two pages. One pair of shoes or a few pieces of clothing, but not both, could be bought per person each year. Food consumption fell below 1,000 calories a day, less than a two- or three-year-old child had needed in peacetime. On the black market, butter sold for 10 times its pre-war price, olive oil even more.

These sacrifices were the result of an armament effort that was far beyond what Italy could afford. Even before war broke out, Italy was spending more money than France on its military, despite being so much poorer. At the peak of the mobilization it supported an army of 91 divisions, more than it could arm. Soldiers fought with weapons from World War I, and some that were even older.

Italian armor was not taken seriously by anyone. The M11 tank—small, slow,

Members of Mussolini's Fascist Youth (standing) welcome a member of the Hitler Youth to a meeting in Italy.

lightly armored and gunned—was considered the worst in the world. Italian aircraft were similarly poor, and Italian warships were notable for their obsolete technology. Bad management and administration—test reports of naval vessels were faked to make ships seem faster than they were, for example—were often responsible for these faulty products.

Between January 1940 and April 1943, the Italian aircraft industry manufactured 10,545 aircraft, with production reaching a high of only 241 units a month. Meanwhile, British aircraft construction during this time exceeded 2,000 a month. Of some 4,500 fighters produced, fewer than 300 were equal to the British Hurricane. In the same period only one battleship, three light carriers, and five destroyers joined the Italian fleet. These were pitifully small numbers for a nation that meant to defeat Britain in the Mediterranean, and more pitiful still considering their lack of quality.

Italy suffered heavy losses in the war. Eight percent of its industrial plants was destroyed, along with 2 million rooms of civilian housing out of a total of 36 million. Sixty percent of its locomotives were destroyed and 90 percent of its trucks. Five thousand bridges were blown up. Agricultural production fell by 60 percent.

The human cost was excessive, too. At peak strength the Italian Army had about 2 million men, the Navy 260,000, and the Air Force several hundred thousand. While fighting on the Axis side, 200,000 Italian servicemen were killed (including 80,000 on the eastern front and 50,000 in the Balkans), an unknown but larger number wounded, and 600,000 made Allied prisoners.

After September 8, 1943, when Italy surrendered, its forces were disarmed by the Germans. Italian units sustained another 19,000 casualties when they attempted to resist. After being disarmed, 600,000 uniformed Italians were sent to Germany as slave laborers. While the civilian losses can only be estimated, perhaps 300,000 were killed in bombing raids; others died while fighting as partisans or as workers in Germany.

After the German occupation began, Italy was doomed to be fought over for the rest of the war. In the north, Germany established a puppet government, called the Italian Social Republic (ISR), led by Mussolini, whom German commandos had rescued. At first many surviving fascists enlisted in Mussolini's armed forces. But before long it became clear that the Germans meant to plunder Italy, not treat the ISR as an ally. The Bank of Italy's gold went to Germany, along with many other assets and resources. Life was unspeakably grim in the ISR and not much better in liberated Italy, to whose people the Allies could provide only the bare necessities.

Italian honor was redeemed somewhat by the lack of Italian anti-Semitism. As long as the Italian Army survived, Jews in Italian zones of occupation were protected. At home, too, although Mussolini issued anti-Semitic decrees, fascists did not kill Jews. It was not until the German occupation of Italy that Jews were murdered there, or sent to the eastern death camps.

The Italian people paid a fearful price for their obedience to Mussolini, however. Although most Italians had followed Mussolini, most had done so with little enthusiasm. The eagerness of Italian soldiers to surrender to the Allies was the result of lack of faith rather than cowardice. Still, the Italians had followed their leader for many years and suffered accordingly.

SEE ALSO

Italian campaigns; Mediterranean theater; Mussolini, Benito; North African campaign; Sicily, Battle of

FURTHER READING

Adams, Henry Hitch. *Italy at War.* Alexandria, Va.: Time-Life Books, 1982.
Lamb, Richard. *War in Italy, 1943–1945: A Brutal Story.* New York: St. Martin's, 1994.
Smith, Dennis Mack. *Mussolini's Roman Empire.* New York: Viking, 1976.
Wiskemann, Elizabeth. *Fascism in Italy: Its Development and Influence.* New York: St. Martin's, 1969.

Italy, surrender of

After the Allied landings in Sicily in July 1943, the Grand Fascist Council of Italy met for the first time since 1939. This meeting established that Benito Mussolini had little support, and on July 25, 1943, King Victor Emmanuel III accordingly had him arrested. He was replaced by Marshal Pietro Badoglio, who assured Germany that Italy would fight on, while at the same time he opened secret talks with the Allies. These talks were slowed by the Allied insistence on unconditional surrender and by Italian attempts to bargain.

A particular sticking point was that Badoglio wanted the Allies to land in Italy with 15 divisions, which was many more than they had available. A German military buildup in Italy was going forward at top speed when General Eisenhower, the Allied commander, announced over public radio that Italy's government had agreed to surrender in principle. This left Badoglio no choice but to take the Allies' terms.

The armistice was announced on September 8. Badoglio fled south from Rome to take shelter with the British, who had already landed in the toe of Italy's "boot." Germany took control of Italy and, with great violence when units resisted, disarmed Italy's armed forces.

The last German troops in Italy were not killed or captured until the war in Europe was over.

SEE ALSO

Italian campaigns; Italy; Mussolini, Benito

FURTHER READING

Davis, Melton S. *Who Defends Rome? The Forty-five Days, July 25–September 8, 1943.* New York: Dial, 1972.
Smyth, Howard M., and Albert N. Garland. *Sicily and the Surrender of Italy.* Washington, D.C.: Department of the Army, 1965.

Iwo Jima, Battle of

The Battle of Iwo Jima was among the worst-planned operations conducted by U.S. forces in World War II. It took place because Iwo Jima, a small volcanic island, only 4.5 miles by 2.5 miles in size, annoyed the U.S. Army Air Forces.

Iwo Jima lay between B-29 bases in the Mariana Islands and their targets in Japan. Japanese fighters based on Iwo Jima forced the American Superfortresses to fly around it, consuming additional fuel at the expense of their bombload. Iwo Jima's radar picked them up anyway, warning the home islands. In U.S. hands, Iwo Jima would instead provide fighter escorts for the B-29s and emergency landing strips, which was why the Joint Chiefs ordered it to be taken.

As it turned out, Iwo Jima was one of the best-defended Japanese positions that U.S. troops would ever be called upon to storm. When the Marines came ashore on February 19, 1945, Iwo Jima became a slaughterhouse.

Although by this time U.S. mastery of the art of amphibious warfare was complete, the assault force was poorly supported. Carriers and battleships pro-

From the crest of Mount Surib-achi, the American flag waves in triumph over Iwo Jima after U.S. Marines had fought their way inch by inch up its steep lava-encrusted slopes.

savageness of the fighting.

When it was over, 6,821 Americans had been killed and almost 20,000 wounded. Most of the enemy—more than 20,000 men—were killed too. But for the only time in the Pacific war, the total Japanese casualties were less than those sustained by Americans. Three marine divisions were used up in this bloodbath, half the corps' total strength. One-third of all marines killed in the Pacific died on Iwo Jima.

The painful truth is that Iwo Jima should have been bypassed. The failure to do so was excused afterward by citing the number of army bombers—2,400— that made landings on the island. Because each B-29 carried a crew of 11, it was later argued that taking Iwo Jima saved more than 25,000 lives. This is a feeble defense, for many of the landings were nothing but scheduled refueling stops. Of the crews that were actually in trouble, some would have made it home. Others that went down in the sea would have been picked up by submarines assigned to that duty or by specialized air-sea rescue units.

In short, there is no way of proving that the lives lost on Iwo Jima were offset by the number of B-29 crewmen who were saved by landing on it. But even if there was some small gain in lives, B-29s played a smaller role in defeating Japan than did the Marine Corps. Had Japan been invaded on schedule, the sacrifice of three assault divisions for the sake of emergency landing strips would have been recognized as the blunder it was.

SEE ALSO

Central Pacific

FURTHER READING

Ross, Bill D. *Iwo Jima: Legacy of Valor.* New York: Random House, 1985.
Thomey, Tedd. *Immortal Images: A Personal History of Two Photographers and the Flag Raising on Iwo Jima.* Annapolis, Md.: Naval Institute Press, 1996.

vided only 4 days of bombardment instead of the 10 that the marines had requested. This was a serious error because, while nothing could reach the enemy's deep bunkers, artillery positions near the surface were vulnerable to naval gunfire. Thus, when the Marines hit the beach many known gun positions remained intact, more so than on any other Pacific island. The U.S. casualties would reflect this.

Iwo Jima is best known for the picture taken by Associated Press photographer Joe Rosenthal of a large U.S. flag being raised atop Mount Suribachi. That event actually took place early in the battle, which raged on until the end of March and featured savage infantry actions in places like the "Meat Grinder" and "Bloody Gorge." Twenty-seven marines and naval corpsmen (medics) won the Medal of Honor on Iwo Jima, a measure not only of U.S. bravery but the

Japan

In 1937, when Japanese forces invaded China bent on conquest, Japan had a population of 70 million. It was the first Asian nation to build an industrial economy, an amazing feat for a country endowed by nature with very few raw materials. Nearly everything industry required—coal, iron ore, rubber, even wood—had to be imported. Japan paid for these imports chiefly by exporting cloth, especially silk goods. As a result, the textile industry employed 38 percent of the work force, more than any other sector.

During the Great Depression of the 1930s, Japan's civilian government gave way to rule by the military. This process was hastened by the so-called Young Tigers, extremist junior officers who were in the habit of assassinating politicians who disagreed with the military.

Because the Army and Navy had different goals, government by the military did not mean quick agreement on national policy. Both services were imperialistic, but looked in different directions. The Navy favored a southern strategy: to gain control of the rich resources of Southeast Asia and make Japan self-sufficient. The Army, which had seized much of Manchuria in 1931, preferred East Asia as a field of conquest. It had forced the issue by invading China without getting the navy's agreement. Army leaders had expected to seize China quickly and exploit its resources, but China turned out to be too big to conquer.

Events finally decided which way Japan was to go. At the same time as it was bogged down in China, Japan clashed with the Soviets. An undeclared Manchurian border war with the U.S.S.R. in 1939 ended when Japan suf-fered a defeat that cast doubt on the Army's East Asian plans. However, Japanese fortunes took a turn for the better when war broke out in Europe. For one thing, the Army-Navy debate over grand strategy came to an end as the Army now saw the value of Southeast Asia.

Origins of war The United States went to war with Japan primarily out of a desire to aid China. Americans had been sympathetic to China for many years, because Christian missionaries operating there had molded public opinion in favor of what was misrepresented as a progressive, modernizing China. Relatively few in number, these missionaries had been sent out by large, powerful churches in the United States whose millions of members formed a kind of lobby on behalf of Chinese interests.

In the 19th century, the main danger to China—at that time an empire itself—came from such European imperial powers as Britain, France, and Germany, which had carved out what were called "spheres of influence" there. By the 20th century, however, and especially after World War I, the greatest threat to China was posed by Japan. Wars with China and Russia had enabled Japan to acquire Formosa (now Taiwan), Korea, and south Manchuria, but had not satisfied the appetites of Japanese expansionists.

The Manchurian "incident" In September 1931 Japan's Kwantung Army occupied the rest of Manchuria, which had been controlled by a Chinese warlord and belonged to China in theory. In fact, however, China, a republic since 1911, was too weak to enforce its rule. The United States regarded the occupation of Manchuria as a violation of various treaties that Japan had signed. To Japan, however, the seizure of Manchuria was not illegal, and in any case, was seen as essential to its own security. Manchuria was the only place to which Japanese citizens could emigrate, as virtually all of the world's major nations denied them permission to enter as immigrants.

Manchuria was also the source of essential raw materials for Japan, such as iron ore and coal, as well as of critical foodstuffs. And it was Japan's buffer against the Soviet Union, which also had designs on Manchuria.

Further, the Great Depression of the 1930s ruined Japan's export trade, and the prohibitive Smoot-Hawley Tariff of 1930 closed Japan's markets in the United States. These events made Manchuria even more important to Japan.

War with China In July 1937 Japan, whose government was now controlled by the Imperial Japanese Army, made an incredible blunder by invading China. The Japanese assumption was that China, where power was shared between Generalissimo Chiang Kai-shek and assorted regional warlords, would be easy to seize and hold. But China's military weakness turned out to matter less than its size.

Japan won every battle in China but could not win the war. Chiang relocated his capital to Chungking, a mountain stronghold deep inside China that the Japanese could not reach. They occupied all the major cities and much of China's coast, but because China refused to surrender, the Japanese found themselves bogged down in a ruinous war.

Apparently thinking that the Chinese people could be terrorized into giving up, the Japanese Army committed terrible atrocities in China. During what became known as the Rape of Nanking, for example, some 250,000 Chinese lost their lives during a six-week orgy of violence. Many of these acts took place in full view of Western journalists and diplomats, for Nanking had been Chiang's capital before he moved it

inland. Japan offended world opinion by behaving in this barbarous way, yet failed to pacify China.

The U.S. reaction War in China presented President Roosevelt's administration with a dilemma. Viewed strictly in terms of American self-interest, there was much to be said for tolerating Japan in the short run. The United States had a large stake in maintaining good relations with Japan, where U.S. investments totaled $466 million, twice as much as in China. Forty-eight percent of U.S. exports to the Far East went to Japan, and 21 percent of the United States's Far Eastern imports came from it—in dollar terms much less than before the stock market crash of 1929, but still a substantial figure. U.S. commerce with Japan was three times that with China and produced a favorable balance of trade. If the United States were forced to choose between the two countries, economics dictated that it side with Japan.

The alternative, which was to challenge Japanese imperialism, meant risking a war that would damage trade and endanger the Philippines—the United States's Far Eastern commonwealth that it could not protect and yet had to defend. Such a war would cost much in lives and money and, if won, still leave East Asia vulnerable to the Soviets. If Japan refused ever to leave China, the United States would someday be forced to act, but to do so later instead of sooner was clearly the wisest path. At first the government and people of the United States were as reluctant to fight Japan as to fight Germany. But as Japan continued to violate China, support for sanctions grew. On July 26, 1939, after Britain made concessions in China as a result of Japanese pressure, Roosevelt decided to give the six-month notice required to cancel a commercial treaty with Japan that dated from 1911. This step met with the approval of 81

Tokyo women help clean up debris in the war-scarred capital some weeks before the Japanese surrender on August 14, 1945.

percent of the Americans polled by the Gallup organization. By 1935 public opinion polls had become frequent and reliable enough to influence public policy. Roosevelt appears to have been guided by them to a considerable extent in his conduct of prewar diplomacy.

The outbreak of war in Europe in 1939 further weakened Britain's position in Asia. Avoiding a Japanese conflict was more important than ever, yet the tight focus of the European imperial powers on Germany created fresh opportunities for Japanese expansion. It was essential to Britain that China continue fighting and thus tie down the Japanese Army. But being stuck in China would lead Japan to seek a solution to its problem by widening the war. That was hinted at on September 15, 1939, when Japan signed an armistice with the Soviet Union, putting an end to the undeclared war between them.

The European war created a temptation for Japan's military leaders that they could not resist. Having failed to crush China, they saw in the weakening of the colonial powers an opportunity to cut

China's links to the outside world. Accordingly, Tokyo demanded that the Allies withdraw their support of China, ordered France to stop all traffic between Indochina and China, and insisted that Britain shut down China's supply lines through Hong Kong and Burma.

Japan also declared the "regions of the South Seas" to be part of its Greater East Asia Co-Prosperity Sphere. The Sphere was a device by which Japan hoped to rally the oppressed peoples of Asia to its side. Represented as a policy of "Asia for the Asians" at a time when much of the continent was still ruled by Europe, the slogan had considerable appeal. Asians knew much about mistreatment by Europeans. Of Japan's far more dangerous aims, they as yet had little knowledge.

The United States Acts to Contain Japan Britain, France, and China called vainly on Washington to assist them against Japan. But Roosevelt and Secretary of State Cordell Hull feared that strong action, such as economic reprisals against Japan, might trigger a war that the United States was unprepared to fight. Some felt that sanctions would be effective, because Japan was so dependent on the United States, which provided it with 80 percent of its oil, 90 percent of its gasoline, 74 percent of its scrap metal, and 60 percent of its machine tools. But Roosevelt was unwilling to gamble on this assumption. Finally, however, after much bureaucratic jockeying, on July 25, 1940, Roosevelt signed an order embargoing aviation fuel and lubricants and the type of scrap metal used in making steel.

Japan was not deterred by this limited embargo. In August and September, Tokyo forced Britain to withdraw its troops from Shanghai, the Dutch to consider making economic concessions in the East Indies, and the French to recognize Japanese claims in Indochina. On September 26, 1940, when it appeared that the Battle of Britain was won and after Japanese troops had entered Indochina, Roosevelt embargoed all iron and steel scrap. The next day Japan signed the Tripartite Pact with Italy and Germany, which specified that they would help each other if any of them went to war with a nation at present neutral.

On April 13, 1941, Washington learned that Japan and the Soviet Union had signed a nonaggression pact, specifying that if one went to war with a third power, the other would remain neutral. The implications were obvious. If the pact held, Japan would gain freedom of action in Southeast Asia. That it would hold became clear after June 22 when Germany invaded Russia. To Washington this attack meant that Japan's rear was safe because the Soviets would not want to fight in both Asia and Europe. The way was now clear for Japan to take Southeast Asia, isolating China from outside aid. Japan could also free itself of dependence on U.S. oil

by acquiring the Netherlands East Indies and their rich oil fields.

Japanese planners had been working on the conquest of Southeast Asia for months, although no target date had been set. They knew that the campaign might lead to war with the United States, but Japan hoped that the United States, which was weak militarily and had its eyes turned toward Europe, would not fight. These were, in fact, compelling motives for a U.S. policy of restraint. The United States was unprepared for war with Germany, Roosevelt's efforts to provoke one notwithstanding, still less for a second conflict with Japan. London and Washington agreed that Germany, as the greater menace, must be disposed of first.

But by the summer of 1941 an Anglo-American war with Japan was looming, despite numerous diplomatic contacts and discussions. The United States was still deadlocked with Japan over China. Japan insisted on retaining a free hand in China, while the United States demanded that it withdraw altogether.

At this time Japan had come to regard war with the United States as unavoidable. This attitude resulted from the U.S. response to its occupation of southern Indochina, which began on July 24. The United States knew something was about to occur, thanks to Operation MAGIC, a triumph of the code breaker's art, which enabled U.S. intelligence to read Japanese radio traffic. The Japanese diplomatic code, named Purple by U.S. code breakers, was yielding up priceless information.

Because of decrypted Japanese diplomatic messages and other forms of intelligence, Washington was aware of Japanese ship movements, although not their destination. Yet, wherever the Japanese were going, it did not appear that they could be stopped, because the combined forces of the Netherlands, Britain, and the United States were feeble compared to those of the Japanese Empire. For this reason the U.S. service chiefs had urged Roosevelt to avoid war in the Pacific.

Steps toward war Nevertheless, on July 26 President Roosevelt federalized the Philippine military and restored its head, retired general Douglas MacArthur, to active duty as commander of U.S. Army Forces in the Far East. Roosevelt also froze Japanese assets in the United States and began licensing the sale of oil to Japan so as to limit its flow.

In September 1941 it was decided to cut off Japan completely. The resulting embargo included Latin America and the Netherlands East Indies, leaving Japan with no source of oil. Given the history of modern Japan, which always preferred fighting to backing down, war was now inevitable.

MAGIC revealed that the Japanese government had established a November 25 deadline for making diplomatic progress. If none was made, military operations were to follow. Yet when Roosevelt and his advisors assembled on the 25th, they confined themselves to discussing how Japan could be manipulated into firing first. On November 26, with full awareness that the deadline had passed and that Japanese troop convoys were in the South China Sea, the administration called again on Japan to withdraw from China. Diplomacy had come to an end.

On November 27 the U.S. Army and Navy sent war warnings to their Pacific commanders. The Navy cautioned that it anticipated a Japanese attack against the Philippines, Thailand, the Kra Isthmus (where Thailand and Malaya meet), or Borneo. In the event of an attack on Thailand alone the United States would not intervene; otherwise, it would.

War with Japan On December 6, Washington time, Roosevelt learned that Japanese convoys were entering the Gulf of Siam. He immediately sent a peace message to Emperor Hirohito, but it was essentially meaningless because it contained no new offer. The next morning, Japanese aircraft destroyed most of the U.S. fighter force in Hawaii on the ground and wrecked the battleship fleet in Pearl

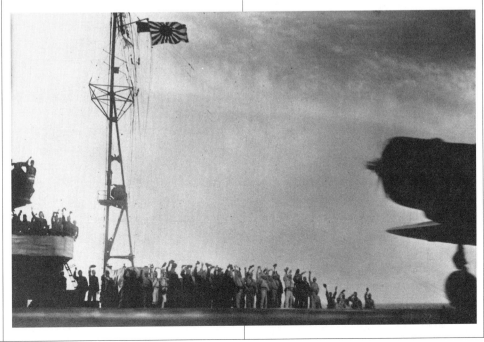

This captured Japanese photograph of a pilot rally was taken on an aircraft carrier before the attack on Pearl Harbor on December 7, 1941.

Harbor. Some hours later Japan struck again, crippling Philippine defenses.

On December 8, 1941, the United States declared war on Japan, and on the 11th Hitler issued a declaration of war against the United States. At last the long wait was over.

Roosevelt's political enemies were soon charging that he had known in advance about the Japanese plan to attack U.S. military bases in Hawaii but allowed the Japanese to go ahead so as to enter the war against Hitler. There is no evidence to support this charge. Thanks to MAGIC, Washington knew that Japan was going to attack, but it believed that Hawaii was safe because it was so far from Japan and so strongly defended.

The real charge against Roosevelt's administration is not that it deliberately allowed Pearl Harbor to be attacked, but that its Far Eastern policy was a shambles. After deciding that Germany was the greater threat to vital U.S. interests, the administration should have bent over backward to reach agreement with Japan. At the very least, it should have stalled for time, since the United States was not yet strong enough to fight Germany alone, still less Japan as well. But Washington did nothing, allowing a Japanese deadline that it knew meant war to pass without making any effort to avoid or postpone the conflict. That this was the popular course and supported by opinion surveys did not make it good policy. Events dictated Roosevelt's course, actions that were too little and too late if boldness was needed, too belligerent if it was not.

The conquest of Southeast Asia
The trouble with the southern strategy, however, was that it meant taking on the great colonial powers. The United States held the Philippines, France held Indochina, Holland held the Netherlands East Indies, and Britain held Burma and Malaya. For Japan to fight three great industrial states plus Holland made little sense until 1940, when the Asian balance of power was tipped by events in Europe.

The early defeat and occupation of Holland and France meant that their lightly defended colonial empires in Asia could not be reinforced. Britain's plan in case of war with Japan had been to send its fleet to Malaya. From "Fortress Singapore" the Royal Navy would then control Southeast Asia. But with Britain fighting Germany, few ships could be spared for service in Asian waters. This left only the United States as an obstacle to Japan.

However, the United States's Far Eastern forces were weak and could do nothing in the short run to stop Japan. Thus, the way was open for Japan to seize the resources of Southeast Asia and, at the same time, cut off China from outside help.

Accordingly, the Japanese Army and Navy agreed to exploit these opportunities. In the summer of 1940, Japan occupied the northern part of French Indochina. Then in July 1941 it secured the south as well. This brought relations between Japan and the United States to a head. Washington demanded that the Japanese withdraw not only from Indochina, but from China too. When the Japanese refused, President Franklin Roosevelt organized an oil embargo. Japan would receive no more oil from the United States, its biggest supplier. And the Netherlands East Indies, Mexico, and other oil producers agreed not to sell to Japan either.

Japan possessed only about a year's supply of oil and had just two ways of responding to Roosevelt's demands. It could either give in on the United

Japan's war with China began in July 1937, more than four years before the United States entered the war. The American public, however, supported the Chinese cause from the very start.

States's terms or seize oil fields on its own. Few were surprised when Japan chose the latter course.

What did surprise Westerners was the speed and ferocity of Japan's attacks, and the ease with which it defeated all the colonial powers. In six months it acquired a vast new empire in Southeast Asia and the western Pacific. The Netherlands East Indies fell, as did Burma, Malaya, and the Philippines, along with miscellaneous islands and territories. In one of the greatest military campaigns of all time, Japan gained the raw materials it needed to go on making war.

Japan's military leaders knew that in the long run the United States's vast industrial advantages would make it impossible to beat. Their hope was that, discouraged by early losses, the Americans would quickly give up. Instead, the U.S. Navy defeated the Japanese at Midway Island in June 1942 and invaded Guadalcanal in August. Japan was now committed to a war of attrition that it could not possibly win. The price of its aggression would be utter ruin.

On the home front The Japanese people were already suffering when Tokyo started the Pacific war. Since the invasion of China in 1937, fuel restrictions had severely hampered civilian travel. Rice, charcoal, clothing, and other essential goods and services were rationed and in short supply. Government price controls failed to stop inflation from destroying the value of money.

The home ministry set up a system that put every village and neighborhood under its direct control. In time every residential area would have meetings at the same time to receive directives and listen to identical radio broadcasts. In this way, the entire population was mobilized and organized, down to and including schoolchildren.

Yet, by 1942, despite its overseas conquests, Japan's military production was falling short. Expecting a brief war, Japanese leaders had not developed their war industries on a large enough scale. Too few ships had been built, and industry remained disorganized. In 1943, with the war going badly for Japan, Prime Minister Tojo Hideki created a new ministry of munitions with sweeping powers that was supposed to eliminate corruption and inefficiency. However, it was sabotaged by military interference and uncooperative industrialists.

Desperate measures did bring some gains in production, though. Draining stockpiles of raw materials, for example, enabled aircraft production to go up. In 1942 the aircraft industry produced only 5,000 planes, but in 1944 it turned out 28,000. This was a feat that could not be repeated, however, because the aircraft and other industries had used up their material reserves. There were plenty of raw materials in Southeast Asia, but the Japanese could not use them because U.S. submarines were destroying their merchant fleet.

The production figures for other industries show how badly the U.S. blockade hurt Japan. In 1941 some 500 medium-sized tanks were built; in 1945 only 89 were completed. Japan built six aircraft carriers in 1942, its best year, and four as late as 1944, but in 1945 production fell to zero. Destroyer production peaked at 31 in 1944, then fell to 6 the next year.

Collapse and defeat By 1944 the fabric of Japanese life was beginning to shred. All kindergartens in Tokyo were closed. Sugar became impossible to buy. Few passenger trains were allowed to carry civilians. Food shortages produced packs of wild dogs in the streets of Tokyo, which some people tracked down, killed, and ate. Then came the firebomb raids. Tokyo was the first to be hit. On March 9 and 10, 1944, it was carpeted with incendiary bombs, which killed perhaps 100,000 people.

As its cities burned, 10 million Japanese fled to the country, flight being Japan's substitute for civilian defense. Workers left their jobs to scavenge for food, which actually did little harm to production, because fuel shortages had closed most of the factories. The U.S. naval blockade, now supported by fighter-bombers from carriers and bases in Okinawa and mines dropped by B-29s, closed off Japan from the mainland.

Even travel between the home islands became difficult, owing to the destruction of ferries. Trains could not run by day, and movement by night was hampered by downed bridges and blocked roads. Japan's collapsing transportation system, as well as its shortages of food and everything else, would have caused massive civilian deaths from starvation and disease had the war lasted much longer than it did. The atomic bombs dropped on Hiroshima and Nagasaki were terrible engines of destruction. But they did force Emperor Hirohito to put an end to the war on August 15, 1945, saving many Japanese as well as American lives.

By then much of Japan lay in ruins, and Southeast Asia and the western Pacific were dotted with Japanese graves. Although Japan never had more than 6 million men in uniform at any given time, a total of 10 million served in the armed forces. Of these, more than 2 million were killed, but only 150,000 were wounded, because Japanese servicemen were supposed to fight to the last man, and usually did.

About 500,000 civilians were killed by U.S. bombers, and more than 600,000 were wounded. In addition, 250,000 troops taken prisoner by the Soviets in Manchuria at war's end never returned to Japan. Total Japanese deaths for the war came to about 3 million. Immense though it was, this death toll was dwarfed by the many more millions of people in China and Southeast Asia, mostly civilians, who were killed by the Japanese or died of disease and starvation as a direct result of Japanese acts of aggression.

SEE ALSO

Atomic bombs; Chiang Kai-shek; China; Hirohito; Hull, Cordell; Japan, surrender of; Japanese Army; Japanese Navy; Pearl Harbor, attack on; Tojo, Hideki

FURTHER READING

Borg, Dorothy. *The United States and the Far Eastern Crisis of 1933–38.* Cambridge, Mass.: Harvard University Press, 1964.

Boyle, J. H. *China and Japan at War, 1937–1945.* Stanford, Calif.: Stanford University Press, 1972.

Chang, Iris. *The Rape of Nanking: The Forgotten Holocaust of World War II.* New York: Basic Books, 1997.

Crowley, James B. *Japan's Quest for Autonomy: National Security and Foreign Policy, 1930–1938.* Princeton: Princeton University Press, 1966.

Heinrichs, Waldo. *Threshold of War: Franklin D. Roosevelt and U.S. Entry into World War II.* New York: Oxford University Press, 1988.

Ienaga, Saburo. *The Pacific War: World War II and the Japanese, 1931–1945.* New York: Random House, 1978.

Toland, John. *Rising Sun: The Decline and Fall of the Japanese Empire.* New York: Random House, 1970.

Japan, surrender of

The main problem facing U.S. leaders when President Franklin D. Roosevelt died on April 12, 1945, was how to bring about a Japanese surrender. Although the U.S. blockade had sealed its fate and firebombs were making Japanese cities uninhabitable, Japan's leaders still would not admit that further resistance was useless. They meant to fight to the last man, woman, and child if Japan was invaded. If the Americans did not come ashore, they were prepared to see everyone starve rather than surrender. The self-destructive course pursued by Japan for years offered little hope that Tokyo would give up within the foreseeable future.

On May 25, 1945, Washington issued an order for Allied forces to assault Kyushu, the southernmost home island of Japan, on or about November 1. This order was given reluctantly, because the closer Americans came to Japan the higher their casualties would be. President Harry Truman had been informed by Admiral William Leahy, his chief of staff, that the casualty rate on Okinawa had been about 35 percent. This meant that with 767,000 men participating in Operation Olympic, the attack on Kyushu, they had to expect that 268,000 men would be killed or wounded—more casualties than had been taken in the entire Pacific war to date. The Army Medical Corps was expecting that Operation Olympic would produce as many as 395,000 casualties. Since the Japanese had assigned more than 3 million troops to defend the home islands, seizing all of Japan would probably have cost the United States 1 million casualties.

On July 26 the Allied leaders set forth the conditions of Japan's surrender in the Potsdam Declaration. The United States, Britain, and China called on Japan to surrender unconditionally or face "prompt and utter destruction." The terms of surrender included an end to Japanese militarism, the punishment of war criminals, an occupation of Japan, the evacuation of all territories except the home islands themselves, and complete disarmament. In return the Allies promised to establish a democratic political order, to allow the rebuilding of Japanese industry, and to end the military occupation when Japan

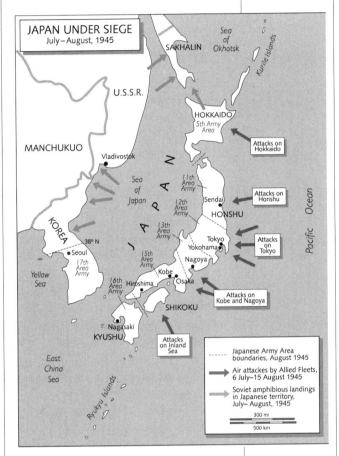

acquired a "peacefully inclined and responsible government." On July 28 Japan rejected this offer.

Meanwhile, the U.S. 509th Composite Bomb Group under Colonel Paul Tibbets was making its final arrangements. On August 6, 1945, the Superfortress *Enola Gay*, with Tibbets at the controls, rose from its runway on Tinian Island in the Marianas carrying "Little Boy," the first uranium bomb. At 8:16 a.m., local time, Little Boy detonated at an altitude of 1,900 feet over the city of Hiroshima, turning it to ashes. Perhaps 70,000 Japanese were killed by the combined effects of the blast and the heavy doses of radiation that followed it, both at the time and over the next few months. Others would die in later years from diseases induced by radiation.

On August 9, Japan having failed to surrender, "Fat Man," the first plutonium bomb, was dropped on Nagasaki. It did not fall on the targeted point, so fewer died in Nagasaki than in Hiroshima. Even so, many thousands perished, then and in later years. On August 10, Washington received word that Japan would surrender if the Potsdam Declaration "did not comprise any demand which prejudices the prerogatives of His Majesty as a Sovereign Ruler." Although this offer involved a condition, there seemed no reason to quibble. Accordingly, just after midnight on August 12, Tokyo learned that its proposal had been accepted. Japan surrendered officially on August 15.

Eventually, the decision to wage nuclear warfare against Japan, which had been highly popular at the time, became controversial. Critics would argue that diplomatic means should have been employed instead. If diplomacy failed, continuing the bombardment and blockade of Japan would eventually have forced a surrender, according to this line of thinking. Some would even maintain than invading Japan would have been a better option and would not have cost all that many lives.

This last position makes no sense, because an invasion would have been bloody beyond belief. Recently declassified intelligence reports show that by the summer of 1945, Japan was even more strongly defended than planners had thought when drawing up Operation Olympic. And diplomacy stood no chance of success. Because U.S. intelligence could read the Japanese diplomatic code, the United States knew that overtures were being made to Moscow to referee a settlement of the war. But the same intercepted messages revealed that Japan's military leaders wanted a peace that involved no occupation of Japan and that would leave them in power. This was so far removed from the terms of the Potsdam Declaration that there was nothing left to talk about.

Continuing to blockade and bombard Japan would have brought it to its knees in time. The problem was that no one could say how long that might take, and during that period, however long it was, Allied troops would go on fighting and dying. The Pacific war was still raging—in the air over Japan, in New Guinea and Burma, in Pacific waters, where Japanese submarines still prowled, and elsewhere in the vast region. After the war, once it became known that a way to end the fighting quickly had been invented but then not used, reputations and careers would have been ruined.

Critics write about the decision to drop the bomb as if U.S. leaders had had a choice. But in a democracy the existence of a weapon that would save American lives—and probably a great many other lives as well—compelled its use. The only real decisions were tactical ones, such as when and where to drop the bombs. They were important questions, however. Since only two bombs were available in August 1945, they had to be employed for maximum effect.

This is why the bombs were dropped only three days apart. The idea was to make Japanese leaders think that the United States had an unlimited supply of atomic bombs that could lay waste to the entire country, which was not true. Atomic bombs were effective only against cities, and most Japanese cities had already been burned out. The few that remained had been saved specifically to demonstrate the bomb's power.

Atomic bombs were all but useless in the field because there were thousands of military targets in Japan, only a handful of which could be destroyed in any given month. The bomb, therefore, was essentially a bluff. If Japan had not surrendered when it did, the military would have found this out and probably prolonged the war.

That nothing less than atomic warfare would have forced a surrender is a

In New York City's Chinatown, celebrations erupted with the news of Japan's unconditional surrender.

conclusion supported by actual events. The Hiroshima bomb had little effect on Japan's military leaders. They were shaken, but did not change their minds, when the Soviet Union declared war on August 8 and entered Manchuria. The Soviets had promised at the Yalta conference in February 1945 that they would join the war against Japan soon after Germany fell. When Hiroshima was bombed, the Soviets were ready to act and promptly did so. These events were followed by the atomic bombing of Nagasaki on August 9, which brought quick results. On the 10th, there was a meeting between the emperor and the Supreme Council for the Direction of the War, which actually ran the country. At this time the Supreme Council was divided over whether or not to surrender, the army still insisting on terms that were obviously unacceptable to the Allies.

Ordinarily, Emperor Hirohito did not even speak at official meetings. But this time he did, ordering his shocked listeners to accept the Potsdam terms. Although in theory the emperor was only supposed to give advice, by coming forward he broke the stalemate. Now civilians who favored peace had the imperial blessing, while the military who wished

to fight on were seriously weakened.

Even so, the surrender was a close thing. Individual military leaders sent out conflicting signals because, in addition to their own varying degrees of fanaticism, they were under heavy pressure from the militaristic Young Tigers, whose "rule from below" was one of the worst features of Japanese politics. To guard against a surrender, junior officers were conspiring to seize Hirohito and take charge of the government, their excuse being that the emperor had been misled by evil advisors and had to be kidnapped for his own good. Notices appeared in public places naming members of the peace party and calling for their deaths.

On August 14, no further steps having been taken, Hirohito called an imperial conference, the first since 1941, when war with the West was agreed upon. At it he once again commanded weeping officials to accept the Potsdam terms. It was the most emotional event in the history of Japanese government. Yet even this was not enough to guarantee obedience.

Early on August 15, a handful of rebellious junior officers demanded that the commandant of the imperial guards division, which protected the emperor, join them in seizing Hirohito and preventing any surrender. When the general refused, they killed him and, using forged orders, took command of the guard and sealed off the palace. Troops led by these Young Tigers then searched the Household Ministry for the recording they knew Hirohito had made to inform his people of the surrender. At the same time, other conspirators seized local radio stations and death squads searched for leaders of the peace party.

This rebellion failed when the general commanding the Tokyo area arrived at the palace and took charge. On August 15 the emperor's recording was aired. Although Hirohito's statement was accepted by most Japanese, it did not prevent further acts of defiance. Isolated kamikaze attacks were made against U.S. ships and positions. Several hundred army trainees seized a Tokyo park for two days, after which the majority surrendered while their leaders committed suicide. Rebellious young warriors dug into the summit of a hill near the palace, where they holed up for four days before all 12 killed themselves.

Diehards made many attacks on government buildings, radio stations, and post offices in the provinces. A conspiracy among naval air officers to keep on fighting was discovered and crushed. Vice Admiral Matome Ugaki led a flight of Japanese planes on a kamikaze attack against the U.S. fleet, with all 11 aircraft mysteriously disappearing at sea.

On August 16, Emperor Hirohito sent three princes away to overseas headquarters, so that no one could pretend that the order to surrender was a fake. Later he dispatched two more princes to restrain military fanatics in the home islands. All the same, more than 1,000 officers and hundreds of civilians took their own lives. Many did so in a plaza before the ruins of the imperial palace, which ran with blood for days after the surrender.

These events took place after the firebomb raids had done their work, after millions had fled to the countryside, after the Soviets had declared war, after two atomic bombs had fallen on Japan, and after the emperor had twice ordered the government to surrender. Many of these acts came after Japan had actually surrendered, the emperor had explained this to the nation, and an imperial order had been sent to all Japanese commands demanding their obedience.

This level of resistance strongly suggests that if the atomic bombs had not forced the emperor's hand, there would have been no surrender, not in August and perhaps not even by November,

when the invasion of Japan was to begin. It also suggests that the timing of the bombings was important as well, for by dropping the two bombs closely together, the United States forced Hirohito and the high command to move so fast that plotters and potential rebels were unable to organize quickly enough. Because emotions were running so high, even a week or two of delay might have made a crucial difference.

Hiroshima and Nagasaki should be remembered as examples of the horrors of war. But the memory of what happened to those cities in 1945 should not be used to indict U.S. leaders as war criminals—which seems to lie behind much of the criticism. Faced with a cruel foe who showed no sign of surrendering, President Truman and his lieutenants took the only course that remained open to them. In doing so they saved not only Allied lives, but many Japanese lives as well.

Millions of Japanese would have perished as the result of an invasion. And millions would probably have died had bombardment and blockade been employed instead, mostly of starvation and diseases resulting from the complete collapse of Japan's transportation system. With no easy choices available to them, the U.S. leaders made the best of a bad situation. They have been acquitted by history, if not always by historians.

SEE ALSO

Atomic bombs; Hirohito; Japan; Japanese Army; Japanese Navy; Kamikaze

FURTHER READING

Alperovitz, Gar. *Atomic Diplomacy: Hiroshima and Potsdam.* New York: Vintage, 1965.
Brooks, Lester. *Behind Japan's Surrender: The Secret Struggle that Ended an Empire.* New York: McGraw-Hill, 1968.
Feifer, George. *Tennozan: The Battle of Okinawa and the Atomic Bomb.* New York: Ticknor & Fields, 1992.

Japanese Americans

The greatest domestic violation of human rights in the United States during the war was its mass internment of Japanese Americans. On the day that Pearl Harbor was attacked, December 7, 1941, there were 117,000 Americans of Japanese origin or descent living on the West Coast, mostly in California. They had been under investigation for being possible spies and traitors by the Office of Naval Intelligence (ONI) since 1935, and since 1939 by the Federal Bureau of Investigation (FBI) as well. In 1940 a committee made up of the directors of the FBI, the ONI, and Army Intelligence drew up a list of alien suspects. Many names on the list resulted from the ONI's having burglarized the Japanese consulate in Los Angeles. The arrest of a Japanese naval officer who had organized an espionage ring yielded additional information.

When the United States went to war, the three agencies were confident that they had identified everyone who might be a threat to national security. Within three weeks of Pearl Harbor, 2,192 Japanese aliens were arrested on the mainland and 879 in Hawaii. Most of them were members of the first generation of Japanese Americans, known as Issei, who had long been residents of the United States. With the completion of these arrests the FBI and the Justice Department were satisfied that Japanese Americans no longer posed any threat to the United States.

Yet, on February 19, 1942, President Roosevelt signed Executive Order 9066 directing Secretary of War Henry Stimson to establish military zones from which anyone could be excluded for security reasons. Lieutenant General

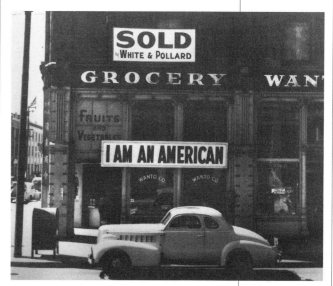

John L. DeWitt, chief of the Western Military Command, had been urging the removal of all enemy aliens from the West Coast to the interior of the United States. He also wanted to raid their homes and confiscate cameras, radios, and weapons that might be used for disloyal purposes. Over the objections of FBI Director J. Edgar Hoover, such mass raids took place but turned up nothing.

Meanwhile, tremendous political pressure was put upon President Roosevelt by Californians and their congressmen to intern all Japanese Americans. The result was his executive order, essentially a blank check authorizing the War Department to do as it pleased. A bill to enforce it then sped through Congress, with Senator Robert Taft of Ohio, who called it the sloppiest criminal law he had ever seen or heard of, making the only protest.

On March 18, FDR signed another Executive Order, 9102, establishing the War Relocation Authority (WRA), which was to share responsibility with the War Department for internees. The result was that by June 7, 1942, most Japanese Americans were behind barbed wire, first in temporary centers and then in more permanent camps, where some 112,000 men, women, and children

The owner of a Los Angeles grocery, a University of California graduate of Japanese descent, had placed the "I AM AN AMERICAN" sign on the storefront the day after Japan bombed Pearl Harbor.

would be held for an average of 900 days under harsh conditions in rural areas and wastelands. There were 10 major camps: two each in California, Arizona, and Arkansas, and one each in Idaho, Wyoming, Utah, and Colorado. All the camps had much more severe climates, both in winter and summer, than the internees were used to.

The camp at Poston, Arizona, was desert country, lacking in shade and whipped by dust and sand. When the internees began arriving in July, many passed out from the intense heat. One said later: "People kept falling down. We thought it was Devil's Island." Seven victims of heat stroke died in the first days. Many internees believed this was intentional, Poston being in their eyes a death camp. The army-style barracks in which they lived offered no shelter from the heat, were overrun with insects, and were impossible to keep clean.

Camp Minidoka in Idaho was hot in the summer but had temperatures that fell to 25 degrees below zero in the winter. Tule Lake in California, despite its pretty name, was a dry lake bed located at an elevation of 4,000 feet. Winter temperatures there fell to 29 below zero. In all the camps, sanitation was poor by any standard and there was a complete lack of privacy. Overcrowding, boredom, and hard work were the rule at all camps.

The national policy of imprisoning and persecuting Japanese Americans was upheld by the Supreme Court because its respect for civil liberties lessened in wartime, and because the government falsely claimed that there was no time to screen Japanese Americans individually, although such a screening had taken place before Pearl Harbor. The government also suppressed the evidence it did have, which was considerable, that undermined the case for internment.

Early on, men and women of con-science began working behind the scenes to undo this injustice. On December 3, 1943, Attorney General Nicholas Biddle requested that President Roosevelt order a liberal "release and return" program. In February 1944 Secretary Harold Ickes, whose Interior Department controlled the WRA, made similar requests. When FDR continued to ignore them, Ickes assigned Undersecretary Abe Fortas to work on the problem. Fortas visited the camps and, horrified by their conditions, brought back strong arguments in favor of early release.

General Charles H. Bonesteel, the new military commander for the West Coast, opposed internment and worked ceaselessly against it, which was probably why he was transferred after serving less than six months at his headquarters in San Francisco. The tide had turned all the same. At the first cabinet meeting after Roosevelt's reelection in 1944, Biddle asked Roosevelt to release all the internees certified by the Justice Department as loyal.

This time, having nothing to lose, FDR agreed. On December 10 the new commanding general issued Public Proclamation No. 21, which was written by Bonesteel, lifting the evacuation and exclusion orders and allowing most internees to return to the West Coast.

Ironically, while their relatives were in prison camps, the elite 442nd Regimental Combat Team, composed entirely of Japanese Americans, was fighting against the Germans in Italy. With an average strength of about 3,000 soldiers, during its 11 months in combat it suffered a total of 9,486 casualties and became the most decorated unit in the Army. All told, some 33,000 Nisei, or second-generation Japanese Americans, served in the armed forces with great distinction, fighting and dying for the sake of a country that had put their families in prison.

SEE ALSO
Internment

FURTHER READING
Collins, Donald E. *Native American Aliens: Disloyalty and the Renunciation of Citizenship by Japanese Americans during World War II*. Westport, Conn.: Greenwood, 1985.
Hoobler, Dorothy and Thomas. *The Japanese American Family Album*. New York: Oxford University Press, 1995.
Ichihashi, Yamato. *Morning Glory, Evening Shadow: Yamato Ichihashi and his Internment Writings, 1942–1945*. Stanford, Calif.: Stanford University Press, 1997.
Irons, Peter. *Justice at War*. New York: Oxford University Press, 1983.
Okihiro, Gary Y. *Whispered Silences: Japanese Americans and World War II*. Seattle: University of Washington Press, 1996.
Smith, Page. *Democracy on Trial: The Japanese American Evacuation and Relocation in World War II*. New York: Simon & Schuster, 1995.
Taylor, Sandra C. *Jewel of the Desert: Japanese American Internment at Topaz*. Berkeley: University of California Press, 1993.

Japanese Army

The Imperial Japanese Army (IJA) fought so well because of the fanatical loyalty of its troops, not because of its leadership. In theory, both of the armed services were commanded by Imperial General Headquarters (IGH). In practice, the IGH Army Section and the IGH Navy Section operated independently of each other and were in fierce competition. Some decisions were made jointly, but much of the time each service went its own way.

Commanders were selected according to seniority, so the best men received the best jobs only by accident. Little attention was paid to such vital areas as intelligence and strategy. Orders from Imperial General Headquarters were frequently mistaken or unclear, which forced field officers to make their own decisions. These were often poor because the Japanese military saw no difference between caution and cowardice. It also rated spiritual strength above material strength, so Japanese soldiers were always being given tasks that they lacked the means to accomplish.

The organization of the Japanese Army was different from that of its Western counterparts. A Japanese division could have as many as 29,000 men, making it the size of two U.S. divisions. In 1941 Japan had a total of 31 divisions. Until 1943 all of these were infantry, because Japan followed the old-fashioned practice of scattering its tanks in small units among the infantry instead of forming separate armored divisions.

The Army had its own troop and supply ships as well as its own warships, including escort carriers. In the same spirit, the Navy had its own infantry units. In 1941 the Army had 151 air squadrons. They were organized into air divisions, which had no fixed size. Most of its aircraft were land-based.

The Japanese Army was poorly armed. Its basic rifle, designed in 1905, had not been improved since. Japanese ammunition was also inferior. Japanese

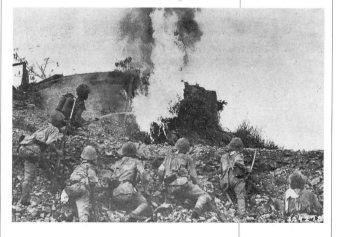

Japanese troops assault a pill-box with flame throwers during their capture of the Bataan peninsula in the Philippine Islands, 1942.

soldiers were poorly led in the field as well as at the top, a favorite tactic of the officers being the suicidal frontal attack. On the other hand, Japanese soldiers were highly motivated and refused to give up.

It has been noted that every army swore to fight to the last man and the last bullet, but only the Japanese actually did so. Despite, or maybe because of, their small stature, Japanese troops could travel and fight for days with only the food and ammunition they carried on their backs.

Against their best traits, it must be said that their cruelty denied these fine soldiers the respect they would otherwise have earned. This trait was deliberately encouraged by army leaders. They believed that people in occupied territories would be easier to rule if they lived in terror. In China the Army had thought that if it raped, tortured, and murdered enough civilians the Chinese government would give up, but these ideas proved both evil and false. Instead, terror promoted the growth of resistance movements in many occupied lands. The Chinese Nationalists, though frequently beaten, refused to surrender.

In the case of prisoners of war, there appears to have been no particular reason for cruel treatment. Prisoners often possessed valuable skills and, since the Japanese used them as workmen, were a labor force with much potential. Yet the Japanese starved, tortured, and murdered them from the start. Some have said that this was because the Japanese regarded surrender as dishonorable, and prisoners of war were therefore viewed with contempt.

However, this does not explain much, because many of the prisoners the Japanese took—the Marines on Wake Island, U.S. and native troops in the Philippines—had fought with great courage. Whatever the reasons for it, the Japanese Army's brutality was shameful.

It not only damaged the Japanese war effort but also caused Allied troops to fight harder than ever, to the death if necessary, rather than risk capture.

In 1943 the tide of battle turned against the Imperial Japanese Army. It lost the Solomon Islands and other territories. Most Japanese units in New Guinea were destroyed. It was able to take the offensive only in China, which in did in 1944, gaining local victories while it continued to lose the war. Elsewhere it fought fierce defensive battles that always ended in defeat. When it lost Okinawa in 1945, the IJA had lost the war, even though large numbers of troops were still stationed in China and Manchuria.

The Imperial Japanese Army raised 170 infantry, 13 air, 4 tank (beginning in 1943), and 4 antitank divisions for overseas service. These units totaled some 2,340,000 men, of whom about 1.5 million were killed. The lucky Japanese soldiers were the 3 million assembled in the home islands in 1945 to repel an Allied invasion that never took place.

SEE ALSO
Central Pacific area; China; Pacific war; South Pacific area; Southwest Pacific area

FURTHER READING
Costello, John. *The Pacific War, 1941–1945.* New York: Rawson Wade, 1981.
Toland, John. *Rising Sun: The Decline and Fall of the Japanese Empire.* New York: Random House, 1970.

Japanese Navy

The Imperial Japanese Navy (IJN) shared many of the army's defects: poor planning, a lack of interest in intelligence work, promotion by seniority rather than by merit, poor control over field officers, and a culture that confused recklessness with bravery. In addition, the navy favored attack plans that were too complex and depended on the enemy's doing exactly what the Japanese expected.

On the other hand, the Japanese Navy was a very big, very high-quality force when the Pacific war began. It was the third largest in the world, and although smaller than to the U.S. Navy, was superior to it in the Pacific. On December 7, 1941, when Japan attacked Pearl Harbor, its Navy had a total of 391 warships, including 10 carriers (to the U.S. Pacific Fleet's 3) and many more cruisers and destroyers than the Pacific Fleet.

In quality the IJN was superior too. Its "Long Lance" torpedo was the best in the world, far stronger, faster, and more reliable than the U.S. Navy's inferior models. Japanese naval aviators were the best in the world as well, having sharpened their skills in combat while the United States was still at peace.

The Japanese Navy had better airplanes also. The IJN's model of the famous Zero fighter outclassed the U.S. Navy's Wildcat in almost every respect. The IJN's torpedo bomber was far ahead of the Devastator, the U.S. Navy's "flying coffin." Furthermore, the IJN excelled at night fighting, as the U.S. Navy would learn to its sorrow in the Solomon Islands campaign.

Although in time the U.S. Navy would dwarf the IJN, at first it had only two advantages over Japan's many superior assets: better intelligence and leadership. The Japanese attack on Pearl Harbor, although a brilliant success, failed to cripple the Pacific Fleet, because the Japanese admiral commanding the attack refused to order a second strike. If it had been launched, it would have taken out oil and gas storage tanks, drydocks, and other supply and repair facilities, thereby forcing the Pacific Fleet to retire to its bases on the West Coast.

This mistake, and others to follow, was a result of many of Japan's best admirals having been purged in the 1930s. With the exception of Admiral Isoroku Yamamoto, who planned the Pearl Harbor attack, Japanese naval leaders tended to be second-rate.

Its superior intelligence and leadership enabled the U.S. Navy to defeat a much stronger Japanese fleet at Midway Island in June 1942. Lacking both, the IJN engaged in costly operations that wore away its strength. The Japanese Navy had planned for a quick victory at sea. Instead it got a war of attrition in which the enemy grew stronger while its own strength declined. Particularly harmful was a policy of using up veteran airmen in combat, rather than sending them home to train others, as the U.S. Navy did. The result was a sharp decline in the quality of the IJN pilots.

The weakening effects of this policy became clear at the Battle of the Philippine Sea in June 1944. When the fight ended, Japan had lost 243 carrier aircraft and most of its pilots. It was the end of Japan's fleet air arm. In the next, and last, great sea battle of the Pacific war, the Battle of Leyte Gulf, Japanese carriers would be used as bait, for lack of air

The first aerial photo taken of one of Japan's Yamato-*class battleships captures it making a sharp turn. The 45,000-ton battleship was sunk on April 7, 1944.*

crews. In this battle, which was actually a series of actions, the Japanese surface fleet was nearly wiped out as well. After that, except for submarine and kamikaze attacks, the IJN was helpless.

The Imperial Japanese Navy commissioned 451 surface warships and submarines during the war. By the time Japan surrendered, 332 of these vessels had been sunk and just 37, or 8.2 percent of the total, remained in use.

SEE ALSO

Central Pacific Area; Leyte Gulf, Battle of; Midway Island, Battle of; Pacific war; Pearl Harbor, attack on; Philippine Sea, Battle of the; South Pacific Area, Southwest Pacific Area

FURTHER READING

Dull, Paul S. *A Battle History of the Imperial Japanese Navy, 1941–1945.* Annapolis, Md.: U.S. Naval Institute, 1958.
Spector, Ronald. *Eagle Against the Sun: The American War with Japan.* New York: Free Press, 1985.

Kaiser, Henry J.

INDUSTRIALIST

- Born: May 9, 1882, Sprout Brook, N.Y.
- Education: left school at age 13
- Died: August 24, 1967, Oahu, Hawaii

Between 1895, when he left school, and 1910, when he entered the construction industry, Kaiser had a variety of jobs and businesses on the East and West coasts. In 1914 he started his own construction business in Vancouver, British Columbia. Until 1940, usually in partnerships with other firms, Kaiser built roads and dams in the western United States and Cuba.

Knowing that the war would make enormous demands on shipping, Kaiser and his partners won a big contract in

December 1940 to build cargo ships for Britain. It was the beginning of a legend for, although he knew nothing about ships, Kaiser was a production genius. He would go on to build 13 types of vessel, but his fame resulted from the class of vessel called the Liberty ship. This was a 10,000-ton merchant vessel that could be manufactured quickly and cheaply.

While other yards took about two months to build a Liberty ship, Kaiser could turn one out in 30 days. In 1942 one of his yards built a cargo ship in 4 days, 15 hours, and 26 minutes. Inventing new methods was the key to Kaiser's success. Among other improvements, his yards were the first to build sections of vessels before final assembly and the first to weld steel plates together instead of using rivets.

Kaiser did his country another important service by persuading the Navy to order escort carriers. The Navy did not want them at first, but Kaiser had enough clout to go over the head of the Department of the Navy. He persuaded President Roosevelt that small carriers, which would be easy to build in quantity, were desperately needed at sea. And they were, as even the admirals, who preferred big ships, would later admit.

By war's end Kaiser had built 1,490 vessels. These included 821 Liberty ships

At the Kaiser shipyards in Richmond, California, Eastine Cowner, a former waitress, works as a scaler to construct the Liberty Ship SS George Washington Carver, launched on May 7, 1943.

and 291 Victory ships, which were slightly improved versions of the Liberty. Although cargo ships were his specialty, Kaiser also built 107 warships, of which 50 were escort carriers.

In addition to being a great builder, Kaiser was a good boss. To the degree wartime shortages allowed, he provided housing for his 200,000 employees. He also gave them what became the Kaiser Permanente medical care program, one of the first and best of the early health maintenance organizations. Kaiser was perhaps the most publicized American industrialist of the war and deserved every bit of praise he received. In the United States, only Andrew J. Higgins, a brilliant maker of landing and assault craft and ships, could be compared with Kaiser. Abroad he had no equal. After the war Kaiser moved from shipbuilding to the manufacture of steel, aluminum, and cement. His only real failure was the Kaiser-Frazer corporation, which manufactured unpopular automobiles.

SEE ALSO
Carriers

FURTHER READING
Adams, Stephen B. *Mr. Kaiser Goes to Washington: The Rise of a Government Entrepreneur.* Chapel Hill: University of North Carolina Press, 1997.
Foster, Mark S. *Henry J. Kaiser: Builder in the Modern American West.* Austin: University of Texas Press, 1989.

Kamikaze

The kamikaze (Japanese for "divine wind") was a pilot who deliberately crashed his airplane into a target. There were other suicide weapons, such as human torpedoes and midget submarines, but kamikazes were far and away the most effective.

The use of kamikazes on a mass basis became Japanese policy late in 1944, when a shortage of pilots was crippling Japanese air power. The first kamikaze waves were launched against ships of the U.S. Navy on October 25, 1944, during the Battle of Leyte Gulf. Kamikazes were employed on a far greater scale after the invasion of Okinawa in June 1945.

When the battle was over, the U.S. Navy had lost 36 ships and landing craft. About 4,900 U.S. sailors were killed by kamikazes and almost as many wounded. This made Okinawa the bloodiest battle fought by the U.S. Navy in World War II. Japan is believed to have lost roughly 5,000 kamikazes.

SEE ALSO
Okinawa, Battle of

FURTHER READING
Lamont-Brown, Raymond. *Kamikaze: Japan's Suicide Samurai.* New York: Sterling, 1997.

Two kamikazes hit the USS Bunker Hill within 30 seconds of each other and set it afire on May 11, 1945, off Kyushu, Japan.

King, Ernest J.

*CHIEF OF NAVAL
OPERATIONS, 1941–45*

- *Born: November 23, 1878, Lorain, Ohio*
- *Political party: none*
- *Education: U.S. Naval Academy, B.S., 1904*
- *Military service: captain, 1918; commander, Lexington, 1930–32; rear admiral, 1932; vice-admiral, 1938; commander, Atlantic Fleet, 1940–41; commander in chief, U.S. fleet, and chief of naval operations, 1941–45; fleet admiral, 1945*
- *Died: June 25, 1956, Portsmouth, N.H.*

A brilliant student, King had commanded submarines as well as air units and aircraft carriers and had served in a variety of staff and shore positions during his naval career before World War II. President Franklin D. Roosevelt did not know him personally. For most officers this ruled out being assigned high command in the Navy, and it is surprising that King advanced as far as he did in the 1930s.

King was assigned to the General Board, a group that advised the secretary of the navy, because he was scheduled for retirement in 1940. But he impressed the outgoing secretary of the navy, who recommended him to Roosevelt. So, instead of being retired, King became commander of the Atlantic Fleet, and then of the entire Navy.

After the Pearl Harbor defeat in December 1941, Roosevelt wanted the Navy shaken up, and the forceful King was the right man for such a job. He was also, in many ways, the officer best qualified to command the Navy, because he had drive, energy, and intelligence. King was one of only a handful of admirals with command experience in the fleet air arm, which was about to become very important. But he was headstrong and arrogant, he seldom sought or accepted advice, and he made little distinction between his personal opinions and naval policy.

By appointing King to the dual position of commander in chief of the U.S. Fleet and chief of naval operations, President Roosevelt made him the most powerful naval officer in U.S. history. These appointments ensured that in the critical opening months of the Pacific war the naval chain of command would be direct and clear. It also meant that King would be able to put his personal stamp on naval policy to an unusual degree. Whether Roosevelt's decision was correct is hard to say. King used his power to accomplish much, but also to force issues in such a way as to achieve his own goals.

The clearest and most important example of his personal style came soon after Pearl Harbor. In planning for a war with Japan, the Navy had always assumed that it would be a naval conflict commanded by an admiral. But Japan's numerous land victories, especially in the Philippines, made the old theories out-of-date. General George C. Marshall, the army chief of staff, therefore proposed that a Southwest Pacific theater be formed with General Douglas MacArthur as supreme commander. He would have charge of all naval forces required to perform his mission. King was furious. He would never allow a general to have supreme command over what the Navy regarded as its private war with Japan.

A compromise was arrived at on March 30, 1942. MacArthur would get his Southwest Pacific Area. It would contain Australia, New Guinea, the Netherlands East Indies, and many other islands—including possibly the Philippines. Everything else in the Pacific Ocean would be reserved for the Navy. This agreement meant having a divided command and two separate war efforts. Duplication, waste, and confusion would be the inevitable results. The two campaigns would be fought so far apart that they would compete for the same resources instead of supporting each other. Only the Japanese and the U.S. Navy benefited from the arrangement.

When it lost the Southwest Pacific Area to MacArthur, the Navy was forced to make the Central Pacific Area its primary theater of war. King ordered a series of amphibious attacks in 1943 against Japanese-held atolls in the central Pacific. The Mariana Islands to the west would be taken in 1944, followed by landings on the China coast.

In 1944, when Japan seized the coastal areas of China, King argued that the island of Formosa should be invaded instead. The Navy, however, did not have the troops required to take Formosa, and the Army would not provide men for an operation that would conflict with its own plans. Accordingly, MacArthur was allowed to liberate the Philippines and both services agreed that Okinawa would be liberated next, followed by Japan itself.

Yet even for the invasion of Japan there was going to be no supreme commander. The army and naval forces would continue to fight under their own leaders. If the two disagreed, bargaining and haggling would presumably settle their differences. Luckily, Japan surrendered before this strange command structure could be put in place.

Some historians still argue that the two-front war of the Southwest and Central Pacific Areas made sense. But the central Pacific drive was extremely wasteful. Huge armadas had to be assembled to invade insignificant islands that were often strongly defended. The resulting casualties were very high in relation to the number of men involved. Months often went by between one operation and the next, during which

time the Pacific Fleet would be essentially idle. Meanwhile, MacArthur's forces were continuously in action and could have made good use of the vast military resources stockpiled in the central Pacific by the Navy.

Because the southwest Pacific contained many Japanese strongpoints, MacArthur employed a variety of methods. He could threaten Japanese positions that he was not in fact going to attack, keeping the enemy off balance. MacArthur might land in the enemy's rear or bypass him entirely. Cleverness and surprise saved many lives in the southwest Pacific.

In the Central Pacific Area, on the other hand, targets were few and far apart. They could not be taken by surprise and had to be stormed, often at great cost. Some admirals, including Chester Nimitz himself, thought that taking unimportant islands in this fashion was wrong. They favored operations that would parallel those of MacArthur and enable the two drives to support each other. King personally put a stop to talks aimed at achieving this result. Responsibility for the central Pacific strategy, therefore, was solely his.

Where interservice rivalries were not involved, King fully supported General Marshall, the figure most responsible for U.S. grand strategy during the war. Although some ships—the vital landing ships tank in particular—were never numerous enough, King always managed to produce some when they were needed in European waters. A good strategist himself, King was against the ill-fated invasion of Italy in 1943. He doubted rightly, as events showed, that air power alone could win the war. He opposed having an independent air force like Britain's RAF, which he saw as a bad use of military resources.

King believed in secrecy to such an extent that if it had been up to him the

Department of the Navy would never have held a press conference. Any information that the Japanese received, no matter how insignificant, was a security threat. When carriers were lost he kept the news even from Secretary of the Navy Frank Knox, who was supposed to be his boss. He tried to keep the great U.S. victory at Midway a secret too, but of course that information could not be kept from the Japanese.

King will always be remembered for having led the Navy to victory in World War II. But all leaders make mistakes, and like many others he fell victim to the intense partisanship that so often put the Army and Navy at odds. King was very much an officer of his time and place, so his likes and dislikes were widely shared. Whether any other admiral could have done better is something we will never know.

SEE ALSO

Central Pacific Area; Nimitz, Chester W.; Pacific war; United States Navy

FURTHER READING

Buell, Thomas B. *Master of Sea Power: A Biography of Fleet Admiral Ernest J. King.* Boston: Little, Brown, 1980.
King, Ernest Joseph. *Fleet Admiral King, A Naval Record by Ernest J. King and Walter Muir Whitehill.* New York: Norton, 1952.

Knox, William Franklin

SECRETARY OF THE NAVY, 1940–44

- *Born: January 1, 1874, Boston, Mass.*
- *Political party: Republican*
- *Education: Alma College, 1893–96*
- *Military service: U.S. Cavalry, 1898; U.S. Army, 1917–18; Secretary of the Navy, 1940–44*
- *Died: April 28, 1944, Washington, D.C.*

Knox was raised in Grand Rapids, Michigan, and served briefly under Theodore Roosevelt as a Rough Rider in the Spanish-American War. In 1902 he entered the newspaper business in Michigan, first as a reporter, then as a publisher. In 1912 he became co-owner and publisher of two papers, the Manchester, New Hampshire, *Union* and *Leader*.

Despite his age (42), Knox joined the Army as a private during World War I. He saw action in France and rose to the rank of major of artillery. In 1931 Knox became part owner and publisher of the unprofitable *Chicago Sun*, which he restored to financial stability. He was the Republican nominee for Vice President in 1936.

As World War II neared, Knox argued for a strong defense. When fighting broke out in Europe in 1939, he favored all possible aid to the Allies short of outright intervention. This stand required courage on the part of a Midwestern publisher, because the region was strongly isolationist.

In the summer of 1940, President Franklin D. Roosevelt nominated Knox to be secretary of the navy, and he joined the cabinet in August. His appointment was made at the same time that another leading Republican, Henry L. Stimson—by coincidence another ex-artillery officer—was nominated as secretary of war. These nominations strengthened Roosevelt's cabinet and gave it a bipartisan flavor in time for the Presidential election of 1940.

As civilian head of the Navy, Knox presided over the greatest expansion in the service's history, seeing it rise from a force of some 200,000 (including Marines) in 1940 to one numbering 3.5 million (with 500,000 Marines) at the time of his death. Knox provided the Navy with important leadership. After only a month in office, he negotiated many of the details concerning an exchange of U.S. destroyers for British bases in the Western Hemisphere. He called for U.S. escorts of Lend-Lease program convoys in the summer of 1941, leading isolationists to demand that he be removed from office. He was never more decisive than in the dark days that followed Pearl Harbor on December 7, 1941.

The day after the Pearl Harbor attack, Knox left Washington for Hawaii. On returning he told reporters that both the Army and Navy had been caught napping. He then relieved Admiral Husband E. Kimmel of duty as commander of the Pacific Fleet, replacing him with a man who was to become one of the Navy's greatest leaders, Admiral Chester W. Nimitz. Knox also made Admiral Ernest J. King, a brilliant if ruthless officer, commander in chief of the U.S. Fleet and chief of naval operations.

Among Knox's best civilian appointees were Adlai E. Stevenson, who served as his special assistant, and Undersecretary James V. Forrestal, who would succeed him. Both were able managers and notable for their integrity and character. A hearty, vigorous, profane man, Knox died in office after a series of heart attacks.

Labor

As war spread across Europe and Asia, no one in the United States worried much about manpower issues, because unemployment remained high as a result of the Depression. In 1940, 9 million men were still out of work, and it was not until 1943 that unemployment came

to an end. This excess manpower enabled President Franklin D. Roosevelt to delay thinking about labor issues for several years.

Instead, the government's manpower policy was aimed at preventing strikes, a problem that could not be avoided or delayed because in 1941 there were 4,228 walkouts involving some 2.4 million men and women. It was the biggest year for strikes since 1919. Although workers usually had good reasons to strike—low wages and poor working conditions, among other issues—they threatened the mobilization effort and could not be allowed to continue.

The 1941 walkouts were hard to handle, because organized labor had become a major ally of President Roosevelt. When he was first elected in 1932, the trade union movement was still dominated by the nonpolitical American Federation of Labor (AFL). But then the Congress of Industrial Organizations (CIO) came along, and most of its leaders were early and constant supporters of Roosevelt. In 1935 Roosevelt had thrown his weight behind the passage of the Wagner Labor Relations Act, which legalized collective bargaining and made possible a great union movement. The CIO supported Roosevelt's reelection campaign the following year by contributing half a million dollars—a huge sum at the time—and supplying thousands of campaign volunteers.

These were the main reasons why Roosevelt's answer to strikes against defense plants would not be a harsh one. Instead, FDR intended to retain labor's support through democratic means. He created the National Defense Mediation Board (later the National War Labor Board—WLB), which developed a mediation process that would outlast the war. The WLB was unusual among war agencies because the general public was represented on it in addition to labor and management groups. For most of its life, the board was directed by William H. Davis, a successful lawyer and Democrat. Under his leadership, the board worked to establish industrywide wage patterns and labor practices. It also sought to prevent strikes by pressuring union heads to calm militant local chapters.

In order to avoid inflation at a time when increased government spending was pushing up prices, Roosevelt had to control wages as well as prices. To do this, on April 27, 1942, he asked for higher taxes, price controls, and a wage freeze to be worked out by the War Labor Board. The board finally decided that wages should be kept at the level existing on January 1, 1941, plus 15 percent. This indexing resulted in average hourly industrial wages rising by more than a quarter, from 66 cents at the beginning of 1941 to 85 cents as of January 1, 1943. Consumer prices increased by 16.4 percent during this period.

The wage freeze reduced inflation, but at the expense of industrial workers. After, Pearl Harbor most labor leaders had pledged not to strike while the war lasted. They believed that unionized workers would be rewarded for giving up the strike weapon. But by freezing wages, the federal government had eliminated the main reason for joining unions, and in 1942 their membership declined—sharply, in some cases.

To save organized labor, the War Labor Board fell back on a practice called the union shop. In return for a no-strike pledge and promises of union cooperation with government, the WLB insisted that employers include in their labor contracts what was called a "maintenance of membership" clause. As defined in June 1942, it stipulated

that workers in organized plants automatically became union members unless they refused to do so within 15 days of being hired. This device reversed the fall in union membership. Largely as a result of the union shop policy, organized labor grew from a total of 8.9 million workers in 1940 to 14.7 million in 1945. Meanwhile, the civilian labor force shrank by 1.8 million workers, to 53.9 million.

The wage freeze remained throughout the war because the government simply could not afford to give industrial workers the increases they wanted. Nor was there any strong reason to do so. Like almost everyone else not in uniform, those employed in manufacturing benefited from the war, with their real wages rising by 22 percent between 1940 and 1944.

This increase was not, however, as large as those others enjoyed. Net farm income doubled between 1941 and 1945. The after-tax profits of corporations had increased by 57 percent between 1941 and 1943. The fact that industrial workers gained less gave them a valid complaint. Yet the wage freeze did not apply when a worker moved to a better job or had his job upgraded. Millions received hourly increases in this way. Many also saw their fringe benefits improve, which benefited them financially even when pay rates remained stable.

But the main reason why workers earned more than before the war was that they spent more time on the job: an average of 45.2 hours per week in 1944 compared with fewer than 38 before the war. As prices had risen as well, it appeared to some that they were working harder but earning less, which was untrue. Still, as the wage freeze grew in unpopularity, strikes became more frequent. There were 2,000 walkouts in 1942, 3,700 in 1943, and nearly 5,000 in 1944, of which 41 involved more than 5,000 workers. The proportion of all workers involved in strikes quadrupled after 1942, returning, in effect, to peacetime levels.

There were differences in wartime strikes all the same. Most of these strikes were "quickie" stoppages that halted work for one shift or less. Congress of Industrial Organization leaders remained faithful to the no-strike pledge, cracking down on locals that walked out and giving the Roosevelt administration more than they received in return. It was a hard war for them, trapped as they were between an irritated membership and a War Labor Board that became more strict over time.

Life was simpler for the AFL, which had not tied itself to the Democratic party and felt no need to punish its locals for breaking the no-strike pledge. This live-and-let-live policy made it more attractive to resentful workers, and AFL unions grew, to some degree at the CIO's expense. Were it not for the WLB's "maintenance of membership" policy, the shift would have been even greater.

Strikes in wartime greatly angered the public. Still, they were almost always brief and did not hurt the war effort. The appearance that workers at home were betraying the boys overseas was far less serious than the reality. If striking workers had gotten what they had asked for, the resulting inflation would have canceled out most if not all of their pay raises. The CIO's restraint was politically wise, but it was also patriotic and in the workers' best interest. Moreover, workers were profiting from the war, if less so than others. Their feelings of being treated unjustly were nothing compared to those experienced by GIs, who saw walkouts as stabs in their backs.

GIs may have felt bitterness toward disgruntled workers on the home front, yet strikes more than anything else symbolized for servicemen the unfairness of wartime. Despite the deep commitment of Americans to the war effort, as a whole it resembled an upside-down pyramid. On top a majority of civilians were living well. Meanwhile, at the bottom a comparative handful of fighting men bore all the suffering. Nothing much could be done about this. Some people called for "equality of sacrifice," but in war that is impossible. Fighting men risk their lives; civilians, at most, some income.

SAVE THEM THIS FATE

don't stay home from work!

BACK UP OUR BATTLESKIES!

A Government propoganda poster implied the terribe fate in store for American families if workers were to strike.

SEE ALSO
Mobilization; Roosevelt, Franklin Delano

FURTHER READING
Lichtenstein, Nelson. *Labor's War at Home: The CIO in World War II.* New York: Cambridge University Press, 1982.
Vatter, Harold G. *The U.S. Economy in World War II.* New York: Columbia University Press, 1985.

Landing ships and craft

Specialized assault vessels were an afterthought in the U.S. war effort. Before the war, U.S. and British planners had not expected that most of their campaigns would begin with amphibious landings. The British started developing landing craft for commando operations in 1940. That same year an American who had invented an amphibious vehicle with caterpillar treads called the Alligator modified it for military use. It would be called the landing vehicle tracked, or LVT. Armored and carrying a tank gun, it would prove the ideal vehicle for storming enemy beaches. The LVT was especially useful against beaches protected by coral reefs, which it simply climbed over. Later an amphibious 2-ton truck was designed that was code named the DUKW, or duck.

In 1941 Andrew Jackson Higgins, a New Orleans boatbuilder, produced an open 36-foot landing craft with a bow ramp, designated the LCVP because it could carry either personnel or vehicles. Easy and cheap to build, Higgins's boats would be manufactured in enormous numbers and were the primary Allied assault craft. Higgins would become one of the production heroes of the war. He was to assault craft what Henry J. Kaiser was to cargo ships.

Most landing craft were small, designed to be carried to the invasion site on "combat loaders," oceangoing cargo and troopships. But it was obvious that larger vessels would be needed. The basic landing craft tank, or LCT, was 108 feet long, although some versions were much larger. Designed by the British, most LCTs were built in the United States. The landing craft infantry, LCI(L)—for

large—was 158 feet long. The oceangoing LCT was actually a ship.

Far and away the most desired assault vessel was the 328-foot-long landing ship tank (LST). Designed with British aid by the U.S. Navy's Bureau of Ships in 1941, the LST was a clever compromise between cargo ship and landing craft. In the front it had a flat bottom so it could be grounded on or close to the beach (it would winch itself off after unloading, using anchors previously dropped astern). Its bow consisted of clamshell doors that opened to let down a ramp connected directly to the tank deck. If necessary, as when under fire, an LST could be emptied in minutes. Though slow and hard to handle at sea, LSTs were invaluable, and every theater commander wanted more of them than he could get.

The basic problem with landing ships and craft was that they were not produced on the basis of a long-range plan. Instead, they were turned out as needed for particular operations. In the case of small landing craft, this lack of system was far from fatal, but major landing craft took more time to build, and LSTs required half a year in production at first.

The invasion of North Africa was delayed for months by a shortage of landing craft. In 1943 and 1944 military operations all over the world continued to be hampered by a lack of assault vessels. The British were especially annoyed that operations they would have liked to stage in the Mediterranean were unable to go forward because they had no LSTs. Britain's dependence on the United States was its own fault. The British had overinvested in heavy bombers, leaving them without the means to build assault vessels of their own. In the entire war, Britain built only 24 landing ships, 21 of them in 1945, too late to matter. It did build 1,264 major landing craft and

2,867 minor ones, but U.S. production totals came to 1,573 landing ships, 2,486 major craft, and 45,524 minor units.

The absence of a long-range plan was responsible for many shortages. Assault vessels, LSTs in particular, were transferred from Europe to the Pacific, but never moved in the opposite direction. The Navy argued, perhaps correctly, that the vast distances of the Pacific made it impractical to transfer LSTs to Europe once they were there. As the Pacific received the lion's share of LSTs, the Navy often used them as ordinary cargo vessels or floating warehouses. Yet even if LSTs and major landing craft were always in short supply, enough remained to win the war.

SEE ALSO

Kaiser, Henry J.

Leahy, William D.

CHIEF OF STAFF, 1942–49

- *Born: May 6, 1875, Hampton, Iowa*
- *Political party: none*
- *Education: U.S. Naval Academy, B.S., 1897*
- *Military service: lieutenant, 1904–9; captain, 1918–27; commander, battleship USS New Mexico, 1926–27; commander, Battleship Divisions, Battle Force, 1935–36; admiral, 1937–39, 1942–44; chief of naval operations, 1937–39*
- *Government service: governor of Puerto Rico, 1939–40; ambassador to France, 1940–42; chief of staff to Presidents Roosevelt and Truman, 1942–49*
- *Died: July 20, 1959, Bethesda, Md.*

When Admiral William Leahy retired for the first time, in 1939, he had been chief of the Navy's two most important bureaus, commander of all the battleship divisions at a time when they were

Leahy and President Roosevelt take time out during a flight to London to look at pictures of Trinadad.

regarded as the main ships of the fleet, commander of the Battle Force (later renamed the Pacific Fleet), and chief of naval operations, which was the Navy's highest position.

Leahy owed his success to great ability as well as the fact that President Franklin D. Roosevelt had known him since World War I, when Leahy served under FDR in the Navy Department. The quiet admiral and the sociable President could not have been more different, but Roosevelt trusted Leahy as he did few others. That is why he insisted on retaining Leahy's services after the admiral retired in 1939.

As Roosevelt's ambassador to France, Leahy found himself in a tricky position, because Vichy France was collaborating with the Nazis. But the French colonial empire was still large, and Roosevelt felt it important to remain on good terms with Vichy anyway. The French Navy (which included a fleet in the Caribbean) remained significant too.

After Pearl Harbor was attacked in December 1941, Roosevelt directed the U.S. Army and Navy, which previously had had no direct link, to form the Joint Chiefs of Staff (JCS) to direct military operations. At first the JCS consisted of three men, Admiral Ernest King, who headed the Navy; General George C. Marshall, the army chief of staff; and General Henry Arnold, chief of the Army Air Forces. Marshall feared that Admiral King, because he was outnumbered on the JCS, might be tempted to go directly to the President when disagreements arose. He solved this possible problem with an inspired solution. He asked Roosevelt to recall Leahy to active service as chief of staff to the President with a seat on the JCS, whose meetings Leahy would chair.

This solved the King problem to the degree that it could be solved, and gave Roosevelt a close and trusted advisor on all military matters. Admiral Leahy had offices in the White House, saw the President every day, and in time was asked by Roosevelt to help with many problems that had little, if anything, to do with military affairs. Although not as close to Roosevelt as Harry Hopkins, FDR's main troubleshooter in civilian affairs, Leahy played a similar role in the military. When Hopkins was too ill to work, which happened several times during the war, Leahy did Hopkins's job as well as his own. Close-mouthed, industrious, and orderly, Leahy was the perfect chief of staff for a President whose habit it was to surround himself with chaos.

Leahy made his greatest contribution to the war effort when Harry S. Truman became President in 1945. Roosevelt had done nothing to prepare Vice President Truman for the Oval Office in case his own health, which was poor, failed. Thus, when Truman was sworn in on April 12, 1945, he knew almost nothing about Roosevelt's foreign and military policies. It therefore fell to Leahy, who knew more about both than anyone else except Roosevelt himself, to brief the new President. Further, unlike Roosevelt, who did as he pleased, Truman not only listened to Leahy but frequently took his advice. Leahy's job

under Roosevelt had been important to the smooth working of the U.S. military machine. Under Truman, however, especially at first, Leahy had real power. Typically, he used it with care.

Leahy was the least known of the nation's top military leaders of World War II. His work was bureaucratic and diplomatic and did not involve making command decisions. He was not associated with any faction or party. He had no pet theories about how the war should be waged. But in his quiet way he was a model officer and did his country a great service.

FURTHER READING

Adams, Henry H. *Witness to Power: The Life of Fleet Admiral William D. Leahy.* Annapolis, Md.: Naval Institute Press, 1985.
Leahy, William D. *I Was There.* 1950. Reprint, North Stratford, N.H.: Ayer, 1980.

LeMay, Curtis E.

COMMANDER OF XXI BOMBER COMMAND

- *Born: November 15, 1906, Columbus, Ohio*
- *Political party: none*
- *Education: Ohio State University, 1924–28, B.S.*
- *Military service: U.S. Army second lieutenant, 1928–37; captain, 1940–41; colonel, 1942–43; brigadier general, 1943–44; major general, 1944*
- *Died: October 1, 1990, March AFB, Calif.*

A tactical genius, Curtis LeMay had trained for years with the Boeing B-17 Flying Fortress before the war. He was given the 305th Bombardment Group not long after Pearl Harbor was attacked in December 1941. The B-17 was the world's first operational four-engined heavy bomber. Heavily armed and armored, it was designed to force its way through enemy fighters in daylight and drop its relatively small bombload exactly on target.

When LeMay took his group to Britain in 1942 he soon discovered that the formation in use there did not enable B-17s to provide each other with overlapping fields of machine-gun fire. Accordingly, he designed the Lead-High-Low combat box. This formation, which permitted between 18 and 21 bombers to give each other maximum fire support, was adopted by all the heavy bomb groups of the Army Air Forces. He pioneered in other ways too, developing methods that won widespread acceptance.

LeMay often led his group into battle and provided it with such effective leadership that he was promoted to command the 3rd Air Division of the Eighth Air Force in 1943. In that capacity he led it in one of the most costly air attacks of the war.

On August 17, 1943, LeMay personally led the 3rd Division to Regensburg, Germany, where it successfully bombed an aircraft plant in an experimental mission before flying on to Tunisia. Twenty-four of the 127 planes he commanded went down that day, giving his division an unbearably high loss rate of some 20 percent.

No one blamed him for this. LeMay had attacked the target accurately and on time, unlike the 1st Air Division, which was supposed to attack Schweinfurt, Germany, at the same time as LeMay's raid on Regensburg. Bad weather over England had delayed it for hours because, unlike the 3rd Division, its pilots had not been trained to take off guided only by instruments. In any case, operations over Germany were making it clear that heavy bombers could not make their way to the target without fighter support. Victory in the air war would have to wait for the arrival of long-range fighters.

After his service in Europe, LeMay was made chief of the XX Bomber Command based in India and China. The XX was equipped with the new Boeing B-29 Superfortress, a much larger, stronger, faster aircraft than the B-17. But its bases were too far from major targets, and its China bases were too hard to supply. Even the long-range B-29 could not bomb effectively under these conditions. When the Allies took the Mariana Islands in 1944, the Army Air Force based its XXI Bomber Command on them. The B-29s of LeMay's XX Bomber Command were then transferred to the XXI, which LeMay took over on January 19, 1945.

The XXI Bomber Command had been trying unsuccessfully to destroy targets in Japan with precision bombing from high altitudes. The trouble was that at high altitudes, the B-29s encountered enormous winds. If the winds were behind them, the aircraft flew up to a hundred miles per hour faster than normal, making accuracy impossible. And if they flew into the wind, their speed was reduced by the same hundred miles per hour, in this case making them easier targets.

LeMay's assignment was to abandon precision bombing and instead burn down Japan's cities. By this stage of the war, the United States's earlier prejudice against terror bombing of civilians had largely faded away. Accordingly, LeMay brought his usual enthusiasm and technical skill to this challenging problem.

Since accuracy no longer mattered, he decided to have his B-29s attack by night at low altitudes. Because they used less fuel at low altitudes than when flying high, they could carry less gas and more firebombs. He further increased the bombloads by removing the B-29s' guns and all but one of the gunners. On the nights of March 11 and 12, 1945, LeMay sent 313 bombers, flying singly because they could not form up in the dark, to set Tokyo on fire. The resulting firestorm was the greatest urban fire in history and killed the most people of any single air attack in the war. It is believed that something like 100,000 Japanese died in the Tokyo firestorm, more than would be killed by either of the two atomic bombs dropped on Japan. More than just a big fire, the firestorm was so hot that it burned up the oxygen around it and suffocated many victims who were never touched by the flames.

LeMay followed this success with other attacks, which destroyed all but five of Japan's urban areas. Kyoto was spared because Secretary of War Henry Stimson, who disliked terror bombing anyway, knew it was a center of Japanese religion and culture and would not let it be touched. The other four cities were reserved for the atomic bomb so that the extent of its destructive power could be accurately measured. Otherwise, LeMay burned urban Japan to the ground, as instructed. Had the war gone on much longer than it did, most of his planes would have been grounded for lack of targets.

These firebomb raids were the moral low point of the U.S. war effort. They contributed little to victory, because the U.S. naval blockade had already brought most of Japan's industry to a halt. They also failed to persuade the Japanese government to surrender. What the firebomb raids did do was to murder at least half a million Japanese civilians for no good purpose. LeMay no doubt accomplished this task faster and more efficiently than anyone else could have.

SEE ALSO

Japan, surrender of

FURTHER READING

Coffey, Thomas M. *Iron Eagle: The Turbulent Life of General Curtis LeMay.* New York: Crown, 1986.
LeMay, Curtis E., and MacKinlay Kantor. *Mission with LeMay: My Story.* Garden City, N.Y.: Doubleday, 1965.

Lend-Lease program

When Britain went to war, its cash reserves were sufficient to cover only a few months of fighting. Somehow the British muddled through, but by the fall of 1940, they were out of money. President Franklin D. Roosevelt had pledged that in 1941 they could buy enough equipment for 10 divisions and 12,000 more aircraft from the United States in addition to the 14,000 already committed, but he did not wish to confront the issue of payment while he was still running for reelection in 1940.

London held its tongue until November 23, 1940, when British ambassador Lord Lothian cheerfully told U.S. reporters: "Well, boys, Britain's broke; it's your money we want." With Britain fighting on alone, everything hung in the balance. American isolationists opposed aid to Britain for fear of being drawn into the war, but Britain had to have aid if it, and the cause of freedom as well, was to survive. The times called for inspired leadership. Roosevelt would provide it.

After a vacation he met with the press and announced his answer to Britain's need, the program that became known as Lend-Lease. This turned out to be simply a method to supply Britain on credit, which was just what the isolationists had feared, but Roosevelt packaged it cleverly. The United States was

Before the United States officially entered the war, the Lend-Lease Act allowed it to assist the Allies with war materiel such as this M-3 Grant tank destined for Africa.

not going to loan the British money, he said, still less would it give away munitions. It was simply going to remove the "silly, foolish old dollar sign," by lending armaments to the British, which they would later pay for in kind, or return.

Roosevelt compared Lend-Lease to a garden hose, which you lend to a neighbor if his house is on fire, receiving it, or a replacement, back once the fire is out. Reporters asked whether this meant escorting goods to Britain, which would involve the U.S. Navy. Roosevelt denied it, possibly even to himself. He acknowledged that Lend-Lease would require congressional approval, but refused to admit that it increased the risk of war.

No one asked what repayment "in kind" meant, although this was the key question. If it referred to leftover weapons after the war, Lend-Lease would actually be a gift. Reporters failed to ask this question probably because they did not wish to hear the answer.

Thanks to the support of the reporters, the press conference was a triumph. Introducing Lend-Lease in this casual way made it seem less significant than it was. That the garden hose comparison worked despite its being essentially untrue could be interpreted to mean that the public of the time was very easy to fool. A better explanation is

that Americans wanted to do the right thing and would act responsibly if offered a face-saving way to ignore the popular isolationist slogans of the day. Years of antiwar propaganda had made it hard to face the truth that Britain's fight was the United States's as well, yet people were waking up.

Roosevelt capped this performance with a fireside chat on December 29, 1940, assuring his radio audience that he was not speaking of war but rather about national security. The issue, he said, was how to keep the nation "out of a last-ditch war for the preservation of American independence and all the things that American independence means to you and to me and to ours." Never in American history had the danger been so great, because the Axis powers were seeking world domination. If Britain fell, all Americans would live at the point of a gun, and to survive, "we would have to convert ourselves permanently into a militaristic power on the basis of a war economy."

This was a great speech in support of a grand decision. The timing was right also, for a Gallup poll released just before his speech showed that 60 percent of the American people favored aid to Britain, even at the risk of war. The Lend-Lease bill, HR-1776, passed with very large majorities in the Senate on March 8, 1941, and in the House three days later, aided by polls showing that thanks to favorable publicity the public now supported it by a margin of two to one.

Although the Lend-Lease program lifted British morale (Churchill called it a "new Magna Carta"), Lend-Lease initially had little effect, because the weapons Britain could buy with its new charge account existed only on paper. Although $14 billion was appropriated under Lend-Lease, in 1941 Britain would receive only $1 billion worth of munitions—all that could be spared, given U.S. unreadiness.

But once U.S. industry shifted into high gear, immense quantities of goods and weapons would go out under Lend-Lease, to Britain and its allies, and to Soviet Russia too after Germany invaded it in the summer of 1941. Ultimately, 38 nations would receive Lend-Lease supplies valued at somewhere between $42 and $50 billion. Britain, and its empire and commonwealth, received about half of this, the Soviet Union some $10 billion worth of aid. A few figures will suggest what these dollars actually bought.

At war's end the Soviet Union possessed 665,000 motor vehicles, 400,000 of them made in the United States. The United States also supplied the Soviets with 2,000 locomotives, 11,000 freight cars, and 540,000 tons of rail, with which the Soviets laid more track than during the last decade before the war. Food shipments alone were equal to the entire wartime consumption of the Red Army. At the same time, the United States was providing Britain with much of its armaments, rising to a peak of 28.7 percent of all British military equipment in 1944. As Roosevelt had predicted in 1941, the United States became the arsenal of democracy, as well as its granary.

Leyte Gulf, Battle of

The greatest naval battle ever fought, the Battle of Leyte Gulf marked the doom of the Japanese surface fleet. This turning point resulted from the U.S. invasion of Leyte, an island in the Philippine archipelago in October 1944 (as shown in map on p. 142.) The Imperial Japanese Navy knew that losing the Philippines would

ensure Japan's defeat if, indeed, its fate was not already sealed.

Since there was no point in holding back, the Japanese Navy determined to make a maximum effort. It still had nine battleships, including the world's largest, the *Yamato* and the *Musashi,* together with a dozen heavy cruisers. It also had four fast carriers, but all told they could launch only about 100 planes manned by green pilots because the Japanese fleet air arm had been destroyed in the Battle of the Philippine Sea in June. Therefore, the Japanese decided to use the carriers as decoys. They would lure away the U.S. Third Fleet, with Admiral William Halsey commanding, while two surface units would meet in Leyte Gulf to wipe out the Leyte invasion force, which Halsey was supposed to be guarding.

At about 1:00 a.m. on October 23, 1944, two U.S. submarines sighted a strong Japanese fleet. Under the command of Vice Admiral Takeo Kurita, it consisted of 5 battleships, including the *Yamato* and the *Musashi,* plus 10 heavy and 2 light cruisers and more than 12 destroyers. Prompt U.S. air and submarine attacks forced it to turn back.

In the meantime, naval aircraft detected a second force under Vice Admiral Shoji Nishimura, including two battleships, a cruiser, and four destroyers, making for the Surigao Strait at the southern end of Leyte. But Halsey and Admiral Thomas C. Kinkaid, commanding MacArthur's Seventh Fleet, were awaiting news of the Japanese carriers before committing themselves. At about five in the afternoon, Vice Admiral Jisaburo Ozawa's carriers were sighted far to the north of Leyte Gulf.

Halsey now took the bait. He and Kinkaid, not knowing that the carriers had few planes and pilots, took it for granted that this was the Japanese main force. On hearing a false report that the enemy carriers were accompanied by battleships, Halsey drove north with all his

General Douglas MacArthur (fourth from right) wades ashore during the initial landings at Leyte, Philippine Islands, in October 1944.

fast carriers and battleships. He would destroy the toothless Japanese carrier force, while Kinkaid's old battleships would similarly sink all but one of the Japanese warships in the Surigao Strait.

Meanwhile, Vice Admiral Kurita, who had doubled back, was passing undetected through the San Bernardino Strait, to the east of Leyte Gulf. Most of his assault fell on Taffy 3, one of three groups of U.S. escort carriers supporting the Leyte operation. Taffy 3 consisted of five escort carriers each mounting a single five-inch gun. With their top speed of 17 knots, they could not outrun a Japanese submarine, much less a battleship. In addition to them, Rear Admiral Clifton T. Sprague commanded only three destroyers and four destroyer escorts. Despite his apparently hopeless position, Sprague launched his aircraft and in a running battle worked his way toward Taffy 2, 60 miles to the south.

Sprague's aircraft had few torpedoes and no armor-piercing bombs. When their torpedoes and bombs were gone, they dropped depth charges and whatever else was at hand. Finally, when they had nothing left, Sprague's pilots made dummy runs on the Japanese ships to draw attention from the invasion force. Meanwhile, his destroyers and destroyer escorts made smoke to screen the carriers and repeatedly charged the enemy ships, firing their guns and making the last torpedo attacks ever executed by destroyers.

Taffy 2 arrived in time to join the battle, sending torpedo planes that helped destroy three enemy cruisers.

So furious were these attacks that Kurita lost his nerve. Even though Sprague had only one destroyer left and the escort carrier *Gambier Bay* was in flames and sinking, Kurita failed to recognize that he was battling escorts, not Halsey's fast carriers. Fearful of additional losses, and believing that the U.S. carriers were outrunning him, Kurita broke off the engagement at 9:30 a.m. on October 25 and swiftly fled the scene.

The Battle of Leyte Gulf had been one of the most astonishing in naval history. Taffy 3, hopelessly outgunned and outnumbered, did not, on the face of it, have a chance of survival. If Kurita had kept his ships together and driven for the beaches he could have sunk the invasion fleet and mopped up Taffy 3 later. The battle showed again how far the Imperial Japanese Navy had declined and how much better the Americans had gotten. Sprague himself summed it up nicely, crediting the result to "our successful smoke screen, our torpedo counterattack, continuous harassment of the enemy by bomb, torpedo and strafing air attacks, timely maneuvers, and the definite partiality of Almighty God." Luck played a part, to be sure, but courage, skill, and leadership were what saved the beachhead.

It was a smashing U.S. victory, and probably would have been almost as great even if Ozawa's air groups had been at full strength. The United States lost the light carrier *Princeton*, two escort carriers, two destroyers, one destroyer escort, and fewer than 3,000 men. The Japanese were deprived of four fleet carriers, three battleships including the mighty *Musashi*, six heavy cruisers, four light cruisers, nine destroyers, and some 10,000 men.

In Leyte Gulf the Imperial Japanese Navy met its end. Leyte Gulf also gave birth to the "divine wind," the kamikaze suicide attacks that were now Japan's only hope, had their beginning.

SEE ALSO
Kamikaze; Halsey, William F.

FURTHER READING
Falk, Stanley W. *Decision at Leyte*. New York: Norton, 1966.

Liberty ships

SEE Kaiser, Henry J.

Lindbergh, Charles A.

SEE Isolationists

Literature

World War II gave birth to a body of literature that is still being written today. Personal and group stories, fictional histories, and novels focusing on the war have been highly popular. For a generation of Americans World War II was the pivotal event of their lives, and a natural interest arose in the less public details of the war, the stories and personal adventures (true or not). The war was a great epic, with intrigue, defeat, revenge, and triumph—an ideal literary setting for a public hungry for war stories. Historians were also busy producing social, political, and economic histories of the war in the years that followed. Together, these fictional and non-fictional works helped people digest the battery of information that had become available. As the war receded into the past, these resources became an aide to reflection and to bet-

ter understanding the world that had resulted.

As for the publishing industry itself, the war spurred economic developments that shook up the genteel book trade and helped democratize American reading. It abetted the paperback revolution, begun in 1939 with Pocket Books' cautious release of ten paperbacks selling for 25 cents each. Wartime paper rationing, which squeezed books into smaller formats, helped make paperbacks respectable, and a mobile public liked the slim, light volumes. The Armed Services Editions became the biggest mass publishing venture in American history. Sixty million books, ranging from Charles Dickens and Joseph Conrad to mysteries and westerns, poured into the hands of soldiers and sailors— free. Charges of censorship flared as zealous officers tried to circumscribe what GIs might read, but the venture was a huge success, shaping both how and what was read after the war.

CLASSIC AMERICAN WORLD WAR II NOVELS

Heller, Joseph. *Catch-22*. 1961. Reprint, New York: Simon & Schuster, 1994.

Hersey, John. *A Bell for Adano*. 1971. Reprint, New York: Vintage, 1988.

Hersey, John. *Hiroshima*. 1946. Reprint, New York: Vintage, 1990.

Jones, James. *From Here to Eternity*. 1952. Reprint, New York: Dell, 1998.

Jones, James. *The Thin Red Line*. 1947. Reprint, New York: Dell, 1998.

Mailer, Norman. *The Naked & the Dead*. 1948. Reprint, New York: Henry Holt, 1998.

Vonnegut, Kurt. *Slaughterhouse-five*. 1959. Reprint, New York: Dell, 1999.

Wouk, Herman. *The Caine Mutiny*. 1951. Reprint, New York: Little, Brown, 1992.

Luftwaffe

The German Air Force, known as the Luftwaffe (literally, "air weapon" in English), was developed from scratch by the Nazis and was Hitler's favorite service. He believed the "air power" theory developed in the 1920s and 1930s, which held that a nation could be defeated by air attacks alone. Curiously, Germany failed to produce four-engine heavy bombers, and as a result it never had a weapon powerful enough to test the theory.

The "air power" believers were in fact wrong. Germany's lack of heavy bombers was not a serious problem, except when Hitler attempted to "blitz" London in 1940 and 1941. The one- and two-engine bombers of the Luftwaffe, which had been designed to support ground troops, could not carry enough bombs to destroy such a huge target. As a ground support force, however, the Luftwaffe had no equal in the early war years.

A bigger problem than its lack of heavy bombers for the Luftwaffe was incompetence at the top of the ranks. Hitler made Hermann Göring, a World War I flying ace, commander in chief of the Luftwaffe and Reich aviation minister. Because of Göring, the Luftwaffe would be badly led and its aircraft production mismanaged. As commander in chief, Göring relied on inexperienced young officers who did not understand the limits of the Luftwaffe.

As a result of his mismanagement, Göring was always promising Hitler goods he could not deliver. He pledged to defeat the Royal Air Force in 1940 and failed. His effort to bomb England into submission that same year failed as well. The German Sixth Army was destroyed at Stalingrad, Russia, largely

because Göring said his pilots would supply it by air, which they could not do. By 1944 Göring was losing interest in the Luftwaffe (thanks to morphine addiction and pursuit of other hedonistic pleasures), while Hitler was interfering more and more, making a bad situation worse.

The Luftwaffe was organized very differently from Allied air forces and included elements usually assigned to armies. Flak (antiaircraft) guns were manned by the Luftwaffe. Parachutists were in the Luftwaffe too, although after the seizure of Crete in 1941 Germany staged no further combat drops. Ultimately, nine Luftwaffe paratroop divisions fought as conventional infantry under Army command. The service had 21 regular field divisions, which also came under the Army's control in 1943.

The Luftwaffe was unconventionally structured internally too. It was divided vertically into air fleets (*luftflotten*), each of which possessed all the various types of aircraft. Each air fleet was responsible for all the operations in a given region. This structure gave the Germans less flexibility than Western air forces had, which were organized horizontally by function.

The most important reason for the Luftwaffe's defeat in the long run was

A German Heinkel III bomber flies over the River Thames in London during an aerial raid in 1940. The Luftwaffe's lightly armed bombers had neither the payload nor the defensive armament to effectively cripple Britain's modern air-defense system.

lack of production. Germany produced relatively few aircraft in 1940 and 1941, because Hitler was expecting a short war. Erhard Milch, a skillful airline executive in private life, gained control of air supply and procurement in 1942, and he increased aircraft production.

Although aircraft production rose sharply, it was never enough. When 1942 ended, German industry was producing 50 percent more aircraft than in 1941. But while Germany turned out an average of 367 fighters a month in 1942, Britain, Canada, and the United States averaged 1,959. Germany averaged 349 bombers a month, the three allies 1,378, many of them four-engine heavies that Germany did not make. German aircraft production, along with weapons manufacturing as a whole, reached its peak in 1944. In April, Germany produced more than 2,000 fighters in a month for the first time. In September, 3,375 fighters were turned out, a German wartime record.

Impressive though they may be, these figures are misleading. Germany was still far behind the Allies in aircraft production. A lack of fuel was crippling the Luftwaffe too. As a result, many aircraft had to be grounded. Training slowed drastically, and early in 1945 it came to a stop.

The Luftwaffe did have a weapon that might have forced the Allies to suspend their daylight bombing attacks on Germany. This was the Messerschmitt 262, the world's first jet aircraft. As a fighter it could have entered squadron service in 1943, when it became operational. The Me 262 was 100 miles an hour faster than Allied propeller-driven fighters. The Allies would not have jets of their own until late in 1945. Thus it was possible that a large-scale deployment of the 262 would have forced the United States to suspend, probably for most of the war, daylight raids on Germany.

Hitler, however, insisted that the jet be reconfigured as a bomber, despite its short range and limited bomb capacity. So much time was wasted attempting to make the 262 perform a function unsuited to it that it did not go into action as a fighter until 1944. There were too few pilots by then, and fewer still with adequate training. Tactics appropriate for a jet fighter were still to be worked out. Units of 262s scored a handful of impressive victories, but these did not affect the course of the war.

German designers produced many impressive propeller-driven aircraft. The Messerschmitt Bf 109 fighter was superior to the British Hurricane, although it was not quite as good as the Spitfire. The newer Focke-Wulf 190 was as fast as or faster than any Allied fighter except for the U.S. P-51 Mustang. The JU 88 medium bomber was highly versatile: it could dive-bomb in addition to bombing in level flight and was useful for reconnaissance and other purposes. The 88 was produced in greater numbers than all other German bombers put together.

In addition to the Me 262, German designers produced air-to-air and ground-to-air rockets, a rocket-powered fighter, and were working on a jet bomber, among other things. But, as German qualitative superiority was not matched by its production capacity, these advanced weapons did the Reich little good. Some never became operational. Those that did were too few, too late.

Had German aircraft production reached its peak in 1942 instead of 1944, and if the resources wasted on the V-2 rocket had been applied to jets and other advanced weapons, things may have turned out differently.

A few incidents suggest what might have been. In April 1945, 6 Me 262s armed with R4M air-to-air rockets destroyed 15 Allied B-17s. A few days later a squadron of Focke-Wulf 190s similarly armed shot down 40 heavy bombers. Luckily for the Allies, the Germans could not overcome years of mismanagement and poor leadership this late in the war.

SEE ALSO
Strategic bombing

FURTHER READING
Galland, Adolf. *The First and the Last: The Rise and Fall of the German Fighter Forces, 1938–1945.* New York: Ballantine, 1957.
Killen, John. *A History of the Luftwaffe.* Garden City, N.Y.: Doubleday, 1968.
Mitcham, Samuel W., Jr. *Eagles of the Third Reich: The Men Who Made the Luftwaffe.* Novato, Calif.: Presidio, 1997.

MacArthur, Douglas

SUPREME COMMANDER OF THE SOUTHWEST PACIFIC AREA, 1942–45

- *Born: January 26, 1880, Little Rock, Ark.*
- *Political party: Republican*
- *Education: U.S. Military Academy, B.S., 1903; U.S. Army Engineering School, 1906–7*
- *Military service: U.S. Army—second lieutenant, 1903; captain, 1911; colonel, 1917; brigadier general, 1918; commander of 84th Infantry Regiment, 1918; major general, 1925; commander in chief of U.S. forces in the Philippines, 1928–30; U.S. Army chief of staff, 1930–35; commander of the Philippine Army, 1936–42; commander of U.S. Army forces in the Far East, 1941–42; general of the army, 1944*
- *Died: April 5, 1964, Washington, D.C.*

Soldiering was in MacArthur's blood. His father, Lieutenant General Arthur MacArthur, had commanded troops during the Philippine insurrection, which took place after the United States bought the Philippine Islands from Spain in 1898 as part of the peace settlement of the Spanish-American War. Young Douglas followed his lead, graduating first in his class from West Point. During World War I, MacArthur became the youngest brigadier general in the Army, enabling him to become the only U.S. commander to serve as a general officer in both world wars. In 1935 he was named military advisor to the Philippine Commonwealth, which, in preparation for its coming independence, was forming its own defense force. In 1936 he was promoted to field marshal in command of the Philippine Army. He retired from the U.S. Army in 1937 but returned to active duty in 1941 as commander of U.S. and Philippine forces in the Far East.

MacArthur's defense of the Philippines when it came under Japanese attack in December 1941 after Pearl Harbor could hardly have been worse. Half his air force was destroyed on the ground 12 hours after the Pearl Harbor attack. The rest soon followed. He failed to fortify or provision the Bataan Peninsula of Luzon, to which he was forced to retreat. Thus, his heavily outgunned forces had to fight without sufficient food, medicine, or ammunition. They fought magnificently even so, delaying the Japanese for months and probably saving Australia. President Roosevelt ordered MacArthur to Australia (so he would not be killed or captured) in March 1942, well before Bataan (April) and Fortress Corregidor (May) were compelled to surrender.

MacArthur should probably have been fired for incompetence. But the courage of his starving men won them great glory, which spilled over onto him. Because the public did not know about

General Douglas MacArthur was a popular figure on the home front, even though he achieved mixed results during the early years of the war.

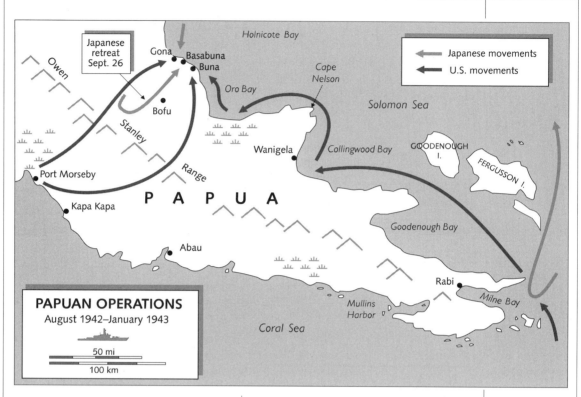

PAPUAN OPERATIONS
August 1942–January 1943

50 mi

100 km

his failures, MacArthur became a great national hero. Roosevelt thus had to give him a job equal to his fame, which is why he became the supreme commander of the Southwest Pacific Area (SWPA). This appointment was part of a deal according to which the Army gained a theater for MacArthur while the Navy got everything else in the Pacific, which was organized by the Navy as the Pacific Ocean Area under Admiral Chester Nimitz. This meant there would be no unified command in the Pacific, rather two different and competing wars against Japan, involving much delay and waste.

MacArthur's first campaign as supreme commander of the SWPA was in the Papuan Peninsula of New Guinea. Papua, essential to the defense of Australia, had been invaded by Japanese forces soon after war broke out. Australian troops had managed to save Port Moresby, its most important harbor, and drive the Japanese back over the Owen Stanley Range. But the Japanese still held the peninsula's northwest coast.

MacArthur resolved to expel them, doing so in a crude and costly way. Again and again he threw his two poorly-trained and prepared National Guard divisions against heavily fortified Japanese strongpoints in the Buna-Gona region. On January 22, 1943, Buna fell. This was the first time the Japanese had experienced a permanent defeat on land.

MacArthur denied that the campaign had been unnecessarily bloody for his troops. But in fact, due to his poor leadership, the troops who took Buna-Gona had a death rate three times as high as the Marines sustained on Guadalcanal, one of the bloodier campaigns of the war. This fact undercut MacArthur's claims that his victory had been won at a reasonable cost. But, although MacArthur went on deceiving outsiders, he and his staff knew better. After the Papuan campaign, MacArthur made a promise, which he kept, that there would be no more Bunas.

MacArthur was learning fast, and the experience would not be wasted.

Over the next two years his troops would suffer fewer than 20,000 casualties in the course of many operations, partly because of tactical lessons learned in Papua that would make later campaigns more efficient. Among other things, MacArthur was learning the many uses of aircraft, whose value he had previously sneered at. And his understanding of sea power was expanding too. MacArthur's need for a sea lift (i.e., troop ships and assault vessels) was glaringly exposed at Buna, where he had almost no ships and thus could not stage landings to outflank or isolate enemy fortifications. His complaints in this regard led the Navy to assign him a specialist, Rear Admiral Daniel E. Barbey, whose VII Amphibious Force would stage 56 operations in the Southwest Pacific Area. MacArthur also learned how to exploit the decoded enemy radio messages provided by Army and Navy intelligence. They would play a key part in future operations by helping to determine which enemy strongholds could be bypassed.

The key to MacArthur's success was his use of tactical air, which was more important in the SWPA than in perhaps any other theater. The southwest Pacific is thick with islands that provided numerous sites for airfields. But, unlike the Germans' defenses in Europe, Japanese air defenses were weak, enabling even heavy U.S. bombers to make precise low-level attacks.

MacArthur also had two outstanding air commanders in General George C. Kenney and Lieutenant General Ennis C. Whitehead. Kenney taught MacArthur what planes could do, starting with an airlift of troops to Buna. Many on MacArthur's staff doubted that men could be flown directly to the battle area. Kenney proved them wrong and saved most if not all of MacArthur's men from having to cross the dreaded Owen

Stanleys. Gradually the air commanders worked out a strategy of blockading enemy strongpoints from the air, covering and assisting Allied ground troops, while, by advancing their forward bases, bringing more and more Japanese targets within bombing range, or what was commonly called the bomb line.

At first, progress was slow, for MacArthur did not have enough of anything. But as his forces expanded and his tactics improved, his troops advanced faster and faster. In April 1944, in his most daring move to date, MacArthur moved his troops 580 miles beyond their lines on the northwest New Guinea coast to seize the town of Hollandia, now Jayapura, in Indonesia. Because this involved bypassing enemy strongpoints, the Japanese were taken by surprise. In less than two years MacArthur advanced almost 2,000 miles, 1,100 of it in the last two months.

After a shaky start MacArthur developed into a commander worthy of his reputation. The sharpness and timing of his operations, his close coordination of land, sea, and air forces, and the boldness and success of his strategy of bypassing enemy strongholds have justly been admired ever since. In the SWPA, his victories were won by cunning and stealth as often as not, saving many U.S. soldiers' lives.

Meanwhile, the Navy's central Pacific drive was proving to be very expensive. Japanese positions in that part of the Pacific were few and small. They could not be outflanked, or taken from the rear. Thus, at Saipan and Iwo Jima, among others, Marines were obliged to make frontal assaults against heavily fortified Japanese positions and suffer terrible losses.

MacArthur argued for much of the war that the Navy's campaign should parallel his own. That way the two advancing forces could readily support each other. The fast carriers and precious landing ships tank (LSTs) needed for amphibious landings could be moved back and forth between MacArthur and Admiral Chester Nimitz as needed, instead of idling in the central Pacific in the off time between operations. Admiral Nimitz apparently thought so too, but was overruled by his domineering superior, Admiral Ernest King.

In 1944, at a conference in Hawaii with President Franklin D. Roosevelt and Admiral Nimitz, MacArthur finally received permission to retake the Philippines. Although he had personal motives for wanting to do so, to erase his earlier defeat, there were good reasons for liberating the islands. The United States needed to show that it cared for the people it had failed to protect in 1942. Furthermore, Luzon was a strategic prize. Missions launched from Luzon air bases would give American forces control of the sealanes between Southeast Asia and Japan, depriving the Japanese of such essential raw materials as oil, rubber, and tin. Taking Luzon certainly made more sense than invading Formosa, which was what Admiral King wished to do. In the Philippines, U.S. forces would be met with open arms, while the Formosan response could not be predicted.

The Philippine campaign won additional laurels for MacArthur. Leyte, the first island to be attacked, was more strongly defended than MacArthur had been led to expect. Luzon was tougher still. In fact, when the war ended, one of MacArthur's field armies was still fighting a strong Japanese force in the mountains of northern Luzon. But MacArthur's forces liberated the other islands with speed and dash.

The Philippine campaign as a whole was a smashing success, even though it was not quite completed by the end of the war. Again, with local exceptions, much had been accomplished at relatively

little cost. MacArthur's forces sustained 62,000 casualties, including 14,000 deaths. While this was a large figure for the Pacific war, it was small when seen in the context of Japanese losses, which came to 350,000. In the central Pacific, however, U.S. casualties were relatively higher. On tiny Iwo Jima, for example, U.S. casualties actually exceeded those of the Japanese defenders.

MacArthur's less admirable character traits loom large in many accounts. A chronic liar, he was likewise boastful, arrogant, remote, and vain. Most communiques from the SWPA named only one man, himself. His commanders soon discovered that he deeply resented any publicity they might receive. They learned to avoid the press, which is why names like Walter Kruger, Robert Eichelberger, and George C. Kenney are unfamiliar today compared to those of General Dwight D. Eisenhower's lieutenants in the European theater. Yet, in the end, MacArthur achieved much. After Buna he learned from his mistakes, took the advice of his generally excellent commanders, and launched a series of brilliant campaigns that were classics of their kind.

MacArthur was hated by most of his men for his lack of apparent concern for them. Yet his skill kept many alive who would have perished under a more conventional leader. The Okinawa campaign, directed by less imaginative generals, was proof of this. There the United States had complete control of the sea and air, making possible numerous amphibious and airborne operations. Instead, soldiers and Marines made one frontal assault after another, battering away at the Japanese lines until they finally collapsed. About 35 percent of the Americans who fought in the Battle of Okinawa became casualties, a ratio exceeding even that of MacArthur's Papuan campaign, which was his worst and never was repeated. In the end,

MacArthur earned his job as supreme commander and made the most of it.

SEE ALSO

Iwo Jima, Battle of; King, Ernest J.; Leyte Gulf, Battle of; Nimitz, Chester W.; Okinawa, Battle of; Pacific war; Southwest Pacific Area

FURTHER READING

Breuer, William B. *MacArthur's Undercover War: Spies, Saboteurs, Guerrillas, and Secret Missions.* New York: Wiley, 1995.
James, D. Clayton. *The Years of MacArthur: Vol. 2, 1941–1945.* Boston: Houghton Mifflin, 1975.
Manchester, William. *American Caesar: Douglas MacArthur, 1880–1964.* Boston: Little, Brown, 1978.
Perret, Geoffrey. *Old Soldiers Never Die: The Life of Douglas MacArthur.* New York: Random House, 1996.
Schaller, Michael. *Douglas MacArthur: The Far Eastern General.* New York: Oxford University Press, 1989.

Machine guns

SEE Small Arms

Malmedy massacre

As a rule, all the forces in western Europe—Axis and Allied alike—observed the Geneva convention, which specified how prisoners should be treated. However, there were isolated instances on both sides of soldiers being murdered after giving themselves up.

The worst atrocities took place in the Battle of the Bulge, in December and January 1944–45. Most of them were committed by Taskforce Peiper, a regiment of the 1st SS Panzer Division under Lieutenant Colonel Joachim Peiper. It led the northern assault on U.S. lines and began shooting U.S. prisoners of war and Bel-

gium civilians almost at once. The worst such event, known as the Malmedy massacre, took place in Belgium on December 17, 1944, and resulted in the deaths of 86 U.S. prisoners.

Manchuria

SEE China; Japan

Manhattan Project

SEE Atomic bombs

Marines

SEE United States Marine Corps

Marshall, George C., Jr.

ARCHITECT OF VICTORY

- *Born: December 31, 1880, Uniontown, Ky.*
- *Political party: none*
- *Education: Virginia Military Institute, B.S., 1901; Army School of the Line, 1906–07; Army Staff College, 1907–08*
- *Military service: U.S. Army—second lieutenant, 1902; captain, 1916; operations officer of the 1st Division, 1917; lieutenant colonel, 1918; chief of staff of VIII Corps; aide-de-camp to General John Pershing, 1919–24; assistant commandant of Infantry School, 1927–32; colonel, 1933; major general, 1938; chief of staff of the army, 1939–45; general, 1939; five-star general, 1944*
- *Died: October 16, 1959, Washington, D.C.*

George Catlett Marshall, Jr., was the greatest chief of staff the U.S. Army has ever had. Although he graduated from Virginia Military Institute rather than from West Point, which is usually seen as a career liability, Marshall's service in

World War I established him as one of the Army's most brilliant staff officers. However, his lack of seniority and the Army's glacial promotion system meant that he did not become a general until he had served 32 years as a commissioned officer.

After World War I, with one exception, he served mostly in obscure posts before becoming chief of staff. During his years at the Army's Infantry School, he invented new doctrines and tactics for the Army. He made the holding attack the tactic of choice. During such an attack, one group of men advanced and pinned the enemy down with fire. Meanwhile, a second group tried to hit the enemy in the flank or rear. If possible, a third group would be held in reserve.

Marshall also experimented with infantry battalions to determine their optimum size, which proved to be about 850 men—the standard still used today in most armies. He disliked the U.S. Army's World War I "square" infantry division of four regiments. His experiments established that a triangular division of three regiments was more mobile and efficient.

To make up for his divisions' smaller size Marshall added firepower: a field artillery battalion to each regiment, a heavy weapons company (mortars and machine guns) to each battalion, and a weapons platoon to each company. Later he attached a tank battalion to most infantry divisions. This addition gave the triangular division several times the firepower of its predecessor. It also met the needs of a holding attack, providing one unit for maneuver, one for fire support, and keeping one in reserve. The result of his labors was the work *Infantry in Battle* (1934), a text produced by the Infantry School that communicated his ideas and methods throughout the Army. It also laid the groundwork for Marshall's transforma-

tion of the Army when he became chief of staff in 1939.

As chief, Marshall rebuilt the Army from scratch. Working with a small core of professional officers, and with ideas tested in the excellent army schools, he built a mighty weapon. Its basis was the 12 million citizen-soldiers who would serve under him during the war, the best-educated men of any army.

Between 1900 and 1920 there had been a revolution in U.S. education, with free public high schools becoming open to nearly everyone. Marshall had seen the results firsthand when he was assigned to Roosevelt's Civilian Conservation Corps in 1933, which put unemployed young men to work on outdoor projects. He was impressed by these youngsters and as chief of staff based the Army's training camps and schools on the assumption that they would make fine troops. A well-educated soldiery would become the U.S. Army's invisible weapon.

Winston Churchill called Marshall "the architect of victory," which was generous, considering how often they were at odds over military planning. Marshall was distinguished by his intelli-

General George Marshall hurries to his car following a conference at Mena House in Cairo, Egypt, 1943.

gence, fairness, strength of character, and integrity. Most who worked for or with him held Marshall in awe and were at least slightly afraid of him, not because he was a bully (although he did have a temper), but because to fail Marshall was unthinkable.

Despite being aloof and formal, Marshall brought out the best in his senior officers. Most owed their appointments and promotions to having previously impressed him. Two hundred men that he met at Fort Benning, Georgia, alone would become generals, their names taken from a little black book in which he recorded his opinions. Even though he lacked the common touch, Marshall was respected by Congress for his knowledge, authority, and directness. This high regard was of immense value to President Franklin D. Roosevelt.

After Pearl Harbor was attacked in December 1941, Marshall wished to focus all the Army's energy on invading France. From the start he resisted Churchill's efforts to involve the Allies in Mediterranean operations. Events and political necessity prevented Marshall from getting his way, however.

Public outrage over the attack on Pearl Harbor meant that the Pacific War would be waged on a far greater scale than Marshall desired. Operations in Europe would suffer accordingly. At the same time, Roosevelt could not wait until 1943—the earliest year when the Allies would be strong enough to land in France—to begin the war against Hitler. Apparently he feared that unless U.S. troops went into action against Germany within a year, the public pressure to put the Pacific war first would become irresistible. If speed was of the essence, then, as it probably was, the British plan to invade French North Africa filled the bill. It could be launched in 1942. It would involve fighting at least a few Germans. And it

would require a buildup of forces that could later be used to invade France.

Marshall fought hard against what became Operation Torch, but he was overruled by Roosevelt. Torch began in November 1942. However, instead of the quick victory that Marshall needed for Operation Roundup, his projected attack on France, the war in North Africa bogged down. Victory finally came in May 1943, perhaps just in time to launch Roundup in August or September. But Roosevelt agreed with Churchill that with all the firepower at hand, the Allies might as well invade Italy, which they did beginning with the island of Sicily in July. The invasion of the Italian mainland in September was by then inevitable.

Marshall and the War Department resented every one of these steps. He rightly guessed that in the end Torch would doom Roundup. But after Italy, Marshall and his planners were strong enough to insist that Operation Overlord, the new code name for the projected invasion of France, go forward without further delay. Churchill tried to drag his feet again, because he always preferred to fight in the Mediterranean, where fewer casualties could be expected. This time, however, the Americans would not be denied. On D-Day, June 6, 1944, the greatest amphibious attack in history was launched by General Dwight D. Eisenhower.

Everyone had expected that Marshall would command Overlord, with Eisenhower replacing him as chief of staff. But when it came to the moment of decision, President Roosevelt wanted Marshall to remain at his side as chief of staff. On December 5, 1943, Roosevelt, who hated to deliver bad news, finally indicated to Marshall that he would be staying in Washington.

Marshall took the blow without flinching and continued to serve as brilliantly as before. Roosevelt had made the right decision, for Marshall really could not be spared. In effect, as the master U.S. planner and strategist he was running the war—and doing it better than anyone else could. Next to Roosevelt himself Marshall was the most indispensable man in the United States.

By the same token, many soldiers had died in the Mediterranean in order for Eisenhower to learn his job. This had been much too expensive an education to waste. He was better qualified than Marshall to be the supreme commander. Having appointed the right men to the right jobs, FDR kept them there.

Because Marshall participated in making almost every strategic decision, his biography comes close to being a history of the U.S. war effort. However, when things went wrong it was rarely because Marshall had erred. More often it was because, for whatever reason, he had not been involved. This was true even in matters far removed from grand strategy and army building. For example, one explanation that has been offered for the failure to provide U.S. troops in Europe with a good tank is that Marshall was not interested in weapons. The implication is that if Marshall had been as interested in weaponry as he was in strategy and tactics, all the U.S. ground and air weapons would have been the best. But Marshall was overworked as it was and had to delegate authority in so many areas that he could not afford to look at any smaller pictures.

A greater pity is that Marshall never took the issue of strategic bombing very seriously. He treated the Army Air Forces as a separate service in most respects. This approach allowed the "bomber barons" of the air force a free hand to kill German and Japanese civilians in great numbers, to little real purpose. Marshall's indifference was shared by Roosevelt, which seems equally strange. Both had fought

hard for air power before Pearl Harbor, at a time when Congress was reluctant to pay for it. But once the great air forces had been built, neither paid much attention to how they were used. At the top, only Secretary of War Henry Stimson worried about killing civilians, and most of his cries fell on deaf ears.

On the big strategic issues Marshall was usually right. He correctly opposed the Mediterranean operation on military grounds. He was convinced that however necessary it was for political reasons to invade North Africa, taking Sicily made little sense and Italy even less. If Operation Roundup had gone forward in 1943 it would have been against a relatively easy target, for France had significantly weaker defenses in 1943 than it would a year later.

Even so, had Marshall not kept everyone focused, there might have been no Operation Overlord at all, or perhaps not until 1945. This seems to be what Churchill had in mind, as by then the Soviets would have all but finished the Nazis off. Of course, they would also have overrun most of Europe as well, a significant drawback to the Mediterranean strategy Churchill favored.

Marshall was right about the atomic bomb as well. Had it not been used against Japan, the Pacific war would have had one of two possible conclusions. One scenario was that the planned invasion would have gone ahead, with hideous casualty tolls for the Allies and worse for the Japanese. The only other alternative was to let the blockade and the air attacks do their work. This tactic would have resulted in victory, no doubt, but would have taken considerable time. During that time Americans would have been getting killed every day in various parts of the Pacific and Southeast Asia. And Japanese civilians would have been dying too, from conventional bombs and starvation and disease as Japan's transportation system collapsed.

Marshall was a great talent scout. Douglas MacArthur had been forced on him by the public. But most of the Army's other commanders were men Marshall knew personally and whose careers he had advanced. Recognizing Dwight D. Eisenhower's worth was certainly his biggest coup.

Eisenhower was a very junior general when Marshall picked him to command Operation Torch, and he seemed an unlikely choice. However, Marshall had watched Eisenhower closely in Washington and given him more and more important jobs. When he finally gave Eisenhower what proved to be the prize appointment of the war, it was because the general had performed superbly.

Likewise, the corps command that Marshall gave George S. Patton for Torch, which seems so obvious an appointment now, was hardly a unanimous choice at the time. Patton had done brilliant work in maneuvers and training troops. Yet many officers regarded him as too unstable and eccentric to lead men into battle. Patton was, indeed, profane, theatrical, and given to making peculiar remarks and gestures. Marshall believed that much of this was only for show, however, and that in the field Patton would be business-like and effective—as he had been in World War I. Patton—and others too, although less spectacularly—would more than repay Marshall's confidence.

Marshall was indeed the "architect of victory" in many ways: a hugely gifted planner and manager, farsighted, incisive, unique. He was a model officer as well, notable for his enormous integrity, selflessness, and devotion to duty—the noblest Roman of them all. In a war led by showoffs of every kind, Marshall's character stood out. As a soldier-statesman (he would serve as secretary of state and secretary of defense in the darkest years of the Cold War following World War II) he was second only to Eisenhower. As a man he was second to none.

SEE ALSO

Eisenhower, Dwight D.; Japan, surrender of; MacArthur, Douglas; Mediterranean theater; Patton, George S.; Roosevelt, Franklin Delano; Strategic bombing

FURTHER READING

Eisenhower, Dwight D. *Dear General: Eisenhower's Wartime Letters to Marshall.* Baltimore: Johns Hopkins University Press, 1971.
Marshall, George C. *Infantry in Battle.* Washington, D.C.: The Infantry Journal, 1934.
Pogue, Forrest C. *George C. Marshall.* 4 vols. New York: Viking, 1963–87.

Medicine

As in most wars, disease and accidents were more common in World War II than battle wounds. Two-thirds of hospital admissions—on both sides—resulted from sickness or injuries not received in combat. Typhus was the scourge of the eastern front, while in North Africa dysentery, hepatitis, malaria, and skin diseases were rampant, especially among the Germans.

Malaria was universal throughout Asia and the South Pacific. There was no cure for it, but antimalaria drugs existed, as did mosquito nets. The failure to provide either of these to U.S. and Filipino troops defending Bataan in 1942 had ruinous consequences. Hospital admissions for malaria ranged from 500 to 1,000 a day. Up to 80 percent of the troops on the line are thought to have been infected with it. Along with shortages of food and ammunition, disease was the main reason why the Bataan garrison surrendered when it did.

Venereal diseases have been a problem throughout history for almost every army, including those of the United States. Prevention was the best approach, especially because penicillin did not become widely available until 1944. The military staged propaganda campaigns designed to create "syphilophobia," and thereby frighten men into abstinence. These drives proved ineffective, however, for troops facing death in battle could not be made to fear a curable social disease.

Rejecting inductees found to be suffering from syphilis, for example, was not workable either. Of the first 2 million men inducted, 48 in every 1,000 had it, and among blacks the rate was 272 per thousand. Most black inductees were from the South, and southern males, black and white, had a venereal disease rate four times that of northerners. Early in 1942, the Army began treating infected men instead of declaring them 4F (physically unfit for induction). By 1945, 170,000 inductees had been cured of syphilis, a process that took about 10 days (before antibiotics became available).

Prevention was effective too. Once the military conceded that enlisted men could not be scared away from having sex, it established hundreds of prophylactic stations in the United States as well as overseas to treat men medically after intercourse. Large quantities of condoms were passed out as well—some 50 million a month—and became so popular that by the end of the war demand outstripped supply.

Although the commonsense approach to social disease offended religious groups, the military could not afford to give it up. Thus, while in 1940 the venereal disease rate for the army was 42.5 cases for every 1,000 men, by 1943 it had fallen to 24. For the entire war it came to 37 per 1,000, about the same rate as among civilians. In 1940, for every 1,000 soldiers, 1,278 days a

year were lost on account of venereal disease, but by 1943 the figure was only 368. This improvement was a public health victory of great importance.

Many medical gains in this period were directly related to the war. Penicillin was still in the research stage when war broke out, which inspired the British scientists involved to redouble their efforts. Because manufacturing the drug was beyond Britain's means, it was arranged for a U.S. firm to do so. As a result of crash programs, wounded soldiers were being treated in the field with penicillin as early as 1943. Progress was also made in surgery and anesthetics.

No achievement was more impressive than the new treatments devised for combat fatigue, known to the army as neuropsychiatric cases, or NP, for short. Although wounded rates were higher in Europe, NP disorders were more frequent in the Pacific, which was a far worse environment in which to fight.

Venereal disease became a serious medical problem as the military spread throughout the globe, and posters such as this one conveyed the message that time lost to disease gave the Axis a winning advantage.

After three months of combat on New Georgia in the Solomon Islands, a force of 30,000 men had 13,000 hospital admissions for illness and injury. Of these, 27 percent were wounded in action, 15 percent were otherwise injured, 21 percent had malaria, 18 percent diarrheal diseases, and 19 percent neuropsychiatric disorders. The incidence of NP cases on New Georgia was not exceptional by World War II standards, however, for it was a rule of thumb that the longer an action lasted the more NPs there would be, regardless of other conditions.

In Europe the Army would experience 110,000 NP cases as a whole, but they were highly concentrated. During one 44-day period of intense combat on the Gothic Line in Italy, 54 percent of all casualties were neuropsychiatric.

The high incidence of NPs caught both psychiatrists and army leaders by surprise, despite the relatively large number of mentally damaged soldiers that World War I had produced. These had been so many and so serious that as late as 1942 some 58 percent of all patients in Veteran's Administration hospitals were World War I "shell shock" victims.

World War II psychiatrists believed they had developed a screening process that would keep most men liable to become NP cases out of the Army. Their confidence in this process was such that of 5.2 million men who appeared at army recruiting stations 1.6 million were rejected for "mental deficiencies." All the same, psychiatric discharges from the Army would be two and a half times as common as in the previous war.

Every army suffered from combat fatigue, which was inevitable given the horrors of modern war. But in addition to war itself, many NP cases resulted from how men were employed in it. The basic problem in the U.S. Army by 1944 was that a military manpower shortage

led to men keeping men in action for excessive periods of time. Even before doctors thought to address the problem, officers had noticed that men reached their peak of efficiency after about 90 days on the line. Then they all started to deteriorate, regardless of their individual strength or courage. A survey of platoon leaders in two veteran infantry divisions carried out by the Army Research Bureau revealed that when asked which soldiers they would most hate to lose, the greatest concentration among enlisted men was those with four to five months of experience (including days spent in rear areas).

Both groups reached their highest level of performance between their third and seventh months, and after eight months they were less effective than men with less combat time. Contrary to the earlier view that some individual types of men were predisposed to break down, it was now found that after enough time in battle—with 200 days being about the maximum, and somewhere between 140 and 180 the average—everyone broke down. Mental health experts recommended that men be given more time behind the lines to ease the stress of battle, and doctors wanted soldiers to be rotated home before they reached the breaking point. But in an Army where there were never enough riflemen to go around, these proposals were out of the question.

Although the Army did not change its way of doing business, psychiatrists did, introducing more aggressive therapies. North African NP casualties had initially been sent to hospitals hundreds of miles to the rear, from which fewer than 10 percent returned to duty. Later, a series of psychiatric care levels were established that started with battalion surgeons operating close to the front. They provided psychiatric first aid, consisting mostly of mild sedation, a good night's sleep, and hot food.

More serious cases went to division clearing stations two to five miles farther back, where they were sedated longer and allowed to bathe. For tough cases the next level of treatment was at "exhaustion centers," where patients might receive actual psychiatric treatment. Then, after a week or 10 days, if all else had failed, the most seriously disturbed went into neuropsychiatric hospitals, from which they seldom returned to combat.

This approach produced impressive results, with about 60 percent of NPs returning to their outfits within five days. Some 70 percent of those hospitalized were later given noncombat assignments, where they replaced men fit for battle. By revolutionizing neuropsychiatric care, U.S. doctors made their biggest contribution to victory.

Improvements in conventional medicine also helped soldiers recover, but they were offset to a large degree by developments in weaponry and munitions. Thus, despite the fact that by World War II medical care had progressed enormously since the 1860s, battlefield death rates remained similar to those of the Civil War. It was only in psychiatry and hospital treatment that doctors made real advances.

FURTHER READING

Herman, Jan K. *Battle Station Sick Bay: Navy Medicine in World War II.* Annapolis, Md.: Naval Institute Press, 1997.

Mediterranean theater

Even before Pearl Harbor, the U.S. Army had been planning to defeat Hitler by invading France. A war with Japan, should it take place, was to be a holding action until Hitler was defeated. General George C. Marshall, the army's chief of staff, wanted that invasion to take place in 1943. In the meantime, troops and munitions would be assembled in Britain until the invasion date. The code name for this planned attack was Operation Roundup.

British prime minister Winston Churchill, on the other hand, wanted to concentrate on the Mediterranean. Because the Axis powers controlled the Mediterranean's western approaches, British ships could not use the Suez Canal and thus had to go the long way to India around South Africa. Furthermore, campaigns in the Mediterranean would support Britain's Eighth Army, which had been fighting Rommel in the western deserts of Egypt for months. Churchill always represented the Mediterranean as a place of wonderful opportunities for the Allies, but the Americans were skeptical.

Many believed that Churchill's enthusiasm derived from the belief that Britain would not sustain huge casualties in the Mediterranean. This relative safety made it preferable to western Europe, which the Germans would fight hard to retain and where big losses could be expected.

However, waging a series of small campaigns in the Mediterranean while Soviet Russia did most of the fighting against Hitler's legions in Europe did not seem like a good idea to General Marshall. Further, the U.S. Army's heritage was one of directly engaging the enemy with maximum force and battering it into submission, not gradually wearing it down. It had done this in the Civil War and World War I and planned to do so again in this one.

The strategic decision was up to Roosevelt, who came down on Churchill's side, ordering that North Africa be invaded in 1942. This cam-

During the invasion of Sicily on July 11, 1943, an American cargo ship is hit by a bomb from a German plane and its cargo of munitions explodes.

paign would be known as Operation Torch. Roosevelt did not deny Marshall's point that making war on the margins of his empire would do little to weaken Hitler. But President Roosevelt had serious political problems. He had promised Stalin to open a second front in Europe in 1942, which the Soviets desperately wanted, and there was no possibility of invading France that year.

Furthermore, if no U.S. troops went into action against Germany until 1943, there would be great pressure on Roosevelt to send additional men and munitions to the Pacific. Americans hated the Japanese even more than the Nazis, and American planners always had to struggle to keep the Pacific war from overwhelming the strategically much more important struggle with Germany. An invasion of French North Africa would be easy, at least if Germany did not come in. Such a drive could be represented, however feebly, as a second front, and would justify a military buildup that could later be used to invade France.

The polls bore out Roosevelt. In February 1943, after U.S. troops had been mauled in Tunisia and the Allies were facing some 250,000 Axis troops there, 53 percent of Americans still thought Japan was the United States's

"chief enemy," with only 34 percent nominating the Germans. Thus, if the North African operations were mainly political, they remained essential for just that reason.

On the larger issue of 1943, Marshall cannot be faulted. The victories in North Africa and the Mediterranean added the equivalent of 2 million tons of shipping when the Suez Canal finally became accessible as a result of them, but they otherwise did little to defeat Hitler. It was clear that Germany had to be beaten in Europe. The more time that was spent on campaigns at the edges of western Europe, the longer the war would last. Hence the importance of Roundup and the danger posed by Torch.

In its final form, Torch, under the command of Marshall's favorite, Lieutenant General Dwight D. Eisenhower, became larger than Marshall desired but was a more cautious affair than if Britain had gotten its way. The plan was for three task forces of 35,000 to 40,000 men each to land simultaneously at widely separated points. A western task force would sail directly from the United States to land near Casablanca, on the Atlantic coast of Morocco. A central task force, also consisting entirely of U.S. troops, would sail from

Britain to Oran, on the Mediterranean coast. And a joint Anglo-American eastern task force would seize Algiers.

The great flaw in this plan, as the British had maintained from the start and Eisenhower soon realized, was that taking Casablanca offered no important benefits. Tunisia, only 100 miles from Sicily and the best place for a German buildup, was the real strategic prize. If the Allies could arrive there first, Hitler would lose General Erwin Rommel's army and with it North Africa. But Marshall was firm about not pursuing this course, thinking Tunisia too much of a risk, so the best chance of making Torch pay off was lost before it started.

Everyone hoped that the French forces in North Africa would welcome the Allies as liberators. The problem was that these forces were under the command of the Vichy occupation government, which collaborated with the Nazis. Complex negotiations designed to win over the Vichyites in North Africa preceded Operation Torch. Admiral Jean Darlan, the head of France's armed forces, which still had a powerful fleet in Toulon, France, that the Allies wanted, was also approached by the Allies. But the Allies, justifiably afraid of leaks, did not entrust their French contacts with the date. Therefore, on November 8, 1942, when the landings commenced, what the French would do was still uncertain.

Admiral Darlan, who by accident was in Algiers on November 8, initially ordered his forces to resist, then that evening announced a cease-fire in Algiers and two days later extended it throughout North Africa. However, Marshal Pétain in Vichy promptly canceled these instructions. Amid the resulting confusion in Oran and Morocco, fighting—some of it heavy—continued for days.

The Moroccan operation turned out to be a shambles, thanks to poor mili-

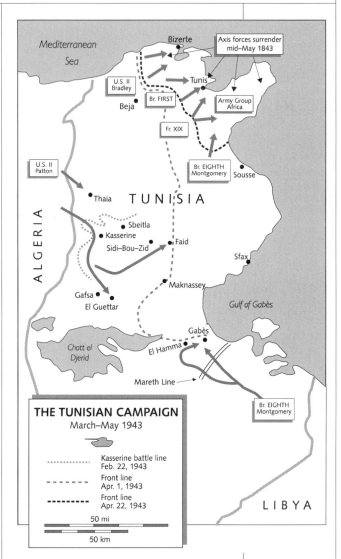

THE TUNISIAN CAMPAIGN
March–May 1943

.... Kasserine battle line
Feb. 22, 1943

– – – – Front line
Apr. 1, 1943

━ ━ ━ Front line
Apr. 22, 1943

50 mi

50 km

tary intelligence and inexperience, although its commander, Major General George S. Patton, Jr., would soon prove himself to be one of the war's outstanding combat leaders. Even so, luck was with the Americans. Along the treacherous Moroccan coast, the landing conditions were ideal, with the seas calmer than usual. The Vichy French could not bring their superiority in manpower to bear because of the lack of transportation and general confusion. Spain, which had 100,000 troops in its part of Morocco, chose not to enter the war. U.S. divisional commanders displayed initiative after failing to make contact with Patton, and American forces quickly gained control of the sea and air. The French defense collapsed after three days.

At this point the Germans immediately occupied the rest of France, ending the pretense that the Vichy government represented an independent country. But they did not secure the French fleet, which was scuttled in Toulon by French admirals. The Allies had hoped it would sail to join them, but destruction was the next best thing and one the Allies could live with.

General Eisenhower put Admiral Darlan in charge of French North Africa. He alone, the theory went, could guarantee an orderly transfer of authority and, most important of all, induce the Vichy troops in Tunisia, where there had been no Allied landings, to cooperate. The chances of this happening were fading fast on November 11 when Eisenhower made the Darlan appointment, but considering the stakes, a slim chance was better than none at all.

The French in Tunisia, however, decided to let German forces land, thus dooming the Allies to a long and bitter campaign instead of the walkover they had hoped for and needed. Had the French in Tunisia responded to Darlan's call, enabling the Allies to arrive there first, the infamous agreement would have been easier to take. Bad as it was in other respects, the worst thing about the "Darlan deal" was that it yielded few benefits. Democratic principles had been sacrificed in vain.

Luckily for the Allied cause, Darlan was soon assassinated by a French civilian. But because FDR hated Charles de Gaulle, the logical choice for leader of the Free French forces, General Henri Giraud was put in Darlan's place instead. Giraud was unacceptable to most of the French in North Africa, however, so de Gaulle brushed him aside and assumed power himself. Then, on November 9, 1943, de Gaulle created a government in exile, which in time would become the real government of France.

While all this intrigue progressed, the war continued. Only a few days before Operation Torch began, Britain's Lieutenant General Bernard Montgomery and his Eighth Army administered a severe defeat to General Rommel at El Alamein in the western desert of Egypt. El Alamein became the farthest point of Germany's advance in North Africa, and Britain's victory there ensured the safety of Egypt and the vital Suez lifeline.

Although it was slow off the mark, the Eighth Army eventually began pursuing Rommel while, from the opposite direction, Allied units advanced to within 12 miles of Tunis. Then the rainy season and stronger German defenses put the offensive on hold and gave Hitler time to send in more troops.

Hitler seems to have reinforced Tunisia because he could not bear to admit defeat or tolerate losses of territory. By doing so, he prolonged the fighting there for up to five additional months. During that time and partly because of the Tunisian campaign, the Allies abandoned their plan to invade France in 1943, thus enabling the Nazi regime to survive for an additional year. From this standpoint, Hitler's refusal to leave Africa proved to be a tactical mistake that, in one of war's cruel ironies, nevertheless brought him strategic benefits.

On May 11, 1943, the last Axis army in Tunisia surrendered, costing Hitler another 250,000 men, in addition to many more killed or evacuated because of wounds. The North Africa campaign had been messy, and long. During it the U.S. Army experienced what would turn out to be its only defeats by the German Army—losing at Sidi bon-Zid and at the Kasserine Pass in Tunisia in February.

Yet Operation Torch had paid for itself in many ways. By committing so many resources to it, Hitler made Africa a significant front that eased the pressure on Russia. And in addition to ending in victory for the Allies, it was a valuable learning experience for U.S. commanders. Politically essential in any case, it might have been strategically important as well had it not led the Allies to invade Sicily and then the Italian mainland.

After Tunisia fell, General Marshall wished to move most of the Allied troops in Africa to Britain. From there they would be positioned to invade France some time in the summer of 1943. Doing so would have been feasible, for France was weakly defended at the time and the Allies already controlled the English Channel and much of the air over France. But U.S. leaders were uncertain about this course, whereas the British were united on the need to take Sicily, which would strengthen the Allied grip on the entire Mediterranean. FDR therefore gave his consent to the invasion, code named Operation Husky.

It might have been possible to have both Husky and Overlord in the same year—if the Allies had moved at top speed. During the months before Tunisia fell, General Patton had been training troops in Morocco. These forces could have been used to take Sicily in May or early June, when it was undefended. Instead, the Allied high command scheduled Husky for July 10, by which time Germany had moved three divisions to the island.

The Sicilian campaign was poorly run. It took 43 days to defeat the Germans, most of whom then escaped to the Italian mainland. As Operation Roundup was now out of the question, the Allies invaded Italy next, partly because the British wanted it but partly through sheer momentum.

This series of bad decisions meant that the war would last for two more

years, whereas if Roundup had succeeded in 1943, it might have been over in one. Italy, which was supposed to have been an easy win, became a horror for the Allies. Some of the worst fighting of the war occurred there and it became a strategic liability, as some Americans had predicted it would. The Italian campaign used up divisions that would have been more useful in France. And, because the Italians under Allied control had to be supplied with food and fuel to stay alive, much of the shipping freed up by Operation Torch went to serve civilian instead of military purposes. The Mediterranean, a sea of dreams for Britain, thus became a nightmare for General Marshall and the U.S. War Department.

SEE ALSO

Casablanca conference; Italian campaigns; Sicily, Battle of

FURTHER READING

Blumenson, Martin. *Kasserine Pass.* Boston: Houghton Mifflin, 1967.
Carver, Michael. *Dilemmas of the Desert War: A New Look at the Libyan Campaign, 1940–42.* Bloomington: Indiana University Press, 1986.
Grigg, John. *1943: The Victory That Never Was.* New York: Hill & Wang, 1980.
Howard, Michael. *Mediterranean Strategy in the Second World War.* New York: Praeger, 1968.
Lucas, James. *War in the Desert: The Eighth Army at El Alamein.* New York: Beaufort, 1983.
Sainsbury, Keith. *The North African Landings, 1942.* Newark: University of Delaware Press, 1976

Midway, Battle of

Midway, the first great U.S. victory of the Pacific war, prevented Japan from renewing its march across the Pacific. It resulted from a decision by the Imperial Japanese Navy (IJN) to draw out the U.S. carriers. Attacking Midway, the westernmost of the inhabited Hawaiian islands, would lure the Pacific Fleet to its doom, Japanese naval leaders believed. Taking Midway would also close a gap in Japan's defensive screen through which a U.S. task force had slipped to launch 16 army medium bombers against Tokyo. This famous raid, led by Lieutenant Colonel James H. Doolittle on April 18, 1942, did little material damage. But in principle it had endangered Emperor Hirohito's life and humiliated the military. As a result, Midway, which some planners had thus far considered unimportant, overnight became an essential target.

On paper the IJN was impossible to beat at this stage of the war. For the attack on Midway, Admiral Isoroku Yamamoto would have at his disposal 11 battleships, 5 fleet carriers and 3 light aircraft carriers, 12 cruisers, 43 destroyers, and some 700 aircraft. The United States would be able to deploy only 3 fleet carriers with 233 combat aircraft, 8 cruisers, 15 destroyers, and a further 121 planes based on Midway Island.

To make matters worse for the Americans, the Japanese carriers were in prime condition and were manned by seasoned crews and aviators. On the other hand, although the USS *Enterprise* was in good shape, the *Yorktown* had been damaged at the Battle of the Coral Sea in May 1942, and the *Hornet* was brand new and its air group lacked experience. Worse still, by this time the Navy knew that its aircraft were inferior to those of Japan. The Grumman Wildcat fighter was no match for Japan's Zero, a splendid fighter plane that came as a nasty surprise to U.S. military leaders (although it shouldn't have because it had been used in China for years).

Even less effective was the obsolete Douglas Devastator, a torpedo plane that lacked self-sealing fuel tanks and was so slow that if unescorted it was easy to shoot down. In addition, the U.S. Navy's Mark XIII aerial torpedo had a small warhead, a tendency to rise to the surface of the water, unreliable firing mechanisms, and so little speed that at long range a Japanese ship could outrun it. The Japanese Long Lance torpedo was literally 10 times better. Japan's torpedo bomber, which Americans called the Kate, was also far superior to the Devastator. Only U.S. dive bombers were up-to-date.

Admiral Yamamoto, who had planned the brilliant attack on Pearl Harbor, this time came up with a poor one for Midway. Some of his vessels, including two light carriers, were to support an invasion of the Aleutian Islands off Alaska to mislead the U.S. Navy, four big carriers of his First Mobile Force were to bomb Midway, then a Midway occupation force was to take it. Far behind them would be the main body with a light carrier and the rest of the surface fleet. Thus, in the decisive carrier duel the odds would be about even, rather than overwhelmingly in Japan's favor if Yamamoto had assembled all his forces into one great fleet.

In addition to Japanese mistakes, the U.S. Navy would benefit from its mastery of cryptanalysis, or the breaking of codes. By April 1942, following a lapse, the code breakers at Station Hypo in Pearl Harbor, plus those in Washington and Australia, were once again reading many of the enemy's radio messages. Thanks to the code breakers, Admiral Chester Nimitz had been able to deploy his carriers to best advantage in the Coral Sea.

Now Naval Intelligence scored its greatest coup of the war, by decrypting Yamamoto's plan for Midway. Luckily, it had been sent over the air in full and the crack code breakers of Fleet Radio Unit, Pacific, headed by Commander Joseph J. Rochefort, could read it chapter and verse. As a result, when the U.S. carriers sailed, they knew exactly where to go. This time they—and not Vice Admiral Chuichi Nagumo, who had commanded at Pearl Harbor and was doing so now at Midway—would do the unforeseen.

On May 27, 1942, *Yorktown* arrived at Pearl Harbor from the Coral Sea with internal damage and serious leaks caused by bomb explosions. The first estimate for repairs was that it would take 90 days. Nimitz gave the yard 72 hours. Fourteen hundred skilled workers immediately swarmed over the ship. On May 29th, on schedule, the *Yorktown* was out of drydock and loading fuel and replacement planes, acquiring an air group composed of elements from three different carriers. The next day, at 9:00 a.m., with hundreds of workmen still aboard (they would be taken off before the battle), it sailed for Midway.

Enterprise and *Hornet* were already at sea, under the command of Rear Admiral Raymond A. Spruance, who had never before been responsible for even a single carrier. Admiral William F. Halsey, an experienced and popular carrier leader, should have led at Midway, but he had come down with a skin disease. In choosing Spruance to replace Halsey, Admiral Nimitz found exactly the right commander, because Spruance would prove himself a master of carrier warfare.

Command of the battle was given to Rear Admiral Frank Jack Fletcher on the *Yorktown,* who made several important decisions, one of them being to have the two task forces operate separately and at a distance from each other. As a result, when the *Yorktown* came under attack the other two carriers would be out of

danger. However, the most important tactical decisions of this battle were made by Spruance, who, if he had done nothing more in his career, would still rank with the greatest U.S. admirals.

The strategic planning for Midway must be credited to Nimitz, who took the risk of placing full trust in his code breakers. He elected not to play it safe, despite the odds, but to defend Midway at all costs. He ordered his task forces to take their station northeast of Midway, out of range of enemy scouts, while aircraft from the island would do their searching for them. As he had hoped, the U.S. carriers retained the element of surprise and were well placed to strike the enemy as soon as it was discovered.

On June 3, a long-range Catalina Flying Boat spotted the Japanese Midway occupation force approaching and it was attacked all day by planes from the island, one of which managed to slightly damage a tanker. On June 4, Nagumo launched a strike against Midway. Soon after, another Catalina spotted his carriers at last. While the Japanese launched their strikes, the U.S. carriers, still undetected, turned southwest to close in on the enemy.

Nagumo's aircraft easily wiped out the obsolete Marine fighters based on Midway, but heavy antiaircraft fire destroyed 38 Japanese planes and put 30 more out of action. Nagumo was deprived of a third of his combat aircraft and now had fewer warplanes than the advancing U.S. carriers. In addition, he had to attack Midway again, because it had still not been put out of action. This meant having to rearm his torpedo planes with bombs and change the bombs of his dive bombers from armor piercing to high-explosive.

While this dangerous procedure was taking place, Nagumo was repeatedly attacked by planes from Midway, which did no damage to his fleet while suffering

TBF Avenger torpedo bombers first saw combat in the Battle of Midway. They were equipped with an electrical powered gun turret and an internal bomb-bay capable of carrying four 500 lb. bombs or an aerial torpedo.

heavy losses. At this point Nagumo was warned of the presence of at least one U.S. carrier. Although he had 36 dive bombers now ready to go, Nagumo, cautious as ever, chose to wait until all his planes had been fueled and rearmed once again with antiship bombs, so he could send out a balanced attack force. He did so in part because the U.S. planes attacking from Midway without fighter protection were being all but wiped out. Thus, by encouraging Nagumo to be conservative, the U.S. fliers at Midway made an important contribution to the battle despite their lack of hits.

Admiral Fletcher gave Spruance, whose task force was closer to the enemy, orders to attack it when he was ready. Given a free hand, Spruance decided to hit the Japanese early and hard, in hopes of catching them with their decks full of planes still being serviced. At the maximum range, his torpedo planes could fly and still have enough fuel to get back, so he launched everything he had—68 dive bombers, 30 torpedo planes, and 20 fighters—retaining only the Wildcats of his combat air patrol.

This bold decision was a difficult one, for it meant that the torpedo planes might not have the fuel to make it back if they had to alter their course. The fighters too were jeopardized: as it happened, all the *Hornet*'s fighters would be forced to ditch in the ocean. After a slow and ragged start, which obliged Spruance to

order his squadrons to attack singly instead of in air groups, his planes were off by 8:00 a.m. Fletcher began launching a much smaller force at 8:30.

The U.S. squadrons were supposed to time their flights so that the dive bombers went in ahead of the vulnerable torpedo planes, which would then attack under fighter protection. But many pilots lacked the experience needed to bring three different types of aircraft with different flying speeds and launching times to the target in formation, and some squadrons lost sight of each other. Because Nagumo had changed course and Midway had neglected to report this to Spruance, the *Hornet*'s fighters and dive bombers never found their targets.

These mistakes left Lieutenant Commander J. C. Waldron's squadron, Torpedo 8, on its own. It was a green unit, with most of its pilots having never taken off with a torpedo aboard, let alone fired one in combat. Although they knew they were flying to almost certain death, not one held back when Waldron led them into battle. All 15 U.S. planes were destroyed, and few if any of them even released their torpedoes. Only one man from Torpedo 8 lived to tell the story.

Torpedo 6, from the *Enterprise*, made the next run. Unlike Waldron's men, these were experienced aviators, but without fighter support all that their skilled piloting could do was to save 4 of the 14 planes that attacked, with none scoring a hit.

The *Yorktown*'s Torpedo 3 arrived last, escorted by six fighter planes of Fighting 3 led by Lieutenant Commander James Thach, whose obsolete Wildcats were heavily outnumbered by the superior Japanese Zeros. Torpedo 3 lost 10 of its 12 Devastators, again without hitting a target. But at that moment, 10:22 a.m.,

Thach recalled, he saw a glint in the sun and then a "beautiful silver waterfall." It was the dauntless dive bombers of *Enterprise* and *Yorktown* screaming down through the empty sky.

By pure accident, the *Yorktown*'s air group had arrived at the same time as Lieutenant Commander Clarence McClusky of the *Enterprise* and his 32 dive bombers, who had finally found the Mobile Force after a desperate search in which they had used up most of their fuel. As the Japanese combat air patrol had been drawn down to sea level by the torpedo plane attacks, all four enemy carriers were for the moment unprotected.

Enterprise pilots delivered lethal blows to *Akagi* and *Kaga,* while planes from *Yorktown* left *Soryu* a flaming hulk. In three minutes the Pacific war had turned against Japan. Only *Hiryu* survived, to launch two waves against *Yorktown,* with her veteran pilots breaking through the U.S. defenses to put three bombs and two torpedoes into the great carrier. But the *Hiryu*'s moment of glory was brief. In the evening, 24 dive bombers from *Enterprise* and 10 from *Yorktown* found the last Japanese carrier and sent her to the bottom of the sea.

Yorktown failed to return from the battle of Midway. The ship survived two air attacks but was almost dead in the water when a Japanese submarine fired a round of torpedoes that sank the ship. Notwithstanding this major loss, Midway gave the IJN a blow from which it would never recover. With heavy odds against them, the Americans had inflicted much more harm than they suffered, losing one fleet carrier to the enemy's four, less than 1,000 men to the enemy's 3,000, and 150 aircraft (including those based on Midway) to Japan's 322.

Japan would desperately miss the more than 100 veteran pilots who were killed at a time when it had only 1,000 carrier pilots and was producing perhaps 100 more a year. The loss was also aggravated by the IJN's self-defeating habit of keeping its veteran flyers in action until they were killed or wounded. As the war progressed, its naval aviators became greener and greener, whereas those of the U.S. Navy, whose veterans were rotated home to train new pilots, became more numerous and skillful. Although Japan would build new carriers, its naval air arm was never again as good as it had been at Pearl Harbor. Midway was the United States's revenge for Pearl Harbor and the assurance of final victory. From that time on, the empire of Japan was forced to fight a war of defense.

SEE ALSO
Coral Sea, Battle of the; Pacific war

FURTHER READING
Barker, A. J. *Midway.* Englewood Cliffs, N.J.: Prentice-Hall, 1983.
Layton, Edwin T. *'And I Was There': Pearl Harbor and Midway—Breaking the Secrets.* New York: Morrow, 1985.
Prange, Gordon W. *Miracle at Midway.* New York: Penguin, 1982.

Mines

The land mine was a new weapon developed between the two world wars to attack tanks. Since antitank mines were large and relatively easy to find, antipersonnel mines, aimed at individual soldiers, were devised to protect their larger cousins.

The first use of mines in World War II was by Italian forces in North Africa. As a rule, mines were most common where tanks were in use, hence their presence in North Africa and on the eastern front. As antipersonnel mines were more likely to cripple than to kill, the Germans invented the "jumping" mine. This fiendish device was spring-loaded so that when a soldier stepped on its trigger, the mine flew up to chest level before exploding.

The Red Army was very short of mines when Germany invaded the Soviet Union in 1941. This lack forced Soviet troops to employ improvised gasoline bombs, known as Molotov cocktails, against German armor. But supply eventually caught up to demand, and by war's end, the Soviets were believed to have laid 200 million mines of all types.

Mine clearing has always been and continues to be a dangerous task. Electronic mine detectors existed as early as 1942 but were not always reliable. Then, too, the Germans began making wooden mines that were undetectable. Steel pipes filled with explosives, called Snakes or Bangalore torpedoes, could be pushed into suspect areas and set off to detonate mines. The British pioneered in developing tank appliances such as plows and drums, for example, to detonate mines quickly and safely.

The most effective British mine-clearing devices were flail tanks, which employed a rotating drum with chains attached to beat a path through minefields. The Soviets sometimes used untrained infantry, or punishment battalions, to clear minefields by marching through them. Other armies, however, employed more conventional methods.

Sea mines went back to the 19th century and were further refined during World War II. Most of the 500,000 sea mines laid during the war were contact mines: steel balls with hornlike detonators that went off when struck by a ship. Acoustic and pressure mines were usually parachuted in by low-flying aircraft. By 1944, however, Allied planes could

The mine sappers (demolition specialists) of the 82nd West African Division move forward on the road to Buthidaung, Burma. Mine detection was a dangerous task because equipment was not always reliable.

deliver mines while flying as high as 15,000 feet. American B-29s mined Japan's harbors and shallow waters so effectively in 1945 that even coastal traffic became severely limited.

Contact mines were cleared by sweep wires, hence the term *minesweeping*. Acoustic mines, which were set to explode when a ship's propellers were heard, could be detonated by sonic sweeps. Magnetic mines were likewise set off by magnetic sweeps, although the best defense was a technique known as degaussing, which removed the magnetic field of a steel ship.

Pressure mines were introduced by Germany in 1944. Against pressure mines, set off by the water pressure generated by a passing ship, there was only one defense—slowness. The only way found to deal with them was to decrease a ship's speed to the point where it did not change the water pressure enough to detonate a mine.

Mobilization

The United States was poorly prepared when it entered World War II. Before November 1940 the lack of preparation resulted from President Franklin D. Roosevelt's decision not to antagonize peace-loving Americans and isolationists who wanted to keep the United States out of the war. But even after he had won reelection for an unprecedented third term and no longer needed to be as concerned about the political effects of increased preparedness, he continued to drag his feet. Roosevelt could be exceedingly cautious politically, doing two contradictory things at once, such as delaying mobilization of the nation's resources while at the same time announcing the Lend-Lease program with Britain in December 1940. At that time the United States had barely begun to convert its industries to war production. It could not arm itself yet, much less anyone else.

Baby steps toward preparation
Roosevelt's method of preparing for war, a baffling one, was to keep creating new agencies without giving them real power. On May 25, 1940, as France fell, Roosevelt created an Office of Emergency Management in the White House. This step seemed to mean that he intended to run the mobilization effort himself, which was obviously impossible. He did appoint prominent men to an advisory commission, but its weakness was such that the usual word used to describe it was *monstrosity*.

When the advisory commission's ineffectiveness could no longer be concealed, Roosevelt replaced it with something called the Office of Production Management (OPM), another monstrosity. A unique feature of the OPM was

that it had two directors, who were to carry out the orders of a four-man board, to which the co-directors belonged. Roosevelt was never able to explain to reporters how this contraption was supposed to work. Further, after the Lend-Lease bill passed, which made inflation a real threat, he created an Office of Price Administration and Civilian Supply instead of giving control of prices to the OPM.

In the meantime, contracts were being signed, production was rising, and shortages were becoming acute. For lack of central direction chaos reigned, and it was every industrialist for himself. Yet, on the other hand, many industries were not converting at all, notably the auto companies. Roosevelt's solution to bureaucratic confusion and production delays was, predictably, another monstrosity, the Supplies Priorities and Allocations Board (SPAB). Created on August 28, 1941, while the Soviet Union was fighting for survival, SPAB was meant to establish the policies that the OPM would then implement.

What mobilization required was a single agency with real power. What Roosevelt established instead was a bureaucratic maze with cross-appointments that bewildered even those who held them. For instance, FDR chose a businessman named Donald Nelson to be the executive director of SPAB, without relieving him of his post with the OPM. Thus, Nelson remained William Knudsen's subordinate as director of purchasing for the OPM, while becoming his superior as head of SPAB.

After Pearl Harbor was attacked in December 1941, it was obvious that a director of mobilization with real power had to be appointed. Thus, in 1942 Roosevelt created the War Production Board (WPB), with Donald Nelson as its head. But the WPB did not have sufficient authority either. The armed services con-

Guns and wingtips have not yet been added to some of the planes on this final assembly line for B-24E (Liberator) bombers at Ford's Willow Run plant.

tinued to place orders themselves, and Nelson was not up to his job. In the first six months of 1942, $100 billion worth of war contracts were placed, requiring levels of output that could not be achieved in one year—or possibly even two. Meanwhile, competition for scarce materials led to crippling shortages. To ease them Nelson put forward a Production Requirements Plan that, by allowing any manufacturer with a contract to set his own priorities, made everything worse.

It was time for yet another agency, the Office of Economic Stabilization, which Supreme Court Justice James F. Byrnes was appointed to direct. His job was to cut the rate of inflation in half, which he did with the Controlled Materials Plan (CMP). The CMP established a strict priority system for three vital materials—steel, copper, and aluminum—which were doled out according to the user's order of importance. This approach gave Byrnes control over production. Thanks to the CMP, munitions production reached a level of $60 billion in 1943 and rather more than that in 1944. Little known at the time and quickly forgotten, the CMP was critical to the entire war effort.

A potentially crippling shortage of rubber was solved after Roosevelt appointed a special committee to investigate the problem. It was headed by Bernard Baruch, a Wall Street speculator who had been the mobilization czar in World War I and was widely respected. It recommended that synthetic rubber be made of petroleum and called for a rubber administrator to be named by the WPB. Nelson was appointed to this position. The committee wanted a national speed limit of 35 miles per hour to save wear and tear on tires and a gasoline rationing program sufficient to bring down the average distance traveled by automobiles from 6,700 to 5,000 miles a year.

Given a green light, Nelson moved quickly for once, and although only 234,000 tons of synthetic rubber would be manufactured in 1943, annual production ultimately rose to 800,000 tons. Meanwhile, gasoline rationing stretched the natural rubber supplies to cover the gap.

Finally, Roosevelt took a decisive step. In May 1943 he created the Office of War Mobilization (OWM), with Byrnes as its head. The WPB remained in place, but under the OWM's direction. To general surprise, the OWM proved to be workable. At long last, the nation finally had a mobilization czar with real authority. Byrnes brought order out of chaos, at least to the degree Roosevelt permitted, and industrial mobilization proceeded at an accelerating pace.

Military mobilization Military mobilization was an easier job than the civilian effort. When the war in Europe broke out in 1939, the U.S. Army had fewer than 190,000 men in uniform. By 1940, after the fall of France, anyone could see that the military had to grow enormously and quickly. Yet, with isolationist sentiment strong, the President was reluctant to act himself and would not let Democratic legislators do so either. Finally, after tireless lobbying by alarmed private citizens, two Republicans—Representative James Wadsworth of New York and Senator Edward R. Burke of Nebraska—introduced a bill providing for a military draft.

That Roosevelt was being overcautious is suggested by the fact that a poll taken just before passage of the Burke-Wadsworth bill showed that 71 percent of Americans favored the bill, including 65 percent of males aged 16 to 25—the very men who would be drafted. Thus encouraged, Roosevelt endorsed the bill, as did Republican candidate for president Wendell Willkie. This act required considerable courage on Willkie's part, because his chances for victory depended to a large extent on winning the isolationist vote.

Roosevelt signed the Burke-Wadsworth bill into law on September 16, 1940. The National Guard and Organized Reserve were called up at that time as well. In this manner an army that numbered 270,000 officers and men in 1940 was five times that size a year later. There was a close call in the summer of 1941 when the House extended the original one-year enlistment of draftees by only a single vote. Still, Burke-Wadsworth did the job. For the next four years, training this new army, not raising it, would be the foremost problem.

SEE ALSO

Byrnes, James F.; Financing the war; Labor; Selective Service System

FURTHER READING

Flynn, George Q. *The Mess in Washington: Manpower Mobilization in World War II.* Westport, Conn.: Greenwood, 1979.
Janeway, Eliot. *The Struggle for Survival: A Chronicle of Economic Mobilization in World War II.* New Haven: Yale University Press, 1951.
Miller, Sally M., and Daniel A. Cornford, eds. *American Labor in the Era of World War II.* Westport, Conn.: Praeger, 1995.
Schwartz, Jordan A. *The Speculator: Bernard M. Baruch in Washington, 1917–1965.* Chapel Hill: University of North Carolina Press, 1981.

Montgomery, Bernard Law

COMMANDER OF THE 21ST ARMY GROUP, 1944–45

- *Born: November 17, 1887, London, England*
- *Political party: Conservative*
- *Education: Royal Military College at Sandhurst, 1908; Staff College, 1920*
- *Military service: British Army— subaltern, 1908; lieutenant, 1914; brigade-major, 1916; lieutenant colonel, 1931; colonel, 1934; major general, 1938; commander of II Corps, 1940; lieutenant general, 1942; commander of Eighth Army, 1942; general, 1943; commander of Allied ground forces, 1944; field marshal, 1944; Commander of the 21st Army Group, 1944–45*
- *Died: March 24, 1976, Alton, Hampshire, England*

Montgomery was the leading British field commander in the Mediterranean and European theaters. Extremely popular with his troops and the British public, Montgomery was despised by most U.S. commanders by his headline-grabbing boasts at their expense. Even by U.S. standards he was unusually cautious and slow-moving.

Efficient, hard working, and a meticulous planner, Montgomery first gained fame as the commander of Britain's Eighth Army in North Africa. His May 4, 1942, defeat of General Erwin Rommel, who had so often defeated British commanders in the past, made Montgomery a world figure. His victory at El Alamein in the western desert of Egypt

Field Marshal Montgomery (left) greets Prime Minister Mackenzie King of Canada in May 1944. Montgomery was much better at internal diplomacy than many of his peers, especially Patton.

was the first major success on land of the British Army in World War II.

Montgomery won El Alamein by battering away at the German lines with overwhelming force until they finally broke. This was typical of his methods, as was the fact that he had no plans to exploit his victory and allowed Rommel to get away. It would take almost another year to seize Rommel's army.

After Montgomery's victory over Rommel, he led the Eighth Army through Sicily in 1943, and then to the Italian mainland. Next he took part in the planning for D-Day, the landing in Normandy to free France. During this campaign, called Operation Overlord, he commanded all Allied ground forces as well as the 21st Army Group, which consisted primarily of British and Canadian divisions. It was supposed to break out of the landing area into the open country beyond Caen, soon after D-Day on June 6, 1944. But his divisions were too slow and the Germans too quick, so Montgomery failed to take Caen. As a result, he ended up playing a supporting role, tying down large numbers of German troops in the north while U.S. forces broke out of southern Normandy.

The U.S. breakout in early August, led by Lieutenant General George Pat-

ton's Third Army, was so sudden, and Patton moved so quickly, that most of the German forces in northern France were caught in what was called the "Falaise pocket." They might have remained trapped there, but again Montgomery's divisions moved too slowly, and by the time they arrived, most of the Germans had escaped.

In the hot pursuit that followed, the 21st Army Group captured Antwerp, Belgium, on September 4, giving the Allies an undamaged port, which they desperately needed. Then Montgomery ordered his forces to halt for refueling. During the two days that elapsed, the Germans fortified the 60-mile-long Scheldt estuary that linked Antwerp to the sea. It would take months of hard fighting for the Canadians to clear its banks, during which time the Allied campaign bogged down for want of supplies and fuel.

Montgomery was bitterly disappointed over being relieved on September 1, 1944, as the commander of Allied ground troops, although this assignment had never been intended as anything more than a temporary job. He was further embittered by Eisenhower's "broad-front strategy." Instead of having the army groups being treated more or less equally, Montgomery wanted to receive most of the available supplies, and at least two U.S. armies, for a single thrust at Berlin.

When Eisenhower refused to play favorites, Montgomery ordered Operation Market-Garden, in hopes of getting his way. The plan was to drop a carpet of airborne troops along the route to Arnheim on the Rhine. Arnheim and its precious bridges would be seized, too, putting the 21st Army Group on the high road to Berlin. But the plan, which was launched on September 17, 1944, was far too ambitious. Lightly armed paratroopers did seize one end of a bridge at Arnheim, but they could not hold it. And they could not be relieved, because Montgomery's XXX Corps, stalled on one-lane roads, failed to break through as planned. Even Montgomery admitted that he was to blame for this defeat.

Throughout the fall of 1944, Montgomery continued to pester Eisenhower with demands for a single thrust on Berlin, antagonizing every U.S. commander with his complaints, demands, and insults. His misbehavior finally came to a head during the Battle of the Bulge. The Germans attacked in the Ardennes Forest on December 17, cutting off General Omar Bradley, the U.S. 12th Army Group commander, from his First and Ninth armies. Eisenhower then gave temporary command of them to Montgomery, which was a big mistake. Montgomery did little during the battle except to spoil Eisenhower's plan for capturing the German force.

Eisenhower's strategy was for General Patton's Third Army to drive north up the base of the Bulge while Montgomery drove south. But once again Montgomery jumped off too late and with too little strength to meet the Third Army in time. Instead, the Bulge was simply flattened by repeated U.S. attacks.

In the course of the fighting Montgomery made such extreme demands, and treated Eisenhower with such contempt, that he nearly lost his job. In no way humbled by this close call, he followed it up by holding a press conference to explain how he had won the battle. This was too much even for Prime Minister Winston Churchill, who at once made a point of describing the Battle of the Bulge as a great *U.S.* victory.

Eisenhower, generous to a fault, planned to give Montgomery priority in crossing the Rhine, the last barrier to an Allied victory. But, as usual, Montgomery spent so long preparing his attack that Bradley's 12th Army Group crossed the Rhine first. By the time Montgomery launched his offensive, the 12th Army Group had crossed the Rhine and was well into an offensive that captured hundreds of thousands of German soldiers and large portions of German territory. So it was that the 21st Army Group ended up playing only a supporting role, yet again.

SEE ALSO

Bulge, Battle of; Eisenhower, Dwight D.; France, battle of; Germany, battle of

FURTHER READING

Hamilton, Nigel. *Monty: The Battles of Field Marshal Bernard Montgomery.* New York: Random House, 1994.

Morgenthau, Henry T., Jr.

SECRETARY OF THE TREASURY

- *Born: May 11, 1891, New York, N.Y.*
- *Political party: Democratic*
- *Education: attended Cornell University*
- *Military service: none*
- *Government service: Chairman of New York State Agricultural Advisory Commission 1928–30; state conservation commissioner, 1930–32; head of Federal Farm Board, 1933; Secretary of the Treasury, 1933–45*
- *Died: February 6, 1967, Poughkeepsie, N.Y.,*

Henry Morgenthau's lack of education (he was a college dropout) and of any business or banking experience led many to claim that he was unfit to head the Treasury Department. However, he was comfortable with the job and, more important, was an old friend and neighbor of President Roosevelt who trusted him completely. That Morgenthau lived up to Roosevelt's expectations is shown by his long tenure in office.

During the war Morgenthau was generally responsible for the complicated programs that froze wages and prices, raised taxes, and sold bonds to cover the annual deficits. Three facts are the measure of his success: Inflation was brought under control; Government revenues covered a larger share of the war's costs than in any previous conflict; and interest rates remained low. Compared to most other war economies, that of the United States was extremely well managed, for which Morgenthau deserves more credit than anyone else.

A humane man, Morgenthau opposed, although he could not prevent, the internment of Japanese Americans. More than anyone else in the Roosevelt administration he drew attention to the Holocaust while it was going on. And Morgenthau was instrumental in the creation of the War Refugee Board, which saved hundreds of thousands of lives.

Morgenthau is perhaps best remembered for a proposal he completed on September 4, 1944. The Morgenthau Plan, as it was usually called, aimed at destroying Germany's ability to make war forever. After its defeat, Germany was to be both demilitarized and deindustrialized. Its surviving armament and heavy industrial plants would be dismantled. Key areas, such as East Prussia, the Saar, and Silesia would be given to neighboring states. The Ruhr basin, the seat of German industry, would be internationalized. What remained of Germany would be divided into two agricultural states.

Although this might have been what the Germans deserved, Morgenthau's plan would have punished much of western Europe as well. Without a strong German economy there was little hope of reviving the economies of Germany's former trading partners. In the postwar years this became common

knowledge, so Morgenthau's plan ended up on the shelf. Morganthau should be remembered for his years of faithful service to the nation, for his humanity, and for the outstanding job he did managing the finances of the United States during World War II.

SEE ALSO

Financing the war; Mobilization

FURTHER READING

Blum, John Morton. *Roosevelt and Morgenthau.* Boston: Houghton Mifflin, 1970.
———, ed. *From the Morgenthau Diaries.* 3 vols. Boston: Houghton Mifflin, 1959–67.
Morgenthau, Henry. *Mostly Morgenthaus: A Family History.* New York: Ticknor & Fields, 1991.

Mortars

A mortar is a weapon that fires only at angles above 45 degrees to the horizon. In World War II, these munitions were mainly smooth-bore as opposed to rifled-barrel weapons used by infantry to provide their own close support. The U.S. Army differed from most in that it had a rifled mortar.

Mortars around the world were much alike, consisting of a steel baseplate, a barrel, and a supporting bipod or tripod. The projectile, usually called a bomb, had a shotgun shell in its tail. When the bomb was dropped down the barrel, a firing pin set off the shotgun shell, which detonated the propellant.

Mortars were small as a rule, except those in the Red Army. Its mortars were up to 9.4 inches in size, equal to a naval gun. They were cheaper and easier to make than artillery, which is why the Soviets liked them.

Motion pictures

Radio and movies were the most important entertainment media during the war years, although radio was also a primary news medium. The government attempted to instruct, or indoctrinate, Americans with motion pictures, but in this effort it had little success.

The outstanding propaganda film was *Casablanca*, a purely commercial product of Hollywood's "dream factory." *Casablanca* succeeded as a movie, and still works today, because its anti-Nazi message is understated and woven skillfully into the plot. Touching at some points, stirring at others, *Casablanca* promoted the war effort by refusing to club its audience over the head. Typically, the government could not see this. It kept *Casablanca* from being shown in North Africa for fear of offending French citizens who had collaborated with the Nazis.

The federal government did sponsor some good documentaries, such as William Wyler's *Memphis Belle*, a film about the first B-17 to complete a tour of duty in Europe. Most of the combat documentaries were made by the armed forces themselves, aided by Hollywood directors and technical personnel. These include Commander John Ford's *The Battle of Midway*; *The Fighting Lady*, a carrier film that did well at the box office; and *To the Shores of Iwo Jima*.

Perhaps the best of these documentaries is *The Battle of San Pietro*, directed and narrated by John Huston. It graphically depicts the fight to take a single Italian village, including rare shots of dead GIs being wrapped in mattress covers. Some officers did not want *The Battle of San Pietro* to be shown to troops in training, for fear it would injure morale. Gen-

eral George C. Marshall overruled them, however, on the grounds that knowing what awaited them could only lead the men to take their training more seriously. Whether it did or not, the film testifies to what could be accomplished when talent was given free rein.

Most of the 2,500 motion pictures that Hollywood turned out during World War II were simply for entertainment. Hollywood never stopped making comedies and musicals, although after Pearl Harbor was attacked in December 1941, the war films increased in number. The peak year for war movies was 1943, after which they became fewer and better.

Except for *Casablanca*, most of the contemporary war films still worth seeing were produced in 1944 and 1945. *Lifeboat*, a political allegory by Alfred Hitchcock about the survivors of an engagement at sea who first rescue, but then are forced to kill, a U-boat commander, is particularly involving. But the most realistic and moving film was *The Story of G.I. Joe*. Based on a column by Ernie Pyle, a newspaperman who was very

Germany had its own propaganda film industry. The German documentary filmmaker Leni Riefenstahl created breathtaking worlds of Nazi domination in her films, yet after the war claimed to be only doing her job. Here she shoots footage for the 1934 classic Triumph of the Will.

popular with the troops, it vividly portrayed the infantryman's way of life and death. Most of the best films about World War II, however, were produced afterward, and long afterward in the case of *Patton, A Bridge Too Far,* and *Saving Private Ryan,* which are among the few that seem likely to last.

Most of the wartime films that people still enjoy are not actually about the war. They include *The Man Who Came to Dinner;* the Preston Sturgis satires *Sullivan's Travels* and *The Miracle of Morgan's Creek; National Velvet,* in which a very young and very beautiful Elizabeth Taylor rides her beloved horse Velvet to victory in the Grand National steeplechase; Bing Crosby's *Going My Way;* and *Yankee Doodle Dandy,* marked by James Cagney's exuberant portrayal of George M. Cohan, the songwriter who penned the song after which the picture was named.

Show business played a very important role in the war effort, lifting morale at home and in the theaters of war. After popular music, no form of entertainment meant more to the troops than American films. War films shown in war zones were likely to cause outbursts of rude GI humor. Otherwise, everything the dream factory produced was welcome overseas. Many men who worked in the film industry were drafted or, like Jimmy Stewart, a real hero, volunteered for combat. But entertainment was never more important than during the war, which justified the special treatment it got. Thus Hollywood was provided with ample film stock even when it was in short supply.

The movie star Betty Hutton visits sailors and Marines in the Marshall Islands in December 1944.

SEE ALSO

Music; Radio

FURTHER READING

Aldgate, Anthony. *Britain Can Take It: The British Cinema in the Second World War.* Edinburgh: Edinburgh University Press, 1994.

Beidler, Philip D. *The Good War's Greatest Hits: World War II and American Remembering.* Athens: University of Georgia, 1998.

Carnes, Mark, ed. *Past Imperfect: History According to the Movies.* New York: H. Holt, 1995.

Koppes, Clayton R., and Gregory D. Black. *Hollywood Goes to War: How Politics, Profits and Propaganda Shaped World War II Movies.* New York: Free Press, 1987.

WORLD WAR II MOVIE CLASSICS

Command Decision. MGM, 1948. The political challenges of an RAF general attempting to stop the production of Nazi jet planes. Starring Clark Gable and Brian Donlevy.

Das Boot. Columbia Pictures, 1981. The claustrophobic world of a German U-boat.

The Desert Fox. 20th Century Fox, 1950. Biopic following Erwin Rommel's career from the Afrika Korps to his part in the assassination attempt on Hitler to his subsequent suicide. Starring James Mason and Jessica Tandy.

Destination Tokyo. Warner Bros., 1944. In order to provide information for the first air raid over Tokyo, a U.S. submarine sneaks into Tokyo Bay and places a spy team ashore. Starring Cary Grant.

The Fighting Seabees. Republic Pictures, 1944. Construction workers in the treacherous Pacific Ocean build Seabees for the U.S. Army. Starring John Wayne.

Mister Roberts. Warner Bros., 1955. Life on a World War II cargo supply ship in the Pacific. Starring Henry Fonda and James Cagney.

Run Silent, Run Deep. United Artists, 1958. A U.S. sub commander, obsessed with sinking a certain Japanese ship, butts heads with his first officer and crew. Starring Clark Gable and Burt Lancaster.

Twelve O'Clock High. 20th Century Fox, 1949. Tenacious U.S. general leads daylight bombing raids over Germany. Starring Gregory Peck.

Munich agreement

SEE Appeasement; Germany

Music

Popular music flourished during the war and did much to raise people's spirits. For the men overseas it was the primary, and sometimes only, form of entertainment. Aboard ship, behind the front, and at home, radio and the 78-rpm record player were everywhere, despite a shortage of shellac, from which phonograph records were made. The banning of recorded music (to be substituted with public performances) in 1942 by the hated James C. Petrillo of the American Federation of Musicians only made records more popular. His was a vain, as well as unpatriotic, effort to save live recording studio bands from the technology that was replacing them.

During the war, people had money to spend but little to buy, which was good for the music business. Before the war, a hit song might sell 400,000 copies of sheet music, whereas during the war sales of 600,000 copies became usual. In 1944 sheet music sales were up 25 percent from the previous year.

Although this was still the golden age of popular music, to which composers like George Gershwin and Cole Porter had made superb contributions, most hits reflected considerably lower tastes. Among those that have mercifully faded from memory are "Goodbye, Mamma, I'm Off to Yokohama," "The Japs Haven't Got a Chinaman's Chance," and "When Those Little Yellow Bellies Meet the Cohens and the Kelleys."

The first hit song of the war was "Remember Pearl Harbor," but Frank Loesser had a much greater success with "Praise the Lord and Pass the Ammunition." It was based on an incident during the attack on Pearl Harbor when a chaplain ("sky pilot") supposedly manned an antiaircraft gun. In reality Captain William A. McGuire did not remember speaking these immortal words and had been passing ammunition himself rather than manning a gun. Whatever the case, the government loved it and even went so far as to ask radio stations not to overplay the song and thereby shorten its life. The most popular war song, "Der Führer's Face," featuring Donald Duck, was kept off the air for a time because censors were offended by sounds suggesting Donald was passing wind.

The later songs became more sentimental, an example being Irving Berlin's "I Left My Heart at the Stage Door Canteen." The most popular song of the war was Berlin's 1942 "White Christmas," introduced by Bing Crosby in the movie *Holiday Inn*. It was the first song in a decade to sell more than 1 million copies of sheet music and led the Hit Parade— music's equivalent of a Nielsen rating— nine times, rebounding again during the Christmases of 1943 and 1944. Songs like this meant much to battle-hardened troops as well as to the folks back home. Over and over, veterans have testified how much one or another song meant to them.

This government poster encouraged people to listen to music wherever they may be for inspiration and courage.

Record companies like Columbia boomed during the war years because Americans had few other places to spend their disposable incomes.

Apart from fear itself, nostalgia seems to have been the nation's strongest emotion during World War II; certainly it was what produced the best music. The most popular song of 1944 was the touching "I'll Be Seeing You," and in that same year "I'll Be Home for Christmas" (with its melancholy coda, "if only in my dreams") was a hit also.

Even novelty songs could elicit a somber mood. Forty-six years later a writer recalled that on his first crossing of the North Atlantic, in 1943, at the height of the submarine war, another young sailor played "Juke Box Saturday Night" over and over on his phonograph. Although it is a bouncy number, being at sea in a dangerous time gave it a "dirge-like quality" to that listener. This must have been a common experience.

SEE ALSO
Home front; Motion pictures; Radio

Mussolini, Benito
PRIME MINISTER OF ITALY, 1922–43

- *Born: July 29, 1983, Predappio, Romagna, Italy*
- *Political party: Fascist*
- *Education: secondary school diploma, 1901*
- *Military service: Italian Army: private, 1905–6; sergeant, 1915–17*
- *Government service: parliamentary deputy, 1921–22; Prime minister, 1922–43*
- *Died: April 28, 1945, Dongo, Italy*

Even as a boy, Mussolini was thuggish and violent. Although his parents had little money, they sent him to boarding schools because of his uncontrollable behavior. His first employment after receiving his diploma was as a teacher, but his drinking, womanizing, and bullying behavior made it difficult for him to hold any job for long. In 1909 he became an editor of a socialist weekly in Trentino, Austria. He soon returned to Italy, where he developed a career as a socialist agitator and editor.

In 1914 Mussolini founded his own paper, *Il Popolo,* using it to support Italian entry into World War I, which the socialists opposed. After being released from the Italian Army in 1917 because of a training accident, Mussolini returned to *Il Popolo,* which he moved from the extreme left to the extreme right politically. It became the organ of his Fascist party, a magnet for violent ex-servicemen. Italy's government was wildly unpopular as a result of its having led the country into a war that produced ruinous defeats and catastrophic economic losses. Having no support, it was easily toppled by Mussolini in 1922. He made himself dictator of Italy in 1925.

Although it is often said that Mussolini came to power as a result of his march on Rome, the mere threat of such a march was sufficient. After he announced that his fascist "blackshirts" would move on Rome and seize power, Mussolini was named prime minister by King Victor Emmanuel III on October 29, 1922. His blackshirts were then ushered into Rome, where they committed unnecessary acts of violence involving 12 deaths. Apparently this was to establish the myth that fascism had come to power by force of arms.

Mussolini ruled with a heavy hand, inflicting violence, torture, and death on his critics and enemies. The only redeeming feature of his regime was that these evils took place on a small scale compared to what went on in Nazi Germany. Also, Mussolini was not anti-Semitic, a result of Italy's being the least anti-Semitic of European countries.

Mussolini made peace with the Catholic Church, signing a concordant and treaty with the Vatican in 1929. His was the first Italian government ever to be officially recognized by the Church. Pope Pius XII said that Mussolini was "a man sent by Providence" to deliver Italy from liberalism.

Mussolini was unable to do much about Italy's poverty and backwardness as an industrial state. Yet, despite its slender resources, the Italy that Mussolini dreamed of would be a new Roman empire, and he would be its leader. This was a fantasy and led to disastrous adventures. In 1935 the Italian Army invaded Ethiopia. Although Addis Ababa, the capital, fell in 1936, fighting continued for three more years. Mussolini spent the equivalent of an entire year's national income on the Ethiopian war, which provided no tangible benefits to the Italian state. Ethiopia remained a drain for as long as Italy occupied it.

This episode alienated the Western democracies and deprived Mussolini of his major diplomatic asset. Before Ethiopia he had been able to play off Britain and France against Hitler's Germany. By first leaning one way, then another, he had inflated Italian prestige. In the future he would become progressively more dependent on Hitler.

The Spanish Civil War of 1936 resulted in another mistake. When General Francisco Franco led an uprising against the Spanish Republic in that year, Mussolini came to his aid with financial and military support. What followed was a three-year war that ended with Franco's victory but cost Italy a sum equal to half a year's revenue and depleted the country's foreign currency reserve by half. Further, setbacks in battle proved that the Italian Army was not very good.

At the Munich conference in 1938,

Mussolini took Hitler's side. The result was that Hitler, who had already seized Austria, gained Czechoslovakia as well. Italy gained nothing. It is true that Italy had seized Albania earlier in the year. But this was a meaningless triumph, for it already controlled Albania's army and economy. Worse was to follow.

In 1940, while Germany was beating France and Britain on the battlefield, Mussolini declared war on the Allies. But Italy's invasion of France was easily stopped, and Italy gained an occupation zone only because Germany provided one. Undeterred by failure, in the fall of 1940 Mussolini ordered his Libyan army to advance into Egypt. Then, in October,

Like Hitler, Mussolini employed banners, ceremonies, rallies, and martial music to build support for his regime.

he ordered an invasion of Greece. The Greeks stopped the Italians cold, then began pushing them back into Albania. In December a small British force attacked the Italians in Egypt, routing them completely. British-led forces also liberated Ethiopia in April 1941.

Germany rescued Mussolini in North Africa by sending over General Erwin Rommel with two divisions in 1941. It also bailed out Italy in the Balkans by seizing Yugoslavia and Greece in that same year. This put Italy very much under the German thumb. Thereafter, it was committed to a Balkan occupation it could not afford and a North African campaign it could not win, even with German help.

By early 1943, three-fourths of the Italian merchant fleet had been sunk and Italy was losing six ships for every one it built. Its economy was collapsing even before the North African campaign was lost in May 1943. The Allies then invaded Sicily.

On July 25, 1943, Mussolini was fired by Victor Emmanuel as prime minister and placed under arrest. No fascists came to his aid, however, because of the party's reputation as well as Mussolini's own, which had been ruined by so many failures.

Mussolini was rescued from prison on September 12 by German commandos and put in nominal charge of a puppet state called the Italian Social Republic in northern Italy. But as real power was now in German hands, Mussolini could do little beyond executing his former advisors. These included Count Galeazzo Ciano, who had been his foreign minister and was still married to Mussolini's daughter.

In 1945, when German power in Italy collapsed, Mussolini wandered about aimlessly until he fell into the hands of communist partisans. They executed him on the spot, along with his mistress, and strung both bodies up by their heels in Milan. So ended the career of one of history's most inept dictators.

SEE ALSO

Germany; Italian campaigns; Italy; Mediterranean theater; Sicily, battle of

FURTHER READING

Carpi, Daniel. *Between Mussolini and Hitler: The Jews and the Italian Authorities in France and Tunisia.* Hanover, N.H.: University Press of New England, 1994.
Hartenian, Larry. *Benito Mussolini.* New York: Chelsea House, 1988.
Hoyt, Edwin Palmer. *Mussolini's Empire: The Rise and Fall of the Fascist Vision.* New York: Wiley, 1994.
Mussolini, Benito. *The Fall of Mussolini, His Own Story.* New York: Farrar, Straus & Giroux, 1948.
Smith, Dennis Mack. *Mussolini.* New York: Knopf, 1982.

Nagasaki

SEE Atomic bombs

Napalm

Napalm was developed by Harvard scientists and introduced by the U.S. Army in 1943. A napalm bomb was created by filling an aircraft fuel tank with a mixture of gasoline and naphthalic and palmitic acids. The result was a "jelled" gasoline incendiary that clung to human flesh upon exploding and was almost impossible to put out. Napalm was also used in flamethrowers, both manually carried and tank-mounted. On Okinawa, U.S. troops poured napalm directly into caves, igniting the fuel with hand grenades. Napalm was used only by U.S. troops.

Navajo code talkers

The first Native American code talkers used in warfare were 14 Choctaw Indian members of the U.S. Army's 36th Infantry Division in World War I. Near the end of the war they were stationed in company headquarters and translated radio, telephone, and written field messages into Choctaw. The Germans were never able to decode these messages, so they were the most secure form of communication employed by the U.S. Army.

In World War II some Choctaws and Comanches were used as code talkers by the U.S. Army in Europe. However, most code talkers in World War II were Navajos, chiefly from New Mexico, who were recruited—and sometimes drafted—by the Marine Corps for service in the Pacific. The idea came from Philip Johnson, an engineer who had been raised on a Navajo reservation as the child of missionaries and knew the language. Because the Navajo language was so difficult and almost never appeared written, Johnson advised the Marine Corps that having Navajos communicate in their own tongue from the front lines to headquarters and back would prove much faster and more accurate than encoding messages. Codes and ciphers were difficult to write under combat conditions, and there was always the risk that they would be broken.

Navajo code talkers were the perfect solution to this problem. It was estimated at the time that only 30 non-Navajos in the entire world, none of them Japanese, understood the language. In a test arranged by the Marine Corps it was discovered that Navajos could encode, send, and decode a three-line message in English in 20 seconds. Marine coding machines required 30 minutes to perform this task. No more proof was required.

About 400 Navajos served in every Marine campaign, beginning with Guadalcanal in August 1942. Each of the six Marine divisions employed code talkers. They worked usually in two-man teams, using field telephones and radios to call in artillery strikes, direct artillery and troop movements, and perform other important tasks. Their greatest achievement was on Iwo Jima early in 1945, which was the bloodiest battle fought by Marines in the Pacific war. The entire operation was directed by orders communicated by the Navajo code talkers. Working around the clock, they sent and received over 800 messages in the first 48 hours alone. Major Howard Connor, head of signals for the 5th Marine Division, said afterward that without the Navajos Iwo Jima could not have been taken.

Japanese intelligence, which often broke U.S. Army codes, was baffled by the code talkers, even though it had access to a Navajo prisoner named Joe Lee Kieyoomia, who had served in the Army and was captured when the Philippines fell in 1942. Although his Japanese captors tortured him, Kieyoomia could tell them nothing because the code talkers had come up with special terms for military purposes that were meaningless to other Navajos. Code talkers did not simply speak to one another in their native tongue, but instead used a code that sounded like gibberish to anyone who had not learned it. The only way to break this code was to capture a code talker. For that reason many believed that it was Marine Corps policy to have code talkers killed if they were in danger of being taken prisoner by the Japanese. In any case, no code talker was ever captured and the code remained secure.

Because code talking was a closely guarded secret, they were unable to tell their families where they were and what they were doing. Anxiety on the reserva-

These Navajo code talkers were part of the first assault wave to land on Saipan in June 1944.

tions owing to lack of information became so great that Johnson finally sent a letter to every family with a code talker in the service describing the code-talking operation and urging them to tell no one else for reasons of security. It was the right thing to do morally, but somehow code talking ended up as a feature story in *Arizona Highways*.

Despite this limited public awareness, the Marine Corps refused to release information on code talking until 1968. Because code talking remained top secret for all that time, not a single Navajo was given an award or medal. Except for readers of *Arizona Highways*, few Americans knew of the Navajos' special contribution until recently. Nowadays, their story is well known and the Navajo code talkers have received many honors and tributes. In December 1981, President Ronald Reagan awarded the Navajo code talkers a Presidential Certificate of Recognition, and proclaimed April 14, 1983, Navajo Code Talker Day.

Because many code talkers fought on the front lines—and in some cases behind enemy lines—they were often in great danger. Like other combat veterans, memories and nightmares based on their wartime experience often disturbed them long after the fighting had stopped. Unlike most other veterans, though, code talkers often turned to using Navajo ceremonies called the "Enemy Way," a ritual designed to help them deal with their memories and the ghosts of dead comrades.

FURTHER READING
Aaseng, Nathan. *The Navajo Code Talkers*. New York: Walker, 1992.

Navy

SEE Japanese Navy; Royal Navy; United States Navy

Nazis

In 1919 Adolf Hitler, then still a soldier on active duty with the German Army, was assigned to observe a meeting held in Munich by the German Worker's party (DAP). This right-wing nationalist group appealed to him at once, and he became its 55th member. In such a tiny band, Hitler's qualities assured him of a rapid rise to the top.

This Nazi bookplate was created specifically for Hitler. Many books that did not support National Socialist ideals, however, were banned and burned.

Hitler began as the DAP's propaganda chairman, but in July 1921 he became party leader. Upon taking charge, he renamed the DAP the National Socialist Worker's party (NSDAP), or Nazi for short. Nazis therefore refers only to members of the NSDAP in its narrowest, original sense. Nazi-like parties in other countries were called fascist, which was specific to Mussolini's National Fascist party, but also became a generic term for any right-wing, undemocratic political organization.

SEE ALSO
Fascism; Germany; Hitler, Adolf

Negroes

SEE African Americans

New Guinea

SEE Southwest Pacific Area

9th Army

SEE France, battle of; Germany, surrender of

Nimitz, Chester W.

COMMANDER IN CHIEF OF THE PACIFIC FLEET, 1941–45

- *Born: February 24, 1885, Fredericksburg, Texas*
- *Political party: none*
- *Education: U.S. Naval Academy, 1905; Naval War College, 1923*
- *Military service: U.S. Navy: ensign, 1905; lieutenant, 1910; lieutenant commander, 1917; commander, 1921; captain, 1928; commander, Augusta, 1933–35; rear admiral, 1938; commander, Battleship Division 1, 1938; admiral, 1941; commander in chief of Pacific Fleet, 1941–45; commander in chief of Pacific Ocean Areas, 1942–45; fleet admiral, 1944*
- *Died: February 20, 1966, Berkeley, Calif.*

Chester Nimitz was the choice to command the Pacific Fleet. He had held many command and staff positions and consistently impressed his superiors. As chief of the Bureau of Navigation (the Navy's personnel branch) from 1939 to 1941, he had frequently met with President Franklin D. Roosevelt. In fact, he had been offered the command of the Pacific Fleet before the war broke out, but Nimitz declined on the ground that he was too junior for such an important post.

This reason was probably not the only one. Nimitz had predicted that when the United States first went to war in the Pacific it would suffer defeats, and those responsible would lose their jobs. This is precisely what happened. Admiral Husband Kimmel, who became commander in chief, Pacific Fleet (CINCPAC) in Nimitz's place, bore the responsibility for Pearl Harbor's lack of readiness and was promptly fired. Thus it was Nimitz who replaced Kimmel, instead of the other way around, as could easily have happened.

It was Nimitz's view that the Pearl Harbor defeat could have happened to anyone. But it is hard to believe that the fleet would have been caught so completely by surprise had he been CINCPAC on December 7, 1941, the date of the attack. In any event, Nimitz proved to be an inspired choice, for his modesty and folksiness concealed a first-class brain. Admiral Raymond Spruance, regarded by Admiral Ernest King as the smartest man in the Navy second only to himself, was one of those who underrated Nimitz at first. However, Spruance later admitted that the better he knew Nimitz the more he admired his intelligence, his openness to new ideas, and his courage.

It was these qualities that lay behind the great U.S. victory at Midway Island in June 1942. As CINCPAC, Nimitz found himself in charge of a battered fleet that was inferior to the Imperial Japanese Navy (IJN) in almost every respect. Yet, when code breakers learned that the IJN was planning to seize Midway in order to lure the Pacific Fleet to certain destruction, Nimitz did not hesitate. Heavily outnumbered though his fleet was, Nimitz sent all three of his carriers and everything else he could spare to Midway—risking everything. Yet it was a calculated risk, for knowing the enemy's plans, Nimitz and his staff had devised a counterplan that might turn the war around.

Luckily for Nimitz, his plan was a success. Thanks to luck, courage, and inspired leadership, the U.S. Navy won a tremendous victory at Midway, despite all the odds against it. There was plenty of credit to go around, but it must go first to Nimitz, who took the risk and would have been held responsible if the Pacific Fleet had been beaten. Hawaii would then have been in deadly danger and Nimitz, almost certainly, would have been finished as CINCPAC.

Nimitz never again took such a dramatic risk, but throughout the rest of the Pacific war he provided his vast theater with the best possible leadership. Shortly before the battle at Midway, Nimitz had been given a second hat as well. In addition to CINCPAC, he became commander in chief of the Pacific Ocean Areas (South, Central, and North). In this role he was responsible for the entire Pacific Ocean, except for the Southwest Pacific Area, which was commanded by General Douglas MacArthur.

Sitting on the bridge of a destroyer, Admiral Nimitz reviews the inspection of a newly acquired base in the Marshall Islands.

An important decision for which Nimitz is remembered was to place Vice Admiral William F. Halsey in command of the South Pacific Area. Late in 1942 the U.S. Navy had gone on the offensive for the first time by attacking the Japanese-held island of Guadalcanal in the Solomons. "Operation Shoestring," as the men called it, went badly from the start. First a Japanese force drove off the U.S. invasion fleet, leaving the Marines stranded. Then it sank an Allied cruiser force at the Battle of Savo Island (August 8, 1942), the Navy's worst World War II defeat at sea. A seesaw campaign followed, marked by frequent Japanese reinforcements of Guadalcanal and numerous fights at sea.

At the end of September 1942, Nimitz went to the South Pacific for a personal look. He discovered that theater commander Vice Admiral Robert Ghormley was exhausted and defeatist, like many of his officers. On Guadalcanal, however, Marine commanders were certain they could win, given decent support. Reluctantly, for Ghormley was an old friend, Nimitz sacked him and put Halsey in charge. Halsey, though impulsive, proved to be a wildly popular commander and soon had put the South Pacific Area on track. Turning defeat, or at least defeatism, into victory in the Solomons would be Halsey's biggest achievement of the war.

Nimitz went on to drive the Japanese out of the Aleutian Islands off Alaska and organize the central Pacific drive that was the U.S. Navy's main effort in World War II. However, unlike Admiral King, Nimitz was never entirely sold on the idea of a main drive in the central Pacific. The area was so far from MacArthur's command that the two theaters competed with each other instead of being mutually supportive. MacArthur wanted the Navy to operate parallel to him in the Southwest Pacific, so that the fast carriers and scarce landing ships tank (LSTs) could shuttle between the two lines of advance as needed. After the bloody fight at Tarawa in the Gilberts (November 20–22, 1943), Nimitz began to think MacArthur was right. After meeting with members of MacArthur's staff, Nimitz tentatively agreed to MacArthur's proposal.

Admiral King shot the idea down at once. Nimitz, who was relieved by the fact that only small losses resulted from seizing the Marshall Islands early in 1944, accepted King's decision and led the Central Pacific drive as best he could. Casualties remained staggeringly high, however. The Fifth Fleet's landing at Saipan in the Marianas turned into another bloody engagement—a much bigger one than Tarawa. Seizing Betio, the principle island in Tarawa's atoll, had cost the Marines 3,000 casualties in 72 hours. On Saipan, Marine and army units would sustain 14,000 casualties during nearly a month of fighting, which ended on July 9, 1944.

After the Saipan campaign, the U.S. command understood and accepted the high rate of casualties that resulted from the inability of land forces to maneuver on the small, scattered islands of the central Pacific. Thus, Saipan was followed early in 1945 by the invasion of Iwo Jima, which resulted in even heavier losses. Iwo Jima caused an uproar at home, but had little effect on Nimitz's strategy.

Nimitz was successful in changing King's mind on one important issue, however. King had originally planned for the central Pacific drive to end on the coast of China, from where a buildup would take place to invade Japan. By late 1944, however, the Japanese had overrun much of China's coastal area, leading King to argue for Formosa instead. MacArthur preferred Luzon in the Philippines, partly because he wanted to liberate the Philippines more than anything else. But he also argued that having air bases in Luzon would let the United States command the South China Sea and would finish the job of cutting off Japan from its supply sources in Southeast Asia. He also pointed out to King that there would be native labor in Luzon to make up for the lack of men in the Army Service Forces. If Formosa were chosen as the launch site, it had to be assumed that native laborers would be unfriendly. King finally gave up the idea of taking Formosa, and the invasion and subsequent operations in the Philippines were highly successful.

Like most naval and air commanders, Chester Nimitz was convinced that Japan could be defeated through strategic bombing and blockades. But the Joint Chiefs believed that Japan had to be invaded, and Nimitz was making plans for such an operation when he learned of the atomic bomb. Nimitz was appalled by the bomb's destructiveness, but he conceded the need for it. Japan had been losing the war for years, yet nothing, including the burning of most of its urban areas, had made it decide to surrender. Nimitz thought that atomic warfare would make the difference, which of course it did. Though he had no voice in the decision to drop the atomic bombs, he supported the action personally.

Saddled with a dubious strategy that he did not always agree with, Nimitz was one of the outstanding U.S. commanders of the war. As commander of the Pacific Ocean areas, he ran his huge theater with outstanding skill. He appointed outstanding officers to lead his mighty fleet and gave them his full support. He richly deserved the five stars that came with his final promotion to fleet admiral. He was also a model officer: modest, considerate, and a gentleman through and through.

SEE ALSO

Central Pacific Area; Midway Island, battle of; North Pacific Area; South Pacific Area

FURTHER READING

Brink, Randall. *Nimitz: The Man and His Wars*. New York: Penguin, 1999.
Hoyt, Edwin Palmer. *How They Won the War in the Pacific: Nimitz and His Admirals*. New York: Weybright and Talley, 1970.
Larrabee, Eric. *Commander in Chief*. New York: Harper & Row, 1987.
Potter, E. B. *Nimitz*. Annapolis, Md.: Naval Institute Press, 1976.

North African campaign

SEE Mediterranean Theater

North Pacific Area

As part of its effort to destroy the U.S. Pacific Fleet in the summer of 1942, Japan seized the islands of Kiska and Attu in the Aleutians off the coast of Alaska. The idea was to force Admiral Chester Nimitz to send warships to Alaska, weakening the Pacific Fleet before its showdown with the Imperial Japanese Navy (IJN).

The Aleutians were in the North Pacific Area, one of three theaters in Nimitz's Pacific Ocean Area. Because U.S.

intelligence was decoding Japanese radio messages, Nimitz knew that Midway Island was where the IJN intended to mass its forces. Nimitz therefore sent only a small fleet to the Aleutians. Japan occupied Attu on June 5, 1942, and Kiska two days later, with sufficient strength to rule out an early liberation by the United States's weakened forces in the Pacific.

For the next nine months, U.S. Army and Navy aircraft bombed these two Japanese-held islands, but to little effect. On March 26, 1943, an attempt by the IJN to reinforce Attu was turned back by a U.S. surface fleet. Attu was then assaulted by 11,000 men of the 7th Infantry Division on May 11. Although the Japanese garrison numbered only about 2,400 men, they put up stiff resistance against hopeless odds. Rather than wait to be hunted down, the Japanese staged one of the biggest *banzai* (suicide) charges of the war on the morning of May 29. After a day of hard fighting, the Japanese made a final, futile assault the following day, with the survivors committing suicide. Only 28 Japanese prisoners were taken. U.S. casualties came to 600 dead and 1,200 wounded.

Rear Admiral Robert A. Theobald, commander of the North Pacific Area, now turned from Attu to the other Japanese-occupied island, Kiska, and invaded it with 34,000 U.S. and Canadian troops on August 15, 1945. They met no resistance, however, because the entire Japanese garrison of more than 5,000 men had been secretly evacuated on the nights of July 28 and 29. This retreat was a rare event in the Pacific war. For the Japanese, last-ditch stands like the one at Attu were the rule, clever escapes the exception.

FURTHER READING

Morison, Samuel Eliot. *History of United States Naval Operations in World War II*. Vol. 7. *Aleutians, Gilberts, and Marshalls*. Boston: Little, Brown, 1951.

Nurses

Army and Navy nurses, almost all of them female, were commissioned officers. In peacetime this made for a life of relative ease marked by eight-hour days, comfortable quarters, travel, and ample relaxation. In wartime everything changed.

Nurses stationed in the Philippines were the first to make the transition from peacetime to wartime nursing. When U.S. troops retreated to the Bataan Peninsula of Luzon to make a last stand in December 1941, the Army Nurse Corps (ANC) went with them. Nurses found themselves working in a jungle "hospital" that was miles long and lacked just about everything except patients. Accustomed to a ratio of 1 nurse to 10 patients, these women now found themselves responsible for up to 300 patients apiece. Desperately overworked, they also shared the hardships of the men: hunger, fear, malaria, and dysentery. They dug their own foxholes and hid in them during Japanese air attacks. Their hospital was bombed twice. By January of 1942, a full day's rations consisted of a few slivers of mule meat in half a cup of soup.

On the night of April 9, 1942, with the Japanese only yards away, the nurses were ordered to retreat to Corregidor ("the rock"), an island fortress that held out for another month. Of the 87 nurses on Corregidor, 21 were evacuated to Australia, but 66 fell into Japanese hands. Though they were not abused or murdered like the male prisoners of war, the nurses were separated from their patients and spent the rest of the war in an internment camp. On February 3, 1945, the half-starved nurses were liberated. Their survival was a tribute to the courage and discipline of the ANC.

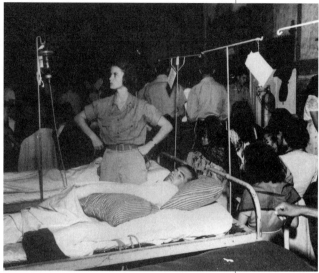

Most military nurses did not suffer like those in the Philippines, but the war was difficult all the same. After what happened to the nurses in Bataan, the Army's leaders decided that nurses had to be trained for field operations. A four-week training program was devised involving 20-mile marches with 30-pound packs. The nurses learned how to pitch tents, purify water, and identify poison gas. Like the male trainees, they crawled through a 75-yard infiltration course with live ammunition firing over their heads at the end of the program.

At the Desert Training Center in California, nurses set up field hospitals in 130-degree heat and coped with scorpions and sandstorms. They practiced setting up a 500-bed field hospital and then, in a day or two, took the whole thing down again to keep up with fast-moving troops. This became valuable experience, for the ANC accompanied U.S. troops when they fought in North Africa.

Considering how many served in combat zones, the army nurses received surprisingly little publicity during the war apart from the heroines of Bataan. In North Africa, Sicily, Italy, France, and Germany they moved just behind the troops, risking—and sometimes losing—their lives.

Phyllis Hocking adjusts a glucose intravenous apparatus for a GI patient during a Christmas Eve service in the Church of the Transfiguration, Palo, Leyte, Philippine Islands. The church had become the 36th Evac. Hospital.

Army flight nurses risked their lives as well, flying on unarmed transport planes without even a red cross to protect them. Usually, nurses flew alone and had to do a doctor's work when emergencies took place. Obviously, they did it well: during 13 months in the South Pacific, army nurses moved 37,000 patients and lost only one.

Navy nurses were less at risk because they were not allowed on combat vessels. Those in the theaters of war were stationed on hospital ships. Emergency care on warships was given by men who had been trained by nurses. Like army nurses, members of the Naval Nurse Corps (NNC) were also teachers and administrators.

The demands of war soon created a nursing shortage. In 1940 the entire ANC consisted of just 700 women. A year later, the corps was recruiting that same number each month. By 1944 the military needed 66,000 nurses, but civilian hospitals needed 300,000 more. The result was a shortage of 100,000 nurses.

Additional trained nurses did in fact exist. Civilian nurses could have been called to action, but most had been paid so poorly that they left the profession to take defense jobs. The statistics tell the story: after graduation from nursing school and three years of unpaid hospital work, a registered nurse earned less than a welder in training.

Military nurses did earn more than civilians, but they still had to qualify as registered nurses (RNs) at their own expense before they could be commissioned. In May 1943 Congress passed Representative Frances Bolton's bill providing support for nursing education, but it came too late in the war to make much of a difference. Thus, in January 1945 President Franklin D. Roosevelt asked that the Selective Service Act be amended so that nurses could be drafted into the armed forces—20,000 of them, to be exact. Such a bill was actually passed by the House and would have passed in the Senate too had Germany not surrendered before it came to a vote.

The sad fact is that there was no need after all to draft nurses. It was prejudice as much as anything else that accounted for the nursing shortage. The military was uninterested in male nurses and rarely gave them commissions. The services did not favor African-American nurses either, accepting only a handful. They refused to take women older than 45, and there was an unofficial tendency to reject women older than 30.

Although by the end of 1942 the Army was allowing nurses to marry, the Navy never accepted already married nurses. And it did not allow single women in the NNC to marry until 1944. The services also refused to accept women doctors. Fewer than 100 female physicians were commissioned in the Army Medical Corps, and then only after overcoming numerous obstacles.

Despite all these stipulations, 60,000 women joined the ANC and 14,000 the NNC. The fact that shortages occurred was the military's own fault for shutting out men and women who wished to serve simply because of their age, color, or sex.

SEE ALSO
Medicine

FURTHER READING
Camp, LaVonne Telshaw. *Lingering Fever: A World War II Nurse's Memoir.* Jefferson, N.C.: McFarland, 1997.
Fessler, Diane Burke. *No Time for Fear: Voices of American Military Nurses in World War II.* East Lansing: Michigan State University Press, 1996.
Poulos, Paula Nassen, ed. *A Woman's War Too: U.S. Women in the Military in World War II.* Washington, D.C.: National Archives and Records Administration, 1996.
Weatherford, Doris. *American Women and World War II.* New York: Facts on File, 1990.

Office of Price Administration

The Office of Price Administration (OPA) began in April 1941 as the Office of Price Administration and Civilian Supply. The OPA's primary job was to control inflation, because defense orders were pushing prices up. Its first head was Leon Henderson, a New Deal economist who at that time was President Franklin D. Roosevelt's budget chief.

A few months later Roosevelt split the two functions, with the OPA remaining independent and the Civilian Supply role being folded into another agency. This change did not solve the problem, however, which was that the OPA lacked enforcement powers and could only nag businessmen about price controls.

After Pearl Harbor was attacked in December 1941, the OPA gained more authority and was assigned the unpopular duty of rationing consumer goods. Its efforts, not always successful, to control prices turned business and Congress against the OPA. As an example, just one of its functions was to apply General Maximum Price Regulations—known as "General Max"—to 1.7 million retailers. On the other hand, while the public believed in price control, it hated rationing and complained incessantly.

Unable to please anyone and pressured from all sides, Henderson resigned as OPA head at the end of 1942. Roosevelt then made a former senator, Prentiss M. Brown, the new chief of the OPA in hopes that he could improve relations with Congress. He could not—nor could anyone else, man or woman, under the circumstances. However, Brown's suc-

cessor, Chester Bowles, an advertising man, did as much as was humanly possible to make the OPA effective.

Office of Strategic Services

In 1940, British intelligence asked President Franklin D. Roosevelt to send someone over to be briefed on its operations. Roosevelt asked an old friend, William J. "Wild Bill" Donovan, a prominent attorney and in World War I a highly decorated officer, to make the trip. At the time, the United States had no intelligence director or central agency. Instead, the various services and government departments maintained their own intelligence units. The success of Donovan's mission, and his report on what the British were doing, convinced Roosevelt that he needed a centralized intelligence operation.

In July 1941 Roosevelt named Donovan as Coordinator of Information (COI). The COI organization grew rapidly, in all directions, and included propaganda as well as intelligence functions. Its structure became unwieldy, and

Allied spies were furnished with false identification papers like these by artists and forgers in the OSS Research and Development Branch in Rome.

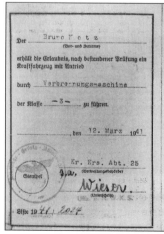

as a propaganda agency it aroused envy and suspicion. Accordingly, on June 13, 1942, the COI's propaganda activities were spun off to become the independent Office of War Information. The rest remained under Donovan's command as chief of the Office of Strategic Services (OSS), which was put under the Joint Chiefs of Staff.

In its final form, the OSS had four intelligence branches, which did everything from running spies to interviewing refugees. The largest of these was the Research and Analysis Branch (R&A). Headed by William L. Langer, a distinguished historian, R&A employed a broad range of specialists and academic experts. Its reports came to be widely admired for their intelligence and fairness.

The OSS's operational branches engaged in sabotage, espionage, and all sorts of covert activities. They supported resistance groups in occupied countries, conducted raids of their own, and planted false information. They were supported in this work by highly skilled technical services, which provided OSS agents with custom-made radios and cameras, as well as other kinds of equipment.

Although it operated in all the theaters of war during World War II, the OSS was most effective in North Africa and Europe, where it had a freer hand. General Douglas MacArthur disliked it intensely, however, and kept it from operating in the Southwest Pacific Area, to the degree that he was able. Admiral Chester Nimitz, too, was far from being an OSS fan.

As always with intelligence, the contribution made to victory by the OSS is hard to evaluate. It operated on a very large scale, conducted numerous operations, and produced countless reports. Because it was not allowed to play a policy-making role, the OSS could offer, in theory at least, unbiased advice. At any rate, although President Harry Truman

dissolved the OSS immediately after the war, it was soon replaced by the Central Intelligence Agency. This suggests that the OSS had done a good enough job in the war to make national security officials feel that they could not get along without it in some form or another.

SEE ALSO
Intelligence, military

FURTHER READING

Chalou, George C., ed. *The Secrets War: The Office of Strategic Services in World War II*. Washington, D.C.: National Archives and Records Administration, 1992.
Corvo, Max. *The O.S.S. in Italy, 1942–1945: A Personal Memoir*. New York: Praeger, 1990.
McIntosh, Elizabeth P. *Sisterhood of Spies: The Women of the OSS*. Annapolis, Md.: Naval Institute Press, 1998.
Morgan, William James. *The O.S.S. and I*. New York: Norton, 1957.
Smith, Richard Harris. *OSS: The Secret History of America's First Intelligence Agency*. Berkeley: University of California Press, 1972.

Okinawa, battle of

Okinawa was the last, and one of the bloodiest, battles of the Pacific war. A 60-mile-long island in the Ryukyu chain, Okinawa was worth having—at least in part. Located only about 350 miles southwest of the Japanese home island of Kyushu and 1,000 miles from Tokyo, Okinawa was within easy fighter bomber range of many targets in Japan. To take it, Admiral Chester Nimitz assembled a great armada: more than 180,000 troops and 1,200 vessels, including 40 carriers of all sizes and 18 battleships.

To defend the island, Lieutenant General Tomohiko Ushijima had some

110,000 troops, centered around the ancient castle town of Shuri in south central Okinawa. In the surrounding mountains the Japanese had built a network of underground strongpoints, the Shuri Line, which bristled with guns and mortars. Ushijima did not intend to resist the landings themselves, a tactic that experience had shown led only to early defeat, but rather to hold the south end of the island with its airfields and harbor.

After uncontested landings on April 1, 1945, the fight for Okinawa turned into a battle of attrition. There were 10 mass kamikaze (suicide aircraft) attacks against the Allied fleet between April 6 and June 22. Hardest hit were the outlying early-warning destroyers, but the big ships took a pounding also. Here the British played an important role for the only time in the Pacific.

A Marine dashes through Japanese machine-gun fire while crossing a valley on Okinawa.

Although Royal Australian and Royal New Zealand Navy ships had fought side by side with the U.S. Navy for years, Admiral Ernest J. King, who hated the British, had not wanted Britain to interfere at all in "his" war and did everything to prevent it. King was forced by President Franklin D. Roosevelt to accept the Royal Navy's contribution, which included not only fighting ships but a supply train that made them self-sufficient.

As it turned out, Admiral Raymond A. Spruance, the naval commander, had fewer fleet carriers than at the earlier Battle of the Philippine Sea, so the Royal Navy's Task Force 57—comprised of 5 fast carriers, 2 fast battleships, 5 cruis-ers, and 15 destroyers—proved invaluable. Best of all, the British carriers had strongly armored flight and hangar decks that could withstand kamikaze attacks much better than their thin-skinned U.S. sisters. British armor was carried at a price, slowing the carriers and reducing the size of their air groups. But when a kamikaze struck a U.S. flight deck it was taken out of action, while a British flattop would simply be dented.

While the Royal and U.S. navies were busy fighting off kamikaze attacks, the soldiers and Marines ashore were engaged in violent combat. Okinawa may have been the most mismanaged battle of the Pacific war. There was no excuse for this, given the great power and expertise that was available by 1945. The Tenth Army's commander, Lieutenant General Simon Bolivar Buckner, presided over a series of grinding frontal attacks, resisting suggestions that he take advantage of his amphibious capability to land in the enemy's rear. Buckner ought to have been relieved of duty for this. He was killed by the enemy, as it happened, but too late to make a difference.

Americans were now far and away the world leaders in regard to all arms and interservice cooperation, capable of uniting land, sea, and air power into a smoothly running, irresistible force. Buckner took this marvelously flexible weapon and used it as a blunt instrument.

The Battle of Okinawa, which began April 1, did not end until June 21, by which time 7,000 Americans had been killed on land and 4,900 at sea. Twenty-nine ships were put out of action—a greater loss than in any previous U.S. naval operation. In addition, 32,000 men were wounded on land, 4,800 sailors at sea. A total of 20 percent of all casualties sustained by the U.S. Navy in World War II were taken off Okinawa. A campaign that was sup-

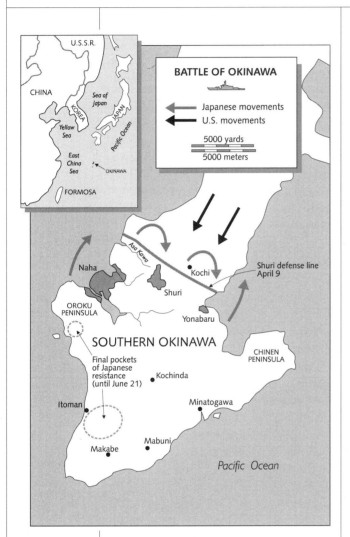

BATTLE OF OKINAWA

→ Japanese movements
→ U.S. movements

5000 yards
5000 meters

Instead, men were thrown against nearly untakeable Japanese defenses. It was World War I all over again, with heavy artillery barrages followed by head-on attacks, sometimes across open ground. The casualty rate, 35 percent of all troops involved, was a result of these ruinous tactics.

Nonbattle casualties, mostly neuropsychiatric (combat fatigue, called NP by the military), were extremely high as well, amounting perhaps to 10 percent of all those who fought. At Sugar Loaf, the key to the Shuri Line, one-third of the Marine casualties were NPs. Of all Marines killed in the war, 14 percent died on Okinawa; and 1 percent of total U.S. casualties in World War II were sustained taking an island of 875 square miles, about 0.6 percent of Japan's total area. There was no excuse for this, but these terrible results had far-reaching consequences.

The casualties on Iwo Jima and Okinawa figured importantly in the decision to make nuclear war on Japan. The Joint Chiefs were planning to invade the home islands on or about November 1, 1945. Given recent experience, this was sure to be costly. Once the atomic bomb became available, however, it offered a way of winning the war without repeating the Okinawa experience many times over. Accordingly, there was no way the bomb could not be used.

SEE ALSO

Atomic bombs; Iwo Jima, Battle of; Japan, surrender of

FURTHER READING

Feifer, George. *Tennozan: The Battle of Okinawa and the Atomic Bomb.* New York: Ticknor & Fields, 1992.
Foster, Simon. *Okinawa, 1945: Final Assault on the Empire.* New York: Sterling, 1994.
Gow, I. T. M. *Okinawa, 1945: Gateway to Japan.* Garden City, N.Y.: Doubleday, 1985.

posed to last 45 days took closer to 80, despite the expenditure of 7.5 million howitzer rounds, 60,000 5- to 6-inch naval shells, 20,000 rockets, almost 400,000 grenades, and 30 million small-arm and automatic weapon rounds.

The Japanese sacrificed 1,465 kamikazes, 150,000 Okinawan civilians (about one-third of the total population), and most of the Japanese garrison—though 11,000 were taken prisoner, by far the largest total of the war, and yet not nearly large enough. General MacArthur severely criticized the land engagement, arguing that after northern Okinawa had been taken, U.S. troops should have dug in and let the enemy come to them.

Operation Overlord

SEE D-Day

Pacific Fleet

Since 1922 it had been U.S. Navy policy to keep the largest part of the U.S. Fleet in Pacific waters. The entire fleet consisted of two main groups. One was the Battle Force, which included the newer battleships, aircraft carriers, cruisers, destroyers, submarines, and a variety of smaller vessels. The second group included the Scouting Force, which was made up of cruisers and destroyers; a Training Squadron in the Caribbean; the Submarine Force, which was divided between the Pacific and Atlantic oceans; and the Base Force, or Train, divided the same way. In addition, there was a small Asiatic fleet that operated largely in Chinese waters. Most of the U.S. Fleet's ships in the Pacific were based in West Coast ports.

In May 1940, as tensions with Japan increased, President Franklin D. Roosevelt ordered the bulk of the U.S. Fleet to be moved to Pearl Harbor in Hawaii as a warning. On February 1, 1941, this force was renamed the Pacific Fleet. Admiral Husband E. Kimmel became the first commander in chief of the Pacific Fleet. Early in 1941 President Roosevelt transferred about 20 percent of the Pacific Fleet to the Atlantic for possible use against German U-boats. This left the Pacific Fleet weaker than the Imperial Japanese Navy (IJN) in every respect. As of May 1941, the Pacific Fleet had 9 battleships, 3 carriers, 12 heavy cruisers, 9 light cruisers, 67 destroyers, and 27 submarines. The battleships were old and slow, many of the

submarines obsolete. In contrast, the IJN possessed 10 battleships, 10 fast carriers, 18 heavy cruisers, 17 light cruisers, 111 destroyers, and 64 submarines. The IJN had qualitative superiority too, many of its ships being newer, bigger, and better than those of the Pacific Fleet. Their night-fighting abilities, events would prove, were far superior to those of the U.S. Navy, and Japanese carrier pilots were much more skilled than the inexperienced U.S. aviators. These great differences in strength, together with U.S. overconfidence and Japanese daring, go a long way toward explaining Japan's early victories.

Ten days after the Pacific Fleet was severely attacked at Pearl Harbor on December 7, 1941, Admiral Chester W. Nimitz was named Pacific Fleet commander. This was the first step on the road to recovery from the attack. With his three carriers and supporting ships, he ordered raids against Japanese possessions. On April 18, 1942, army planes launched from the *Enterprise* and *Hornet* bombed Tokyo, doing little damage but raising U.S. morale.

In May 1942 a carrier task force of the Pacific Fleet operating in the Coral Sea stopped Japan's advance toward Australia. That set the stage for the great U.S. victory at Midway Island in June, where the IJN lost four carriers, the Pacific Fleet only one. Only months after Pearl Harbor, the balance of power now began to tilt in favor of the United States.

Until 1943 Admiral Nimitz directly commanded the Pacific Fleet, while as commander in chief of the Pacific Ocean Areas, he was also theater commander of all military operations for the whole of the Pacific except the Southwest Pacific Area, which was commanded by Army General Douglas MacArthur. The War Department feared that Nimitz could not effectively direct both the fleet

Landing Ships Tank pour army equipment ashore on Leyte Island in the Philippines, 1944.

and the theater, which included a growing number of army and army air units, and requested that he appoint an admiral to command the fleet. Doing so would allow him to concentrate on his duties as commander of the Pacific Ocean Areas. Admiral Ernest J. King, chief of naval operations, would not hear of this initially, but a compromise was eventually arrived at.

While Nimitz remained commander of the Pacific Fleet, the Central Pacific Force, which contained most of the fighting ships in the Navy's Pacific Fleet, was renamed the Fifth Fleet in March 1943. It would be named the Fifth Fleet when led by Admiral Raymond A. Spruance and the Third Fleet when under Admiral William F. Halsey, with the two taking turns as commander. Subject to Nimitz's policies, operational control was now in these two admirals' hands. In addition, a Pacific Fleet joint staff was established in September 1943 with four sections, two headed by army officers.

These arrangements were generally satisfactory to all involved. The great problem still was that General Douglas MacArthur's Southwest Pacific Area (SWPA) and Nimitz's Pacific Ocean Areas were entirely separate commands. But except for MacArthur's SWPA, there was now an effective command and staff structure that would last for the rest of the war.

SEE ALSO
Central Pacific Area; Coral Sea, Battle of the; Midway, Battle of; Nimitz, Chester W.; Pearl Harbor, attack on

FURTHER READING
Hoyt, Edwin Palmer. *MacArthur's Navy: The Seventh Fleet and the Battle for the Philippines.* New York: Orion, 1989.
Lundstrom, John B. *The First South Pacific Campaign: Pacific Fleet Strategy, December 1941–June 1942.* Annapolis, Md.: Naval Institute Press, 1976.
Spector, Ronald H. *Eagle Against the Sun: The American War with Japan.* New York: Free Press, 1985.
Winslow, Walter G. *The Fleet the Gods Forgot: the U.S. Asiatic Fleet in World War II.* Annapolis, Md.: Naval Institute Press, 1982.

Pacific Ocean Area

General Douglas MacArthur's arrival in Australia after his escape from the Philippines in March 1942 forced all the services to arrive at a unified Pacific strategy. Japan's success had cancelled the prewar plans of the United States, yet the speed of events left little time for thought. Now, as MacArthur demanded men and munitions, and with the nation expecting action in the Pacific, the service chiefs could no longer avoid laying plans for the middle distance.

The chiefs had assumed that a Pacific war would be fought by the Navy. However, Japan's vast territorial conquests meant that the Army would be involved as well. A new strategy was required, and the question of supreme command was closely linked to it. The need to resolve this thorny issue complicated everything, for the Navy would not allow the Pacific Fleet to be commanded by a general, and the Army would not allow MacArthur to take orders from an admiral.

The different services' pride and rivalries dictated the outcome of the problem, which was to reshape strategy in such a way as to avoid having a supreme commander. Admiral King proposed setting up strongpoints in preparation for an advance through the New Hebrides Islands, the Solomons, and the Bismarck Archipelago. Such a movement would secure Australia and pave the way for a return to the Philippines. The land forces required for this offensive would be directed by Admiral Chester W. Nimitz, King's newly appointed Pacific Fleet commander.

Army General George C. Marshall and his planners countered with a plan of their own. They wanted a Southwest Pacific Area to be commanded by MacArthur. In one stroke the Army took over King's strategy, while also reaching for the means to make it work.

After heavy negotiations, a deal was struck on March 30, 1942. King agreed that MacArthur should have his theater, to consist initially of Australia, the Netherlands East Indies, and New Guinea. The Navy got everything else: a vast region designated as the Pacific Ocean Area, which it subdivided into the South, Central, and North Pacific areas. By forcing the issue, Marshall had gained the Army a theater of its own while also taking over King's strategy, for Australia was the key to any advance up the South Sea island chains that led to mainland Asia. King's response would be to devise a new strategy using the central Pacific that would compete with his original scheme as executed by MacArthur.

Installing two separate commands in one region was among the worst U.S. decisions of the entire war. It led to major strategic errors, the most important of these was the Navy's decision to make costly attacks on small islands of little value. It also meant that for much of the war, MacArthur would be denied the men and supplies he needed for his much larger campaigns.

SEE ALSO
Central Pacific Area; Pacific War; Southwest Pacific Area

Pacific war

The Imperial Japanese Navy's (IJN) attack at Pearl Harbor on December 7, 1941, was less of a victory than it appeared. Tactical gains had been won, but Japan failed to grasp the strategic

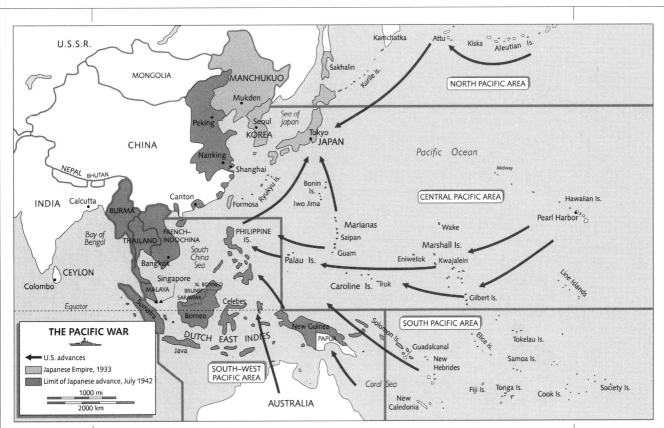

THE PACIFIC WAR

← U.S. advances
▢ Japanese Empire, 1933
▢ Limit of Japanese advance, July 1942

1000 mi
2000 km

advantage. The United States lost many aircraft, ships, and men, but because its aircraft carriers were at sea at the time of the attack, the Pacific Fleet retained its offensive punch. This advantage doomed Japan's hope for a quick end to the war, and made the attack on Hawaii a poor long-term decision.

To make matters worse for the Japanese, Vice Admiral Chuichi Nagumo denied his air commander permission to launch a second strike against Hawaii, thus sparing the shipyards, drydocks, machine shops, and especially the fuel storage tanks, on which the whole military effort depended. Had these been wiped out, the Pacific Fleet would have withdrawn to its mainland bases and there would have been no triumph at Midway Island to redeem Pearl Harbor. Even the battle damage at Pearl Harbor was less serious than it looked: except for the *Arizona* and the *Oklahoma*, the battleships would be repaired, modernized, and put to useful service.

Despite these silver linings, the clouds of war hung heavily over the United States in the aftermath of Pearl Harbor. While its enemies were fully armed, the United States was almost unprotected. The Army still did not have a single combat-ready division. The U.S. Army Air Forces had lost most of its front line planes. The Pacific Fleet was heavily outnumbered in every type of ship. To avoid antagonizing Japan, the United States had failed to develop a naval base on Guam, which meant that for want of a supply train the fleet was tied to Hawaii. The IJN, in contrast, had built a string of island bases and could go wherever it pleased.

Japanese planners had devised a complex and far-reaching network of operations designed to win the Pacific war in short order. The raid on Hawaii was accompanied by landings in southern Siam and northern Malaya. These were followed by other attacks that quickly reduced most of Southeast Asia. Air strikes against the Philippines were supposed to coincide with those against Pearl Harbor. They did not, however, because pilots of Japan's Eleventh Imperial Air Fleet based on Formosa were grounded by a heavy fog. Having lost the element of surprise, Japanese airmen were prepared for heavy casualties. Yet when they arrived over Clark Field, the main U.S. bomber base in the Philippines, they met little resistance. A hundred aircraft were destroyed at Clark and its neighboring fighter base—including 18 Flying Fortresses, half the strategic bomber force that was supposed to make the Philippines defensible. At a single blow the Japanese had reduced U.S. air power in the Philippines by more than 50 percent.

In the weeks that followed, Japan attacked other U.S. possessions in the Pacific. Guam in the Mariana Islands, a refueling stop for Pan American flying boats, was the first to fall. Its tiny garrison was overrun on December 10, 1941, by 5,400 Japanese soldiers. At Wake Island, 2,300 miles west of Hawaii, a small force of Marines actually sank two destroyers of an invasion fleet on December 7, forcing the Japanese to retreat. To avenge their loss of face, they returned in greater strength on December 23 (December 22 Hawaiian time) and overran the U.S. garrison.

To make December 22 an even darker day, 43,000 Japanese troops came ashore at Lingayen Gulf at dawn with orders to take Luzon and then the other Philippine Islands. To defend them, General MacArthur commanded a force three times as large, but his army consisted mainly of some 100,000 Philippine reservists, who were ill trained, poorly armed, and usually fell apart under fire. One U.S. general described them simply as a "mob."

MacArthur's effective forces consisted of miscellaneous army units, the 4th Marine Regiment, and 12,000 well-trained Philippine Scouts, about 30,000 regulars in all. The Japanese not only outnumbered MacArthur's combat-ready force but had total air and naval mastery. On that basis, their plan realistically allowed 50 days for seizing the islands.

MacArthur waited too long before deciding to concentrate his troops in Bataan, a 30-mile-long peninsula that, together with the island of Corregidor, controlled Manila Bay. Bataan was covered with mountains and jungles, making it highly suitable for a stand. But it had not been fortified or provisioned either beforehand or during the several weeks between the first air strikes and Japan's invasion. This oversight occurred because MacArthur planned to attack the Japanese at their landing points and in his arrogance regarded preparations to hold Bataan as defeatist. When he finally did give the order to retreat on December 23, it was too late to stock Bataan with even the barest essentials.

Japanese forces occupied Manila on January 2, 1942, and the evacuation to Bataan, superbly directed by Major General Jonathan Wainwright, was largely complete by the 6th. The garrison on Bataan consisted of about 15,000 U.S. and 65,000 Filipino troops, who were short of ammunition, medical supplies, and especially food. Bataan, with its swamps and jungles, was a hotbed of malaria, and so thousands of soldiers were soon racked by chills and fever.

Even so, against all odds, the garrison fought a tremendous delaying battle. When its first line of defense was outflanked, it fell back to a second line halfway down the peninsula, stopping Lieutenant General Masaharu Homma's Fourteenth Army in its tracks. When the 50 days he had allowed for the campaign were up, Homma had taken 7,000 casualties, lost an additional 10,000 to 12,000 men to malaria and other diseases, and could not launch another assault. He was therefore obliged to pull back and seek reinforcements.

Not counting the minor action at Wake Island, this was the first setback Japan experienced in its spectacular round of conquests, giving the Americans and Filipinos in Bataan almost two more months of freedom. Since Japan controlled the western Pacific, U.S troops could not be reinforced or resupplied. Thus they were steadily worn down by starvation, disease, air attacks, and Japanese raiding parties. On February 23 President Franklin D. Roosevelt sought to lift their morale with a radio broadcast. Unhappily, in doing so he disclosed that no help was to be expected.

On March 11, 1942, MacArthur, his wife, his son Arthur, and Arthur's Chinese nurse boarded PT-41 for a rough and dangerous 500-mile passage to Mindanao, in the southern Philippines, followed by a long flight to Australia. Upon arrival he gave a press conference and a promise, saying: "I came through, and I shall return."

Meanwhile, the Bataan front crumbled under renewed Japanese attacks. On April 9 some 76,000 men, most too weak to fight, laid down their arms. The great fortress of Corregidor, just off Bataan and the key to Manila Bay, held out under continuous bombardment until May 6, when Japanese landings forced Wainwright to surrender all the Philippine and U.S. forces throughout the islands.

The valiant U.S. defense of Bataan held up Japan for only a few months, but this delay was just enough for Australia to organize a successful defense. Other than Bataan, the Japanese swept all before them, seizing Burma, Malaya, the Netherlands East Indies, the Philippines, and islands without number. In the six months following Pearl Harbor, Japan made itself master of Southeast Asia, an area comprising 1 million square miles and 150 million people.

Yet at the very peak of Japan's success, two battles managed to turn the tide of the war. The first of these, the Battle of the Coral Sea, put an end to Japanese expansion. The following battle at Midway Island shattered its main attack force. These defeats resulted in part from "victory disease," the overconfidence and carelessness of Japanese commanders. Intoxicated by success, they proceeded at once with further offensive actions rather than consolidating their gains.

The first expansion effort of the Japanese was to occupy Tulagi in the Solomon Islands and other points in the region, notably Port Moresby, New Guinea, so as to gain control of the Coral Sea and threaten Australia. As usual the enemy plan was too complex, not only requiring that the IJN employ great skill but also that the U.S. Navy act exactly as the Japanese expected. Moreover, the Japanese paid little attention to security, a dangerous failure because the U.S. Navy had an overwhelming intelligence edge.

Thanks to information supplied by code breakers, Admiral Nimitz was able to send a task force to intercept the

A tired member of VF-17 pauses under a squadron scoreboard at Bougainville. Each Japanese flag represents a downed enemy plane.

Japanese invasion fleet steaming for Port Moresby. They met in the Coral Sea on May 7, 1942, where the first naval engagement fought entirely by aircraft took place. When it was over the U.S. Navy had suffered a tactical defeat, losing the vitally needed fleet carrier *Lexington*. Japan lost only a light carrier, while its two participating fleet carriers were damaged but not sunk.

Strategically, however, the Battle of the Coral Sea was a win for the United States because a line was drawn there that Japan would never cross. Furthermore, the damage done to the two Japanese carriers was so serious that they were unavailable on June 4 when the Pacific Fleet won its most important victory in the waters off Midway Island. Had they been present, the battle might well have been lost.

After Midway, the United States went on the offensive. Their progress can be measured by referring to the discussions under each separate theater of war, and also to the major battles.

SEE ALSO

Central Pacific Area; Coral Sea, battle of the; MacArthur, Douglas; Midway Island, battle of; Nimitz, Chester W.; North Pacific Area; South Pacific Area; Southwest Pacific Area

FURTHER READING

Bischof, Günter, and Robert L. Dupont. *The Pacific War Revisited.* Baton Rouge: Louisiana State University Press, 1997.
Fahey, James J. *Pacific War Diary.* Seattle: University of Washington Press, 1993.
Mason, John T., ed. *The Pacific War Remembered: An Oral History Collection.* Annapolis, Md.: Naval Institute Press, 1986.
Spector, Ronald H. *Eagle Against the Sun: The American War with Japan.* New York: Free Press, 1985.

Paratroops

SEE Airborne warfare

Patton, George S., Jr.

COMMANDER OF THE THIRD ARMY, 1944–45

- *Born: November 11, 1885, Pasadena, Calif.*
- *Political party: none*
- *Education: U.S. Military Academy, B.S., 1908; U.S. Army Cavalry School, 1923; U.S. Army Command and General Staff School, 1924; Army War College, 1932*
- *Military service: U.S. Army: second lieutenant, 1909; captain, 1917; major, 1920; lieutenant colonel, 1934; colonel, 1938; brigadier general, 1940; major general, 1941; commander, 1st Armored Corps, 1942; commander, II Corps, 1943; lieutenant general, 1943; commander, Seventh Army, 1943; Commander of the 3rd Army, 1944–45; four-star general, 1945*
- *Died: December 21, 1945, Heidelberg, Germany*

George S. Patton, Jr., was born to a wealthy California family and married into a richer one. Even as a child he dreamed of becoming a soldier. In 1909 he graduated from West Point and during World War I trained and commanded the first brigade of U.S. armor to fight in France. Although tanks were still primitive and unreliable, Colonel Patton quickly grasped the importance of this new weapon.

Patton became, along with Major Dwight D. Eisenhower, an early supporter of armored warfare. Both were silenced by the army brass, however, which favored horses, and Patton spent the next 20 years serving in cavalry units. The time was not wasted, though, for Patton was a scholarly and intelligent officer, an expert on military history and tactics, and a superbly qualified soldier who graduated with distinction from three service schools and colleges. Patton had dyslexia, a learning disability that impairs the ability to read, which

Patton (left) discusses military strategy with Lyle Bernard, a prominent figure in the daring amphibious landing behind enemy lines on Sicily's north coast in 1943.

nearly kept him out of West Point, but in later years it ceased being a handicap. His professional experience was immensely broad. By 1944 Patton had served at every level of command from platoon to field army and had also been a divisional, corps, and War Department staff officer.

Patton rose rapidly once the Army committed itself to tank warfare, and soon became commander of the newly formed 2nd Armored Division. In peacetime maneuvers during 1941, the 2nd Armored established Patton as the Army's leading tanker. He was soon given a corps and also asked to create the Desert Training Center in California.

Patton was one of the ablest trainers of troops in the U.S. Army, and training was the solid foundation on which his battlefield achievements rested. As part of Operation Torch, the invasion of North Africa in 1942, Patton commanded the Western Task Force that landed in Morocco.

While he was training troops in Morocco, the II Corps was taking beatings at Sidi-Bou-Sid and the Kasserine Pass in Tunisia. Eisenhower, now a general and the Allied supreme commander, sent Patton to turn the situation around, which he did in 40 days, leading the II Corps to victory and restoring its self-confidence. Patton distinguished himself again in Sicily, as commander of the Seventh Army. The only bright spot in a poorly planned campaign was Patton's boldness and drive and his imaginative use of amphibious landings behind the German lines.

Sicily, however, was almost the graveyard of Patton's ambitions. He was eccentric, perhaps slightly mad, and very emotional. Although some of his outrages were staged performances, Patton had poor self-control and at times lost his head. Contrary to all the medical evidence, he did not believe that combat fatigue was a mental disturbance, regarding it as cowardice instead. Twice in Sicily, after visiting field hospitals, Patton slapped enlisted men who were being treated for combat fatigue. When news of this got out, it was all Eisenhower could do to keep Patton from being removed from command.

Eisenhower helped Patton survive many inappropriate incidents, including one in Britain in which he allegedly insulted Russia during a speech to a ladies' group. Although Patton caused Eisenhower more trouble than all his other commanders combined, he was the best of them, and Eisenhower knew it. The Germans knew it too, which enabled Eisenhower to use Patton to deceive them. The Germans realized that the invasion of France was coming, but did not know when or where. The Allies wanted Hitler to think the attack would be at the Pas de Calais, the narrowest point of the English Channel, although the real target was Normandy. Thus, Eisenhower made Patton commander of a fictitious 1st U.S. Army Group (FUSAG) across from the Pas de Calais. Because the Germans could not believe that Eisenhower would keep his best commander out of the invasion, Patton gave FUSAG great credibility. As a result, Hitler was completely deceived, while Patton, once taken off the bench, performed up to his usual standards.

In his breakout from Normandy and his drive to the West Wall, Germany's frontier defenses, Patton would perform feats that his colleagues could only dream of. No other commander could have made the breakout from Normandy such a success because it required him to do the impossible. The task in August 1944 was to push an entire army through the Avranches bottleneck at the base of the Cotentin Peninsula in Normandy. With only a single road open to him, Patton drove 200,000 men and 40,000 vehicles over it in a matter of days—at one point personally directing traffic. Fed into the road piecemeal, Patton's divisions came out at the other end fully intact and ready for battle.

Patton performed what seemed to be another miracle at the Battle of the Bulge, which began when the Germans attacked in the Ardennes Forest of Belgium on December 16, 1944. Most of the commanders had been caught off guard because the Germans were supposed to be too weak by this time to launch a major offensive. But Patton had been worried that the First Army's VIII Corps, immediately to his left, was sluggish and wide open to a surprise attack. Therefore, he had plans drawn up in case the Third Army had to come to its rescue. On the 18th Eisenhower met with his senior officers and asked Patton what he could do to help stem the German tide. Patton replied that he could attack with three divisions in 72 hours. This involved pulling three divisions out of combat and turning them at a 90-degree angle to move directly across Third Army's lines of supply and

communication—a seemingly impossible task. An operation so complex would take days to plan and even more days to accomplish. But because Patton had already formulated his plans, his divisions were smashing into the German flank within the promised time. Even General Omar Bradley, commander of the U.S. 12th Army Group and not a fan of Patton's, called the action "magnificent" and "one of the most brilliant performances by any commander on either side in World War II."

As the Allies neared the Rhine River, Germany's last defense, they made elaborate plans for Britain's 21st Army Group to cross it with enormous air and artillery support. The U.S. armies were under orders to assist the British commander Field Marshal Sir Bernard Law Montgomery by distracting the Germans' attention. Two events made this plan obsolete. The first was that when the Germans blew up the bridges across the Rhine, their explosives failed to destroy the railroad bridge at Remagen, which was crossed by elements of the U.S. Ninth Army. The second resulted from Patton's leadership. Believing that the German-held riverbank facing the Third Army was held weakly, he slipped a division over the Rhine at night on March 22, 1945, without benefit of air, artillery, or any other form of support. When the massive British assault began, the Third Army was already on the other side. Because of his initiative, the Americans led the final drive into Germany, with the British playing a supporting role. This brought the war to a quicker conclusion and gave Patton, who was very competitive, great satisfaction as well as added glory.

Patton was the best U.S. field general because he was a superb professional and a master at combining all available arms to achieve maximum force, not because of his swaggering and

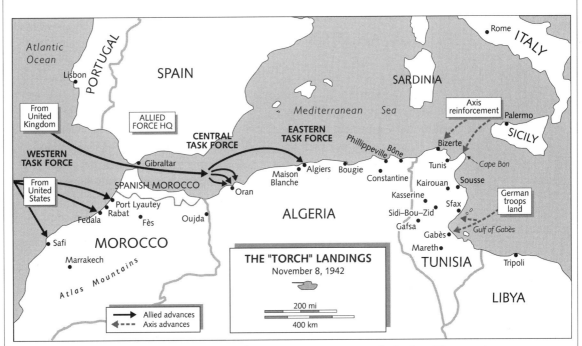

showmanship, his immaculate uniforms and ivory-handled pistols, or his profane speeches to the troops. Among the Allied commanders in Europe, Patton was the only one who understood strategic maneuver, a system used to outflank an army and totally destroy it. Most of the other Allied commanders were concerned primarily with limiting their risks, which also meant restricting their gains.

Patton, who was quick to see possibilities and was a master of exploiting breakthroughs, was the reverse of a cautious general like Montgomery. He was unorthodox and daring—but seldom rash, having calculated the odds. No Allied commander understood armored warfare as well as Patton did, and none had his ability to "read" a battle. Amid the fog of war, he had a unique gift for judging accurately what was going on and what the enemy was likely to do next.

Had it not been for the slapping incidents, Patton might have become commander of the 12th Army Group instead of Omar Bradley, who was junior to him and lacked Patton's bril-

liance. Patton was crushed when Eisenhower passed him over, but he understood the reason why and was grateful for being allowed to keep the Third Army. Bradley could be counted on not to embarrass Eisenhower nor antagonize the British, whereas Patton was likely to do both.

In this sense Patton's career demonstrates the wisdom of holding one's tongue, but this is not why he is remembered. Patton remains one of the most admired commanders of World War II because he had a genius for war.

SEE ALSO

Bulge, Battle of the; France, Battle of; Germany, surrender of; Mediterranean theater; Sicily, Battle of

FURTHER READING

Blumenson, Martin. *Patton, the Man Behind the Legend, 1885–1945.* New York: Morrow, 1985.
———, ed. *The Patton Papers.* 2 vols. Boston: Houghton Mifflin, 1972, 1985.
D'Este, Carlo. *Patton: A Genius for War.* New York: HarperCollins, 1995.
Patton, George S. *War As I Knew It.* Boston: Houghton Mifflin, 1947.
Province, Charles M. *Patton's Third Army: A Daily Combat Diary.* New York: Hippocrene, 1992.

Pearl Harbor, attack on

In 1941 the Japanese high command decided to expand into Southeast Asia, a decision it knew meant war with the United States. Since the United States's war-making potential was far greater than Japan's, the plan was to destroy the U.S. Pacific Fleet at anchor in Pearl Harbor at the outset. Then the Philippines and the U.S. possessions in the western Pacific could be easily taken. These actions, the Japanese naively hoped, would create a mood of defeatism in the United States and with it a willingness to let Japan have its way.

Strategically this plan could not have been more wrong-headed. Anyone with the slightest knowledge of the United States and its history could have predicted that the nation, far from caving in, would demand revenge. In taking such a foolish step, Japan's leaders had doomed their empire.

Tactically, however, the attack on Pearl Harbor was brilliantly planned

and executed. A harbor in Japan similar to Pearl became a training ground that paid big dividends during the actual attack. To allow for the shallow waters of Pearl—which U.S. Navy leaders thought protected the fleet from torpedo attack—Japan modified its torpedoes so that they would stay near the surface. The attack fleet of six carriers slipped out of Japan unnoticed and kept radio silence while at sea. Thus the U.S. radio network that located Japanese ships by their transmissions had no idea where the carriers were.

On the morning of December 7, 1941, the Japanese carriers launched a first wave of 180 aircraft in 15 minutes against Pearl Harbor. A second and equally powerful wave followed an hour behind it. All Japan's aircraft were in the air within 90 minutes, a feat no other navy could match at that time. United States Navy personnel first received news that Hawaii was under attack when Japanese bombs and torpedoes started exploding at 7:55 a.m. In a matter of minutes battleship row was in chaos.

Two hours later, when the attack ended, the United States had lost 188 planes, with 159 others damaged. A total of 18 warships were sunk or disabled, including seven battleships. A total of 2,403 Americans lost their lives, while 1,178 were wounded. Japan lost 29 planes and pilots, five midget submarines, and one fleet sub, plus their crews. In the history of war, few victories have been more lopsided.

This sudden and sweeping defeat led to charges that President Franklin D. Roosevelt or his commanders must have orchestrated this battle to lead the United States into World War II. No evidence to support this theory has ever been discovered. Instead, what two congressional investigations and a library of books have uncovered was a mountain of complacency and incompetence.

On December 8, 1941, one day after the attack on Pearl Harbor, Congress issued this joint resolution declaring war on Japan.

Pearl Harbor was taken completely by surprise when the Japanese arrived in the early morning of December 7. A total of 247 planes were either destroyed or damaged during the two-hour attack.

Although the fleet trained hard on weekdays, it still took weekends off. The ships at Pearl Harbor were sitting ducks, with no steam in their boilers, no gunners on watch, ammunition for the guns locked up, and many of the men ashore on leave. The battleships were not protected by torpedo nets. No long-range air patrols were being conducted, yet the Army's fighter planes required four hours' notice to take to the air. Furthermore, as the Army was worried abut sabotage, the aircraft were clustered together, which made them easy targets for the Japanese. Radar was available, but not in use—except for training purposes.

No precautions had been made against an attack because no one thought it likely, despite the war warnings sent to Hawaii. As a result of the attack, the army and navy commanders in Hawaii were fired. Hawaii had been given enough fighter planes and antiaircraft guns to defend itself if given sufficient warning. It had long-range patrol planes too, which, if they had been in the air could have provided that warning. There is no need to look for elaborate conspiracies when the evidence of leadership failures is so obvious.

Humiliating and costly as the Hawaiian defeat was, things were not as bad as they seemed. The three carriers stationed at Pearl Harbor were away delivering airplanes when the base was attacked, so they returned untouched. Vice Admiral Chuichi Nagumo, who commanded the attacking force, refused the request from his air commander for a second strike. Thus, the shipyards, drydocks, machine shops, and especially the fuel storage tanks, which were essential for servicing the fleet, were largely intact. Without them the fleet would have been forced to return to the West Coast and the Pacific war would have taken a different course.

Even the damage itself was not as bad as it looked. Except for *Arizona* and *Oklahoma*, all the battleships would be raised, modernized, and restored to useful service. The Pacific Fleet was in business still, and would soon put a stop to the Japanese advance.

SEE ALSO

Coral Sea, Battle of; Japan; Midway, Battle of; Pacific Fleet; Pacific war

FURTHER READING

Black, Wallace B. *Pearl Harbor!* New York: Maxwell Macmillan, 1991.

Prange, Gordon W. *At Dawn We Slept: The Untold Story of Pearl Harbor.* New York: McGraw-Hill, 1981.

Raymer, Edward. *Descent into Darkness: Pearl Harbor, 1941: A Navy Diver's Memoir.* Novato, Calif.: Presidio, 1996.

Toland, John. *Infamy: Pearl Harbor and Its Aftermath.* Garden City, N.Y.: Doubleday, 1982.

Willmott, H. P. *Pearl Harbor.* Englewood Cliffs, N.J.: Prentice-Hall, 1983.

Perkins, Frances

SECRETARY OF LABOR, 1933–45

- Born: April 10, 1889, Boston, Mass.
- Political party: Democratic
- Government service: Member, Industrial Commission of the State of New York, 1919–26; chairperson, Industrial Board of the State of New York, 1926–29; Industrial commissioner of the State of New York, 1926–33; secretary of labor, 1933–44
- Died: May 14, 1965, New York City

Although her given name was Fannie Coralie Perkins, throughout her career she preferred to be called Frances. She devoted her life to public service, first as a teacher, then as a settlement house worker and reformer. Beginning in 1919, she served the Industrial Commission of New York State as a commission member, chairperson of the commission, and finally as the commissioner. This commission served as the judicial and legislative branch of the state Department of Labor, and labor issues were her chief concern throughout her working life.

Although Perkins entered government service with the support of New York state governor Al Smith, she was closely associated with the administration of Franklin D. Roosevelt from the time he became governor of New York in 1929 until his death in 1945. When she became secretary of labor in 1933, she became the first woman ever to serve as a member of a President's cabinet.

Energetic and forceful, Perkins was a highly visible secretary who involved herself in many pieces of New Deal legislation that affected labor. During the war she was less prominent than in the New Deal years, because reform took a backseat for the duration of the war. She became a controversial cabinet member because of her strong defense of labor's rights, and Roosevelt preferred that she maintain a low profile. Although she offered to resign on several occasions, Roosevelt trusted her and refused to dispense with her services. Her most important contribution to the war effort came in 1942 when she helped create the National War Labor Board, an agency that mediated disputes between labor and management and did much to keep the production lines running smoothly throughout the war.

SEE ALSO

Labor

FURTHER READING

Martin, George. *Madam Secretary: Frances Perkins.* Boston: Houghton Mifflin, 1976.

Perkins, Frances. *The Roosevelt I Knew.* New York: Viking, 1946.

Philippine Islands

SEE Pacific war, Southwest Pacific Area

Philippine Sea, battle of the

On June 15, 1944, U.S. troops went ashore on Saipan in the Mariana Islands. By nightfall 20,000 troops had landed, despite the usual fierce resistance. Within hours Admiral Raymond Spruance had learned that the Imperial Japanese Navy (IJN) was going to make an all-out effort to destroy the Fifth Fleet, which was there to protect the invasion force. The IJN had assembled a great armada, including nine new carriers, in hopes of gaining a decisive victory.

Vice Admiral Jisaburo Ozawa knew his force to be weaker than the Fifth Fleet, but he counted on two advantages. Because his planes lacked armor and self-sealing gas tanks that would prevent loss of fuel and explosions, his planes had more range than the U.S. fighters, enabling them to attack from 300 miles out compared to 200 for the Americans' aircraft. In addition, Ozawa thought he would have the assistance of some 200 aircraft based on Guam and Tinian in the Marianas. What he did not know, because the Japanese commander of those two islands misled him, was that U.S. carrier planes had wiped out the airfields he was depending on for support.

At Midway, Japan's pilots had been the best. But this was no longer true—most of Japan's veterans had been killed in action. Along with superior firepower, the superior skills of its crews gave the U.S. Navy an ever-growing advantage. Since Midway, radar had been refined so that it could give 45 minutes' notice of an attack, and Carrier Task Force 58 could launch 300 fighters in less than half an hour. Since a Hellcat could climb 20,000 feet in seven minutes, even the last ones off the decks would reach combat altitude before the first Japanese fighters arrived.

Japan's search planes discovered the Fifth Fleet late on June 18, 1944, and Ozawa ordered a full attack. The U.S. Navy's response was overwhelming. Fewer than 100 of 373 Japanese planes that flew into battle made it back to their carriers, three of which were sunk

and one badly damaged. The Americans lost only 29 aircraft in what they came to call "the Great Marianas Turkey Shoot."

At the time, there was considerable grumbling that Admiral Spruance had held Task Force 58 back when it could have sunk most or all of the Japanese carriers. But Spruance believed that guarding the landing force took priority over chasing enemy ships. What was not understood at the time was that by destroying most of Ozawa's planes, TF58 had put Japanese naval aviation out of business anyway. The IJN could replace its lost aircraft, but not its pilots. When the IJN fought its last great battle, at Leyte Gulf in October 1944, they would use their carriers simply as bait, since they could no longer launch effective air strikes.

SEE ALSO
Central Pacific Area; Leyte Gulf, Battle of; Spruance, Raymond A.

Poland

Few countries suffered more during World War II than Poland. When it was invaded by Germany on September 1, 1939, Poland had a population of 36 million. At a minimum, 6 million Poles had been killed by the end of the war.

In the 1930s, Poland was governed by a quasi-dictatorship led by the military. This leadership aroused much anger in the West by taking a chunk of Czechoslovakia in 1939 when it was dismembered by Hitler. Although it profited briefly from German aggression, Poland became the next to fall. While Britain and France had promised to come to Poland's side, and did declare war on Germany when it crossed the Polish border on September 1,

1939, they provided little tangible aid. Poland was too far from Britain for the Royal Air Force to provide support. The French Army was afraid to move beyond its Maginot Line, allowing the Germans to concentrate their forces in the east, where they deployed 60 divisions.

There was little Poland could do to stem the German advance. It had no defensible frontier. Its regular army of 280,000 was no match for the German Wehrmacht (military). It did have a large reserve, but mobilization problems prevented it from being fully effective. Poland's small navy and air force were quickly destroyed. To make matters worse, the Soviet Union invaded Poland on September 17, putting the Polish Army between two jaws of a nutcracker. Warsaw fell on September 27, and all organized resistance was over by October 5.

Defeat did not end Poland's role in the war, however. Some 90,000 Polish soldiers escaped through neighboring states. Many made their way to the west, to fight again under Allied leadership. In addition, many Poles taken prisoner by the Soviets would be released after Germany invaded Russia in 1941. These former prisoners of war also fought again, notably in the Italian campaigns. A handful of small vessels became the basis of a Polish naval force that eventually numbered 4,000 men, and they fought alongside the Royal Navy. Some of the best squadrons in Britain's Fighter Command were Polish as well. A Polish government in exile was headquartered in London throughout the war.

In addition, Poland developed the biggest resistance movement of any conquered state. The main Polish underground army was organized to help liberate Poland when Allied forces arrived on the scene. As a rule it avoided making attacks on German positions for fear that reprisals would be made against the civilian population. An exception to this rule came in late 1942 and early 1943 when Germany began mass expulsions from the Lublin and Zamosc region. Germany's plan to resettle the area with German immigrants was defeated by the Polish Home Army, which attacked the German settlers and made resettlement impossible.

The resistance sought to counteract German propaganda with its own newspapers and leaflets. It gathered intelligence, which was passed on to Britain. As German pressure on Polish Jews worsened, the resistance established a Committee for Aid to Jews. The broad reach of the resistance made it a shadow state, with its own courts, schools, universities, and cultural life. In the face of terrifying dangers, Polish patriots kept the flame of freedom burning.

The best-remembered events in the history of occupied Poland were the two Warsaw uprisings. The first of these took place in the Warsaw ghetto, where Jewish leaders had been stockpiling arms to make a last-ditch stand against what became known as the Holocaust. The Allies were still far away. Some 300,000 out of the ghetto's 360,000 inhabitants had been sent to the Treblinka death camp. This left the remainder with only two choices: to die passively in gas chambers or with guns in their hands in the ghetto.

On April 19, 1943, about 3,000 Germans with armored vehicles and artillery stormed the ghetto, which was defended by 1,000 Jews, who fought back with small arms and other hand weapons. Though heavily outnumbered and outgunned, they managed to hold out until May 16, when they were overrun. Elements of the Home Army, and the Communist People's Guard, attempted to break into the ghetto and open an escape line, but could not get through. Thus, nearly all the survivors were sent to the Treblinka and Majdanek death camps. Although the ghetto rising failed, the heroic defenders

Polish soldiers march out of Warsaw to a prison camp after surrendering the partly demolished capital in 1939.

inspired other uprisings, notably in the Treblinka and Sobibor death camps.

The second Warsaw uprising took place on a much greater scale. When it broke out on August 1, 1944, the Red Army was nearing Warsaw. The Home Army had long prepared for this day, for which it had political as well as military goals. It hoped to hand the Germans a defeat. More important, it meant to take control of Warsaw before the communists got there and installed their own government. To that end, the Home Army mustered 37,600 fighters, of whom only 14 percent had weapons. The rest were to arm themselves with weapons parachuted in by the Allies or taken from German corpses.

The Home Army's leaders expected the fight to last 10 days, but it actually took the Germans several months to retake the city. During that time the Soviet offensive came to a halt—because of German pressure, or so the Soviets claimed. Small quantities of arms were dropped on Warsaw by Allied, and even Soviet, aircraft. But aircraft losses were high and the quantity of supplies dwindled. Except once, Stalin would not let Allied planes land on Soviet fields, which made supplying Warsaw by air all but impossible.

The Home Army surrendered on October 1. During the months of savage fighting, 83 percent of Warsaw was destroyed and perhaps 250,000 civilians (out of a total of 1 million) were killed in addition to 15,000 Home Army irregulars.

Stalin was the real winner of the second Warsaw uprising. By the time the Red Army reached Warsaw the Home Army had been fatally weakened. Polish confidence in the government in exile, which had not been able to organize sufficient help, was seriously eroded. All this made it that much easier to turn Poland into a Soviet satellite after the war.

Germany divided its share of Poland into two parts. The western half, which the Nazis called Wartheland, was ruthlessly Germanized. Most Poles were expelled from it, and all traces of Polish culture erased. The eastern half, called the General Government, became a kind of reservation for the Polish people. But here too extreme anti-Polish measures were employed. Millions of Polish men and women were sent to Germany as slave laborers. Many of those who remained became forced laborers in German camps. Although all Jews were already scheduled to be exterminated, the German hope was to eliminate the

Slavic population too. By 1941 the food ration for Warsaw's Poles was 669 calories a day, which ensured that malnutrition and disease would take many lives.

Soviet-occupied Poland fared little better. It was absorbed into the Soviet Union from September 1939 to June 1941 and was ruled by terror, every effort being made to abolish Polish culture and murder Polish leaders and resisters. All private property was seized, and all important government offices filled with Soviet citizens. Polish publications were suppressed. Ukrainian and Byelorussian became the official languages, with Russian also compulsory in schools and universities. One and a half million Poles were deported to beyond the Ural Mountains. Perhaps 30 percent of them died in the Soviet Union before being released in the fall of 1941.

After Germany invaded Russia in June 1941, the former Soviet zone of Poland was divided between the Government General and the Baltic states of Estonia, Latvia, and Lithuania. If Germany had won the war, Hitler's plan was to turn the Government General area into German soil and eliminate the Polish people. Even though he ultimately lost the war, he still eliminated millions of Poles. The accepted estimate is that 6 million Polish people died, fewer than half being Jewish victims of the Holocaust.

Some non-Jewish Poles were murdered by the Soviets, but most fell prey to Nazism. For its suffering Poland deserved a better fate in the postwar period than it actually received.

SEE ALSO

Germany; Eastern front

FURTHER READING

Engel, David. *Facing a Holocaust: The Polish Government-In-Exile and the Jews, 1943–1945*. Chapel Hill: University of North Carolina Press, 1993.

Gross, Jan Tomasz. *Polish Society Under German Occupation*. Princeton, N.J.: Princeton University Press, 1979.

Lukas, Richard C. *The Forgotten Holocaust: The Poles Under German Occupation, 1939–1944*. Lexington: University of Kentucky Press, 1986.

Sagajllo, Witold. *Man in the Middle: A Story of the Polish Resistance, 1940–45*. London: Leo Cooper, 1984.

Potsdam conference

Code named Terminal, this was the last wartime conference of the Grand Alliance, which consisted of Britain, the Soviet Union, and the United States. It met in Potsdam, Germany, from July 17 to August 2, 1945. The United States was represented at the conference for the first time by President Harry S Truman, who had succeeded to office in April following Franklin Roosevelt's death. The conference began with Prime Minister Winston Churchill heading the British delegation, but his party was defeated in the British general election and Clement Attlee came to Potsdam on July 28 as the new Prime Minister.

The terms on which Japan was to surrender were discussed at Potsdam, as were the peace terms for Europe. A great deal of time was spent on the thorny question of Poland's future, as well as on drawing the boundaries between many of the states of Eastern Europe. Because no agreement could be reached on these issues, they were never resolved.

The Japanese surrender terms were the easiest to agree on, and issuing them became the conference's main achievement. Japan's unconditional surrender remained the basic demand, but the details had to be spelled out. Japan's armed forces were to surrender without conditions and be disarmed. Japan was to be occupied by the United States. Japanese sovereignty would be confined to the four home islands. Its war criminals would be punished. The citizens of Japan were to receive the blessings of democracy, including freedom of speech, thought, and respect for individual rights.

Prisoners of war

The Geneva convention of 1929 spelled out the conditions under which prisoners of war (POWs) were to be held. POWs were to be promptly removed from the battle area, if wounded they were to receive medical attention, and they were to be fed and housed in the same way as troops of the capturing power. They were not required to disclose any information except for their name, rank, and identification numbers. They had the right to correspond with families and friends. If they escaped and were recaptured their punishment could not exceed a month's solitary confinement. The International Red Cross had the right to inspect the camps in which they were held.

All the warring powers in World War II had signed this convention, except Japan and the Soviet Union. In actual practice, the degree to which the convention was observed varied enormously. The United States and Britain upheld it faithfully in most respects. Germany, too, generally observed the convention where Western POWs were concerned. However, it treated captured Soviet troops with extreme brutality. Of some 5 million Soviet POWs taken by Germany, only one-sixth are believed to have survived the war. On the eastern front, the Waffen SS took no prisoners at all. This monstrous crime also turned

out to be a serious blunder on Germany's part, for it had acute labor shortages throughout the war that Soviet POWs could have eased.

The Soviet Union replied in kind, working to death a large proportion of the German prisoners it took. This was the policy of Japan too. The Japanese regarded surrender as dishonorable and treated POWs as criminals or worse. All the POWs in Japanese hands were subject to torture and murder at the whim of camp commanders, as well as being underfed and overworked. U.S. POWs, most of them taken in the Philippines during the war's early months, had little more than a 50-50 chance of going home alive. Had the war lasted much longer, all would have died.

The luckiest POWs, mostly German, were those imprisoned in the United States. They performed healthful agricultural duties for the most part and were well treated and fed. The farm areas in which they worked tended to greet them warmly and were glad for their help. When they traveled in the South, German POWs rode and ate in superior whites-only facilities, to which black Americans were denied entry. This complicated the job of teaching POWs democratic values, which was a vain effort in most cases anyway.

The American Red Cross provided standard care packages such as this one to American prisoners of war.

PT boats

The United States had only 12 Patrol Torpedo (PT) boats when World War II broke out, although large numbers of them were constructed after Pearl Harbor was attacked in December 1941. The PT boat was 77 feet to 81 feet long and powered by three Packard V-12 gasoline engines. These engines, along with its plywood hull, gave the PT a top speed of 45 knots, making it faster than any destroyer.

In theory the PT boat's two to four torpedoes made it a ship killer. But in practice, with its gasoline tanks, wooden hull, and lack of armor plate, the PT was a floating coffin. Nor, in practice, was it as fast as advertised. Its engines were balky, and the boat seldom achieved anything near its maximum speed.

PT boats became famous early in the war because the half-dozen stationed in the Philippines did heroic work. They also carried General Douglas MacArthur and his party to safety when he was ordered to leave Corregidor and escape to Australia. After the war, PT boats became famous again because, as a young officer, John F. Kennedy had commanded PT-109 and performed bravely when it was sunk by a Japanese destroyer.

Although movies showed PT boats attacking enemy warships, in reality they were mostly used against barges and other small craft, serving in effect as gunboats. For these duties deck guns, not torpedoes, were needed, and PT boat skippers made every effort to add to their firepower. Young Kennedy obtained a 37-mm anti-tank gun from the Army and mounted it on his bow, a common solution. The Navy would have been better off to copy Germany's E-boat, which, with its diesel engine and steel hull, was reliable, hard to sink, and powerful for its size.

Race riots

SEE African Americans

Radio

World War II brought record levels of income to radio stations and networks because they wanted to spend more on advertising, which they could deduct from their high wartime taxes. Further, paper shortages established limits to the amount of print advertising that could be purchased. Magazines, for example, were given paper quotas equal to 75 percent of what they had consumed in peacetime. As a result, in 1944 the nation's 836 full- and part-time radio stations earned $68.9 million, a 125 percent increase over 1942.

The greatest growth of sponsored programs during the war was in detective-mystery dramas, comedy-variety shows, and news. The so-called dramatic shows included such light fare as "The Man from G-2," "The Whistler," "The Man Called X," "David Harding—Counter-Spy," and "The FBI in Peace and War," which was supposedly based on real cases.

As in peacetime, the majority of money was spent on comedy-variety shows. Most of these continued to use the formulas that had worked so well in the 1930s—Jack Benny's alleged stinginess, for instance. "Fibber McGee and Molly" was unique in that its writer, Don Quinn, built whole shows around war themes ranging from black marketeering to the recruitment of nurses' aides. This show had consistently high ratings, which suggests that others could have been topical too, with no loss of popularity.

Bob Hope, who had been just another comedian before the war, became a national institution during the early 1940s by traveling around the world to military camps and bases. Virtually all the broadcasts of his weekly show were performed live before audiences of servicemen. It may have been exhausting, but the formula proved to be good business. His show set an all-time high in ratings for a continuing series, and his face appeared on the cover of *Life* magazine, a rare distinction for a comic.

As an entertainment medium, radio was highly successful. But as an educational medium it fell short. In war, as in peace, the more serious and ambitious shows were often dropped or were aired at unpopular hours. Of the sponsored shows, only "Town Meeting of the Air" had a large audience.

As a news medium, on the other hand, radio did an outstanding job. CBS reported after the war that war-news programs made up 38.7 percent of the total network air time from Pearl Harbor to V-E Day. Thanks to Edward R. Murrow and his brilliant team of reporters, CBS's news was the best, but the other networks stepped up their news coverage as well.

All the radio news organizations refused to allow recorded material to be broadcast, requiring everything to be aired live. Although the recording technology of the day was clumsy and not easily portable, it did exist. This mobility enabled the British Broadcasting Company, which employed recordings, to bring the sounds of war to its listeners, sounds that Americans would have rarely heard otherwise.

Everyone appreciated the tremendous efforts made by CBS and other news organizations to keep the public abreast of current events. But critics justifiably complained of radio's failure to deal with issues in depth. These complaints were much the same as those made about network television today.

Serious documentaries were expensive to produce and usually received poor ratings. Airing them was a public service, but bad business—even in a time of soaring profits.

Local stations took a similar view. Writing was the key to good radio, yet in 1944 the 747 full-time stations in the United States employed fewer than 600 writers. Their average pay was $40 a week, about half what was paid to the stations' salesmen. Quality suffered as a result.

SEE ALSO
Home front

Rationing

Rationing (limiting the quantity of products a family could buy in a given period) was essential to the war effort but a terrifying prospect for public officials. They feared that voters would not tolerate sharp restrictions on what had in peacetime been regarded as essential goods. As it turned out, politicians misjudged the public's reaction.

Gasoline rationing is a case in point. No one had expected that war with Japan would mean the loss of most of the world's natural rubber supplies. The United States had failed to stockpile natural rubber when it had the chance, and now it would have to do without it. Synthetic rubber would meet the military's needs, but because rubber

Different home front activities provided for different rations of gasoline. A "C" card, issued for one of the reasons listed at the bottom, granted a car owner more than the standard four gallons of gas per month.

R-558.—Rev. 10 1 42

C

MILEAGE RATION

☐ Official Gov't or Red Cross business.
☐ School official traveling school to school.
☐ Transportation 4 or more to school.
☐ Transportation of United States mail.
☐ Wholesale newspaper delivery.
☐ Carrying newsreel photographic equipment.
☐ Physician, surgeon, veterinarian.
☐ Public Health nurse or interne.
☐ Embalmer.
☐ Minister, priest, or rabbi.
☐ Transportation of farm workers, marine workers, or farm materials.
☐ Essential hospital, utility, or war worker.
☐ Labor conciliation, recruiting, training workers.
☐ Construction, repair, maintenance services or production specialist.
☐ Members of Armed force to duty.
☐ Telegram delivery.
☐ **Essential scrap agent.**

would always be in short supply, it would have to be rationed.

The easiest way to do this was to ration gasoline, which was not scarce (except in the Northeast). By restricting gasoline use, rubber would automatically be conserved, simply because fewer miles would be driven.

President Franklin D. Roosevelt hesitated to act, but Congress forced his hand in 1942 by establishing a Rubber Supply Agency to make rubber out of alcohol. FDR vetoed the bill but then got to work on the problem. The result was a combination of gasoline rationing and a national speed limit of 35 miles an hour that saved enough natural rubber to meet essential needs. Once the public became aware of what was at stake, it accepted these restrictions.

Many other items had to be rationed as well, leading to endless complications. Irritation over rationing was continuous and so heated that in 1943 Leon Henderson, one of the most brilliant New Deal politicians, had to resign as head of the Office of Price Administration even though he was one of the "unsung heroes of World War II" and a greater organizer than Albert Speer, the German production genius.

Urban Americans eventually grew used to standing in lines. Not only were many types of food and clothing rationed, but the number of ration "points" (the units used to determine what could be purchased) required for specific items fluctuated, obliging every housewife to update her calculations on

a weekly, or even daily, basis. Consumers were issued coupon books and paid for their purchases of rationed goods with coupons as well as cash. This procedure made shopping, which was a nightmare in wartime anyway, even more difficult. A certain amount of black marketeering was inevitable under these circumstances. Most Americans, no matter how angry or frustrated they might get, abided by the complex rules as best they could. In short, rationing worked. United States fighting men and women never lacked for essentials because of shirking or cheating on the home front.

SEE ALSO
Home front; Mobilization

Red Army

SEE Soviet Union (U.S.S.R.)

Refugees

Few aspects of World War II were sadder than the refugee crisis. At the outbreak of war in Europe, Poles fled from the advancing Germans, only to find themselves trapped by Soviet forces approaching from the rear. In France and Belgium, masses of people took to the roads in May 1940 when the German blitzkrieg (lightning war) struck. With civilian and military traffic mixed together many civilians died in strafing attacks.

In 1944, with Allied armies closing in on all sides, millions of Germans became refugees themselves. As death camps and concentration camps were liberated, and slave laborers were released from bondage, millions more took to their feet. By war's end more than 30 million people had become refugees, a tide of human misery so vast as to be almost beyond belief.

The United Nations Relief and Rehabilitation Administration (UNRRA) was established in 1943 to deal with this catastrophe. Refugees, now labeled "displaced persons" (DPs, for short) were housed in makeshift camps all over western and central Europe. Volunteers provided much of the effort needed to operate these camps, while the United States provided the funds. Under such extreme circumstances, the program did as much good as it could. The UNRRA distributed 25 million tons of food in 17 countries between 1945 and 1947.

Most survivors eventually found their way home or were resettled in new homelands. This was a slow and difficult process, because most European countries were having trouble meeting the needs of their own people, let alone those of refugees. A lucky few made it to the United States or, in the case of Jewish displaced persons, to Palestine. But others remained in camps for years, living a kind of half-life until death or emigration solved their problem.

Of the millions of Chinese refugees, whose displacement went back to when Japan invaded China in 1937, little is known.

Relocation camps

The so-called relocation camps were actually concentration camps in which the entire Japanese-American population of the West Coast was confined. Almost 120,000 people were interned, or forcibly held, in these camps between 1942 and 1946.

Most relocation camps were placed on barren sites in six western states, although two particularly unpleasant camps were built in Arkansas. While the inmates were not maltreated physically as a rule, they lived harsh lives in their bleak camps, which were cold in winter and hot in summer. In the worst camps, entire families constructed dugouts beneath their barracks to obtain some relief from the searing heat. A special trial for female inmates was the absolute lack of privacy.

The camps were surrounded by barbed wire and armed guards and were administered by the newly created War Relocation Authority. This mass internment was popular with Americans at the time, but it became a source of shame shortly thereafter.

SEE ALSO

Japanese Americans

FURTHER READING

Gesensway, Deborah. *Beyond Words: Images from America's Concentration Camps.* Ithaca, N.Y.: Cornell University Press, 1987.
Okihiro, Gary Y. *Whispered Silences: Japanese Americans and World War II.* Seattle: University of Washington Press, 1996.
Smith, Page. *Democracy on Trial: The Japanese-American Evacuation and Relocation in World War II.* New York: Simon & Schuster, 1995.
Tateishi, John, ed. *And Justice for All: An Oral History of the Japanese American Detention Camps.* New York: Random House, 1984.

Resistance movements

Every country occupied by the Axis powers had some type of resistance movement. Patriotic undergrounds (groups of citizens secretly acting against their occupiers) gathered information for the Allies, hid wanted individuals, Jews, and downed Allied airmen, and performed acts of sabotage.

A nation's courage bore no relation to its size. The resistance movement of Luxembourg (population 300,000) helped some 4,000 Allied military personnel escape from the Nazis. In some countries, resisters formed paramilitary units, such as the French Maquis and the Polish Home Army.

Women played a prominent role in the resistance, even in partisan bands (illegal military units). In World War II women typically did not serve in combat, but partisan bands had trouble recruiting and could not afford to discriminate against women. As a result, many women took part in the dangerous fight for victory and even rose to positions of leadership. Nancy Wake, an Australian married to a Frenchman, became *chef du parachutage*—the organizer of arms and equipment supplied by Britain—for 7,000 resistance fighters in central France.

Resistance tactics also included industrial strikes and slowdowns, being as uncooperative or inefficient as possible, and other forms of civil resistance. Underground presses turned out anti-Nazi posters, pamphlets, newspapers, and even books. At its simplest, resistance was expressed—frequently—by scrawling or scratching Churchill's V-for-victory sign (or, in France, de Gaulle's Cross of Lorraine) on German posters, as well as other forms of patriotic graffiti.

In Norway, civil resistance was so widespread that the Nazi leader Vidkum Quisling (whose name became a synonym for Nazi collaboration) was unable to form a puppet national legislature. One of the most justly celebrated resistance coups took place in Denmark. In October 1943, learning that the Nazis were planning to seize Denmark's Jews and send them to death camps, the resistance ferried almost the entire Jewish population to Sweden and safety. Out of some 8,000 Jews, fewer than 500 remained behind.

Another striking example took place in Bulgaria. When its fascist government attempted to send Bulgaria's Jews to the death camps, massive popular opposition forced the move's cancellation. Holland was too small for armed resisters to operate safely. But the Dutch staged three massive strikes against their occupiers. The first was in February 1941 to protest the arrests of Jews. The second, in the spring of 1943, was a response to the call-up of former prisoners of war for forced labor in Germany. The third was a rail strike in September 1944 to support Operation Market Garden, a doomed Allied effort to seize bridgeheads on the Rhine. Savage reprisals followed each of these actions but did not break the Dutch spirit. Some 15,000 Dutch Jews survived the war because

French resistance fighters march on patrol in the Eire and Loire region in France.

their fellow countrymen concealed them throughout the occupation.

The French underground was exceptionally large and well organized. It reached its peak of effectiveness after D-Day (June 6, 1944), when rail workers and the Maquis combined to sabotage the railways and prevent the German Army from sending reinforcements to Normandy. Their efforts were so effective that it required two weeks to move a single German armored division from southern France to the Normandy battlefields. As the Allies neared Paris, the Maquis went into the streets and battled with the occupiers.

The Polish Home Army was less fortunate. In 1944, as the Red Army approached Warsaw, the underground attempted to seize the city. But German forces crushed the uprising as the Red Army ground to a halt. The Soviets did not resume their offensive until Warsaw had been flattened and the resistance wiped out.

Except in Yugoslavia, where partisans led by Joseph Tito ultimately beat the Germans, no resistance movement was strong enough to liberate its own country. But resistance movements in many cases provided the Allies with significant help. Their mere existence sustained national pride both during and after the war.

SEE ALSO
France; Poland

FURTHER READING

Camus, Albert. *Between Hell and Reason: Essays from the Resistance Newspaper Combat, 1944–1947.* Hanover, N.H.: University Press of New England, 1991.
Chevrillon, Claire. *Code name Christiane Clouet: A Woman in the French Resistance.* College Station: Texas A & M University Press, 1995.
Foot, M. R. D. *Resistance: An Analysis of European Resistance to Nazism, 1940–1945.* New York: McGraw-Hill, 1977.
Mastny, Vojtech. *The Czechs Under Nazi Rule: the Failure of National Resistance, 1939–1942.* New York: Columbia University Press, 1995.
Michel, Henri. *The Shadow War: European Resistance, 1939–1945.* New York: Harper & Row, 1972.

Riots

SEE African Americans; Zoot-suit riots

Rommel, Erwin

GERMAN FIELD MARSHAL; "THE DESERT FOX"

- *Born: November 15, 1891; Heidenheim, Germany*
- *Political party: National Socialist (Nazi)*
- *Education: Royal Officer Cadet School, Danzig, 1911*
- *Military service: German Army— second lieutenant, 1912; first lieutenant, 1916; captain, 1918; major, 1933; lieutenant colonel, 1935; colonel, 1937; brigadier general, 1939; commander of 7th Panzer Division, 1940; commander of Afrika Korps, 1941; major general, 1941; lieutenant general, 1941; commander of German-Italian Panzerarmee, 1942; general, 1942; field marshal, 1942; commander of Army Group Afrika; commander of Army Group B, 1943*
- *Died: October 14, 1944, Germany*

Although he is not particularly esteemed by German historians today, Rommel was extremely popular in Germany during the war. He was also admired by the Western Allies, who called him the Desert Fox.

As an infantry commander in World War I, Rommel won Germany's highest decoration, the Pour le Mérite. One of the few professional soldiers to be kept on in Germany's tiny postwar army, Rommel came to Hitler's attention as a

Erwin Rommel pauses for a photograph in Libya with the 15th Panzer Division, one of the two founding divisions of his Afrika Korps.

result of his highly successful book *The Infantry Attacks* (1937).

In 1939 Hitler put Rommel in charge of security at his headquarters. The following year Rommel was given a panzer division. During the armored battles that defeated France in May and June 1940, Rommel led his division with great dash and ingenuity, and became a national hero.

In 1941 Hitler sent Rommel and two divisions to North Africa, where his Italian allies were being flattened by the British. Ordered to remain on the defensive, Rommel attacked instead, driving the British almost out of what is now Libya. The rest of the year he devoted to weathering three separate British offensives, but in January 1942 Rommel attacked again. It was during this offensive that Prime Minister Winston Churchill, speaking in the House of Commons, said of Rommel: "We have a very daring and skillful opponent against us, and, may I say across the havoc of war, a great general."

In June, Rommel captured Fortress Tobruk, which had withstood his offensive the previous year, and drove the

British back into Egypt. Rommel won his victories despite continual shortages of men, tanks, and fuel. But there was a limit to how much could be achieved by cleverness in the face of his enemy's ever-growing superiority in men and materials.

That limit was reached at El Alamein in the western desert of Egypt, where Rommel was badly defeated by Britain's Eighth Army under the command of General Bernard Law Montgomery in November 1942. Rommel saved his force with a masterful fighting retreat, but was forced to withdraw all the way back to Tunisia.

Thanks to Operation Torch, the Allied landings in Morocco and Algeria, the Allies were now closing in on Tunisia from the west as well as the east. Rommel's advice to Hitler was to pull out, but Hitler ignored his advice and poured men into Tunisia for a last stand. A fraction of the force assembled there, if given to Rommel in 1941, would have enabled him to seize Egypt and the Suez Canal. Now all it could do was buy time. Rommel won one last victory, against U.S. forces at the Kasserine Pass, but his final efforts were futile. He left Africa on extended sick leave in March 1943, two months before the Axis surrender.

Like those of the Third Reich itself, Rommel's glory days were now behind him. When his health improved, Rommel was sent by Hitler to Italy and then to France. He was assigned to defend the English Channel coast. Although he strengthened Germany's defenses, when D-Day arrived, they proved to be inadequate. Rommel was not even there on D-Day, having gone home for a visit. He returned to France, only to be badly wounded in an air attack on July 17.

Although he had had almost nothing to do with it, Rommel was accused of joining in the plot to kill Hitler. Faced with a choice between taking poison or being tried for treason, he took his own life.

Rommel was noted for his gallantry

and courteous treatment of prisoners of war. His war in the western desert was a "clean" one in that few civilians were killed and both sides observed the rules of war. Relatively small forces contended over vast stretches of desert there, making it ideal country for an inventive tactician like Rommel. Whether he would have done as well had he commanded a great army on the European Continent will never be known, since he was never given that chance. But on his own in the desert, commanding what was essentially an army corps, Rommel was unmatched.

SEE ALSO

Afrika Korps; D-Day; Mediterranean theater

FURTHER READING

Irving, David. *The Trail of the Fox*. New York: Dutton, 1977.
Mitcham, Samuel W. *The Desert Fox in Normandy: Rommel's Defense of Fortress Europe*. Westport, Conn.: Praeger, 1997.
Rommel, Erwin. *The Rommel Papers*. B. H. Liddell-Hart, ed. 1948. Reprint, New York: Da Capo, 1982.
Rutherford, Ward. *The Biography of Field Marshal Erwin Rommel*. Oregon, Ill.: Quality Books, 1981.

Roosevelt, Anna Eleanor

FIRST LADY, 1933–45

- *Born: October 11, 1884, New York, N.Y.*
- *Political party: Democratic*
- *Died: November 7, 1962, New York, N.Y.*

Eleanor Roosevelt was the fifth cousin of Franklin Delano Roosevelt, to whom she was married on March 17, 1905, during the presidency of her uncle Theodore. Unlike Franklin, who was an adored only child, Eleanor had a difficult early life.

Her mother, Anna Hall Roosevelt, died of diphtheria in 1892 when Eleanor was not quite eight. Her brother Elliott died of the same disease in 1893, and her father, Teddy Roosevelt's brother, died of alcoholism in 1894, all three passing away within a period of 21 months. Other than Eleanor, only her brother Hall survived, and he eventually become an alcoholic like his father. Until she was 15, Eleanor was raised by her Grandmother Hall, whose stern regimen deprived her of much-needed affection.

In 1899 Eleanor was sent to Allenswood, a boarding school in England, where she spent the happiest part of her youth. In New York society Eleanor, who had no money of her own and believed (wrongly) that she was unattractive, had felt inadequate. But at Allenswood, an outstanding institution where a girl was judged by her character, she came into her own, enjoying both academic achievement and popularity. This first experience with success planted seeds that would one day flower beyond anyone's expectations. Yet she remained sensitive and needy in ways her husband Franklin could not meet. It was a mixed blessing for both of them that they fell in love and were married.

In short order, Eleanor had five children. Franklin studied law at Columbia University, was admitted to the bar in 1907, elected to the New York State Senate in 1910, and appointed assistant secretary of the navy by Woodrow Wilson in 1913, a post he held until nominated for Vice President by the Democrats in 1920.

The marriage of Franklin and Eleanor did not follow this same upward course. Too many babies, too much interference—however well meant—by her mother-in-law Sara, and too-frequent absences by Franklin made marriage something less than the joyful state

Eleanor Roosevelt (center) and Mary McLeod Bethune (second from left) greet guests at the opening of Midway Hall, one of two residence halls built by the Public Buildings Administration in 1943 for black women in government service.

Eleanor had pictured. In 1918 she learned that Franklin was having an affair with her own secretary and friend, Lucy Mercer. The marriage survived, but only because divorce would have ruined Franklin's political career. Eleanor never forgave him for this betrayal, even though she herself was unable to provide Franklin with the same adoration as Lucy Mercer had.

If no longer a love match, the Roosevelts' marriage was more than one of convenience. This became clear when Franklin was struck down by poliomyelitis in 1921. He almost died and was left a paraplegic. With his legs heavily braced, he could only move horizontally for short distances. From this point on, Eleanor performed not only the duties of a politician's wife but served as Franklin's eyes and ears—and sometimes his voice as well—in all the places he would have liked to go.

Eleanor helped Franklin resist the temptation to retire from active life and threw herself into furthering his career.

Already well informed on social issues because of her close association with social workers and reformers, she became a skillful politician too. Always more liberal than Franklin, she served as his conscience—especially on issues relating to women, children, and African Americans. During World War II she served briefly in the Office of Civilian Defense (OCD), the only government job she held during Franklin's lifetime. This proved to be a mistake, for Eleanor's liberalism had made her many enemies, who now extended their often-vicious attacks to include the OCD.

After Pearl Harbor was attacked on December 7, 1941, Eleanor's real war work was as the President's representative on both the home and fighting fronts. Her tours often took her to hospitals and military bases at home and abroad, most notably to the South Pacific in 1943. Admiral William Halsey, commander of the South Pacific Area, like most who did not know

Eleanor, dreaded her arrival. He was too busy to shower attention on visiting VIPs, and her reputation as a reformer and general "do-gooder" did not recommend Eleanor to conservative military leaders.

By the time she left the area under his command, however, Halsey had become one of Eleanor's warmest admirers. He later wrote that in a single day she inspected two navy hospitals, had lunch at an officers' rest home, reviewed the 2nd Marine Raiders Battalion, made a speech at a service club, attended a reception, and was guest of honor at a formal dinner. Although Halsey did not know it, that night she wrote her daily newspaper column—pecking it out herself on a portable typewriter.

Halsey's own description of Eleanor's methods cannot be bettered. "When I say that she inspected those hospitals," he wrote, "I don't mean that she shook hands with the chief medical officer, glanced into a sun parlor, and left. I mean that she went into every ward, stopped at every bed, and spoke to every patient: What was his name? How did he feel? Was there anything he needed? Could she take a message home? I marveled at her hardihood, both physical and mental; she walked for miles, and she saw patients who were grievously and gruesomely wounded. But I marveled at their expressions as she leaned over them. It was a sight I will never forget."

Eleanor made good on her promises too, carefully writing down the men's names and messages and religiously delivering them when she got back home. This was a practice that she continued throughout the war. At other times she inspected kitchens, stood in chow lines with the men, and rode with them in jeeps. Once she came across a convoy of armed troops heading for the front and

walked down the long line saying good-bye and good luck to every truck.

In the course of this one trip, she visited 17 islands plus Australia and New Zealand, and was seen by an estimated 400,000 servicemen. Among the islands she went to was Guadalcanal, which was bombed the night before she arrived and the night after she left. Admiral Halsey said that in his entire time as South Pacific Area commander, Eleanor did more good than any one person or group of civilians who visited his theater.

In other tours she visited Britain and numerous places in the Caribbean and South America. During the 1944 Presidential campaign, when FDR was too tired and busy to go on the stump, Eleanor filled in for him on many occasions. She also pushed him to hit the campaign trail himself, which he did late in the season, with great success.

As before the war, Eleanor continued to represent her husband at numerous functions, to serve as a link between the President and numerous other people, and to write a great deal, not only her regular column but magazine articles as well. For some time she also had a weekly radio broadcast. Although liberalism and reform took a backseat during the war, she continued to speak for the young, the poor, the disadvantaged, and African Americans.

SEE ALSO

Roosevelt, Franklin Delano

FURTHER READING

Freedman, Russell. *Eleanor Roosevelt: A Life of Discovery.* New York: Clarion, 1993.
Goodwin, Doris Kearns. *No Ordinary Time: Franklin and Eleanor Roosevelt: The Home Front in World War II.* New York: Simon & Schuster, 1994.
Lash, Joseph P. *Eleanor and Franklin.* New York: Norton, 1971.
Vercelli, Jane. *Eleanor Roosevelt.* New York: Chelsea House, 1994.

Roosevelt, Franklin Delano

PRESIDENT OF THE UNITED STATES, 1933–45

- *Born: January 30, 1882, Hyde Park, N.Y.*
- *Political party: Democratic*
- *Education: Harvard College, A.B., 1903; Columbia University Law School, 1904–07*
- *Military service: none*
- *Government service: New York Senate, 1911–13; assistant secretary of the navy, 1913–20; governor of New York, 1929–33; President of the United States, 1933–45*
- *Died: April 12, 1945, Warm Springs, Ga.*

As the son of James Roosevelt, a wealthy gentleman farmer in New York, and Sara Delano, whose family was even richer, Franklin Delano Roosevelt was born into wealth and privilege. Although his mother was very possessive, Roosevelt managed, with difficulty, to have himself sent to one of the top prep schools, Groton, and then to Harvard College. He failed to distinguish himself at Groton but did better at Harvard, where he became editor of the student newspaper. He did not excel in law school, but it was as a law student that he married a fifth cousin, Anna Eleanor Roosevelt, on March 17, 1905.

Franklin was admitted to the bar in 1907, but politics was his first love, and he won election to the New York State Senate in 1910. His name, and the fact that he had won election in a solidly Republican district, marked him as a rising figure in the Democratic party. As a result Woodrow Wilson appointed him assistant secretary of the navy in 1913, a post he held until nominated for the Vice Presidency by the Democrats in 1920. No

blame was attached to him for the ticket's defeat in that election. Indeed, he benefited from the exposure and from the opportunity to campaign all over the country and establish ties with prominent Democrats.

Franklin was struck down by poliomyelitis (polio) in 1921. He almost died at first, and suffered great pain for a long time, eventually being crippled by it. The supreme crisis of his life, it was also his making as a leader. He showed immense courage from the start, not only in fighting for survival but having an attitude so positive as to seem scarcely believable. Far from merely brushing off sympathy or sorrow, he made his bedside a place of good cheer and high spirits. Nothing in his life better became him than the manner in which he almost left it, and he would be brave and gallant about his disability ever after.

A lesser man would have been driven from public life by so great a misfortune. But Franklin, aided immensely by Eleanor, was able to conceal the full extent of his disability and remain actively involved in Democratic party affairs. In 1928 he gave a powerful nominating speech for Governor Al Smith of New York. When offered the gubernatorial nomination by Smith, he accepted. He would have preferred to wait, for people assumed that the Republican nominee, Herbert Hoover, would serve two terms. That would make 1932 the year for Roosevelt to run for governor and 1936 his year to be elected President.

Nonetheless, Roosevelt ran for governor in 1928 and, in the face of a Republican landslide, managed—by a tiny margin—to win. Two successful terms, during which he coped as best a governor could with the Great Depression, earned Roosevelt the Democratic Presidential nomination in 1932 from which he ascended to the Presidency. During his first two Presidential terms

President Roosevelt addresses a joint session of Congress on May 16, 1940.

Roosevelt established what became known as the New Deal.

Although it failed to bring economic recovery (World War II did that), the New Deal was highly successful in other respects. Legislation, such as the Social Security Bill, laid the basis for what would become a reasonably effective social safety net for poor Americans. Other acts created the Tennessee Valley Authority (which brought cheap power through public construction projects to many states and raised their standard of living), the Securities Exchange Commission, the Federal Deposit Insurance Corporation, the Home Owners Loan Corporation, the Works Progress Administration (which hired unemployed men to do many kinds of work), and numerous other programs and agencies. Together they put millions to work, enhanced the safety and well-being of millions more, and greatly improved the nation's infrastructure. The number and importance of the bills Roosevelt pushed through Congress has never been equaled.

By the late 1930s the worsening world situation forced Roosevelt to concentrate more on foreign affairs. In this area, however, he was greatly handicapped by the overwhelming reluctance of Americans to be drawn into another war. This mood, usually called isolationism, became more and more of an obstacle after war broke out in Europe in September 1939. FDR had once been an isolationist himself, but after the fall of France in June 1940, it was clear to him that the United States's interests, and perhaps national security itself, was threatened by the advance of Nazism and, to a lesser extent, of Japanese imperialism.

Until he won reelection to an unprecedented third Presidential term in 1940, Roosevelt hesitated to act. He was more decisive after the election, although he remained handicapped by the popular view that the United States should not enter the war unless it was actually attacked. But in 1941 he did secure passage of the Lend-Lease program, which provided essential aid to Britain and the Soviet Union.

In that summer Roosevelt met with Prime Minister Winston Churchill of Britain and issued the Atlantic Charter with him. This document was a statement of democratic principles that would govern the Allied war effort, although the United States was still at peace and as yet had no formal allies. He also expanded naval operations to the point where the U.S. Navy was actually engaged in combat with German U-boats. At the same time, he took a hard line against Japan, cutting off its oil supplies until the Japanese agreed to withdrawal from China (a proposition that was out of the question for Japan's military rulers).

Roosevelt seems to have hoped that Germany would declare war as a result of the fighting in the North Atlantic. Instead, it was Japan that broke the stalemate by attacking Pearl Harbor, Hawaii, on December 7, 1941, and seizing U.S., British, and Dutch possessions in the Pacific and Asia. Hitler declared war shortly after, and the United States finally became an active player in the world conflict.

In the early war years, Roosevelt kept a close eye on military affairs, and his foreign relations centered on reaching agreements about strategy with the British. He successfully clung to Europe as the first priority for U.S. arms, despite an enormous popular demand for revenge against Japan. Even so, the Pacific war was expanded far beyond what General George Marshall and other planners had wanted.

The war in the Pacific would likely have grown even larger if Roosevelt had not ordered that North Africa be invaded in 1942. War strategists believed this was the wrong place to fight Hitler, wishing instead to invade France as soon as possible in order to establish a second front in Western Europe. It would take much of the pressure off the Soviets, who were battling Germany in the east, and open the way to seizing Germany's industrial bases, without which Hitler could not wage war.

Although this was the best strategy, it could not be activated until May 1943 at the earliest. By that time the pressure to concentrate on the war with Japan might have become irresistible. Perhaps North Africa was not the right place, but November 1942 was the right time to launch a campaign that would put U.S. troops into battle against the Germans before Americans lost interest in them. Just as Marshall had feared, fighting in the Mediterranean forced the postponement of D-Day to 1944, but it may very well have saved the European priority, on which everything depended. Marshall did get his cross-channel invasion of France in 1944, later than he wanted but not too late for the Allies to help defeat Hitler and liberate Western Europe. Thus, Roosevelt seems to have done the right thing by forcing Marshall to fight in the Mediterranean first.

From mid-1943 on, with victory over Hitler becoming ever more certain, FDR concerned himself mainly with the shape of the postwar world. At major conferences with Soviet leader Joseph Stalin and Prime Minister Churchill, he struggled to design a new world order that would be fair, democratic, and peaceful. Although European colonialism did not fit into this vision, the main obstacle to a just peace was the Soviet Union.

In later years Roosevelt would be criticized for "giving away" Eastern Europe and other areas to the Soviet Union. But to treat the Soviets as a new enemy after having jointly defeated Hitler not only seemed unfair but could create a self-fulfilling prophesy. In an attempt to avert what would someday become known as the "Cold War," Roosevelt made every effort to assure the Soviets of

A 1940 campaign banner supports an unprecedented third term for Franklin Roosevelt.

U.S. goodwill and to meet the Soviet Union's legitimate security requirements.

At the Teheran conference in 1943, and again at Yalta in 1945, the Big Three (Britain, the Soviet Union, and the United States) agreed on occupation zones in Germany, on the future of Europe, and on certain territories that the Soviets would be allowed to keep in Europe and Asia. At Roosevelt's urging, the Soviets signed a "Declaration on Liberated Europe" in which all three parties promised that free elections would be held to determine each country's future.

Roosevelt has been accused of being too trusting, or worse, in supposing that Stalin would live up to such an agreement. But doing so would have been in the Soviets' best interests, which gave some reason for hope. If the United States and the U.S.S.R. worked together, they could ensure peace and prosperity for both in the postwar era. If, on the other hand, the nations of Eastern Europe, which the Red Army largely controlled at the time of Yalta, were denied the right of self-determination, the results would be very costly. The Soviets would have to occupy these states for years to come, maintain large armed forces for the purpose, and also, because of the United States's certain anger, would be denied the postwar U.S. loans and aid they desperately needed.

To make the latter point very clear, Roosevelt refused to discuss postwar aid with Stalin during the war. He also did not share the United States's nuclear secrets, or even tell Stalin that the United States was building an atomic weapon. Thanks to his spies, Stalin knew about the plans to build such a bomb, which meant he also knew that Roosevelt was

holding out on him. Roosevelt offered both a carrot (potential aid) and a stick (the threat of the atomic bomb). It was up to the Soviets to choose.

Events later proved that Stalin was prepared to pay almost any price to keep Eastern Europe firmly under his thumb—but there was no way for Roosevelt to know that in advance. The lands that the Soviets gained from the war were mostly territory the Soviets had fought for and that could not have been taken from them. The only way that Stalin might have been kept out of Poland would have been for the United States to enter the war much earlier than it did. Given the United States's late start, Roosevelt did everything he could for the people who fell under Stalin's rule.

Unfortunately, it was not good enough. When Stalin chose to ignore the Declaration on Liberated Europe, only war, or perhaps the threat of it, could have changed his mind, and that was out of the question.

Roosevelt made mistakes, as even the greatest do, but he provided the United States with the best possible leadership. One has only to think of the Presidential candidates of his era to appreciate the difference. Wendell Willkie and Thomas E. Dewey, the Republican nominees in 1940 and 1944, were good enough men, to be sure, but utterly lacked knowledge of the world. Henry Wallace, who would have become President if Roosevelt had died a year earlier, believed in appeasing the Soviets. Senator Robert Taft, who understood neither foreign affairs nor grand strategy, had been an isolationist before Pearl Harbor and was therefore hopelessly wrong about the greatest issue of the century. Roosevelt towered above them all, and it was the country's good fortune to have him at its head before and during the war.

When Roosevelt died, on April 12, 1945, the war in Europe was virtually over, the Pacific war already won—although the Japanese refused to admit it. The United States was safe and rich. It would soon have the atomic bomb. U.S. casualty rates were lower than those of any other great nation. In the real world, where people make mistakes and things go wrong, leadership does not get much better than this.

SEE ALSO

Atlantic, Battle of the; Atlantic Charter; Casablanca conference; Home front; Mediterranean theater; Mobilization; Roosevelt, Anna Eleanor; Teheran conference; Truman, Harry S.; Unconditional surrender; United Nations; Yalta conference

FURTHER READING

Ben-Zvi, Abraham. *The Illusion of Deterrence: The Roosevelt Presidency and the Origins of the Pacific War.* Boulder, Colo.: Westview, 1987.
Burns, James MacGregor. *Roosevelt: The Soldier of Freedom, 1940–1945.* New York: Harcourt, Brace, Jovanovich, 1970.
Cashman, Sean Dennis. *America, Roosevelt, and World War II.* New York: New York University Press, 1989.
Dallek, Robert. *Franklin Roosevelt and American Foreign Policy, 1932–1945.* New York: Oxford University Press, 1979.
Kimball, Warren F. *The Juggler: Franklin Roosevelt as Wartime Statesman.* Princeton, N.J.: Princeton University Press, 1991.
Newton, Verne W., ed. *FDR and the Holocaust.* New York: St. Martin's Press, 1996.

Royal Air Force

Unlike the United States Army Air Forces, the Royal Air Force (RAF) was an independent service with its own cabinet minister (secretary of state for air), who presided over the policy-making Air Council.

At the time World War II broke out, the RAF was divided into separate branches, with Fighter, Bomber, and Coastal Commands being the combat arms. For most of the war, the Coastal Command was controlled by the Royal Navy, an arrangement that made the British antisubmarine campaign better coordinated than that of the United States.

Overseas the RAF was organized vertically, with all types of aircraft operating under a single command. The most important of these were the Middle East Command and Air Command Southeast Asia. Beginning in 1943, RAF units in the Mediterranean served with U.S. aircraft under the combined Mediterranean Air Command. In 1943 the RAF formed its Second Tactical Air Force to support British ground troops on the European continent during and after D-Day, June 6, 1944.

Dominion air forces—Australian, Canadian, New Zealand, South African—served as part of the RAF, as did units made of refugees from occupied Europe. Some, notably the Czechs, had their own separate national squadrons. RAF squadrons were much larger than those of the U.S. Army Air Forces (USAAF), being comparable in size to a U.S. air group. They were supported by Princess Mary's RAF Nursing Service and the Women's Auxiliary Air Force (WAAF), who were put at greater risk than U.S. servicewomen. Most notably during the Battle of Britain, WAAFs served in heavily bombed installations.

Although ground personnel were often draftees, as in the United States, all RAF airmen were volunteers. Many were trained overseas in Canada. Unlike the USAAF, whose pilots, bombardiers, and navigators were always commissioned officers, RAF airmen were often sergeants. And while the pilot was always the aircrew commander in U.S. planes, in the RAF command rested with the man who had the highest rank, whether he was the pilot or not.

Like the USAAF, the Royal Air Force had committed itself before the war to strategic bombing. This doctrine held that an enemy could be defeated by destroying its war plants and infrastructure from the air, making ground warfare obsolete. In practice the RAF quickly discovered that bombing Germany by day was too costly, because its small undergunned aircraft were no match for the Luftwaffe (Germany's air force). Accordingly, Bomber Command shifted over to night operations and area attacks.

Since precision bombing was impossible when attacking at night, the RAF abandoned strategic bombing for terror attacks that were supposed to break the Germans' morale. They never did manage to break the German spirit, although Bomber Command lost 56,000 crewmen and thousands of planes in a vain effort to bring about a civilian collapse. Bombing Germany consumed more than a quarter of the British war effort but achieved only modest practical results. It was, therefore, a blunder as well as a crime, given that most people killed or wounded on the ground were civilians.

On the other hand, Fighter Command won the all-important Battle of Britain in 1940, which made ultimate victory possible. The fighter-bombers and medium bombers of the Second Tactical Air Force gave tremendous support to Allied ground forces after they invaded the Continent. In time, Bomber Command acquired the skill and equipment to bomb accurately, making genuine strategic bombing possible. However, its commander, Air Marshal Sir Arthur Harris, believed passionately in terror raids and seldom allowed Bomber Command to make precision attacks. British historians have been the most severe critics of Bomber Command, often comparing it unfavorably to the USAAF, which remained committed to strategic bombing and was sometimes successful at it.

SEE ALSO
Britain; Britain, Battle of; Strategic bombing

FURTHER READING
Hastings, Max. *Bomber Command*. New York: Dial Press, 1979.
Richards, Denis. *Royal Air Force, 1939–1945*. London: H.M.S.O., 1974.

Royal Navy

Called the "senior service" in Britain, the Royal Navy (RN) was founded in the reign of Henry VIII. Its civilian minister was the First Lord of the Admiralty, while operations were directed by the First Sea Lord in his role as chief of naval staff. The Royal Navy was divided into regional commands which, since the British Empire was still intact, operated in all the world's oceans. Commonwealth navies and—from 1940 on, those of the various governments in exile—served as units of the RN. The main exceptions were warships of Australia and New Zealand, which, after 1941, came under U.S. command in the Pacific.

The RN's offensive power was located in its battle fleets. At the outbreak of World War II there were two main fleets: the Home Fleet, which protected Britain; and the Mediterranean Fleet,

The British destroyer HMS Oakley *heads out to sea.*

based in Egypt. In 1941 an Eastern Fleet was created, with its headquarters in Singapore. Much of it was destroyed in the early days of the Pacific war, with the survivors withdrawing to Mombasa in British East Africa. These survivors eventually grew into the British Pacific Fleet, the largest British Fleet of the war, which fought with distinction in the Okinawa campaign.

The officers and men of the Royal Navy fell into three categories: the standing regular navy (RN); the Royal Naval Reserve (RNR), consisting of officers and men with previous RN service as well as former officers of the merchant fleet; and the Royal Naval Volunteer Reserve (RNVR), consisting of officers who had volunteered and draftees who had been promoted to commissioned rank. The RNVR was called the Wavy Navy, because RNVR officers had waved rings on their cuffs to distinguish them from RN and RNR officers.

Enlisted draftees had no service insignias at all. Although there were historical reasons behind these distinctions, to Americans they seemed artificial and snobbish. In the U.S. Navy all enlisted men dressed alike, and although the U.S. Navy differentiated between regular and reserve officers, both categories wore identical uniforms and markings.

Because British forces made few amphibious assaults compared with those of the United States, the Royal Marines had only one division. It was formed in 1940 but was later broken up into smaller, specialized units. On the other hand, the Women's Royal Naval Service (whose members were called Wrens) was relatively larger than its U.S. counterpart, known as the WAVES. In addition to shore duties, a few Wrens served on motor torpedo boats. Of the 73,642 RN personnel who died in the war, 124 were Wrens.

The RNVR's officers made up three-fourths of the officer corps, and they bore the brunt of the antisubmarine war as commanders of small escort vessels. The high ranks and prestige, however, went to those who commanded battleships and carriers. But everything would have been lost if the RNVR-officered corvettes, frigates, destroyers, and aircraft had not defeated the U-boats.

Because Germany did not have an important surface fleet and the Italian Navy avoided battle, the RN did not fight any great naval actions in the Atlantic or Mediterranean. There were some spectacular incidents, such as the pursuit and sinking of the *Bismarck* in 1941, but the RN's main job in the war was the unglamorous but absolutely essential task of keeping the sea-lanes open.

Although it was small at first, the Fleet Air Arm came to play a vital role in both oceans and the Mediterranean. When war broke out, the RN had 232 obsolete aircraft and only five carriers. Even so, the Fleet Air Arm won a remarkable victory against the Italian Navy. On November 11, 1940, 21 Swordfish-class biplanes launched from the carrier *Illustrious* torpedoed three battleships and a cruiser at anchor in Taranto, Italy. In one stroke the naval balance of power in the Mediterranean shifted in Britain's favor.

Taranto also marked the end of the battleship era, although this was not fully apparent until the much bigger Japanese victory at Pearl Harbor a year later. By war's end, the Royal Navy had more than 50 carriers of various sizes and 1,336 front line aircraft, half of which were built in the United States.

SEE ALSO

Atlantic, battle of the; Central Pacific Area; Britain

Russia

SEE Soviet Union

Saipan, battle of

Saipan, in the Mariana Islands, was assaulted by the U.S. Fifth Amphibious Corps on June 15, 1944. This attack was a continuation of the Navy's drive across the central Pacific that had begun with the seizure of the Tarawa atoll the previous year. The chief strategic value of the Marianas was as a site for the Army's heavy B-29 bombers.

Admiral Chester Nimitz, who commanded the Pacific Ocean Area, initially had been opposed to the Saipan operation. He and his staff feared another bloody engagement like Tarawa and did not think bomber bases were worth their probable cost. But Nimitz's superior, Admiral Ernest King, the chief of naval operations, was dedicated to the central Pacific strategy and insisted on taking the Marianas. After the January 1944 Marshall Islands campaign, in which U.S. casualties were light, Nimitz raised no further objections.

But the Marianas, unlike the tiny Gilbert and Marshall atolls, were substantial islands, and on Saipan there were more than 30,000 Japanese troops, about twice the number expected. Some 20,000 U.S. troops went ashore on Saipan the first day and met the usual fierce resistance. The result was, as Nimitz had feared, another bloody battle. When it ended, on July 9, there were 14,000 U.S. casualties and 30,000 Japanese dead.

The Japanese had abandoned their original technique of trying to defend beaches, and much of the fighting consisted of rooting out or destroying clusters of Japanese in underground bunkers and tunnels. At Stalingrad in 1942 and 1943, Germans had called their underground battle a *Rattenkrieg*, or war of the rats, which described Saipan perfectly. The rest of the Marianas, however, proved much easier to seize.

American troops mourn the death of their fellow soldiers during the burial services after the battle of Saipan.

ILLUSTRATED CURRENT NEWS

SERVICES FOR SAIPAN DEAD

A Navy chaplain reads burial services for Marines who died on Saipan before they were sent to rest at sea from this troop transport. Buddies of the dead Leathernecks act as pall-bearers. Troops on Saipan have suffered three times the casualties of Tarawa to date.

Apart from the high cost of taking it, Saipan was notable for being the first conquered island with a large Japanese civilian population. Of its 12,000 non-combatants, most of them women and children, about two-thirds committed suicide, because they thought honor demanded it or because they had been led to believe that their captors would treat them atrociously. It sickened GIs to see whole families jump off cliffs or blow themselves up with grenades. This was a chilling foretaste of what the expected invasion of Japan would bring.

Whether the Saipan campaign was worth the cost depends on how much value is attached to the firebomb raids against Japan that were staged from the island. Many argue that these raids contributed materially to the defeat of Japan, but some historians believe they had little effect, because Japanese industry had already been brought to its knees by the U.S. naval blockade.

SEE ALSO

Central Pacific Area; Philippine Sea, Battle of the

FURTHER READING

Crowl, Philip A. *Campaign in the Marianas.* Washington, D.C.: Center of Military History, United States Army, 1993.
Gailey, Harry A. *Howlin' Mad vs the Army: Conflict in Command, Saipan, 1945.* Novato, Calif.: Presidio, 1986.

Schweinfurt, bombing of

There were two separate bombing attacks on Schweinfurt, Germany, in 1943 that resulted in very heavy U.S. losses and put an end, temporarily, to the daylight air war against Germany.

The campaign began on June 10,

1943, when enough heavy bombers were available for the U.S. Eighth Air Force to attack strategic targets in Germany with daylight precision bombing. Schweinfurt was considered an important target at the time, because so much of Germany's ball-bearing industry was located in the area. It was believed that if the five ball-bearing plants in the Schweinfurt region could be destroyed Germany would run out of ball bearings and therefore lose the war.

The first attack was made on August 17, 1943, by two separate air divisions, which struck Schweinfurt and the city of Regensburg. Of the 315 heavy bombers that reached their targets 60 were destroyed by German fighters and flak guns. This rate of loss cast doubt on the theory that heavily armed and armored B-17s and B-24s, unaccompanied by fighter escorts, could fight their way to targets deep within Germany and make it home again without suffering heavy casualties.

Because so much had been invested in this form of strategic bombing, air force leaders were reluctant to admit defeat. On October 14, 1943, the Eighth Air Force launched another attack, with Schweinfurt as the only target. Of 291 heavy bombers that took off for this attack 60 were again lost, leaving the concept of the self-defending bomber force in ruins. The second Schweinfurt attack was the fourth on German industrial areas that had been staged in a single week, during which 148 bombers were lost. After "Black Week," as it was called, the Eighth Air Force in effect admitted defeat. There were no more deep penetration raids into Germany for the rest of the year. They did not resume on a regular basis until February 1944, when long-range fighter escorts at last became available.

SEE ALSO

Spaatz, Carl; Strategic bombing

Seabees

Seabees was the nickname given to the men of the U.S. Navy's construction battalions. Unlike other sailors, the Seabees were all volunteers drawn from civilian life because of their skills as construction workers or their qualifications as engineers.

Established on December 8, 1941, the Seabees reached a peak strength of 8,000 officers and 250,000 men in 1945. They worked all over the Pacific, building roads, air bases, and whatever else the Navy needed. Although they were neither soldiers nor sailors, the Seabees operated close to the action and sometimes came under fire. As semicivilians they were better paid than sailors, the basic wage being that of a noncommissioned officer. Their insignia was a bee in flight, wearing a sailor's cap and carrying a submachine gun, a wrench, and a hammer.

FURTHER READING

Huie, William Bradford. *Can Do!: The Story of the Seabees.* Annapolis: United States Naval Institute, 1997.

The promotional material on this Seabees songbook reads, "Here is a real OPPORTUNITY for two-fisted, red-blooded Americans to serve shoulder-to-shoulder with the combatant forces in the 'SEABEES,' the newest arm of Uncle Sam's Navy."

Kimmel, Jay. *U.S. Navy Seabees: Since Pearl Harbor.* Portland, Ore.: Cory/Stevens, 1995.

Second front

This term came into use after Germany invaded the Soviet Union in June 1941. The Soviets demanded that a "second front" be opened in the west to relieve the pressure Germany was exerting against them in the east. Specifically, the Soviets and their sympathizers wanted the Allies to launch a major invasion of France.

When the United States entered the European war on December 11, 1941, such a front became possible in theory, but in fact it was not until D-Day on June 6, 1944, that the second front became a reality. The problem was not America's lack of desire for a second front. From the start, leaders such as General George Marshall, the Army's chief of staff, wanted a new western front in Europe at the earliest possible date.

Two things prevented the second front from happening earlier. One was that Britain and the United States did not have the means to invade Europe in 1942. The other was that, for different reasons, Prime Minister Winston Churchill and President Franklin D. Roosevelt wanted to begin the ground war against Hitler in the Mediterranean.

Thus, the opening of that war took place in North Africa in November 1942 and proceeded from Africa to an invasion of Sicily and Italy in 1943. These operations made it impossible to stage Operation Overlord, the invasion of Normandy, until 1944, although Roosevelt had unwisely promised Stalin a second front in 1942.

Churchill and Roosevelt tried to represent the North African campaign as the equivalent of a second front.

Churchill also tried to argue that the Allied air war against Germany was a kind of second front. Neither of these substitutes met Soviet Russia's basic need, but as Stalin could not direct Allied operations himself, he had no choice but to wait for the real thing.

SEE ALSO
Mediterranean theater

Selective Service System

Otherwise known as the draft, the Selective Service System was established by an act of Congress in September 1940. Initially, conscription (the act of drafting) applied only to men aged 21 to 36 and the term of enlistment was limited to one year. In 1941, by a margin of only one vote in the House of Representatives, the term of service was extended. The next year the age limit of those eligible for the draft was widened to include men 18 to 46 years of age. Student exemptions, which were part of the original Selective Service Act, were also dropped. In all, some 10 million men were drafted, a majority into the Army. Women were not drafted at all. Enlisted draftees served an average of 33 months, officers about 6 months longer.

Draftees were called up as the result of decisions made by thousands of local draft boards that reflected local as well as national prejudices. Most boards preferred to draft single men, which meant that in the early war years, young fathers were being exempted while single men younger than 40 were called to active service. By 1944 a military manpower shortage developed that required boards to cast their nets more broadly and stop giving exemptions for fatherhood. Selective Service was generally regarded as fair, in part because conscription was not as rigorously applied in the United States as in most other belligerent nations.

In January 1944 President Franklin D. Roosevelt asked Congress for a National Service Bill. It would have subjected civilian men and women to mandatory work assignments, as well as making the military draft more productive. Similar legislation had been highly effective in Britain, and polls showed considerable support for it in the United States. But Congress feared that in practice National Service would be unpopular and therefore refused to enact it.

Sicily, battle of

As Tunisia fell to the Allies in May 1943, an Allied conference was convening in Washington. Known as Trident, the conference's discussions were often stormy, because U.S. Army chief of staff General George Marshall had begun to tire of letting Britain direct the war effort. The British had been able to force Marshall to accept Torch, the invasion of North Africa, but they could not make him like it. And now that more time was being lost while the British continued to come up with proposals for landing in various places on the margins of Europe, the Americans were becoming irritated. General Alan Brooke, chief of the Imperial General Staff, would not admit that the Americans would never share Britain's view of the Mediterranean, and he always seemed taken aback that putting off the invasion of France led the United States to divert resources to the Pacific.

This aerial photograph captures the view from a B-17 Flying Fortress intent on destroying shipping and harbor installations at Palermo, Sicily. The explosions below, and the bomb on its way, indicate a successful mission.

The Trident conference began with Churchill arguing for an Italian campaign to follow the conquest of Sicily, while Roosevelt worried that it might delay the cross-channel attack into France he planned for the coming year. After days of tough bargaining, during which each side promoted its own sideshows in the Mediterranean and the Pacific, a compromise was hammered out. After taking Sicily, the Allies would eliminate Italy from the war by means of unspecified actions. These actions would come to an end on November 1, 1943, after which troops would be concentrated in England for a cross-channel assault on May 1, 1944.

Soviet leader Joseph Stalin responded angrily to these decisions because the Germans were gearing up for a great offensive at Kursk, in the Soviet Union (which did happen in July 1943), and needed to be diverted. Although Stalin committed a series of unfriendly acts—including recalling his ambassadors from Washington and London—Operation Husky, as the invasion of Sicily had been code named, had been set into motion.

On July 10, 1943, the greatest fleet ever assembled to that date—an armada of 3,200 ships—arrived off the coast of Sicily. In three days 150,000 troops hit the beaches, soon followed by 300,000 more. Sicily was defended (on paper) by 350,000 Axis troops; however, most were Italians who wished only to surrender. The real opposition was a German Army corps that never exceeded 60,000 men. The Allies ought to have brushed it aside, but instead the campaign lasted for 38 days and ended with the entire German force escaping to Italy after suffering fewer battle deaths than the Allies.

Given the lack of enemy strength, the Sicilian campaign was poorly executed. The British War Office went so far as to called it "a strategic and tactical failure." It took too long to execute and only gained air bases that could have been obtained more easily by taking Corsica and Sardinia, which would have had the additional effect of neutralizing

Italy by air and thus avoiding the need to invade it.

Operation Husky was poorly executed because it was poorly planned. Eisenhower unwisely left the Sicilian campaign in the hands of General Sir Harold Alexander, who, although well-liked by Americans, had been promoted above his merits. The planning for Husky was sloppy and late, with little effort being made to exploit the Allies' superiority in air and naval power.

There was no planning beyond taking the beachheads, so the Allies followed up their landings with too many unimaginative frontal attacks and a campaign of attrition. The air commanders went their own way, failing to provide adequate ground support or anticipate that the Germans would withdraw across the Strait of Messina (although it was the only escape route). As Husky was a combined operation, both Britain and the United States shared the blame for it.

Politically and strategically the results were even grimmer. On July 17, General Eisenhower decided to invade Italy as soon as the Sicilian campaign was over. This step was almost inevitable once the Army abandoned the idea of invading France in 1943. For the leisurely Sicilian campaign had ended too late in the year to organize an invasion of France and left substantial military resources assembled in the Mediterranean. Thus the misbegotten, and strategically unnecessary, Italian campaigns were born.

SEE ALSO
Italian campaigns; Mediterranean theater

FURTHER READING
D'Este, Carlo. *Bitter Victory: The Battle for Sicily, 1943.* New York: Dutton, 1988.
Mitcham, Samuel W. *Battle of Sicily.* New York: Orion, 1991.

Siegfried Line

SEE Germany, surrender of

Small arms

This category of weapons includes pistols, rifles, submachine guns, machine guns, and antitank rifles. Pistols as a battlefield weapon had long since become obsolete by 1939. United States combat officers seldom used them, preferring the light M-1 carbine instead. Antitank rifles were not very useful either, and heavily armored tanks soon made them obsolete as well.

The rifle, the basic infantry weapon, had changed little since World War I. It required a soldier to unlock a bolt, move it back and forth, and relock it every other shot. The exception to this rule was the U.S. Army's superb Garand, or M-1, rifle. It was an accurate semiautomatic weapon that held an eight-bullet clip, which could be emptied as rapidly as a soldier could squeeze the trigger.

Another exception, although it was not issued until 1943 and did not, in most cases, replace the obsolete Mauser, was the German assault rifle. In order to achieve a greater rate and volume of fire, the assault rifle was lightweight, compact, and fired a light bullet with a short case. It was fully automatic, and its long magazine carried a much larger number of rounds than the Mauser. Called the Machine Pistol 43, it was later renamed the Assault Rifle 44 and was the model for the next generation of military rifles developed after the war.

The submachine gun was a light, fully automatic weapon that fired pistol ammunition. Developed by the Germans in World War I, they used it widely in

A sailor checks over the small arms in a guard room in England in anticipation of the Battle of France, 1944.

World War II. The British equivalent was called the Sten gun, while America had the Thompson submachine gun. Popular with gangsters before the war in its drum-magazine version, the Thompson, now fitted with a 20- or 30-round box magazine, was in great demand by Allied ground troops throughout the war.

Apart from being a bit heavy and expensive, the Thompson was a splendid weapon, sturdy and absolutely reliable. In addition, its .45-caliber rounds gave it plenty of stopping power. Although 2 million Thompson guns were made, the troops would have liked millions more. The Soviet Army used more machine guns than any other. They developed a cheap model made from stamped out, rather than machined, parts that suited their method of close-in fighting extremely well.

The Allies employed both heavy and light machine guns. The heavy gun—belt-fed, water-cooled, and mounted on a tripod—was similar to World War I models. Light machine guns were generally newer designs. The U.S. Army issued a Browning automatic rifle (BAR) to every rifle squad. An air-cooled gun with a bipod near its muzzle, the BAR was heavy but provided a considerable increase in firepower.

The Germans developed an all-purpose machine gun that could be altered as needed. With a shoulder stock and bipod, it served as a light machine gun. When heavy fire was required, the gun received a tripod and long-range sights. This concept was widely implemented by other armies after the war, because having one type of machine gun instead of two greatly simplified the problems of supply and repair.

Solomon Islands

SEE Guadalcanal, Battle of; South Pacific Area

South Pacific Area

In April 1942 the Joint Chiefs of Staff agreed that the Southwest Pacific Area was to be a separate Army theater of war. The rest of the Pacific became the Pacific Ocean Area, directed by navy Admiral Chester Nimitz, whose vast command was subdivided into three areas: South, Central, and North. Once the spheres of control had been defined, everyone understood that the first thing to be done was to save Australia from the Japanese threat.

Japan was overextended and probably lacked the means to invade Australia, but the Allies could not be sure of this, and Australia's strategic importance meant that it had to be protected. The question was by which armed service. Most Japanese bases fell within General

Douglas MacArthur's Southwest Pacific Area. However, to seize or neutralize the bases would require naval support, and Admiral Ernest King, the Navy's head, would not allow the Army to control his fast carriers.

After a serious struggle, the Joint Chiefs arrived at a compromise. The effort to protect Australia was divided into three parts, or "tasks." Task One was to establish a position in the southern Solomon Islands. Because this would require an amphibious landing that only the Navy could mount, its South Pacific Area was moved one degree west so as to include these islands. Task Two would be an army advance along the northeast coast of New Guinea together with a naval drive up the Solomons. Task Three was to be an assault on Rabaul, a great Japanese air and naval base on New Britain, from which it controlled the Solomons and the Bismarck Archipelago. Tasks Two and Three would be under MacArthur's command, with the Joint Chiefs determining the forces' composition and timing.

Turf having been staked out and honor preserved, King was eager to seize Guadalcanal (code named Cactus) in the Solomons, where a Japanese airfield was under construction. MacArthur favored doing so as well, for operations in the Navy's South Pacific Area supported his own, unlike the subsequent central Pacific campaigns, which were too far away to help him.

The War Department reluctantly went along, despite well-grounded fears that the Navy was too weak to mount such an offensive and would soon be calling for assistance. The Joint Chiefs ordered Operation Watchtower—assaults on Tulagi and Guadalcanal—to commence in early August 1942. Just as the Army feared, King was barely able to patch together an expeditionary force.

The marines went ashore on August 7,

meeting little opposition. Then Rear Admiral Frank Jack Fletcher sailed away, only 36 hours after the marines had landed and before they were half unloaded. Fearing a Japanese attack, he wanted to save his fast carriers. He left only cruisers and destroyers to defend the invasion force.

But even as he fled, Japanese heavy cruisers were moving down the "slot" formed by the Solomon Islands. At 1:30 a.m. on August 9, they took the Allied cruisers by surprise, destroying four of them: three American and one Australian. This encounter, dubbed the Battle of Savo, was the U.S. Navy's worst defeat at sea and did much to prolong the Guadalcanal campaign. Since Rear Admiral Richmond Kelly Turner, who commanded Amphibious Force South Pacific, now had no air cover, he sailed away at noon, leaving the Marines stranded.

By a narrow margin, the expeditionary force on Guadalcanal was saved, and the island finally taken after a costly campaign lasting six months. Watchtower was a mistake all the same, for if King believed that by forcing the operation on Marshall he had a guarantee of boundless support he was seriously mistaken. Watchtower had to compete not only with MacArthur's theater but with the North African campaign as well.

Guadalcanal might have been lost if Japan had made a maximum effort. Instead, the Japanese sent reinforcements in small numbers and never assembled a large enough force to win the battle. Even so, the Navy was reduced at one point to a single carrier in the Pacific as a direct result of Watchtower.

The U.S. Army was dismayed because Admiral King was soon demanding more and more support from it. He had forced the operation on Marshall by threatening to seize Tulagi, which was at first considered more important than Guadalcanal, with naval power alone if the Army did not assist

In the early morning light on Bougainville, a tank and infantrymen scout out Japanese soldiers who may have infiltrated American lines the night before.

him. However, when the fighting started he immediately began calling for land-based air support. King later said that the Battle of Savo Island was the blackest day of the war for him. After Savo, which showed that the Navy had over-reached itself, King's demands became relentless. To hold Guadalcanal would cost America 24 ships and make the waters between the Guadalcanal, Savo, and Florida islands—Ironbottom Sound to Allied sailors—the largest naval graveyard of the war.

The South Pacific Area's first theater commander was Vice Admiral Robert Ghormley. He did not function well in a job that entailed trying to do too much with too few resources. In September 1942 he was replaced by Vice Admiral William Halsey, the Navy's most aggressive commander. Halsey restored morale and, after being given more men and munitions, launched Operation Cartwheel in June 1943.

Cartwheel's job was to implement Task Two by taking a series of steps up the Solomons and toward the Bismarcks, isolating Fortress Rabaul. Task Three, the plan to storm Rabaul, now began to fade away as planners consid-

ered blockading and neutralizing it from the air, which would free up resources for other operations.

As the climax of Operation Cartwheel, Halsey's forces invaded Bougainville in the Solomons on November 1, 1943. The Japanese first sought to prevent the landings by attacking the invasion fleet with four cruisers and six destroyers. They were driven off by a U.S. task force composed of four new light cruisers and eight destroyers. The Japanese then sent down a large force from its main fleet anchorage in Truk. But code breakers in Hawaii decrypted the order and warned Halsey that seven heavy and one light cruiser plus four destroyers were making for Rabaul, which would put them within easy striking distance of his landing site in Bougainville.

Halsey had no battleships or heavy cruisers with which to protect his invasion force, because every available large warship had been assigned to the Central Pacific Area. What he did have on temporary loan were the fast carriers *Saratoga* and *Princeton*. Carrier planes had never attacked a Japanese base as strong as Rabaul, which was believed to have 150 aircraft besides the newly arrived cruisers. But the situation was so desperate that Halsey ordered Rear Admiral Frederick C. Sherman to throw every plane he had against Rabaul.

Halsey feared that Sherman's air groups would be cut to pieces, yet the potential losses had to be borne if necessary to save the Bougainville beachhead. Sherman launched two strikes on Rabaul that left the Japanese commander with only half his carrier planes, which for their safety he had to send back to Truk along with the cruisers. The threat to Bougainville was over. By May 1, 1944, except for Japanese fugitives, the island had been secured. All the other Cartwheel objectives in the South and Southwest Pacific areas were similarly reached.

With the completion of Cartwheel, operations in the South Pacific came to an end. The South Pacific Area command was dissolved, and Halsey went on to command the Third Fleet in the Central and Southwest Pacific areas. His best work of the war was done in the South Pacific, where he turned a dispirited command around, took the Solomons, and helped isolate Rabaul, where 100,000 Japanese would spend the rest of the war waiting for an invasion that never came.

Invading Guadalcanal may have been a mistake, but in the end U.S. soldiers and sailors in the South Pacific Area fought a successful war of attrition that cost the Japanese dearly.

SEE ALSO
Guadalcanal, Battle of; Halsey, William F.; Southwest Pacific Area

FURTHER READING
Morison, Samuel Eliot. *History of United States Naval Operations in World War II: Breaking the Bismarck Barrier, 22 July 1942–1 May 1944*. Boston: Little, Brown, 1950.
Morris, Mack. *South Pacific Diary, 1942–1943*. Lexington: University Press of Kentucky, 1996.
Potter, E. B. *Bull Halsey*. Annapolis, Md.: Naval Institute Press, 1985.

Southwest Pacific Area

Before Pearl Harbor was attacked in December 1941, the Navy had assumed that in case of war with Japan, it would be in complete control of all of the Pacific war effort. But Army General Douglas MacArthur's valiant, though hopeless, defense of the Philippines made him a national hero. Once he escaped from the Philippines to Australia he had to be given a suitable command. After heavy negotiations between the Army and Navy early in 1942, they arrived at a compromise that would make a command position for MacArthur possible.

MacArthur was given what the Joint Chiefs of Staff called the Southwest Pacific Area (SPA). This theater consisted of Australia, New Guinea, the Philippines, the Solomon Islands, the Bismarck Archipelago, and most of the Netherlands East Indies. The Navy was given almost all the rest of the Pacific, which it named the Pacific Ocean Area. The great defect of this arrangement was that it meant there would be no supreme commander in the Pacific and thus no unified effort could be mounted. Instead, the Army and Navy would, for the most part, fight two separate wars against Japan.

The first challenge facing the United States within the SPA was to save Australia, which was being threatened by Japan's huge gains in the Southwest Pacific. The Joint Chiefs decided to protect Australia by launching three separate operations called "tasks."

Task One was to invade the southern Solomon Islands. As this would require an amphibious landing, the Navy's South Pacific Area was enlarged to include these islands. Task Two would have the Army advance up the northeast coast of New

Red Cross workers prepare to ship gift boxes to servicemen fighting on islands in the Philippines. Each soldier was to receive a gift package on Christmas Day.

Guinea, at the same time as the naval campaigns in the Solomons. Task Three entailed an attack on Rabaul, Japan's most important naval and air base in the region and the key to victory. Tasks Two and Three would be under MacArthur's command, with the Joint Chiefs determining when and on what scale they would be undertaken.

On July 22, 1942, at the same time as the Navy was preparing to invade Guadalcanal, 16,000 Japanese troops landed at Buna on the north coast of Papua, New Guinea. Their objective was Port Moresby, an important strategic site for launching an Australian campaign. If the Papuan Peninsula had been level, Port Moresby would have been easy to take, for only a handful of Australian soldiers stood between the Japanese and their target.

What made Port Moresby's defense possible were the Owen Stanley Mountains, which rise to a height of 13,000 feet from their roots in a steaming jungle. The Kokoda Trail over the mountains was only a path, adequate for barefoot natives but not for armed soldiers. The Japanese troops who landed at Gona and Buna on the Solomon Sea were obliged to march from tropical heat and filth to freezing mountain passes. For Australians, the Kokoda Trail was a hell on

earth too, but they stubbornly defended it yard by yard despite appalling hardships.

All who fought in New Guinea were tormented by its horrors. The perils of the jungle war were severe, but were outweighed by "jungle rot"—dreadful ulcers that formed all over soldiers' bodies—clouds of insects whose bites quickly became festering sores, leeches that attached themselves to genitals and rectums, and diseases like malaria and dysentery, which struck down five men for every one that was wounded in battle. But the Australians hung on, and their gallantry and sacrifices paid off. They occupied Milne Bay at the tip of Papua and held it, preventing Japanese flanking movements. They slowed the Japanese drive on Port Moresby as well, which became weaker as it advanced, because the enemy could not bring enough supplies over the terrible mountains.

Meanwhile, the Australian force had a shortening support line, and as more men and supplies were fed into it they became progressively stronger. The enemy was stopped 25 miles from Port Moresby, then gradually driven back on supply lines so slim that by October Japanese soldiers on the Kokoda Trail had been reduced to cannibalism.

MacArthur's counteroffensive did not get off to a brilliant start. For the reconquest of Papua, MacArthur had only two U.S. divisions, both of them National Guard outfits that had not gone through the Army's new training program and were completely unprepared to fight. Experience would show that, unlike the Army's regular divisions, which had officers promoted on merit and no bad habits to unlearn, National Guard divisions required extra training. But they were all that MacArthur had, and he was forced to use them. The 32nd Infantry Division was considered the better of his two guard units. On September 15 MacArthur's air officer, Major General

George Kenney, began flying the 32nd to Papua—the first large-scale airlift ever undertaken by the U.S. Army.

The hardest fighting took place in the Buna-Gona area. It was the scene of one of the worst-directed U.S. battles of the war, largely because MacArthur had little understanding of the Army's new triangular division formation, an infantry-artillery team which had tremendous firepower. Unfamiliar with the triangular division, MacArthur broke up the 32nd and sent it to Papua without heavy artillery or tank support. Its luckless commander, Major General Edwin Forrest Harding, was obliged to separate the division into undergunned task forces and throw them against defenses that were nearly impossible to take.

In the Buna-Gona area, MacArthur repeatedly ordered costly frontal attacks that had no chance of success. His chief of staff, the much hated Major General Richard K. Sutherland, inspected the battle area and reported back that guns, not leadership, were needed. MacArthur then relieved Harding and put Lieutenant General Robert L. Eichelberger in command, saying: "I want you to take Buna, or not to come back alive."

Buna fell on January 22, 1943, the first time Japan had sustained a permanent defeat on land. But a very heavy price was paid for victory in Papua, which MacArthur refused to admit, saying instead that no campaign in history had gained so much at so little cost. This was an absurd boast that the facts proved to be hollow.

In Papua some 40,000 Allied troops were committed, and the Army suffered 8,546 casualties, including 3,095 killed—a death rate more than triple that of Guadalcanal. The 126th Infantry Regiment was completely wiped out, and whole battalions were reduced by disease and casualties to a tenth of their normal strength.

Yet MacArthur was learning fast, and the experience would not be wasted. After the Papuan campaign he made a promise, which he kept, that there would be "no more Bunas." During the next two years his troops would suffer fewer than 20,000 deaths in the course of many operations, partly because of tactical lessons he learned in Papua that would make his later campaigns more efficient. Among other things, he was learning the many uses of aircraft, whose value he had previously sneered at.

MacArthur's understanding of sea power was expanding too. His need for troop transports was glaringly exposed at Buna, because he had almost no ships and thus could not stage landings to outflank or isolate enemy fortifications. His complaints led the Navy to assign him a specialist, Rear Admiral Daniel E. Barbey, whose VII Amphibious Force would stage 56 operations in the Southwest Pacific Area. MacArthur also learned how to exploit the decrypted enemy radio messages provided by army and navy intelligence. They would play a key part in future operations by helping determine which enemy strongholds could be bypassed.

MacArthur still did not have enough of anything—during the first year of campaigning in Italy the United States shipped 2.3 million tons of provisions to the Italian people alone, which was roughly equal to the volume of supplies provided to MacArthur's entire theater. The Australians made up some of the difference, but his command would never be supplied as well as U.S. troops in Europe. Nor would he ever have enough warships. Even so, MacArthur worked wonders.

In 1943 the Southwest Pacific Area campaign concentrated on the advance to Rabaul. MacArthur was disappointed when the Joint Chiefs canceled his assault on that fortress. However, in a series of amphibious and air attacks

American troops wade ashore the heavily mined beaches during the invasion of Cebu Island in the Philippines.

MacArthur isolated it and laid the basis for his brilliant bypassing strategy. Operation Cartwheel required him to attack west along the coast of New Guinea, north to the Admiralty Islands, and east into New Britain while Admiral William Halsey's South Pacific Area forces were working their way up the Solomons.

Some at home were discouraged by the campaign's slow progress. In August 1943 *Life* magazine noted sourly that it had taken a year of fighting to advance from Guadalcanal to the tip of New Georgia, a distance of 200 miles. At that rate the United States would invade Japan sometime in 1957.

But these early efforts were about finding solid footing. As U.S. power built up, the pace quickened. In February 1944 a daring surprise attack put MacArthur in the Admiralty Islands (literally, because on this occasion he accompanied the troops, which was a rare event), and he secured them a month later. This completed the encirclement of Rabaul and ensured Japan's defeat. The United States now had air control over a vast region, which the Japanese vainly contested until their air strength was wiped out.

The key to MacArthur's success was his use of tactical air, which was more important in the Southwest Pacific Area than perhaps any other theater. The Southwest Pacific is thick with islands capable of providing numerous sites for airfields. But unlike in Europe, the enemy's air defenses were weak, enabling even heavy bombers to make precise low-level attacks.

MacArthur also had an outstanding air commander in General George C. Kenney. Kenney taught MacArthur what planes could do, starting with the airlift to Buna that had encountered so much skepticism. Gradually, Kenney's team worked out a strategy of blockading enemy strongpoints from the air, covering and assisting Allied ground troops while, by advancing their forward bases, bringing more and more Japanese targets within bombing range, or inside what was commonly called the bomb line.

By 1944 MacArthur had the means for his most daring effort yet, a long leap up the New Guinea coast that would carry his forces 580 miles beyond the enemy's lines and into their rear. This campaign would become widely admired as one of the most beautifully planned and executed of the war.

The conventional wisdom in April 1944, in both Japan and the United States, was that Wewak or Hansa Bay in northeast New Guinea had to be the next target. They were inside the bomb line and the Japanese occupation force of 55,000 men had to be destroyed, according to orthodox doctrine, before U.S. forces could move farther along the coast.

The idea of bypassing Wewak developed after bombing attacks on airfields in and around Hollandia destroyed the Japanese air cover. Intelligence reported that unlike Wewak, Hollandia was lightly defended. When one of MacArthur's planners brought this to his attention, MacArthur decided to cancel the planned attack on Hansa Bay and leap over it to Hollandia.

All went according to plan. The Fifth Air Force performed so well that the Japanese were left with only 25 planes in the whole of New Guinea. Admiral Barbey's amphibious force, the largest yet seen in the southwest Pacific, consisted of 217 vessels carrying 80,000 troops, which had been brought together from three different staging areas located up to 1,000 miles away.

The plan unfolded as air and naval attacks on Wewak and Hansa Bay convinced the enemy that they were MacArthur's targets, so that when on April 22 his fleet changed course the element of surprise was total. This operation hastened the liberation of New Guinea by several months and provided the Allies with a magnificent harbor that became one of their most important bases. All this was gained at an initial cost of 159 U.S. dead. Of 7,000 Japanese who escaped into the jungle barely 1,000 survived.

Flushed with success, MacArthur's forces then moved quickly forward, seizing one island or coastal base after another. Only on Biak, where the Japanese were strongly entrenched and did not charge the beaches and expose themselves to naval gunfire, were there problems. All the same, on August 20, at a cost of 600 U.S. casualties, Biak was secured. In less than two years MacArthur had advanced almost 2,000 miles, and 1,100 were covered in the last two months.

There was only one drawback to this splendid achievement—many bypassed Japanese garrisons still had to be taken. Thus, while U.S. forces went on to bigger things, the Australian Army spent the rest of the war mopping up the Japanese in New Guinea—an unglamorous task that cost it many casualties. Typically, MacArthur gave the Australians no credit for this effort.

MacArthur had wanted to liberate the Philippines ever since he had been forced to abandon them in March 1942. Sentiment, politics, and personal vanity all played a part in this, but there was a sound military reason, too, for retaking at least the northernmost island of Luzon. Its Manila Bay was a great harbor, and aircraft based in Luzon would command the South China Sea and finish the job of cutting off Japan from its Southeast Asian empire.

Admiral King thought otherwise, however. He wanted the Navy's central Pacific drive to end with the seizure of Formosa, which did not have as good a harbor as Manila Bay but otherwise would serve the same purpose as Luzon. A final decision was deferred, but an agreement was reached that MacArthur's next move should be to take the southern Philippine island of Mindanao.

Accordingly, in September 1944

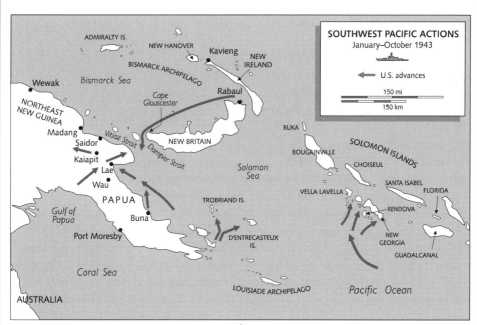

Admiral Halsey, now commanding the Fifth Fleet, raided the Philippines and encountered little resistance. He therefore advised Admiral Nimitz to bypass Mindanao and invade the central Philippines. The Joint Chiefs, then in Quebec for a conference, promptly directed that operations planned for the Talauds, Mindanao, and Yap be canceled and everything thrown at Leyte—except for a small force that was to take the Palau Islands. (When assaulted, the main island of Peleliu in Palau would cost U.S. forces some 10,000 casualties, to no real purpose). Leyte was about to be assaulted by the greatest naval strength ever assembled, for the Seventh and Third fleets together deployed some 17 fast and 18 escort carriers, 12 battleships, 28 cruisers, 150 destroyers, and hundreds of other vessels.

Once the United States was committed to Leyte, opinion soon turned in favor of Luzon over Formosa. MacArthur informed the Joint Chiefs that seizing Leyte would enable him to invade Luzon two months ahead of schedule. Formosa could not be attacked that soon, and before long, planners decided that Formosa could not be invaded at all until after victory in Europe,

because Nimitz would require up to 200,000 army service troops for the operation and they did not exist.

But there were enough troops for operations in the Philippines, whose friendly inhabitants would provide much of the needed labor, and for Okinawa also. Meanwhile, in China the advancing Japanese were seizing more and more U.S. air bases. This ruled out the possibility of land-based air support from China for an assault on Formosa. It also eliminated the value of Formosa as a staging area for landings on the China coast, as these were now out of the question. In the end, almost no one except King liked Formosa as an objective, and on October 3 he finally gave in. The Joint Chiefs then directed MacArthur to assault Luzon in December.

Although the initial landings in Leyte on October 20, 1944, were easy, the invasion fleet was almost sunk by a strong Japanese surface force which, after Admiral Halsey and his Third Fleet were lured away by decoy ships, nearly broke through the U.S. escort carrier screen. In the end, however, what became known as the Battle of Leyte Gulf ended with such a decisive Allied victory that the Imperial

Japanese Navy was, for all practical purposes, destroyed.

Leyte proved a much tougher nut to crack than expected because of weather conditions that deprived the invading troops of land-based air cover and allowed the Japanese to reinforce their garrison. This forced a delay in attacking Luzon, but on January 9 when MacArthur's troops went ashore at Lingayen Gulf they were as strong as they had ever been, amounting to 10 divisions, 5 regimental combat teams (enlarged regiments comparable to brigades), and various other units—more U.S. troops than would fight together anywhere else in the war except on the western front in Europe.

So many Japanese troops and weapons had been lost defending Leyte that General Tomoyuki Yamashita, famed as the conqueror of Malaya, had decided not to defend Lingayen. Thus, the landings were no problem. Simply getting there was the hard part, for some 200 Japanese suicide planes took a heavy toll on the invasion fleet, sinking 24 ships, seriously damaging 27 more, and inflicting more than 2,100 casualties, of whom 738 were killed. The Seventh Fleet's little escort carriers did not have the fighter strength to break up these kamikaze attacks, and the fleet carriers of Task Force 38 were not there to do it for them. Once again, having a divided command resulted in extra losses. The good news was that after 200 Japanese suicide planes had gone down, there were no more kamikaze attacks.

On February 3, advance units of the 1st Cavalry Division were in Manila's northern suburbs, liberating Santo Tomas University and nearly 4,000 Allied internees. But because the Japanese commander put up a ferocious defense, it took a month to secure Manila, during which time 70 percent of the city's factories, 80 percent of its southern residential area, and 100 percent of its

business district were destroyed and 100,000 civilians died. Among the other world cities involved in the war, only Warsaw is believed to have sustained more damage.

During this time MacArthur sent Lieutenant General Eichelberger to liberate the rest of the archipelago in a campaign that made little military sense and that the Joint Chiefs did not want, but that delivered many Filipinos from enemy hands and was a masterpiece of dash and daring. Eichelberger's Eighth Army, Barbey's VII Amphibious Force, and Lieutenant General Paul B. Wurtsmith's Thirteenth Air Force came together to pull off 14 major and 24 minor amphibious landings in 44 days, freeing most of the Philippine islands.

Operations did not go so well in northern Luzon, however, where Yamashita's troops had withdrawn to the mountains. The fighting there was bitter and went on for the rest of the war, with some 50,000 Japanese holding out until V-J Day, August 15, 1945. Some have criticized MacArthur for not beefing up the 6th Army and crushing Yamashita. Yet the slower approach saved many lives in a situation where haste was unnecessary. Even on its reduced scale, Luzon was the biggest campaign in the Southwest Pacific Area, with 8,300 Americans, 1,100 Filipino guerrillas, and 205,000 Japanese dying during its course. Liberating the entire archipelago cost the United States some 48,000 casualties and 14,000 deaths, the great majority sustained on Leyte and Luzon.

Considering the scale of the fighting, the number of casualties was actually moderate. The enemy lost 350,000 troops in the archipelago, making it far and away the most crushing defeat Japan would sustain in the Pacific. On Okinawa, by comparison, 7,000 U.S. troops would be killed fighting an enemy force less than a third the size of Japan's

Philippine garrison. Had MacArthur assaulted Yamashita in the headlong central Pacific style his losses might well have been similar.

Except for Yamashita's last stand, and clean-up operations in New Guinea, the liberation of the Philippines completed the work of Allied forces in the Southwest Pacific Area. After a shaky start, the Southwest Pacific Area's strategic planning, tactical inventiveness, and skillful execution set a standard of excellence rarely matched in any other theater of war.

SEE ALSO

Leyte Gulf, Battle of; MacArthur, Douglas; South Pacific Area

FURTHER READING

Bergerud, Eric. *Touched with Fire: The Land War in the South Pacific.* New York: Viking, 1996.

Cannon, M. Hamlin. *Leyte: The Return to the Philippines.* Washington: Office of the Chief of Military History, Department of the Army, 1954.

James, D. Clayton. *The Years of MacArthur.* Vol. 2. *1941–1945.*

Smith, Robert Ross. *Triumph in the Philippines.* Washington, D.C.: Department of the Army, 1963.

Soviet Union (U.S.S.R.)

When it was invaded by Germany on June 22, 1941, the Union of Soviet Socialist Republics (U.S.S.R.) had a population of about 170 million. This figure does not include those living in the eastern area of Poland, which the U.S.S.R. had acquired in 1939 as a result of the Stalin-Hitler Pact. That agreement, which opened the way for Germany's invasion of Poland, allowed the Soviets to take much of Poland, the Baltic states (Esto-

nia, Latvia, and Lithuania), Bessarabia, and, after a short but bitter war, the Karelian Isthmus of Finland. It also required the Soviets to supply Germany with large quantities of raw materials, which they did right up to the day they were invaded.

Although Americans have commonly referred to the U.S.S.R. as Russia, the Russian Federation, which was the largest of 11 republics that were independent in name only, actually made up only 64 percent of the Soviet population. But because many of the U.S.S.R.'s inhabitants were not of Russian descent, the Russian population of the U.S.S.R. as a whole amounted to 58.4 percent. The Ukrainian Republic was the next largest, with about 16.6 percent of the entire population. The rest of the Soviet Union was home to a dizzying variety of peoples, including Byelorussians, Uzbeks, Tatars, Kazakhs, Armenians, Georgians, and on and on, speaking more than 80 different languages and numerous dialects.

In 1941 Soviet citizens were still recovering from years of bloodshed inflicted on them by the savage regime of Joseph Stalin. From the late 1920s through the early 1930s, millions of peasants were shot, died of starvation (mostly as a result of government policies designed to achieve that end), or died in forced labor camps. Millions more fled to the cities or were deported to Siberia. Additional millions of people, including most leaders of the original Bolshevik Revolution and almost the entire senior officer corps of the Red Army, were killed during the Great Terror of 1935–39.

The exact number of deaths by execution, starvation, and being overworked and underfed in the vast chain of forced labor camps known today as the Gulag Archipelago is unknown. But a common figure is that 20 million Soviets perished as a result of Stalin's orders. All this occurred before a single Soviet citizen was killed by the invading Germans.

Understandably, many Soviet citizens, especially those in the Ukraine, which had been hardest hit by the famines, initially welcomed the German soldiers as liberators. Wholesale confiscations and massacres soon made it clear, however, that—impossible as it seemed—Hitler's rule would be even worse than Stalin's. This realization united the Soviets as Stalin could never have done and made possible an almost miraculous national recovery. Stalin exploited this national will to survive by naming the Soviet struggle the Great Patriotic War.

Only a united and determined people could have survived the terrible losses of 1941. Many millions of Soviet soldiers were killed or captured. Germany occupied Soviet territories that included 40 percent of the country's population, 60 percent of its armaments industries, 63 percent of its coal, 58 percent of its steel production, and similar large shares of its industrial and agricultural output.

The key to Soviet survival in the face of these staggering losses was relocation. Even as the fighting raged, not only did millions of people flee the invaded regions, but they removed much of their industry as well. A total of 2,593 plants relocated to new sites in the Volga region, beyond the Ural Mountains, and elsewhere. Some 40 percent of the workers and technicians relocated as well. A second, though smaller, relocation was made necessary in 1942 as a new German offensive threatened the Volga and Caucasus regions.

Meanwhile, military production in unaffected areas increased at such a rate that even while the relocation was going on, target levels set before the war were actually exceeded. Production still did not meet requirements, but Soviet industry manufactured about as many weapons as Germany did in the second half of 1941. In 1942, and for every year thereafter, Soviet production of aircraft, tanks, and other important weapons exceeded Germany's output. This was accomplished even though Germany's steel and coal production was much greater than that of the Soviets through 1944. The Soviets also received substantial Lend-Lease aid from the United States, although this program's assistance did not become important until 1943, when the tide of battle had already turned in the U.S.S.R.'s favor.

The miracle of Soviet military production was achieved by sacrificing civilian goods production almost completely. Agricultural production was hard hit too, not only from the loss of farmlands but because the agricultural workforce fell by a third (compared to a 12.5 percent decline in the industrial workforce). Because few able-bodied men of military age remained on the farms, most work was done by women, minors, and the aged. The loss of horses, oxen, and tractors meant that women had to serve as draft animals to an astonishing degree. Women made up a large part of the industrial work force as well, and 800,000 served in the military, some in combat jobs.

Under these conditions, Soviet agricultural output fell drastically. Because of German advances the total population—including Poles—fell from 194 million to 130 million. But while the population of the native Soviets alone fell to 67 percent of its prewar size, potato production fell to 31.3 of what it had been, grain to 27.9 percent, and meat and fats to 38.3 percent. This meant that most Soviet citizens went through the war in a state of malnutrition, a condition worsened by the fact that most of them, including children and the aged, were working harder and for longer hours than before. Calorie allowances for dependents were set at 780 a day and for nonindustrial employees at 1,074 to 1,176. To encourage people to work in factories, industrial workers had a ration that provided up to 4,418 calories a day, though this quota was seldom met.

The conditions in Soviet factories were extremely harsh. This was particularly so in the relocated plants, which often lacked roofs and whose workers slept in the open at first. New housing, when it was available, consisted mainly of hovels. This held true for relocated plants and the nation as whole.

As might be expected, civilian mortality rates under these conditions were very high. It is estimated that the total population decrease, including indirect losses resulting from premature births, desertion, and emigration, may have been as high as 48 million. Many deaths resulted from Stalin's policy of removing entire peoples to Siberia whose loyalty was suspect. These groups included the Volga Germans, who had been there for centuries, the Tatars of Crimea, and others.

Many deaths also resulted from Stalin's order of August 16, 1941, which defined surrender as treason. Any soldiers who surrendered and later fell into Soviet hands were to be shot on the spot. The families of those who surrendered were to be arrested or deprived of all state allowances and assistance, which was frequently a sentence of death. Because millions of soldiers became prisoners of war, millions of families suffered accordingly.

The Red Army had been professionalized during the 1930s and equipped with a substantial number of weapons. The share of the national budget going to the military rose from 9.1 percent in 1927–28 to 43.4 percent in 1938. But although it was better trained and equipped as a result of these expenditures, the army suffered from numerous defects. Because the senior officer corps had been slaughtered in Stalin's earlier purges of people he suspected—often

without reason—to be his enemies, most commanders had been promoted above their experience and ability. Soviet military doctrine emphasized infantry tactics to the neglect of armor and air power. It also concentrated on offense and did little to prepare the Red Army for the defensive battles it would be called on to fight. Although it had a great many tanks, most were obsolete and few had radios. Soviet aircraft were not much better.

What seemed at first to be another obsolete feature of the Soviet war engine was the large number of cavalry units attached to the Red Army. In fact, because the Soviet Union had few good roads, the horses were invaluable and gave the Soviets scouting and raiding capabilities that the Germans greatly envied.

At the time of the German invasion, the Red Army had 5.37 million men under arms, and another 5 million were mobilized within 10 days. On paper they should have been more than a match for the 3 million German and other soldiers in the invasion force. But the Soviets were short of transport, their communications soon broke down for lack of radios, and their prewar training and tactics proved to be out of date. As if this were not enough, incompetent leadership resulting from the purges ensured disaster.

Throughout the war, Stavka, the Soviet high command that worked directly under Stalin, introduced numerous changes. What was an army group in the

Three Soviet women with guns plan guerilla fighting strategies. The sheer number and determination of the Russian people, as well as severe winter weather, proved to be too much for the Germans.

West was known as a "front" to the Soviets and was named after the military district to which it was assigned. Each front had a varying number of armies of varying sizes, depending on its mission. In 1942 the first tank corps were formed, and then the first tank armies, which were designed as offensive units. In the same year, entire artillery divisions were created to provide massive concentrations of firepower, above and beyond the guns provided to each rifle (infantry) division. In 1943 artillery corps were formed with 700 guns apiece. At war's end there were 10 of these corps.

Stalin never accepted the concept of the strategic retreat. And he insisted on massing troops so that defeats became catastrophes. However, once the Red Army went over to the offensive in 1943 these mistaken ideas no longer mattered.

Although the Red Army's performance improved enormously during the course of the war, some of its problems were never solved. German optics and electronics were always better, as was German leadership, especially on the middle and lower levels. Stalin squandered men by insisting, for example, that the infantry attack without tank support, with Soviet armor being kept in reserve to exploit breakthroughs. It appears also that on at least some occasions minefields were cleared by having low-grade troops or punishment battalions march through them.

These unfortunate tactics led to huge and avoidable losses. By one estimate the Red Army lost more men taking Berlin alone than the U.S. Army lost in action in the entire European theater. In all, it appears that some 11 million Soviet servicemen and women were killed in action or died of their wounds. This figure compares with fewer than 300,000 U.S. battle deaths for the entire war.

Despite these horrendous losses, which led to severe manpower shortages in Soviet defense plants, the Soviets out-produced the much more advanced German economy in almost every important category of weapons. Although accurate figures are hard to come by (which is true throughout Soviet history), a few facts are suggestive. In December 1941, the low point of the Soviet war effort, the Soviet and German forces each had about 2,500 combat aircraft. By January 1945, when both countries were close to their peak production levels, the Soviets had at least 14,500 aircraft, the Germans not quite 2,000.

For tanks and self-propelled guns, the 1941 figures were 1,700 Soviet and 1,500 German. The 1945 figures in this category were 11,000 and 4,000, respectively. Most Soviet tanks were comparable to the best German tanks, something that was never true on the western front.

No other state—not even Germany and Japan—suffered losses on the immense scale that the Soviets did. And no other nation made as great a contribution to the defeat of Germany. A few simple statistics make this clear. Germany's armed force suffered more than 13 million casualties—killed, wounded, captured, and missing in action—in the entire war. Of these, 10 million were sustained fighting the Soviets on the eastern front.

SEE ALSO

Eastern front; Finland; Germany; Japan, surrender of; Stalin, Joseph; Stalingrad, Battle of

FURTHER READING

Dunn, Walter S. *Hitler's Nemesis: The Red Army, 1930–1945.* Westport, Conn.: Praeger, 1994.
Erickson, John. *The Road to Berlin.* Boulder, Colo.: Westview, 1983.
Salisbury, Harrison. *The Siege of Leningrad.* New York: Avon, 1969.
Temkin, Gabriel. *My Just War: The Memoir of a Jewish Red Army Soldier in World War II.* Novato, Calif.: Presidio, 1998.
Werth, Alexander. *Russia at War, 1941–1945.* New York: Avon, 1970.

Spaatz, Carl A.

COMMANDER OF THE UNITED STATES STRATEGIC AIR FORCES EUROPE, 1944–45

- *Born: June 28, 1891, Boyertown, Pa.*
- *Political party: none*
- *Education: U.S. Military Academy, B.S., 1914; Air Service Tactical School, 1924–25; Command and General Staff School, 1934–35*
- *Military service: U.S. Army—second lieutenant, 1914; major, 1917; commander, 13th Aero Squadron, 1918; commander, 7th Bombardment Group, 1928–31; lieutenant colonel, 1935; colonel, 1939; brigadier general, 1940; chief of the Air Staff, U.S. Army Air Forces, 1941; commander, Eighth Air Force, 1942; major general, 1942; air commander, N.W. Africa, 1943; lieutenant general, 1943; commander of the United States Strategic Air Forces Europe, 1944–45; general, 1945*
- *Died: July 14, 1974, Washington, D.C.*

The model "Bomber Baron," General Carl Spaatz was one of those airmen who embraced the doctrine of strategic bombing after World War I. As outlined by General William "Billy" Mitchell and others in the 1920s and 1930s, this theory held that in the future it would be possible to defeat an enemy nation solely through air power. By destroying its defense plants and infrastructure, the argument went, an enemy would be deprived of the means to wage war and would have to surrender without ever being invaded.

Leaders of Britain's Royal Air Force believed in strategic bombing too, but found themselves unable to put theory into practice. Because bombardiers had to see their targets, German objectives had to be attacked in daylight to be accurately hit. This tactic proved to be impossible to carry out, however, because bombers operating by day were sitting ducks for German fighters.

Accordingly, the RAF's Bomber Command was forced to attack at night. Because for years the smallest target that could be found at night was a large city, strategic bombing had to be abandoned. Instead, Bomber Command made what were called area attacks, on the theory that by killing civilians and burning their homes German morale would be destroyed.

In 1943 the first U.S. heavy bomber groups began attacking German targets. Initially, United States air commanders were not deterred by the RAF's dismal experience, because they believed that their heavy bombers were armed and armored strongly enough to fight their way through the German fighter screen. America's four-engine bombers, the B-17 Flying Fortress and the B-24 Liberator, carried many heavy machine guns and plenty of armor plate. Even so, the Eighth Air Force discovered that it could not fight its way through German fighters without taking unacceptable losses. In the fall of 1943, therefore, strategic attacks on Germany came to a halt.

Having invested so much in strategic bombing, the U.S. Army Air Forces were unwilling to give up on it. Major General Ira Eaker, who commanded the Eighth Air Force, based in Britain, was

General Carl Spaatz (right) presents a gold loving cup he received in London to General H. H. Arnold (left) while the British ambassador looks on. The cup is symbolic of friendship between the Royal Air Force and the U.S. Army Air Forces.

relieved of his job and made the senior air officer in the Mediterranean theater. General Spaatz, who had been commanding in the Mediterranean, was sent to Britain as commander of a newly formed entity, the United States Strategic Air Forces Europe (USSTAF). His command included the Eighth Air Force and a newly formed Fifteenth Air Force based in the Mediterranean. In addition, Spaatz was put in charge of all other U.S. air units in the European Theater of Operations. Since Eaker tended to defer to Spaatz, Spaatz became, in effect, the director of all U.S. air operations in both theaters.

In practice, however, Spaatz was primarily concerned with strategic bombing. In February 1944 the USSTAF resumed its attacks on Germany, this time with the support of long-range fighter escorts that previously had not been available. This cover enabled USSTAF to gain control of the daylight skies over Germany and reduce the German fighter force, for the most part, to night operations. That was the major contribution made by heavy bombers to the success of Overlord, the Allied invasion of Normandy on June 6, 1944.

During the preinvasion period, and for a time afterward, Spaatz fought hard to keep his bombing attacks confined to strategic targets. The ones he most wished to destroy were oil plants, refineries, and factories that turned coal into synthetic gasoline. This campaign was known as the Oil Plan. But General Dwight D. Eisenhower, the Allied supreme commander in Europe, who had gained direct control of USSTAF and the RAF's Bomber Command during the invasion period, disagreed. He and other Allied commanders had too often seen heavy bomber commanders make claims for strategic bombing that were not borne out in practice. Thus he insisted that the heavy bomber forces attack rail marshaling targets in France as part of what was called the Transportation Plan. The idea behind it was to disrupt the French rail and road systems so that Germany could not reinforce and resupply its forces in Normandy.

Although Eisenhower's desire to see some visible support from the heavy bomb groups was understandable, in this instance Spaatz was right. There was in fact no need for USSTAF to attack transportation targets in France, because Bomber Command, which by mid-1944 had achieved a high degree of accuracy, could attack rail yards as well or better. Also, the Allies had big tactical air formations that were extremely effective against transportation targets.

Spaatz persisted, however, bootlegging oil attacks as often as the Transportation Plan allowed. By the fall of 1944 he was finally free to concentrate on oil targets. Eventually the Oil Plan would succeed, but the problem was that oil plants had to be bombed visually, and clear days came only about once a month. Thus, in practice USSTAF was forced to bomb blind most of the time, using H2X radar sets that could not find a target smaller than a city.

Because visibility was too poor for precision bombing, the attacking aircraft would bomb cities as their secondary targets. These bombings were area attacks, and therefore in their effects little different from the terror raids made by the RAF.

The USSTAF terror raids became a public issue after the bombing of Dresden in 1945. Bomber Command attacked this previously unbombed city on the night of February 13–14, creating a firestorm that virtually leveled it. On the 14th, USSTAF made two separate attacks on Dresden, aiming, as usual, at its marshaling yards, not knowing that they had already been destroyed. Unlike most such attacks, the bombing of Dresden became an issue in the United States.

Its apparent brutality and pointlessness sparked reports that the Allies were now committed to terror attacks. Spaatz strongly defended USSTAF's policies, arguing that precision bombing was still the goal, with the area attacks being made only out of necessity. Most Americans seemed to have accepted this position.

It became apparent that the USSTAF's strategy was successful at the time of Germany's surrender. By then its rail system had been put out of commission by attacks on the rail yards. Its oil industry was defunct as well. Still, the fact remains that Germany surrendered not for these reasons but because it had been overrun by Allied and Soviet forces. Spaatz's legacy was, therefore, ambiguous, both morally and with respect to the value of strategic bombing.

SEE ALSO

Arnold, Henry H.; Berlin, bombing of; Royal Air Force; Schweinfurt, bombing of; Strategic bombing

FURTHER READING

Davis, Richard G. *Carl A. Spaatz and the Air War in Europe.* Washington, D.C.: Smithsonian Institution Press, 1992.
Mets, David R. *Master of Airpower: General Carl A. Spaatz.* Novato, Calif.: Presidio, 1988.

Spruance, Raymond Ames

AMERICAN ADMIRAL, VICTOR OF THE BATTLES OF MIDWAY AND THE PHILIPPINE SEA

- *Born: July 3, 1886, Baltimore, Md.*
- *Political party: none*
- *Education: U.S. Military Academy, B.S., 1914; Air Service Tactical School, 1924–25; Command and General Staff School, 1934–35*
- *Military service: U.S. Navy: midshipman in U.S. Naval Academy,*

July 1903–08; ensign, 1908; lieutenant, j.g., 1911; lieutenant, 1913; lieutenant commander, 1917; commander, 1918; captain, 1932; rear admiral, 1940; commander of carrier task force at Battle of Midway, June 4–6, 1942; vice admiral, 1943; commander Fifth Fleet, 1943; admiral, 1944.
- *Died: December 13, 1969, Pebble Beach, Calif.*

Raymond A. Spruance was the best American seagoing admiral of World War II, and perhaps in the entire history of the United States. In his time he was less famous than his outspoken partner, William Halsey, who became a five-star fleet admiral, while Spruance retired with only four stars. But Spruance was a better seaman than Halsey, and made better decisions in the heat of battle. He was also a quiet man, highly intelligent, courteous, and publicity-shy.

Spruance worked his way up the ladder of promotion as a commander of surface ships. When the Pacific war broke out on December 7, 1941, he was in charge of Cruiser Division 5, part of Halsey's carrier task force. In May 1942 naval intelligence learned that the Japanese main fleet was going to attack Midway Island, the westernmost one of the Hawaiian chain. Its purpose was to lure the U.S. Pacific Fleet's carriers into a trap and destroy them.

Admiral Chester Nimitz, commander in chief of the Pacific Fleet, decided to meet the Japanese force because even though the Americans would be outnumbered and outgunned in every type of ship and weapon, they would have the advantage of surprise. Halsey should have been in command of this battle, but he was hospitalized with a skin condition. When Nimitz asked Halsey who should take over his command, he picked Spruance. This was unheard of because the Navy believed that only aviators could command aircraft carriers and task forces, and Spruance was not a pilot. But except for Rear Admiral Frank Jack Fletcher, who would command the fleet at sea, there were no other carrier admirals available. Nimitz therefore put his faith in Spruance, and would be richly rewarded.

Spruance and Fletcher commanded separate task forces. Spruance had two carriers, *Enterprise* and *Hornet*, while Fletcher had only one, *Yorktown*. When the enemy fleet was sighted on June 4 by a Midway search plane, Spruance, who had been given a free hand by Fletcher, made one of the most important decisions of the war at sea. He attacked the Japanese immediately with all his strength at the maximum range of his torpedo bombers. Fletcher attacked an hour later.

The battle did not go as expected. All the air groups had trouble locating the Japanese force, which consisted of four carriers and a number of supporting ships. The torpedo plane squadrons found the carriers first and, attacking with little or no fighter protection, were nearly wiped out without scoring a single hit. Land-based aircraft from Midway also failed to damage the Japanese. Although the dive bombers from *Hornet* never did find the enemy and had to land on Midway for lack of gas, the other two dive bomber squadrons found all four enemy carriers, their decks crammed with aircraft, and their defensive fighter patrol, which had been shooting down torpedo planes, flying at low altitudes. At once the Americans began their bombing runs and within minutes three Japanese carriers were aflame and sinking.

Later that day Spruance sent a mixed force, including planes from *Yorktown*, which had been attacked and could not recover its aircraft, against the remaining Japanese carrier, which was then destroyed. The battle continued for several

more days. *Yorktown*, already damaged by Japanese planes, finally was sunk by an enemy submarine. Spruance's aircraft sank a Japanese cruiser. Finally, low on fuel and planes, Spruance, who now had operational command of the fleet, turned its ships toward home.

Until Midway the Japanese had enjoyed seven months of unbroken success. But the defeat suffered by the Imperial Japanese Navy (IJN) on June 4 was a blow from which it never recovered. After Midway Japan was forced to assume a defensive position and would never have anything in the future but local successes that changed nothing. Midway, the most strategically important battle of the Pacific war, was won by U.S. courage and luck, but also to a large extent because of Spruance's good judgment and willingness to take calculated risks.

After serving as chief of staff to Nimitz from August 1943 to November 1945, Spruance was made co-commander of a fleet of ships that had previously been known as the Pacific Fleet. Command of the fleet alternated between Halsey and Spruance; while one man took it out to sea, the other planned its next operation. It was called the Third Fleet under Halsey and the Fifth Fleet under Spruance. The Fifth Fleet, and its companion, the amphibious Central Pacific Force, successfully assaulted the Gilbert Islands (November 1943), the Marshalls (January 1944), the Marianas (June 1944), Iwo Jima (January 1945), and Okinawa (April 1945).

The most important of these was the attack on the Marianas—Spruance's second most important victory against the IJN. When the Fifth Fleet began its air attacks on the Marianas on June 11, 1944, Japanese naval leaders intent on achieving a decisive victory sent the largest fleet they could assemble from bases in the Philippines. Spruance learned of its approach on the 15th and

313

• S S (S C H U T Z S S T A F F E L N) •

made plans to receive it. His first concern was for the invasion force of transports and support ships, which he assumed the Japanese planned to attack. Therefore he placed Task Force 58, which had all his fast carriers, and his fast battleships and cruisers in front of the enemy fleet, but limited them to the waters near Saipan.

The Japanese, however, did not attack the invasion force on June 19. Instead, they assaulted Task Force 58 with both land-based and carrier aircraft. Unlike the battle at Midway, U.S. planes and pilots were now superior, and the result was a slaughter. The Japanese lost about 375 planes while Task Force 58, commanded by Vice Admiral Mark A. Mitscher, lost only 25. This fight was informally named "The Marianas Turkey Shoot."

The enemy fleet, now in retreat, was not located until late the following day. Mitscher then launched his air groups at maximum range, and with the light fading they managed to sink one more Japanese carrier in addition to two that were destroyed by U.S. submarines on the 19th. Many planes ran out of gas on the long flight back to Task Force 58, but most of their crews were later rescued. In this two-day engagement, known as the Battle of the Philippine Sea, the Japanese lost 476 planes and 445 aviators, Spruance, 130 planes and 43 men. Even though most of the Japanese carriers got away, the Japanese Fleet Air Arm was destroyed because of the loss of so many aviators who could not be replaced, although the Allies did not realize this at the time.

Spruance was much criticized, both at the time and later, for not sending Task Force 58 and his fast battleships to meet the enemy as soon as it was sighted. In hindsight, however, this was clearly the right course because the Japanese were after Mitscher's carriers, not the invasion force. If Mitscher had been given a free rein, all nine Japanese carriers would probably have been sunk. Strategically, though, this would have made little difference because without air crews the remaining carriers were nearly useless. Although his victory could have been even greater, Spruance won a crucial battle with little risk to his own men. Faced with a similar decision at the Battle of Leyte Gulf in October 1944, Halsey went on the attack at once and nearly lost an entire U.S. landing force.

SEE ALSO

Central Pacific Area; Halsey, William F.; Midway, Battle of; Philippine Sea, Battle of

FURTHER READING

Buell, Thomas B. *The Quiet Warrior: A Biography of Admiral Raymond A. Spruance.* Annapolis, Md.: Naval Institute Press, 1987.

SS (Schutzsstaffeln)

The SS (Schutzsstaffeln, literally "protection squads") began as Hitler's squad of personal bodyguards in 1923. In 1929 command of it was given to Heinrich Himmler, who expanded it from a few hundred men to over 200,000 by 1933. Known as the "black order" because of the color of its uniforms, the SS became Hitler's elite organization with its own political police, the dreaded Gestapo. It ran the concentration and death camps, owned its own businesses, and was a great empire that penetrated many areas of German life.

The largest department of the SS was its field army, the fierce and feared Waffen-SS, which, by the end of the war consisted of 800,000 men organized into 38 divisions. The first 3 divisions

Gestapo officials record data on incoming prisoners at a German concentration camp. Those waiting to be questioned are seated on the ground (left) under guard.

were formed in 1939, against the will of the German Army, which saw the Waffen-SS as a rival for men and resources. In time the Waffen-SS was fully integrated into the Army on the command level, while remaining under Himmler's authority in other areas, such as personnel and replacement training. Competition was further reduced by severe restrictions on the Waffen-SS's ability to recruit inside Germany. Although friction never died out, army commanders came to appreciate the Waffen-SS for its dedication, drive, and willingness to take high casualties.

Because of the limits placed on it, the Waffen-SS depended heavily on recruits. It often forcibly enrolled men from ethnic German communities outside the Third Reich. In addition, volunteers were obtained from other Nordic countries such as Norway and Holland. Manpower needs were so great, however, that by 1943 the SS also included men from all over Eastern Europe and the Balkans. These non-Germans frequently volunteered because of threats or false promises, and therefore they lacked motivation. As a result, the Waffen-SS lost much of its elite character. Only about a dozen Waffen-SS divisions were really effective. They were used as troubleshooters, moving from front to front wherever the need was greatest.

Although its best divisions were excellent fighting units, the fanaticism of the SS led it to commit many atrocities. These took place not only in the east, where vicious acts were common, but also on the western front, where the regular army generally observed the rules of war. Thus, efforts to make moral distinctions between the "bad" SS of the death camps and the "good" SS that only fought for its country must be viewed with suspicion.

SEE ALSO

Bulge, Battle of the, Eastern front, German Army

FURTHER READING

Lumsden, Robin. *The Waffen-SS*. London: Allan, 1994.
Stein, George. *The Waffen-SS: Hitler's Elite Guards at War*. Ithaca, N.Y.: Cornell University Press, 1966.

Stalin, Joseph
ABSOLUTE RULER OF THE SOVIET UNION

- *Born: December 9, 1879, Gori, Georgia*
- *Political party: Communist*
- *Military service: Red Army: political commissar, 1918–20; marshal of the Red Army, 1943; generalissimo, 1945*
- *Government service: Commissar of nationalities, 1918; member, Central Committee of Communist party; member, Political Bureau of the Communist party (Politburo), Organizational Bureau of the Communist party (Ogburo) and commissar of state control, 1919; general secretary of the Central Committee, 1922–1952*
- *Died: March 5, 1953, Moscow, Russia, U.S.S.R.*

Despite his two years as a political commissar with the Red Army and his lofty titles, Iosif Vissarionovich Djugashvili, who named himself Stalin in 1912, was never a serving soldier. He regarded himself as a military genius, however, and all important military decisions and plans had to have his approval.

Stalin spent virtually his entire adult life as a politician, first as a Bolshevik revolutionary, then as a leader of the Communist party of the Soviet Union. He held many titles and offices, but it was as general secretary of the party that he managed to defeat his rivals to become leader of the U.S.S.R. after Lenin's death in 1924. By 1927 he had acquired dictatorial powers, which he used to launch a series of famines and purges that made his rule the bloodiest in world history.

A conservative estimate is that Stalin had put 20 million people to death by the time World War II broke out. Among those he had killed in the course of preparing the Soviet Union for war included most of the senior officer corps of its armed forces. Not only was this a terrible crime, it was also a serious mistake that contributed to the many Soviet defeats in 1941 and 1942.

Stalin made another mistake when he signed a pact with Hitler in 1939. Under the terms of this agreement, the Soviet Union acquired about half of Poland, all of the Baltic states (Estonia, Latvia, Lithuania), and parts of Finland and Romania. In return Stalin pledged to remain neutral in the coming war and provide Germany with foodstuffs and raw materials. Apparently Stalin made this deal because he anticipated that Germany's war in the west would be long and difficult, as it had in World War I. But Hitler's stunning victory in 1940, which drove Britain from the Continent, proved Stalin's calculations wrong. Because Hitler no longer faced much of a threat in the west, he was able to draw on practically all of the resources of Europe when he invaded

Stalin (center in white jacket) arrives at the Potsdam residence of former British prime minister Winston Churchill, who was hosting a state dinner for the "Big Three" leaders.

the Soviet Union in June 1941.

That the Soviets survived their devastating defeats that year was partly because Hitler made mistakes but also because Stalin had done some things right in the prewar era. Hitler's most important mistake was to launch a reign of terror in the occupied regions of the U.S.S.R., alienating the anticommunist inhabitants there and uniting the entire nation behind Stalin in a struggle for survival. Stalin's biggest contribution to victory was that he had, through brute force, created an arms industry that would prove to be superior to that of the Germans, although Soviet industry as a whole was much behind Germany's.

Nonetheless, Stalin contributed to the Soviet losses by insisting on carrying out offensives before the Red Army was strong enough to defeat Germany on the battlefield. He survived numerous debacles by ruling with an iron hand while at the same time wrapping himself in the mantle of patriotism.

During the war Stalin also eased some forms of repression, such as allowing the Orthodox Church to operate more freely. But these freedoms were offset by Stalin's infamous order of August 16, 1941, that Soviet military personnel taken prisoner by the Germans were to be regarded as traitors. When Lieutenant General Andrey Vlasov was captured in 1942—as a result of Stalin's refusal to allow him to retreat from a hopeless position—he offered to lead Soviet prisoners of war in battle as German allies on the eastern front.

Hitler foolishly failed to take advantage of this opportunity. Vlasov did form a small army of Soviet prisoners of war, but they were not sent to the eastern front. Most Soviet prisoners of war were simply brutalized and neglected by Nazi Germany, which made little use of them either as fighters or workers.

As time went on, Stalin's military leadership improved. He made fewer mistakes, appointed able men to positions of command, and gave them greater freedom. Just to be on the safe side, however, Stalin made sure that most Soviet leaders had at least one relative held hostage in the vast and terrible prison camp system known as the Gulag. While generals that lost battles were sometimes shot, winners were showered with medals and privileges.

Soon after the German invasion, Stalin began demanding aid from Britain, and from the United States too, once it entered the war. Most of all, he demanded that the Allies open a second front by invading France. He continued to make this demand even after the Soviets gained the upper hand over Germany in 1943. After the war anticommunists in the United States would charge that President Roosevelt, as a negotiator, had lost to Stalin, but this was untrue. Stalin possessed no special gift for diplomacy and was not particularly farsighted. His constant demand for a second front was proof of this, since the later the Allies arrived in Europe the more territory Stalin would be able to seize. Certainly after 1943 he did not need a second front and could have taken all of Europe if the Western Allies had not invaded France.

At the Teheran and Yalta conferences in 1943 and 1945, it was agreed that the Soviets would have a sphere of influence in Eastern Europe. The Allied hope was that Stalin would allow internal self-government in the states he liberated. But the main reason why Stalin gained a free hand in the region was not because of bad Allied diplomacy. What Stalin ruled after the war were territories that the Red Army had taken from Germany and its allies. No amount of brilliant diplomacy on Roosevelt's part could have prevented this from happening. The only way to have saved Eastern Europe from communist rule was for the United States to have entered the war, and thus opened the second front, much sooner than it actually did.

It is also unclear how much Stalin actually gained by turning his newly acquired Eastern European territories into communist police states. To keep them in his empire they had to be occupied by the Red Army on a permanent basis. And to keep their economies from collapsing altogether, they had to be supplied with raw materials, oil and gas especially, at low prices. With Germany eliminated as a military power, the Soviet Union was going to dominate the region in any case and could have done so much more profitably if it had treated the eastern states as it did Finland.

The Finns had sided with Germany in 1941 to regain their Karelian Isthmus, which Stalin had taken from them after the Winter War of 1939–40. When Finland surrendered, it was forced to pay an indemnity and trade with the Soviets on highly unfavorable terms. The Soviets also retained a veto over Finland's foreign policy. Otherwise, Stalin left Finland alone. Giving the Finns internal freedom at a high economic price satisfied the security requirements of the Soviet Union while also enriching its coffers.

Stalin's failure to "Finlandize" Eastern Europe turned out to be not in the best interests of the Soviet state. "Stalinizing" the east was a disastrous choice. It guaranteed that World War II would be followed by a cold war, which would prove to be ruinously expensive for the Soviets. Probably Stalin dealt harshly with the east for personal reasons rather than reasons of state. It extended his power, which he loved to exercise.

Furthermore, the cold war gave Stalin an excuse for maintaining the Soviet Union as a police state, which in the absence of enemies would have been harder to do. The United States and Britain were eager to have good relations with Stalin after the war. Had he Finlandized Eastern Europe there would have been no important barriers to good relations between East and West. This suggests that the Stalinization of Eastern Europe was designed to provoke the West, thereby creating the permanent enemies that would justify Stalin's dictatorship.

The legend of Stalin as a master of statecraft is therefore largely false. The collapse of Germany and Japan left the Soviet Union and the United States as the only remaining great powers. Stalin then had a choice between alienating the United States and maintaining the two countries' wartime alliance. Had he chosen the latter, the Soviet Union would have gotten Marshall Plan aid and would not have needed to maintain great armed forces.

Under these circumstances the Soviet Union might have enjoyed enough economic success to have survived in some form or other. While claiming to act in the name of the Soviet Union and communism, Stalin launched policies that were ultimately destructive to both—hardly the mark of a great leader. Like Hitler, Stalin did as he pleased, regardless of the cost or the consequences.

Stalin's reputation as a blood-soaked monster is not legend but fact. He per-

sonally ordered untold millions of Soviet citizens put to death before, during, and after World War II. He insisted on military strategies and tactics that caused millions of Soviet soldiers to die who otherwise would no doubt have lived. Cruel as he was to the peoples of Eastern Europe, he was crueler still to his own people. It cannot be denied that without the Soviets, Nazi Germany would not have been defeated. The Soviet Union's victory was achieved under Stalin's leadership; this too cannot be contested. But the price of victory was terribly high—for the Soviets most of all.

SEE ALSO

Eastern front; Finland; Germany; Roosevelt, Franklin Delano; Soviet Union (U.S.S.R.); Teheran conference; Yalta conference

FURTHER READING

Barros, James. *Double Deception: Stalin, Hitler, and the Invasion of Russia.* DeKalb: Northern Illinois University Press, 1995.
Bialer, Seweryn. *Stalin and His Generals: Soviet Military Memoirs of World War II.* New York: Pegasus, 1969.
Ulam, Adam. *Stalin: The Man and His Era.* New York: Viking, 1973.

Stalingrad, Battle of

Stalingrad is usually regarded as the turning point of the European war. In 1942 the Wehrmacht (the German military) was weaker than in 1941 when it had failed to capture Moscow. Just the same, Hitler ordered another offensive in Russia that was supposed to be decisive. Known as Operation Blue, it was intended to defeat the Soviets by, among other things, cutting them off from their oil supplies in the Caucasus.

The mission of General Friedrich Paulus, who commanded Germany's Sixth Army, was to take the city of Stalingrad. This would support the Caucasus drive and give Germany control of the lower Volga region. The Sixth Army reached the outskirts of Stalingrad on September 12, 1942. Because of its value, and fearing a loss of prestige if the city named after him fell, Stalin decided to hold it at all costs. Accordingly, he poured reinforcements into Stalingrad while at the same time planning vast Red Army movements to encircle the Sixth Army. This was accomplished on November 23 after Soviet forces destroyed two Romanian armies.

When Germany's relief efforts failed, the obvious response was for the Sixth Army to break out of its pocket while the Soviet lines were still weak enough to make escape possible. But Hitler once again refused to authorize a retreat. Instead, the Luftwaffe (Germany's air force) was to supply the Sixth Army by air. Germany's air commander, Reichsmarshal Hermann Göring, pledged to deliver 300 tons a day of supplies to the pocket. But the Sixth Army required a minimum of 500 tons of supplies a day, a total that was reached just once. And on most days the Luftwaffe, despite heavy losses, delivered far less (an average of 90 tons). Starving and running low on all supplies, the Sixth Army fought in the cellars and ruins of Stalingrad. The German soldiers called this a *Rattenkrieg,* or war of the rats, and they steadily lost ground.

There could be only one end to what had become such a lopsided battle. On January 30, 1943, as the end neared, Hitler promoted Paulus to field marshal. Presumably this was so that he would kill himself, because no German marshal had ever before been taken prisoner. Paulus, however, became the first, surrendering on January 31. The Ger-

mans' resistance came to an end a few days later.

The Germans lost some 250,000 men at Stalingrad, the Soviets at least that many. Stalingrad marked the end of the German blitzkrieg (lightning war), which had once swept all that lay before it. The balance of military power on the eastern front now tipped in the Soviets' favor for good.

SEE ALSO
Eastern front

FURTHER READING

Erickson, John. *The Road to Stalingrad.* New York: Harper & Row, 1975.
Hoyt, Edwin Palmer. *199 Days: The Battle for Stalingrad.* New York: Tor, 1993.
Jukes, Geoffrey. *Stalingrad: The Turning Point.* New York: Ballantine, 1968.

Stimson, Henry Lewis
SECRETARY OF WAR, 1940–45

- *Born: September 21, 1867, New York, N.Y.*
- *Political party: Republican*
- *Education: Yale, B.A., 1888; Harvard, M.A., 1889; Harvard, L.L.B., 1890*
- *Military service: U.S. Army—colonel, 1917–19*
- *Government service: U.S. attorney, 1906–08; secretary of war, 1911–13; governor general of the Philippines, 1927–29; secretary of state, 1929–33; secretary of war, 1940–45*
- *Died: October 20, 1950, Huntington, N.Y.*

Henry Stimson was the oldest and most distinguished of President Franklin Delano Roosevelt's civilian war leaders. Well before he entered the cabinet in 1940 he had helped set in motion the chain of events that led to the December 1941 attack on Pearl Harbor. As President Hoover's secretary of state, he was responsible for the policy of not recogniz-

Secretary of War Stimson draws the first number in the Selective Service Lottery held in the departmental auditorium on October 15, 1940.

ing Manchukuo, the puppet state Japan had set up after seizing Manchuria in 1931. This was the beginning of a steady decline in American-Japanese relations that resulted in the Pacific war.

Although a lifelong Republican, Stimson was asked by Roosevelt to serve in his cabinet because he was an outspoken enemy of isolationism and could be counted on for support if Roosevelt ever wished to enter the European war. That he was a Republican mattered too, for Stimson would give Roosevelt's policies a bipartisan flavor. Finally, he was highly qualified for the job by virtue of his previous government service and because he was well informed on military matters.

A man of outstanding good judgment and integrity, Stimson supported aid to Britain and was urging Roosevelt to use the Navy to escort Lend-Lease convoys well before the President decided to do so. He was one of very few Presidential advisors who agreed with Roosevelt's decision to provide the Soviet Union with Lend-Lease aid when it entered the war.

Stimson continued to favor taking a hard line against Japan even if it meant war, but when war came he supported the decision to concentrate on Europe first. To that end he, like General George C. Marshall, was opposed to the Mediterranean campaigns that delayed the invasion of France.

On other issues Stimson was less wise. He went along, however reluctantly, with the imprisonment of Japanese

Americans in so-called "relocation," or internment, camps. He agreed with the policy of not diverting U.S. air power to bomb Hitler's death camps. Because of this policy, many died in the Holocaust who might otherwise have been saved. (Though some prisoners in the camps would have been killed in the raids, the bombs might well have destroyed the Germans' efficient machinery of death—the crematoriums and gas chambers—without which the mass murders could not continue.) He also opposed admitting refugee Jews to the United States above the existing quotas.

Stimson was an excellent administrator and, for a man of the 19th century, remarkably aware of the value of science. One of his major contributions was to urge the traditionally conservative military leadership to take advantage of what scientists had to offer. He ardently supported the atomic bomb project and was the principal civilian advisor to both Roosevelt and Truman on nuclear issues.

Stimson regretted the need to drop atomic bombs on Japan, and he succeeded in having Kyoto, a religious and cultural center, removed from the target list. He also had reservations about the conventional bombing of cities, especially the Japanese fire bomb raids, which were undisguised terror attacks. In fact, Stimson was the only civilian war leader to have serious doubts about the morality of making war against civilians.

SEE ALSO

Atomic bombs; Japan; Japanese Americans; Mediterranean theater; Strategic bombing

FURTHER READING

Hodgson, Godfrey. *The Colonel: The Life and Wars of Henry Stimson, 1867–50.* New York: Knopf, 1990.
Stimson, Henry Lewis. *On Active Service in Peace and War.* New York: Octagon Books, 1948.

Strategic bombing

The Allied air forces arrived at their common destiny by different means and from different starting points. Unlike the British Royal Air Force, which had been independent since 1918, the U.S. Air Force remained a branch of the Army throughout World War II. But it yearned to be a separate service and as early as 1935 had embraced an idea designed to bring that about—the doctrine of strategic bombardment.

According to this theory, an enemy could be bombed into submission by attacks on its industrial base. Victory through air power was advanced by Air Marshal Hugh Trenchard, founder of the RAF, by the Italian general Giulio Douhet, and was promoted ardently by Brigadier General William "Billy" Mitchell of the United States—who resigned his commission after being court-martialed in 1925 for going outside official channels to promote his cause. Despite Mitchell's punishment, air officers continued to keep the faith, although with greater discretion.

When war came, both the U.S. Army Air Forces (USAAF) and the RAF were committed to strategic bombing as their primary mission. The USAAF had acquired the first real heavy bomber in history for this purpose, the four-engine Boeing B-17 Flying Fortress. Britain lagged behind, with its first strategic bombers being two-engine aircraft incapable of accomplishing their mission.

Not surprisingly, the first RAF attempts at daylight precision bombing under combat conditions were miserable failures. In September and December 1939, it attacked German naval targets with 159 bombers, losing 29. A loss rate of almost 19 percent was intolerable. Thus, when the RAF began subjecting Germany to strategic bombardment it had to do so by night, when the enemy's fighter force was less effective.

From May 1940 until the end of 1941, Britain attacked strategic targets in Germany with feeble results. The War Cabinet ordered a study that found that only one in four air crews who claimed to have hit their target had actually dropped their bombs within five miles of it. The RAF's own casualties were higher than those it inflicted on enemy civilians.

Britain might have called off its air war against Germany at this point and been little the worse for doing so. Instead, it decided to continue bombing Germany under different principles. In February 1942, under a new commander, Air Marshal Sir Arthur Harris, known to his men as "Butch," for butcher, Bomber Command began to attack German cities. Its purpose was what Lord Cherwell, the prime minister's science advisor, called "de-housing the workers," a policy that aimed to destroy German morale by destroying that country's civilians. This strategy was forced on the RAF; a city was the smallest target that could be located at night by bombers.

The United States joins the air war
In 1942, when the U.S. Eighth Air Force dropped its first bombs on Europe, several facts were alarmingly clear. Germany's air attacks on Britain in 1940 and 1941 had failed. And the RAF's attempts to destroy strategic targets in Germany had failed also. Britain was now engaged in a program of area bombing that was extremely expensive in men and machines and yet seemed to have little effect on German war production. Not even the introduction of RAF four-engine heavy bombers with big bomb loads had changed this equation.

The aerial view of fields and roads creates an abstract pattern in this photograph taken above Czechoslovakia. The clouds over the industrial facility in the center are bombs that have hit their target.

U.S. generals argued that the experience of other air forces was not relevant, because only B-17s, and the newer B-24 Liberators, had been designed for daylight precision bombing. Both types were heavily armed and armored, payload being sacrificed to defensive capability. Thus, while Bomber Command's splendid Avro Lancaster carried immense 10-ton "blockbusters," the U.S. heavies could drop only 2 or 3 tons of bombs on distant targets.

Lancasters had but five puny .303-caliber machine guns, while the B-17Es that attacked Rouen were armed with a dozen .50-caliber guns. Three pairs of these were mounted in power turrets (rotating gun chambers), and the later G model added another power turret with two more guns under the nose. By flying in close formations that provided overlapping fields of fire, the U.S. heavies were supposed to be capable of fighting their way across Germany and back again. In any case, there was no point in adding U.S. bombers to the RAF's night attacks, because their small payloads

made them unsuitable for area bombing. As bombers, the 17s and 24s could be effectively used only for daylight precision attacks.

But the U.S. generals were wrong. It was not until June 10, 1943, that the order was given to attack German targets, with the U.S. Eighth Air Force concentrating especially on the Luftwaffe (Germany's air force) and its supporting aircraft industry. Despite efforts to provide fighter planes with extra fuel capacity, on their deep penetration raids the bombers still had to go it alone, resulting in terrible casualties. A climax was reached on August 17 when two separate air divisions attacked Regensburg and Schweinfurt. Of the 315 heavies that reached their targets, 60 went down, resulting in a loss rate of 19 percent.

Too much had been invested in strategic bombing at this point to admit defeat. On October 14, Eighth Air Force bombed Schweinfurt again and lost another 60 aircraft out of 291 that were launched. Including Schweinfurt, a total of 148 bombers had been lost in four attacks mounted during a six-day period.

"Black Week," as the airmen called it, stopped the Eighth Air Force in its tracks. German fighters had destroyed the theory of the "self-defending bomber force." Without admitting defeat, the Eighth staged only one more bombing attack between the second Schweinfurt attack and February 1944.

The Allied aircrews' extraordinary losses also destroyed the theory that air forces would limit casualties on the ground by substituting aircraft for men, a key rationale for air power in the first place. The USAAF, with about one-fourth of the Army's manpower, took only one-ninth of its battle casualties. However, the comparison is misleading, because it includes wounded men, of which the Army's ground forces had many and the air forces relatively few. When a U.S.

bomber went down, half its crew usually perished.

Out of 291,557 U.S. battle deaths in World War II, 52,173 were army airmen. This is an enormous number considering that bomber crews made up a small part of the military as a whole. Their non-combat death rate was higher as well, because of the hazardous nature of air operations. A total of 35,946 airmen were killed accidentally, 43 percent of all such deaths in the Army. During the worst months of the air war in Europe, a study tracked 2,051 airmen through their duty tour of 25 missions, and only 559, or 26.8 percent, completed it, with 1,195 being killed or missing in action.

The odds improved somewhat for U.S. airmen once the Luftwaffe was beaten as a daytime force (though not for Bomber Command, because German night fighters remained active to the end). Still, bombing Germany was never safe, and overall a high price was paid by American youth in support of the USAAF's faith in daytime precision bombardment.

Victory in the air The USAAF responded to its defeat with very little delay. In December 1943, General Henry "Hap" Arnold—whose nickname belied his impatience, hot temper, and ruthlessness—replaced the Eighth's commander, Major General Ira Eaker, with Major General James H. Doolittle, hero of the first bombing raid on Tokyo in 1942. This change was part of a general reorganization that merged the Eighth Air Force with the Fifteenth Air Force (a new command operating from Mediterranean bases) to create the U.S. Strategic Air Forces in Europe (USSTAF). Lieutenant General Carl Spaatz was made chief of USSTAF, with Eaker taking over all Allied air forces in the Mediterranean.

A more important development was the arrival of the desperately needed long-range P-51 Mustang, the last and greatest propeller-driven fighter. It was originally built by North American Aviation for service with the RAF, which on delivery found it to be underpowered. The British then fitted it with their own superb aircraft engine, the legendary Merlin. Thus equipped, it could outperform any propeller-driven fighter, but it still lacked the range to accompany deep attacks. The solution to this problem came from an intervention by Robert A. Lovett, the U.S. assistant secretary of war for air.

Unlike Arnold, whose "hands were tied by his mouth," Lovett said later, he was not limited by having previously championed the idea of a self-defending bomber. He demanded results from Arnold, who dropped the problem on his new chief of staff, Major General Barney M. Giles. The decisive Giles had North American Aviation take out a big radio from behind the pilot's seat and replace it with a 100-gallon fuel tank, while also installing bulletproof tanks in the wings. Fears that 300 additional gallons of fuel would be more than the wings and landing gear could support were proven wrong when a test showed that the rugged little Mustang could take it. Thanks to Lovett and Giles, bomber crews would now have a good chance of survival.

In February 1944 the strategic air forces—reorganized, reinforced, and defended by a large number of fighter groups—were ready to take on the Luftwaffe once again, this time in Operation Pointblank. On February 20, when bad weather over Germany finally lifted, "Big Week" began. The Eighth Air Force committed 16 combat wings (a battle formation consisting of 63 heavy bombers) and 17 fighter groups, most being equipped with P-47 Thunderbolts and P-38 Lightnings, whose ranges had been extended with belly and wing tanks.

These aircraft had varying combat ranges, but two groups consisting of

Mustangs and could go most, and soon all, of the distance to the target. In addition, the RAF's fighter command threw in 16 squadrons of Spitfires and Mustangs. The targets of this immense force were aircraft and ball-bearing factories in the Reich, most of which were struck, at a cost of only 25 U.S. bombers and 4 fighters. The bomber loss rate was just 2.5 percent—a far cry from the attacks on Schweinfurt. Fighter-bomber attacks on German airfields were equally effective.

When Big Week was over, the Eighth Air Force had made 3,300 bomber runs and the Fifteenth more than 500. Together they dropped 10,000 tons of bombs, more than the Eighth had delivered in its first full year of combat operations. Together the VIII and XV fighter commands and the Ninth Tactical Air Force made 3,773 runs. The cost was heavy—2,600 airmen were killed, wounded, or missing—but for the first time something important was gained. Within a few months, the German daylight fighter force was broken. The Luftwaffe remained active at night, but the United States ruled the skies over Germany by day.

The Transportation Plan On April 1, 1944, Operation Pointblank came to an end, and the Allied strategic air forces came under General Eisenhower's control for the first time. He used his authority to order attacks on rail marshaling yards and related targets specified by the Transportation Plan, which proposed to isolate Normandy from the rest of Europe so that during the invasion of France, Germany would not be able to reinforce and resupply its troops in the combat zone. In order to conceal the landing site, it was necessary for air attacks to be made all along the Channel coast, not just in Normandy.

General Spaatz argued that this was a misuse of his bombers, because Transportation Plan targets could be destroyed by tactical air strikes and did not require his heavy bombers to take them out. He

preferred the Oil Plan, according to which USSTAF would concentrate on eliminating Germany's supply of liquid fuel. But Supreme Headquarters Allied Expeditionary Forces (SHAEF) had lost confidence in the air marshals and generals whose promises had seldom been kept, and insisted that the British and U.S. heavy bombers concentrate on transportation targets.

Even so, Spaatz secretly kept the Oil Plan going throughout this period, making attacks supposedly in support of the Transportation Plan that actually struck petroleum targets. USSTAF had estimated that 90 percent of Germany's liquid fuel and lubricants was produced by 54 oil refineries and synthetic petroleum plants, of which 27 were especially important.

The Oil Plan On June 10, 1944, when he regained his independence, Spaatz announced that oil targets would have first priority in strategic bombing efforts. USSTAF then began attacking targets in the Ruhr Valley and around Ploesti in Rumania. They were fiercely defended and had the virtue of putting more pressure on the German

A formation of B-29s releases incendiary bombs over Japan in June 1945. On August 1, a fleet of these planes dropped 6,871 tons of explosives on Japanese strategic targets, the largest air raid of the war.

fighter force, which was now desperately short of pilots.

These attacks were costly, especially for the 15th Air Force, since Ploesti was the third-best-defended target in Europe (the first was the Ruhr). The Fifteenth also attacked Vienna, which had the second-best air defense. Accordingly, Fifteenth's losses were higher than those of Eighth Air Force and Bomber Command, amounting to a loss of 318 heavy bombers in July, Fifteenth's worst month. During August it actually lost more men than the Allied armies in Italy. But when the Red Army reached Ploesti a month later it found that oil was no longer being produced there—an exploit that had cost the Fifteenth Air Force 350 bombers.

By September 1944 Germany's petroleum output was reduced to 23 percent of the pre–Oil Plan levels, ending German tank training altogether and drastically reducing the training time of Luftwaffe pilots. At the end of 1944 Germany had only four crude oil refineries in operation and five or six synthetic plants running. By February 1945 air attacks had brought industry to a halt completely.

On April 7 the RAF discontinued area bombing, and on the 16th Spaatz informed his commanders that the bomber offensive was over. Except for tactical targets there was nothing left to attack. By this time Germany's transportation system had been destroyed as well, since it was the habit of USSTAF to have its bombers attack cities when the weather did not permit raids on Oil Plan targets—which was most of the time. As a result of frequent area attacks by U.S. and British bombers, all of Germany's cities were eventually burned out, including their precious rail yards.

Analysis of the bombing of Germany British air historians, embarrassed by the record of Bomber Command, tend to hold up the USAAF as the model that ought to have been copied. And, undeni-

ably, for sheer mindless violence Britain's Bomber Command took first place. It began to carry out terror bombing because it could not attack Germany in any other way. But under Air Marshal Harris, it went on raiding German cities long after it was capable of accurately bombing real strategic targets.

Bomber Command committed the two worst crimes of the European air war: the bombings of Hamburg in 1943 and Dresden in 1945. Both attacks, the second deliberately, created huge firestorms that consumed oxygen faster than it could be replaced, killing thousands of people by carbon monoxide poisoning who were untouched by flame or blast. Furthermore, Dresden had limited strategic value and the war was nearly over. The USAAF, in contrast, made serious efforts to bomb precisely and killed far fewer German civilians.

But the differences between the two air forces were greater in theory than in practice. More than half of all U.S. attacks ended up with the bombs being dropped through "undercast" (clouds and fog seen from above in a plane), which was in fact area bombing, whatever the military called it. In time Americans employed terror bombing intentionally. One series of such attacks, on February 22 and 23, 1945, code-named Clarion, was aimed at small cities and towns that had little or no military importance. The "Thunderclap" bombing of Berlin on February 3, which was purely a terror raid, killed up to 25,000 civilians. Four other attacks on Berlin were similar in character.

USSTAF also supported Britain's attack on Dresden in February and, when criticism of area bombing developed, issued a statement saying that there had been no change in policy, an obvious falsehood, since it was policy to area bomb whenever precision bombing was impossible. Ultimately, U.S. air strikes killed fewer Germans than those of the British, mainly because they dropped smaller bomb loads. The touch of moral superiority over the RAF that may remain after noting these exceptions leaves little to celebrate.

Not just a crime, the air war was also a blunder. Even the official historians of the USAAF admit that daylight attacks on Germany should not have been undertaken before February 1944, when long-range fighter escorts became available. Although they did not admit this, the constantly shifting rationales of the bomber barons gave their game away. Strategic bombing was supposed to defeat the German nation, but in actual practice the bomber campaign became a war of attrition between the Allied air forces and the Luftwaffe.

Control of the skies was supposed to be won by destroying Germany's aircraft industry. Because this proved impossible, control was won by raids whose principal function was to attract German fighters, with the supposedly war-winning Allied heavy bombers serving simply as bait.

The air war succeeded in the sense that virtually all the strategic targets in Germany were destroyed by war's end. But this achievement came so near to the end of the ground war that it actually made little difference. Bombing Germany had other uses as well, mainly the diversion of German resources to air defense. Yet victory could have been achieved as quickly, and perhaps even sooner, had the huge Allied investment in strategic bombing been put into the ground war instead.

None of this criticism applies to the fighters and medium bombers (known as tactical air) directly supporting the ground troops, which were an outstanding success. This support enabled Allied armies that would otherwise have been too small for the job to prevail over the German Army.

Japan The strategic bombing of Japan was even more futile and mindless than that of Germany. It began in 1944 when the new Boeing B-29 Superfortress was based in China for long-range attacks on the Japanese home islands. This campaign failed because all the supplies for the bombing effort had to be flown in from India over the "Hump," a series of mountain ranges. This expensive and dangerous enterprise cost many planes yet never managed to deliver enough fuel and munitions to make air raids from China effective. So the effort was canceled and the planes sent to bases in the Mariana Islands.

Few senior officers outside the air force were enthusiastic about strategic bombing by this time, and there was constant pressure to use heavy bombers in direct support of troops. This was why General Henry H. "Hap" Arnold had persuaded the Joint Chiefs of Staff to make B-29s independent of theater commanders in the Pacific. He would personally direct the Twentieth Air Force, to which all Superfortresses were assigned, with operations to be run by the heads of its bomber commands.

Given the vast resources that had been committed to the B-29, and considering the Navy's skepticism in particular about it, the USAAF had much at stake in its bombardment of Japan. Although the Marianas were far superior to China as a base of operations and Tokyo was only 1,200 miles from Saipan, the XXI Bomber Command (the principal striking force) accomplished very little.

The B-29 still suffered from technical difficulties, its maintenance was poor to begin with, and the long flights to Japan consumed more fuel than expected, leaving little margin for error. The USAAF had not been prepared for the tremendous winds and heavy cloud cover frequently found over Japan. Its very first attack, launched from the Marianas on November 24, 1944, was made by 111 aircraft. Of these 17 aborted and returned to base,

Miniatures of Japanese targets, such as this model of Tokyo Bay in the background, were constructed on sound stages and used to brief crews preparing to bomb Japanese targets.

6 could not bomb because of mechanical failures, and those that made it to Tokyo could not see the target because of undercast and were swept along by 120-knot winds that made even radar useless. A mere 48 bombs fell on the primary target. Although only one Superfortress was lost to enemy air defenses, 29 ran out of gas and had to ditch in the ocean. This futile attack was followed by others. As a result of poor visibility and winds as high as 200 knots an hour, accuracy was nearly impossible.

Arnold solved the problem by firing Major General H. S. Hansell, the chief of the XXI Bomber Command and a believer in precision bombing. His offense seems to have been failing to launch firebomb raids against Japanese cities. Hansell did not understand that the USAAF was now committed to area bombing, its prewar theory of strategic bombardment having been proven wrong. His replacement, Major General Curtis E. LeMay, the tactical wizard of the Eighth Air Force, understood that he was supposed to terrorize Japan.

Firebomb raids Once accuracy became unimportant, a battery of new methods could be used to burn out Japanese cities, which were especially vulnerable because of their flimsy construction. Area bombing could take place after dark, because Japan had few night fighters, and could be carried out at low altitudes, where the B-29 consumed less fuel and could carry heavier bomb loads.

The skies over Japan were more often clear at night than during the day, the winds at low altitudes were not as great as at higher ones, and loran, a radio navigation system, also worked better at night. This was an important point, because at night bombers could not fly in formation and every plane had to find its own target by itself.

The first firebomb raid on Japan took place on the night of March 9–10, 1945, when 334 Superfortresses carrying six-ton bomb loads attacked Tokyo. The resulting devastation consumed almost 16 square miles of the city and one-fourth of its buildings. One million people were made homeless and at least 100,000 killed. It was the single most destructive air attack of the war—including the atomic bombings—and was followed by many others.

When Japan surrendered, 40 percent of its 66 major cities had been destroyed, perhaps 400,000 people killed, some 9 million forced to move to the country, and 13 million made homeless. The XXI Bomber Command had practiced terror bombing on an entirely new scale, far surpassing the RAF's attacks on German cities. Little effort was made to determine the usefulness of firebombing, the policy being simply to smash and burn until Japan gave up.

As with Germany, the bombardment of Japan was both morally wrong and a waste of U.S. resources. It is true that legitimate targets were sometimes destroyed, but most were marginal. Even the official USAAF history is candid about this, admitting that it was the blockade rather than the bombing that destroyed Japan's defense effort. By April 1945 the flow of oil into Japan had been cut off completely. It was only a matter of time, and not much of it at that, before the wheels of Japanese industry stopped turning.

On June 26, the XXI Bomber Command launched an "oil plan" of its own, similar to the one employed with such success against Germany. But after the war it was found that the Japanese refineries were operating at only 4 percent of their capacity when the campaign against them started. Thus, though it was hugely destructive, firebombing contributed little to the defeat of Japan and alone would never have produced a surrender. The most effective Allied military campaign against Japan was the blockade, originally conducted by submarines, but after January 1945 by the surface navy and tactical air units.

Minelaying The blockade of Japan was completed by the Army Air Forces. There was considerable irony in this, because the XXI Bomber Command's greatest success was forced on it by the Navy. By 1945 Japan's open-ocean convoy routes had been closed by a mix of naval and tactical air power. Much of what traffic remained went through Shimonoseki Strait, and experience had shown the Navy that heavy bombers could do this best.

The USAAF agreed to do so, and General Arnold ordered a mining campaign to begin on April 1, 1945. Mining the Tsushima and Shimonoseki straits and the ports of Kobe and Osaka proved in fact to be sensationally effective. The tonnage of shipping received in Kobe declined from 320,000 tons in March to 44,000 in July. Once Major General Curtis LeMay realized this, he stepped up the effort, overwhelming Japan's minesweeping force. By this time Japan had given up trying to import anything but foodstuffs and was failing even at that.

In the last four and a half months of the war, mines accounted for half of all Japanese shipping losses. The Army Air Force's mining operations played an important role in completing the blockade and did more to secure victory than the celebrated firebomb raids. They were also more humane. Only 16 aircraft were lost out of 1,528 sent out to plant mines. While it is not known how many Japanese seamen were killed, the number had to be small, because mining was done in shallow waters close to land, giving crews a good chance of survival.

Had the atomic bomb not become available, the combined blockade and bombardment of Japan would have forced a surrender in time, although it is impossible to know how much time would have been required.

SEE ALSO

Aircraft; Dresden, bombing of; Germany, surrender of; Hamburg, bombing of; Japan, surrender of; Royal Air Force; Schweinfurt, bombing of; United States Army Air Forces; United States Strategic Bombing Survey

FURTHER READING

Craven, Wesley F., and James L. Cate. *The Army Air Forces in World War II.* 7 vols. Chicago: University of Chicago Press, 1948–58.

Levine, Alan J. *The Strategic Bombing of Germany, 1940–1945.* Westport, Conn.: Praeger, 1992.

MacIsaac, David. *Strategic Bombing in World War Two: The Story of the United States Strategic Bombing Survey.* New York: Garland, 1976.

Messenger, Charles. *"Bomber" Harris & the Strategic Bombing Offensive, 1939–1945.* New York: St. Martin's, 1984.

Schaffer, Ronald. *Wings of Judgment: American Bombing in World War II.* New York: Oxford University Press, 1985.

Sherry, Michael S. *The Rise of American Air Power: The Creation of Armageddon.* New Haven, Conn.: Yale University Press, 1987.

Submarines in the Pacific

Japan owed its desperate state in 1945 chiefly to U.S. submariners. Few expected such success, given the service's depressing record of failure against Japanese ships in 1942. There were many reasons for this poor start. As part of its obsession with big ships, the Navy had neglected submarines, so the force consisted mostly of small, obsolete boats, including many with defective engines.

Worse still, the Navy's Mark XIV torpedo, which had never been tested at sea, turned out to be riddled with defects. The Navy's tactics were defec-

tive as well, assigning the boats to patrol huge areas instead of the Luzon Strait and other places where enemy shipping was concentrated. They hunted singly rather than in groups, despite the success Germany was enjoying with its "wolf packs."

The U.S. Navy acted in the Pacific as if U-boats did not exist, neglecting the rich store of knowledge about submarine tactics that had been accumulated while fighting them in the Atlantic. U.S. skippers were too old and cautious, having acquired their commands through seniority at a time when conserving torpedoes was an important leadership requirement. Finally, the submarine fleet was divided into three commands, two based in Australia and the largest in Pearl Harbor, an arrangement that encouraged them to compete with each other instead of cooperating.

Early on it became clear that the Mark XIV was ineffective, but the Naval Bureau of Ordnance, known as the Gun Club, refused to admit error, insisting month after month that it was the skippers who were at fault and not their torpedoes. After many months of unsuccessful torpedo attacks, tests in the field proved conclusively that the Mark XIV was in fact no good. Its magnetic detonator did not work, it ran too deep, and even when a torpedo made a perfect hit at a 90-degree angle the firing pin crumpled instead of triggering the detonator. Machinists built sturdier pins, and at last, after 21 months of war, the submarine fleet had a reliable weapon. The Gun Club finally went down to defeat.

Together the three submarine commands mounted 520 war patrols in 1944 and sank 603 enemy vessels totaling 5.1 million tons. This was a level of damage that Japan could not hope to sustain and still survive. In the previous year Japan had imported 16.4 million tons of bulk commodities, but in 1944

Sailors run drills in this submarine off the coast of North Carolina in preparation for combat in the Pacific.

that was reduced to 10 million tons. In a single year the Japanese merchant fleet, excluding tankers, was cut in half, bringing it down to 2 million tons. Tanker capacity remained constant at 860,000 tons, but only because Japan built 204 additional ships. Without them the tanker tonnage would have fallen by about two thirds. Even so, at the end of the year oil imports were down to 200,000 tons a month from 700,000 in September. At that rate there would be none at all very soon.

To all intents and purposes the submarine war came to an end in December 1944, when Japanese merchant ships abandoned the open ocean. From then on, they kept to the narrow waters of the Sea of Japan or the Yellow Sea, sailing close to shore and anchoring in harbors at night.

While this protected Japanese ships against torpedo attacks, it also drastically limited their usefulness. During the Okinawan campaign not a single Japanese supply ship reached the island. After the war it was calculated that U.S. sub-

mariners had destroyed 1,314 enemy vessels, including one battleship, eight carriers, and eleven cruisers. A force of 16,000 men accounted for 55 percent of all enemy ship losses, driving its merchant fleet from the high seas and putting Japanese industry out of business for lack of oil.

In doing so, 3,500 U.S. submariners perished, the highest loss rate of any U.S. combat arm, and yet a very low figure compared with the number of Americans being killed on land. Despite almost two years of bungling, the submarine was far and away America's most effective Pacific weapon.

FURTHER READING

Blair, Clay, Jr. *Silent Victory: The American Submarine War Against Japan.* New York: Bantam, 1976.

Calvert, James F. *Silent Running: My Years on a World War II Attack Submarine.* New York: Wiley, 1995.

Galantin, I. J. *Take her Deep! A Submarine Against Japan in World War II.* Chapel Hill, N.C.: Algonquin, 1987.

Mendenhall, Corwin. *Submarine Diary.* Chapel Hill, N.C.: Algonquin, 1991.

Supreme Headquarters Allied Expeditionary Force (SHAEF)

Formed in February 1944, several months after General Dwight D. Eisenhower had been named supreme commander, Supreme Headquarters Allied Expeditionary Force (SHAEF) was located in Bushy Park, just outside London. SHAEF's naval commander in chief was Admiral Bertram H. Ramsey, of the Royal Navy, its air commander another British officer, Air Chief Marshal Arthur W. Tedder, who also served as deputy supreme commander. A key figure who accounted for much of SHAEF's efficiency was U.S. Lieutenant General Walter B. Smith. He did much of Eisenhower's administrative work and protected him from seeing unwanted visitors.

In May 1944 a command post nearer to the action was established with a small staff at Portsmouth, known as SHAEF Forward. As the Allies advanced, so did Eisenhower's headquarters. On August 7 he established himself at Tournieres, near Bayeux in Normandy. At the end of August, SHAEF Forward moved to Jullouville, and on September 19 it relocated to Gueux near Reims. It was at Reims that the Germans surrendered unconditionally on May 7, 1945. By this time the entire headquarters, including SHAEF Main, to which the bulk of Eisenhower's staff was assigned, numbered some 16,000 persons, of whom about 6,000 were British.

SHAEF is generally considered to have been the most effective joint command ever assembled for any war. The Axis powers had nothing like it. A great deal of credit for this goes to Eisenhower himself, who bent over backwards to give the British equal treatment even though they weren't making an equal contribution to the fight against Hitler. Some U.S. commanders were annoyed at this, but it was crucial to the success of SHAEF.

Tarawa, battle of

Tarawa was the site of the first battle in the U.S. Navy's Central Pacific campaign. Although savage fighting was taking place in the South and Southwest Pacific Areas, instead of supporting these campaigns, the largest fleet in the world was poised to strike at Tarawa and Makin atolls in the Gilbert Islands.

On November 21, 1943, after a brief bombardment, Marines assaulted Tarawa's Betio Island. What followed was a bloody and difficult engagement. In three days of fighting on Betio, where the Japanese had dug in, the Marines suffered 3,000 casualties (40 percent of the assault force), including 1,000 dead, while Japan lost 4,500 men—all on an island of less than 3 square miles.

Although many Marines died on Betio because the Navy was in a rush, many sailors died off Makin because the Army wasn't. Since Makin was lightly defended, the U.S. assault force of 6,500 men consisted mostly of soldiers who were opposed, it turned out, by only some 800 Japanese and conscripted Korean laborers. Although the Americans prevailed in the end by sheer force of numbers, it took them four days to secure Makin. On the fourth day, the escort carrier *Liscomb Bay* was sunk by a Japanese submarine at a cost of more than 600 lives.

This serene sunset was captured just moments before the Marine attack on Tarawa.

Naval officers were not slow to point out that had Marines been sent to Makin they would have taken it by storm and the *Liscomb Bay* would have been safely at sea when the Japanese sub arrived. This argument was probably unfair, since Makin was taken according to a timetable agreed to by the Navy.

Lessons learned at Tarawa were applied to subsequent landings. The fact remained that assaulting fortified strongpoints would always be bloody work no matter how well the troops were supported. Americans were horrified that such heavy casualties had been sustained on Betio in only three days of fighting. But because the Navy remained committed to its strategy of making frontal assaults on strongly defended islands, worse was to come.

SEE ALSO
Central Pacific Area

Taxation

SEE Financing the war

Teheran conference

In September 1943 Soviet leader Joseph Stalin, who previously had found ways around meeting with Roosevelt and Churchill, finally agreed to a conference. More than likely this was because of Russia's victory at Kursk in July 1943, where the last German offensive on the eastern front was crushed. Stalin had breathing room now and could not be forced into making unwanted concessions in return for Overlord, the impending invasion of France. To the contrary, Overlord's success would depend on having the Soviet Union launch a supporting offensive to prevent Germany from reinforcing France with troops drawn from the eastern front.

Furthermore, by playing hard to get Stalin had moved President Franklin D. Roosevelt to signal that he might make concessions on the Polish boundary and recognize Soviet annexation of the Baltic states (Estonia, Latvia, and Lithuania). In short, Stalin was gaining the upper hand, and a meeting with the other Allied leaders would enable him to exploit it. Roosevelt confirmed this belief by agreeing to Stalin's demand that the meeting be in Teheran, Iran, a site that was highly convenient for the Soviet premier but not for the ailing President.

Before he arrived in Teheran, Roosevelt held meetings with the British at Cairo, but instead of using them to prepare for hard bargaining with Stalin, Roosevelt saw to it that most of the time was spent discussing China. This emphasis was partly because he was still trying to build up operations there but also partly, it seems, because he wanted to avoid discussing Teheran with the British, intending to handle Stalin by himself.

At Teheran, each of the Big Three nations—the United States, Britain, and the Soviet Union—had a different agenda. Churchill, to the despair even of British diplomats, was still trying to stop the Overlord invasion planned for France and promote his Mediterranean strategy. Stalin was determined to have a second front opened in France and would not discuss anything else until its main features had been agreed upon. Roosevelt was most interested in the postwar settlement, which he believed depended on establishing a good relationship with Stalin.

As a result of Churchill's stubbornness, most of the Teheran conference was given over to wrangling about Overlord. For days the Big Three argued about when it should take place, about who should be in command if and when there should be a supporting invasion of southern France, and over prospective operations in the Mediterranean. At various times both Churchill and Roosevelt attempted to curry favor with Stalin at the other's expense.

Stalin, for his part, issued the customary veiled threats to make a separate peace if Overlord were canceled. Churchill gave in finally, agreeing that Overlord would take place in May 1944 and that there would be landings in the French Riviera associated with it. There was never any doubt of this once Stalin made it clear, as he did almost immediately, that he backed the U.S. position.

After rushing through many subjects, the Big Three ended their talks with a flurry of pledges and pronouncements. They issued an ambiguous statement on the future of Iran. They promised to support the Yugoslav partisans in various ways in their fight against the Germans. Turkey would be encouraged to enter the war. Stalin was to launch an offensive in support of the invasion of France and enter the war against Japan within months of V-E Day.

In Europe, Russia would gain Konigsberg, Germany, half of East Prussia, a third of the Italian fleet, and a free hand with Finland. During a conversation with Stalin, FDR revealed that he would not challenge a possible Soviet annexation of Latvia, Lithuania, and Estonia.

In East Asia, Darien would be a free port, while Russia would acquire the southern half of the Sakhalin Islands in addition to the Kuriles. Most of all, Russia would move its European boundary west to the so-called Curzon Line, at the expense of Poland, despite the opposition of Poland's government-in-exile in London. Stalin agreed to join a global collective security organization after the war. He gave his blessing to Roosevelt's plan for partitioning Germany.

Turkey never entered World War II, despite heavy British pressure on it to do so, and it was lucky for the Turks that they didn't. If an Allied force had been sent to Turkey this would only have provided Stalin with an excuse to follow suit. And once in, the Soviets would have been difficult to get out. Otherwise, the understandings arrived at in the Teheran conference determined the postwar settlement. The Yalta conference of February 1945 mainly confirmed what had already been agreed upon.

SEE ALSO
Yalta conference

FURTHER READING
Dallek, Robert. *Franklin D. Roosevelt and American Foreign Policy, 1932–45*. New York: Oxford University Press, 1979.
Eubank, Keith. *Summit at Teheran*. New York: Morrow, 1985.
Mayle, Paul D. *Eureka Summit: Agreement in Principle and the Big Three at Tehran, 1943*. Newark: University of Delaware Press, 1987.

Tojo, Hideki

PRIME MINISTER OF JAPAN, 1941–44

- *Born: December 30, 1884, Tokyo, Japan*
- *Political party: none*
- *Education: Military Academy, 1905; Staff College, 1912–14*
- *Military service: Imperial Japanese Army—second lieutenant, 1905; first lieutenant, 1907; captain, 1915; major, 1925; colonel, 1929; brigadier general, 1931; major general, 1933; lieutenant general, 1936; chief of staff of Kwantung Army, 1937; vice war minister, 1938; minister of war, 1940; general, 1941*
- *Died: December 23, 1948, Tokyo, Japan*

Apart from Emperor Hirohito himself, Hideki Tojo was the Japanese leader most often attacked by U.S. propagandists. He did not owe this distinction to any remarkable traits of character. Tojo was not a Hitler or Stalin, or even a Mussolini. Rather, he was a typical Japanese general of his time, which is to say hard-working, brutal, narrow, imperialistic, and loyal—to the emperor in theory, but to the Imperial Japanese Army in practice. He was a prominent figure in the war party and held the office of prime minister when Japan attacked Pearl Harbor, and for most of the war. Therefore, he came to symbolize everything Americans hated about Japan.

Tojo was a leader of the imperialistic "control faction" in the Army. He ardently promoted all the major Army initiatives that led Japan to destruction and inflicted intense suffering on the peoples of East and Southeast Asia. Among the actions he supported were the military's, and especially the Army's, seizure of power in Japan during the 1930s, the invasion of China in 1937, and the seizure of French Indochina in 1940–41

that led to the oil embargo of Japan. He argued successfully that Japan should respond to the embargo by launching the Pacific war.

Given the style of Japanese decision making, in which a consensus is sought for every major decision, Tojo was not an absolute dictator. He had dictatorial powers, but in exercising them he was answerable to the military clique that had made him prime minister.

When the war turned against Japan in 1944, he was forced to resign as prime minister and retire from the army, even though the policies that were leading the Japanese Empire to its doom had not been his alone but those of the ruling faction. However, a scapegoat was needed and, loyal to the end, Tojo always insisted that he personally was responsible for everything Japan did during his years in power.

After the war, and after a failed suicide attempt, Tojo was tried as a war criminal and sentenced to death by hanging. Even though the war crimes trials had an arbitrary quality in that only a few individuals were punished for the crimes of many, Tojo's sentence was not unjust. As prime minister, he led Japan into a war that caused millions of deaths. He also approved of the brutal acts committed by the Japanese military and had personal knowledge of many atrocities. He himself gave the order that starving Allied prisoners of war be put to heavy work, a policy that killed them by the thousands and probably would have killed them all if the war had lasted much longer.

SEE ALSO
Japan; Japanese Army

FURTHER READING
Brown, Courtney. *Tojo: The Last Banzai.* New York: Holt, Rinehart, 1967.
Palmer, Edwin. *Warlord: Tojo Against the World.* Lanham, Md.: Scarborough House, 1993.

Tokyo, bombing of
SEE Strategic bombing

Torch, Operation
SEE Mediterranean Theater

Truman, Harry S.
PRESIDENT OF THE UNITED STATES, 1945–53

- *Born: May 8, 1884, Lamar, Mo.*
- *Political party: Democrat*
- *Education: high school*
- *Military service: U.S. Army: captain, 1917–19*
- *Government service: road overseer, Jackson County, Mo., 1914; postmaster, Grandview, Mo., 1915; Jackson County judge, 1922–24, and presiding judge, 1926–34; U.S. Senate, 1935–45; Vice President, 1945*
- *Died: December 26, 1972, Kansas City, Mo.*

Like so many leaders of the period, Harry Truman came from the midwestern heartland of the United States. He was born in a small town near Joplin, Missouri, raised near Independence, and was about as typically American as you could get. Yet, like Eisenhower, his "plain vanilla" exterior concealed a formidable personality.

A poor speaker whose seat in the Senate was his reward for loyalty to a political leader, "Boss" Pendergast, Truman had previously been best known for his careful grooming ("dapper" was the word always used) and modest friendliness. These appearances were deceptive. While he had no education beyond high school, Truman was a serious reader of history, biography, and the classics, about

Franklin Roosevelt (right) hosts his new running mate Harry Truman at a lunch on the lawn of the White House.

which he knew more than most college graduates. A member of the Missouri National Guard, he had been elected captain of an artillery unit in World War I, leading it with distinction. The "boys" of Battery D, mostly Irish Catholics from Kansas City, would be the core supporters of this small-town Baptist when he entered politics—early evidence of his ability to rise above the prejudices of his youth.

Western Missouri was at the time dominated by the political machine of T. J. Pendergast. Truman would not have had a political career if he had failed to go along with it, yet he remained completely honest. He served eight years as presiding judge of Jackson County, an administrative post similar to that of county executive elsewhere, which provided many opportunities for graft in the awarding of contracts for roads, bridges, and other public works. But when the 50-year-old Truman arrived in Washington in 1935, he was literally broke. After renting a modest apartment for himself, his wife, and daughter, he had to take out a bank loan to pay for the furnishings.

People initially thought little of Truman when he arrived in Washington, calling him the "senator from Pendergast." But they found, as his fellow Missourians had, that he was hard-working and honest, which, with his other good qualities, made him popular in the Senate. Truman was allowed to form his Special Committee to Investigate the National Defense Program out of courtesy more than anything else, few sharing his belief that corruption in defense spending could be dealt with by legislators.

The skeptics were wrong. Truman's committee could not detect every scam, but it did a remarkably good and honest job of discovering waste, incompetence, and fraud. This was a direct result of Truman's determination, his efforts to create policy by including Republicans as well as Democrats, and his experience in Missouri, which had taught him where to look for the dirt. Within a year, citizens respected his congressional committee more than any other. Newspapers called him the "billion-dollar watchdog," which proved to be a considerable underestimation of what he would eventually save taxpayers.

Truman, unlike Henry A. Wallace, his predecessor as Vice President, was everything party leaders wanted. Well known and admired, he was acceptable to labor and northern liberals because of his pro–New Deal voting record and to southerners because he was, or at least appeared to be, one of them. Few if any delegates to the Democratic National Convention in 1944 seem to have asked if he was qualified to run the nation, yet in selecting Truman the delegates were also unwittingly naming the next President. All knew that the likelihood of President Franklin D. Roosevelt's dying in office was great. But they chose to ignore this for the sake of a balanced ticket. Not since 1864, when Lincoln's vice president was chosen, had the Vice Presidential decision been so important.

No thanks to the political process, Truman would prove to be a better than average President. He was sworn in quickly on April 12, 1945, after FDR's sudden death. By that time Roosevelt's appointees were doing well in their jobs, and Truman retained them. He tried as best he could to follow Roosevelt's conciliatory policy toward the Soviet Union. However, because Truman had a quick temper, this was not natural to him and he was soon responding to tough talk by the Soviets with sharp language of his own.

Truman's best-remembered wartime decision was to make nuclear war against Japan. Actually, he made no decision as such, but rather he allowed military leaders to go forward with their plans to drop the first two available atomic bombs on Hiroshima and Nagasaki. Characteristically, however, Truman accepted responsibility for employing atomic bombs and always maintained that the decision to drop them was his alone. Technically he was correct in that he had the power to cancel the drops had he chosen to do so.

However, Truman followed General George C. Marshall's lead in this and other matters. Like Marshall, Truman worried most of all about the many Americans who would surely die if Japan had to be invaded. Under the circumstances, he felt that no other decision was possible. Truman was convinced that he had done the right thing and never regretted it.

SEE ALSO

Atomic bombs; Japan, surrender of; Potsdam conference

FURTHER READING

Hamby, Alonzo L. *Man of the People: A Life of Harry S. Truman.* New York: Oxford University Press, 1995.
McCullough, David. *Truman.* New York: Simon & Schuster, 1992.
Truman, Harry S. *Memoirs.* Garden City, N.Y.: Doubleday, 1955.
Wainstock, Dennis. *The Decision to Drop the Atomic Bomb.* Westport, Conn.: Praeger, 1996.
Walker, J. Samuel. *Prompt and Utter Destruction: Truman and the Use of Atomic Bombs Against Japan.* Chapel Hill: University of North Carolina Press, 1997.

U-boats

U-boat stood for *Unterseeboot*, the German word for submarine. From 1940 until mid 1943, U-boats were the scourge of the Atlantic, as they had been in World War I.

The basic U-boat was the Type 7c, which in its final version could cruise on the surface for 12,600 nautical miles and dive to a depth of 1,000 feet. Like all operational subs of the period, U-boats were diesel-powered surface vessels that dived only when they had to. On the surface their top speed was about 17 knots, more than enough to overtake merchant ships, but underwater, running on batteries, their best speed was only 7 knots. Even that rate could not be sustained for long, nor could their crews, whose air supplies were good for only about 24 hours. U-boats could operate far from home, thanks to the big Type XIV "Milch Cow" submarines that resupplied boats operating in the South Atlantic and Indian oceans.

Near the end of the war, the Germans came close to deploying a true submarine, the "Walter," which had a turbine propulsion system supplied with oxygen and steam created by the breakdown of hydrogen peroxide. It was tested in 1944 but, fortunately for the Allies, never became operational. Germany did deploy a very long range underwater cruiser, the Type IXD, which had a top speed of better than 19 knots and a range of 32,000 miles. But it suffered from the same defect as the Type 7c in that it was primarily a surface boat. Both types were equipped with the *Schnorchel* pipe beginning in 1944, which vented exhaust gases and brought in fresh air. This device enabled a U-boat to cruise just beneath the surface but did not change the nature of undersea warfare.

Despite the excellent quality of Germany's U-boats and crews, they were no match for the Allied hunter-killer task forces introduced in 1943. These units were built around escort carriers whose planes wreaked havoc on the U-boat "wolf packs." Together with Allied land-based, long-range aircraft and improved antisubmarine weapons and tactics, they won the battle of the Atlantic and virtually destroyed Germany's U-boat force.

SEE ALSO
Atlantic, Battle of the

FURTHER READING
Von der Porten, Edward P. *The German Navy in World War II*. New York: Crowell, 1969.

These three German sailors were picked up by the Coast Guard after their U-boat was sunk in Atlantic shipping lanes.

ULTRA

SEE Intelligence, military

Unconditional surrender

The unconditional surrender of the Axis powers was announced by President

Franklin D. Roosevelt at a press conference during his Casablanca, Morocco, meeting with Prime Minister Winston Churchill in January 1943. Although the doctrine of unconditional surrender had been implied by earlier statements, as when FDR said that his goal was "total victory," this was his first use of a phrase that would quickly become routine.

Taken for granted during the war, when most people believed that you could not negotiate with regimes as evil as those of Nazi Germany and Imperial Japan, it later became controversial. In particular, critics would charge that the doctrine of unconditional surrender prolonged the war by undermining the anti-Nazi movement in Germany.

It probably did not. To avoid, or delay, having to pay for their crimes, the blood- and guilt-drenched leaders of Germany and Japan would have fought to the bitter end regardless. Italy's surrender was delayed by some weeks while the regime that succeeded Mussolini's tried to negotiate better terms. While it dithered, German forces were able to seize most of the Italian peninsula. But most likely the Germans would have done so anyway, because they were in Italy in strength and the Allies were not.

Japan was allowed one condition in the end—that the emperor be treated with respect. This took only a few days to arrange, so the demand for unconditional surrender would seem to have had little effect on the Pacific war.

SEE ALSO

Germany, surrender of; Italy, surrender of; Japan, surrender of

FURTHER READING

Armstrong, Anne. *Unconditional Surrender: The Impact of the Casablanca Policy Upon World War II*. New Brunswick, N.J.: Rutgers University Press, 1961.
O'Connor, Raymond Gish. *Diplomacy for Victory: FDR and Unconditional Surrender*. New York: Norton, 1971.

Union of Soviet Socialist Republics

SEE Soviet Union (U.S.S.R.)

United Nations

In 1942 the United Nations Declaration was signed by 45 Allied states. No formal organization existed, however, until representatives of 50 states met in San Francisco from April 25 to June 26, 1945, to draw up the United Nations Charter.

The UN was divided into two parts, a Security Council consisting of five permanent members (China, France, the United Kingdom, the United States, and the U.S.S.R.) and six temporary members, and a General Assembly. At San Francisco a Trusteeship Council was also formed to oversee the colonies and mandates of the former Axis powers as well as other non-self-governing territories. The Trusteeship Council was phased out shortly after the last trust territory, Palau, gained independence in 1994.

Some hoped that the UN would evolve into some sort of world government, or at least be a mechanism for enforcing world peace. These hopes were not only unrealistic but were rendered impossible by the Security Council, each of whose permanent members had the right to veto resolutions. President Franklin D. Roosevelt, who died just before the conference met, had been the moving spirit behind the UN and appears to have intended it to be a way of dividing the world into "spheres of influence."

It had been Roosevelt's intention

that peace would be maintained in the future by what he called the "Four Policemen" (China, the United Kingdom, the United States, and the U.S.S.R.), or at least the "Three Policemen" (the previous four minus China). Before long, however, it became clear that the postwar world would have only two policemen, who would be rivals in the cold war rather than partners. Thus, the UN evolved in ways unanticipated by any of its planners.

FURTHER READING

Hilderbrand, Robert. *Dumbarton Oaks: The Origins of the United Nations and the Search for Postwar Security.* Chapel Hill: University of North Carolina Press, 1990.

Hoopes, Townsend, and Douglas Brinkley. *FDR and the Creation of the UN.* New Haven: Yale University Press, 1997.

Patterson, Charles. *The Oxford 50th Anniversary Book of the United Nations.* New York: Oxford University Press, 1995.

Roberts, Adam. *Presiding Over a Divided World: Changing UN Roles, 1945–1993.* Boulder, Colo.: L. Rienner, 1994.

United States Army

In September 1939 the U.S. Army consisted of only 190,000 officers and men. Behind this minuscule force was a National Guard of 200,000 civilian volunteers who trained on weekends and for two weeks in the summer. The guard was mobilized in 1940 at the same time as the Selective Service System was created to supply soldiers through a limited military draft of civilians. In practice, National Guardsmen proved to be poorly trained and required extensive training to perform well in combat.

Although the regular army was underequipped and far too small, the groundwork that would turn it into a mighty force had been laid before war broke out. When General George C. Marshall became chief of staff in 1939, he brought to his job a vision of a new army based on his experience as a trainer and leader of troops. The old "square" division consisting of four regiments and some 20,000 men was replaced by a "triangular" division consisting of three regiments and about 15,000 men. Leaner and more flexible than the square division, it also possessed greater firepower, because of its artillery battalions. In time, the typical infantry division would also have a tank battalion attached to it. Because of their many vehicles, most infantry divisions were actually motorized. In addition to high mobility, self-propelled guns enabled U.S. divisions to start fighting immediately upon arriving at the battlefield.

The three regiments of an infantry division consisted of three battalions of about 850 men each, which were subdivided into three rifle companies and one heavy weapons (mortars and machine guns) company, a headquarters company with six 105-mm howitzers, a service company, and an antitank company.

It was not accidental that a division came to have three regiments and the regiments three battalions. Marshall believed in the holding attack, according to which one unit would fix the enemy in place, a second would seek to flank, or go around, the enemy, and a third would be held in reserve ready to support the other two or take advantage of opportunities as they arose.

The first armored divisions, of which there would ultimately be 16, consisted of two regiments of tanks and one of armored infantry, supported by three artillery battalions. However, in practice U.S. armor rarely made massive "blitzkrieg-style" assaults, and in 1943 the armored divisions were reorganized

This mammoth 274 mm railroad gun captured during the U.S. Seventh Army advance near Rentwertshausen easily holds the 22 men lined up on the barrel.

to achieve greater flexibility. The regiments were replaced by three battalions each of infantry, tanks, and artillery. These units were assigned as needed by divisional headquarters to two smaller field headquarters known as combat commands.

In 1943 Marshall decided to cap the Army's size at 90 divisions. In all, the Army would deploy 11 field armies. Each army consisted of two or more corps, which typically were made up of two infantry divisions and one armored division, plus supporting units. By the war's end, 26 corps would be deployed, with a total of 68 divisions going to Europe and 22 to the Pacific.

Marshall's decision to limit the Army to 90 divisions turned out to be a mistake because it meant, particularly in Europe, that there would never be a strategic reserve and divisions could not be rotated out of combat on a regular basis. This put a great burden on the U.S. combat soldier, who spent more time in battle than his British, and even German, counterparts.

Although Eisenhower in particular never had enough manpower, what the U.S. Army did have instead was superb air and artillery support. Although prewar artillery officers often had to train without guns, the plans they made proved to be tremendously effective when war came. Eventually there would be 326 artillery battalions armed with highly effective 105-mm and 155-mm guns.

The services' radio communications were first rate, and the introduction of small planes made artillery spotting highly effective as well. Army gunners specialized in the technique of time-on-target (TOT) method of bombardment, according to which all guns fired their first rounds at intervals timed to bring every round on target at the same moment. The resulting storm of fire that broke without warning was the U.S. tactic the Germans feared the most.

Of the approximately 16 million Americans who served in World War II, some 10 million were in the Army Ground Forces. Unlike sailors and airmen, most soldiers were draftees, and the Army's makeup was heavily influenced by Selective Service priorities.

Wool field jackets (this one with a discharge emblem on its lapel) worn by Army personnel were nicknamed "Ike" jackets because Eisenhower was rarely seen without one.

Americans did not think fathers should be drafted, as a result of which the average age of soldiers in 1944 was 26, while it was 23 for sailors and 22 for Marines.

The Army found itself drafting single men in their forties but sparing married men half their age. This practice had to change as casualties mounted. Thus, although fathers made up only 6 percent of those drafted in October 1943, by the following April more than half the draftees were fathers.

Another change as the war developed was the process of "skimming," whereby the Army Service Forces (the noncombat support branch of the Army) got most of the men with technical skills and the Army Air Forces (AAF) received the pick of those who scored highest in qualification tests. As a result, combat soldiers were less educated than other military personnel (having a year of high school on average), and were also shorter and lighter.

In 1943 the AAF lost its skimming privileges. In 1944 General Marshall closed down the Army's specialist academic programs and the training of air cadets as well. The transfer of personnel—some 30,000 air cadets alone—to the infantry was one reason, in addition to experience, why U.S. divisions improved with time, whereas almost everyone else's were worn down.

Most U.S. soldiers saw little or no combat, because they played supporting roles to the men who actually fought. The U.S. Army fought at such a distance from its bases at home, it had to devote more of its resources to transportation and logistics. But because so many men were working to provide goods and services to the troops, U.S. soldiers enjoyed a higher standard of living than those of other nations.

The Army sustained 949,000 casualties, of which 175,000 were killed in action. Thus the chance of being hit was less than 1 in 10, and of being killed less than 1 in 50. But in a combat unit, the odds underwent a radical shift, with the infantry suffering 264 casualties per 1,000 men per year and the armored units 228. Combat engineers, field medics, and tank destroyer groups had similar casualty rates.

Even this summary understates the risk, because casualties were not spread throughout an infantry division but were concentrated in its rifle companies. Additionally, these figures are for the entire war, while the heaviest ground fighting took place between June 1944 and June 1945. For the last six months of 1944, between 12,000 and 18,000 GIs were killed each month and 40,000 to 60,000 wounded. In a typical rifle company, combat losses would normally equal the number of men originally assigned to it. Few riflemen escaped unharmed.

Even though the greatest number of casualties was sustained in Europe, men preferred it to the Pacific. Overall casualty rates were lower in the Pacific, chiefly because 60 percent of all casualties were caused by shells and the Japanese had inferior ammunition. There were actual cases of Japanese who attempted to commit suicide with hand grenades and only bruised themselves. In Europe the "lethality" rate for shrapnel wounds was 25 percent but in the Pacific only 16 percent.

However, the Pacific was a much less healthy place to fight in than Europe, which resembled home to some extent and had towns and liquor and women. Except for beer and illegally distilled spirits, the Pacific had little to offer. Most fighting took place in jungles where heat and humidity were high and the disease rate enormous. Malaria was everywhere, as were dengue fever, parasites, scrub typhus, diarrhea, swimmers' itch, tree sap dermatitis, and every other skin ailment known to man, plus a mysterious disease called "blue nail," which the doctors never did figure out.

When first sent into battle, U.S. divisions composed of draftees and National Guardsmen were not very impressive, the inevitable result of mobilizing too little and too late. But with experience, more realistic training, more and better weaponry, and the abandonment of the practice of skimming, U.S. soldiers became as good as, if not better, than those of any other nation.

As evidence one may offer the experience of the 99th Infantry Division. It was a green division that went on the line in Belgium only weeks before the Battle of the Bulge began in December 1944. Yet, despite its absolute lack of experience, and though heavily outnumbered and outgunned, the 99th stopped the Sixth SS Panzer Army dead in its tracks. It destroyed the German plan of attack and won the precious time needed for Eisenhower to redeploy his forces and turn defeat into victory. Many such stories could be told, all demonstrating the point that the U.S. Army prevailed on the battlefield not because it heavily outnumbered the enemy, which it seldom did, but because of its men and its methods.

SEE ALSO

France, Battle of; Germany, surrender of; Marshall, George C.; Southwest Pacific Area

FURTHER READING

McManus, John C. *The Deadly Brotherhood: The American Combat Soldier in World War II*. Novato, Calif.: Presidio, 1998.
Perret, Geoffrey. *There's a War to Be Won: The United States Army in World War II*. New York: Random House, 1991.
Province, Charles M. *Patton's Third Army: A Daily Combat Diary*. New York: Hippocrene, 1992.

United States Army Air Forces (USAAF)

In June 1941 the U.S. Army Air Corps became the U.S. Army Air Forces (USAAF). However, most people called it the Air Force, as if it were a separate service equal to the Army and Navy. After the war it would become a separate branch of the military, but even during the war it maintained a great deal of independence from the army command, because General George C. Marshall, the Army's chief of staff, usually went along with the USAAF's commander, General Henry Arnold, on air matters. Furthermore, Arnold had a seat along with Marshall on the Joint Chiefs of Staff.

Although all the services grew enormously during the war, none equaled the USAAF in percentage terms. In 1939 the Air Corps had 20,000 men. In 1945, 1.9 million men and women served in the USAAF. By then it had risen from 11 percent of the Army's total strength to more than 22 percent. In 1939 the air corps possessed 2,470 aircraft, nearly all of which were obsolete. In 1944, when it reached its peak, the USAAF had 80,000 aircraft in service, most of which had been built after Pearl Harbor was attacked in December 1941.

In addition, the USAAF employed 422,000 civilians, including female ferry pilots, who were known as WASPS, and the Civil Air Patrol, which performed a variety of duties, including searches for German U-boats. Some 1.5 million men and women are estimated to have served in the Ground Observer Corps, which turned out not to be needed because the enemy aircraft they were supposed to spot never arrived.

The USAAF included a great number of services and commands, which existed to support the 16 separate air forces raised during the war. They were numbered according to the order in which they were formed. The First, Second, Third, and Fourth Air Forces remained in the continental United States for training and defense purposes. The Sixth Air Force protected the Panama Canal, while the Eleventh was based in Alaska. All the rest were deployed overseas.

The Twentieth Air Force, to which all the USAAF's B-29 very heavy bombers belonged, was unique also. It was commanded by General Arnold himself. This was a maneuver designed to prevent B-29s from being diverted to duties other than bombing Japan. In practice, the Twentieth's operations were directed by Arnold's representative in the field.

The USAAF's greatest achievements in the war were providing air support for ground troops and transporting men and materials all over the world. But Arnold and the air generals were dedicated above all to the theory of strategic bombardment, according to which Germany and Japan would be defeated by daylight precision bombing of essential military and industrial targets. Although USAAF bombers destroyed large parts of Germany and Japan and killed many civilians, ultimately strategic bombing failed to persuade either country to surrender. Nonetheless, it consumed the largest part of the USAAF's resources.

The basic air unit was the squadron, which ranged in size from 7 B-29s to 25 single-engine fighters. The typical group consisted of three or four squadrons. As of February 1945 the air force had a total of 26 very heavy bombardment groups and 72.5 heavy bombardment groups. Each very heavy group had 45 aircraft and 2,000 men, while heavy groups flying B-17s and B-24s had 72 aircraft and 2,300 men. By comparison, there were 71 single-engine fighter groups, each with fewer than 1,000 men, 28.5 medium bombardment groups with 1,800 men apiece, and 32 combat cargo groups, each with fewer than 900 men. In addition, there were miscellaneous squadrons of light bombers, twin-engine fighters, troop carriers, and such specialized units as mapping and photo-reconnaissance squadrons. Even so, the imbalance is clear; strategic bombing got much more than its share of resources.

Heavy and very heavy bombers were often useful, especially in the Mediterranean Theater and the Southwest Pacific Area, where targets were plentiful and lightly defended as a rule. But the majority of the heavy bombers, and all the very heavy ones, were devoted to bombing Europe and Japan, with results that did not justify the cost in planes and men—especially in Europe. The USAAF was, therefore, both lopsided and excessively large.

Although strategic bombing was supposed to save lives, as compared to the heavy costs of ground warfare, it did not. Some 40,000 airmen were killed in the war, plus an additional 35,000 who died in training or other noncombat missions. Considering that the great majority of men and women in the USAAF were ground personnel, this was a very high total.

SEE ALSO

Arnold, Henry H.; Spaatz, Carl A.; Strategic bombing

FURTHER READING

Craven, Wesley F., and James L. Cate. *The Army Air Forces in World War II*. 7 vols. Chicago: University of Chicago Press, 1948–58.

McLachlan, Ian. *U.S.A.A.F. Fighter Stories*. Osceola, Wis.: Motorbooks, 1997.

Perret, Geoffrey. *Winged Victory: The Army Air Forces in World War II*. New York: Random House, 1997.

Schaffer, Ronald. *Wings of Judgment: American Bombing in World War II*. New York: Oxford University Press, 1985.

Sherry, Michael S. *The Rise of American Air Power: The Creation of Armageddon*. New Haven: Yale University Press, 1987.

Watry, Charles A., and Duane L. Hall. *Aerial Gunners: The Unknown Aces of World War II*. Carlesbad, Calif.: California Aero Press, 1986.

United States Marine Corps (USMC)

A separate service within the Navy Department, the U.S. Marine Corps had the distinction, and the advantage, of being the only Marine force in the world with its own air arm. Although the Marines had their own commandant and headquarters, he was not represented on the Joint Chiefs of Staff, and marine operations served the Navy's needs and required naval approval.

The USMC was the first service to recognize the need for amphibious operations and established the Fleet Marine Force (FMF) in 1933 for that purpose. It consisted of two brigades and a Marine aviation group. Although numbering only 20,000 men, and with little support from the Navy, the Marines worked to obtain specialized landing craft that would make beach assaults easier.

In 1941 the two FMF brigades became the 1st and 2nd Marine Divisions, which later were joined by four more. They were organized into two amphibious corps. Marine aviation expanded similarly, growing from 641 pilots and 13 squadrons in 1941 to more than 10,000 pilots and 128 squadrons by war's end.

Because the Navy's Central Pacific strategy required the marines to storm small but heavily defended islands with little room for maneuver or finesse, their losses were very high. Marine casualties, nearly all sustained by its six infantry divisions, totaled 92,000, including 24,500 dead. Although the corps was 500,000 strong at its peak, a majority of Marines occupied noncombat positions.

A better sense of what combat cost the Marines may be gained by looking at a few figures. Like the U.S. Army, a Marine division was comprised of three regiments, plus attached and supporting units. Because divisional strengths varied considerably, the Regimental Combat Team (RCT)—an overstrength regiment—is the best unit for comparison with the Army. An RCT had an average strength of about 7,500 officers and men, many of whom had jobs that entailed little risk. On Peleliu the 1st Marine RCT had 1,749 casualties. On Iwo Jima the 26th RCT sustained 2,675 casualties. On Okinawa the 29th RCT suffered 2,821.

In Europe it was almost impossible for a combat soldier to serve throughout the 11 months of fighting that began on

Skillful and experienced jungle fighters, these Marines gather in front of a Japanese dugout they helped to take at Cape Totkina on Bougainville, Solomon Islands, in 1944.

D-Day without becoming a casualty. In the Pacific, by 1945 it was unusual for the average Marine rifleman to go through a single operation unscathed.

SEE ALSO

Central Pacific Area; Guadalcanal, Battle of; Iwo Jima, Battle of; Okinawa, Battle of; Saipan, Battle of; South Pacific Area; Tarawa, Battle of

FURTHER READING

Berry, Henry. *Semper Fi, Mac: Living Memories of the U.S. Marines in World War II.* New York: Morrow, 1996.
Hough, Frank, Verle Ludwig, and Henry Shaw. *History of U.S. Marine Corps Operations in World War II.* 5 vols. Washington, D.C.: U.S. Marine Corps, 1958–71.

United States Navy (USN)

Like the U.S. Army, when war broke out in 1939 the U.S. Navy was poorly equipped for the task that lay ahead. It had 15 battleships but only 5 aircraft carriers, which, although naval leaders did not know this yet, was a ratio that should have been reversed. All the battleships were too slow to keep up with the fast carriers that would soon become the basis of naval power.

Otherwise, the Navy had 18 heavy and 19 light cruisers, 61 submarines—most of them obsolete—and a variety of destroyers, gunboats, and the like, all of which were too few and mostly too old. A large majority of the Navy's big ships were in the Pacific Fleet, the rest in a small Asiatic Fleet and an Atlantic Squadron. In 1941, although it had grown only a little, the basis for a two-ocean navy was created by upgrading the Atlantic force to fleet status, with Vice Admiral Ernest King becoming commander in chief of the Atlantic Fleet.

After the Pearl Harbor disaster in December 1941, President Roosevelt cleaned house. He replaced the commander in chief of the Pacific Fleet with Admiral Chester Nimitz, a brilliant choice. The old position of commander in chief of the U.S. Fleet was revived, and King was appointed to it. In a few months he was named chief of naval operations as well, becoming the only man then or since to hold the Navy's two highest positions simultaneously.

The U.S. Navy experienced the same explosive growth as the Army, rising from a prewar strength of 161,000 officers and men to 3.4 million men and women in 1945. Some 75,000 aircraft were delivered to the Navy between mid-1940 and August 1945, while aviation personnel increased during the same period from 11,000 to about 440,000 persons. In June 1940 the Navy possessed 1,099 ships of all types. In August 1945 it had a strength of 67,952 vessels. The Navy completed or acquired 10 battleships in this period, plus 27 fast carriers (fleet and light), 111 escort or "jeep" carriers, and 217 submarines. By far the greatest part of the fleet, from the standpoint of numbers, was its landing ships and craft, of which it acquired no fewer than 66,055.

This was not the type of force that naval leaders had planned on having when the war first broke out. Most believed that the battleship was still the principal weapon of naval warfare. They expected that its function in the event of war with Japan would be to win a decisive battle at sea. In reality, nothing went as planned. Pearl Harbor established that carriers were not auxiliary vessels but the backbone of the fleet. Battleships, if they were slow, were relegated to bombarding enemy-held islands and, if fast, providing antiaircraft support for carriers.

Submarines, previously all but ignored, played a critical role in the war by destroying most of Japan's merchant marine. Antisubmarine warfare, completely ignored in peacetime, became one of the Navy's most critical missions and its chief contribution to the defeat of Hitler. Amphibious operations, also ignored by the prewar navy, started every major land campaign in Europe and North Africa as well as in most of the Pacific.

There never was a decisive naval engagement. After the Solomon Islands campaign, the Navy won every battle at sea. But even when their fleet was gone the Japanese continued to fight on.

In a sense, therefore, the Navy's achievement was greater than that of the Army, because it had to unlearn so much. Army leaders made mistakes and failed to forsee the unknowable. But the war against Germany went much as the Army had expected it to after the fall of France in 1940 (except for politically motivated diversions in North Africa and the Mediterranean), while almost nothing in the Pacific war conformed to the Navy's expectations.

The Navy got better and better technically as the war went on. It filled its routine but all-important role as the carrier of men and materials to remote theaters of war. And it learned to do a great many things skillfully that it started out doing badly. The submarine war in the Pacific was almost a joke to begin with, handicapped by poor commanders, bad tactics, and defective torpedoes. But in the end, a force that never exceeded 50,000 men swept Japan's merchant fleet from the seas and sank a great many warships.

The war against the U-boats, pathetic at first, ended with the Navy's putting together a huge and complicated antisubmarine campaign that, with much help from the British and other allies, ended in complete victory. In the Pacific the U.S. Navy assembled the greatest fleet the world had ever seen or will likely ever see. This mighty force, alternately

named the Third or the Fifth Fleet, depending on who was commanding it, became a well-oiled machine that utterly crushed the Imperial Japanese Navy.

Planning, however, remained the Navy's weakness. In part this resulted from President Franklin D. Roosevelt's failure to name a supreme commander for the Pacific, thereby allowing the services to fight two separate wars. When General Douglas MacArthur was given command of the Southwest Pacific Area, the Navy had to invent a new mission for itself. The result was the Central Pacific drive, which kept the fleet from aiding MacArthur's Southwest Pacific Area most of the time, although that was where most Japanese forces in the Pacific were located.

Instead, the Navy launched a series of usually brief but, for the Mmarines, extremely bloody island campaigns. Not only was the strategy wrong, but the planning of the land battles was poor as well. At Tarawa Atoll in 1943, the intelligence was so bad that many landing craft became hung up on reefs, forcing the Marines to wade long distances in the face of heavy fire. In 1945 Iwo Jima, although it ended in victory, began with an overoptimistic plan, followed by a too brief bombardment. When it was finished, three Marine divisions had been

Recruitment posters with slogans such as "Fighting Fish and Fighting Men" contributed to the explosive growth of the Navy during the war.

destroyed (half of the corps) to acquire emergency landing strips for the Army Air Force.

While the Navy did many things supremely well, it committed itself to a costly and unwise strategy. After the bloody battle at Betio Island in Tarawa Atoll, naval planners came up with better tactics while clinging to the strategy that would produce additional, unnecessarily bloody battles at Saipan, Peleliu, Iwo Jima, and Okinawa.

SEE ALSO

Atlantic, Battle of the; Central Pacific Area; King, Ernest J.; South Pacific Area; Submarines in the Pacific

FURTHER READING

Davidson, Joel R. *The Unsinkable Fleet: The Politics of the U.S. Navy Expansion in World War II.* Annapolis, Md.: Naval Institute Press, 1996.
Gunter, Helen Clifford. *Navy WAVE: Memories of World War II.* Fort Bragg, Calif.: Cypress House, 1992.
Hoyt, Edwin Palmer. *Now Hear This: The Story of American Sailors in World War II.* New York: Marlowe, 1994.
Morison, Samuel Eliot. *History of United States Naval Operations in World War II.* 15 vols. Boston: Little, Brown, 1947–62.
———. *The Two-Ocean War: A Short History of the United States Navy in the Second World War.* Boston: Little, Brown, 1989.
Spector, Ronald. *Eagle Against the Sun: The American War with Japan.* New York: Free Press, 1985.

United States Strategic Bombing Survey (USSBS)

The United States Strategic Bombing Survey was launched in late 1944 to evaluate the air wars against Germany and Japan. It was led by Franklin D'Olier, a former commander of the American Legion and an insurance executive. For some reason, lawyers played important roles in the survey, which also included young men such as George Ball, Paul Nitze, John Kenneth Galbraith—and even the poet W. H. Auden, who had not yet become famous.

After Germany's defeat, the USSBS made a quick study of bombing results and in mid-June returned home. Survey experts recommended to the U.S. Army Air Force, on the basis of what they had seen in Germany, that the system of targeting Japan be changed. At the time Major General Curtis LeMay was firebombing Japanese cities in a terror campaign that was forcing Japanese civilians to move into the countryside but which had not yet persuaded Tokyo to surrender.

Instead of this approach, called area bombing, the USSBS recommended that LeMay concentrate on railways and coastal shipping or what was left of it, as well as oil, chemical, and electrical power plants. Their advice was ignored, however, because the Air Force had attempted daytime precision bombing in late 1944 and early 1945 and failed. The strong winds that prevailed over Japan made accuracy impossible, hence the terror attacks.

Little controversy surrounds the USSBS report on bombing results in Germany, but its report on Japan is still debated. That is because, after an examination lasting not quite two months, the USSBS announced that Japan would have surrendered by November 1, 1945, or December 31 at the latest, even if the atomic bomb had not been used and there had been no Allied invasion. This report has played a key role in the continuing historical argument over whether the United States was justified in waging nuclear warfare against Japan.

But the USSBS report was seriously flawed. Although some 1,000 USSBS staff members participated, none of them were experts on Japanese culture and history, and no such experts advised them. Furthermore, the survey relied heavily on interviews with 14 leaders of wartime Japan who, it claimed, agreed that Japan was on the verge of surrender when the atomic bombs were dropped. But transcripts of these interviews do not bear out this claim—in fact, 13 of those interviewed actually said that Japan intended to fight on to the end.

The differences between the interviews and how they were reported appear to be the work of General Henry H. Arnold, chief of the Army Air Forces. In the immediate postwar period, air officers feared that nuclear weapons would doom their plans for a large and independent air force. Thus it was important to establish the value of conventional bombing even in a nuclear age. Their fears were groundless. Atomic weapons have never been employed since World War II, and the Air Force has never lacked bombers. Accordingly, the USSBS could have told the truth about Japan without endangering the Air Force's future.

SEE ALSO
Atomic bombs; Japan, surrender of; Strategic bombing

V-1 flying bomb

The V-1 flying bomb was a small, unmanned aircraft carrying an explosive warhead and powered by a jet engine. It was the first example of what are today called cruise missiles. The current U.S. Tomahawk, for example, is a jet-powered missile like the V-1, but it has greater range and more explosive power.

The most important difference between them is that the Tomahawk is highly accurate because of its computer guidance system and on-board radar.

The V-1 was developed by Germany for use against Britain as a response to Allied bombing attacks. But because it lacked a real guidance system, the V-1 was mainly a terror weapon of little military value.

Germany began launching V-1s against London in June 1944. By the end of the war about 10,000 V-1s had been fired at England. Most of these were shot down before reaching their targets, but 2,419 fell on London, 30 on Portsmouth and Southampton, and one on Manchester. They killed 6,184 people and wounded another 17,981. V-1s were also launched against the vital port of Antwerp and did some damage to it.

Because V-1s were so inaccurate their chief effect was political. Londoners in particular were upset by these "buzz bombs," and many Allied aircraft were diverted to make wasteful and almost always unsuccessful attacks on V-1 launching sites, which were small and hard to hit. Otherwise, though, the V-1 was a waste of scarce German resources.

V-2 rocket

The first true ballistic missile, the V-2 was an astonishing technical achievement. It was first launched against Britain in September 1944 and ultimately 1,054 V-2s fell on English soil, about half of them on London. Another 900 were fired at the port of Antwerp, Belgium.

Against this liquid-fueled rocket,

which reached speeds of 2,500 miles per hour, there was no defense. Since this rate far exceeded the speed of sound, the V-2 gave no warning. The first indication of danger was the explosion that blew you up. However, like the V-1 flying bomb, the V-2 could not be targeted against anything smaller than a city and so had little military value. Furthermore, the V-2 was far more complicated and expensive to build than the V-1 and strained Germany's technical resources to the limit. Had Hitler not been so committed to these frightening but largely useless weapons, the Germans might well have developed an atomic bomb. At the very least, the highly advanced conventional weapons the Germans were introducing—a submarine that could stay underwater for weeks at a time, a wire-guided antitank missile, the first ground-to-air missile, among others—could have been made operational in time to affect the course of the war.

The V-2 put Londoners on the front line again, as during the blitz of 1940–41. But the development of the V-2 greatly reduced Germany's ability to defend itself. About 2,700 Londoners were randomly killed by the V-2, but a far larger number of Allied soldiers survived the war who would otherwise have been killed had Germany's resources been more intelligently employed.

Vichy France

After its defeat in June 1940, France was divided up and greatly reduced in size. Large sectors on the German frontier were either directly annexed by Germany or reserved for future coloniza-tion. A sizable strip along France's Italian border, including the major port of Marseilles, was occupied by Italy. The most industrialized and populous area, which included Paris and the English Channel and Atlantic coasts of France, was occupied by Germany. What remained, a largely rural area including most of southern France and part of the Mediterranean coast, had a limited amount of self-rule. Marshal Henri Petain, a hero of World War I who came out of retirement to preside over France's surrender to Germany, established his seat of government in the resort town of Vichy in central France.

From Vichy, Petain's government exercised direct control over what was called the *zone libre,* or "free zone," while it administered occupied France under German control. The Vichy regime broke sharply with France's republican past and attempted to stage what it called a national revolution based on traditional and authoritarian values. It replaced all elected officials with appointees loyal to itself and perse-cuted Jews, communists, and its real, or potential, political enemies.

On November 11, 1942, following the Allied invasion of French North Africa, Germany occupied the *zone libre.* But it did not acquire the sizable fleet, moored in Toulon since the Armistice of June 1940, which was scut-tled by the French Navy. Now directly under German control, Vichy retained its administrative functions and, as resis-tance to it mounted, conducted ever

Henri Philippe Pétain headed France's Vichy government. A military hero from World War I, Pétain was convicted of treason after World War II for his collabo-ration with Nazi Germany.

more savage campaigns against the Jews and its armed opposition, known as the Maquis.

After the liberation of France, the Vichy leaders were removed to German-held territory. After the war, some went into exile, but others, like Petain himself, returned to France, where they stood trial for treason. Vichy's active collaboration with the Nazis, and its brutal acts of repression, left a legacy of shame that troubles France even today.

SEE ALSO

France; France, Battle of; France, fall of

FURTHER READING

Novick, Peter. *The Resistance Versus Vichy: The Purge of Collaborators in Liberated France.* New York: Columbia University Press, 1968.
Paxton, Robert O. *Vichy France.* New York: Knopf, 1972.

Victory gardens

Food production and conservation had been strongly encouraged by U.S. leaders in World War I, and many families who did not ordinarily grow their own produce established kitchen gardens in response. Americans took it for granted that food would be short this time as well. Accordingly, they began planting vegetables in the spring of 1942, despite receiving no encouragement from the Department of Agriculture, which initially dragged its feet. By April at least 6 million gardens were being cultivated, inspiring Secretary of Agriculture Claude Wickard to call for 18 million Victory gardens, a goal that was easily reached.

In 1943 more than 8 million tons of produce was grown on 20 million individual plots, many of them very small.

In cities with populations above 100,000, Victory gardens averaged 500 square feet in size, or about 20 by 25 feet, but they amounted collectively to 7 million acres—an area the size of Rhode Island.

Victory gardens appeared everywhere, not only on private lots but in parks, before the San Francisco city hall, in the yards of schools and prisons, wherever there was arable soil and hands to do the tilling. The Agriculture Department reported that the amount of vegetables grown in Victory gardens exceeded "the total commercial production for fresh sale for civilian and noncivilian use." This level of production was all the more impressive because after being grown, much of this produce still had to be canned in family kitchens—no small thing, because a mistake could result in glass canisters exploding—or even in bacterial growths that could be potentially lethal. A real help to the war effort, Victory gardens also demonstrated the commitment of ordinary people and their willingness to do more than was asked of them.

A London couple plants a victory garden in this bomb crater. Americans also kept Victory gardens, on both public and private grounds.

WACs

SEE Women's Army Corps (WAC)

Wage and price controls

With mobilization came inflation, the obvious solution to which was price controls, a policy few objected to in principle, although every seller believed the prices set for goods he sold were never high enough. Beginning in 1942, the War Labor Board's (WLB) biggest headache was pay. Since price controls did not become effective until 1943, and then were fixed for as long as the war lasted, union leaders soon found themselves under pressure from the rank and file to negotiate higher wages. But if wages rose, prices would too. In a war economy, if the population's income exceeds the supply of civilian goods, inflation results. Ideally, government could have raised taxes or in other ways locked up all surplus income, thus keeping the supplies of money and goods in balance. Doing so would not only have prevented inflation but distributed the sacrifices of war more fairly—among civilians but also between them and the armed forces.

However, to do so would have angered the typical voter, who, government believed, preferred to have any financial sacrifices borne by someone else. Consequently, President Franklin D. Roosevelt's administration felt that it had to erect a complicated structure of taxes and controls that gave the impression of being, or at least could be defended as, both fair and effective, while at the same time making the fewest possible demands on civilians.

Wages, prices, and taxes could not be controlled except in relation to each other. In the early war years there were heated debates within the administration about how to balance wages, prices, and taxes. Raising taxes did limit inflation

and was essential in any case to help finance the war. It cost $304 billion to wage World War II, of which 45 percent was paid for out of current revenues, or in other words taxes. This ratio, which was a much higher one than in any previous war, was accomplished by raising the percentage of national income that went to pay federal taxes from 7.1 percent in 1940 to an impressive 24.2 percent in 1945. To avoid inflation altogether, this tax rate should have been higher still, but Congress ruled that out. Congress also ruled out making purchases of war bonds compulsory, which would also have curbed inflation.

Given these limitations, the administration had no choice except to hold down both wages and prices. Some, including Leon Henderson, who headed the Office of Price Administration, wanted higher taxes and compulsory savings too. Roosevelt took everyone's advice in his stabilization address of April 27, 1942, which called for a seven-point program involving higher taxes, price controls, and a wage freeze to be worked out by the War Labor Board.

The board finally decided that wages should be pegged at the level existing on January 1, 1941, plus 15 percent. This decision resulted in the average hourly industrial wage rising by more than 25 percent, from 66 cents at the beginning of 1941 to 85 cents as of January 1, 1943, while consumer prices increased by 16.4 percent. In July 1942, the board confirmed its policy in a decision affecting the smaller steel producers. What became known as the "Little Steel formula" would determine wage policy for the balance of the war.

The wage freeze, as it was called despite being less drastic than the term implied, reduced inflation at the expense of the industrial unions. After the December 6, 1941, attack on Pearl Harbor, acting on the assumption that

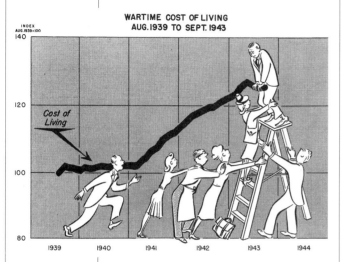

WARTIME COST OF LIVING
AUG. 1939 TO SEPT. 1943

The cost of living in the United States rose during the war until measures by the government to keep it in check became effective.

unionized workers would be rewarded for their restraint, most labor leaders had pledged not to strike while the war lasted. But by freezing wages, government had eliminated the main reason for joining a union, and in 1942 their membership declined—sharply in some cases.

To save organized labor, the WLB agreed to help the unions hold and recruit members. In return for a no-strike pledge and assurances of union cooperation with government, the WLB insisted that unionized employers include in their labor contracts what was called a "maintenance of membership" clause. As defined in June 1942, it stipulated that workers in organized plants automatically became union members unless they refused to do so within 15 days of being hired. Thanks to this device, the fall in membership was halted and organized labor grew from a total membership of 8.7 million in 1940 to 14.3 million five years later. Workers continued to resent the wage freeze, but on the whole it worked well and did not cause undue hardship.

SEE ALSO

Financing the war; Labor; Mobilization; Office of Price Administration

FURTHER READING

Lichtenstein, Nelson. *Labor's War at Home: The CIO in World War II.* New York: Cambridge University Press, 1982.

Vatter, Harold G. *The U.S. Economy in World War II.* New York: Columbia University Press, 1985.

Wallenberg, Raoul

RESCUER OF JEWS

- *Born: August 4, 1912, Stockholm, Sweden*
- *Education: University of Michigan School of Architecture, 1935*
- *Military service: Swedish Army, 1930–31*
- *Government service: Secretary to Swedish legation in Hungary, 1944–45*
- *Died: Time and place of death unknown*

Raoul Wallenberg was one of the greatest heroes of World War II and the foremost savior of Jews. Little in his early life suggested he would play such a role. His family was one of the richest and most influential in Sweden but was also devoted to public service. After his graduation from the University of Michigan, Wallenberg traveled widely, holding various jobs in Europe and elsewhere. He returned to the safety of neutral Sweden after the war in Europe broke out.

A few things about Wallenberg seem important in retrospect. He was an early critic of Adolf Hitler. His great-great-grandfather was Jewish. He had worked for six months in Haifa, Palestine, which was largely Jewish. These few personal details do not go very far, however, toward explaining the fantastic courage and zeal he would bring to the task of saving Hungarian Jews.

Many currents met to bring Wallenberg to Budapest, Hungary, on July 9, 1944. The Allied and neutral states had done little about the Holocaust previously, but in 1944 the American War Refugees Board was formed and charged with, among other things, saving Jews if it could. Sweden, which cooperated with

Hitler in many ways in order to maintain its neutrality, was growing bolder, because numerous German defeats were making it clear that the Axis powers were losing the war. Thus, when the plight of Hungary's Jews became known, Sweden and the United States were willing to take action on their behalf.

Although Hungary was a member of the Axis, its ruler, Admiral Miklos Horthy, did not support the Holocaust. Because of Horthy's protection, in the beginning of 1944 most Hungarian Jews were still alive. But Hungary's role as a safe haven ended on March 19, 1944, when Germany occupied Hungary to prevent it from surrendering to the Soviet Union. The roundup of Jews began the next day, under the supervision of Adolf Eichmann, a leading exterminator. By July 7 the provinces had been cleared of Jews, hundreds of thousands having been shipped to death camps in Poland.

Several hundred thousand Jews were still alive in Budapest, and the U.S. War Refugees Board, the Swedish Red Cross, and the Swedish government resolved to save them. Since Sweden was to front the operation, because of its neutral status, the rescue supervisor had to be Swedish. In the small world of Sweden's elite, Wallenberg stood out at once. He was young, single, his family name was famous and would afford him some protection, and he was available and willing to go.

Wallenberg's job as secretary of the Swedish legation enabled him to issue protective passes and other documents to Jews that in theory should, and in practice often did, save them from the Holocaust. Wallenberg counted on the German respect for paperwork and procedure, and it did not fail him.

Under Wallenberg's leadership an extensive network of rescuers was developed that included Jewish youth, friendly legations (notably that of the papacy),

"safe houses," where Jews could stay until they could be taken out of the country, and much more. These methods worked in part because Horthy, who was still regent of Hungary and retained some authority, let them go ahead.

However, on October 15, 1944, Horthy announced over the radio that Hungary was prepared to surrender to the Soviets. The Germans immediately put a puppet in his place, the leader of the Hungarian fascist movement called the Arrow Cross. Wallenberg and his colleagues now redoubled their efforts, Wallenberg personally pulling Jews off death trains and demanding that their documents, usually provided by his organization, be respected. He risked his liberty, and perhaps his life, time and again in daring trips into the very heart of the Nazi death machine. Arguing that Germany had lost the war and continuing with the killing of Jews would only make it worse for the losers after the war, Wallenberg tried to persuade Eichmann to call off the slaughter. But Eichmann and his fellow butchers were already so drenched with innocent blood that they had nothing to lose.

Eichmann left Budapest on December 23, 1944, when the Red Army was knocking on its gates. He left orders that the central ghetto was to be cleared of Jews. But Wallenberg prevented that, pointing out to the SS officer in charge that when he went to trial for crimes against humanity after the war, sparing the ghetto would count in his favor. No one knows how many Jews were saved by Wallenberg and his operation, but it cannot have been less than 100,000.

Wallenberg was eager to make contact with Soviet authorities to arrange for the completion of his rescue work. He left Budapest on January 17, 1945, with two Soviet officers, and was never seen again. After years of international agitation on Wallenberg's behalf, during which the Soviets denied any knowledge of him, Soviet authorities announced in 1957 that he had died of "natural" causes a decade earlier. That seems unlikely.

He was probably executed, for a host of reasons. The Soviets distrusted Sweden and thought the Swedish legation in Budapest to be a nest of Nazi spies. It would have been easy for them to see Wallenberg as the spymaster of this imaginary espionage ring. Then, too, after the war he was going to be hailed throughout the world for his heroic acts on behalf of humanity and would, by his very existence, be a symbol of freedom and an embarassment to the Soviets, who intended to replace Hitler's tyranny in the East with another of their own. Maybe they had hoped to turn Wallenberg into a spy for them, and finding themselves unable to do so shot him out of frustration. Whatever their reasons, the act was criminal. But, in killing Wallenberg, the Soviets only made him a martyr to the cause of freedom as well as even more of an international hero.

SEE ALSO
Holocaust

FURTHER READING
Adachi, Agnes. *Child of the Winds: My Mission with Raoul Wallenberg*. Chicago: Adams Press, 1989.
Marton, Kati. *Wallenberg*. New York: Random House, 1982.
Rosenfeld, Harvey. *Raoul Wallenberg*. New York: Holmes & Meier, 1995.

War bonds

Of all the methods used to raise funds for the war effort, Secretary of the Treasury Henry Morgenthau, Jr., favored bonds especially. He wanted bonds sold widely and in such a way as to make Americans "war minded." He believed that this was even more important than helping finance defense purchases. To sell bonds was to sell the war, so bond drives were aimed at the average American rather than wealthy investors, which

A young woman sells war bonds and stamps and distributes War Production Drive literature.

meant, in turn, drawing heavily on the popular culture.

The war-bond drives, of which there were seven, entertained Americans as well as raised money. Movie stars played important parts, with Hollywood organizing seven tours that played in some 300 communities. Dorothy Lamour, the star of many movies, was credited with selling $350 million worth of bonds. Carole Lombard, another popular movie actress, gave her life to the cause, dying in a plane crash on her way home from a bond tour. In addition to bonds, war stamps costing only pennies were sold—mainly to children. Every form of salesmanship was employed in this cause, and few Americans managed to escape it.

War-bond purchases were voluntary, although some thought that apart from the "educational" value of war-bond drives it would be more effective to make them mandatory. Morgenthau shrank from this, however, believing (no doubt correctly) that Congress would simply reduce the income tax to offset the added burden. Even so, war-bond sales to individuals amounted to $49 billion, one-sixth of the war's total cost.

SEE ALSO
Financing the war; Office of Price Administration; Wage and price controls

WAVES

SEE Women Accepted for Voluntary Emergency Service (WAVES)

Western front

Western front was a term carried over from World War II to describe the com-

bat zone in which the Western Allies and Germany fought. In World War I, the front was a continuous line of trenches running from Switzerland to the English Channel. In World War II there was no single fortified line, but the invasion of Normandy by Allied forces on June 6, 1944, established a new western front. To the U.S. Army there was no western front in World War II, but rather a European theater of operations. "Western front" was, therefore, an unofficial term.

SEE ALSO
France, Battle of; Germany, surrender of

Willkie, Lewis Wendell

REPUBLICAN NOMINEE FOR PRESIDENT, 1940

- *Born: February 18, 1892, Elwood, Ind.*
- *Political party: Republican*
- *Education: Indiana University, B.A., 1913, LLB, 1915*
- *Military service: U.S. Army, 1917–19; captain, 1919*
- *Government service: none*
- *Died: October 8, 1944, New York, N.Y.*

Wendell Willkie was a power company executive. He had never previously run for office and, until 1939, he had been a Democrat. Any one of these factors should have prevented him from getting the GOP nomination in 1940. Although they were beloved by many Republicans, big businessmen were not greatly admired during the years of the Great Depression. In addition, changing parties was rare and tended to be looked down on. In any case, Presidential nominees were usually selected at conventions run by political bosses.

Wendell Willkie (left) delivers a personal message to Winston Churchill from President Roosevelt while inspecting conditions in war-torn Britain.

Willkie won the Republican nomination all the same, because the GOP had not recovered from its two huge defeats by Franklin D. Roosevelt in 1932 and 1936 and was desperate. Unknown before the New Deal launched the Tennessee Valley Authority project in 1933, Willkie led his industry's attack against publicly owned electrical power, a central feature of TVA. But he did so in such a refreshingly down-home way that the Republican rank and file warmed to him immediately and forced him on the party bosses, who would have preferred a professional but wanted to win above all else.

Although most Americans wished the United States to stay out of the European war, neutrality was becoming harder and harder to maintain; therefore, 1940 was a crucial election year. After the fall of France in June 1940, many prominent Americans called for aid to Britain. Doing so would compromise U.S. neutrality, however, and might well end by bringing the country into the war.

In addition to foreign policy, rearmament was a key issue in the 1940 election. Interventionists such as Henry Stimson, Roosevelt's secretary of war, held that being able to defend the United States was simple self-preservation. Isolationists like aviator and popular hero Charles A. Lind-

bergh feared that having arms would inspire the President to use them.

At first Willkie's position on most issues was not much different from that of President Franklin D. Roosevelt. Like FDR, he wanted Britain to survive and believed that the United States should be able to defend itself. As Willkie was not giving people much reason to prefer him over Roosevelt, he trailed in the polls. In October, reason having failed, Willkie made a last-ditch effort to win by smearing FDR as a warmonger. This almost worked, because the polls showed that the more mud Willkie threw the more popular he became. In self-defense FDR was obliged to make promises that he knew he might not be able to keep. One of these affirmations was that "our boys" would never fight overseas. FDR won his third term, but the election itself was a disgrace, with both candidates lying about their true positions.

That Willkie is still respected results not from the dirty finale of his campaign but from the support he gave to the right side of several important issues. Before the election, FDR worked out a deal with Britain in which some 50 overaged U.S. destroyers would be exchanged for long leases on British bases in the New World. Isolationists were furious about this step away from neutrality. But Willkie, who had agreed not to criticize the arrangement, kept his word, arguing instead against the way the decision was made.

Willkie also ended up supporting the Burke-Wadsworth Act, which established the first peacetime civilian draft in American history, which isolationists also hated. Perhaps he would have lost the election anyway, but Willkie did not do himself any good by antagonizing his most important supporters.

After the election Willkie gave up his chance at another nomination by showing his true colors, supporting Lend-

Lease, rearmament, a bipartisan defense effort, and other policies loathsome to isolationists. Then, after Pearl Harbor was attacked on December 7, 1941, he generally supported FDR's war policies and championed what would become the United Nations. He did so knowing the political risks but hoping to overcome them. However, he had angered too many conservative Republicans and party bosses to be nominated again, so he withdrew from the race in 1944 when that became clear. He died suddenly a few months later, having sacrificed his political career for the sake of his country.

SEE ALSO

Roosevelt, Franklin Delano; Selective Service System

FURTHER READING

Ellsworth, Barnard. *Wendell Willkie: Fighter for Freedom.* Marquette: Northern Michigan University Press, 1966.
Johnson, Donald Bruce. *The Republican Party and Wendell Willkie.* Westport, Conn.: Greenwood, 1960.
Moscow, Warren. *Roosevelt and Willkie.* Englewood Cliffs: Prentice-Hall, 1968.
Neal, Steve. *Dark Horse: A Biography of Wendell Willkie.* Garden City, N.Y.: Doubleday, 1984.

Women

Among the most conspicuous failures of the mobilization process was the federal government's failure to take advantage of American women's eagerness to serve. This was true even before Pearl Harbor was attacked in December 1941. Thus, in August 1941 the president of the General Federation of Women's Clubs—an old, large, and conservative body—complained that women were being discriminated against "intolerably" in the civil defense program. The Office of Civilian Defense did not even have a women's division.

At the time, there were only seven women in the entire federal government at the policy-making level. Women were excluded from serving in Civil Aeronautics Authority programs for training student pilots. The female assistant national civilian defense director had just resigned, because Director Fiorello La Guardia disapproved of her efforts to have the Works Progress Administration survey and catalog volunteer associations around the country, many of them women's groups, as possible contributors to civil defense.

Women were joining the Red Cross and other emergency-related bodies in large numbers, but not because government was encouraging them to or promising that if war came it would use their services. This lack of interest on the government's part would not change very much after Pearl Harbor. In the age of total war, the United States would make only a partial effort at enlisting the aid of its female population. This prejudice against women would seriously weaken the war effort.

It was obvious that vast numbers of men in uniform would be performing clerical tasks and other duties that were not gender specific. Yet military leaders were slow to admit that women could do

Women slide markers onto a grid map to track airplane movements at an intelligence center in Virginia. These volunteers worked four- to five-hour shifts, sometimes after getting off their regular jobs.

these jobs as well as, if not better than, men, thus freeing able-bodied males for combat. Early in 1942, the Army agreed to accept 10,000 volunteers for a Women's Army Auxiliary Corps—later renamed the Women's Army Corps (WAC)—only because a bill introduced in Congress by Representative Edith Nourse Rogers (Republican–Mass.) forced its hand. The Navy went on refusing to accept women in any capacity. There were plenty of men who were as yet not drafted, the military's reasoning went, which was true at the time, but this surplus did not last, forcing a later change of heart.

Washington's attitude toward women was particularly annoying in light of the popular support for a more serious war effort. In January 1942 a Gallup poll reported that 68 percent of the public favored a labor draft for women aged 21–35—among women the majority in favor rose to 73 percent. The women in the suggested age group were the most enthusiastic of all: fully three-quarters of those questioned asked for such a draft.

In March 1942 another poll disclosed that the support for registering all adults and assigning as many as needed to war work—what later would be called national service—was supported by a ratio of almost two to one. It seems clear that a selective labor draft, focusing on young women but including other women (and men as well) who met certain criteria, had all the support it needed. Magazines regularly predicted the enactment of legislation to that effect. But Congress refused to pass such a bill, even in 1944 when President Franklin D. Roosevelt finally got around to asking for it.

Lacking official outlets for war work, women formed numerous paramilitary groups of their own, including the Powder Puff Platoon of Joplin, Missouri, the Home Guard of Kalamazoo, Michigan, and the Women's Defense School of Boston, which taught a course in field

cooking modeled on that of the Army. Some 25,000 women volunteered for the Women's Ambulance and Defense Corps of America, whose slogan was "The Hell We Can't." Its more than 50 chapters trained women to serve as air-raid wardens, security guards, and messengers for the armed forces. However, most who wished to contribute joined the Red Cross, which, with 3.5 million female volunteers, was by far the most important outlet for patriotic women.

Some government agencies recognized opportunity when they saw it. The Office of Civilian Defense employed a number of female volunteers. The Office of Price Administration used 50,000 women in five states to conduct a three-day canvass in July 1942 during which they briefed 450,000 retailers on the new price regulations. For the most part, though, except for defense contractors, who gradually warmed to the idea of hiring women workers, volunteer organizations remained the main outlets.

Of these, the most controversial was the American Women's Voluntary Services (AWVS), founded by a group of society women in 1940 to prepare women for emergency work in the event of a London-style blitz. It soon enrolled 350,000 members in almost every state. To refute mockers who accused them of being social butterflies out on a spree, the AWVS cast a remarkably broad net for the times, organizing several units in Harlem, at least one Chinese chapter, a number of Hispanic units, and one affiliate consisting entirely of Taos Pueblo tribeswomen in New Mexico. Defying local taboos, the New Orleans chapter bravely included African-American women.

When it became evident that the United States was not going to be attacked by German bombers, the AWVS took on new assignments. In New York its members sold $5 million worth of war bonds. In California there were AWVS "chuck wagons" that delivered food, including late-night snacks, to Coast Guard stations and remote military sites. In San Francisco, AWVS women taught Braille to blinded veterans. Others organized agricultural work camps in California and Colorado. Some New York suburbs had ambulances staffed entirely by AWVS members.

Although it was the biggest such agency, the AWVS was by no means the only volunteer women's organization that made a place for itself in the war effort. At least three other women's groups provided land and air ambulance services. There were also volunteer groups of working women, such as WIRES (Women in Radio and Electric Service), WAMS (Women Aircraft Mechanics), and WOWS (Women Ordnance Workers), who collectively by 1943 had a membership of 33,000 in dozens of munitions plants.

As part of an elaborate recruiting campaign, Oldsmobile created WINGS (also known as the "Keep 'Em Winning Girls"), workers who were given uniforms with a torch and wing insignia on the front pocket. So that housewives should not feel excluded, the *Ladies' Home Journal* organized WINS (Women in National Service), saying that housewives were "the largest army in the nation fighting on the home front." The outpouring of female volunteers in a host of organizations enabled women to accomplish much, and suggested how much more they might have done had there been a system in place to take full advantage of their enthusiasm. Even as it was, in April 1942, when 10,000 women volunteers marched down Fifth Avenue in New York, there were so many different uniforms that no one could identify them all.

Probably women's greatest contribution to national well-being in wartime was the efforts of the millions of wives and mothers who fed and clothed their families and kept their children in school, sometimes under extremely difficult conditions. Rationing, including that of gas, made everyday life much harder than before. Shortages, a complex rationing system in which the number of "points" required to buy rationed items was constantly changing, long lines, and an overburdened transportation system could make shopping and getting children to school and to appointments a nightmare by prewar standards. Housewifery, never an easy job, was never harder in modern times than during World War II.

Working women had to do all those things plus toil long hours at what were frequently hard and demanding jobs, especially in defense plants. The government did little to make things easier for them, an astonishing oversight considering the seriousness of the manpower shortage. This was a problem to which women presented the obvious solution.

A few figures make this clear. Of the 9 million additional persons who entered the labor force during World War II, some 3.3 million represented a natural increase, with the balance coming from people who would not otherwise have been employed. Boys and girls left school early to work in factories, or at least replace those who had given up lower-paying jobs to do so. Old men came out of retirement to fill in for youths who had been drafted. But the most numerous new adult workers were married women, despite the prejudice against them.

In 1936 a Gallup poll disclosed that 82 percent of the men questioned, and 75 percent of the women, believed that wives with employed husbands should not work. War did not change these attitudes as much as might be supposed, for U.S. democracy had not yet reached the point where women were seen as having the same rights as men.

Fortunately for the war effort, married women joined the labor force anyway. Between 1940 and 1944, the number of employed women rose by half, reaching a high of 19 million, and for the first time in American history, married women outnumbered single ones. This was a matter not of choice but of need. When the supply of white male and single white female workers was exhausted, employers had no alternative but to hire married women and blacks.

However, unlike today, and despite the fact that the basic allotment for a serviceman's wife was only $50 a month, young mothers remained at home. The number of women workers younger than 35 increased just one-half of 1 percent more than if there had been no war. The Women's Bureau, part of the U.S. Department of Labor, found that only 32 percent of the married, widowed, or divorced women in the work force had any children younger than 14, and in half of these cases only one. Women older than 35 years of age accounted for 60 percent of the increase.

There were several reasons for this. For one, the government did not want young mothers to work. In 1942 Chairman Paul McNutt of the War Manpower Commission issued a directive saying that "no women responsible for the care of young children should be encouraged or compelled to seek employment which deprives their children of essential care until all other sources of supply are exhausted." Few efforts were made to assist employed mothers of young children. Although some department stores, led by Bloomingdale's of New York, set up defense plant branches, most stores kept the same hours as in peacetime. This left women coming off the day shift with little or no time to shop.

Only 130,000 children were served by the Lanham Act, which provided federal subsidies for child care. Part of the

These women welders were trained for a typically "male" occupation, challenging gender conventions of the day.

reason was that mothers mistrusted, and often rightly so, the quality of these hastily assembled facilities. In other cases the nursery fees were so high that working women could not afford them. Notable exceptions were the Kaiser Corporation's shipyard care centers, which were open 24 hours a day and staffed by child development experts. The excellence of these centers and their success in persuading young mothers to use them was, for the most part, an example that persuaded few employers.

Britain, where the labor crunch was more severe, showed how much more could have been done. Britain conscripted women between the ages of 19 and 30, offering them a choice between the armed services and essential war work. Although this program was not rigorously enforced, the country expected most women younger than 60 to contribute in some way to the war effort. Child care support was provided on a much larger scale in Britain than in the United States, stores there were required to remain open late, and in other ways the nation did a good deal to make motherhood and employment compatible. As a result it was estimated that 8 married women out of 10 between the ages of 18 and 40 were either in the armed services or industry.

Although U.S. support for women workers was never this good, the work force changed anyway. In 1940 about half of the 11 million working women held poorly paid clerical, sales, and service jobs. The one-fifth engaged in manufacturing were concentrated at the low end, mostly in textile and clothing factories. Four years later, the percentage of the female labor force in clerical, sales, and service jobs had declined to 34 percent—because 3 million women had taken jobs in industry. Of these, about half had not worked at all before the war, while about a quarter had transferred to manufacturing from the service industries.

Officially, the U.S. view was that married women were only working for the duration of the war and would return home when it was over. There were many exceptions to this rule even in 1940, when 15 percent of married women held outside jobs. But after that the proportion of married women who joined the labor force increased to one in four in 1950, and then to more than half in 1980. The proportion who were active mothers rose as well, so that by 1980 three out of five married women with children aged 6 to 17 were in the work force, and so were two out of five with children younger than 6.

By June 1987 more than half of all women, 51 percent to be exact, who had given birth during the previous year were gainfully employed. Thus, while the prominent role played by married women in wartime was seen as a temporary expedient, it marked an historic change from a relatively small female work force dominated by young singles to an immense force comprised for the most part of older, married, or formerly married women.

For U.S. industry as a whole, female employment patterns varied widely during the war. In Detroit women held 20 percent of the jobs in aircraft factories, while at Boeing's facilities in Seattle they made up 47 percent of the workforce. Also in Seattle women held 1.8 percent of the jobs at one shipyard but 21 percent at another. Yet, despite regional differences, the total number of women in the war industries soared, in Detroit alone the figure rising from 46,800 to a high of 215,000 female industrial workers.

Apart from patriotism, the chief reason why women poured into factories—dirt, noise, and danger notwithstanding—was money. Even without wage equality, women earned more as factory workers than in their previous jobs. By 1945 at Ford's Willow Run plant in Michigan, one-third of the women workers had experienced pay raises of 100 percent since the war began, compared to one-ninth of the men.

Although the prejudice against working women declined, or was at least suspended for the war, one thing that did not change was a refusal to take full advantage of women's potential. Black women were discriminated against in war plants even more than white women, not only by employers but by workers. During one two-week period in Detroit there were five "hate" strikes caused by the employment of black women. Yet black women were even more eager than whites to work.

While the participation rate of all women in the Detroit workforce rose from 29.5 in 1940 to 39.7 percent in 1944, the rate for nonwhite women went from 31.6 to 48.8 percent. By 1945 the percentage of employed black women who were in private household service had declined from 60 to 45. One black woman told an investigator that it was Hitler who had gotten them out of white folks' kitchens. They would not go back.

Even when labor was in shortest supply, little was done to relieve women of domestic duties that impaired their job effectiveness. In Seattle's war industries during 1943, women workers were more than twice as likely to be absent from work as men. The War Manpower Commission believed that 100,000 worker hours were lost per month in Detroit alone because women took days off to do their laundry. In Baltimore the quit rate for women workers was 6.16 percent, compared to 4.78 for men. If shopping and laundry services, hot take-out meals, and more and better nurseries had been more widely available, all these losses could have been cut. It would probably have made some difference too if women workers had been promoted and paid equally with men, which seems not to have happened anywhere. This discrimination helps to account for their much lower wages, $31.21 per week in 1944 compared to $54.65 for men. Even the high degree of unionization during wartime had no effect, since union leaders developed little interest in the special problems of women.

Given the stereotyping and the prevailing bias against employment of women, and the mass media's habit of trivializing what they did, what is remarkable is that so many women did find jobs in defense plants. They were essential to the war effort, yet, like racial minorities, they could have contributed even more but for the prejudices against them. Here, as well, American democracy had far to go and much to learn.

SEE ALSO

Mobilization; Women Accepted for Voluntary Emergency Services (WAVES); Women's Army Corps (WAC)

FURTHER READING

American Women in a World at War: Contemporary Accounts from World War II. Judy Barrett Litoff and David C. Smith, eds. Wilmington, Del.: Scholarly Resources, 1997.

Anderson, Karen. *Wartime Women: Sex Roles, Family Relations, and the Status of Women during World War II.* Westport, Conn.: Greenwood Press, 1981.

Campbell, D'Ann. *Women at War with America: Private Lives in a Patriotic Era.* Cambridge, Mass.: Harvard University Press, 1984.

May, Elaine Tyler. *Pushing the Limits: American Women, 1940–1961.* New York: Oxford University Press, 1994.

Poulos, Paula Nassen, ed. *A Woman's War Too: U.S. Women in the Military in World War II.* Washington, D.C.: National Archives and Records Administration, 1996.

Weatherford, Doris. *American Women and World War II.* New York: Facts on File, 1990.

Women Accepted for Voluntary Emergency Service (WAVES)

The Navy called its female sailors Women Accepted for Voluntary Emergency Service, so that they could be called WAVES. At first the U.S. Navy did not want women in the service, but when Congress began working on a bill to that end in 1942, the Navy benefited from the Army's mistakes and insisted that women be admitted to service on the same terms as men. However, WAVES were held to higher standards than the army's Women's Army Corps (WAC). They were required to have a college degree or two years of college and at least two years of work experience in areas of use to the Navy. This made the average WAVE far better educated, and older too, than most enlisted men.

The Coast Guard, which was controlled by the Navy Department during wartime, followed suit. Its female personnel were known as SPARS, from the

WAVES were required to have at least two years of college and another two years of work experience in areas of use to the Navy.

Guard's Latin motto, *Semper Paratis,* and its English translation, "always ready." SPARS were only required to be high school graduates, or to have comparable business experience. The Marines were last to enroll women, waiting until January 1943. When it did, the Marine Corps announced that there would be no special designation for its women reserves, who would simply be called Marines. Unlike the WAC, whose members served in both Europe and the Pacific, SPARS and WAVES were restricted to service in the United States. In the last year of the war, they could be assigned to any base in the Western Hemisphere, which still kept them far from danger.

Like WACS, WAVES, SPARS, and female marines were never very numerous, and for similar reasons. Members of the press slandered them repeatedly, claiming they were "loose" women or lesbians who had joined the service for sex. Their low pregnancy rate, compared to the national average for single women, had little affect on the prejudices of men, and indeed on women of traditional beliefs. Every service came to appreciate its women volunteers, who on average were abler than men at a great many clerical and technical tasks. But the prejudice against uniformed

women was impossible to overcome. Polls consistently showed that women of draft age would have welcomed conscription. Being drafted on an equal footing with men would have meant that women were in the military for the same reasons as men, making it more difficult to slander them. However, Congress would not pass such a bill, which would have released millions of men in uniform for active duty and prevented the military manpower crisis of 1944.

SEE ALSO

Women; Women's Army Corps (WAC)

FURTHER READING

Weatherford, Doris. *American Women and World War II*. New York: Facts on File, 1990.
Wingo, Josette Dermody. *Mother Was a Gunner's Mate: World War II in the Waves*. Annapolis, Md.: Naval Institute Press, 1994.

Women's Army Corps (WAC)

The Women's Army Corp was established to meet a pressing need—the Army's manpower shortage—which became acute after the Allies' invasion of France in 1944. But the WAC, although it did valuable work, never lived up to the hopes entertained for it.

The War Department was not to blame for this failure. Army chief of staff General George C. Marshall and Secretary of War Henry L. Stimson were early and enthusiastic backers of the effort to recruit women. In 1941 when First Lady Eleanor Roosevelt and Representative Edith Nourse Rogers (Republican–Mass.) urged that women be enlisted, the Army drew up a bill establishing the Women's Auxiliary Army Corps (WAAC), which

Mrs. Rogers introduced in Congress. But opposition to having women in the military was immediate, and worsened as time went on. Some thought the WAAC would be too expensive, others that it would hurt discipline. As finally enacted, the bill discriminated against women soldiers by making their pay structure lower than that of men.

A War Department study established that fully half of the Army's jobs could be performed by women, for behind the front was a huge weaponless army of uniformed clerks and laborers whose work was not gender specific. The Navy, hostile at first to having women, finally came to similar conclusions. It then outdid the Army by creating its WAVES, who made twice as much money as WAACs and had a smarter uniform to boot.

In addition to pay inequities, the WAAC was put into the Army Service Forces, which made every mistake possible in recruiting, training, and deploying women. In 1943 a new Women's Army Corps came into being, to which most WAACs transferred. It was placed directly under the General Staff, after which conditions improved. What could not be improved, however, was the widespread contempt for women in the military, which resulted in endless amounts of bad publicity and slanderous whispering campaigns.

WACs were said to be promiscuous—indeed, to have volunteered so that they could have sex. Army and civilian newspapers ran many cartoons making fun of women in uniform. Surveys found that many soldiers were convinced that 90 percent of WACs were prostitutes, even though their venereal disease rate was minimal compared to that of male soldiers, and pregnancies in the WAC were one-fifth those of single civilian women in the same age group. Even so, servicemen continued to warn

their girlfriends against joining up, on the ground that WACs were whores or, alternatively, lesbians, and in either case unfit associates. Women in the other services were similarly smeared.

The War Department racked its collective brains to counter this negative propaganda, although an early recruiting campaign with the theme "Release a Man for Combat" backfired, because it implied that women who enlisted could be condemning their loved ones to death. Some believe the WAC never recovered from this recruitment mistake. In any case, the whispering campaign was so vile and widespread that it could easily have been fatal by itself. The result was that while Marshall hoped for a WAC of 500,000 women, it never exceeded 100,000.

If Congress had been willing, there would have been an easy solution to this problem, for Gallup polls taken throughout the war showed that a majority of women aged 21 to 35 supported the idea of a female military draft. Conscription would have put the morality issue to rest, for while one could defame volunteers, it would be difficult to slander conscripted women who would, like male soldiers, have the same sexual preferences as

Major Charity Adams and Captain Abbie Campbell inspect the women of the 6888th Central Postal Directory group in England, the first black Women's Army Corps members to be sent overseas.

civilians. In light of the double standard, according to which men who joined up freely were patriotic but women who did so were sluts, the draft would have been just as important for the WAC as it was in fact for the regular army.

Congress's failure to enact a female draft proved to be a serious blow to the war effort. The limited number of women who braved public scorn to volunteer released the equivalent of seven divisions of men for active service. But the army ground forces did not make the best use of their women. Too many were employed at clerical tasks that could as easily have been done by civilians. But some were used as decontamination experts in the Ordnance Corps, as photographers and cryptanalysts, and in other specialized jobs. The Army Air Forces, which enlisted half of all women, employed them to the fullest. General Henry H. Arnold opened every noncombat assignment and school to women, who performed superbly.

Ultimately, 10,000 women served in the Europe and 6,000 in the Southwest Pacific, where they quickly proved their worth. Eisenhower could not get as many women assigned to his forces as he wanted. MacArthur called the women who served in his forces "my best soldiers." Women nurses, who encountered little resistance, served nobly in all theaters, and intrepid civilian women ferried military aircraft across some of the most dangerous transoceanic routes.

Thus, long before the Persian Gulf War in 1990–91, women had proved that they belonged in uniform. If only the War and Navy departments could have overcome prejudice and congressional opposition, women soldiers would have solved the military manpower problem. Perhaps even more than discrimination, the failure of democracy to recognize women as equals jeopardized the war effort.

SEE ALSO
Women Accepted for Voluntary Emergency Service (WAVES)

FURTHER READING
Flint, Margaret. *Dress Right, Dress: The Autobiography of a WAC.* New York: Dodd, Mead & Company, 1943.
Green, Blanche. *Growing up in the WAC.* New York: Vantage, 1987.
Gruhzit-Hoyt, Olga. *They Also Served: American Women in World War II.* Secaucus: Carol, 1995.
Meyer, Leisa D. *Creating GI Jane: Sexuality and Power in the Women's Army Corps During World War II.* New York: Columbia University Press, 1996.
Weatherford, Doris. *American Women and World War II.* New York: Facts on File, 1990.

Yalta conference

The last meeting of the Big Three—Churchill, Roosevelt, and Stalin—was held at Yalta in the Russian Crimea during February 1945. It was purely a great power summit. Not only were the smaller Allied states excluded as usual, but so were France and China—despite Roosevelt's having at times named the latter as one of the "policemen" who were supposed to maintain world peace after the war. For the most part, Yalta confirmed what had earlier been suggested at the Teheran conference in late November 1943.

On the public level, agreement was reached at Yalta about the occupation zones in Germany and central Europe, a new provisional government in Poland, free elections in the other liberated states, their representation in the United Nations, and a formula for the veto authority to be exercised by the great powers in the UN Security Council.

Secretly, Roosevelt and Stalin also arranged for the Soviet Union to enter the war against Japan within two or three months of V-E Day. In return the Soviets would gain the Kurile Islands, the southern half of Sakhalin, the restoration of rights and privileges in Manchuria lost during the Russo-Japanese War of 1904–05, and the recognition of its puppet state Mongolia.

Most historians agree that the Soviets were allowed to take only what they could not have been kept from seizing. The Asian territories, although often regarded as a bribe to obtain help against Japan, were beyond Allied control and ripe for Soviet picking. Since there was no way to keep them out of the Soviets' grasp, Roosevelt and Churchill made a virtue of necessity for the sake of cordial relations.

In Europe too the settlement was determined by Soviet power. The Allies, having waited so long to invade France, were in no position to demand that the Soviets retreat from positions they had won by hard fighting. It was not sympathy for communism but the lack of prewar preparedness, aggravated by bad strategy, that were responsible for the Allies' weak hand at Yalta.

At Yalta, the United States and Britain realistically recognized the limits of their power. Rather than taking a hard line, the two countries bent over backwards to satisfy the Soviet Union. This was a popular position at first, with even ardent anticommunists like Herbert Hoover and John Foster Dulles praising the Crimean settlement.

The only mystery about Yalta is what Roosevelt really understood the Declaration on Liberated Europe, a part of the final agreement, to mean. The language is plain enough, the Big Three affirming the Atlantic Charter and calling for provisional governments in Eastern Europe representative of all democratic elements in the population and committed to early, free elections.

In his history Churchill claimed that the Declaration meant exactly what it said. And he believed that if only Stalin had lived up to it there would have been no cold war. Both Churchill and Roosevelt feared that the Soviets would renege on the promise of free elections, as in due course they did. But with the war still raging, the Allies had to behave as if Stalin could be trusted, because there was no real alternative.

Nonetheless, after the war Roosevelt would especially be blamed for "selling out" to the Soviets and "giving away" Eastern Europe. Eastern Europe was not Roosevelt's to give, but the sentiment was politically potent anyway. Thus Yalta would come to have the same distasteful meaning for the cold war that Munich did for World War II, despite their lack of any real similarity.

Roosevelt (center) meets with British prime minister Winston Churchill (left) and Soviet premier Joseph Stalin in Yalta to discuss war strategy.

SEE ALSO

Atlantic conference; Foreign policy; Teheran conference

FURTHER READING

Clemens, Diane Shaver. *Yalta*. London: Oxford University Press, 1970.
Fenno, Richard F. *The Yalta Conference*. Boston: Heath, 1955.
Snell, John L., ed. *The Meaning of Yalta: Big Three Diplomacy and the New Balance of Power*. Baton Rouge: Louisiana State University Press, 1956.
Sulzberger, Cyrus Leo. *Such a Peace: The Roots and Ashes of Yalta*. New York: Continuum, 1982.

Yamamoto, Isoroka

COMMANDER IN CHIEF OF THE COMBINED FLEET OF JAPAN, 1939–43

- *Born: 1884, Nagaoka, Niigata Prefecture, Japan*
- *Political party: none*
- *Education: Japanese Naval Academy, 1905; Navy Staff College, 1916*
- *Military service: Imperial Japanese Navy—ensign, 1905; lieutenant, 1914; lieutenant commander, 1915; commander, 1921; naval attaché at Japanese embassy in Washington, 1926; commander, cruiser Isuzu, carrier Akagi; captain, 1926; head, Technical Division of Aeronautics Department, 1930; rear admiral, 1930; commander, First Carrier Division, 1933; vice admiral, 1934; head, Aeronautics Department, 1935; navy vice minister, 1936; admiral, 1940*
- *Died: April 18, 1943, Bougainville Island, South Pacific*

Isoroka Yamamoto was the most brilliant Japanese naval leader of World War II and the architect of Japan's victory at Pearl Harbor. His talent was recognized early, hence his rapid promotions.

Yamamoto was unusually well traveled even by the standards of the Imperial Japanese Navy (IJN), whose officers knew the world far better than did the provincial army leaders. He served two tours of duty in the United States. The first, from 1919 to 1921, was as a student and observer, the second as a naval attaché. He also toured Europe in 1923 and was a delegate to a London naval conference in 1930. Because he knew the strength of the West, and that of the United States in particular, Yamamoto belonged to the peace party in the IJN, which was known as the "treaty" faction. (The officers who favored war were called the "fleet faction.") As navy vice minister he so antagonized the fleet faction that his life was in danger. It was

in part to prevent him from being assassinated by radical young officers, which often happened in the Japan of the 1930s, that he was appointed commander in chief of the Combined Fleet. Apart from his being the obvious choice, the job kept him out of Tokyo and often at sea.

Although Yamamoto opposed waging war on the West and predicted that Japan would be defeated if the conflict lasted more than a year, he did his duty when the decision to fight was made. It was his idea to begin the Pacific war by attacking U.S. bases in Hawaii, a plan that met with outstanding success. But he knew that the failure of his conservative subordinate Vice Admiral Chuichi Nagumo to destroy the port facilities at Pearl Harbor with a second strike was a mistake that could cost Japan dearly.

Yamamoto also planned the failed attack on Midway Island in June 1942. Part of that blame went to Admiral Nagumo again, but Yamamoto's plan for Midway was too complex and involved too much dispersal of his forces. Thus, despite its overwhelming superiority in ships and aircraft, the IJN was defeated by a much smaller U.S. force that had the advantage of surprise, better planning, and superior leadership.

From August 1942 until his death in April 1943, Yamamoto was preoccupied with the struggle to prevent Allied forces from seizing the Solomon Islands and undermining Japan's position in the South Pacific. This was already a losing battle when Yamamoto's transport plane was shot down by a U.S. fighter squadron while he was making an inspection tour. United States intelligence had learned the details of his flight plan and prepared an ambush. He was the only high commander in the war to be assassinated in this way, a tribute of sorts to the regard in which he was held by his enemies.

SEE ALSO

Japan; Japanese Navy; Midway, Battle of; Pearl Harbor, attack on; South Pacific Area

FURTHER READING

Agawa, Hiroyuki. *The Reluctant Admiral: Yamamoto and the Imperial Navy.* New York: Kodansha, 1979.

Davis, Burke. *Get Yamamoto.* New York: Random House, 1969.

Hoyt, Edwin Palmer. *Yamamoto: The Man Who Planned Pearl Harbor.* New York: McGraw-Hill, 1990.

Yamashita, General Tomoyuki

JAPANESE COMMANDER IN MALAYA AND THE PHILIPPINES

- *Born: November 8, 1885, Osugi Mura, Shikoku, Japan*
- *Political party: none*
- *Education: Central Military Academy, 1908; Staff College, 1914–17*
- *Military service: Imperial Japanese Army—2nd lieutenant, 1908; captain, 1917; assistant military attaché to Japanese Embassy in Switzerland, 1919–22; major, 1922; attaché to embassy in Austria, 1927–30; colonel, 1930; commander, 3rd Regiment, 1930; chief of military affairs and major general, 1936; lieutenant general, 1937; commander, 25th Army, 1941; commander, 1st Army Group, 1942; general, 1943; commander, 14th Army Group, 1944*
- *Died: February 23, 1946, Manila, Philippines*

Tomoyuki Yamashita was the ablest commander in the Japanese Army. He proved this after the Japanese invasion of the British colony of Malaya on December 7, 1941. Although his small force of some 60,000 men was heavily outnumbered by the British imperial and commonwealth garrison, Yamashita won a stunning victory.

In a series of amphibious landings, Yamashita worked his way down the Malayan Peninsula, outflanking or landing behind the British time and again. His troops moved on foot, in commandeered trucks, and on bicycles, never giving the British a chance to build a strong defensive position. By January 31 all of Malaya had been taken, and its surviving defenders were besieged in the fortress of Singapore, an island just off the peninsula. On February 8 Yamashita invaded Singapore, and on the 15th it surrendered.

Yamashita's victory was based on the superior experience of his veteran troops, his daring tactics and inspired leadership, and on Japanese control of the sea and air. But he was lucky, too, in that half of Britain's force consisted of poorly trained and motivated Indian troops who were quick to surrender or even desert. Added to that was the incompetence of Britain's Lieutenant General Arthur Percival, who surrendered Singapore at a time when Yamashita was running out of everything and might well have been forced to withdraw if the British had attacked him.

Still, the facts speak for themselves. In 54 days, at a cost to himself of fewer than 10,000 casualties, Yamashita's army killed, wounded, or captured 138,708 enemy troops. Of these, more than 130,000 became prisoners of war. As a result of his victory Yamashita became known all over the world as the "Tiger of Malaya."

Instead of being honored for this stunning achievement, Yamashita was quickly exiled to a command in Manchuria, where he sat out much of the rest of the war. This was apparently because he belonged to a different army faction from that of Prime Minister Tojo, who mistrusted Yamashita and may have seen him as a possible rival.

When Tojo fell from power in 1944, Yamashita was brought back from exile to defend the Philippine Islands against General Douglas MacArthur. By October, when he reached Manila, the Philippines were no longer defensible, but even if they had been Yamashita arrived too late to make a major difference. Although he believed Japan had lost the war and ought to be suing for peace, he did his best to make the U.S. seizure of the Philippines as difficult as possible. But the best he could do after a string of defeats was to withdraw his main force on Luzon to its northern mountains, where it held out until Japan surrendered. On September 2, 1945, he gave up himself and his army to the Americans.

Although many atrocities had been committed by troops under Yamashita's command in Malaya and the Philippines, they had not been done at his orders, or perhaps even with his knowledge. However, Yamashita was tried as a war criminal on the grounds that he should have prevented any illegal acts committed by troops under his command. This doubtful rule had never before been applied to a commander. Further, the most egregious crimes were committed by Japanese naval infantry defending Manila under the direct command of an admiral who disobeyed Yamashita's order to abandon the city. His trial, which was hasty and in which he was poorly defended, has been severely criticized by historians. It was also criticized at the time by two justices of the U.S. Supreme Court—although a majority of the Court voted that it had no authority to hear Yamashita's appeal. His conviction and execution have always been viewed by critics as General Douglas MacArthur's revenge for the defeat Japan had handed him in 1942.

SEE ALSO

Japanese Army; Southwest Pacific Area; Tojo, Hideki

FURTHER READING

Barker, A. J. *Yamashita*. New York: Ballantine, 1973.
Reel, A. Frank. *The Case of General Yamashita*. New York: Octagon, 1971.

Zhukov, Georgi K.

MOST HONORED SOVIET COMMANDER OF WORLD WAR II

- *Born: December 2, 1896, Strelkovka, Kaluga Province, Russia*
- *Political party: Communist*
- *Education: primary school, 1915; Cavalry School, 1924–26; Command School, 1928–30*
- *Military service: conscripted into Russian Army, 1915; Red Army volunteer, 1918; commander, 39th Buzuluksk Cavalry Regiment, 1923; commander, 2nd Cavalry Brigade, 1930; commander, 4th Cavalry Division, 1933; commander, 3rd Cavalry Corps, 1936; commander, 1st Army Group, 1939; general of the army, 1940; chief of the General Staff, 1941; deputy defense commissar, 1941; varied assignments, 1941–44; marshal of the Soviet Union, 1943; commander, 1st Byelorussian Front, 1944*
- *Died: June 18, 1974, Moscow, Russia, U.S.S.R.*

A child of poverty, Georgi Zhukov owed everything to the Red Army, hence his loyalty to it and the Communist party. He was a ruthless, hard-driving commander who abused his subordinates and was widely disliked. However, he also got results, and rose rapidly in the Red Army (which did not adopt Western-style ranks until 1940) and his assignment to the Far East in 1939, where the Soviets and Japan were fighting an undeclared war on the Manchurian border.

Events did not go well in the Far East for the Soviet forces initially, and Zhukov was sent out to turn things

During the fall of Germany, Georgi Zhukov led the 1st Byelorussian Front into Berlin, a triumphant march that signaled victory for the Allies.

around—the first of many times when he would be called on to do so. As commander of what became the 1st Army Group, he reorganized the Soviet force and led it to victory. This move had an effect that went beyond simply bringing peace to the Manchuria frontier. Zhukov's victory helped persuade Japanese leaders that it would be easier to expand to the south than to take on the Soviets again. Thus, in 1941 Japan and the U.S.S.R. signed a nonaggression treaty that freed Japan to launch the Pacific war. The treaty, and the war, guaranteed that when Germany invaded the Soviet Union in June 1941 the Soviets would not have to worry about being attacked by Japan as well.

At the time of the German invasion of the Soviet Union that began in June 1941, Stalin formed a new high command for the armed forces, known as the Stavka, of which he and Zhukov comprised one third of the total membership. Thus, Zhukov would be involved throughout the war with strategic planning at the highest level. In addition, he served as Stalin's troubleshooter. In 1941 he organized the successful defenses of Leningrad and then of Moscow. In 1942 he played a crucial role in the defense of Stalingrad and the annihilation of Germany's Sixth Army.

For these and other valuable services Zhukov became the most decorated Soviet officer, as well as the first Soviet general to be promoted to the rank of marshal during World War II. In 1944 Zhukov was given command of the 1st Byelorussian Front (the equivalent of a U.S. army group). This was the prize Soviet military appointment of the war, for it meant that Zhukov would capture Berlin and win the most glory of any commander.

SEE ALSO

Soviet Union (U.S.S.R.); Stalingrad, Battle of

FURTHER READING

Chaney, Otto Preston, Jr. *Zhukov.* Norman: University of Oklahoma Press, 1971.
Fugate, Bryan I. *Thunder on the Dnepr: Zhukov-Stalin and the Defeat of Hitler's Blitzkrieg.* Novato, Calif.: Presidio, 1997.
Le Tissier, Tony. *Zhukov at the Oder: The Decisive Battle for Berlin.* Westport, Conn.: Praeger, 1996.
Spahr, William J. *Zhukov: The Rise and Fall of a Great Captain.* Novato, Calif.: Presidio, 1993.
Zhukov, Georgi Konstantinovich. *Marshal Zhukov's Greatest Battles.* New York: Harper & Row, 1969.
———. *The Memoirs of Marshal Zhukov.* New York: Delacorte, 1971.

Zoot-suit riots

Not all race riots were directed against blacks. In California the riot victims were usually Mexican-American youths, known as "zooters" or "zoot-suiters" because of their colorful apparel, the zoot suit.

This garment had a very long jacket, heavily padded shoulders, and balloon trousers with tight cuffs. In June 1943 mobs of servicemen, egged on by civilians, began beating zoot-suiters in Los Angeles and San Diego in a series of riots that lasted for several days.

APPENDIX 1

IMPORTANT DATES DURING WORLD WAR II

1939

Sept. 1
Germany invades Poland

Nov. 4
United States Neutrality Act passed

1940

May 10
Germany attacks in the west

June 22
France signs armistice with Germany

1941

March 11
U.S. Lend-Lease Bill becomes law

June 22
Germany invades the Soviet Union

Aug. 9
Conference in Newfoundland between Churchill and Roosevelt begins and results in Atlantic Charter

July 26
The United States freezes Japanese assets and restricts oil sales to Japan, a restriction that soon becomes an embargo

Dec. 7
Japan attacks American military targets in Hawaii, including Pearl Harbor

Dec. 8
The United States declares war on Japan

Dec. 11
Germany and Italy decare war on the United States

Dec. 23
Japan invades the Philippines

Dec. 24
Wake Island falls to the Japanese

1942

Apr. 9
Bataan peninsula in the Philippines falls to the Japanese

May 6
Corregidor Island falls, and the Philippines surrender to the Japanese

May 4–8
Battle of the Coral Sea

June 4–7
Battle of Midway

Aug. 7
American troops land on Guadalcanal

Nov. 8
Allies land in Morocco and Algeria (Operation Torch)

1943

Jan. 14–24
Casablanca Conference

Feb. 2
Soviets win the Battle of Stalingrad

May 13
Axis forces surrender in North Africa

July 10
Anglo-American forces invade Sicily

Aug. 17
Sicily falls to Allies

Sept. 3
Allies land in Italy

Nov. 20–23
Battle of Tarawa

Nov. 28–Dec. 1
Teheran Conference

1944

Jan. 22
Americans land at Anzio in Italy

Jan. 25
Allies secure Papua

Feb. 20–25
"Big Week," Allied offensive turns tide of the air war over Germany

June 4
Rome falls to Allies

June 6
D-Day, the Allied invasion of France (Operation Overlord)

June 15–July 9
Battle of Saipan

June 19–20
Battle of the Philippine Sea (The Great Marianas Turkey Shoot)

July 28
Americans lead the breakout from Normandy

Aug. 15
Allied landings in southern France (Operation Dragoon)

Aug. 25
Allies liberate Paris

Sept. 17–25
Operation Market Garden

Oct. 20
Americans land on Leyte in the Philippines

Oct. 24–26
Battle of Leyte Gulf

Dec. 16
Germans launch the Battle of the Bulge

1945

Jan. 28
Battle of the Bulge ends

Feb. 4–11
Yalta Conference

Feb. 19–March 26
Battle of Iwo Jima

Mar. 9–19
Americans initiate first firebomb raids on Japan

April 1–June 21
Battle of Okinawa

April 12
President Franklin D. Roosevelt dies

April 28
Italian partisans shoot Benito Mussolini

April 30
Adolf Hitler commits suicide

May 2
Berlin falls to Allies

May 2
German troops in Italy surrender

May 8
V-E Day (Germany surrenders)

July 16
American scientists test atomic bomb at Alamogordo in New Mexico

July 17–Aug. 2
Postdam Conference

Aug. 6
United States drops the atomic bomb "Little Boy" on Hiroshima

Aug. 8
Soviet Union declares war on Japan

Aug. 9
United States drops the atomic bomb "Fat Man" on Nagasaki

Aug. 15
V-J Day (Japan surrenders)

Sept. 2
Japanese sign instrument of surrender aboard USS *Missouri*

APPENDIX 2

MUSEUMS AND HISTORIC SITES

There are many facilities of various kinds devoted, wholly or in part, to World War II. The first category listed below consists of institutions devoted solely to World War II. The second consists of more general military museums or displays that include other wars as well. Both lists are suggestive rather than inclusive, as the United States and its possessions contain a host of memorials, exhibits, and preserved weapons—including armor, aircraft, and naval vessels—as reminders of the national effort in World War II. The many internet sites devoted to the war include digital exhibitions and guides to a host of museums. You can tour the Intrepid Sea-Air-Space Museum, for example, at its location in New York City or on the internet at www.intrepid-museum.com.

World War II History Sites

Admiral Nimitz Museum and Historical Center
P.O. Box 777
304 East Main Street
Fredricksburg, TX 78624
(830) 997-4379

Allied Air Force, Inc.
1730 Vultee Street
Allentown, PA 18103
(610) 791-5122

American Airpower Heritage Museum of the Confederate Air Force
P.O. Box 62000
Midland International Airport
9600 Wright Drive
Midland, TX 79711-2000
(915) 563-1000
fax: (915) 567-3047
www.avdigest.com/aahm/aahm.html

National Atomic Museum
P.O. Box 5800
Albuquerque, NM 87185-1490
(505) 284-3243
www.sandia.gov/museum/main.htm

Saipan Museum
American Memorial Park
National Park Service
P.O. Box 5198-CHRB
Saipan, MP 96950-5198
(670) 234-7207
www.nps.gov/amme

USS Bowfin Submarine Museum and Park
11 Arizona Memorial Drive
Honolulu, HI 96818-3145
(808) 423-1341
www.aloha.net/~bowfin

United States Holocaust Memorial Museum
100 Raul Wallenberg Place, SW
Washington, DC 20024-2150
(202) 488-0400
www.ushmm.org

USS Arizona Memorial
1 Arizona Memorial Place
Honolulu, HI 96818
(808) 422-0561
www.nps.gov/usar

USS Massachusetts Memorial
Battleship Cove
Fall River, MA 02721
(508) 678-1100
www.battleshipcove.com

USS North Carolina Battleship Memorial
P.O. Box 480
Wilmington, NC 28402
(910) 251-5797
www.city-info.com/battleship/main.html

War in the Pacific National Historical Park
Box FA
Agana, Guam 96910
(011) 671-477-9362
www.nps.gov/wapa

Military History Sites that include World War II

Arlington National Cemetery
Arlington, VA 22211
www.arlingtoncemetery.com

Intrepid Sea-Air-Space Museum
Intrepid Square, 46th Street
  and 12th Avenue
New York, NY 10036
(212) 245-2533
www.intrepid-museum.com

National Air and Space Museum
Smithsonian Institution
Washington, DC 20560
(202) 357-2700
www.nasm.edu

National Infantry Museum
US Army Infantry Center
Fort Benning, GA 31905
(706) 545-2958

National Museum of Naval Aviation
1750 Radford Boulevard
Pensacola, FL
(800) 327-5002
namfmktg@naval-air.org

Patton Museum of Cavalry and Armor
P.O. Box 208
4554 Fayette Avenue
Fort Knox, KY 40121-0208
(502) 624-3812

United States Air Force Museum
1100 Spaatz Street
Wright-Patterson AFB, OH 45433-
  7102
(937) 255-3286
www.wpafb.af.mil/museum

United States Marine Corps Air-Ground Museum
Brown Field
Marine Corps Base, Quantico
Quantico, VA 22134
(703) 784-2606

United States Marine Corps Museum
Washington Navy Yard, Building 58
Washington, DC 20560
(202) 433-3840

Women's Army Corps Museum
3rd Street and 5th Avenue
Fort McClellan, AL 36205
(205) 848-3512

DOING RESEARCH ON WORLD WAR II: FURTHER READING AND WEBSITES

Further Reading

Ambrose, Stephen A. *Citizen Soldiers: The U.S. Army From the Normandy Beaches to the Bulge to the Surrender of Germany.* New York: Simon & Schuster, 1997.

Ambrose, Stephen A. *D-Day, June 6, 1944: The Climactic Battle of World War II.* New York: Simon & Schuster, 1994.

Bergund, Eric. *Touched with Fire: The Land War in the South Pacific.* New York: Viking, 1996.

Cohen, Stan. *V for Vicotry: America's Home Front During World War II.* Missoula, Mont.: Pictoral Histories, 1991.

Dallek, Robert A. *Franklin Roosevelt and American Policy, 1932–1945.* New York: Oxford University Press, 1979.

Dawidowicz, Lucy. *The War Against the Jews, 1933–1934.* New York: Holt, Rinehart, and Winston, 1975.

Dear, I.C.B. & Foot, M.R.D., eds. *The Oxford Companion to World War II.* New York: Oxford University Press, 1995.

Goodwin, Doris Kearns. *No Ordinary Time: Franklin and Eleanor Roosevelt: The Home Front in World War II.* New York: Simon & Schuster, 1994.

Keegan, John. *The Second World War.* New York: Penguin, 1991.

Lewin, Ronald. *American Magic: Codes, Ciphers, and the Defeat of Japan.* New York: Farrar, Straus & Giroux, 1982.

Lewin, Ronald. *Ultra Goes to War.* London: Hutchinson, 1978.

Lyons, Michael J. *World War II: A Short History.* 3rd ed. Upper Saddle River, N.J.: Prentice Hall, 1999.

Mauldin, Bill. *Up Front: The Classic Portrait in Text and Drawings of the American Combat Soldiers in World War II.* New York: Norton, 1991.

May, Elaine Tyler. *Pushing the Limits: American Women, 1940–1961.* New York: Oxford University Press, 1994.

Morrison, Samuel Eliot. *The Two-Ocean War.* Boston: Little, Brown, 1963.

O'Neill, William L. *A Democracy at War: America's Fight at Home and Abroad in World War II.* New York: Free Press, 1993.

Perrett, Geoffrey. *There's a War to be Won: The United States Army in World War II.* New York: Random House, 1991.

Polmar, Norman. *World War II: The Encyclopedia of the War Years, 1941–1945.* New York: Random House, 1996.

Shirer, William L. *The Collapse of the Third Republic.* New York: Simon & Schuster, 1986.

Shirer, William L. *The Rise and Fall of the Third Reich: A History of Nazi Germany.* New York: Simon & Schuster, 1960.

Spector, Ronald H. *Eagle Against the Sun: The American War With Japan.* New York: Free Press, 1985.

Stokesbury, James L. *A Short History of World War II.* New York: Morrow, 1980.

Time-Life books, Editors of. World War II. Alexandria, Va.: Time-Life, 1976-83.

Toland, John. *Rising Sun: The Decline and Fall of the Japanese Empire.* New York: Random House, 1970.

Tuchman, Barbara. *Stillwell and the American Experience in China, 1911–1945*. New York: Macmillan, 1970.

Tuttle, William M. *Daddy's Gone to War: The Second World War in the Lives of America's Children*. New York: Oxford University Press, 1993.

Weigley, Russell F. *Eisenhower's Lieutenants: The Campaigns of France and Germany 1944–1945*. Bloomington: Indiana University Press, 1981.

Weinberg, Gerhard L. *A World at Arms: A Global History of World War II*. Cambridge: Cambridge University Press, 1994.

Werth, Alexander. *Russia at War, 1941–1945*. New York: Avon, 1970.

Websites

There are many websites about World War II, and a large number of these include bibliographies, guides to sources, and archives of valuable information and research. The few listed below are good examples of the quality and quantity of information available. In addition, Access Indiana Teaching and Learning Center offers a categorized index of general World War II websites for educational use at tlc.ai.org/wwii.htm.

American Memory
www.loc.gov/amhome.html
Exhibition of photographs, documents, and sound recordings at the Library of Congress

German Surrender Documents
www.law.ou.edu/hist/germsurr.html
From the University of Oklahoma Law Center.

Hiroshima
www.khm.uni-koeln.de/~akke/hiroshimaproject
A guided tour, personal accounts, and analysis

Holocaust Sites
www.lib.muohio.edu/inet/subj/history/holoc.html
A guide to links.

The Home Front
hyperion.advanced.org/1551
Educational site about life in the United States during the war.

Official Government Publications
www.smu.edu/~sshort/ww2home.htm
Includes documents, posters, and maps issued by the government during the war.

Oral History Archives
history.rutgers.edu/oralhistory/orlhom.htm
A large oral history archive of Rutgers University alumni who served in World War II.

Powers of Persuasion
www.nara.gov.exhall/powers/powers.html
Newly expanded government poster exhibit from the National Archives.

Soviet Archives Exhibit
sunsite.unc.edu/expo/soviet.exhibit/entrance.html#tour
The Soviet experience of World War II.

Those Who Served
www.nara.gov/exhall/people/people.html
Exhibition highlighting the contributions of thousands of Americans, both military and civilian, who served during the war.

INDEX

PICTURE CREDITS

American Red Cross: 271; Archive Photos: 43, 93, 121, 159; courtesy of The Army Museum collection: 22, 88, 136, 157, 340; Corbis: 307; Corbis/National Archives: 169, 345; Dwight D. Eisenhower Library: 89; Express Newspapers/Archive Photos: 369; Franklin D. Roosevelt Library: 11, 107, 117, 203, 285, 349, 353, 356; Hulton-Deutsch Collection/Corbis: 59, 175; Imperial War Museum/Archive Photos: 32, 99, 144, 207; Library of Congress: 19, 31, 40, 49, 62, 68, 77, 79, 81, 83, 83, 91, 102, 108, 110, 135, 138, 155, 163, 183, 199, 231, 236, 240, 244, 266, 269, 274, 283, 287, 299, 301, 309, 314, 315, 319, 321, 323, 331, 351, 348, 365; Los Almos Scientific Library, courtesy of the Harry S. Truman Library: 32; National Archives: cover (top left), cover (top right), cover (bottom), frontispiece, 6, 9, 15, 17, 18, 23, 24, 27, 29, 33, 35, 37, 39, 44, 45, 47, 51, 52, 64, 66, 70, 73, 74, 87, 104, 112, 113, 115, 123, 125, 127, 130, 147, 148, 151, 153, 161, 167, 172, 178, 177, 185, 187, 189, 190, 191, 193, 197, 205, 209, 214, 218, 221, 229, 233, 237, 238, 244, 245, 248, 250, 252, 255, 259, 261, 264, 265, 278, 280, 289, 291, 295, 297, 299, 326, 329, 333, 334, 336, 339, 343, 355, 359, 363; National Museum of Naval Aviation: 141, 192, 227, 362; National Park Service, courtesy of the Harry S. Truman Library: 57; Tallandier/Archive France/Archive Photos: 276; Gary Tong: 13, 26, 34, 55, 97, 133, 142, 165, 181, 210, 222, 253, 257, 263, 303; The Raul Wallenberg Committee of the United States: 351; UPI/Corbis: 13

William O'Neill is a professor of history at Rutgers University, New Brunswick, New Jersey, where he teaches courses on 20th century American history and the two world wars. Among his books are *A Democracy at War: America's Fight at Home and Abroad in World War II* and *American High: The Years of Confidence, 1945–60*. He has written articles and book reviews for a wide range of scholarly and general publications, including *The Boston Globe*, *The New York Times*, and *The Washington Post*; has lectured at numerous colleges and universities, including the National War College in Washington, D.C.; and has participated in many documentary films and videos. He is a member of the board of *Gender Issues*. One of William O'Neill's daughters served in the U.S. Army.

William H. Chafe is Alice Mary Baldwin Distinguished Professor of History and Dean of the Faculty of Arts and Sciences at Duke University. His numerous publications include *Civilities and Civil Rights: Greensboro, North Carolina and the Black Struggle for Freedom* (winner of the Robert F. Kennedy Book Award); *A History of Our Time: Readings in Postwar America* (edited with Harvard Sitkoff); *The Unfinished Journey: America Since World War II*; *The Paradox of Change: American Women in the Twentieth Century*; *Never Stop Running: Allard Lowenstein and the Struggle to Save American Liberalism* (winner of the Sidney Hillman Book Award); and *The Raod to Equality: American Women Since 1962*. Professor Chafe is courrently the president of the Organization of American Historians.